SANDCASTLES

SANDCASTLES

The Arabs in Search of
the Modern World

MILTON VIORST

Alfred A. Knopf   NEW YORK   1994

This Is a Borzoi Book
Published by Alfred A. Knopf, Inc.

Copyright © 1994 by Milton Viorst

Portions of this work were originally published in somewhat
different form in *The New Yorker*.

Library of Congress Cataloging-in-Publication Data
Viorst, Milton.
Sandcastles: the Arabs in search of the modern world / by Milton
Viorst. — 1st ed.
p.   cm.
Includes index.
ISBN 0-679-40599-2
1. Arab countries—Description and travel.   I. Title.
DS49.7.V56   1994
909'.0974927082—dc20   93-2540   CIP

Manufactured in the United States of America
First Edition

This book is dedicated to the children of the Middle East,

who deserve peace

CONTENTS

Acknowledgments   ix
Introduction   xi

Chapter 1 Iraq
I   The Abbasid Flavor   3
II   Tug-of-War   9
III   Searching for Order   19
IV   Freedom Is   28
V   Pouring In Fire   41
VI   An Understanding with Washington   46

Chapter 2 Turkey
I   Melancholy City   53
II   Islam and Europe   57
III   Empire in Decline   62
IV   Never a Renaissance   67
V   Ataturk's Republic   70
VI   Headscarf and Miniskirt   75

Chapter 3 Egypt
I   Meeting Mahfouz   83
II   Disappointment in the Liberal Age   90
III   Despair in the Alleys   96
IV   Dictator Years   102
V   The New Era   106
VI   The Brotherhood and the Mosque   110
VII   The Mahfouzian President   116

Chapter 4 Syria
I   Saladin's Scion   122
II   The Reality of the State   128
III   Assad as Leader   136
IV   The *Mukhabarat* State   141
V   The Jews of Damascus   149
VI   Assad on Peace   153

Chapter 5 Lebanon
I   The Christian Enclave   158
II   Meeting the Maronites   163
III Down from the Mountain   171
IV   Bashir   174
V   East Beirut, West Beirut   181
VI   Amin   186
VII Since Amin   190

Chapter 6 The Palestinians
I   The Mountain Village   194
II   The Tragedy Unfolds   201
III Gaza   205
IV   Abdullah's Dream, Arafat's Vision   210
V   Baramki and Rada   219
VI   Who Decides   226

Chapter 7 Kuwait
I   Carrying a New Flag   233
II   Out of the Desert   237
III Utopia in the Sands   242
IV   Strange Negotiations   248
V   Kuwait Under the Iraqis   257
VI   The Government of Exiles   261
VII Postliberation Normality   270
VIII Holding to Account   275

Chapter 8 Jordan
I   Friends of Saddam Hussein   285
II   American Queen, Arab Home   293
III Democracy and Fundamentalism   300
IV   Critical Days   308
V   King, from Boy to Man   312
VI   Meeting the Israelis   318

Chapter 9 Iraq Revisited
I   Overland to Baghdad   322
II   Baghdad in Pain   327
III The Survivor   330
IV   Tariq Aziz Speaks   337
V   Provincial Spring   346

Epilogue   357
Postscript   361
Bibliography   387
Index   401

ACKNOWLEDGMENTS

It would be impossible to acknowledge all of the people who have helped me in the preparation of this book. Many are American. Many more are Middle Easterners, who have sat patiently with me, over countless cups of coffee and tea, sharing their experiences, their fears and prejudices, their interpretations, their hopes. I have cited some by name in the text, but left many others anonymous. They include scholars, officials, diplomats, journalists, rulers, clerics, politicians, merchants, students and—those garrulous bellwethers—taxi drivers. I thank them all. Let me mention just a few friends who have been especially kind: Hazem Mushtak in Baghdad, Mehmet Isvan in Istanbul, Tahsin Bashir and the late Lewis Awad in Cairo, Sadiq al-Azm in Damascus, Samir Fares in Beirut, Mahdi Abdul-Hadi in Jerusalem, Najat Sultan in Kuwait, Musa Keilani in Amman. At home, I would like to note the encouragement given to me by Mary King, Sharon Russell and Nameer Jawdat. I want also to thank Betsy Folkins at the library of the Middle East Institute in Washington and my inspired literary agent, Andrew Wylie. It goes without saying that I am most grateful of all to my rigorous editor, quick-witted companion and fetching bed partner, Judy, my wife.

Milton Viorst
Washington, July 1993

INTRODUCTION

The liberation of the Arabs, after four centuries of Ottoman rule, came suddenly. During the nineteenth century, when the empire was already in steep decline, the Ottomans' Christian provinces grew increasingly conscious of their separate identities and embarked on campaigns to free themselves. Not so the Arabs. They saw themselves not in ethnic but in religious terms, as Muslims like their rulers, and were without the resentment that foreign control normally breeds. The few Arabs with a separatist vision commanded no following. The overwhelming majority, with no interest in liberation, gave little thought to what independence might bring. Unprepared for the Ottoman collapse in 1918, the Arabs were in no position to seize power for themselves, and so the Europeans took control of their lands.

The ailment of the Arabs, in an era when nationalism served as a channel to the modern world, was that their nationalist roots had long since withered. In contrast to, say, the Greeks and the Serbs of the Ottoman empire, the Arabs had not regained a sense of special identity. The Arabs shared a language, a way of life strongly shaped by Islam, and a range of historical experiences. But these elements had not sufficed to create a sense of nationhood. Only in the decade or so before World War I did Arab thinkers begin the attempt to fuse the jointly held cultural elements into a theoretical basis for unity. Their efforts produced the idea of one eternal "Arab nation," encompassing the Arabic-speaking peoples from the Atlantic to the Gulf. No such nation had ever in fact existed, not even during the centuries of grandeur in the last millennium, when Arabs dominated much of the Mediterranean region. Nonetheless, this was the vision that came to pervade the Arab world. Under the most favorable of circumstances, it was probably too grand to be attainable; but at the time of liberation the circumstances were not favorable at all.

By the eve of World War I, Europe already ruled the Arab lands on the north coast of Africa and was waiting impatiently for the remaining Arab provinces to fall from feeble Ottoman hands. The occasion arose out of the debris of the war. In the postwar settlement the Allies, notwithstanding the pledges of independence they had given the Arabs in return for their help against the Turks, divided up the Middle East among themselves. The Arabs, leaving the familiar embrace of the Ottomans, entered the modern world as colonies of Europe. Their Arab identity, long before surrendered, was restored, but it was received with little enthusiasm. Though they were again players in the arena of world affairs, they were without preparation, while nursing grievances against both the Ottomans for abandoning them and the West for its betrayals. It might be argued that to this day, the Arabs have not recovered from the shock of the transition.

The colonial era was mercifully short for the Arabs; in the decades after World War II, they rode the global wave of decolonization to achieve their independence. It took the form, however, not of one "Arab nation" but of twenty-one Arab states, the borders of which had been drawn in London and Paris. Internally and externally, none was very strong, and for all of them the ensuing years constituted an era of questing and of struggle, of arduous toil to shape institutions that were culturally authentic on the one hand, yet strong enough to meet the demands of the age on the other. Though the sense of community—tribalism, some would call it—remained alive among the Arabs, few signs pointed to a realization of the ideal of an "Arab nation." Each of the twenty-one states embarked on its own course in its search for an accommodation with modern times.

By most standards, the search has not been successful. The states have been as fragile as sandcastles. They have produced tyrants and secret-police agencies and corrupt bureaucracies that rule over restive populations by imposing a suffocating conformity, both intellectual and political. Save for the few with the luck to have oil, they have provided little economic security for their citizens. They have squabbled among themselves over preeminence and power, and though they formed an Arab League to contain their differences, their impotence in dealing with either one another or the non-Arab world has simply underlined their weakness. They have repeatedly failed in diplomacy and lost wars.

Scholars note that the Arabs have produced a "defensive culture," resorting to old ways in response to new challenges. One study describes the Arab dilemma as that of "a preindustrial culture in the scientific-technological age." It is no surprise, of course, that the Arabs, so abruptly thrust onto the global stage, have had trouble coming to terms with values, whether social or scientific, that are not their own. To Arabs, democracy and human rights are imported notions; authoritarianism is indigenous. Secularism, and the separation of religion and the state, are ideas born in the Christian world; Islam, which holds that politics must be guided by religion, is embedded in the culture. The result of these old ways, which many Arabs deplore, is that much of Arab society today is torn between secular despotism and religious fanaticism. Meanwhile, Arabs debate reforms that may one day create a more open and democratic culture but such an achievement seems very distant.

Still, whatever its shortcomings, Arab society has not been stagnant, and the signs of change are intriguing. In population—a mixed blessing, to be sure—the Arab world has leaped from twenty-two million a century ago to nearly two hundred million today. Elementary school enrollment rose from single-digit percentages in the colonial era to 40 percent by 1960, and currently stands at more than 90 percent. Arab governments have built universities, as well as roads, harbors and communications systems. Clean water and electricity have been provided nearly everywhere. Infant mortality is down, life expectancy is up. The status of women has been generally improved. Such evidence suggests an Arab civilization that is seeking to reshape itself for a new assault on the complexities of the modern world. Certainly, it leaves no doubt that the search goes on.

This book examines that search. It is the product of a long-standing fascination with the Middle East, based in the first instance on my emotional interest in the Arab-Israeli struggle. Being Jewish, I was raised with a natural bias toward Israel, but I learned very early that the truth about the conflict could not be grasped by listening to the proponents of only one side. Over the course of dozens of visits to the Middle East, during which I have been treated as graciously by one side as by the other, I have asked countless questions and acquired a deepening involvement with two very different societies. In 1987, I published *Sands of Sorrow: Israel's Journey from Independence,* an examination of the political culture of the Jewish state. The Arab world, with its twenty-one countries, required more stops, and its diversity has led to a different kind of book. Nonetheless, *Sandcastles* is meant as a counterpart and a sequel.

The geographical emphasis of *Sandcastles* is on the Arab heartland: Egypt, and the region that the Arabs call the Mashreq ("East" in Arabic), extending from the eastern shore of the Mediterranean to the Gulf. On these lands, in past centuries, the Arabs built great empires. These are also the lands in which the core of the Arab history of our own time—from the fall of the Ottomans to the Arab-Israeli wars to the liberation of Kuwait—has been fashioned. It is here that Arabs and Jews must reach agreement if there is to be Middle East peace. *Sandcastles,* reflecting the conviction that each has much to learn about the other, is at least indirectly about Middle East peace. Without peace, furthermore, I believe that neither Arabs nor Israelis are likely to succeed in the modern world.

Much of *Sandcastles* emerged out of assignments to the Arab world from newspapers and magazines, beginning with my first eye-opening trip to Egypt shortly after the October war of 1973, when I wrote for the *Washington Star*. In recent years, I have traveled extensively in the region for *The New Yorker*, and much of the book has been drawn from the resulting articles. During the course of my *New Yorker* work, Iraq invaded Kuwait, precipitating a bitter split among the Arabs, and the first major deployment of Western forces in Arab lands since World War II. *The New Yorker* enabled me to return repeatedly to the area, and from my reporting I acquired an understanding of the crisis that diverges significantly from convention. The final portions of the book, based largely on this reporting, deal with a war that revealed much about Arab society, and the West's still troubled relationship with it.

Sandcastles is not meant to be a systematic or comprehensive work. Its aim is to convey a sense—perhaps a *feel* for—Arab society today. It meanders toward its destination, much like a caravan passing across the desert, calling at oases along the way. It is part scholarship and part journalism, with doses of travelogue, impression, anecdote, reflection, analysis. Its intended audience is the reader who is interested in the Middle East, but is also patient enough to follow along when the caravan digresses into history, literature or religious philosophy. I have tried not to be excessively Western—or, to use the term currently favored by critics, too "Orientalist"—in my perspective. Yet I cannot deny that the work is infused with liberal values, a product of the West, for which I make no apology. Some will say the book is too tough on the Arabs; others will call it too soft. My answer to both is that I have tried to inform, and to be fair.

SANDCASTLES

CHAPTER ONE

IRAQ

I THE ABBASID FLAVOR

THE FIRST TIME I saw Baghdad was in the mid-1980s, in the heat of the struggle with Iran. I had expected to find—as I had in Damascus and Cairo, the other great cities of the Arab heartland—a metropolis that bristled with soldiers, manning artillery in the parks or sitting behind machine guns in sandbag kiosks, guarding public buildings. But Damascus and Cairo at peace had seemed more on edge than Baghdad at war. I knew that Arab cities, routinely squeezed between an oppressive state and a smothering religion, were not by nature carefree, and Baghdad, in our own generation, has spilled its blood in revolutions, ethnic and ideological strife, in the wantonness of tyrants. Can Baghdadis, I wondered, be so accustomed to the violence that flows through the arteries of the society that they dismiss it with a shrug? Iranian armies were hammering at a frontier barely a hundred miles away. Yet Baghdad, whatever fears it was hiding, presented a face surprisingly free of tension, even playful.

My visit was in summer, when midday temperatures reach 110 degrees or higher. Sensibly, street life takes the afternoon off and resumes about six, when the heat abates. That is when Baghdadis awake from their naps, return to the bazaars, settle into seats in the coffeehouses. By the time the sun has vanished, central Baghdad has widened its diversions. Parents play with their children in the parks, and lovers stroll hand in hand on the promenade along the Tigris. By ten or so the avenues are noisy with traffic and dazzling with lights, the sidewalks dense with pedestrians. (During my visit, many were soldiers still in battle fatigues.) In street-corner restaurants, young men in brightly printed shirts sit in groups over beer or soft drinks. At midnight, the nightclubs, their music booming through the streets, welcome their first patrons. At two or three in the morning, kebab is still cooking over hot coals in dingy shops along the boulevards.

To be sure, the street scene changes from one district in Baghdad to the next. Once a small community clustered on the east bank of the Tigris, Baghdad has become a collection of diverse neighborhoods, stretching a dozen miles from north to south along the river's serpentine turns, and a half-dozen miles east to west on both sides of the river. Its population, only one hundred forty thousand at the turn of the century, has soared to more than four million. In growing, it has reached out not just to pave over farmland but to swallow neighboring towns and villages, each with its own name and distinct identity. Much of the space in between now contains agglomerations of high-rise apartments, urban scapes so commonplace to the eye that they could belong to almost any Third World city. But the towns and villages themselves were never completely digested, and as neighborhoods they have retained not only their historical names but much of their unique character. Together they make of Baghdad a multicolored mosaic of Iraqi history, the record of a people in the era of Islam.

In 762, the caliph al-Mansur of the Abbasid dynasty—the title "caliph" signifies successor to the Prophet Mohammed, and thus Islam's supreme authority, both temporal and religious—laid the first brick of his new imperial capital on the Tigris. By that time, hardly more than a century after Mohammed's conquest of Mecca, Muslim rule had spread along the southern shore of the Mediterranean to Spain, through Anatolia to the Caspian Sea in the north, and to Persia in the east. In establishing Baghdad, al-Mansur transferred the center of rising Arab power from the desert oases of Damascus and Mecca (Cairo did not yet exist) to the rich plains known as Mesopotamia. Legendary home of the Garden of Eden, the lands between the Tigris and Euphrates were already rich in history. The Sumerians had flourished there. Hammurabi and Nebuchadnezzar had reigned in Babylon, fifty miles to the south, and Alexander the Great, campaigning to extend his hegemony, had died in that city. The Persians had ruled an empire of their own from nearby Ctesiphon (al-Mada'in to the Arabs), from which they were driven in 637 in a battle that Iraqis today call the opening campaign of the eternal Arab-Persian wars. The victory at Ctesiphon turned the geographic perspective of the Arabs eastward, away from the Mediterranean, and in time Islamic armies would spread the faith to the Ganges, while Islamic ships would make converts as far away as the Pacific islands.

No less important, the Abbasids' decision to pitch their stakes on the Tigris exposed the Arab world to Persia's rich artistic and literary culture. While Muslim armies continued to advance, the influence of Persia caused a shift in social dominance among the Arabs from the austere and ardent warriors of the desert to a new class of merchants, craftsmen and scholars, who urbanized for all time the culture of Islam. By the ninth century, Baghdad not only was the capital of a great empire but was celebrated the world over for its intellectual and artistic creativity. Europe, having never fully recovered from the collapse of Rome, was still in the Dark Ages, its major cities no match for Baghdad. Caliph Harun al-Rashid presided over a court which far outshone that of the Frankish king Charlemagne, the most eminent of the Western monarchs. For the Arabs, it was a unique era, in which Muslim thinkers, as familiar with the philosophy of the Greeks as with the Koran, fought—ultimately, in vain—to bring Hellenistic rationalism into the interpretation of Islam.

Save for some decades in Samarra, the Abbasid dynasty reigned in Baghdad for five hundred years. Its dynamism, however, was exhausted centuries before that. The end came in 1258, when invading Mongols, encountering little resistance, sacked the city and slaughtered the last of the Abbasid caliphs. And so Baghdad retreated into oblivion, to play no real role in world affairs until the advent of the present era.

Unfortunately, few reminders of Abbasid glory remain in Baghdad. Part of the blame can be laid upon the Mongols and the other plunderers who followed them, but the fault is in larger measure nature's. Unlike Europe, or the hills around Jerusalem, Mesopotamia is not blessed with stone. The only building material offered generously by the land is mud, and until recently nearly every structure—dwellings, mosques, palaces, city walls and gates, bazaars—was built of mud brick. One of the consequences has been to give Iraq's cities and towns a bland sameness, a dull beige uniformity that blends into the generally flat terrain, offering little pleasure to the eye. Another has been to impose severe limits on the life span of its buildings.

It is true that, as long ago as Babylonian times, builders had learned that by baking the brick in kilns, they could make it nearly as durable as stone itself. But the process required fuel, and before oil the only fuel they knew was wood, which had to be imported at great cost, and often at great peril, from India or Lebanon or Africa. Moreover, once imported, wood was more economical to build with than to burn, which meant that most structures were framed in timber, then clothed in mud. Though Baghdad's architects knew how to shape bricks into complex domes and arches, they generally reserved the practice of this skill for public buildings. Most buildings unfortunately fell prey, in time, to termites, which ate the timbers, and weather, which eroded the mud. So, apart from a few noble brick structures, little remains in Baghdad that is more than a century old.

Still, the city has never fully lost its Abbasid flavor. What was the core of Baghdad a millennium ago, a community called Rusafa hugging the east bank of the Tigris, remains the core today. An earlier site, the so-called Round City, a fortress built by al-Mansur, was later abandoned and lost, even to archeologists. Settled by the Abbasids on returning from Samarra, Rusafa is known to visitors today as Old Baghdad. Like most Islamic cities, it has no central square, no parks and little open space. It is a warren of narrow, crooked thoroughfares clustered around the surviving brick buildings dating to the thirteenth century, the era of Abbasid decline. After the Mongol conquest, the face of the city changed very little. Philip K. Hitti, the eminent historian, notes in his book *Capital Cities of Arab Islam* that a map drawn by a Frenchman who visited Baghdad in 1651 was nearly identical to the maps the British drew when they seized the city from the Turks in 1917.

Rusafa's hub is the Mustansiriyah, built in 1234 as a university for studies in Islamic law, as well as in mathematics, astronomy and medicine. The main gate is elaborately decorated with calligraphy, Arab culture's most distinguished art form, but the true artistic emphasis was placed on the interior, a two-story rectangle embracing a courtyard the size of a football field, with a high arch on each face. Behind the double-tier of galleries that make up the interior walls are eight lecture halls, ninety small chambers designed for student quarters and a large library. Local lore holds that when the Mongols under Hulagu Khan, the grandson of Genghis Khan, swarmed into the city, he ordered all the books in the Mustansiriyah library thrown into the Tigris, which for days ran black from the print. The building, however, somehow survived. Even Hulagu, nicknamed the Prince of Destruction by Iraqis, could not raze its two-foot-thick brick walls. After Baghdad passed under Turkish rule in the sixteenth century, the Mustansiriyah was put to use variously as a secondary school, an inn, a military academy, a hospital and an army barracks. During my visit, the government's Department of Antiquities was renovating the building to return it to its original, Abbasid condition.

Surrounding the Mustansiriyah are ancient mosques, their domes and minarets visible from within the courtyard. The chant of the muezzins, meant to be audible to the students inside their chambers, is in our own day amplified by loudspeakers that carry it through the quarter. Just to the north lies the Abbasid palace, a few years older but of less certain parentage; historians are unsure which caliph built it, or how it was used, though it served the Turks as a fortress during their four hundred years of occupation. Designed to keep its interior rooms cool on the most fiercely hot days, the palace has three-foot-thick walls, pierced by vertical shafts that capture breezes from the roof and dispatch them below. Its arches, highly ornamented on both ceiling and facade, rise thirty feet from the level of the huge courtyard, creating galleries that provide sun-free access to any part of the building. Outside the palace is a promenade along the Tigris for strolling in pleasant weather. It looks downstream over the market area—the *souk*, among the most pervasive institutions of Arab culture—that lies adjacent to the Mustansiriyah's southern wall.

As an institution the Baghdad *souk* is probably unchanged since Abbasid

days, and in appearance only slightly modified. Standing on the ramparts
of the Mustansiriyah, I could see the crumbling plaster pillars with their
eroded capitals that fixed the market's boundaries. From above, the *souk*
is a square mile of small domes built by the Turks to cover the stalls inside.
Between them are tattered awnings, layered with dust, which appear to
have provided shade to generations of shoppers, and ugly sheets of cast-
iron to help keep out the rain. As I watched, crowds moved in and out.
Most of the women wore the traditional black *abaya*. Many of the men
were dressed in turbans and robes; later I learned they were Egyptian
peasants, working at jobs vacated by Iraqis who had been called away to
military service.

Inside the *souk*, the aisles are dark and narrow, the floors damp and
dirty. Most of the shops are tended by a single proprietor, listening to
music on a transistor radio or reading a newspaper or checking his stock
. . . on a small computer. The shoppers shuffle by slowly, stopping frequently to finger an item, the price of which is established by hard bargaining. Young boys slip through the crowd, carrying trays of coffee.
Occasionally, a donkey loaded with cardboard boxes comes by, a keeper
leading him lightly by the tether. Though the look is anarchic, the organization of the *souk* actually follows a familiar logic. The shops are clustered
into specialized sections, much like a Western department store—statio-
nery, toiletries, plumbing supplies, shoes, fruits, bolts of fabric for men's
suits, jewelry, housewares. There is a ladies' underwear *souk*, past which
the men are expected to hurry discreetly, and a doctors' and dentists' *souk*.
My favorite was the spice *souk*, with its open burlap bags displaying
powders of golden shades of brown and emitting heavy, pungent odors.
There is also a gold *souk*, where products are weighed, then sold, according
to the international price, with little or no bargaining. I had often wondered, in a society with no obvious class of conspicuous consumers, who
bought this gold. The answer, I was eventually told, is rural women, who
know they may, under Islamic law, be divorced at any time it suits a
husband's fancy, and so keep gold as an insurance policy for old age.

Just beyond the *souk*, parallel to the Tigris River, is Baghdad's celebrated
Rashid Street, the city's first modern thoroughfare and still its most intriguing. Construction began under the Ottomans in 1915, the year the
railroad arrived from Istanbul, and was completed under the British when
they took over after World War I. At the price of many leveled buildings,
the street was driven through the densest, most heavily populated section
of Old Baghdad, straight as the Champs-Elysées, wide enough for two
vehicles to pass. It was a street of arcades, shaded by overhanging balconies,
sheltering modern shops. Initially called New Street, it was renamed in
1921 on the occasion of the founding of the Hashemite kingdom, Baghdad's

first Arab government in seven hundred years. The new name commemorates Harun al-Rashid, greatest of the Abbasid caliphs. (Al-Rashid, an honorific title, means "follower of the right path.") In recent years, Baghdad has acquired busier and more stylish thoroughfares, and the shops along Rashid Street have grown shabby. Now it is the street of banks and old mosques, coffeehouses and schools and art museums. But it has remained, withal, the spine of the modern city.

Adjacent to Rashid Street lies a web of alleys wide enough only for the passage of two men or a loaded donkey, the principal vehicle of transport in Islamic cities until modern times. The worn structures that line both sides evoke bourgeois life of a century ago. Squeezed against one another, Baghdad's old homes reveal only a flat, windowless wall to the passerby. The traditional Islamic city showed little concern for exterior aesthetics; even now, Arabs seem not to notice their streets and cover them with litter. Some observers explain this indifference to public space as an outgrowth of Islamic culture's fixation on privacy, on conducting social life only inside the home. The major exterior charm of these narrow streets is on the second level, where screened, overhanging balconies, called *shanashils*, cast shadows on the pavement below. *Shanashils* are the source of much Baghdadi legend. Often elaborately adorned with carved or paneled wood, they have evoked tales of secret signals between lovers, of daring escapes, of vigilant women collecting gossip. Handsome *shanashils* are still visible in some of Baghdad's older quarters but are poorly maintained; most are in advanced states of deterioration.

Baghdad's traditional houses, like its palaces, were invariably arranged around a courtyard, where there was always some shade; it was the only space used in common by men and women. Until economic factors forced them to move to modern homes and apartments, Baghdadis used space far differently than Westerners. The traditional house was sharply divided into the *diwankhana*, for the men and their guests, and the *haram* (the "sacred" or "forbidden" precinct) for the women, who rarely if ever left their domain. The men took their meals together, seated on the floor; the women served them; family ceremonies in which the sexes participated together were rare. Virtually without furniture, these houses had only rugs and cushions to adorn bare floors and walls. Family members slept not in assigned rooms but wherever the search for comfort led. Carrying their mattresses, they moved to the roof on hot nights, to the *shanashil* in winter, to the courtyard in spring, and to rooms off the courtyard or even to vaulted basements to nap on summer afternoons. Scholars attribute these practices to a bedouin heritage, lost to modern Baghdadis, most of whom now live like Westerners in dwellings where air-conditioning overrides the climate. Generally women still remain apart from men, though even this practice seems to be fading with the generations.

Abu-Nuwas Street is another index of change in Baghdad's ways. Just as Rashid Street was the city's response to the invasion of the automobile, Abu-Nuwas Street—which begins at the al-Jumhuriya Bridge, where Rashid Street ends—was its response to the invasion of Western secular values. Appropriately, the street is named for the Abbasid era's favorite poet, a friend of Harun al-Rashid and the son of a Persian washerwoman, a composer of erotic and bacchanalian songs and a bon vivant. Though by Western standards Abu-Nuwas Street is tame, by Islamic standards it is naughty, far naughtier than anything on public display in Cairo or Damascus, and for that Baghdadis love it.

In the parks that extend between Abu-Nuwas Street and the Tigris, young men and women have been known to kiss. In spacious open-air cafes, men of diverse ages, and even a few women, sit until the morning hours beneath strings of bare lightbulbs drinking not just tea and soft drinks but whiskey and beer, while listening to American rock music or Arab love songs piped over loudspeakers. The street is also celebrated for colorful restaurants, improvised of straw mats attached to trees, but with tile tubs in which fish swim while waiting to be grilled on the wood fires that burn on the floor. Though shabby, the restaurants are expensive, a tribute to the delicacy of the dish, called by Baghdadis *mazgouf*, a fish said to be unique to the Tigris. Even more than for the outdoor cafes and restaurants, Abu-Nuwas Street has won fame for its nightclubs, honky-tonk showcases for buxom belly dancers, nestled among three or four blocks of seamy bars and shady hotels. It occurred to me that Abu-Nuwas, unlike any other Arab street I knew, was Iraq's way of proclaiming its defiance of old-fashioned religious strictures and its quest for a place in the modern world.

II   TUG-OF-WAR

THE TUG-OF-WAR between secularism and religion is, perhaps, the central issue the Middle East faces today. Even before the breakthrough in the peace talks in 1993, it came to supersede in importance the long, obsessive conflict with Israel. In doctrinal terms, the Islamic religion does not acknowledge that there is a secular side to life. Religion, to Muslims, is more than human beings' relationship with God; it governs their entire relationship with society. A true Muslim recognizes no human activity that is independent of celestial guidance. Politics and sex, the bonds of family and friendship, eating and drinking, business and the conduct of war, all are subject to religious rules. Islam asserts that its jurisdiction is absolute, that its laws are all-encompassing. Muslims who argue that the modern world makes its own demands, grouped under the heading of secularism, stand on shaky theological ground. Many Muslims, in fact, regard such a belief as tantamount to a rejection of Islam. The "modern" Muslim is thus on the defensive. It is the extremists, claiming to carry God's banner, who today define the Islamic way of life.

The extremists have another advantage. Unlike Judaism—whose doctrines emerged only after the exile in Egypt and the wandering in the desert—and unlike Christianity—which started as a small and persecuted Jewish sect, improvising its theology as it grew—Islam was born, so to speak, full-blown. Mohammed was recognized from the start as prophet and leader. The Koran was revealed to him in its totality by God and provided all the doctrine that was needed. The era of his personal leadership was one of virtually uninterrupted triumph. Islam, within a few decades of his famous *hegira* from Medina to Mecca, not only rose to the status of a major religion but served the Arabs as the vehicle for creating an empire, spreading a language, building a culture. It is small wonder that Arabs regard their first days together as their Golden Age, from which they have ever since slipped steadily downhill.

With Islamic dogma buttressed by a triumphant history, Arab thought is uncomfortable with the notion of a better future—at least in this world. In contrast to Judaism and Christianity, it has difficulty absorbing the idea that mankind is destined to progress, or that innovation can bring improvement to life. On the contrary, conventional thinking, lamenting the loss of Arab preeminence, holds deviation from the true and revealed faith to blame for the decline. The Islamic concept of reform rejects what is new in favor of a model based on the lost utopia. The *hajj* to Mecca, one of the few duties rigorously imposed on the believer, is meant as a palpable reminder of that utopia. Islam's indifference to the idea of human progress generally permits "modern" Muslims to make their case only with arguments external to the faith, and encourages in extremists a fanaticism which insists that a higher order of life may be found only by going backward.

These extremists—called fundamentalists in the West—have organized in every Arab country with the aim of taking control of the state. Their organizations vary in size, in temperament and in tactics, but they are a dynamic force everywhere in the Arab world, and they share a determination to impose their definition of Islamic life on the society as a whole. The people arrayed against them are not necessarily antireligious, much less anti-Islamic, but they tend to perform their religious duties more casually and see fundamentalism as a major threat to economic and social development. These people tend to come from the educated classes, esteem Western values and support secular government, even when it is oppressive. Marx would not recognize the divisions in Arab society. They create not a class but a culture war, and it is a war in which the secularizing forces are at a serious disadvantage. Most Arabs perceive the war as a contest between modernism and medievalism, and recognize that its outcome will establish for decades or more the character of the world in which they live.

Religion was surely at the heart of the war that Iraq, a secular state, fought against Iran, a fundamentalist state, from 1980 to 1988. In saying this, I do not dismiss the importance of the personal ambitions of Saddam Hussein and the ayatollah Khomeini, or the imperatives of the historical rivalry between Iraq and Persia. These factors notwithstanding, however, most Arabs understood that at stake was not just which state would prevail but the social and cultural system that the victor was likely to impose on the region as a whole.

Complex as the conflict between secularism and fundamentalism is throughout the Arab world, in Iraq it contains elements that are not present elsewhere. In, say, Egypt or Syria, almost all of the population is Sunni, that is, members of Islam's mainstream sect. In contrast, though Iraq's population is 95 percent Muslim, more than half is Shiite, that is, members of a dissident Islamic sect. The situation is complicated further in that a majority of Iraq's Sunnis are Kurds, who inhabit the hills in the north of the country and are ethnically and culturally distinct from the Arabs. Iraq's Kurds consider themselves to be part of a people who occupy a large and contiguous area which they call Kurdistan and which extends into Iran, Turkey, Syria and even the Muslim republics of what was the Soviet Union. The Kurds nearly attained nationhood in the peace settlement after World War I, when the colonial powers were redrawing the map of the Middle East. But the dream vanished after the discovery of oil on Kurdish lands, which persuaded the British to incorporate them into its Iraqi mandate. Since 1920, the Kurds' reluctance to be assimilated into Iraqi political life has been a challenge to Baghdad, taking its place next to the Sunni-Shiite rivalry as an obstacle to national cohesion.

The schism between Sunnis and Shiites began thirteen hundred years ago in a doctrinal dispute that, even then, was political in substance. In the absence of a Koranic doctrine of succession, two rival factions sought to assume leadership on the death of the Prophet. The Sunnis—whose name is taken from the word for "tradition"—were led by the Omayyads, an aristocratic family from Mecca, which favored selection of a successor by a *shura*, a kind of electoral college. (Arab democrats today seek to legitimize their beliefs by pointing to the historical precedent of the *shura*.) The

Shiites—from the word for "partisan"—were led by Ali, Mohammed's son-in-law, whose followers argued that keeping the caliphate in the Prophet's family would keep the new religion free of political intrigue and manipulation and assure its spiritual purity. When Ali, who became the fourth caliph, was murdered in 661, his supporters contended that the succession should pass to his sons. In losing the contest to the Omayyads, the Shiites became perpetual dissidents within Islam. Iraq, unlike any other Arab country, is burdened by the weight of the Shiites in its population, as well as by the proximity of Iran, the leading Shiite nation, as its principal historical enemy.

Although social and economic issues have in the course of thirteen centuries widened the breach between Sunnis and Shiites, politics remains at the heart of their differences. Islam, recognizing no government outside the faith, has long had difficulty in defining government's role. The Koran provides little guidance. While Muslim governments throughout history have had secular leaders, they have traditionally based their claims to legitimacy on their faithfulness to the *shari'a*, the code of Islamic law. Sunnis have been satisfied with this arrangement. Shiites, more ardent practitioners of the faith, have never been comfortable with it, preferring clerical rule.

For as long as the caliphate linked the state with the faith, fundamentalism was unknown among Sunnis. An exception occurred in Arabia, where the triumph of the Wahabi sect two centuries ago imparted an austere fundamentalist cast to what is now the Saudi regime; but Wahabism never passed into the Arab world at large. Sunni fundamentalism was born only after the collapse of the Ottoman empire and the attendant abolition of the caliphate in 1924, which left the Islamic community of believers—the *umma*—without universally recognized leadership. Since then, Sunni fundamentalists have joined the Shiites in leaning toward theocracy, and have borrowed heavily from Shiite doctrine to bolster their own dogmas.

During the four centuries that they occupied Iraq, the Ottomans relied heavily on local Sunnis to help them rule. As Sunnis themselves, they were more comfortable with their local counterparts; they also distrusted the Shiites for their constant trafficking with Iran. This Ottoman favoritism intensified the estrangement of the Shiites from the state. Though individual Shiites prospered, the community as a whole became Iraq's permanent underclass. Meanwhile, Iraq's Sunnis (more precisely, its Sunni Arabs, not its Sunni Kurds) emerged as a ruling elite, a status they never gave up. To this day—under the rule of Saddam Hussein—they make major exertions to retain it.

The rivalry of Sunnis and Shiites—along with that of Arabs and

Kurds—lies at the heart of Iraq's long-standing reputation as a country difficult to govern. These strong subcultures make modern Iraq the most heterogeneous of the Arab countries. One Thursday evening in 1987, this heterogeneity was dramatized to me in visits to Kadhimiyah and al-Mansur, two of Baghdad's most sharply contrasting neighborhoods. On Thursday after dark, Baghdad is at its liveliest, especially in the summer, when everyone lives out-of-doors. Though Islam does not recognize a sabbath—that is, a day endowed with special holiness—Arab countries generally designate Friday as a day of rest. Most Arabs use the free time for contemplation or retreat, in the company of family and close friends. But Baghdadis, both Sunni and Shiite, being less devout than other Arabs, know they can sleep late on Friday, and set aside Thursday evening for frolicking.

I spent half of that Thursday evening in al-Mansur, an upper-middle-class neighborhood that might be called "trendy" Baghdad. It is totally, or nearly totally, Sunni. Named for the Abbasid caliph who founded the city, it contains embassies, a few small government ministries, a race track, a bustling business district, clusters of elegant homes, and rather little history. The mosques are undistinguished in design and seem to have few patrons, and the chant of the muezzin is practically inaudible in the din of traffic. Al-Mansur, though hardly a rival to Paris or Rome, is the only section of Baghdad that claims to be chic. The war had deprived its shops of imports but merchants made good use of local manufacturers in trying to be stylish, not only in men's and women's dress but even in the handsome outfits laid out in the shop windows for children. Al-Mansur had art galleries and video shops and the only stores in the city that sold running shoes and bathing suits (though no bikinis). It also had an ice cream parlor, in front of which young and old Baghdadis stood in orderly lines, to walk away licking chocolate and vanilla cones.

I arrived at al-Mansur at about 10 p.m. that Thursday, when the main avenue was bumper-to-bumper with Toyotas and Brazilian-made Volkswagens, Iraq's most popular cars. At the wheel of many of them were young men who waved at friends, tooted their horns and scanned the sidewalk for girls. Apart from a few Saudis in white robes, all the strollers on the tightly packed sidewalks were in Western dress. Teenagers generally favored T-shirts and jeans; pushing strollers, young parents wore well-groomed sports clothes; the soldiers on leave looked crisp in khaki and olive-drab; smartly clad couples hurried by, as if late for their dinner reservations at some swank private club. Al-Mansur was known for fine restaurants, as well as for small cafes where kebabs were grilled over white-hot coals. It was also notable for the three or four McDonald's-like fast-food shops, down to the bill of fare posted above the counter in English. Inside, adolescent boys and girls loitered about, sipping soft drinks from paper cups, smoking, flirting.

After an hour or so of enjoying the street scene, I sat down for a coffee on the terrace of a cafe whose name translated as "The Garden" and struck up a conversation with a neatly dressed young man seated at an adjacent table. He told me he was a student and, with obvious pride, that he was soon to marry a "modern girl," a research scientist in a government lab. He was quick to add, however, that being modern had no bearing on her virtue, which he expected to be intact on their wedding night. He also expected his family to be faithful to tradition, by requiring him to produce a bloody handkerchief by morning. Many young Iraqis, he acknowledged, "play tricks," like drawing blood from a finger, to placate the family. He added that he had a friend in medical school who would donate a vial or two of blood, in case of need. Brides, he informed me, still ran personal risks in the absence of such proof, and in the countryside might even be killed, though he assured me that in Baghdad killings were rare. As we both rose to leave, I asked him whether he and his fiancée would join me one evening for dinner. He hesitated, then ruefully declined. She was not so modern, he said, that her parents would permit her to go out after dark with him, much less with a man they did not know.

From al-Mansur, I taxied to Kadhimiyah, the city's bastion of traditional Shiism, which dazzled me with people and light. About five miles upriver from the Mustansiriyah, a half-hour cab ride from al-Mansur, Kadhimiyah had grown as a town around a cemetery for the Quraysh, the Prophet's clan, predating Baghdad by more than a century. As a Shiite burial place, the town was from its earliest days a center of religious devotion. In the sixteenth century, an elaborate mosque was built there, with two huge domes and four minarets coated in gold leaf. Today, the mosque adjoins a *souk* whose alleys contain some of Baghdad's most beautiful (albeit tragically dilapidated) *shanashils*. Night and day, I had observed earlier, the Kadhimiyah Mosque is a hub of intense activity. But on a Thursday evening in summer, under the glow of green neon lights festooning the minarets and flashing bulbs strung between the domes, with water soaring from an illuminated fountain in the public square, everyone in the ancient town seemed to be out, either relaxing in the courtyard of the mosque or promenading on the adjacent streets.

The crowd within the walls of the mosque, mostly women, differed in character from the promenaders on the street. Dressed uniformly in black *abayas*, the women looked worn from overwork, bad diet, poverty. Most wore veils. Those who did not, when they saw me looking, reproachfully raised a black scarf to their faces, momentarily concealing bad teeth and tattoo marks. Surrounded by children, many of them nursing babies, they gossiped in alcoves built into the courtyard wall, or rested their backs against the marble sides of the shrine itself. They smoked, drank water from thermos jugs or dozed. Some spread blankets on the pavement and picnicked with their families, consuming chickens and flat bread and watermelon, leaving behind the remains to be swept up later. The women seemed also to have taken charge of commerce at the mosque. Squatting on straw mats at the main gate, they assumed from the drape of their *abayas* the shape of cones, selling nuts and candy, balloons, soft drinks and tea. A few held their hands out to beg and seemed to bring in as many coins as those who were in business.

The women who strolled in the streets were clearly of another social class. They were younger and healthier, and they carried themselves more stylishly, even when they were leading children. Few were veiled, and I saw no tattoos. Many wore lipstick and makeup, particularly around the eyes. Although they, too, had on *abayas*, they draped them loosely, revealing colorful dresses and jewelry underneath. Many showed high heels and slim ankles below their hemlines. Though most women grouped themselves into twos and threes, some walked at the side of men, though rarely arm in arm, and never hand in hand. The shops they passed, unlike the windows in al-Mansur, were poor but the promenaders, examining one another instead, seemed no less cheerful.

Profoundly Shiite as Kadhimiyah is, it is an island in the overwhelmingly Sunni sea that is Baghdad and its environs. To reach the Shiite heartland, one must venture south across the fertile plains of Mesopotamia. The road I took, newly paved and four lanes wide, passed through the center of busy market towns and along the edge of mud-brick farming villages that wore haloes of television antennas. The land was relentlessly flat, too flat to be beautiful, but, despite a rainless summer, irrigation had turned much of it a lush green. There were no forests, but groves of trees periodically appeared. Children tended flocks of sheep or goats. Small herds of cattle and, occasionally, water buffalo collected in and around the irrigation canals. Tractors, standing in the fields, announced the adoption of modern cultivation techniques while antiaircraft batteries, pointing skyward atop high mounds adjacent to bridges and overpasses, were reminders of the presence of the war. The tractors and guns joined the heaps of trash along the roadside— abandoned automobile carcasses, tires, oil drums and plastic bags, the detritus of economic development—to proclaim the intrusion of modern man upon ancient Mesopotamia.

Karbala and An Najaf, respectively sixty-five and one hundred miles south of Baghdad, are the sacred cities of the Shiites, nearly as holy to them as Mecca itself. An Najaf is eternally linked to Ali, the son-in-law of Mohammed. Shiite tradition holds that Ali's dying wish, after receiving fatal stab wounds in 661, was to be placed on a loose camel and interred wherever it knelt. An Najaf became his burial place. His sons, Hussein and Abbas, were buried at Karbala. Throughout the Iraq-Iran war, the ayatollah Khomeini, claiming to be the guardian of Ali and his descendants, exhorted his troops to liberate the holy cities, to save them from the desecration of the enemy infidels. Compared to Baghdad, I found Karbala and An Najaf somber cities, where the people seldom smiled. Poverty was the prevailing human condition. Indoors and out, few women appeared without veils and *abayas* which, hot as it was, they wrapped tightly around themselves.

In both Karbala and An Najaf, the great Shiite shrines are at the end of a long avenue, which makes the initial view—the domes and piercing minarets in silhouette—startling, even awesome. Though the shrines differ slightly in design, all are in style and scale similar to the Kadhimiyah Mosque. Once inside the walls, my eye explored a courtyard the size of a grand piazza, then focused on the sides of the mosque, covered in brightly colored, inlaid mosaic tiles, arranged in intricate patterns, predominantly in hues of blue. Pillars support a roof that leans over to shade the high, arched entrance. Above it is a cupola of small mirrors deftly arranged to catch the sunlight. Not being a Muslim, I was forbidden to enter the shrine. But, having removed my shoes, I was permitted to stand at the door and peer inside, to see a tomb about the size of a railway car, with men and women in dark-colored robes crowding around to touch, even to kiss, its surface of hammered gold.

Late one morning, in the courtyard of the Hussein Mosque in Karbala, I watched a grim procession wind through the main gate carrying the caskets of three soldiers killed in the war. The Iraqis call their war dead *shaheed*, which translates as "martyr." Unlike other dead, I was told, a martyr is buried unwashed and fully dressed, a symbol of his inherent purity as defender of the homeland, the family and the faith. The army placed martyrs' bodies in flag-draped coffins, which were sent home for burial on the roofs of taxis; on any day, it was normal to see many such taxis on the road headed north from the battlefields around Basra. While I watched in the courtyard the three bereaved families played out the funeral rites. The women huddled together shrieking, doing terrible contorted dances, chanting dirges, pulling their hair. Standing not far away, the men slapped themselves sharply on the cheeks. I was told that the government now bans Shiite mourners from flagellating themselves with whips, a practice once common in Iraq and still common in Iran. Nonetheless, the scene was noisy, intimate, painful. After a quarter hour of public display, the mourners disappeared into the mosque, where the bodies were blessed in a ceremony which I was not permitted to witness. Within a half hour they emerged, each casket carried on the heads of two young pallbearers. An irregular line formed again and, to a backdrop of persistent moaning, the procession made its way slowly out the main gate and on to the cemetery.

Later that day, I visited the Ali Mosque in An Najaf, where I met the guardian, who was addressed as "imam" and who told me proudly that he was the ninth generation of his family to hold that post. He wore a turban in the style of the Iranian *mullahs*. As we talked, it occurred to me that this shrine, like the Hussein and Abbas mosques, was covered with scaffolding, and I asked the imam by what authority renovation work was taking place simultaneously on all three. He answered that the government provided the funds, on the orders of Saddam Hussein, who had generously approved not only the regilding of the domes and refinishing of the ceramic facings but the installation of modern air-conditioning in all the buildings.

As the imam and I spoke, I noticed on his wall a genealogical tree, and in response to my question, he told me that recent research had revealed Saddam to be a descendant of the Prophet. Saddam, I knew, would by no means have been the first to fabricate such a claim. Genealogical links to desert chieftains have always been important to Arabs, and descent from Mohammed is at the pinnacle of the hierarchy. Arabic even has a title, *sharif*, for the Prophet's descendants and, as one historian has noted, in Baghdad alone in the ninth century, the title had four thousand claimants. When I smiled skeptically, the imam seemed irritated, and insisted that the chart on the wall was conclusive proof of Saddam's genetic credentials.

It was at the Ali Mosque that the ayatollah Khomeini prayed during his thirteen years of exile in An Najaf. This was the period between his expulsion from Iran by the shah and his brief residence in France, which ended with his triumphant return to Teheran in 1979. When I asked where Khomeini had lived, the imam first insisted he did not know, then relented and led me about a hundred yards down a main street and into a network of alleys. The neighborhood was old but well preserved, and full of handsome *shanashils*. Large numbers of Iranians once lived there, the imam said, but most were expelled at the start of the war. The presence of Khomeini, who came every day to the mosque to pray, went largely unnoticed by Iraqis, who knew little of his political activities. His neighbors, however, strongly disliked him, the imam said, because he shouted at women and hit children. The story is told, according to the imam, that one day a neighbor's child struck Khomeini's grandson during a game and, in Iraqi fashion, the father appeared at Khomeini's door to apologize. Spurning the apology, Khomeini demanded vengeance and the opportunity for his grandson to strike back. True or not, the story spread far beyond An Najaf, to serve Iraqis as a parable on Khomeini's vindictiveness in pursuing the war against their country.

Not long after visiting Karbala and An Najaf, I traveled north into Kurdistan to see what I could of the third major group in the Iraqi community. Like that of the Shiites, the Kurds' commitment to the central government was diluted by other loyalties. Having never surrendered their yearning for a Kurdish state, they remained reluctant partners in the Iraqi mix. In the decades after World War I, they rose up repeatedly in quest of their independence, and they resumed the practice after World War II. In 1970, Saddam Hussein, then second-in-command of the Baath regime, put a temporary end to the Kurdish wars by negotiating an agreement permitting the exercise of Kurdish political rights. Under the agreement, Iraq established an autonomous Kurdish region, and though Saddam never really yielded the political autonomy he had promised, he delivered far more concessions—Kurdish as an official language, Kurdish administration of the local schools, the establishment of a Kurdish university, equal access by Kurds to government services—than they had ever had before. The concessions were also far more than the Kurds of Turkey, Iran or Syria had ever enjoyed.

My first stop in Kurdistan was Arbil, capital of the Kurdish autonomous region, which consists of three northeastern provinces. Though war raged along the border less than a hundred miles away, the city, populated by one hundred thousand Kurds, was considered safe. Architecturally, it looks much like Iraq's other cities, though, being higher and a bit cooler than the Tigris valley, it seemed on a summer day to exhibit more energy than either Baghdad or the Shiite cities. The men on the street left no mistaking their identity. Nearly all wore the traditional Kurdish costume of baggy pants, a short jacket, a cummerbund and sandals. Around their heads they wrapped a scarf into a loose turban, often positioned at a rakish angle. Some carried rifles, but nearly all wore in their belts the curved ceremonial dagger long associated with Kurds.

When the autonomy agreement negotiated by Saddam collapsed after only a few years, the Kurds justly blamed Baghdad's false dealing, but neither had they themselves been innocent parties. In clear violation of its terms, Kurdish leaders had maintained clandestine military relations across the mountains with Iran, which continued to supply their forces with weapons. In 1974, the Kurds rose up again and were suppressed a year later when the shah, in a deal with Saddam, abruptly turned his back on them. Under the agreement, the Kurdish forces withdrew into Iran, where they lived quietly until Khomeini resumed resupplying them, then turned them loose to renew guerrilla activity at the start of the Iraq-Iran war. Kurdish units in the field fought the Iraqis with limited success, but

Kurdish rebels also served as auxiliaries in the Iranian army, making the mountains east of Arbil into a danger zone.

During my visit in Arbil, I talked with Sirwan Abdullah Jaff, chairman of the executive council for the autonomous region, in one of the city's modern government buildings. Though a Kurd, Jaff had forsworn baggy pants for olive drab, the uniform of Baathi officials; his post was equivalent to provincial prime minister. Pompous in his style, Jaff claimed that his people overwhelmingly supported the autonomy system, and that Kurdish rebels were paid agents of Persian imperialism. "They have very few members," he said, "and they are pursued like criminals." Most of the pursuing forces were themselves Kurds, he said, fighting in Kurdish units loyal to Baghdad, wearing Kurdish insignia on uniforms with baggy pants. Diplomats in Baghdad had told me that at night the rebels were in control, particularly in the mountains, but the tranquillity that I saw in Arbil and the surrounding plains seemed to confirm Jaff's contention that, as a people, the Kurds were basically loyal to Iraq. As long as the enemy was Iran, the evidence was strong that most Kurds, like most Shiites, favored an Iraqi victory. But, as events in the spring of 1991 were to show, that was hardly the end of the story.

III   SEARCHING FOR ORDER

IRAQIS ARE FOND of saying that for seven hundred years they did not choose their own government, but even that is an understatement. For most of those centuries, there was no identifiable country called Iraq. After the Mongol conquest, even the name fell into disuse. In the countryside, the inhabitants divided themselves into tribes, hostile to one another and to the inhabitants of the cities. Under the Ottomans, Baghdad, Mosul and Basra became provincial capitals, but they were scarcely oriented toward the Sultan's court in Istanbul. The Sunnis of Baghdad looked west, in the direction of the Arab heartland. Mosul, a largely Kurdish city, was oriented northward, toward the Kurds of Turkey. The Shiites of the center depended on Persia, while those of Basra maintained ties with the Arabs of the Gulf and with India. None of the population, not even the favored Sunnis, thought of themselves as Ottomans, much less as Turks, but neither did they identify themselves as Iraqis. The only loyalty they shared, save for the few Christians and Jews who lived among them, was to Islam.

Nationalist ideology, imported from Europe via Istanbul, did not appear among Iraqis until the twentieth century. Moving south to Beirut, then eastward to Damascus, nationalism reached Baghdad, the most remote of the Arab capitals, only on the eve of World War I. It took root first among the Sunnis, leaving the others largely untouched. (Some say they are still untouched.) When an Iraqi state was created, after the Ottoman collapse, Great Britain governed it, under a mandate from the League of Nations, and being infidels, the British were considered more objectionable than the Turks. Iraq at last existed, but the struggle to create an Iraqi nation lay ahead; it is still far from over.

By 1920, the Iraqis—Sunni and Shiite together—had already risen up once against British rule. A year later, to appease demands for more local power, the British declared Iraq a monarchy and crowned as king the Hashemite prince Faisal, whose family had come out of Arabia to lead the celebrated Arab Revolt against the Turks and whose brother, Abdullah, the British had already placed on the Jordanian throne. With his unimpeachable nationalist credentials, Faisal was personally esteemed by Iraqis, but he had no illusions about the task that lay before him. In his classic study *The Old Social Classes and the Revolutionary Movements of Iraq*, Hanna Batatu quotes a memorandum written in 1922 by Faisal: "There is still—and I say this with a heart full of sorrow—no Iraqi people but unimaginable masses of human beings, devoid of any patriotic idea, imbued with religious traditions and absurdities, connected by no common tie, . . . prone to anarchy, and perpetually ready to rise against any government whatever. Out of these masses we want to fashion a people. . . . The circumstances being what they are, the immensity of the efforts needed for this (can scarcely be imagined)."

Unfortunately, Faisal was unequal to the task that he so eloquently described. Though Arab, he was identified more with the Arabian desert than with Iraq. More burdensome was his total dependence on the British, and though he gallantly resisted them, he could not escape their domination. They not only controlled his decisions; they also established a parliament weighted in favor of the landowning class, which was indifferent to the national cause and obediently legislated in behalf of British interests. Without commitment to the people, the regime did little to ameliorate the living conditions of the country's poverty-stricken masses. Only the rich—mostly Sunnis—acquired some stake in the Hashemite system. The Kurds wanted independence; the Shiites wanted theocracy. In this atmosphere, popular animosity to the mandate intensified, without popular allegiance to the monarchy ever taking root.

By the end of the 1920s, Nuri al-Said, an Ottoman officer who had defected to the British in World War I, had emerged as King Faisal's closest associate and the most powerful figure in Iraqi ruling circles. Under a treaty he negotiated in 1932, the British withdrew their forces from the country, acknowledging a nominal Iraqi sovereignty; Iraq was to have a national army, but it was still expected to do Britain's bidding. Some regarded the treaty as scarcely more than an exchange of the mandate for an indirect dependency. Opposition to British rule was the one popular issue among Iraqis, creating a proto-nationalism with an unpredictable dynamic. The soldiers of the Iraqi army, drafted under universal conscription, seethed with anti-British feeling, which turned them as well against the king, who under Nuri's influence was seen as hardly more than Britain's surrogate.

By the eve of World War II, Iraqis were demanding a political and social order that was authentically their own. They were not alone in the Middle East in their yearnings. Such feelings were shared by all the Arab states that had received their nominal independence in the decades after World War I. All resented the foreigners who exploited and humiliated them. Four centuries of Ottoman rule had left them without viable political institutions, or even much political experience. The Arabs at this stage still knew politics only as victims. Neither their religion nor their history provided constructive political guidance. Their models for the exercise of power were authoritarian, and their precedents for the transfer of power were violent. When independence finally arrived, not surprisingly they turned for leadership to their armies, their most cohesive institution.

In 1936, Iraq experienced its first military coup against the monarchy. It failed, but in 1941, with the British preoccupied by war in Europe, it had another. When a highly nationalistic clique within the army seized power, Iraqis considered it only natural that it should turn for support to the Nazis. Britain's response was to dispatch an expeditionary force to Iraq, and what became known as the second British occupation began. The throne that the British restored was occupied by young Faisal II, grandson of the dynasty's founder, but power was exercised by Nuri and the crown prince, Abd al-Ilah. They proceeded to hang or imprison the coup's leaders, an act of vengeance that only confirmed the monarchy's association with British colonialism. It triggered a feud between Nuri and the nationalists that, a few years later, ended in tragedy for the Iraqi throne.

The decade after World War II is remembered by Iraqis for riots and strikes, for the defeat of the Arab armies in Palestine and for a surge of militant nationalism, particularly among the Sunnis. It was also noteworthy for the rise of the Communist Party, based largely among Shiites and Kurds, the alienated underclasses. For several years, the Communists were Iraq's best-organized civilian institution. The monarchy, meanwhile, was rotting under the weight of political and economic corruption. By the early 1950s, talk of reform was giving way to a growing prospect of radical revolution.

In 1954, yielding to urging from the West, Nuri made the fatal misstep of joining the anti-Soviet alliance known as the Baghdad Pact, two of whose members were Britain and Iran. That Iraq should take sides in the Cold War, particularly in the company of its worst enemies, was intolerable to nationalists and to Communists alike. In Cairo, meanwhile, a new pan-Arab nationalism was flourishing under the leadership of Gamal Abdel Nasser, whose anti-Western rhetoric had won him the military support of Moscow. In 1956, Nasser took on heroic dimensions for many Arabs by emerging from the attack in the Sinai by Britain, France and Israel—paradoxically, with the help of the United States—with its territory intact. Nasser's demagogy intoxicated the Iraqi masses, eating away at the foundations of the Iraqi monarchy. Moscow's attraction to Nasser, meanwhile, left Iraq's Communists isolated. When Nasser, in the name of pan-Arabism, proclaimed Egypt's unification with Syria in 1958, Nuri countered by announcing Iraq's federation with Jordan, whose throne was occupied by King Faisal II's cousin, King Hussein. To Arab eyes, Nuri's move looked like a desperate effort to defend the pro-Western throne against the revolutionary force of Nasser's pan-Arab ideology.

The nationalists in the Iraqi army struck on July 14, 1958. They seized the palace in Baghdad and executed King Faisal II and Crown Prince Abd Al-Ilah. The next day, Nuri was discovered in disguise on a Baghdad street and promptly shot. After his burial, the mob disinterred his body and dragged it through the streets. The army's blood feud with Nuri and the monarchy had been consummated.

Abd al-Karim Qasim, head of the cabal that carried out the coup, declared Iraq a republic, and at first pledged to unite the country with Egypt and Syria. But almost immediately, he broke from the pan-Arab mainstream, by refusing to subordinate himself to Nasser, and outmaneuvered his rivals to make himself Iraq's president. He then turned to the Communists, who helped him put down a bloody military uprising in Mosul. Two weeks later, Qasim withdrew Iraq from the Baghdad Pact and signed an economic agreement with the Soviet Union. Iraq's Communists thought they had an ally, and Moscow was convinced it was a step closer to controlling the Middle East.

At the time, the Baath party was an obscure underground organization, largely Sunni, which supported Nasser's vision. On October 7, 1959, a young Baathi zealot named Saddam Hussein al-Tikriti tried to kill Qasim, firing shots on Rashid Street at a presidential motorcade. Qasim was wounded and Saddam escaped, but seventy-eight party members were rounded up and put on trial. The episode put the Baathis on Iraq's political map. Four years later, the Baath Party was strong enough to bid for power itself, and before the 1960s were over, it had won permanent control of the government.

In my visit to Iraq in 1986, I asked Tariq Aziz to explain to me this

astonishing rise. Aziz, a Christian, had been a Baathi since his student
days in the 1950s, and before entering government had worked as a journalist and a teacher of English. In April 1980, when he was minister of
information, a Khomeini supporter threw a grenade which wounded him
and killed several students, accelerating the rush to war. When I met Aziz,
he was the foreign minister and the most sophisticated member of Saddam
Hussein's circle.

"At the time of the revolution in 1958," Aziz said, "it is true the people
did not know or care very much about the Baath. Then, when it appeared
that Qasim's regime was being manipulated by the Communists, people
began to worry. The Communists were taking over a revolution they did
not make. In contrast to the Chinese Communists, who were always
Chinese, the Arab Communists were Soviet, and they referred to Arab
nationalism as 'chauvinism.' Most of their leadership was from minorities.
It was mainly Jews at the start, not only here but in Syria, Lebanon
and Egypt. Then, after the Jews left Iraq, it was Christian, Kurdish and
Armenian. This made the Communists an alien element. They were well
organized and knew how to seize opportunities but they were isolated from
the people.

"Qasim was not a Communist. He was a patriotic military adventurer
with great personal ambition. But in trying to use the Communists, he
made a strategic error. The reactionaries of the old regime were against
the Communists, of course, but so were the nationalists and most of the
progressives. The first priority of the established parties of the left—the
Communists, nationalists and progressives—was to maintain a loose unity
to avoid a restoration of the old regime, and so the others stood by while
Qasim gravitated into the embrace of the Communists. We were the only
party that took the Communists on. The Baath was small but well organized and bold, and could not be intimidated. It appealed to the patriotism
of the nationalists and to the social goals of the progressives. Old ladies
called themselves Baathists because it was prorevolution and anti-Communist. Gradually, the Baath came to be seen as the savior of the nation, even
by those who had little involvement in politics."

Committed to overthrowing Qasim and moving in secret, the Baath
recruited heavily in schools and universities, while infiltrating key units
in the army and building a civilian militia. Unconstrained by an aversion
to bloodshed, it made its first bid for power in February 1963, assassinating
the chief of the air force, then attacking the main radio station, the ministry
of defense and a series of military installations. The Communists fought
back bravely but hundreds of them, lacking firepower, were mowed down
by army tanks. On the second day of the coup, Qasim was captured and
summarily executed, and the Baath took charge. Its first move was to

embark on a campaign of terror, killing hundreds of opponents, mostly
Communists, while resuming the ongoing war against the Kurds. Notwithstanding their pan-Arab dogma, however, the Baathis emulated Qasim in
refusing an accommodation with Nasser. Some of the Baath leaders objected, and the party split into rival radical and moderate camps. Within
six months, party leaders were fighting among themselves and their rule
collapsed. The Baath government was replaced by a military cabal under
Abd al-Salam Arif, who organized a regime much like Qasim's.

"To understand why so much blood flowed in those days," Tariq Aziz
continued, "you have to remember that Iraqi history has no tradition of
political dissent. Nuri Said did not tolerate opposition. I was a student in
Nuri's day, and we had to smuggle books to read—I'm not talking about
Das Kapital but about Dostoyevski, Victor Hugo, Rousseau and Voltaire,
the kind of liberal books that are in any home library in New York or
Paris. In fact, as Baathis, we were far more influenced in those days by
liberal than by Marxist ideas. We had respect for the ideas of the French
Revolution and the Industrial Revolution. We simply wanted to get rid of
a reactionary regime. Nuri Said, who was a product of Ottoman times, set
the tone by executing and torturing many Baathists, in fact almost anyone
who opposed him.

"The Communists under Qasim continued this practice. The ideas of
the Baath were at first democratic. We wanted to reach our goals democratically, but under the monarchy there were no means to do it, no electoral
system to achieve power by legal procedures. Revolution was our only
choice. The Communists used killing and torture, and we retaliated. When
they took to the streets in 1963, we had to stop them. It was not our policy
to use force. But we were its first victims, and the Communists left us no
other means for dealing with them.

"Our weakness when we took power in 1963 was that we were inexperi-
enced and incapable of running a government. Remember that most of our
party members were very young men. The Arif regime, which succeeded
us, was rightist, militarist, nationalist, pan-Arab and not much stronger
than we had been. It was also reactionary, in the South American sense,
meaning corrupt. We reacted to it by going underground to rebuild our
support but, justifiably, Iraqis remained skeptical of us. We had to prove
that we had matured, that we would not make the same mistakes if we got
back into power. In the succeeding years we replaced our old leadership
with a totally new leadership, and when we returned in 1968, we were
ready to govern."

Debilitated by dishonesty and drift, the Arif regime—like every other
in the Arab world—was humiliated in June 1967 by the catastrophic defeat
that the Arabs suffered at the hands of Israel. In its wake, the Communists

resumed their active quest for power, while the Baath, purged of its hard-line leadership, adopted more pragmatic positions. On July 17, 1968, supported by dissident military units, the Baathis conducted a coup which was so well organized—a "white revolution," they called it—that Arif's military government fell without a shot being fired. But, predictably, the revolution's pristine character was soon marred. Within months, nearly one hundred Iraqis, of whom some were Communists, some right-wingers and some Jews accused of spying for the Israelis, were summarily tried and executed, most of them in Baghdad's main square.

"We have never asked for a monopoly of power," Aziz said. "The democratic tendencies among us are still alive. But we have a vision to protect, and we do not intend to adopt the British or American system of government to do it. After the revolution of 1968, we proposed to establish a national front, and we opened a dialogue with the Communists, the Nasserites, the Kurds and others. We were ready at that point to have normal relations with them. We were willing to let the Communists reorganize their party and have a newspaper, but they also wanted power inside the army. They wanted a secret organization, which would permit them to plot another coup d'état. We would not permit it, and when they insisted, we had to punish them.

"The Communists were not the only threat to the revolution. We are equally ready to punish a member of Al-Dawa [a fundamentalist, Shiite group linked to Iran], because he is not a patriot. We will not tolerate someone who cries 'Down with the government.' But that does not mean we will tolerate no dissent. We will not punish a professor who criticizes the ministry of higher education. If someone doesn't like the way we are running the government and wants to discuss alternative ideas with us, we will listen. But we did not then and we do not now tolerate conspiracies. We will not allow a foreign government"—the reference was to the Soviet Union—"to send a penny to help Iraqi Communists substitute their revolution for ours."

Within a few months of the coup of 1968, Saddam Hussein, though officially second in command, had emerged as the dominant member of the new regime. Saddam was born in poverty in 1938 in the small Sunni city of Tikrit, about a hundred miles north of Baghdad. Orphaned at a young age, he spent most of his youth in the home of an uncle, Khairallah Talfah, an army officer whom the British had jailed for five years for participating in the nationalist uprising of 1941. Saddam idolized his uncle, whose son, Adnan Khairallah, was his best friend and later his defense minister, and whose daughter, Sajida, later became his wife. At eighteen, having attended school only sporadically, Saddam moved to Baghdad, where he was caught up in the pan-Arab fervor against the Baghdad Pact.

He joined the Baath Party, probably at the suggestion of Khairallah's cousin, Ahmad Hassan al-Bakr, who would later be Iraq's president. Saddam became known as a tireless activist, and in 1959 he willingly joined the plot to assassinate Qasim. During his ensuing exile, he visited Damascus, then took up residence in Cairo, where he completed high school and enrolled in the university to study law. At age thirty, he returned home, and again attached himself to Bakr, who was then prime minister. Though meagerly educated, lacking polish and with a limited knowledge of the outside world, Saddam moved up rapidly in the Baathi hierarchy. He was intelligent and charismatic, showed an aptitude for resolute action in the violent world of Iraqi politics and was willing to play the game of power for high stakes.

As the strong man of the regime, Saddam compiled an impressive record in the 1970s. He outmaneuvered the army to concentrate decision-making in the civilian wing of the Baath party. He negotiated the autonomy agreement with the Kurds. He presided over the nationalization of the oil fields, the last remaining symbol of foreign hegemony in Iraq and the source of its future wealth. He went to Moscow and returned with a treaty establishing a strategic alliance which brought Soviet arms without significant domestic intrusion. He poured subsidies upon the Shiites, presided over the development of a socialist economy and a welfare state and made significant progress in getting both children and adults, female as well as male, into schools. He also purged the bureaucracy, imparting to it a reputation for integrity beyond anything Iraq had known before and, to demonstrate the party's seriousness, he routinely executed officials, including ministers, accused of financial corruption.

At the same time, Saddam reshaped the party from an underground elite into a huge security apparatus, operating in secrecy to monitor every Iraqi in virtually every aspect of life. In the key positions he placed only his most loyal supporters, chiefly his blood kin from Tikrit. Their presence in high positions became so conspicuous that prudence ordained the adoption of a lower profile. Since Arab surnames are often taken from the family's home city, Saddam ordered all Tikritis to drop their last names. That is how Saddam Hussein al-Tikriti became simply Saddam Hussein. His concentration of power made Iraq the most totalitarian of the Arab regimes, and though many Iraqis resented the hegemony of the Tikritis, most delighted in the accomplishments produced by unprecedented national prosperity, as well as in the clear rise in Iraq's international standing.

"The rules are strict, very harsh by our standards, but they are not arbitrary," said a Western diplomat who had spent many years in Baghdad. "The government does not go around brutalizing people for its own sake. The security services are tight. The telephones are tapped. Most Iraqis will not talk to foreigners without official authorization, and we are never invited to their homes. The war against Iran has demanded greater discipline, but I see little resistance to it. Every Iraqi knows the rules, and as long as he does not challenge them, he is unlikely to get in trouble.

"This government is authoritarian, but it is not necessarily unjust. Executions have taken place since I've been here, on charges of corruption, but I think the charges have been corroborated. The rule of thumb is that the higher the office, the greater the likelihood of being hanged for corruption. The other side of the coin is that you don't see officials driving around in big limousines, as in Russia. Saddam himself is said to live rather modestly, and the people like him for that.

"It is true that the middle class, which has grown tremendously under the regime, yearns for more freedom, but the freedom it wants is to travel and consume rather than to dissent. I see very little demand for civil liberties. No one advocates restoring the parliament, because the pro-British landowning class left the last parliament with such a bad reputation. The comparison may be thin but, whatever the criticisms, the regime is unquestionably the best Iraq has had for centuries. It has a sense of purpose, a direction. It is honest, it is efficient, it is paternalistic, in that it has demonstrable concern for the poor. It has even mellowed over the years. But it is certainly not soft."

In 1979, Saddam maneuvered his former patron, Ahmad Hassan al-Bakr, out of office and took the title of president, thus gaining officially the powers he already exercised in fact. And before long he initiated a cult of personality around himself. His picture appeared in the press every day. He was forever on television, not only for official pronouncements but even to urge children to study hard and brush their teeth. His role in the attempted assassination of Qasim in 1959 was transformed into legend. His style of dress, his manner of speech, his mustache, were widely imitated among party members. Many Iraqis even wore wristwatches with his face on the dial. When he began to slim down after putting on a middle-age belly, half of Iraq went on a diet. Even in private conversation, he was routinely referred to as "Our great president Saddam Hussein," a formula usually followed by "May God preserve him." He had the newly built airport and a working-class suburb named for himself, as well as the new art center. Monuments to his glory went up throughout the city. And, as every visitor to Iraq has noted, his portrait became ubiquitous, on display not just in public buildings but in cafes, in the living rooms of private homes, along roads, in hotel lobbies, in the town square of even the remotest village.

"I know you won't believe me when I say that nearly all of this is spontaneous," Tariq Aziz said, giving some clue to how Saddam Hussein could lose all sense of his own limitations. "You Americans have a different experience. Since Hammurabi we have lived without ever electing a head of state, so we have a different feeling toward leadership. In this part of the world, we have an instinctive love for our leader, if he really is a leader. The people in Egypt loved Nasser. They made poetry and sang for him. Iraqis loved and respected King Faisal I—though never Nuri Said. They loved Qasim for a while. Then they found Saddam Hussein, the symbol of their aspirations, who really cares for them. He is strong, he is an Iraqi like us, he raised himself from poverty and he leads the first government since the Abbasid era that is doing something for the people. He is also a romantic figure. There is something chivalrous about him which attracts both women and men.

"It is not within our capacity to manufacture a cult of personality. We can control what is hung in front of a government building, but we cannot order parents to hang a photo of Saddam Hussein in a child's bedroom. [But, according to Iraqis I know, they can—and do—apply considerable pressure through the party and the schools.] And yet it happens. Of course, the mass media make a contribution to Saddam's popularity. But it is the Iraqi people, not the press, that has made Saddam what he is. Saddam Hussein is in their hearts. That's why this government is secure. That's why Iraq today is stable."

IV   FREEDOM IS

IF SADDAM HUSSEIN is the Lenin of the Iraqi revolution, Michel Aflaq was its Karl Marx. Aflaq was a Christian from Damascus who, in the years before World War II, pondered how the Arabs, with their ethnic and religious diversity, could work together to build a modern society. Educated in Paris, he drew heavily from ideas then popular among French intellectuals. Aflaq's solution was Baathism—the word translates roughly as "renaissance." It was a political philosophy that he and a handful of his friends developed in secret party cells, in an era of growing disillusionment with the unrepresentative regimes of the Arab world. In 1949, a delegation of Aflaq's Syrian adherents founded the Baath party in Iraq.

Baathism was a set of ideas, never reduced to a coherent system, which Aflaq articulated over the course of many years in speeches and essays. These notions, rarely precise and often inconsistent, mixed analysis, mysticism and practical advocacy. Aflaq's transcendent vision was "one Arab nation with an eternal mission," an image that exalted Arabism over Islam—thereby leaving room for Christian Arabs—and fused nostalgia for Arab grandeur with the pan-Arab ideal. It never mattered to the Baathis that, save during the few years of the Prophet's life, there had never been Arab unity. Even during the Abbasid ascendancy, Arab Spain was ruled by the rival Omayyads, and Egypt by the rival Fatamids. But unity, touched by martial glory, remained lodged in the Arabs' historical memory, and the notion of its inevitable return, cultivated by Arab nationalists, became embedded in Arab dreams. Aflaq's rallying cry for the Baath Party was "unity, freedom, socialism," a philosophical triad which he spent much of his life trying to define; it is to this day the central tenet of Baathi sloganeering.

But Aflaq the thinker was no less a political activist, and in that capacity he fell out in 1966 with Syria's Baath regime, which proceeded to expel him from the country. Aflaq fled to Baghdad and, when the Baathis returned to power there in 1968, he took charge of a party headquarters dedicated to overturning Syria's preeminence in the Baath movement. Acting as the revolution's chief theoretician, Aflaq in Baghdad imparted ideological legitimacy to the regime of Saddam Hussein.

At the time of my first visit to Baghdad, Aflaq was already eighty and disinclined to appear in public. He had ceded the function of chief party ideologist to his deputy, Elias Farah. A Ph.D. in philosophy from the Sorbonne, Farah was a tiny, elegantly dressed man who received me in his large book-lined office at party headquarters. His answers to my questions resembled an academic lecture. Farah, like Aflaq, was a Christian, which was an indicator of the welcome that Baathism claimed to extend to all Arabs, Muslim and non-Muslim alike, and even to Kurds. It was this inclusive character which offended many Shiites, who took the superiority of their Islam more seriously than did most Sunnis, and it was the tenet that persuaded the ayatollah Khomeini that Baathism was heresy.

"Baathism," Farah told me, "is a secular philosophy, but it is not anticlerical, as secular ideas tend to be in Europe. It does not reject Islam. It could not. Islam is not just a religion, like Christianity. It is our civilization. It has forged the unity of the Arab world. In the cultural sense, I think of myself as Islamic, and so does Aflaq. Baathism respects Islam, as it respects all religions, for their spirituality. Islam is at the base of Baathism, but contemporary Arab society, divided and underdeveloped, needs to modernize itself. Baathism's goal is to strike a balance between cultural authenticity, of which Islam is the central element, and modernity. What we cannot accept is abuse of power by religion for political ends."

In his quiet, scholarly style, Farah drew upon Baathi ideology to discredit, even to delegitimize, Iraq's principal enemies, Syria and Iran. Syria's regime, though Baathi in name, was a deformation of Baathi philosophy, he said, a distortion to permit the Alawites, a religious minority, to rule through the instrument of the armed forces. As for the Khomeini regime, he argued not only that it was "the antithesis of modern civilization," but that it exploited Islam to serve Persian nationalism, largely by using Shiism as an instrument of Persian ambitions. Iraq's leaders, Farah said, worked tirelessly to erase distinctions between Sunnism and Shiism and have largely succeeded in unifying the nation. Now all Iraqis, he said, recognize Khomeini as a threat not just to the nation and to modernism but to Islam as well.

"To achieve the end of modernizing Iraqi society without violating its traditions," Farah continued, "Baathism cannot be rigid. We acknowledge a dependency on ideas coming from the outside, and we willingly draw from other ideologies current in the world today. We have much in common with Zionism, whose goal is a Jewish renaissance. Ours is an Arab renaissance, based on the creation of a new man and a new woman, liberated not only from colonialist dependency but from the shackles within our own civilization. Baathism has also drawn on Marxism, especially for its concepts of socialism, but we do not think of ourselves as a closed system, as the Marxists do. We are wary of dogmatism and we believe the Marxists are trying to substitute one set of theological absolutes for another. As for modern Western thought, its openness and sense of practicality are an important model. We reject Western colonialism but, unlike Khomeini, we do not confuse it with Western civilization, which we admire. Western liberal ideas are a guide for us. As Baathists, we are trying to build a society in a state of permanent evolution, and we will build it by engaging in permanent dialogue with other societies, and particularly with the West."

Farah explained that, in the decades after World War II, forward-looking Arabs faced a choice between Communism, Nasserism and Baathism, all competing for the Arab soul. Communism regarded nationalism as an obstacle to the rise of the international proletariat, and so rejected the concept of Arab national unity, he said, which is a fundamental value to the Baath. Nasserism strongly endorsed national unity but, focused as it was on a charismatic leader, was burdened with a shallow ideology, particularly in the economic realm. Baathism, while as strongly nationalistic as Nasserism, did not seek to impose a rigid uniformity on Arab society. "Baathism's position is that Arab unity has always been enriched by diversity," Farah explained, which is a very convenient tenet for Iraq, a society that is itself highly diverse and concerned with objectives of the Iraqi state more than those of the Arab world.

"Nothing is more important than personal freedom for all Iraqis—men and women, Sunnis and Shiites, Arabs and non-Arabs," he said. "This freedom is an essential goal, because we cannot think of the individual as a number, without a role in history. We don't believe democracy is simply placing ballots in a ballot box, or that freedom is the right to reverse the revolution. Our commitment is to a democracy that is socially involved, in which the masses participate in determining the nation's future. It is based on the national will, on the confidence of the people. Democracy and freedom are for us a response to the alienation of the individual."

I did not find it easy to grasp what Farah meant by "freedom," a term that seemed incongruous when applied to a state as oppressive as Iraq. Farah did not acknowledge any inconsistency in this regard in Aflaq's writings, but it was apparent that Aflaq himself had problems with the concept of freedom. In his writings, he sometimes used the term to mean individual freedom in the Western sense. More often, he used it to refer to freedom for Arab society from colonial domination. Sometimes, he spoke specifically of freedom for the Arabs from the bondage of old tribal, religious or regional loyalties. What emerged rather late in his thinking was a notion of freedom *for the state* to mobilize the citizenry, in any way that it saw fit, for what Aflaq called "the higher Arab national interest." Insofar as Saddam Hussein may be said to subscribe at all to the tenets of Baath ideology, this last definition, a rationale for virtually any abuse by the state of the individual, is surely the one he prefers.

Ironically, Michel Aflaq, in his grave, became himself a victim of the search for a "higher Arab national interest." When he died in 1989, the Iraqi government announced that, some time earlier, Aflaq had secretly converted from Christianity to Islam, and it proceeded to give him an Islamic burial. Some Arabs told me they were convinced Saddam had lied about the conversion and had inflicted on Aflaq a posthumous humiliation. Saddam, these critics said, no doubt reasoned that by Islamizing Aflaq, he would avoid reminding Iraqis of Baathism's Christian sources.

ONE OF THE COMMITMENTS of Baathism is to bring women into the mainstream of Arab life, rectifying the sexual discrimination, conventionally attributed to Islam, that has historically pervaded Arab society. Indeed, Arab fundamentalists have made male dominance, which they consider intrinsic to their religious beliefs, a central tenet of their political program. Yet historians generally agree that, in the early days of Islam, when women's work was vital to the society, the Prophet Mohammed took considerable pains to reform pre-Islamic practices that were oppressive to women. He enunciated women's rights to education and property, to choose a marriage partner, to attain sexual satisfaction, to earn and manage an income, to receive compensation in the event of divorce. On the other hand, he himself was not only polygamous but kept concubines, hardly a precedent for the equitable treatment of women. Furthermore, he did not leave behind a clearcut doctrine of women's rights, and when he died the erosion began. Men very soon barred women from voting to elect the Prophet's successors and from praying as equals in the mosque.

Changing conditions accelerated the decline. Military triumph inundated Arab society with the booty of conquest, not the least of it in the form of slaves. By the time the caliphs left the desert and moved to Damascus, then to Baghdad, women's work had lost its importance and, under Persian influence, women were reduced to sexual ornaments, veiled and sent into seclusion, to serve as a status symbol for men. An Englishwoman, visiting Istanbul in the nineteenth century, noted that an Ottoman's several wives (though not his concubines) had greater rights, particularly over their property, than did monogamously married Victorian women, but this was less an accolade to Islam than a comment on the status of women in Europe. Over the centuries, without specific religious sanction, the *haram* system increasingly isolated and degraded Muslim women, and in substance it has persisted throughout the Arab world until the present day.

It was the responsibility of Menal al-Yunis to preside over the dismantling of the *haram* culture in Iraq. Head of the General Federation of Iraqi Women, she was among Iraq's most prominent political figures when I first visited in the mid-1980s; and when I visited again, after the Gulf war, I saw no indication that she had lost influence. The federation, an official body, had branches in every city, town and village in the country, and action groups in nearly every neighborhood. More highly organized than the party itself, it had a speedy communications network which reached out to women on virtually every street corner in Iraq. Certainly this made it an invaluable source of intelligence for Saddam's Big Brother system, and this accounted for much of Yunis's power. But to stop there would be unfair to Menal al-Yunis's commitment, and the Baath Party's, to the rights of Iraqi women. Her mandate covered what is perhaps the most difficult issue that policymakers face in the Arab world. Women, no less than men, are not yet comfortable with the notion of women's rights. I met Menal al-Yunis in the federation's cheerless downtown office. At the time, she was stirring up controversy by her defense of Iraqi widows and marriageable young women—frequently against threats of bodily harm, and even death—who had established relationships with Egyptian workers during the long absences of Iraqi men at the battlefront. With dark eyes and a warm smile, she was handsome, by no means petite, yet feminine, and obviously strong. It struck me that she was one of the few Iraqi women who, in talking, looked me straight in the eye.

Clearly, I got off on the wrong foot with Yunis by asking the obvious Western question of why so many Iraqi women still wore the *abaya* and the veil. She instructed me patiently.

"Maybe you consider the *abaya* and the veil a sign of backwardness," she said, "but that is a Western criterion. Or maybe you think development means every girl should have a boyfriend before she marries. That might be all right in Europe, and I even defend the practice when it occurs, but in our country it is considered immoral. You cannot apply Western criteria to measure development in Iraq. American and European societies are already one hundred years ahead of us, socially as well as economically, and their lead is widening. So we cannot allow ourselves to be distracted by superficial concerns. We must get down to the substance of change, and our government tries very hard not to get diverted by offending morality, as we would if our first target were the veil.

"In the countryside, we avoid mixed activities for men and women, which reduces the resistance of men to participation by their wives and daughters in our programs, especially education. We want development to grow naturally, like a plant in a natural environment. So when I measure its progress, I must use not your indicators but indicators that are important to us, like the number of women in education and employment, the enthusiasm of women for change, the response of the society to amended social laws, and the level of women's participation in political life. To be honest, women do not hold many positions of leadership in Iraq. But that, too, will change."

When I asked Yunis why Iraq had failed to eliminate the obvious disparities in development between Sunni and Shiite women, as well as between urban and rural women, she wrinkled her brow for a moment, then informed me that my question was too narrowly focused. She said she would answer me on a broader level.

"We began our development only after our revolution, in 1968, when political will combined with the arrival of financial resources from the oil boom," she said. "We call our policy *comprehensive* development. That means we are trying to eliminate the differences between urban and rural development. We understand that, socially speaking, not all of Iraq is developing at the same speed, and this is a practice and not an ideological consideration. Many factors determine the pace of development, such as the distance from city centers, the available communication and transport facilities and the nature of development itself. The countryside, after all, is more traditional, more conventional.

"But by now, we have built much of the infrastructure. We have adopted a system of compulsory education, and it is one system for all—Sunni and Shiite, city and country, boys and girls. Anyone who refuses education is penalized. Television now covers eighty-six percent of the country. That means development will move more quickly. Rural women are cooperating enthusiastically with the federation and are making increasing use of the services we provide. City women are too busy, too tired. Country women, with more time, are quick to take advantage of our vocational training, health training and adult education."

When I asked Yunis whether the clergy, seeing a threat to social tradition, was an obstacle to development, she answered:

"In making these changes, the religious establishment has been a less serious problem than we once feared. We began talking to the clergy when we initiated our programs, and through repeated meetings their resistance has progressively weakened. Even now, we continue the dialogue with them. But, frankly, I don't think there is a place here in Iraq for the kind of fundamentalist movement that triumphed in Iran. Iranian women gave in to Khomeini because the shah had neglected them, using a small intelligentsia to Westernize the society against its will. Iran had only the very rich and the very poor, and the leadership was doing nothing to solve that problem. Religious movements prosper on frustration. The wealth in our society is spread around much more evenly. Iraqis are meant to feel part of the society, to feel a share in what they are asked to defend."

Had the war against Iran, I asked, been a major obstacle to advancing the condition of women?

"The war has been such a part of our lives for so long that it is actually hard to say what the impact is," she answered. "With less money for development, we have had to put more emphasis on the mind and will of individuals. With so many men away at the battlefield, maybe it has enabled women to *think* of themselves as more valuable. Our textbooks used to say the job of women was to cook and clean. Now there is enthusiasm among young women, in both the city and the countryside, to defend the country, even to join the army. Women are working at jobs they never had before. University graduates are moving all over the country to find work. This is a society that relies heavily on family and family ties. Women don't choose their husbands by themselves, and the same applies to men. The whole family participates, and we Iraqis think a good marriage is one made with the full cooperation of both families. Men and women don't separate from their families after marriage. Still, it's not like the old days, in which men and women married within the tribe, or at least within the extended family. Now it is settled in Iraq that a woman can take the job she wants and, similarly, she cannot be forced to marry against her will. There is less marriage within the family than before. Sunni and Shiites are marrying one another more and more. But I think these changes— and they are quite profound—are the result of government policy at least as much as of the war. These changes are the natural fruit of development."

It was apparent to me after a few days in Iraq that the effort to bring women into the mainstream of national life had indeed made considerable progress. Far from being hidden in the *haram*, women staffed the offices, crowded the bazaars, worked on the assembly lines. Their paintings and sculpture were on display in museums and galleries. According to United Nations data, female enrollment in primary school was nearly 100 percent, and though it dropped off at the higher levels, it remained only slightly behind that of boys. Women made up a third of Iraq's young scientists and engineers and nearly half of the physicians.

One afternoon in Karbala, I stopped, at Menal Yunis's suggestion, at the office of the General Federation of Iraqi Women, which was decorated with posters of women, some of them veiled, marching to war. In a room full of women, the director insisted that I not be misled by the prevalence of the veil and the *abaya* in Karbala and argued that Shiite women are not only as modern as others in Iraq but have taken the lead among women in training for battle against Iran. I knew that, in the early days of Islam, women had fought at the side of the Prophet, a recollection that fills Muslim women with pride. The director confirmed that women were not yet permitted to fight on the battlefield, but she added belligerently that if Khomeini ever came near Karbala, he would get a good dose of fire from armed women. As if on cue, a tall woman in an *abaya* stood up and shouted, "I want them to turn me loose so I can go to the front to defend my country." I do not know whether she had rehearsed the line, but even if she did, I had the feeling that she really meant it.

ON THE DAY I visited Karbala and An Najaf, I interrupted the return trip to Baghdad for a look at Babylon. Apart from the awe evoked by the name itself, I had found the site during an earlier visit to be a bore. The famous Lion of Babylon, a basalt carving displayed atop a pedestal, was an inspiring symbol of Babylon's power in the ancient world, but the rest seemed like a collection of archeologists' mounds and holes, of which my eye made little sense. I returned because I had heard that some restoration was going on there; nonetheless, I was unprepared for what I saw.

I arrived late on a very hot afternoon and found teams of laborers— from their costumes I knew they were Egyptians and Sudanese—working frenetically, pouring concrete, laying bricks. Streets had suddenly appeared and walls were rising to frame them. My first reaction was to be appalled at what seemed like the transformation of the ruins into an archeological Disneyland, but I had to admit that, compared to my previous visit, what I encountered had more meaning. Unable to find anyone in authority on the site, I resolved that in Baghdad I would find out what was going on.

A few days later I talked with Dr. Bahram Abu-Alsouf, a retired field archeologist who was for many years in charge of excavations in Iraq's northern region. A Cambridge Ph.D., Abu-Alsouf was a large man with a thatch of white hair and an open face. He acknowledged that it was Westerners who introduced Iraqis to the historical grandeur to be found through archeology. The first excavations in the Middle East took place in the nineteenth century, he said, when Bible societies in the West began looking for confirmation of the Old Testament stories. British and French teams were the first to dig in Iraq, and in 1899 a German expedition went to Babylon. The foreign expeditions took home all the archeological treasures they could get their hands on, and in some measure it was to avoid future losses that Iraq, when its own government was set up, became involved in archeology. In 1926, the Iraqi Department of Antiquities was formally established, and within a few years Iraqis were studying archeology at universities both at home and abroad.

"Archeologists can get very emotional about their work," Abu-Alsouf said. "I went into archaeology because I was brought up in Mosul and played on the ruins of Nineveh. As a kid, I lived with gods and heroes. I spent my life working at archeological sites, dealing with the dead, trying to re-create the past, and I can confirm that archeologists like to show their work. The critics who argue against touching these ruins are romantics. They are simply not practical people. I am one of those archeologists who want people to enjoy these excavations, to appreciate the heritage they represent, to learn the lessons of history from them, not just to weep over them."

For decades, a fierce debate raged within the government and among archeologists, Abu-Alsouf said, over what to do about Babylon. Many meetings were held, attended by international as well as Iraqi experts. The technical problems in excavating Babylon were serious. The remains of the Hammurabi age, about 1800 B.C., are now below the water table, probably because at some time in the past the Euphrates spontaneously altered its course. Above them are the ruins of the Nebuchadnezzar era, which came twelve hundred years later. Over the centuries, nearly all of the construction material above the foundations of Nebuchadnezzar's city had been pillaged; much of it went to build nearby towns, where the bricks were still identifiable. German teams, working from 1899 until World War I, skillfully unearthed and mapped the foundations of Babylon, Abu-Alsouf said, which were all that remained of its ancient splendor. Inevitably, he noted, these foundations were a disappointment to casual visitors.

By now, archeology in the Middle East had become more than an intellectual endeavor. Nationalist governments had learned to exploit its potential to cultivate patriotism and promote political loyalty. The Jews in Palestine probably started the trend, digging at Old Testament sites to provide evidence of their historical connection to the land. In Egypt, the government supported Pharaonic excavations, particularly after Sadat's falling out with the Arab world over the peace with Israel, to prove the deep and separate roots of Egyptian nationhood. Iraq and Syria sought to elicit pride in the remains of ancient civilizations—not only pre-Islamic but pre-Arab—which was paradoxical, in view of the two regimes' pan-Arabist ideology. Iraq's decision late in the 1970s to restore Babylon along the lines of the research of the turn-of-the-century Germans certainly had nationalist ends. In the mid-1980s, in the heat of the war against Iran, the government advanced the funds to step up the pace of the work. What I saw in my most recent visit to Babylon was its approaching culmination.

The force behind the acceleration of this work, however, was not in the Department of Antiquities. It was Munir Bashir, Iraq's most acclaimed musician. Bashir was the acknowledged world master of the oud, a stringed instrument that is shaped like a half watermelon and dates back to ancient Mesopotamia. Born in Mosul in 1930, he was compared as a musician to the late Andrés Segovia, whom he physically resembled. But, as director of the music department at the ministry of culture, Bashir was also a bureaucratic dynamo. He supervised music education throughout Iraq and promoted concerts of traditional Iraqi music throughout the Arab world. When Bashir talked, it was said, even Saddam listened, and when he declared that Iraq ought to sponsor an international music festival in a restored Babylon, the wheels of government began to turn.

"I started thinking of a great music festival a few years ago," Bashir told me in his bare-walled office in the ministry, "and I took it to Saddam. Babylon, after all, belongs not to Iraq but to all the world. When he accepted, we got to work. We'd like the people of the world to know more about Iraqi music. Iraqi culture is part of international culture. Of course, I myself will play, probably at the opening. But getting Babylon ready in time is a challenge. It is like the Americans setting a deadline for getting to the moon. Dealing with the nation's heritage is very sensitive and very dangerous. I agree with the Department of Antiquities that the authenticity of the work is more important than speed, but we did serious research, and I insisted on high standards. Believe me, we're not going to destroy Babylon."

That same afternoon I made the one-hour drive back to Babylon, where I met with Donnie George, the field director of the renovation project. An Iraqi, George told me he was a Nestorian Christian. He said Nestorians often have Western names, and noted that his children were Stephen and Mary. Discharged from the army after spending four years at the front, he took a master's degree in archeology at the University of Baghdad. He had worked in Babylon for nearly a year and oversaw construction of a small factory to produce bricks using the same processes and materials as the ancients used. One of his main responsibilities, George said, was to mediate between archeologists and engineers in disputes over the issue of authenticity versus structure. His instructions from the ministry, he said, were insofar as possible, to decide for authenticity.

In the temporary shack that George used for an office, he and I huddled over a copy of the map first drawn by the draftsmen of the German expedition some seventy-five years before. He said the current work depended on these Germans not just for the location of buildings but for imaginative sketches they drew of the buildings themselves. Superimposed over the map on transparent paper were the city walls, palaces, temples, theaters, a grand avenue for processions and an artificial lake, all of which were to be built. When we left the office, George took me on an inspection tour of the site. It was only a segment of the original Babylon, he pointed out, the total archeological dig being much larger. But from what I saw, I was willing to testify that this was no Disneyland of papier-mâché and plaster but, for better or worse, a serious effort at Babylon's re-creation.

Back in Baghdad, I called on Munir Bashir again and asked how he and the government justified the expenses of the Babylon restoration and the festival at a time when Iraq was bearing the burden of an extremely costly war. "This is not just a military war," he answered. "It is also a cultural war. Khomeini has his own idea of what culture is. He believes music is heresy, that it is an offense against God. He has no sympathy for dance. He is trying to destroy our culture, Arab culture. This struggle is more a cultural war than it is over a piece of land. Babylon is basic to our culture, and I believe life is worthless without culture. The festival will give balance to the war effort. The government is spending this money as part of the weaponry of war. If we retreat on this battlefield, it will symbolize the end of our national life."

THE SADDAM ART CENTER is part of the new Haifa Street development in downtown Baghdad. A handsome complex of apartments and offices, Haifa Street (the Arabs have a peculiar predilection for commemorating lost cities and lost battles) fuses traditional Islamic themes with the simplicity of contemporary architecture. The Iraqis took credit for the style; a Korean company did the construction. The art center, which opened in 1986, replaced a small museum which the oil baron Calouste Gulbenkian donated to Iraq in the 1960s. According to official statements, it was a personal project of Saddam, to whom has been credited the observation that "A modern nation that cannot develop great poets and artists will not be able to develop great political leaders." Eight stories high, the art center surrounds a courtyard that serves both as entryway and as a garden for contemporary sculpture. The galleries, suffused with sunlight during the day, cover the entire ground floor. The floor above contains a library and documentation room. The rest of the building will be devoted to classrooms and lecture halls, studios, special exhibition areas and whatever other uses will promote Iraqi art.

Two exhibits were on the walls the day of my visit. The first was a retrospective of the work of Zaid Mohammed Salih, who was a Pioneer—a term used by Iraqis to designate members of an artistic vanguard of the 1930s, whose works hung in the Pioneer Museum, a traditional house with a fine *shanashil*, lovingly restored, on Rashid Street. Salih, an army officer as a young man, painted military scenes, many of them in the style of the French Impressionists. The second exhibit was a competition named in honor of al-Wasiti, an artistic genius of the Abbasid era. The works included oils, watercolors and graphic designs, as well as sculpture in metal, plaster and stone. The styles ran from totally abstract to vividly representational, with themes ranging from inspirational to nostalgic. Only a few of the works referred to the war, and even fewer to politics. The painting that made the strongest impression on me was a subtly rendered, long-haired nude, half-concealed in a grove of leafless trees. It seemed so delicate, yet so defiant of a culture that subjugated its women. Titled *Alienation*, it was the work of Leyla al-Attar, who I learned later was the Center's director.

Leyla al-Attar was the most stylish woman—and, perhaps, the most modern—I have ever met in the Arab world. Small, then in her mid-forties, she possessed a silky femininity. She had chestnut hair, fastened in a ponytail, and as we talked she removed a pin and let it fall across her shoulders. She wore a flowing, elbow-length lavender jacket over a white blouse, matching harem pants and high-heeled sandals. Around her neck was a gold necklace, and high on her arm a gold bracelet. Her eyes sparkled beneath heavy make-up and long lashes, and though she laughed as we talked, I sensed that they veiled a certain sadness, a clue to which I thought could be found in her haunting work. Later, she took me to a room where were hung a dozen of her paintings, all in fragile shades of black and white, each of a nude woman whose back was turned, nearly lost in enveloping foliage. They were her series on women's loneliness, she said. When I asked whether she considered them to be in the Arab tradition, she replied, "They are not Islamic," but would not elaborate.

Attar told me that her own mother had been a painter who studied in Beirut in the 1920s; her sister was a full-time painter in London. She herself had studied art only in Baghdad, and did her painting in a studio behind her house in al-Mansur. Her husband, she said, was a successful businessman, and she had three grown children. She had been director of the Gulbenkian Museum before coming to the Saddam Center, and she told me that she liked working as an administrator, with other artists. After all, she observed, painting was lonely work.

But Attar seemed to enjoy talking more of Iraq's art than her own. Sitting on gray-and-white overstuffed chairs in the museum salon, she told me that after Baghdad's sacking by the Mongols, Iraq produced no art, save Koranic calligraphy, for hundreds of years. Then, in the 1930s, Iraqi artists, introduced to ideas circulating in European circles, awakened. The Pioneers, who painted in European styles, were followed by Iraqis trained in the art institutes of London and Paris, who reached out in search of an authentic national style. They looked back, she said, to the Abbasids and beyond, to the Sumerians and Assyrians, and into folk art, native handicrafts, calligraphy and illuminated manuscripts. The Saddam Center, Attar told me, was built to encourage them, and to assert Iraq's membership in the international art world. It had been given a generous budget, she said, to acquire paintings, bring foreign artists to Iraq and send Iraqi art for exhibit abroad. Meanwhile, her staff—almost all women, I noticed—was spreading the word worldwide about Iraqi art. She expressed the hope that the Center would soon be well enough known and trusted to become a regular stop on the international circuit of touring masterpieces.

Attar did not want to discuss politics with me, but some Iraqi friends told me later that neither she nor her husband ever belonged to the Baath Party. They had survived in the constricted atmosphere of Saddam's despotism, I was told, by being scrupulously nonpolitical. The people she entertained in her home were Western-oriented artists, writers and musicians, who paid for a measure of artistic freedom with political silence. Saddam, yearning to be regarded as a patron of culture, indulged them, I was told, in the conviction that they would help bring him international approval and political legitimacy.

But Attar's hopes for Iraqi art foundered on the aggressive policies followed by Saddam after the Iraq-Iran war. In January 1991, six months after Iraq seized Kuwait, Attar's house was struck from the air in the American bombardment that launched the Gulf war. Many of her paintings were destroyed. During the rebuilding, she and her husband moved temporarily to her sister's house, also in al-Mansur. But as if she were being pursued, in the American raid of June 1993, which Washington described as retaliation for Saddam's attempt to assassinate former president George Bush, a stray missile demolished her sister's house. Attar, her husband, one of their children and a housekeeper were all killed. I never learned whether any of her paintings portraying the loneliness of women survived.

V POURING IN FIRE

AMONG THE HEROIC poses assumed by Saddam Hussein on billboards around the country, perhaps the most dramatic had as a background the battle of al-Qadisiyah. Saddam usually wears an olive-drab uniform, but often he is in the costume of a bedouin warrior. Sometimes he is mounted on a stallion; at other times he poses next to a tank or an artillery piece. Spread out behind him is the scene of a four-day desert battle in A.D. 637 between the fervent armies pouring out of Arabia and the Persian defenders of an empire which, at its peak, had hammered at the gates of Alexandria and Constantinople. The battle took place outside of Ctesiphon, the small town near Baghdad that once served as Persia's capital. The town still displays a marvelous vestige of Persian glory, a single-span brick arch more than one hundred feet high, built in the mid-third century, presumably as the gate to a now vanished palace. Near it, a squat, undistinguished brick building contains a circular reenactment in sand and oils of the Arab victory there, some three hundred and fifty linear feet of clashing cavalry, archers and elephants. Saddam Hussein personally commissioned the work, as a monument to what he has called the eternal Persian-Arab struggle.

Debate still rages among diplomats and historians over the responsibility for starting the Iraq-Iran war—or, as Saddam would have us believe, the most recent phase of the unending conflict. It is not disputed that Iraq sent its armies across the Iranian frontier in late September 1980; the unresolved question is whether Iraq was legitimately provoked. In January 1979, the ayatollah Khomeini had returned in triumph to Iran after fifteen years in exile. Iraq promptly recognized the new regime and extended friendly overtures, but Khomeini was not impressed. He blamed Saddam personally for his expulsion from An Najaf and left no doubt that he regarded Saddam's state not just as anti-Shiite but as anti-Islamic, heretical and illegitimate. At stake was whether the secular Baathism of Suddam or the radical Shiism of Khomeini would prevail in Iraq, and perhaps in the Middle East. Khomeini made it unmistakably clear that, having disposed of the shah, he considered Iraq his next target.

As early as the summer of 1979, Khomeini repudiated the 1975 treaty between the shah and Iraq in which the two states pledged noninterference in each other's internal affairs. He proceeded to supply arms to Kurdish guerrillas fighting Baathi rule in the north, and in An Najaf he financed the Shiite leader Ayatollah Baqir al-Sadr, who provoked disorders to the end of replacing the Baathis with a fundamentalist theocracy. Saddam's response to these provocations was the arrest of Ayatollah Sadr and the deportation of thousands of Iranian Shiites. In early 1980, after the assassination attempt on Tariq Aziz, he had Sadr executed. These events set a pattern of escalating violence, which included border incursions by both sides and artillery exchanges. Then, on September 23, Iraqi forces invaded.

In its initial advance, Iraq announced that it had no territorial aims. The case can be made that Saddam intended a limited war to coerce Khomeini into ending Iranian meddling, though he no doubt hoped for a victory that would bring Khomeini down. By the end of 1980, however, Iraq's forces had been stopped cold, and by the following spring the Iranian army was counterattacking, employing waves of young zealots, without air cover, and with little regard for their lives. Barely saving their army, the Iraqis fell back and, within weeks, none of their forces remained on Iran's soil. Acknowledging that a quick victory was impossible, Saddam initiated what became a long diplomatic campaign to end the fighting. Khomeini answered that Iran, the victim of unprovoked aggression, would remain on the battlefield until the Baathi revolution gave way to his own Islamic vision. By attaching the religious imperative, he ensured that the war would not end until one side or the other dropped from exhaustion.

But then the tide turned again, as Iran's armies proved incapable of carrying their advance into Iraq. After 1980, Iran's only real victory was the capture in 1986 of Fao, a small port on the Gulf. Otherwise, the two armies remained strung out along the old international border. Every year, the Iranians, willing to take huge losses, launched one or two major offensives, the immediate objective of which was the southern city of Basra. Khomeini proclaimed each "the final offensive," certain to destroy the enemy's power to resist. But the Iraqis used their superior air and fire power skillfully and, with morale holding steady, proved tenacious at defense.

Many asked during these years why the Iraqis, badly divided as they were, accepted the sacrifices that the war imposed on them. Defenders of a secular revolution, they did not have their enemy's otherworldly zeal. In place of the good life they had been promised, they mourned hundreds of thousands of sons. Yet they went on dying. Were there serious discontent within Iraqi society, would not there surely have been signs—however repressive the regime—of rebellion, strikes, flight from the trenches?

Whatever one's opinion of Saddam, one must grant him much of the credit for Iraq's resoluteness. His leadership might not have been inspirational but it was, at the least, intelligent and forceful. He used the instruments of tyranny at his disposal, but he also maintained a functioning economy, spread the suffering fairly among the different social classes and paid attention to the wants of the separate religious and ethnic communities. He was also vigilant in thwarting corruption and favoritism, morale-

breakers in any war, and in general fostered a sense that Iraq was compe-
tently governed. The willingness of Iraqis to follow him was seen by some
as evidence that Saddam had at last forged Iraq's disparate population into
an authentic nation, with common values and a common purpose. Now,
with the hindsight of the 1991 war over Kuwait, it seems more accurate
to say that Iraqis fought not so much to preserve the Baathi state as to
preserve the country from becoming a satrapy of Iran.

During my visit to Iraq in 1986, a few months after the fall of Fao, I
was given a tour of military installations on the southern front. I was first
struck by the feeling of war just north of Basra, six or seven hours' drive
from Baghdad. The congestion of army trucks, the tents pitched in neat
rows at the side of the road, the checkpoints manned by tense military
police and the hitchhiking soldiers filled the air with the electricity of battle.
Basra itself was heavily damaged from recent artillery bombardments, and
Egyptian workmen were clearing debris. Entire residential quarters had
been decimated, forcing the inhabitants to abandon their homes. Young
men in bandages and on crutches, apparently clean and well cared for,
seemed to be omnipresent. Military policemen in red berets with weapons
slung casually over their shoulders patrolled the sidewalks.

Having spent the night in a half-functioning hotel, I was irritated at not
starting my tour of the front until eleven o'clock, but when I learned that
the troops routinely remained awake during the hours of darkness to guard
against surprise attack, my attitude necessarily softened. Led by a recently
awakened colonel, an escort team picked me up at the hotel at the appointed
hour. As I approached the battle lines south of Basra, I saw units of tanks
concealed within palm groves along the bank of the Shatt-al-Arab, the
waterway that separated the hostile armies. Pontoon bridges linking several
islands with the mainland were positioned behind high, well-maintained
levees, hidden from Iranian guns. The officers I encountered were vigilant,
the soldiers alert. Shaven and neatly dressed, they saluted smartly as the
jeep carrying the colonel and me made its way along the dirt roads that
ran between unit positions. The bivouacs were clean and food appeared to
be ample, and the sandbag walls of the sentry posts were in excellent
repair. The Iranians were threatening another end-the-war offensive in
the fall, some months away, but I saw no reason to believe they had a
greater chance to succeed than in their earlier attacks.

The offensive actually started at Christmastime and it battered the Iraqis
until April. The lines around Basra bent but they did not break. Afterward,
Iraqi soldiers were said to be more confident than ever of their ability to
defeat the best Iran had to throw at them.

During my visit a year later, I met with Adnan Khairallah, the minister
of defense, for a talk about Iraq's military strategy. Khairallah was more

than an official; he was Saddam's boyhood friend and brother-in-law. A year after the war, he would be killed in a helicopter crash, which many Iraqis believed was linked to a scandal within Saddam's family. Khairallah, it was said, had sided with his sister, Saddam's wife, in these family troubles. Officials, predictably, denied that Saddam had staged the crash. One of them offered me what he said was conclusive evidence: Khairallah had died in a new American-made helicopter; had Saddam ordered the killing, he would surely have used an old, expendable Russian model. Khairallah, being a Tikriti, had never been personally popular. But being identified with an army that knew how to win battles, he had been held in great respect.

On the morning of my appointment, I delivered myself to the defense ministry, a European-style palace of many wings near the Mustansiriyah. Begun under the Ottomans and enlarged over the years, it had been used as the presidential residence by Abd al-Karim Qasim. At the main gate I was subjected to the most rigorous security check I had encountered in Iraq, after which a military policeman drove me across an acre of formal gardens to the main entrance. Inside, I was joined by a uniformed escort and climbed a marble staircase to the second floor, passing on each landing a saluting soldier and a selection of paintings and sculpture on patriotic themes.

When I entered the cavernous office, Khairallah, a round-faced man in battle dress, greeted me with a soft voice and surprising warmth. After coffee, I asked him to discuss the reasons for Iraq's stubborn adherence to a defensive strategy in the ground war against Iran. Western military experts had repeatedly written that Iraq could not win by defensive measures alone, and they speculated that the Iraqi army, notwithstanding its high performance, remained short of confidence. Some reasoned that Saddam lacked the political support he needed for an offensive, which would have increased already heavy casualties. I had heard reports that Iraq's generals were getting impatient to move forward, but that Saddam was holding them back.

Khairallah started by pointing out that Iran, with three times as many inhabitants as Iraq, had an advantage in fighting a war of attrition, with one-for-one losses. Iran was also favored by geography, in that its capital and its principal economic centers were, in contrast to Iraq's, at great distances from the fighting front. Not only distant, they were also extremely spread out, he said, thus difficult targets for offensive warfare. It was a problem faced not just by the Iraqi army but by the air force, in that long distances favored defense. Nonetheless, he said, Iraqi aviation was on the offensive, pounding economic and military targets, especially oil installations in the Gulf. For the ground forces, he said, the decision was more difficult.

"Iran is known for attacking in human waves," Khairallah continued. "The military philosophy that currently guides us is based, first, on obstructing the enemy forces prior to their attack, to reduce their strength before they reach the battlefield. It is, next, imperative to reduce the power of their offensives once they begin, until the attack exhausts itself and we can counterattack to get the land back. Our objective is to inflict as many casualties as possible.

"To do that, we have taken advantage of a psychological factor. Iranians are known for obstinacy. When they hate, they become blind and lose their reason. We have found this hatred a consistently weak spot in their attack plans. Take, for instance, their most recent attack on Basra. They chose a place where the front, limited by obstacles to the left and right, is barely two miles wide and about three miles deep. In this small area, we concentrated the firepower of three divisions, as well as aviation and helicopters. Despite this firepower, the Iranians persisted, continually pouring in reinforcements, and from December twenty-fourth to April seventeenth they advanced about two miles toward Basra. But by their own admission, they took two hundred thousand casualties. If we decided to undertake a limited offensive operation within Iran, we could not hope to get such positive results.

"In the spring, we had a similar experience in the north, where we had two divisions in the mountains near Sulaimaniya. The Iranians were at the end of three parallel mountain chains and attacked the central chain to separate the right and the left wings of our forces. They thought if they reached the end of the chain, our forces would fall. Our calculation was that the left and the right would hold, and that they were putting themselves in the center of powerful fire from three sides. They put eighty regiments into the advance, plus two divisions of *pasdaran*, the elite Revolutionary Guards, and they captured a foothold of two or three square miles, which was not much. But, by our estimates, we destroyed sixty-five to seventy-five regiments, the equivalent of more than nine divisions. If we had been on the offensive, we could not have achieved anything like the favorable ratio of casualties that we got on the defense.

"I can understand their trying to get Basra. It is a strategic point, and if they took it they would have an important card for negotiations. But the territory in the north is uninhabited terrain, the complexity of which gives the defense a major advantage. What can they tell their people after losing nearly eighty regiments there? Our experience indicates that they will keep pressing. They have proclaimed that this is the 'final year' of the war. But where are the forty-eight brigades they sent into a two-mile area east of Basra? We had four thousand weapons—mortars, cannon, tanks, guns—pouring in fire, not including the planes and the helicopter gunships. My information is that the air force dropped twelve thousand bombs of two hundred and fifty to five hundred kilograms. Unbelievable killing!

"So you see why the defensive is, at this stage, more important to us than any offense. If our calculations are correct, Iran cannot wage war at this rate much longer. For the first time, we are finding Iranian troops who surrender without fighting, sometimes holding up the white flag without a battle. We are capturing soldiers who insult Khomeini without our even asking. We are in the seventh year of the war, and nowhere are they more than a few miles from the border. They were unable to reach Baghdad when they were at top strength. They surely cannot do it now, after seven years of losses. As soon as our field calculations indicate that they are weak enough for us to go through, we will take the offensive. Then we will expel them from the Iraqi ground on which they have a foothold."

Khairallah's words proved prescient. In the spring of 1988, the Iraqi army went on the offensive in both the north and the south. In a lightning operation, the Iraqis retook Fao and in four months of relentless fighting won victories along the entire 730-mile frontier, driving the Iranians out of the country. Its forces shattered, the Khomeini government agreed in August to a cease-fire. By this time, Adnan Khairallah was dead but, according to some observers, it was his success which persuaded Saddam Hussein two years later that he could hold off the combined armies of the United States and its allies. My own judgment is that Khairallah would have appreciated the huge difference between the armies of the allies, which fought with state-of-the-art technology, and those of Iran, which squandered manpower prodigiously. But Iraqis can only speculate—and many do—whether the course of events would have gone differently had Khairallah remained alive.

VI   AN UNDERSTANDING WITH WASHINGTON

I DON'T WANT to lecture your people on their interests," Tariq Aziz said, "but certainly American strategists understand that stability in this region of the world is important to the United States." In the summer of 1986, when he pronounced those words, Washington's position was that an Iranian victory over Iraq would be harmful to the security of the United States. Vice-President George Bush had recently visited the region, and in Saudi Arabia, Oman and Bahrain, with which the United States had military-cooperation agreements, he pledged America's support to combat aggression, presumably Iran's. When Bush became president, he carried out his anti-aggression pledge—against Iraq. Yet, even in 1986, Aziz was dubious about American intentions. "We reached an understanding with the United States several years ago to limit the flow of arms to Iran," he said. "It affects Iran's ability to carry on the war. Nevertheless, a flow of arms from the West continues. It is one of our main problems."

Aziz insisted in our talk that night that Israel was delivering weapons to Iran, and he showed me photographs that had appeared in Baghdad newspapers of captured American equipment. Iraq had protested to Secretary of State George Shultz, he told me, and was assured that America had long before persuaded Israel to stop the shipments. I recall having questions about Aziz's claim, and on my return to Washington, I inquired at the State Department and the Pentagon, and received the stock reply that the allegations were untrue. It took the Irangate scandal, which broke in November 1986, to demonstrate that Aziz had been correct, while Shultz and the other Americans who thought they knew better were wrong. That this double-dealing was motivated not by malice toward Iraq but by Iran's potential for containing the Soviet presence in Afghanistan and freeing the American hostages in Lebanon, both important matters to the United States, did not make it any easier for the Iraqis to swallow. Subsequently, it was revealed that Shultz's predecessor, Alexander Haig, first authorized Israel to sell arms to Iran in 1981 and that the shipments went on without significant interruption until the end of the Iraq-Iran war.

Notwithstanding the arms shipments, Washington's proclaimed policy, initiated in 1979, was to establish warmer relations with Iraq. In 1967, the Iraqi government had joined with other Arab countries in holding the United States responsible for the Arab defeat in the Six-Day War. Diplomatic relations were broken, and for a dozen years Baghdad courted the Soviet Union, while Washington moved steadily closer to the shah of Iran. In the early 1970s, Secretary of State Henry Kissinger actually encouraged Iran's mischievous promotion of the Kurdish uprising in the north of Iraq. It took Khomeini's revolution to break the pattern of mutual hostility between Washington and Baghdad. Washington made its first overture on the eve of the seizure of the U.S. embassy in Teheran, nine months after Khomeini came to power.

Washington initially responded to the Iraq-Iran war by announcing a rigorous neutrality. But American officials were soon meeting regularly with highly placed Iraqis and in 1982, the United States gave the first public signs of a "tilt" by extending credits to Iraq to buy U.S. agricultural products. In 1983, President Reagan sent a special envoy to Baghdad to meet with Saddam Hussein, and in the same year Washington said that it would seek to persuade its allies to stop their arms shipments to Iran. In

November 1984, Washington and Baghdad formally resumed diplomatic relations and in a policy paper a few months later, the United States stated that though its objective was to preserve the sovereignty and territorial integrity of both belligerents, it looked with disfavor on Iran's rejection of a negotiated end to the conflict. Over the next few years, Baghdad bought arms from the West, though not from the United States, and increasingly distanced itself from Moscow. At the same time, Washington encouraged friendly nations to embargo arms to Iran, even though it made a secret exception for the Israelis.

Throughout the war, Israel spoke openly of its preference for an Iranian victory. Its reasoning had an oddly self-delusive ring. Israel, accustomed to close relations with the shah's Iran based on a shared hostility to the Arabs, seemed unable to take Khomeini at his word when he said that his overriding goal was to destroy Zionism. Israel failed to grasp that Iraq was now its forward line of defense against a rampaging Iran. In 1981, the Israeli air force destroyed an Iraqi nuclear reactor in an attack on Baghdad. Without Israeli parts, Aziz told me, Iran's air force and anti-aircraft systems would have ceased to function. Israel's hostility was obviously something the Iraqis would not soon forget.

Yet Iraq, presumably to gain favor with Washington, officially changed its hard-line stance toward Israel in the early 1980s. Its new position was that it would accept any settlement of the Arab-Israeli conflict to which the other Arab parties, and particularly the Palestinians, agreed. At the same time, it began to move away from the "rejectionist" Arabs and to seek warmer relations with the moderate governments of Egypt and Jordan. Israel did not respond to these changes. A few secret meetings were held between Israeli and Iraqi diplomats, but on the Israeli side they had no official backing—and much later Aziz denied that they had ever taken place at all.

"In the 1970s, it is true that we had a much harder line and, as minister of information, I often delivered it," Aziz told me in 1987, when I asked him about the policy shift. "But we are more mature than we were then. We long ago stopped giving lectures to the Palestinians, Jordanians and Syrians about what to do about the conflict with Israel. If the Palestinians accept an accommodation, why should we object? Unfortunately, we are not optimistic about Israel's interest in peace, but we will not, for tactical or any other reasons, retreat on our position." (Early in 1993, Saddam Hussein as an overture to the new American president, Bill Clinton, restated this position. The United States did not react.)

Whatever his feelings toward Israel, Aziz expressed shock at our meeting in 1987 at Washington's duplicity. "Until Irangate," he said, "we thought we had a full understanding with the United States. Afterward, we wondered. Were the arms sales an isolated phenomenon or was that the *real* policy? I have since explained to the American government that the damage it did was much greater than the equipment it sent. Iran cannot defeat us on the battlefield. But Khomeini still has expansionist ideas. He toppled the shah and humiliated President Carter. And with America's arms sales he could say to himself, 'Look, our policies are working. Even the Americans are coming to us to reach an accommodation.' God has not yet created a country, except for Israel, that is fool enough to want Iran to win the war. But America encouraged Iranian arrogance to new extremes, while demoralizing the Arabs. It was the *political* damage of the arms sales that was serious and will have a lasting impact."

Even though Tariq Aziz and I talked until midnight, I ran out of time for the last round of questions I had intended to ask about the government's postwar plans. But I did find in my notes some relevant comments. "We will tolerate dissent," he said at one point; and at another: "I assure you that when the war ends, we will not stick to the one-party system." I recall being skeptical when I heard him but, in retrospect, I suspect that he believed his assertions. It is possible, of course, that Aziz's job within the official structure was to deceive visitors like me. It is also possible that he was engaging in some wishful thinking. But I believe Aziz belonged to a Western-oriented clique within the ruling circle that looked forward to cordial relations with Washington after the war as a vehicle for liberal reforms.

Another member of that clique was Saddoun Hammadi, who in 1987 was president of the National Assembly, the body that passes for a parliament in Iraq. American-educated and a former foreign minister, Hammadi was the highest ranking Shiite in the regime. He was known as a cautious, sensible man, who spoke without flamboyance. In fact, Iraqis joked that he never smiled. Looking back, I suspect he told me what he *hoped* would happen after the war, and in rereading his comments, it seems clear that even he had apprehensions about whether it would.

"We have to start thinking now what we will do when the war is over," he said, "what the region will ask of us. Heavy as the costs have been, Iraq will have reaped major psychological benefits from the war. It will be self-confident and self-assured, and we will be in a position of unprecedented prestige. Our resources will be relatively plentiful, and we don't have huge gaps in class or wealth, so we shall have something to contribute. The question is, what will we do with what we have?

"We don't have a ready theory for all of the Arabs' problems, but there is nothing in our thinking that is pushing us toward expansionism or interference in the affairs of others. We know now what war means. Fortunately, our ideology as Baathists will serve as a control. Our concept as Arab nationalists does not call upon us to demand one sovereign Arab state, and certainly not an Arab nation subject to our rule. Our interest, rather, is in a federation in which local characteristics would remain. We don't believe one country or one leader should dominate the Arab world. It has been tried and failed.

"We want to approach the Arab world constructively, while at the same time allowing our own system to grow and develop. We have much to do right here in Iraq. I believe we will play a stabilizing role in the region after the war. I think we will use what we have constructively, though *we will have to be careful about excesses,* because we are human beings."

When the war ended in 1988, Saddam as victor was riding high. In shattering the armies of the ayatollah, he had eliminated a threat not only to Iraq but, by their own testimony, to the Arab states of the region, perhaps even to the industrial states of the West. He had reason to believe this service had earned him a claim to their assistance in the rebuilding of his country and in the resumption of a program, largely suspended during the war, of economic development. His oil wealth was intact, as was most of the modern infrastructure that Iraq had built as the foundation for industrialization. As the only Arab in modern times to win a foreign war, Saddam was now preeminent among Arab leaders. The problem created by Washington in Irangate had elicited in him a deep resentment, but the Americans had expressed remorse, and he said he was willing to start the relationship over again. The dark cloud seemed to be passing.

But in the last weeks of the war, Saddam began the drift toward excess against which Hammadi had warned. With it, Iraq's prospects for the future retreated ominously.

In March of 1988, Iraq and Iran had fought a battle over Halabja, a small Kurdish city in the mountains separating the two countries. By then, both sides had used chemical weapons in battle, Iraq perhaps more often, having learned that even in small quantities poison gas would sow panic among field troops, helping to equalize Iran's superiority in numbers. Neither side used chemicals for the kind of mass killing that took place in World War I; still, at Halabja some five thousand Kurds died. Each side blamed the other, and a later study by the U.S. Army War College held that the Iranians were probably responsible. But Iran had leveled the charge first, and international public opinion seemed to hold the Iraqis responsible. Most of the world, then, was prepared to believe that the Iraqis had once again resorted to chemicals in August 1988, to put down the insurrectionary Kurds who had fought throughout the war at Iran's side.

Though the details of the poison gas dispute are mired in rhetoric, what is known is that Saddam, after the cease-fire, sent in his army to stamp out Kurdish insurgency once and for all. He ordered his troops to go as far as the Iranian border and depopulate a swath of territory eight or ten miles deep, neutralizing for all time an area that had served the rebels as a sanctuary.

Saddam's objectives were understandable; his tactics were characteristically brutal. The army dynamited dozens of villages into rubble and dispatched thousands of inhabitants from their ancestral homes to newly built "resettlement villages" far in the interior. In the process, sixty thousand Kurds crossed the border into Turkey, where they told journalists they were fleeing from attacks of gas. The Iraqis angrily denied the charge, but Secretary of State Shultz claimed it was true, and the Senate Foreign Relations Committee, without investigating, proposed a bill to impose heavy sanctions on Iraq. With the pro-Israeli lobby fanning the fire, the bill nearly passed. But in the Turkish refugee camps, international teams of doctors were more skeptical of the refugees' claims, saying their examinations did not confirm the use of gas at all.

I was in Iraq shortly after the incident. I had gone to write about the second Babylon music festival, which Munir Bashir in the ministry of culture had organized to celebrate the war's end and Iraq's return to the cultural mainstream. But the poison gas story broke before the festival opened, discrediting Iraq so badly that hardly anyone showed up, and the festival was a total flop. Instead of going to Babylon, one day I accepted a government offer of a ride in an army helicopter flying over Kurdistan, and along the border, from a few hundred feet, I saw barren terrain without signs of life—no people, no animals, no smoke curling from chimneys. Few walls were standing, and even fewer roofs remained, though it was easy to identify the remains of villages from the clusters of foundations that, from the air, made up maplike mosaics. Later, I toured one of the relocation towns on the flat land, ugly clusters of cement-block buildings that had become the homes, schools, clinics and mosques of displaced Kurds. Obviously, the Kurds did not like them but the Iraqis maintained that what they offered was a fair exchange: the Kurds were provided with decent amenities, in some cases better than they had enjoyed in their villages; in return they no longer presented a threat to Iraqi security.

Over the next few days in Baghdad, I talked to Red Cross, United Nations and Western embassy officials, and all said they knew of no proof that chemicals had been used on the Kurds. On returning home, I interviewed academic experts; none unequivocally ruled out the use of gas, but the most reliable among them were doubtful. It was only Washington, and particularly Congress—although, conspicuously, not the U.S. embassy in Baghdad, which was in the best position to know—that stuck stubbornly to the original story, and this persistence bewildered the Iraqis. Some Iraqi friends I had made, all without illusions about their government, had looked forward to the war's end, in the hope that America's influence would rub off, persuading Saddam to loosen up on his oppressive practices. They did not understand the American animosity on the Kurdish issue. Saddam's government had already dropped some travel restrictions, but prospects for further reforms seemed to depend on a rapprochement with the West. Iraqi officials said the government felt unjustly defamed by Washington, and made clear that such a rapprochement was now unlikely.

A few weeks later, France's President Mitterrand proposed, as a way to break the impasse, to convoke a conference to review, within the context of modern battlefield practice, the traditional limitations on the use of chemical weapons. The conference met in Paris in January 1989, with one hundred fifty nations, including Iraq, in attendance. The Iraqis did not dispute that they had used chemicals against Iran. Adnan Khairallah, the defense minister, even stated that Iraq reserved the right, under similar circumstances, to use them again. Tariq Aziz, as foreign minister, made a different argument. Stipulating Iraqi apprehension over Israel's nuclear capacity, he said, "Iraq feels any appeal for total prohibition of chemical weapons should be joined to an identical appeal for total prohibition of nuclear weapons." Unwilling to acknowledge chemical and nuclear arms as equivalent deterrents, the United States rejected the argument, and the conference adjourned with little accomplished. The United States took the failure at Paris as a sign of aggressive Iraqi intentions; Iraq took it as proof of Washington's refusal to treat its security concerns seriously. The deadlock cast over United States–Iraqi relations a deeper pall, which had not dissipated as the Middle East entered the critical months of 1990.

CHAPTER TWO

TURKEY

I MELANCHOLY CITY

STRUGGLING TO COME TO TERMS with lost grandeur, Istanbul is a melancholy city. Or so, at least, it seemed to me during my visit in the gray and rainy weeks of winter a few years ago. Was only the weather to blame? I suspect that the weight of the centuries imparts a solemnity to the city, whatever the season. Istanbul was the jewel of great empires; their relics—a Roman aqueduct, Byzantine churches and ramparts, Ottoman mosques and luxury palaces—litter the landscape. Much of its past was triumphant, but much was tragic, and in my memory, the glamour of empire fades into the crowds of dark-eyed men and women dressed in somber raingear who shuffled silently along the streets, circumventing puddles, unsmiling.

For most of the twentieth century, Istanbul has been a provincial capital in a workaday republic, feeding on nostalgia, often floundering, yet refusing interment in the catacombs of history. I had the feeling that, like Turkey itself, Istanbul seeks to recapture departed splendor, though not by turning back to what has failed. Istanbul stands out in the Islamic world by looking ahead to see what remains to be mastered.

I write of Istanbul in a book about Arabs because it was the hub of authority—political, religious and intellectual—of the universe inhabited by the Arabs before the occupation of their lands by the West. From the beginning of the sixteenth century until the beginning of the twentieth, the Arabs made contact with the rest of the world through the vehicle of the Ottoman empire. Although the empire's triumphs brought little glory to the Arabs, its failures were deeply felt. Arab culture in our own time cannot be understood, I believe, without knowing something of Ottoman history and experience. Moreover, a look at the Turks since the fall of the empire offers an intriguing insight into a path that, in its widest limits, might also have been taken by the Arab world—but which, for many reasons, it chose not to take.

In the eleventh century, the Turks, moving across the steppes from

Mongolia, entered the Middle East, and in time were converted to Islam. Certain Turkic tribes established themselves in Anatolia—among them the Ottomans, who in 1453 succeeded where Arab conquerors had failed: taking Constantinople and so putting an end to the Byzantine empire. Thenceforth, while Christianity would remain in the Middle East, Christian power there was at an end.

Over the ensuing half century, the Ottomans conquered the Arabs, taking Damascus, Cairo and Baghdad. Their domination lasted until the end of World War I, when the empire fell, and Turkish and Arab societies rushed off in different directions. With few exceptions, neither Turks nor Arabs these days express any nostalgia for the era of sultanic rule. Yet much of the civilization of the Ottomans remains with them both, while the different social and intellectual paths they have selected now keep them fervently apart.

Dogan Koban, a Turkish architectural historian, argues that the Ottoman mentality remains imbedded in the pavement of Istanbul. Koban met with me in a dusty office littered with architectural drawings off the great hall of Istanbul Technical University, established by the sultans in the eighteenth century to train military engineers. Son of an army officer, educated in Europe, Koban is a student of the social changes that have created contemporary Istanbul. In our talk, he did not find the Arabs blameless. The city's commercial and administrative elite, he maintained, was until recently crippled by Arab ways of thinking which had been absorbed by the Ottomans. Thanks to lessons learned from the West, he said, the leadership has since acquired a sense of responsibility, and a belief that its own commitment can shape Istanbul's economic, social and artistic future.

"According to Islamic custom, which we inherited from the Arabs, the city—in fact, all land—belonged to the sultan," he explained. "The idea of citizenship did not exist, as it did in Paris or Florence. The people, under law, were slaves of the sultan. They thought of themselves as the city's tenants. They had no notion of how to organize themselves to achieve common goals. The concept of private organization is still unfamiliar in Islamic societies. The state was the only legitimate organization.

"The sultan, responsible for administration of the city, turned it over to a functionary who had a small office in the palace. The city had no government of its own until late in the nineteenth century, when the idea of the municipality was imported from the West. It had nothing resembling a city plan until the twentieth. It had no codified law through most of its history. All growth was organic. People built houses in relation to a neighbor, and streets emerged around them. Only fires—which were frequent enough, since most homes were built of wood—changed street patterns.

"The sultans had no sense that they owed anything to the city or its inhabitants. European monarchs were often as powerful as the sultans, but Europe was softened by the liberal ideas which had been circulating since the Renaissance. The Ottoman empire had no comparable development. If the French Revolution had an impact, it was more in promoting reorganization of the state administration than in changing public philosophy. There was no Rousseau promoting the sovereignty of the people in Ottoman history. The people believed in God's will and divine rule. They accepted their fate.

"It's revealing that whatever we know about how Istanbul looked in the Ottoman era comes from Western writers and artists. The inhabitants did not seem to be interested in the objective world, an outlook which characterizes Islamic thought, even today. Muslims produced subjective thinking, which defined things only in relation to their spiritual needs. Westerners noticed the city; the Turks hardly ever did. The Turks' identity was linked to the Islamic religion and to the sultan who, in his capacity as caliph, claimed the rulership of Islam."

Not all of Istanbul's inhabitants were Turks, however. From the first settlers who arrived in the seventh century B.C., calling their settlement Byzantium—for Byzas, their founder—until modern times, Greeks dominated the city and the adjacent region. In A.D. 196, Rome took the city, and a century later the Roman emperor Constantine, his homeland besieged by barbarians, transferred his capital there, renaming the city Constantinople, for himself, and bringing with him Christianity as the state religion. Rome's domain at the time extended from Western Europe to Persia, but it was soon to divide into two segments. Rome, seat of the papacy, ruled the west. Constantinople presided over the Eastern Empire, where it shaped a separate rite called Eastern Orthodoxy, which spread westward into the Balkans, eastward through Anatolia, and southward as far as Egypt. Byzantine civilization, remaining predominantly Greek in speech, developed over the centuries into a unique mixture of east and west, and in time surpassed Europe in the richness of its literature and art.

It was in the seventh and eighth centuries that Constantinople held out against the Arab invaders who had come out of the desert. But the city did not prove so sturdy in the thirteenth century, when it was besieged by Crusaders from Western Europe, loyal to the pope of the Roman church. En route to the Holy Land, they captured and brutally pillaged the city, widening the breach within the Christian fold. They also left the Byzantine empire irretrievably weakened, and within a century, the Ottomans had taken not just Anatolia but much of the Balkans. In 1453, they captured Constantinople itself.

In contrast to the Crusaders, the Ottomans made no effort to stamp out religious or cultural diversity. In fact, they invited the Byzantines—by now a mix of Greeks, Armenians, Italians and other Europeans—to remain in the city to help in its reconstruction. At the end of the fifteenth century, with the Inquisition raging in Spain, they took diversity a step further by welcoming the Jews who had been expelled. In time, Constantinople became known as Istanbul—a name derived from the Greek words *tin poli*, meaning "to the city"—and in imperceptible steps its character grew increasingly international and cosmopolitan.

"Under the Ottomans, Constantinople's commerce was mostly conducted in Galata, a town outside the city walls," Dogan Koban continued. "Galata was much like the other port cities of the Eastern Mediterranean—Alexandria, Beirut, Izmir, Jaffa. That is, it was populated by Europeans who were known as Levantines, a very large proportion of them Italians and most of them Roman Catholics, though among them were plenty of Jews, Greeks and Armenians. They were excellent sailors. They had played a critical role in Constantinople's unsuccessful defense; yet the victorious Ottomans did not interfere with their way of life. As Muslims, the Ottomans had never shown much taste for commerce and diplomacy, which they considered beneath them. They also held the West in contempt. The fact that infidels controlled the empire's economy and its relations with Europe never bothered them.

"So Galata thrived as a community of merchants and bankers, craftsmen and shopkeepers, with a reputation for material well-being, romance and intrigue, not unlike the milieu described by Lawrence Durrell in his *Alexandria Quartet*. Turkish was hardly spoken there at all; Italian was the *lingua franca*. In time, theaters, restaurants and fine shops grew up, and Western-style schools were founded for the children. Merchant-capitalists made large profits and built grand houses, where their wives conducted elegant salons.

"The Muslim quarter of Istanbul, profoundly traditional in its ways, mixed very little with Galata. It had no art beyond folk music and storytelling. The few Turks who, for one reason or another, settled in Galata became very cosmopolitan, very Europeanized, and very distant from their own society. Yet, the separation was relative. The Ottoman empire was at the frontier of Europe, a fact of crucial importance to understanding subsequent developments, and Galata was the Ottomans' permanent window on the West. This gave the local Turks far more exposure to Western culture than the Arabs, the Persians or even the Turks of Anatolia. Europe's impact was slow, but over time the exposure made a big difference."

In the present century, Koban pointed out, Istanbul experienced another major demographic transformation. After World War I, when Turkey became a republic, the Levantines left. The Greek and Armenian communities, having sided with the Christian states during the war, all but vanished. Their departure, he said, cost Istanbul its cosmopolitan flavor. Arriving to take their place were Anatolians from the countryside. Istanbul was now more Muslim, and more provincial, than ever before in its history, and it was likely to remain that way in the decades to come.

"It was only after the Ottomans fell that the Anatolians were introduced into Istanbul's life," Koban said. "Before, they were incidental participants at best. Urban migration began, here as in other societies, when schools and roads and clinics were built. In Turkey, it has been slower than elsewhere, however, and even now, nearly two-thirds of our people are in agriculture, which is a much higher proportion than in Europe. But since World War Two, Istanbul's population has gone from six hundred thousand to nearly seven million, and it's still growing by two hundred thousand a year. Most of this demographic growth has been in the immigration of peasants from the countryside.

"The newcomers are not yet urbanized. They retain an Islamic mentality, which means they have difficulty separating objective problems from old traditions. They do not plan ahead. Their sense of time and social relations are guided by nonurban rules. They drive cars but they treat them like horses. Traffic in Istanbul moves like flocks of sheep. Their relationship with their physical environment is not that of an experienced urban population. Only if you understand that Istanbul is inhabited by Anatolian peasants will you understand how difficult it is to make it into a modern international city. The change may take a very long time."

II ISLAM AND EUROPE

SEVEN CENTURIES before the Ottomans, the Arabs—in the name of Islam—embarked on a massive invasion of Europe. Halted at the gates of Constantinople, they detoured southward across the top of Africa and crossed the Strait of Gibraltar into Spain. They then advanced north across the Pyrenees into France, where finally, in 732, they were defeated by the French at Tours and turned back. Europe, however, never fully recovered from the fright of the invasion.

Gibbon, in *The Decline and Fall of the Roman Empire*, wrote that had the Arabs triumphed at Tours, "the interpretation of the Koran would now be taught in the schools of Oxford and her pupils might demonstrate to a circumcised people the sanctity and truth of the Revelation of Mahomet. . . . From such calamities was Christiandom delivered." In the time of Charlemagne, a century later, troubadours made a cult figure of the French knight Roland for his courage in the Pyrenees against the Arab armies; the *Chanson de Roland* remains to this day a staple in the education of French children. "This heroic literature," wrote the French historian André Maurois, "contributed greatly to shaping the French soul." The legends of Christianity's rescue from Islam are still deeply rooted in European culture.

In *Orientalism*, the Arab-American writer Edward Said, himself a Christian, has acknowledged that Christianity had good reason to feel provoked by Islam. The two faiths were geographically close and shared enough doctrine to generate a bitter competition. Christians were alarmed at the inherent aggressiveness of Islam, which founded an empire in its very first years, and were shocked as Islam took over the heartland of the Bible. "Not for nothing did Islam come to symbolize terror, devastations, the demonic hordes of hated barbarians," Said wrote. "For Europe, Islam was a lasting trauma. Until the end of the seventeenth century the 'Ottoman peril' lurked alongside Europe to represent for the whole of Christian civilization a constant danger, and in time European civilization incorporated that peril and its lore . . . as something woven into the fabric of life." That Islam, as the scholar Bernard Lewis pointed out in *The Muslim Discovery of Europe*, was no less impregnated with myth relating to the permanent menace of Christianity, only exacerbated the climate of tension.

Behind both Christian and Islamic fears was a conviction that whichever faith triumphed in their titanic struggle would gain universal recognition as the one true religion. In the grand waves of history, Islam advanced following the Arab flag for the three centuries that began with Mohammed, after which Europe counterattacked under the banner of the Crusades; when the Crusaders exhausted themselves, the Ottomans went on the offensive, and Islam once more hammered at Europe's gates; there then followed the era of European colonization of the Middle East. The vision of religious struggle has been a permanent theme of European and Islamic history and has had a profound impact upon the shaping of both the Western and the Eastern mind. In our own day the excesses of fundamentalists, who pose a far greater threat to Islamic than to Western society, have touched a raw nerve in the Christian psyche. In *Moses and Monotheism*, Freud speculated that mankind has a gift for historical memory, a cultural disposition to pass along myths, if not facts, from one generation to the next. It would be naive to contend that the theme of religious struggle does not to this day influence the political practices of both the West and the Muslim world.

Turks are convinced that the West's reflexive fear of Islam is a major factor in Europe's resistance to their admission into the Common Market. They are probably right. I recall discussing one evening the question of Turkey's prospects for admission at a reception given for American and

European business leaders at the U.S. consulate in Istanbul. The business-men pointed out a number of practical obstacles to Turkey's membership, but they also mentioned—under their breath, as if to acknowledge that such talk was not for public consumption—that Europe felt uncomfortable at the prospect of admitting an Islamic country into the European Community. They said that Germans in particular had cultural, if not racial, problems in dealing with Turks, a contention seemingly confirmed by subsequent anti-Turk outbreaks in Germany. Europeans would never admit it, they said, but a combination of racial and religious prejudice might, in the end, be too much for Turkey to overcome.

When I was visiting Turkey, a brief incident—over a soccer match—laid bare the underlying tensions. The Galatasaray team, the Turkish underdog, had beaten a highly rated Swiss team by a score of five to zero, advancing thereby to the quarterfinals of the competition for the European Champions Cup. A few days later, however, the disciplinary committee of the Union of European Football Associations (UEFA) voided the results on the grounds that Turkish spectators had thrown coins from the stands, striking a referee and a Swiss player. European soccer officials had been penalizing teams for the misconduct of their supporters since British fans rioted at a match in Brussels in 1985, killing thirty-nine people. Still, the feeling was widespread that in this case the penalty was disproportionate. The Turks roared in outrage. The president of the republic and the prime minister solemnly protested, and angry crowds demonstrated in front of the Swiss embassy. The Turks filed an appeal and, while it was being decided, the nation held its breath.

Of the reams of newspaper commentary that appeared on the subject, I quote from a column by Haluk Sahin of *Dateline*, who seemed to me to capture the essence of the moment.

> Obviously the UEFA disciplinary committee touched an open nerve in the Turkish psyche with its ruling. It certainly produced a national reflex. People coming from very different ideological corners jumped up and screamed in unison: "See, didn't I tell you? They don't like us."
>
> For instance, the decision provided the Islamic groups with a golden opportunity. "Just as you cannot make leather from pig hide, you can't make friends with the West," one fundamentalist paper screamed. The message: Why waste your energy and time in vain? Return to the fold of Islam.
>
> This kind of reaction was not confined to the believers, though. Other more-secular voices also spoke of a plot hatched in the "Crusaders' spirit." The implication was that Galatasaray had been singled

out because it was a Turkish team. Since Turks are overwhelmingly Muslim and since Europeans are just as overwhelmingly Christian, what can you expect? They will repel the infidel, no matter what.

Others viewed the cancellation as a signal of the European rejection of Turkey's full membership in the European Community. "They don't want us, but can't say so," was the refrain, "so they are humiliating us in other ways."

Fortunately for international order, Turkey won the appeal and the victory was restored. The appeals body imposed a small fine, which the Turks gladly paid. "Justice has prevailed," declared the president of the republic. On the evening of the decision, traffic throughout Istanbul was stopped by crowds celebrating in the streets. This time, the demonstrators that gathered in front of the Swiss embassy joyfully waved Galatasaray's red-and-yellow colors and uncorked bottles of champagne. "I am delighted," said the prime minister on hearing the news as he emerged from a meeting with the West German chancellor in Strasbourg. The spokesman for the Galatasaray team was quite modest: "This success is not only ours. We have shown the world what we can do when we cooperate as a nation." But a respondent to a man-on-the-street interview in one of the papers took another view: "Okay, we take the whole thing seriously because as a nation we are still considered in Europe to be second-class people. But I condemn Switzerland for their dirty tricks."

Turkish intellectuals, normally more reserved, do not necessarily express a different view. "Europe has always had this prejudice against us," said Sevki Adali, foreign editor of the Istanbul daily *Hurriyet*. "Portugal was admitted to the [European] Community, and it's not more developed than we are. Greece is nothing, and yet it was accepted easily. It would not be a problem for the Community to admit Israel. But when it comes to Turkey—or, for that matter, the Arabs—it's hopeless. It's got to be religion. We're not Islamic like Iran. We're not even strict, but we're ninety-five percent Muslim. That's the difference.

"In my job, I see the European newspapers every day and I keep reading about the Armenian massacres. We were in a war then, and the Armenians were supporting the enemy. I'm sure something awful happened to them. But it was 1915, a very long time ago, and I still see articles all the time, more than I see about Israel killing the Palestinians. Is it because the Armenians were Christians and the Palestinians are Muslim? The Europeans say the Germans are civilized but, not long ago, they killed far more people than we are even accused of killing, using their highly organized bureaucracy, and they talk about Turkish genocide as if what we did was no different. The Germans show prejudice against the Turkish workers in

Germany. We feel the discrimination when we go there. But Germany is in the European Community and we are not.

"The Turkish government should insist more on our dignity but it does not want to see us isolated. The problem is that Turks have nowhere to turn. We have nothing in common with the Soviet Union and we don't want to be identified with the Islamic world, particularly the fundamentalist countries like Saudi Arabia and Iran. As for the Arabs, they lived under our domination for hundreds of years, and neither of us benefited from it. Now the Arabs think of us as fallen-away Muslims. Our relations with them are correct, but we don't want closer ties, and neither do they. Practically speaking, Europe is our natural partner. Haven't we been in NATO from the start? I know the prime minister feels humiliated, and so do Turkish businessmen, and I wonder sometimes why we want to get into the European Community so badly. The answer is, where can a modern Muslim country go?"

Historians acknowledge that, over five hundred years, the Ottomans dealt far more tolerantly with the Byzantine Christians than had their co-religionists the Crusaders. Going back even further, the Arab conquerors of Spain put no Christians or Jews to the sword for their religious beliefs—the way the Catholic monarchs later did with both. If Islam was oppressive, how does one explain the fact that Greece and the Balkans remained Christian after centuries of Ottoman occupation? "The Ottomans," wrote Lord Kinross, the British historian, "contrary to the image of Islam projected abroad since the earlier Arab conquests, dealt with their enemies in a spirit free from religious fanaticism."

In fact, Islam, like Christianity and Judaism, has its share of self-righteousness, just as its believers have by no means been free from cruelty. The sultans were ruthless in dealing not only with their enemies but with those within ruling circles whose performance fell below expectations. Since the line of succession among Ottomans was never as clear as it was in European kingdoms, newly elected sultans were actually authorized to murder their brothers to avert usurpations. (Given the many mothers available in the *haram* culture over which the sultans presided, brothers were usually numerous.) But in religious matters, the Ottomans were faithful to the Koranic stricture to treat Christians and Jews—in recognition of the contribution that their doctrines made to Islam—as *dhimmis*, that is, as members of a protected faith.

In newly conquered Constantinople in the fifteenth century, the sultan decreed that the Greek Orthodox patriarch, the Armenian patriarch and the Jewish chief rabbi live side by side with the *ulema*, the Islamic authority. They live side by side, albeit as relics of an earlier age, to this day. Sensitive to the admonitions of the Koran, the Ottoman empire devised a structure—with some modification, it is the law today in Israel and the secular Arab states—which recognized the Christian and Jewish communities as each a separate *millet* (from the Turkish word for "nation") and authorized their self-rule in most matters of personal status, community affairs and education. This autonomy left Muslims with a higher rank; the protected minorities were required to pay a special tax and wear special headgear and shoes. But, for the most part, Christians and Jews regarded these burdens as a tolerable price for the right to preserve their own customs under a responsible religious leader of their own choice.

Since the collapse of the Soviet Union a few years ago, the imperial idea—"neo-Ottomanism," some have called it—has had a rebirth among Turks. To Turkey's east, whence came the original migrants to Anatolia, lie a cluster of Asian states, former Soviet republics, inhabited by Islamic peoples who are ethnically and culturally Turkic and who speak Turkic dialects. That these lands were never a part of the Ottoman empire has not stopped the spread of what has been called pan-Turkic fever. "Turkey is facing an historic mission," a prominent journalist wrote recently. "We must develop an imperial vision." Government officials express more modest goals, but the country quickly produced champions of pan-Turkic power through which Turkey might exercise further influence in the region. At the same time, the problems created by the Soviet collapse have diverted Europe's attention from the building of a strong Western community. The talk of Turkish membership in the European Community has become less audible. It now seems possible that in the coming years, the Turks will decide that joining Europe was not such a good idea after all, and will turn their attention to bonding with the eastern lands with which they already have much in common.

In either event, the cultural animosity between Christianity and Islam is likely to remain, generally hidden behind a facade of cordiality but a powerful influence nonetheless in relations between East and West.

III   EMPIRE IN DECLINE

WITH THE PASSAGE OF YEARS, the Ottoman sultanate strayed farther and farther from its Turkish roots. Its overriding doctrine held that the empire, far from being an extension of Turkey, was a multinational, multiethnic, private possession of the ruling dynasty. Once they succeeded in freeing themselves from dependence on the Turkish aristocracy, the sultans governed through a household staff of highly trained slaves, generally Christians converted to Islam. Even in the *haram*, they preferred

Christian women, which Westernized the Turkish blood in the royal veins, and persuaded some sultans that they were European themselves.

The sultans often named Jews to high posts and chose Christians to man their bureaucracies and their armies. For the Janissaries, their elite fighting corps, they preferred young Balkan Christians, whom they converted to Islam but trained to be loyal servants of themselves rather than of the Muslim faith. "The driving force of the empire, ostensibly Islam, was in reality conquest," Vahit Halefoglu, a retired foreign minister, said to me. "Whatever the Europeans believed, the Turks had no sense of mission to promote their religion, much less their culture. Conquest was its own reward." The Ottoman provinces, both Christian and Muslim, were allowed a large measure of local government and, unlike the imperial Romans or the nineteenth-century British, the Ottomans did not impose their legal system, their artistic values or even their language on their conquered subjects. They actually showed so little interest in their own tongue that over the centuries the language as used by the empire's ruling classes became too corrupted with expressions from Persian, Arabic, French and Greek for the ordinary Turk to understand.

With no special recognition or privilege, Turks were treated by the empire as just another subject people, less indulged in practice than the Christians of the Balkan provinces. The name "Turk" itself fell into disuse, except as a term of derision, referring to Muslim peasants. In a state so thoroughly oriented toward war, the government's chief concern was the collection of taxes to fight the next military campaign—and, to this end, the Turks were squeezed into appalling poverty. Many left Anatolia and resettled in the empire's European provinces. Yet the Turks, faithful to Islam, were also faithful to the dynasty that embodied it. Without discernible complaint, they paid in blood and money in the sultan's wars, convinced that these were wars for Muslim glory.

By the sixteenth century, however, the glory was stretched thin. In the two centuries before, the Ottomans had enjoyed a virtually uninterrupted series of triumphs, extending their domains to the Persian border in the east, to Arabia and the upper Nile in the south and to the edge of Morocco on the African littoral. The Ottoman navy dominated the Mediterranean, and Ottoman ships carried the flag of Islam as far as the Atlantic and the Indian Ocean. In the West, Suleyman the Magnificent, the most celebrated of the sultans, reached the gates of Vienna in 1529, confident that its fall would open the way to Central Europe. But the outskirts of Vienna—the Ottomans' Tours—was as far as the empire ever got.

In 1683, Ottoman armies made a second vain attempt on Vienna, but their cause effectively had been lost. Their navies were sunk in the Mediterranean by the Portuguese, the Venetians and the other rising maritime powers. In Africa, their advance was halted by desert and mountain, and in Russia they were blocked by the military power of the upstart Romanovs. Strong military and bureaucratic traditions sustained the Ottomans, but by the start of the nineteenth century, notwithstanding gallant efforts at renewal, it was obvious that the empire was in decline.

The Ottomans' weakness was not at the frontiers, however. When they first overran Anatolia and Thrace in the fourteenth century they had clear tactical superiority over their enemies. A century later, they successfully adapted artillery, a European invention, to their own military doctrines and used it brilliantly before the walls of Constantinople. But soon afterward, decline set in. While Europe moved into the age of the industrial revolution, Ottoman craftsmen continued to cast guns, mix gunpowder and build ships in outdated workshops. While literacy spread in Europe, schools in the empire remained few in number, and concentrated on Koranic studies. Three hundred years after Europe adopted the printing press to disseminate knowledge, the Turks were still copying books by hand. In the sixteenth and seventeenth centuries, repeated military reverses warned the Ottomans of their weakness, and to overcome it they recruited European teachers. But the curriculum they adopted was limited to military remedies. It took another century, and further setbacks on the battlefield, for the Ottomans to admit that they needed a transformation of the society itself.

The French Revolution in 1789 triggered a major effort. The Ottomans had long enjoyed good relations with France, their on-and-off ally in wars against the Hapsburgs. Though they disapproved of the revolutionary mobs, and understood nothing of the rights of man, they warmed to the revolution's hostility to the Catholic church, Islam's traditional nemesis. Under French guidance, the Ottomans adopted some important legal and economic reforms. But the greatest impact on the empire came uninvited: it was the idea of nationalism, which the revolution aggressively promoted. In time, it forced the Ottomans to recognize that a family enterprise, held together by the thin paste of religious doctrine, could not be forged into a modern nation-state.

Early in the nineteenth century, the Ottomans established new military and naval colleges under the direction of the French, who imposed an unaccustomed academic rigor. The language of classroom instruction was French, which gave students access to ideas that had never before penetrated popular circles. The sultans suffered periodic setbacks in their program of renewal; one of them, at the demand of the *ulema*, was actually deposed for his efforts. But the reformist spirit persisted. Education spread, particularly for army officers. Doctors and architects returned from study in Europe in possession of up-to-date techniques. The first newspapers in

Turkish were published. Gradually, corrupt bureaucracy was cleansed and the power of the *ulema* curbed. In 1826, the celebrated Janissary corps, backbone of the empire for centuries, was disbanded and replaced with an army equipped and trained along European lines. Entering its ranks was a generation of Anatolian Turks, prepared to implement the Western ideas they were learning. The sultanate imposed on this new army the mission of reclaiming its lost grandeur.

"The officer candidates were selected at age thirteen from the most promising youths in the empire, both Muslim and Christian," said Professor Ersin Kalaycioglu, a historian at Bosporus University. "They were isolated from society and given systematic schooling and tutoring. While most students still went to religious schools, these young men were given a modern education, in physics, chemistry, biology and math. They became well read—in French—studying philosophy and sociology. By midcentury, they were exposed to nationalism by serving among the Christians in the Balkans, then by the European refugees of the 1848 revolutions who settled in Istanbul. This army was not Turkish yet and it was not nationalistic but it was moving that way. It was an army that was becoming more professional as the sultanate got weaker."

Europeanization also had a negative side, however. The same spirit that rebuilt the army served to destroy the institutions that for centuries had limited the sultanate's excesses. To show how Western he was, Sultan Abdul Mecit in 1853 transferred his residence from Topkapi, an Oriental palace in the Muslim quarter of Istanbul, to Dolmabahce, a palace he built at huge expense on a landfill of the Bosporus on the European side. Emulating Versailles, he ordered formal gardens, lavish interior appointments and a ludicrous rococo facade. Imagining himself a kin of Hohenzollerns and Hapsburgs, he had Italian masters train Turkish musicians, and he hosted balls at which he himself danced. Yet he was traditional enough to retain a harem, whose members he adorned in fashionable Western clothes. Such practices were costly, and under a succession of sultans the empire borrowed heavily for their personal pleasures from European banks. In 1881, the sultan was forced to permit his creditors to collect the state's revenues, which further impoverished the people. The scholar Bernard Lewis quotes a Turkish lament penned in 1870: "I passed through the lands of the infidels, I saw cities and mansions; I wandered in the realm of Islam, I saw nothing but ruins." In the end, Europeanization became a burden that the empire could not survive.

Throughout the nineteenth century, the empire's boundaries retreated. Napoleon started the process, arriving on the Nile in the guise of a liberator; though he was driven out by the English, he left behind Mohammed Ali, an ambitious Ottoman official who effectively made Egypt independent. In 1821, Greece rose up and, after nine years of sporadic but bloody fighting, won its freedom. By now, the colonial powers were nibbling at the European frontiers. "Minorities were their point of entry," said Professor Kemal Oke, a noted historian at Bosporus University. "The British, the French, the Russians sent in missionaries, diplomats, tradesmen—even poets like Lord Byron—to organize nationalist societies, declaring 'we're your champion.' The Albanians, Greeks, Armenians, Circassians, Serbs, all the minorities became their tools. The empire would have been divided earlier but for conflicts among them over the spoils."

Turkish intellectuals, seeking to save the empire and calling themselves Young Ottomans, appealed in the 1860s for the adoption of a constitutional monarchy with a democratically elected parliament, and they attracted a substantial following, even within ruling circles. In 1876, the wastrel Sultan Abdul Aziz was overthrown and a liberal constitution was actually promulgated. A year later, the first Ottoman parliament was elected—democracy's first appearance among the Turks and the Arabs—in what appeared to be the consummation of nearly a century of reform. But within a few months, Sultan Abdul Hamid, successor to Abdul Aziz, dismissed it without resistance, and, though badly weakened, the sultanate behaved more arbitrarily than before.

As the twentieth century approached, a movement called the Young Turks, more nationalist than the Young Ottomans, gained strong support in the army with a promise of restoring the 1876 constitution. Its leaders were, for the most part, Anatolian Turks of modest background, educated in modern ideas and pledged to reform. In 1908, the Committee of Union and Progress, the political arm of the Young Turks, forced Abdul Hamid to reconvene the parliament. On learning that he was secretly rallying support to regain his authority, the Committee overthrew him and replaced him with a more compliant sultan. The Committee then revised the constitution, leaving the sultanate formally in place but transferring effective sovereignty to the parliament; the revision also nullified for all time the Ottoman concept of a multinational commonwealth. What the Young Turks established instead was a regime committed to nationhood for the Turks.

The Young Turk revolution speeded the disintegration of the empire, inviting demands for freedom from Turkish rule not only from Balkan Christians but from a few Arab Muslims who had caught the nationalist contagion. Beginning in 1911, a series of Balkan wars further shrank the empire's control over its European provinces. As World War I approached, the Committee of Union and Progress, overriding the parliament to become a military oligarchy, allied the empire with Germany and Austria. The war, undertaken with foreboding, ended in catastrophe, with the Christian provinces emancipated and the Muslim provinces in European hands. As for the Turks, they were driven back into Anatolia, whence they had gone forth on their wave of glory seven centuries before. Only now they were fighting to save Turkey from extinction altogether.

IV NEVER A RENAISSANCE

THE DECLINE AND FALL of the Ottoman Empire has been attributed to a range of causes, among them the Ottomans' monarchical decadence and fiscal mismanagement, the overextension of lines of communication and supply, and the shift in international commerce to the New World, which left the eastern Mediterranean an economic backwater. But the crucial explanation, historians agree, was the technological backwardness, in agriculture and industry on the one hand and in military weaponry on the other, into which the empire increasingly fell. Many observers, both Muslim and non-Muslim, consider this intellectual weakness a by-product of a basic antagonism to creative thinking that had come increasingly to characterize Islam. Whether or not this is true, the Ottomans, in their last centuries, were unable to hold their own against the intellectual dynamism of the Christian powers, whose engine was an aggressive, secular nationalism rather than an old-fashioned faith in God.

Though the Ottomans were the dominant force within Islam when the West edged into its lead in the fourteenth or fifteenth century, the intellectual race may well have been lost several hundred years earlier, by the Arabs of the Abbasid era. It was an era that began auspiciously. A desert people with almost no previous exposure to the outside world, the Arabs who settled Baghdad in the eighth century were attracted to the ideas of Greek thinkers, fragments of whose writings had been left behind when the Byzantines abandoned Damascus. Some historians speculate that the Abbasids, searching for treatment of their ailments in Greek medical writings, came by chance upon the Greek philosophers. Whatever the explanation, Caliph Harun al-Rashid saw to it that his conquering armies transported Greek manuscripts back to Baghdad as booty, and in A.D. 830 a successor caliph established the Beit al-Hikmah (House of Wisdom), a combination library and translation bureau, which the historian Hitti called "the most important educational institution since the foundation of the Alexandrian Museum in the first half of the third century B.C."

These manuscripts were initially translated by Christians and Jews and, within a few decades of the dynasty's founding, had provided the Arab world with access to Homer, Galen and Euclid, as well as Aristotle and the Neo-Platonists. They served as the starting point of an age in which

Baghdad was the world's leader in the study of mathematics, astronomy, geography, medicine and chemistry. At the time the Arabs were reaching these stunning intellectual heights, Europe, dominated by ecclesiastics, was still in the Dark Ages.

While some Arab thinkers were breaking new ground in the sciences, others were engaged in a serious reexamination of Islamic doctrine. Faithful Muslims, they struggled to reconcile the process of rational thought, exalted by the Greeks, with a belief in the literalness of God's revelation, as expressed in the Koran and in the statements of the Prophet. "We should not be ashamed to acknowledge truth from whatever source it comes to us, even if it is brought to us by former generations and foreign peoples," wrote Yaqub ibn Ishaq al-Kindi, a student of Aristotle who became known in this era as "the philosopher of the Arabs." "For him who seeks the truth, there is nothing of higher value than truth itself." The early caliphs themselves favored a school of theologians called the Mutazilites, who argued that Islamic texts should agree with the judgments of reason. These caliphs did not hesitate to persecute as heretics those who professed a theology which held that the Koran, being of celestial origin, had necessarily to be the only truth.

But the rationalists were not preeminent for long. Within a century, the dominant scholarship had shifted in favor of an orthodoxy which maintained that human behavior had to be governed not by reason but by divine will alone. Its proponents argued that the Koran was meant to be the final word, which could not be improved upon and so could never be subject to review. Although the debate dragged on, it took only another century or two before the *ulema* and the jurists had shaped the *shari'a* into a rigorous body of rules based exclusively on the scriptures, effectively expunging reason as a factor in the doctrine of Sunni Islam. "My community will not agree on an error," is one of the celebrated statements attributed to Mohammed, its implication being, according to the orthodox interpretation, that whatever is should continue to be, without challenge.

"In theology and law, in science and philosophy, in literature and the humanities, Islam is today what it was nine centuries ago," wrote Hitti, with obvious regret, in his *History of the Arabs*. Islam became, and remained, a calcified system of thought. In one of the great ironies of history, the philosophical spadework done by Islamic thinkers in the Abbasid age, along with the texts of the Greeks, made the journey from Baghdad to Western Europe, where they were instrumental in terminating the Dark Ages by ushering in the intellectual explosion known as the Renaissance.

Muslims, both Arabs and Turks, readily acknowledge that, judged by a range of intellectual criteria, their civilization does not measure up to that of the West, and it is common to hear them lament, "We never had a

Renaissance." Many say it without knowing quite what it means. Europe, starting with Italy in the fourteenth century and moving northward, broke away from medieval orthodoxies by virtue of the willingness of exceptional individuals to reexamine the truths passed on to them in the name of Christianity. Among them were artists, inventors, poets, philosophers. Some were even businessmen, explorers or politicians. Together, they began to replace a priest-ridden civilization with secular societies committed to unraveling, through reason and observation, the mysteries of life on earth. They were not necessarily antireligious; generally, they proclaimed man's right to worship as he chose. The value held in common by these rebels was, above all, the free exercise of the intellect.

In the preface to the book which argued that the earth revolved around the sun, transforming mankind's concept of its relation to the universe, Copernicus stated, "I can well believe that, when what I have written becomes known, there will be an uproar. . . . A philosopher's ideas may conflict with those held by the common people—since the philosopher's goal is truth within the bounds set by God to human intelligence—but I do not believe they should be rejected for reasons of prejudice."

It is difficult to imagine many Muslims even today, willing to write those phrases. Islam—the very word means "surrender" or "submission" to God's will—succeeded where Christianity failed in shackling man's powers of reasoning. It was a success for which Muslim society has continued to pay heavily. Individuals persuaded that God's word has been set down for all time face problems when trying to depart from customary thinking or conventional deeds. Arabs have often noted an intrinsic disposition to conservatism, if not to fatalism, within their culture. They are uncomfortable with intellectual challenge. Gustave von Grunebaum, an esteemed European scholar, wrote that Islam, mistrustful of free will, "inclines to a deterministic solution. . . . The Muslim deeply feels man's insignificance, the uncertainty of his fate, and the omnipotence of the uncontrollable power above him." Few Arabs would disagree with Grunebaum's conclusion that the Muslim is far readier than the Westerner to accept his destiny, however unsatisfactory, as the will of God.

In the West, of course, free thought has had its martyrs. Copernicus was one of them, and the battle between free thinkers and orthodoxy goes on, which is perhaps as it should be. The explanation is hardly that Western religion, historically, has been more tolerant of dissent than Islam. It is rather that the church failed in its effort to stifle the revolution that the mind of the Renaissance had ignited. The Muslim community never had a Copernicus. Nor did it have, as Dogan Koban pointed out, a Rousseau. In our own time, it cannot abide the challenges to religious orthodoxy of a Salman Rushdie. Orthodox Islam deprived the Ottomans not of cannon but of the power to overturn dogma, a more vital weapon. In the years when Europe was setting the stage for modern times, the Ottoman empire was closing the curtain on its future.

V ATATURK'S REPUBLIC

WELL BEFORE the end of World War I, the Allies had reached a consensus in principle on carving up the Ottoman empire, stripping away both its Balkan and its Arab provinces. These peripheral territories, however, were not enough to satisfy the victors' appetites. Russia wanted Istanbul itself and the Straits, to satisfy its long-held dreams of access to the Mediterranean, as well as some of northeast Anatolia. Italy insisted on a piece of southwest Anatolia, around the city of Adalia (now Antalya), and France claimed the region called Cilicia to the north of Syria, which it was seeking as a mandate. Athens, visualizing its own empire, proposed moving its border in Thrace to the gates of Constantinople; it also had an eye on Turkey's Aegean coast, inhabited by Greeks since antiquity. In addition, the Armenians and Kurds demanded independent states in Anatolia. As for Britain, which already ruled over Ottoman Egypt, it planned to take its booty in the oil fields of Iraq, while presiding regally over the disposition of its allies' competing claims. In public, however, it took a more lofty position, joining with America's President Wilson in supporting Turkey's sovereignty within the historical Turkish homeland.

When the war was over, the Turks had little to say about the settlement. The sultan remained on his throne in Istanbul; but the city was occupied by the Allies and, with much of his army disbanded, he was totally subject to their whims. The Bolsheviks had recently taken power in Russia, and Allied leaders, with relief, cancelled Moscow's claims. In fact, after the Soviet revolution, they pondered whether it was better to keep Turkey intact as a bulwark against Bolshevism, but they never reached that decision.

In the spring of 1919, while the victors were meeting at Versailles, the Italians, distrustful of their allies' intentions, seized Adalia. Furious, Britain and America authorized Greece to land in Smyrna (Izmir) to stop the Italians from advancing. The Turks, who had barely reacted to the Italians, became aroused by the appearance of the Greeks, their historic enemy, and spontaneously formed guerrilla units to harass the Greek beachhead. By now the Turks understood that if their country was to avoid dismemberment, their local resistance had to be transformed into a national movement, and for this they needed a leader. Fortunately for them, a leader appeared in May 1919, in defiance of both the Allies and the sultan, declaring his intent to raise an army to beat back the Greeks. His name was Mustafa Kemal, later to be known as Ataturk—"Father Turk."

Son of a minor official, Kemal belonged to the generation of Ottoman army officers trained in secular Western ways. Born in 1880, he was like most Turks of the period in having no surname; given Mustafa, he took Kemal in cadet school. Later, he attended the military academy and the staff college, where he joined protests against the sultanate and was once briefly jailed. But he was never involved with the Young Turks, and in 1914 he opposed their decision to enter the war. As a colonel in 1915, he commanded the successful defense of Istanbul against the British armies at Gallipoli, and as a general in 1916 he won a series of victories against the Russians in the east. Though he was by then the Ottomans' most illustrious commander, his reputation for fractiousness consigned him late in the war to relative idleness. He was in Istanbul when Turkish irregulars attacked the Greeks, and was ordered by the sultan, who feared both Turkish nationalism and the Allied occupiers, to hasten to Anatolia to quell the military revolt. Kemal went, but he defied his orders. At Samsun on the Black Sea coast, he declared that the sultan was a captive of the Allies, and proclaimed his intention to preserve national independence. The course he adopted led to the end of the empire and the establishment of a Turkish republic.

Resigning his commission, Kemal set up a headquarters in Ankara, a small town in the Central Anatolian hills. In April 1920, after the sultan dismissed the parliament, Kemal convoked a provisional governing body, which he called the Grand National Assembly. The sultan's response, in compliance with Allied orders, was to sentence him and his followers to death. In August, the sultan signed the Treaty of Sèvres, a peace settlement whose terms were harsher than those imposed by the Allies on Germany. It not only ended Turkish sovereignty in the Balkan and Arab provinces but transferred to France, Italy and Greece virtually all the land they coveted in Anatolia and Thrace. In addition, Armenia and Kurdistan were to become independent. The treaty, in effect, left as Turkish territory only Istanbul and its immediate surroundings. For many Turks, the sultan's signature on this document decisively ended the ambivalence they had felt until then. Turks everywhere rallied to Kemal.

Whereas the Treaty of Sèvres made the sultan the symbol of national dismemberment, Kemal now became the instrument of Turkish nationhood. Istanbul was soon without authority, and over the next three years, Kemal rebuilt the army and won a series of battles, and, as head of the recognized government, signed treaties with the Soviet Union, France and Italy, which had lost their appetite for war and agreed to give up their territorial claims. Meanwhile, Turkish forces repeatedly met and defeated the Greeks. In September 1922, the Turkish army crossed the Straits into Europe to face the Allied occupation forces, which chose to withdraw from Istanbul rather than fight. Now positioned to recapture much of the old empire, Kemal laid aside that temptation, announcing that the republic would not extend its boundaries beyond the traditional Turkish homeland. In October, the Greeks acceded to an armistice, and a few days later Kemal took possession of Istanbul; but as a sign of a new day, he chose not to reestablish the government there. Instead, he designated Ankara as the capital, and so it has remained.

With its enemies routed, the Turkish government passed a law abolishing the sultanate, though, as a sop to traditionalists, it bestowed the caliphate—provisionally—on a cousin of the sultan. Conservatives protested Kemal's high-handedness, but he would accept no other course. In November 1922, the last of the dynasty, Sultan Mehmet VI, boarded a British warship and sailed to Malta, bringing the Ottoman age formally to an end. Three days later, Turkish and Allied delegates met in Lausanne to affirm Turkish sovereignty over Anatolia and Thrace, within the pre-1914 boundaries. Both Armenians and Kurds lost the states promised to them. Under the treaty signed by the parties, the Ottoman empire vanished, and "Turkey" joined the family of nations.

Kemal's nationalism was concerned with more than borders, however. In a 1923 speech quoted by Bernard Lewis, he warned: "The successes which our army has gained up to now cannot be regarded as having achieved the real salvation of our country. . . . Let us not be puffed up with military victories. Let us rather prepare for new victories in science and economics." By "science," his biographers tell us, he meant the enlightened laws of human behavior. His Westernized education had convinced him that the empire's increasingly dismal record was the product of Ottoman despotism and Islamic obscurantism, and without apology he resolved that Turkish society, once and for all, would shift its orientation from East to West. Guided by his belief in "science," Kemal took upon himself the responsibility to make Turkey—in politics, religion, law, education, social relations, economics, even in dress—into an enlightened Western state.

Kemal's state was a constitutional republic governed by a democratically elected parliament. During his lifetime, the parliament generally bowed before his autocratic temperament, but since his death in 1938, the practice of democracy—though with periodic setbacks—has continued to advance. Kemal established the Republican People's Party as the governing instrument of the state. He failed to open the system to competing parties, and specifically barred the formation of religious parties. But he laid the groundwork for the multiparty political structure that evolved in Turkey in later years.

In 1924, Kemal abolished the caliphate—Islam had long since ceded the powers of the office to Istanbul—and at the same time nullified the *shari'a* as the law of the land, replacing it with an adaptation of the Swiss civil code. He relieved the *ulema* of responsibility for the schools, which he placed in the hands of secular authorities. To emphasize church-state separation, he also imposed a constitutional ban on Islamic political organizations.

To facilitate Westernization, Kemal substituted the Roman for the Arabic alphabet in written Turkish, adopted the Western calendar and decreed Sunday instead of the Muslim Friday as the weekly day of rest. He required all Turks, for the first time, to adopt surnames—which was when he was given the name Ataturk by the Assembly—and he extended to women the right both to vote and to sit in parliament. Though even he did not have the courage to ban the veil for women, he consistently attacked it as a barbarous religious relic. He was more daring with the men, prohibiting the fez, a distinctively Muslim headgear (it was designed to permit the touching of the forehead to the ground in prayer), calling it "an emblem of ignorance, negligence, fanaticism and hatred of progress and civilization."

Elected president in 1923, Kemal continued to rethink and reshape the society. He had, almost single-handedly, created a revolution, and though it was far less violent than its French and Russian counterparts, it was also more radical, particularly in its social and cultural ramifications. Kemal transformed a civilization, leaving practically nothing of the old orthodoxy undisturbed. His revolution, no doubt, built upon a century of Ottoman reform; Kemal was himself one of its offspring. Yet, no social metamorphosis ever owed more to the vision and action of one man. Turks today remain in awe of what Ataturk did to them and for them. Though the practice of modernization has in many ways lagged behind the spirit of the laws that he instituted, he generated a momentum which the Turks, with few exceptions, have shown no disposition to reverse.

"What you must understand about contemporary Turkey is that Ataturk was first of all a soldier, and that the army saw itself as the instrument of Westernization and modernization," a history professor said during a symposium on Kemal that I attended at the Bosporus University. "The army was the only institution that emerged out of the ruins of the Ottoman empire with a grasp of the West. It was—and this is not normal for an army, much less an Islamic army—the nation's intelligentsia, its source of creative thinkers. Its arms liberated the national territory from foreigners after the Treaty of Sèvres, but it also deposed the sultan and established the republic. In most other countries, the army is seen as a right-wing instrument, a servant of the ruling class, maybe fascist, certainly conservative. The Turkish army is conservative, but only by Kemalist standards. The conservatism of the army is Ataturkism, which goes beyond nationalism to include secularism and democracy. For these reasons, the people have confidence in it.

"Remember, the Turkish army predated the state, and it still asserts its seniority. It is much more autonomous than, say, the central bank, the universities or even the parliament. In that sense, Turkey departs from the West, where the army is kept more strictly under civilian control. The Turkish army justifies its resistance to such control by asserting responsibility for the preservation of Ataturk's work. The army is anti-Communist and anti-*ulema*, but it is beholden to no political party. Three times since World War Two, it has intervened to supplant governments, both right and left of center, but in each case, the republic was in danger—or, at least, so it seemed, both to the army and to most Turks. Each time, after it restored order and applied correctives to the system, it went back to its barracks. Westerners consider such an arrangement dangerous to democratic rule. It is a paradox to the West, but Turks have more confidence in the army as a democratic institution than in the state itself."

What the Ataturk revolution did not do, however, was change the citizen's relationship to the power of the state. Kemal's quarrel with the Ottomans was not that their regime was oppressive—though it was—but that it had served the Turks badly. In justifying the termination of the dynasty, he sometimes extolled the sovereignty of the people, but he meant this as a denial of the sovereignty of God, the conventional Islamic concept. Islam's designation of God as sovereign was, as he saw it, simply a cover for the reactionary rule of the *ulema*. Ataturk's real belief was in the sovereignty of the nation, a formulation that placed individual rights on a tier below the needs of the community. Central to Ataturk's thinking—a concept imbued in him by his Ottoman training—was always the supremacy of the state.

Scholars generally agree that had Ataturk shown a fastidious regard for democracy as the term is understood in the West, his revolution would have been stillborn. To be successful, democracy requires that the voting population identify with the nation, permitting voters to make choices within a civil context. In Turkey after World War I, nearly all voters identified themselves less as citizens than as Muslims; many still do. Notwithstanding Ataturk's immense personal prestige, Islamic traditions were too strong for most Turks to have acceded voluntarily to his notions of change. Kemal was an authoritarian. Suspicious of the popular will, he claimed that during the centuries of despotism the people had been deprived of their capacity to determine their self-interest. Even today, Turkey's liberals have reservations about lifting restrictions on religious parties, and it is the country's Islamic leaders, confident of having the popular support needed to pull the society back toward the *shari'a*, who now call most vigorously for more democracy.

The Turks never asked for Ataturkism; it was Kemal who bestowed it upon them, through the instrument of the state. Public opinion, as he understood the concept, was not for consulting but for shaping. He was a teacher, who explained to the Turks in detail the rationale for each of his reforms. But when he could not shape opinion as he wanted, he rode roughshod over it, citing "science" as his authority. Turks, having for centuries willingly followed the strictures of the sultans, raised little protest to following the strictures of Ataturk. He promoted democracy, but not as an end in itself, as it is in the West; he saw it as the best means to modernize Turkey quickly. Kemal had little patience for the rights of individuals in relation to the state, and it is a concept the Turks still have trouble grasping.

VI HEADSCARF AND MINISKIRT

WITH A POPULATION that is 98 or 99 percent Muslim, Turks say theirs is an Islamic country—but they quickly add that it is not Iran or Saudi Arabia, countries that serve up the faith undiluted. So just how Muslim is it? The nature and degree of commitment demanded by Islam is a question that Muslims wrestle with throughout the Middle East today. Checking out the restaurant scene in Istanbul, for example, one does not encounter much that looks traditionally Islamic—that is, austere, exclusively male, nonalcoholic. It is possible to spend a week in Ankara, the most republican of Turkish cities, and never see a headscarf, at least in the stylish downtown area where the civil servants work and shop. The Turkish countryside, barely distinguishable from rural Syria or Egypt, is another matter. It is a land of the veil and the *abaya*, and of crippling poverty. Are the veil and the *abaya* the measure of Islam? Perhaps it is more relevant to ask whether the trend in Turkey is toward the conquest of the countryside by modern secular values or the takeover of the cities by traditional Islam. There is evidence of both. Secular Turks worry, and many often ask: Is Ataturkism currently yielding to the surge of fundamentalist Islam?

Few Turks imagine the country will go the way of Iran or Saudi Arabia. Most think the prospect of a fundamentalist revolution is farfetched. Overwhelmingly Sunni, Turks find little positive to say about the Shiites of Iran and, having acquired an appetite for democracy, they are offended by the autocratic powers of the Saudi monarchy. Almost all of Turkey's Islamic thinkers express a nationalist doctrine, arguing that Iran and Saudi Arabia have corrupted Islam. Even under the Ottomans, Turkey was rather casual about its Islamic practices, and the society is certainly unlikely to succumb to fundamentalism today.

Still, a struggle is underway between secularists and traditionalists and, in a society changing as fast as Turkey's, the outcome is by no means certain. It is worrisome to the secularists, for example, that religion recently established a beachhead within the state educational system; moreover, schools for Islamic clergy are turning out as many as fifty thousand graduates a year. But, as a Turk with a taste for American football said to me, if we take Iran or Saudi Arabia as the standard, the contest in Turkey between religious and secular visions is currently being waged within the forty- or forty-five-yard line. Whatever Ataturk's goal, Turkey's secularists have come to recognize that stamping out Islam is impossible. Similarly, even the most committed traditionalists acknowledge that the country has come too far to revert to Koranic rule. So the two sides, with a few exceptions, have become reasonably tolerant of each other and have tacitly accepted rules that limit their jousting to a quest for minor and usually symbolic rewards.

A few years ago, the country went through a joust over headscarves on university campuses. It raised tempers perilously but was surely minor and symbolic. During several visits I made to campuses, most students I saw dressed in blue jeans and sweaters. But three or four years earlier, some women at the University of Istanbul had taken to wearing headscarves to cover their hair, as a sign of their Islamic commitment. Since Ataturk's day, regulations have forbidden headscarves among government workers, but the rules for students were unclear, and in 1986, the Higher Education Council, which supervises the universities, ended the equivocation by banning them outright. After that, young women were sporadically disciplined for violating the code, and a few were expelled. It was the expulsions that set off the tempest, not just on the campuses but in parliament, the state bureaucracy and the newspapers.

In the national assembly, a coalition of conservatives put together a majority to pass a bill which lifted the ban and reinstated the dismissed students. Kenan Evren, then Turkey's president, promptly vetoed it. Evren was an ex-general who sometimes gave in to the Islamics but who nonetheless saw himself as the upholder of the army's traditions of Westernism and Ataturkism. "Modern garb is an inalienable requisite of the modernizing principles and reforms of the founder of the republic," he wrote in his veto message, and he went on to say that should an unlimited freedom of dress be recognized, professors and students would show up in school in "veils, baggy trousers, shorts, fancy evening dresses, knee-britches, long hair or beards." The last reference was to the short, neatly clipped beards which young Muslim men had made the male counterpart of the headscarf.

The Higher Education Council overrode the president, a procedure authorized by law. But in reversing its own ban, the council said it would continue to require dress that "does not contradict civilized norms," adding that, after a serious study, it had concluded that "a modern style headscarf is civilized." Muslims declared a victory. But so did Hasan Cemal, a secular columnist who promoted civil liberties. "Ataturk's reforms," he wrote, "envisaged changing ways of thinking. When he introduced the hat [to replace the fez], he did not believe that in itself the hat would change people's thinking. Meddling with people's clothing, their hairstyles and beards on the threshold of the twenty-first century has nothing to do with Ataturk."

Ayla, a sweet-faced, brown-eyed girl of eighteen, was a student who wore a headscarf. She and Nilufer, a pretty nineteen-year-old with flowing golden hair, had met as classmates at the University of Istanbul. An intern at the daily newspaper *Gunes*, Nilufer arranged for Ayla to meet me, on condition that I not use her last name, for fear of embarrassing her traditionalist family. The three of us had coffee at the *Gunes* office; Nilufer, who spoke excellent English, translated.

Ayla wore a blue-checked scarf on her head, from which not a hair protruded. She also wore a light blue sweater and an ankle-length skirt and had on no makeup. Obviously shy, she told me she was the only one of five children in the family to attend the university. She had hoped to be a lawyer but fell below the qualifying marks for the law faculty, so she chose journalism. Though her family had been loath to have her exposed to the temptations of Istanbul, she said, she won them over to her desire for an education and a career. With ten other girls, all serious Muslims, she was currently renting a house in one of the city's strictly religious neighborhoods.

Ayla told me that, though she had always been a believer, her study of the Koran had only recently convinced her that wearing a headscarf was the right thing to do. She denied that wearing it was in any way a political act. "Wearing a scarf or a long skirt is less important than having inside you a belief in God," she said. "That belief is what makes me feel happy." When I asked her how she planned to pursue a career in journalism, she replied, "I want to work for a Muslim magazine that will take me as I am. A newspaper like this"—meaning *Gunes*—"wouldn't take me in these clothes, and if I give up wearing this scarf, I'll be another person. I don't want a career for myself but only to serve God. I want to be a journalist who transmits God's will."

Ayla acknowledged that she was comfortable only with people who shared her commitment to Islam, and, indeed, she seemed quite uncomfortable with me. Referring to Nilufer, she said she was troubled at being so fond of someone who lacked her strong religious beliefs, and she said she wished she could help her friend to become a believer. When we finished talking, I reflexively reached out my hand to thank her and say good-bye, and I sensed a dilemma as she drew back a half-step. But in an instant she resolved the dilemma by brushing her fingers quickly across mine. Then, with dignity, she stood up and left.

Later, Nilufer confirmed that Ayla found physical contact, even hand-shaking, distasteful and said she had been brave to meet me at all. It had taken hours, Nilufer said, to persuade Ayla to talk to me. "Finally she trusted me," Nilufer said. Then, on arriving at *Gunes*, it took an hour to find a pin she insisted she needed to hold her scarf more tightly under her chin. But fond as she was of Ayla, Nilufer challenged the assertion that the headscarf was not meant politically. "She's not militant," Nilufer said, "and she doesn't try to convert me, like so many of the religious students. Maybe the scarf isn't political for her, but for the other girls, it's a sign of protest against the government, which they say is hostile to Islam. For them, the headscarf is a very big deal.

"My friends and I often discuss the difference between girls like her and our own crowd," Nilufer said. "I wear miniskirts and hats. I date boys. I make up my hair. I asked Ayla if she envied me because of that, and she said what matters is what's inside. I don't know what she means. Sometimes we see girls our age wearing the *abaya*. In summer, they wear these long things down to their ankles, even gloves, and we don't understand it. These are good times for women in Turkey. We can study what we want and choose our career. There are plenty of good jobs, especially if a girl knows a foreign language. Some girls have jobs that their boyfriends can't get. It's true that a girl like Ayla can't get a job in a place like *Gunes*. Her clothes would make the people who work with her too uncomfortable.

"My grandmother, who is sixty-five, gets more upset than I do at girls like Ayla. She doesn't want the government to allow any religious dress at all. She says Ataturk taught us to go forward, so why are we going back to the sultans?"

The late Turgut Ozal, who became Turkey's president in 1989, had fought against the ban on headscarfs. Ozal was often said to be soft on religious symbolism, so soft that secularists maintained that his goals exceeded the symbolic. The Motherland Party, of which he was the leader, had a religious wing with which he was said to be in sympathy. Prime minister at the time of my visit, Ozal was the first of his rank to attend the mosque and openly say prayers, practices that had been scorned by

Ataturk. He had been on a *hajj* to Mecca. He was even said to be a member of a secret Sufi society called the Naksibendis, something like an Islamic Masonic order. Ozal himself was far too Western to favor Turkey's Islamization. But being a practical man, he understood that religious symbolism was important to the small-town Anatolians who were his most faithful constituency.

Actually, Ozal's wife Semra was regarded as the family's secularist, which was counter to convention in Turkey, and in most of the Third World, where women are generally more religious than men. Semra Ozal was a favorite of most of Turkey's feminists, a small but dedicated band, for publicly and aggressively asserting her individuality. Some feminists, however, criticized her for failing to move beyond Ataturk's vision, which lifted many of the disabilities imposed by Islam on women but left in place a legal system badly skewed in favor of men. Semra Ozal smoked, spoke up in public and held her husband's hand on television to advertise her equality in the marriage. Turks gossiped that she had barred her husband's extremely religious brother, Korkut, from the house, on the grounds that he was a bad influence on the children. More important, she took her feminism into the countryside, traveling from village to village urging women to defend their rights within the family. Said to have political ambitions of her own, Mrs. Ozal, in contrast to her husband, openly aligned herself with the Motherland Party's liberal wing.

Semra Ozal received me at the official residence in Ankara one afternoon, greeted me in English, then switched to Turkish as she got into the subject of women in Turkey. "Turkish women are very fortunate," she said. "Women in Europe had to fight for their rights. In Turkey, Ataturk gave them these rights voluntarily. There are no problems with the system in Turkey that would not be cured if women were persuaded to exercise these rights." She insisted that her husband, notwithstanding his religious practices, supported her work among rural women, including family planning. One of her major achievements, she said, had been to convince traditional women—along with their husbands and fathers—that Islam permitted them to be examined by male doctors. This change, she said, had already helped to bring down the high rate of infant mortality in the countryside.

"I have not encountered serious resistance from the clergy," she said, responding to a question I raised about the Islamic reaction. "In fact, I've succeeded in enlisting the imams on my side. Even the fundamentalists respect the work I am doing. Remember, we are a Muslim society but we are not Iran. We are the world's most modern Islamic country."

Mehmet Kececiler, the former mayor of Konya, an Anatolian city with deep Islamic roots, was the formal leader of the Motherland Party's religious wing. Though he was said to be the dominant force within the party, his followers complained that their influence was not equal to their numbers, and they blamed Ozal. Kececiler, a heavyset man in his mid-forties, acknowledged his religious commitment. He told me he believed in God and abstained from alcohol, but he added with a chuckle that he was modern enough to have only one wife. Since his election in 1983, he said, he had been a spokesman for Turkey's Muslims but, whatever the opposition's claims, he was not an extremist. He thought of himself, he said, as a democrat, a political more than a religious man, and a thorough opponent of a theocratic state.

"We are realists," Kececiler said in his tiny office in the complex built by Ataturk in Ankara for the body that is still officially called the Grand National Assembly. "I cannot abandon my religious convictions but I was educated in lay schools in Turkey and in France, and I sincerely accept the laicism in our constitution. Our wing of the party believes in some Islamic education in state schools but thinks that extended religious training should be paid for by voluntary funds. I oppose pornography and beer sales to students, but I have no interest in banning alcohol. We are completely committed to the West, of which Turkey is a part. Our group wants to be on good terms with the Islamic world, but we don't want to resurrect the Ottoman mentality."

Not all of Turkey's religious thinkers, however, talked in such conciliatory terms, though the extremists tended to be at the margins of politics. One of them was Fehmi Koru, a thirty-eight-year-old columnist for a small Islamic newspaper called *Zaman*. I met him in a shabby office in a working-class quarter of Ankara.

"We have figures that say sixty percent of Turks practice Islam, and the other forty percent identify with it," he said. "In this neighborhood, everyone practices. I believe the majority are fed up with the present situation. The politicians who have been governing us for sixty years still figure that anything Ottoman, and that includes Islam, has to be bad. But we Turks have an extraordinary past. We once lived at the apex. Why not again? Imitating foreign ideas cannot get us back to where we were. The present government takes the ideas for its economic system from Western professors. Why not adopt a system that's nearer to our roots? Islam is the key to our past, and we believe it is the key to our future."

Ismail Kara, a slim, soft-spoken man of thirty-three, was a writer, but one little known except in religious circles. "When the Ottomans fell and the army established the republic, Islam was discarded," he told me during a talk in the back room of a religious bookstore in downtown Istanbul. "Since then, the army has perpetuated a one-sided secularism, in which religion has no role in the state but the state can interfere in religious affairs. We don't have real democracy. Our movement thinks that drinking alcohol is a sin, but no religious authority can say it. We cannot even observe our day of rest on Friday. In my judgment, if the Turkish people could express themselves freely—that is, if they could vote for religious parties—they would say that they want a restoration of conditions that would enable them to live according to their Islamic beliefs."

Notwithstanding the ban on Islamic parties, religion's strongest voice in Turkey belongs to a political party named Refah, which pushes its program to the edge of what the state will tolerate. Refah—the word means "prosperity"—is heir to the National Salvation Party, to which the two Ozal brothers once belonged. Oguzhan Asilturk, its secretary-general, was a cabinet minister in the 1970s, when he succeeded in enacting laws enlarging the religious school system. Asilturk and I talked at Refah's headquarters in an Ankara suburb, part of a complex that had its own mosque. The office workers I saw shuffled about Islamic-style, in their stockinged feet.

Asilturk, a small, clean-shaven man, ridiculed the notion that Turgut Ozal was a good Muslim. He criticized Ozal's failure to extend the religious school system beyond where he himself had left it more than a decade before, and to subsidize the building of mosques. Asilturk argued that the government was actually anti-Islamic and he urged real laicization, which he defined as state neutrality in relations with religion. Though he denied that Refah had any plan to impose the *shari'a*, he said it was immoral that Turkish law, in banning religious parties, denied people the political means to seek religious goals. Islam's failure to expand its popular support, he said, was the consequence of its exclusion from the state-owned television channels. Asilturk was the only major political figure I met in Turkey who departed from the national consensus in favor of membership in the European Community.

"The European Community," he said, "is a Christian union, and we are a Muslim country. They tell us openly there is no part there for us. It is very difficult for Muslims to be together with Christians. We are different, our way of life is different, our customs are different. We are part of Eastern thought. We can increase our economic and cultural relations with the Christians but we cannot be intimately linked with them in one state, like the states of the United States, and that is their goal. It would not give us the freedom we need to develop our Islamic character. We would live in perpetual crisis."

IN TURKEY, Ataturk did more than build the foundations of a modern state. He also narrowed the huge intellectual gap with the West that began with the Renaissance. But there are dissenters, like Asilturk, from the consensus in favor of Ataturk's work. Asilturk and his comrades in the Islamic movement leave no doubt that many Turks still reject the secularism that Ataturk imposed on them. They question whether Turkish society can be modern without secular values, and they make clear that if it cannot, they prefer not to be modern. At the moment, their view seems to be gaining ground in the Islamic world. Will it determine the course that Arabs take?

The Arabs have never had an Ataturk. They have had a Nasser and a Saddam Hussein—secularists yet also leaders whose attraction to a quickfix vision of grandeur overrode their commitment to social and intellectual transformation. The lesson, perhaps, is that there are no shortcuts to the modern world. Whatever their charisma, the vision of these leaders proved to be a mirage. Forswearing grandeur, Ataturk set Turkey on a course of hard work to attain economic and social transformation. He made mistakes. He certainly had an impaired view of democracy and human rights. But he had the courage to challenge orthodoxies that were deeply rooted among the Turks. The same orthodoxies exist among the Arabs. More than a half century after Ataturk's death, Turkish society is still struggling to lighten the burdens imposed by traditional Islam but Turkey is moving ahead. Can the same be said of the Arabs?

Ataturks are rare in history, and the Arabs can scarcely expect one to appear among them anytime soon. A question that Turkey's experience raises is whether the Arabs can ever truly enter the modern world without one. Can they afford to dismiss the Turkish experience as inapplicable? Will they reject an Ataturk if he does appear? In the absence of such a figure, Arab societies slog along on their own, progressing fitfully, a step forward inevitably followed by a half-step back. It is not certain, given the handicaps, that even Turkey's achievement will be equal to its ambitions. It is still less certain for the Arabs.

CHAPTER THREE

EGYPT

I MEETING MAHFOUZ

CROSSING TAHRIR SQUARE each morning to meet Naguib Mahfouz, the Nobel laureate in literature, was not easy. The hub of modern Cairo, Tahrir—Arabic for "liberation"—is a few steps from the east bank of the Nile. Along its periphery are the city's principal hotels, the offices of the major government ministries, the Egyptian Museum and the airline offices. The busiest shopping streets radiate from it in a half-circle. At its southern end stands a sprawling thirteen-story eyesore called the Mugamma, central workplace of the state bureaucracy, where, Cairenes like to say, more bodies are at rest than in all the tombs of ancient Egypt. Just to the west is the now rehabilitated headquarters of the Arab League, vacant between Egypt's expulsion for talking peace with Israel in 1977 until the Egyptians' restoration to their fellow Arabs' good graces a dozen years later.

Egypt had been the preeminent member of the Arab League since its founding in 1945. Indeed, throughout the modern era, Egypt has been the standard-bearer among the Arabs. Its population, currently nearly sixty million, makes it the largest of the Arab states, but that is not the only measure. It was Egyptians, the first Arabs seriously exposed to the West, who led in aspiring to European-style nationhood. Egyptian thinkers broke new ground in attempting to reconcile traditional Islam with the values of the contemporary West. Egyptian universities produced a stream of well-trained professionals and artists who fanned out to serve the Middle East region. Egypt offered the first Arab challenge to colonialism. An Egyptian friend recalls his grandfather solemnly reminiscing that when Japan defeated Russia in the war of 1905 and took its place among the modern nations, he and his friends believed that Egypt would be the next in line. It had, however, stumbled along the way. And, not surprisingly, the other Arab peoples were no more successful. When Egypt was expelled from the Arab League, an official predicted boldly to me that it would soon be back, since the Arabs needed Egypt. The League's return to Cairo vindicated his boast.

When I first saw Tahrir Square in 1973, the smiling face of Anwar Sadat, recently triumphant in the October war, beamed down from a huge painted panel upon the hordes of passersby. Eventually his appeal faded, and in 1981 he was gunned down by Islamic terrorists. I found it hard not to think of Sadat when I saw Tahrir, and I was relieved to see that he had not been forgotten: the Tahrir station of Cairo's new subway bears his name. His successor, Hosni Mubarak, is a more prosaic figure. Without the flamboyance of Sadat, much less of Gamal Abdel Nasser, he is said to be like the typical protagonist of a Mahfouz novel: bumbling, a bit smaller than life. The Egypt over which he rules has reined in the nervous energy of the Nasser and Sadat eras and subordinated its taste for glory to a search for equanimity. Yet to cross Tahrir belied that equanimity. It was a task no less frenzied than I remembered it from my first encounter.

Leaving my hotel each morning, I made my way loftily past hucksters of Pharaonic-style papyruses, exotic native perfumes and guided tours of the pyramids. I navigated through an open-air terminal, where hordes of half-shaven men, whose street-length *galibiyas* proclaimed their rural origins, descended from battered buses to begin their morning's work at God-knows-what menial jobs. I cast an eye at the journals on the newsstand, with their headlines in loose, looping Arabic script, and I took in the pleasant odors of newly baked bread, meat and rice, and grayish hot cereals, offered for sale by elderly women, some of them tattooed, sitting cross-legged on the pavement. Finally, I reached the heavily trafficked boulevards that ring Tahrir, over which, I remembered, a Y-shaped iron footbridge, never painted and rarely swept, once crossed; no doubt it was removed to drive pedestrians into the network of underground passages that make up the subway, but the effort has been only partially successful. Cairenes clearly enjoyed defying oncoming traffic, some of it powered by horses or donkeys but most approaching at remarkably high speeds. Under the indifferent gaze of shabbily uniformed policemen, pedestrians even leaped the picket fences erected to keep them on the sidewalk. I was faced with a decision and, the first few mornings, I followed the underground route, but the psychology of the crowds won me over. On subsequent days I joined them in dashing mindlessly across the thoroughfares.

As I approached the Ali Baba Cafe, I would see Mahfouz sitting next to the upstairs window. On arriving in Cairo a few weeks before, I had turned to intermediaries for an introduction, and the word came back that Mahfouz had been used up by the hordes of journalists who descended after he was awarded the Nobel Prize. So I decided to approach him directly and learned that each Thursday evening he met with young writers at the Kasr-el-Nil, a heavily patronized cafe overlooking the Nile on the upper-income island of Zamalek. Sure enough, that was where I found him, in a downstairs room, surrounded by disciples who looked at me with some suspicion while I engaged the master in talk.

After hearing me out, Mahfouz agreed to meet with me, expressing some regret that he would have to put off a little longer getting back to the rigorous writing routine that for so many decades had dominated his life. He has written a few short stories, he told me, but the only regular writing he did now was a weekly column, usually on politics, for *Al-Ahram*, the Arab world's most celebrated newspaper. "The prize disturbed my life," he said to me, and no doubt he missed the tranquillity he had put to such creative use. Yet, when I knew him better, it was clear to me that this warm and sociable man, so long unknown outside the Arabic-speaking world, enjoyed the attention he was receiving from all points of the compass and that he was ambivalent about getting back to the lonely discipline of composing novels. That evening at the Kasr-el-Nil, Mahfouz invited me to join him the next day at the Ali Baba, where each morning he took his coffee.

In contrast to the neon-lit Kasr-el-Nil, the Ali Baba is a dark recess among the shops that face the square. It is one of a handful of cafes in Cairo and, in the summer months, in Alexandria, where writers gather. Though he had forgotten, I had met Mahfouz at one of them before, in 1982, shortly after I was introduced to his work. I was researching an article which, I thought, needed a literary source, and I decided to approach Tewfik al-Hakim, who was then Egypt's first-ranking man of letters. I was told I would find him drinking coffee on the seaside in Alexandria, a four-hour drive from Cairo across the lush Nile Delta, which for five or six thousand years has been the source of Egypt's riches.

With some difficulty, I found the Champs-Elysées, a small, weathered hotel on the boulevard that ran along the sea. Across from it was the beach, crowded with vacationing Egyptians, the men strutting about in dark suntans, the women seated passively, fully dressed, beneath umbrellas. Inside was a shabby cafe furnished with worn wooden tables and chairs. It was the haunt in the summer season of a group of writers known for their democratic and secularist views. Hakim was their leader. A blue-eyed octogenarian with a white walrus mustache, he spoke elegant French and habitually wore a beret, a vestige of his days as a student at the Sorbonne. The scene over which he presided made me think of a bistro painting by Cézanne, and from midmorning to early afternoon, he graciously orchestrated an exchange between me and the half-dozen men seated around him.

As the hour for the midday meal approached, some of the men drifted off, and when the circle finally broke up, I witnessed what I suspected was a daily ritual, with each member insisting it was his turn to pay the check. In the disarray, I struck up a conversation with a man in dark glasses who had not said a word all morning; he introduced himself as Naguib Mahfouz and he offered me his phone number in Cairo. I still had the slip of paper on which it was written. Later, in recalling the encounter, I asked why he had been silent. After a moment, he replied that he had always found it difficult to express himself around Hakim, who was his mentor, his professor and his literary idol.

For me, however, Mahfouz's work was more important than Hakim's. I was a beginner in the study of Egypt, and he offered me a clear look at the hidden dynamics of Egyptians' social and personal relations. Such relations, in any country, are usually impenetrable to a foreign observer. I found his view free of either apology or ideology. Though sympathetic to the characters he created on his pages, most of them everyday Egyptians, he was unrelenting in dissecting their flaws. He has frequently been called Egypt's conscience; his work, without heroes, made me wonder how Egyptians could read his stories without anguish.

Scholars of Middle East literature say that, as a stylist, Mahfouz writes with remarkable precision. Arabic, a florid language, requires most writers to choose between poetry and clarity; Mahfouz's choice makes his prose easy to translate. He is also a tireless experimenter in literary forms. Even his admirers often acknowledge that Mahfouz is not a great writer (Mahfouz, characteristically, says of himself that, judged on an international scale, he is third-rate), and is certainly not the peer in technique of a Dickens or a Balzac, to whom he has been compared. Yet few question that he deserved the Nobel Prize, in recognition of the unremitting honesty of his work, which sets a standard for other writers, in Egypt and throughout the Third World. For myself, I was grateful to him for bringing to me an Egypt that I could never have hoped to discover on my own.

Mahfouz's deference to Hakim in the Champs-Elysées revealed much about his perception of himself. Unlike the sophisticated Hakim, he was not educated abroad. Mahfouz was born in 1911, the last of seven children, in the rundown quarter of Gamaliya in the Islamic—that is, non-Western—part of Cairo. He attended Islamic elementary schools, earned a place in a secular high school, then attended Cairo University (called, in those days, King Fuad I University), where in 1934 he was awarded a degree in philosophy. To earn a living, he entered the civil service, and remained in the bureaucracy until 1971, when he retired. Only then did he become a full-time writer.

As a bachelor, Mahfouz, like most men of his generation, lived in his parents' home and only married when he was forty-three. He rarely traveled, and had never even seen Upper Egypt, the site of the great Pharaonic monuments, though the Pharaohs were ostensibly the subject of his early novels. (The real subject, lightly veiled in symbolism, was Egypt's struggle against colonialism.) "I didn't travel because I was poor," he told me. "If I had traveled like Hemingway, I'm sure my work would have been different. I understand that my work was shaped by my being so Egyptian." Since the 1930s, he has written almost exclusively about life in Cairo, with scenes occasionally set in Alexandria. In contrast to the Europeanized Hakim, he is considered a pure Egyptian and, since he has experienced little of life in the countryside, a quintessential Cairene.

Mahfouz declined to go to Stockholm to accept the Nobel Prize; his friends told me he was reluctant to travel so far and put on tails to be received by the Swedish king. "I'm very introverted," he said to me in one of our talks, "I don't enjoy leaving my milieu." His refusal created a dilemma in Egypt's literary establishment until he gave in to his wife's urging to send his two daughters—Um Kalthum, then thirty, and Fatma, twenty-seven—to represent him. To chaperone them, he chose the playwright Mohamed Salmawi, one of his acolytes. The two women, dressed in traditional Egyptian gowns, accepted the award on their father's behalf, and Salmawi delivered Mahfouz's Nobel lecture. In it, Mahfouz said how proud he was to be the first to address the Nobel assembly in Arabic, which he called "the real winner of the prize." Hakim was now dead, and the prize ratified Mahfouz—though one or two others claimed the title—as Egypt's first man of letters. It also made him Hakim's heir as the leader of the democratic, secular circle in Cairo's literary cafes.

Each morning Mahfouz would wave when he noticed me on the sidewalk outside the Ali Baba, and his smile would still be on his face when I reached him. He rose in courtly fashion and extended his hand to greet me. He was then seventy-eight years old and fragile. Thin, and with an unusually narrow face, he wore glasses that appeared opaque. His hair was brushed straight back from his high forehead. On most mornings he wore a leisure jacket of wool over a turtleneck shirt. An untouched cup of coffee sat on the table next to several newspapers, of which he said he read only the headlines because of his poor eyesight. Mahfouz answered my questions freely, except on the subject of his personal life. He was extremely private, I was told, even with longtime friends—and he rejected, politely but firmly, all my efforts to visit him in his home or to meet his family.

Mahfouz reached the Ali Baba on foot each morning, about two miles from his apartment in the middle-class quarter called Agouza, on the west bank of the Nile; it was an experience which contained hazards that went beyond the racing traffic. For most of his life, he told me, one of his joys has been to roam Cairo's streets. The habit has made him a familiar figure

to many Cairenes who would otherwise know him only from his books—
or, more likely, from the movies based on his books. It was also a habit
which made him vulnerable when the terrorist wing of Egypt's Muslim
fundamentalists—the people who assassinated Sadat—responded to his
winning the Nobel Prize in the fall of 1988 by threatening to kill him.

Mahfouz's falling-out with orthodox Islam went back to 1959, when he
published the novel called in English *Children of Gebelawi*—Gebelawi
being a symbolic representation of a rather unpleasant God. A departure
from his normal preoccupations, which are worldly, the novel was a meta-
physical allegory, scrutinizing the social codes practiced in the name of
Judaism, Christianity and Islam; ultimately, it found them all profoundly
wanting. That he was evenhanded toward the three faiths brought him no
indulgence in the Islamic community, however. Serialized in *Al-Ahram*
prior to publication, the novel scandalized the orthodox, and before it
appeared in book form it was banned by the authorities of the Al-Azhar
Mosque, which is Egypt's equivalent of the official church. In 1967, a
Beirut publisher began smuggling in a bootlegged version, slightly expur-
gated, which was still available in a plain brown wrapper at a few downtown
bookshops. I obtained a copy after spending an hour persuading a shop
owner—who pretended at first never to have heard of such a thing—
that I needed it for my research; most Cairo intellectuals also have their
bootlegged copies. The fundamentalists feared that the Nobel award would
become a pretext for Al-Azhar to lift *Gebelawi* from the proscribed list.
But, more important, they had never forgiven Mahfouz for writing it, and
they decried his receipt of the prize as an evil Western plot to discredit
Islam.

The controversy took on another dimension a few weeks after the Nobel
announcement, when Iran's Ayatollah Khomeini pronounced a death sentence on Salman Rushdie, an Anglo-Indian Muslim, for the allegedly
sacrilegious content of his novel *The Satanic Verses*. The record shows that
Mahfouz reacted promptly to defend Rushdie's right of expression, calling
Khomeini a "terrorist." But, predictably, his position inflamed the fundamentalist *sheikhs*, who, in terms circumspect enough to stay within the
law but fiery enough to permit the faithful to draw dangerous conclusions,
denounced him in the mosques. The Islamic press added ominous warn-
ings. In London, a writer in a Muslim newspaper that was much read in
Cairo declared, "If only we had behaved in the proper Islamic manner with
Naguib Mahfouz, we would not have been assailed by the appearance of
Salman Rushdie. Had we killed Naguib Mahfouz, Salman Rushdie would
not have appeared." Meanwhile, a high-ranking Egyptian cleric linked to
Muslim terrorists told a Kuwaiti paper that, according to Islamic law,
Mahfouz should have been killed when *Gebelawi* appeared, on the grounds

that he had abandoned his religion. By the time the statement was picked up by the Cairo papers, the cleric had softened it with a proviso that execution could be waived if Mahfouz repented.

In fact, Mahfouz did repent—or, at least, he distanced himself from Rushdie. In a press conference at the Kasr-el-Nil cafe a few weeks after Khomeini's pronouncement, he rejected a comparison between *The Satanic Verses* and *Children of Gebelawi*, which he called "my illegitimate son," the product of a phase in his life that had ended thirty years before. He said that his early defense of Rushdie had been quoted out of context and, furthermore, had been made before he had read Rushdie's novel, which as a Muslim he found disgusting. A few weeks later, he gave an interview to one of Cairo's Islamic newspapers in which he said that while he might defend an author's prerogative to misinterpret Islam, he could not tolerate Rushdie's "insults and calumny against Islam and the Prophet."

During the course of our talks at the Ali Baba, which took place about six months later, Mahfouz said he considered himself a Muslim. But he declined to reply when I asked whether he prayed; it was the only question of mine that he flatly refused to answer. He acknowledged that after the death threats he shifted to what had become the standard position of Muslim "liberals" on the Rushdie affair. It held that Islam has no immunity from criticism, and that Khomeini had no power to impose a death sentence, but it accepted the idea that Rushdie might appropriately be tried in a court of law for slandering Islam and the Prophet—much as any citizen would be tried for slandering a fellow Egyptian.

"I had to take the threats on my life seriously," Mahfouz said to me. "These people killed President Sadat and have tried to kill others. They could kill me." (In 1992, they assassinated a well-known secular Muslim writer, Faraj Foda.) Though the Egyptian government took no official position on Khomeini's pronouncement, the Mufti of the Republic—a high state bureaucrat, responsible for interpreting Islamic law—declared that any Muslim who sought to assassinate Mahfouz had to be insane. On a more practical level, Cairo's police offered bodyguards and asked Mahfouz to refrain from his long walks alone. They stationed guards outside his apartment and at that very moment, Mahfouz said, there might be guards standing in the crowd outside the Ali Baba.

"I could not change my routine," Mahfouz said to me. "When the police gave me the choice of staying home with my wife and daughters or facing the dangers of going to my cafes, I decided it would be less painful"—he smiled at what was meant as a male joke—"to take my chances in the outside world. I just try not to think about the danger."

I asked Mahfouz if he was disappointed that Al-Azhar, after his worldwide recognition, refused to lift its ban on *Children of Gebelawi*. He shrugged. Some had hoped that Egypt's politico-religious establishment, embarrassed at appearing medieval, would respond to the Nobel Prize by restoring Mahfouz's Islamic legitimacy. But the Rushdie fuss, if nothing else, made it impossible for the government and Al-Azhar to risk such an audacious action.

II   DISAPPOINTMENT IN THE LIBERAL AGE

THOUGH A PRODUCT of what is called Egypt's Liberal Age, Naguib Mahfouz—like all Egyptians—often talks of being shaped by Pharaonic forces, going back seven thousand years. (A less vainglorious count is five thousand, since historians know little about what happened in Egypt before the establishment of the Old Kingdom, about 3100 B.C. Though it faded badly in its last centuries, Pharaonic government—by far, history's most enduring political system—lasted for at least three thousand years.) In the Nobel address in Stockholm, Mahfouz cited the importance of the Pharaohs to contemporary Egyptian culture, apologizing for belaboring with "worn-out pride" their art and literature, as well as their architectural miracles. In his writing, he asserts that today's Egyptians are the same people who inhabited the Nile valley in the Pharaonic era, and that their nature has not been transformed by the traumas of history, not even by the Muslim conquest of the seventh century. In his talks with me, he pointed out that the Islam which Egyptians practice still contains such Pharaonic elements—Egypt's fundamentalists recently embarked on a campaign to extirpate them—as elaborate burials and the veneration of saints. These primitive practices, he said with obvious delight, scandalize such Islamic purists as the Saudis.

Mahfouz also pointed out, more pertinently, that today's Egypt has inherited from the ancients a sense of nationhood that is unknown to other Arab peoples. Isolated by desert from neighbors to the east and west, endowed with the Nile as a source of agricultural wealth and a channel of communication, Egypt was forged very early into a cohesive society, with one government, one religion, one artistic style, and one language, written as well as spoken. Unlike other Arab lands, Egypt has no nomadic tradition, and its economy has always been agricultural. Egyptians often note, with a mixture of boastfulness and bemusement, that they have the world's oldest bureaucracy, spinning red tape for thousands of years before the Arabs arrived with the sword and the Koran.

Though the Arab conquest made the Egyptians into Muslims, it is not fully clear whether it made them into Arabs. The Arabs, ruling first from Damascus and then from Baghdad, succeeded in imposing their language in place of the old Pharaonic tongue and the Greek that had arrived from Byzantium. In the tenth century, with Baghdad's rule in disarray, Egypt fell to the Fatamids, who founded Cairo and Al-Azhar, then to the Ayyubites, the Mamluks and the Ottomans—dynasties that were Islamic but not Arab.

Egypt today thinks of its culture as more worldly than that of its Arab neighbors. Even its spoken vernacular is a dialect that other Arabs have difficulty understanding. (Mahfouz, like most writers, avoids the dialect in his work in favor of classical Arabic, which is more widely comprehensible.) Physically, most Egyptians look more like the cream-colored figures on the walls of their ancient temples than the swarthy descendants of the Semites from the Arabian desert. And though, under Nasser, the Egyptians led the call for Arab unity, their enthusiasm seemed to come not from an Arab heart but from a calculation that begs to be called imperial. It is interesting that Anwar Sadat, while president, entitled his autobiography *In Search of Identity*. As Mahfouz's words to the Nobel assembly suggest, Egypt's thousands of years of culture imbue it with a feeling if not of superiority then of uniqueness. Other Arabs resent this attitude.

Yet, despite their deep-seated sense of nationhood, Egyptians for centuries passively accepted being governed—usually misgoverned—by foreigners. From Alexander the Great in 332 B.C. to King Farouk, descendant of an Albanian freebooter, the country was ruled without interruption by non-Egyptians. The conventional explanation for this passivity is that, after the Arab conquest, Muslim identity diverted the yearnings that, in modern times, are associated with nationalism. But, even by Islamic standards, Egyptians have historically been submissive. In contrast to the Iraqis, for example, who are said to be ungovernable, Egyptians have rarely risen up against oppressors. Some say the gentle, bounteous Nile bred rebelliousness out of them. One expert suggests that any taste for rebellion inevitably died in the flat, narrow Nile valley, which was easily policed, and in the merciless desert beyond, which contained no place to hide. Egyptians of Mahfouz's generation take pride in what is called the Revolution of 1919, though it was more a series of anti-British street demonstrations than a genuine revolution. Whether or not this general docility dates back to the Pharaohs, it is a factor which Egypt's rulers take for granted. Its other face is that Egyptians, having been so long alienated from their rulers, do not even now have very high expectations of the state.

The seed of today's Egypt, in which Western values merge with the Pharaonic-Muslim mix, was sown in 1798, when Napoleon arrived by sea and astounded the population by the ease with which he defeated the local army. Egypt was ruled at the time by the Mamluks, a fraternity of ex-slaves, in the name of the Ottoman sultans. The French, in their three years in Egypt, introduced new concepts in law, administration, public health and technology, and left behind a strong hunger for Western knowledge, particularly in the urban circles with which they came into contact.

In the vacuum created by their departure, Mohammed Ali, one of history's more fascinating characters, brutally exterminated the Mamluks and maneuvered his way to the throne. Albanian-born and allegedly illiterate, he had shown unusual powers of command in the Ottoman army and had been dispatched to Egypt to lead the fight against the French; he stayed to rule for four decades and founded a dynasty free of Ottoman control that lasted one hundred and fifty years. Contemporary drawings reveal a clear-eyed man with a bushy white beard. Though artists also imbued him with a benign smile, Mohammed Ali followed the tradition, all too familiar to Egyptians, of unmitigated despotism. What distinguished him from his predecessors was his recognition that Europe offered a special wisdom which it was willing to share, and which could make or break his rule.

Mohammed Ali resolved to bring Egypt into the modern world. With French advisors, he adopted European technology, applied modern methods to agriculture and founded state industries. Breaking the monopoly of Al-Azhar over education, he established a state school system, and sent Egyptians to Europe, and particularly to France, to bring back a new and modern curriculum. His efforts produced a Westernized intellectual elite, from which emerged in time Naguib Mahfouz and the restless society that he chronicles. Egyptians still debate whether Mohammed Ali was the first nationalist, or simply a tyrant with the vision to overturn tradition. Whichever, he laid the groundwork for Egypt's economic development, as well as for the present-day Egyptian state.

Under Ismail, Mohammed Ali's French-educated grandson, the country made a leap toward genuine nationhood. Acceding to power in 1863, Ismail declared, "My country is no longer in Africa. It is in Europe." He took the title of "Khedive," which was closer to royalty than the "Pasha" of his predecessors, and embarked on a grandiose program of Europeanization. To execute it, he brought in hundreds of thousands of Englishmen, Frenchmen and Italians; to house them, he authorized erection of wholly new, European-style quarters in Cairo and in Alexandria. Remembered chiefly for presiding over the construction of the Suez Canal, Ismail also created irrigation networks, brought pure water to the cities, built bridges across the Nile and laid out telegraph and postal systems. He encouraged the founding of newspapers, patronized playwrights and artists and built an elegant opera house, which for a century was the city's cultural hub.

In his early years, Ismail's ambitions thrived on the high prices paid for Egypt's cotton in international markets, a consequence of shortages produced by the American Civil War; when, however, the war ended and the market collapsed, his spending only grew. By the mid-1870s, Egypt was bankrupt. The European powers, which had once vied to finance him, now used his indebtedness as a wedge to promote their colonialist aims. Britain was the most skillful, not only in outmaneuvering the French to acquire ownership of the Suez Canal but in establishing control over the management of Egypt's financial affairs. In his last years, Ismail thrashed about vainly to salvage Egypt's independence, but in 1879 the Europeans forced him to abandon his throne and take refuge abroad. The contributions Ismail made to the modernization of Egypt were remarkable, but the state he left behind was a shambles. Its weakness made Egypt an easy mark for incorporation as a province of the British Empire.

In July 1882, British warships shelled Alexandria to suppress a military rebellion against the submissive Khedive Tewfik, Ismail's successor. A few months later, British forces took possession of the Suez Canal, defeated the rebels on the battlefield and seized Cairo. Tewfik became the first in a series of weak Khedives who acknowledged Britain's stranglehold and, in the face of rising nationalism, identified with the occupier. Curiously, the fiction of Ottoman sovereignty in Egypt remained intact until World War I, when Britain declared Egypt a protectorate, with a promise of independence. But decade after decade passed and Britain stayed on, its army enforcing the rule that its civil servants exercised in the name of Mohammed Ali's hapless descendants.

The British were teachers, however, as well as autocrats. Once they had walled off Egypt from its neighbors, interrupting a thousand years of Islamic cross-fertilization, they filled the gap by transmitting a tantalizing set of European ideas. On the one hand, Egyptians grew increasingly resentful of foreigners during these years, both those who ruled and those who, as émigré workers, dominated the life of Cairo and Alexandria. On the other, they were drawn to British notions of representative government, free expression, political parties and popular suffrage. Egyptian intellectuals, faithful to Ismail's vision, embraced secular European ideals in place of dedication to the *shari'a*. With innocence and optimism, many Egyptians were convinced that democracy was at hand and that it would somehow emancipate them from colonialism. This was Egypt's Liberal Age, and it was ridden by ambivalence toward Britain. It reached its climax in the 1919 uprising, the product of Egyptians seduced by London's ideals and abandoned to its lies. This was when the generation of Naguib Mahfouz grew to adulthood.

Mahfouz's *Cairo Trilogy*, considered his masterwork, chronicles the age through the experiences of the Al-Jawad family, who live in one of the alleys of the Gamaliya quarter, a short walk from the Al-Azhar Mosque. Born nearby, Mahfouz writes fondly of these alleys, which make up the heart of Islamic Cairo. In the trilogy, his most autobiographical work, he acknowledges modeling the Al-Jawads' youngest son after himself. The family he portrays is hierarchical in structure, middle-class in status and fiercely protective of its position in the community. The tyrannical Al-Sayyid Ahmad, and Amina, his timid wife, try valiantly to save it from the assaults of British ideas, which penetrate each successive generation more deeply. Inevitably, they fail.

The trilogy went virtually unnoticed in the West until Mahfouz's Nobel Prize, when it was finally translated and published. The title of the first volume, *Palace Walk*, recalls a famous ceremonial ground, now a thoroughfare in Gamaliya, that linked two mansions of the Fatimid caliphs. Vintage Mahfouz, it treats the Revolution of 1919 without romanticism. Led by the liberal hero Sa'd Zaghlul, the uprising was anticolonial and democratic in its impulses, but Mahfouz reminds us that it was also irresolute in execution. Fahmy, the only Al-Jawad to participate, dies near the end, not in an act of heroism but shot by "mistake," during a demonstration to celebrate what Egypt incorrectly took for a victory.

Mahfouz describes Fahmy's futile efforts to exact permission to join the protests from his powerful father, a patriot who is ready to have only other men's sons risk their lives. His mother cannot understand protesting against the British at all.

" 'I can scarcely believe my ears. How can you expose yourself to danger when you're such an intelligent person?' " Mahfouz has her say. "Fahmy did not know how to answer her. . . . He was closer to the heavens than he was to convincing her that he had a duty to expose himself to danger for the sake of the nation. In her eyes, the nation was not worth the clippings from his fingernail. . . . Whenever the subject came up in a conversation she would remark quite simply, 'Why do you despise them, son? Aren't they people like us with sons and mothers?' Fahmy would reply sharply, 'But they're occupying our country.' She would sense the bitter anger in his voice and fall silent. There would be a veiled look of concern in her eyes . . . Once when he was exasperated by her reasoning, he had told her, 'A people ruled by foreigners has no life.' She had replied in astonishment, 'But we're still alive, even though they've been ruling us for a long time. I bore all of you under their rule. Son, they don't kill us and they don't interfere with the mosques. The community of Mohammed is still thriving.' "

Mahfouz is no less critical of the other family members. "While Fahmy was outraged and attacked the English with lethal hatred, yearning for Sa'd so much it brought tears to his eyes, Yasin [his older brother] discussed the news with calm concern and quiet sorrow that did not prevent him from continuing his normal routine of chatting, laughing and reciting poetry and stories following an evening on the town that lasted until midnight. . . . Zaynab, his brother's wife, was the most disconcerting of them all. She was frightened by the course of events, and the only person she could find to vent her anger on was Sa'd Zaghlul himself, whom she accused of having caused all the evil. 'If he had lived the way God's children should, meekly and peacefully, no one would have harmed him in any manner and this conflagration would not have broken out.' "

As for Kamal, the youngest, he is actually the mascot of a British unit stationed in their neighborhood. Learning of his activities, Fahmy sneers, "What a traitor you are. They bought you with a piece of chocolate. You're not so young you can be excused. . . . Pupils in your school are dying as martyrs every day. May God grant you failure."

But, sadly for Egypt, the failure was Fahmy's. The Egyptian monarchy successfully excluded the leaders of the uprising from negotiations with the British, and no deal was struck. Instead, in 1922, Britain issued a unilateral declaration which abolished the Protectorate and recognized Egyptian sovereignty, but the British also retained the right to keep their army in Egypt, which left their representatives with the last word on most matters. Zaghlul and the nationalists were not alone in condemning the result as not being sovereignty at all, but Khedive Ahmad Fuad, great-grandson of Mohammed Ali, accepted the declaration. In naming himself King Fuad I, he tied the dynasty more tightly than ever to the occupation, and in doing so assured Egypt a future of domestic strife.

The new constitution, proclaimed by the king after Britain exiled Zaghlul, established a parliamentary system tilted heavily in favor of the monarchy. Nonetheless, the Wafd, Zaghlul's party, won a huge majority in the election of 1924, and Zaghlul became prime minister. His election seemed to promise realization of the European-style society of which liberals had so long dreamed, but in power Zaghlul was vindictive, intolerant of opposition and a self-serving dispenser of party patronage. When the king dismissed him in 1925, he had few supporters left, and the parliamentary principle itself was in serious crisis. Zaghlul died two years later, and in the ensuing years, during which the struggle between the monarchy and the nationalists dominated Egyptian politics, violence became increasingly common. Though Britain made concessions to nationalism in a new treaty signed in 1936, the downward spiral continued. The great war that was approaching would delay the final confrontation between the people and the king, but it could not avert it.

"Maybe my generation, the generation of 1919, was the last one that really believed in democracy," Mahfouz said to me in one of our morning talks. "I was proud of our revolution and proud to be a Wafdist. Our top priority was to get rid of foreign rule, but democracy was a close second.

Egypt was the first country in our century to rise up against European occupation. The people, led by the Wafd, ended the Protectorate, but once the Protectorate was gone, the Wafd lost its purpose. It did not know how to govern in a democracy.

"It is true that democracy is not deeply rooted in our culture. The people would make sacrifices for independence but not for democracy, and so, step by step, our system fell apart. The generation that came after mine blamed democracy for the corruption of the monarchy and the privileges of the rich. I don't believe that. I believe the blame belongs to Britain's colonialism and the Egyptian kings. But whoever was responsible, when we tried it in the years after 1919, most Egyptians concluded that it offered nothing—not social justice, not freedom, not even full independence. They laughed at democracy."

III   DESPAIR IN THE ALLEYS

WHILE THE LIBERAL AGE was winding down to an ignominious end, life in Cairo's alleys became only worse. For Western sightseers, the charm of the alleys was never easy to discern. An English traveler in the 1820s, when Cairo was *only* alleys, noted that, "In a city containing three hundred and fifty thousand inhabitants, there is not one tolerable street. Splendid mosques, some of which surpass, in my estimation, those of Constantinople, are built in . . . filthy lanes; the public thoroughfares are hardly twelve feet wide, darkened by mats to impede the rays of the sun, and choked with putrid vegetables and reeking offals, from the various stalls which line the streets. The first thing that astonishes a stranger in Cairo is the squalid wretchedness of the people." Mahfouz would not contend that the aesthetics of the alleys had since improved; what he loved about them was their revelation of life, their intimacy. Yet, eternal as they seemed, the alleys could not hold off the impact of Egypt's changing ways.

The modernization of Cairo, which began with Khedive Ismail, brought the alleys electricity, a few schools and running water; it also brought higher material expectations. Mahfouz's novels dwell heavily on the hopes and ambitions of the alley-dwellers, particularly the young, who almost invariably wind up disappointed, victims of Egypt's perpetually stagnant economy. Routinely, bleak prospects drive the most talented among them into criminality or, like Mahfouz, into the state bureaucracy, where they can count, at least, on a regular income, a little power, a retirement pension and—important in a status-conscious society—a measure of social prestige.

In an earlier era, the alleys were socially integrated; the homes of the rich, though bigger, were close by the homes of the poor. The Europeans, in establishing new quarters near the Nile, introduced Cairo to the notion of good and bad neighborhoods. Well-to-do families like the Al-Jawads moved from the alleys, leaving behind a culture of concentrated poverty. Then, when World War II came, *fellahin* responded to the British army's demand for labor by leaving the fields and moving into the space that the rich had vacated. When no more space remained, the newcomers subdivided houses, built additions on roofs, doubled up in tiny rooms and then doubled up again. The functions served by spacious courtyards—casual socializing, family celebrations, doing the laundry—were transferred outside the walls to the alley itself. Women became an accepted part of the street scene. ("Why, they even go to Fishawi," noted Mahfouz, referring to a cafe well known to his readers.) As unfamiliar faces replaced old friends, life in the alleys substituted more-distant relationships for the personal interdependence that had once softened physical hardship. The government's response to the crowding was to freeze rents, which discouraged maintenance, leaving roofs to leak and trash to go uncollected.

Yet, despite Cairo's postwar explosion from two to fourteen million inhabitants, traditional social controls remained largely intact. The Islamic values held in common by new and old residents kept discipline in line. Though physical privacy diminished, a sociologist said to me, the extended family remained strong. Psychologically, even the *haram* system was preserved. Mahfouz makes clear in his work that alcohol was always pervasive in the alleys, notwithstanding Islamic strictures, as were prostitution and drugs; moreover, life in the alleys was never totally free of violence. But shopkeepers routinely maintained a tight surveillance over strangers, and vice and crime were not allowed to devour the society. Houses decayed, but their inhabitants seem somehow to have avoided the kind of self-destructiveness associated with the breakdown of social controls in contemporary America's urban slums.

For me, Mahfouz's Gamaliya, with its gorgeous old mosques and madrasas, is still a wondrous place. In the courtyards of the mosques, old men in rags lie on the pavement, taking the afternoon sun; in the madrasas, students cluster around their imam, absorbing the Koran. Some of the sites date back to the Mamluks of the thirteenth century, others to the Fatimids a century earlier; almost all are in serious disrepair, if not ruin. A few wear the sagging scaffolding of decades-old restoration work, performed lackadaisically by Egyptians, likely as not with financing from private sources in the West. As reminders of the wealth that Gamaliya once enjoyed, the government has restored several handsome houses, built by long-departed merchants. Their gardens are lush, and their upper windows remain covered with latticed *mashribiyas*, the shutters through which sequestered women once looked out upon the street. But the beauty of Gamaliya, and the reminders of vanished riches, cannot veil the evidence of today's economic distress.

One walks in Gamaliya along crowded streets with charming names— Street of the Judge's House, Sugar Street (title of the final volume of the *Trilogy*), Street of the Tobacco Merchants. The pavement is muddied with water running from unrepaired sewers; the trash heaps require detours. A building graced by pointed arches on the ground floor rises to three or four stories in unsightly cement blocks. A man washes at an Ottoman-era *sabil*, a public fountain decorated in colored marble; behind him stands a heavy, middle-aged woman waiting her turn to fill a pitcher for the evening's cooking. A misty-eyed mother in a *galibiya* sits on a doorstep, feeding bits of bread to her unwashed babies. Persistent young men hustle souvenirs or postcards in accomplished English, and a peddler hawks hot roasted corn from a pushcart. One small shop offers coal for sale by the chunk, weighed on a primitive scale, while in another a tailor presses pants with an iron he heats in an open fire.

"There are moments in a man's life when he feels a certain spiritual dryness," Mahfouz said. "When I come to Gamaliya, all sorts of images rush to my mind and I feel full again. A man must have someplace to hold on to, something that can move him emotionally." Mahfouz is not alone in his nostalgia. It is said that every Cairene, wherever in the city he has been raised, has—for better or worse—some of the alley left within him.

One morning I asked Mahfouz why, given his deep attachment, he portrays the men of the alley so negatively. The women of his novels are, generally, not only dutiful but strong. The men are almost invariably self-centered, exploitative, whining, weak. They are always ready to sacrifice substance for appearances. Few of them are even likable.

Mahfouz's best-known character is Al-Sayyid Ahmad, father of Fahmy, who has become a metaphor like, say, Hamlet or Scrooge in our own culture. In Egypt, his name is a synonym for a man who is a hail-fellow among his friends and a despot and hypocrite to his wife and children. Others among Mahfouz's famous characters are no more engaging. In *Respected Sir*, Othman Bayyumi, a lifelong functionary—some say Mahfouz satirized his own career as a civil servant in this work—dedicates all of his attention to his career, sacrificing love and integrity to position, recognizing only on the eve of his death how much he has wasted. In *Autumn Quail*, two promising young officials are destroyed, one for lack of adaptability, the other for lack of honesty, by a shift in political winds. Most contemptible of all is surely the impoverished Hassanein Kamel Ali of *The Beginning and the End*, whose hunger for social recognition strips him of all qualms about abusing others.

Mahfouz conveys his contempt for Hassanein very early, in a scene set after his father's death. "When it was nearly time for the funeral," he wrote, "Hassanein became very depressed. Deeply disturbed, he forgot his grief. He had hoped for a magnificent funeral, appropriate to his father's position and prestige. His brothers were not of a type to be much concerned about such a matter, but to Hassanein a degrading funeral seemed as much a catastrophe as death itself."

Later, Hassanein muses about the brother who has paid for his (Hassanein's) schooling with the proceeds of a criminal career, and who has been wounded in a gun battle. " 'I'm the one who's really injured,' Hassanein told himself. 'As for him, he's sound asleep in a happy state of unconsciousness. . . . Recovery would be more serious than death. If his condition becomes worse, the police will be informed. And if he improves, his existence will continue to weigh heavily upon me until his enemies inform the police. So scandal is inevitable. Is there no escape? I loathe this wounded man. I loathe myself and even life itself.' " The book ends with Hassanein's forcing his sister, a prostitute, to commit suicide, after which, in a fit of despair, he kills himself.

Once I asked Dr. Nawal el-Messiri Nadim, a sociologist whose dissertation was based on two years of living on Sugar Street, whether such values persisted. It was impossible, I said, not to note the preoccupations of Egyptian men with appearances. Even Mahfouz, a modern man, could not imagine permitting his unmarried daughters, both of whom have jobs, to leave home to take an apartment of their own. It would not be acceptable, Mahfouz told me, it would not *look* right. The same concern had emerged during a talk I had had over a glass of whiskey with a prominent, Western-trained journalist, who lamented having to go deeply into debt to buy an apartment for his newlywed daughter, whose husband was a professional with a lucrative position. When I asked why, he explained that not only his children but his relatives and friends expected such generosity of him, and as an Egyptian he would be shamed if he failed to fulfill this traditional responsibility.

Dr. Nadim explained that, in the culture of the alleys, what people think of you is more important than individual achievement. An alley-dweller is not just a person; he or she is part of a social network. Hassanein, Mahfouz's detestable character, understood that if his brother was exposed as a criminal, or his sister as a prostitute, it did not matter what he did: his career was ruined and he had no prospect of marrying into a good family. "This is real, this is not imagined," she said. "Mahfouz's characters are very true. The quality of the furniture that your friend buys for his daughter's apartment is considered the community's business. Relatives and friends come to visit, and they check up on the fabric. Everybody knows. Your friend's accomplishment in life is measured by how well he meets the obligation."

Though it began in the alleys, Dr. Nadim said, the value system behind this conduct is intrinsic to all Cairo. Notwithstanding the soaring population, she said, the values have neither changed nor softened. The acceptance of these rigorous rules, she added, is what keeps the social structure of the city together.

My talk with Dr. Nadim gave me more sympathy for Mahfouz's men. But if such men were representative, I wondered what Egypt's prospects were of becoming a first-class country. When I pressed Mahfouz, he smiled enigmatically and was slow to respond. He insisted that the traits he sketches will not neutralize Egypt's promise. Then he added, "I guess I did much of my writing during an era when Egypt felt defeated. That has been the case throughout most of my life. Mine has not been an era of heroism. My characters were poor. The economic system did not give them much hope. I suppose I specialized in writing about the weak people on earth. I have no doubt Hassanein would have been a better man under better conditions. Yet it is true that I admire Egyptian women more. Al-Jawad's wife Amina may have been mousy. She was kept by her husband in a permanent state of terror but, because of her, in crisis the family stayed together. It may be the women who save Egypt."

READERS OF *PALACE WALK* will remember the yearning of Amina, whom Al-Jawad kept sequestered in the house, to visit the famous Hussein Mosque, the minarets of which she could see from her window. The mosque, at the edge of the labyrinthian Khan el-Khalili bazaar, is dedicated to Mohammed's grandson, who was killed at the battle of Karbala in Iraq in 680. Five hundred years later, a head said to be his was brought to Cairo and placed in a shrine. (The body is said still to be in Karbala.) To house the shrine Khedive Ismail built the mosque, one of Cairo's largest, and every autumn, after the harvest, hundreds of thousands of *fellahin* flock to Cairo to spend a few days at a *moulid*, a religious street festival, that celebrates the head's arrival. Few sophisticated Cairenes will even get close to the Hussein Mosque at *moulid* time. They look down on the whole affair as a carnival for peasants.

I arranged to attend the *moulid* with my friend Ali, a poet, whose mystical verses reminded me a little of haiku. We arrived early in the evening, when many families were still eating or dozing on the grounds around the mosque, and Ali suggested we visit with some of his friends at Fishawi until the festivities got underway. Mahfouz has made Fishawi a fixture in his stories; in his younger days, he told me, he often sat there for hours smoking the narghile, or waterpipe, ruminating on his life and work. Fishawi is located in a passage of the bazaar festooned with strings of colored bulbs. Ali chose a table outdoors. The traffic, composed of Egyptians of every station, was heavy. Passing by were men in turbans, scarves, skullcaps and woolen hats, and women varying from citified teenagers in blue jeans to bedouins in black *abaya* and veil. A man in a *galabiya* led a cow on a leash; young boys, presumably heading for nearby restaurants, hurried past with wooden trays of freshly baked, steaming bread on their heads; a girl of five approached the table, swinging an incense pot, to beg for coins; a handsome woman wearing a tattered jacket, accompanied by a man playing a trombone, serenaded us in a monotone with songs in praise of Hussein. Mixed with the smoke of narghiles, for which our waiters every few minutes brought hot coals and fresh tobacco, was the unmistakable odor of garlic and unwashed bodies. Meanwhile, Ali and I drank tiny glasses of heavily sugared tea, some of it with mint and some without.

When we returned to the mosque, the square in front was overrun by men, nearly all with mustaches, wearing *galibiyas* of rough, homespun fabric. A few had women with them; some carried children on their shoulders. Decorated stands at the edges of the square displayed souvenirs, party hats, candy, cheap jewelry and photographs of Egyptian movie stars. With Ali, I circled the exterior of the mosque, where giant drapes hung in sequence, making compartments ten or twelve feet wide. The *moulid*, Ali said, is a favorite gathering place of Sufis, Muslims whose worship consists of inducing in themselves a mystical trance; each compartment was the meeting place of a different Sufi order. Inside several of them, men played instruments that sounded like bagpipes, while others danced slowly to the music. But most were being used by families, for eating supper or bedding down. Later in the evening, Ali said, all the space around the mosque would be alive with Sufi ceremonies.

Ali then led me inside the mosque, which was stuffy, noisy and dazzlingly lit. A dozen *sheikhs* were leading rites for clusters of followers seated on the stone floor before them. Here and there, an armed soldier watched silently, presumably to enforce order, though no one in the sweaty, pushing throng seemed at all quarrelsome. With some difficulty, Ali and I made our way through the bodies into the shrine of Hussein's head, a narrow side room where a tomb stood, framed in wood and glass, and decorated with hammered silver. Moving with the crowd, I circumnavigated the tomb, occasionally stumbling over the feet of worshippers seated against the wall. Once I pressed my face against the glass and saw what I took to be a small casket inside.

Later, Ali led me down a long corridor, past dingy rooms where men sat on their haunches eating, to a small, smoky chamber that looked to be a storeroom of records. There, a dozen men in Western dress—neighborhood dignitaries, I was later told—were seated around a table finishing off plates of rice and meat. Ali greeted them warmly and told me that, in the tradition of the *moulid*, the mosque offered food to all travelers, and that I was welcome to partake. But somehow I was not hungry. The heat, the smoke and the smells of the evening had taken their toll of my appetite and, as politely as I could, I declined. As soon as it seemed decent to do so, I fled toward fresh air and hailed a taxi on the crowded street back to my hotel, leaving Ali behind to wait for the next sitting of dinner.

The following morning, the *Egyptian Gazette*, the local English-language newspaper, spoke of a million believers at the mosque for the *moulid*, which it called "a perfect example of how the power of belief can mobilize people to serve an idea." Later, I described the scene to Mahfouz, and we drifted back to an earlier discussion about whether such profoundly Islamic people were ready for secular democracy. Mahfouz insisted—rather too facilely, I thought—that they were, citing the well-worn argument that democracy is embedded in Islamic doctrine. "The autocrats who have ruled the Arabs over the centuries," he said, "have not drawn from our Islamic heritage. They have created their own traditions." But for the cruel tricks that history has played on the Muslims, he said, democracy might well be identified now not with the West but with Islam.

IV DICTATOR YEARS

EGYPT CAME OUT of World War II with both the monarchy and the nationalists discredited. Threatened by Axis armies moving across North Africa, Britain had coerced both the king and the Wafd into doing its bidding, and neither one ever recovered. After the victory, the British made matters worse by insisting on staying in Egypt—while in retreat elsewhere in the empire—to stand watch over the Suez Canal. Their intransigence, in the context of their declining power, encouraged the rise of antidemocratic extremists on both the right and the left, all of them eclipsing the Wafd in the ardor of their anticolonialism.

Neither the Communists nor the fascistic Young Egypt Society drew a mass following; both followed ideologies of foreign inspiration. The Muslim Brotherhood, however, had nativist appeal, in relentlessly condemning Western culture, and it attracted hundreds of thousands of followers in both the city and the countryside. The Brotherhood used a campaign of terror, which undermined the political system and fanned a fervor that brought Egypt into war against Israel in 1948. The subsequent defeat only exposed the government's irresolution and corruption, weakening it further. By the early 1950s, industrial strikes, political assassinations and student demonstrations followed in unending succession, while attacks against the British forces increased. On January 25, 1952, British soldiers killed fifty Egyptians in a retaliatory shelling at the Suez Canal. The next day, angry mobs set fire to Cairo, unleashing chaos.

That Egypt's debauched King Farouk and its bumbling parliament were overthrown a few months later came as no surprise; the surprise lay in who overthrew them. Hardly anyone at that time had heard of the Free Officers, an association of young conspirators within the army. Anwar Sadat, a junior officer who had at different times flirted with the Brotherhood, Young Egypt and even the Marxists, had been a key organizer, but he gave up leadership when the British imprisoned him in 1942 for making contact with German intelligence. Gamal Abdel Nasser, his successor, was a man of equally nationalistic convictions but had until then shown much less interest in politics. Of lower-middle-class origins, both had turned eighteen the year the British, mindful of the approaching war, authorized the expansion of the Egyptian army. The decision to open the Royal Military Academy offered to the two young men a career never before available to members of their class. It was at the academy that the two became avid nationalists, for whom the army was a way to serve not Britain but Egypt. Both saw the army as an instrument of political and social revolution.

Nasser, in the front lines against Israel while Sadat was in prison, personally witnessed the incompetence of the regime. But neither he nor his coconspirators seemed to have a political vision that went beyond a distaste for Britain and the Egyptian establishment. Few Egyptians at that time perceived the army as a contestant for power. Egypt's thinking had been shaped by a century of parliamentary politics; if there was any alternative at all, it appeared to lie in traditional Islam. The country had not had a military regime since the Mamluks. Yet, Nasser and the Free Officers took over without opposition, bloodlessly.

"For years, we asked ourselves what the way was out of the monarchy and the corruption of the regime," Mahfouz said to me. "We asked, when will the people revolt? Then one morning we woke up and our entire past was gone."

At the time, no one knew Gamal Abdel Nasser. In the first days after the revolution, both the old-style politicians and the Muslim Brotherhood dismissed his importance and debated how they would use the junta— officially called the Revolutionary Command Council—to serve their own political ends. Their illusions quickly vanished.

In its first two weeks, the RCC set the tone of the regime by hanging the leaders of a workers' strike. It purged the officer corps and higher ranks of the civil service. After briefly jailing the old political leaders, it barred them from politics, while it cracked down on the municipal councils, the bar association and the press. It organized a major security apparatus and dissolved the Muslim Brotherhood, its chief rival. Following an attempt on Nasser's life in 1954, the RCC tried more than a thousand persons for high treason, including two hundred and fifty military officers, and, growing increasingly intolerant, it arrested more and more intellectuals, particularly of the left, routinely torturing many. In 1955, the regime executed six Muslim Brothers, while holding more than three thousand political prisoners. Meanwhile, the collective responsibility of the Revolutionary Command Council gave way to the one-man rule of the charismatic Nasser, who in 1956 took the title of president. To their astonishment, and with mixed feelings, Egyptians found that their revolution had produced a rigid despotism.

Egyptians, however, also had reasons to applaud the regime. On the domestic side, it decreed a major land reform which broke the back of feudalism and dramatically improved the conditions of rural life. It nationalized financial institutions, en route to socializing most of the economy, and established a structure of state enterprises whose aim, at least partially achieved, was Egypt's industrialization. It also instituted, for the first time, heavy taxes on the rich. These policies ended the much resented economic domination of the foreign communities—Greeks, Italians, Lebanese, Jews, French—and effectively drove them out of the country. But unfortunately, native Egyptians, whether for lack of training or aptitude, never succeeded in filling their role.

In foreign affairs, the RCC reached an agreement with London, after seventy years of Egyptian effort, which removed all British troops (eighty thousand were still at the canal) from its territory. The regime also helped to found a movement of nonaligned states. At the same time, it ended its military dependency on the West by agreeing to a purchase of heavy arms from the Soviet Union.

The crucial year for Nasser was 1956, when the arms from the Soviet Union began to arrive. After the West reneged on a promise to build a high dam at Aswan, he retaliated by accepting Moscow's offer and by nationalizing the Suez Canal. When Britain and France joined Israel in an attack aimed at seizing the canal, President Eisenhower forced the withdrawal of their troops from the Sinai, and Nasser claimed a victory over imperialism. Vowing a rematch with the Israelis, he launched a campaign to assert his personal leadership over the entire Arab world. But by now Nasser was overreaching. His designs trapped Egypt into diverting badly

needed resources from internal development and they led to two devastating military defeats, one in Yemen in the mid-1960s, the other against
Israel in 1967. Egyptians, however, were slow to recognize Nasser's negative side. It had been a century since Egypt, under Ismail, could boast
of authentic achievements, and the vision of national glory that Nasser
proclaimed was like dust in their eyes.

"The generation of intellectuals that came after me," Mahfouz told me,
"was thrilled by Nasser. They didn't like the dictatorship, but they were
excited by his heroism in the fight against imperialism and by the social
justice that the revolution had brought. I had a serious break with my
mentor, Hakim, over the revolution. Having long before lost his patience
with Egyptian democracy, he was lenient toward Nasser. Even intellectuals
gave no public support to the continuation of our democracy. Its roots in
Egypt proved to be remarkably shallow. Frankly, I was surprised at how
easily Egyptians accepted the dictatorship. But Nasser gave them what
they wanted—free education, land, jobs—and dictatorship was a price they
willingly paid. The people who had gains from the revolution quickly
forgot everything else.

"I was also impressed by the revolution's accomplishments but, unlike
Hakim, I was frightened of the dictatorship from the very first day. My
friends and I who met for coffee in the Cafe Riche were angry but not
brave. We were very careful in our conversations. We knew the walls had
ears, that spies were listening to us. We were persuaded to keep our
opinions to ourselves by what we saw all around us. We kept democracy
in our hearts but we didn't even dream of opposing the regime."

Twenty years after the coup, when Nasser was dead, Hakim made a
public confession. "Where were the thinkers of the country," he wrote.
"And where was I, who loved freedom of thought? The fact is that we—
and to the fullest extent of the word I mean myself and my feelings—felt
no constraint. On the contrary, I was happy with the coming of these
young men and dazzled by what they had undertaken in throwing out the
king. . . . I welcomed this revolution and did not grieve for the loss of the
constitution. This, then, is my responsibility. . . ." Hakim's confession
was received with little sympathy, his critics noting how little courage it
took to attack Nasser when he could not retaliate.

In our talks, Mahfouz made no boasts about his own conduct. He published the first segments of the trilogy in 1952, the year of the coup, and
did not produce another novel until *Gebelawi* in 1959. Critics have wondered about his silence, and Mahfouz has said that he was waiting to see
what direction Nasser would take. Did his subsequent work reveal opposition to the dictatorship? An Israeli specialist insists that it did. (The top

experts on Mahfouz, interestingly, are Israelis, no doubt because he was one of the early advocates of Arab-Israeli peace.) In *Sugar Street*, which appeared as the trilogy's final volume in 1957, Mahfouz wrote, "Fiction contains unlimited artifices. It is a cunning art" for expressing political criticism. From this, the Israeli concludes that Mahfouz regularly used allegory to condemn the Nasser regime.

Yet, apart from *Gebelawi*, with its overarching antiauthoritarianism, Mahfouz's work under Nasser remained focused on everyday life, with no obvious political message. Mahfouz told me he was once questioned by the secret police for a novel called *Chitchat on the Nile* but, unlike so many fellow writers, he was never sent to jail. Egyptians know he was left alone, though at no time did I hear it suggested that Mahfouz had knuckled under to the state.

"It is true that I was symbolic when I attacked the dictatorship," he told me. "What saved me, I suppose, was that I had no impact on the masses. Since I belonged to no party and had no connection with any foreign embassy, I was not a threat to Nasser. I was only a writer, and Nasser was generally lenient toward artists. Still, I never felt secure during the Nasser era. My wife used to say that when she went out shopping, she was sure someone was watching her. I always worried that one night someone would come knocking at the door. Whom the authorities took away could be a very arbitrary matter. I was lucky."

V   THE NEW ERA

THE NASSER ERA ended in a few bloody days in 1967, when Israel decimated the Egyptian army, the backbone of the revolution, and positioned its units on the Suez Canal, some sixty miles from Cairo. Mahfouz, like all Egyptians, still expresses humiliation and anger when he talks about the war. It revealed, he said, that corruption had pervaded the Nasser regime, as it had pervaded the monarchy. Everything had been politicized. The army was under the command of small men, favorites of Nasser; the soldiers, poorly motivated, lacked discipline. No one fought, he said, everybody ran. The war was over so fast that those of his friends at the Cafe Riche who were in the reserves never had time to change into their uniforms. Mahfouz complained that Egypt still does not have the full story of what went wrong. The government, under both Sadat and Mubarak, has refused to release the records. It appoints committees to study the events and they do nothing. The defeat took all the wind out of the regime, and all the will out of its leader. When Nasser died three years later, however, Egyptians recalled the grandeur, forgave the blunders and cried over his bier.

But they did not object when Sadat dramatically reversed Nasser's course. Disposing harshly of Nasser's minions, Sadat quickly established his authority, then embarked on a policy of distancing Egypt from the Soviet Union and the Arab world, while moving closer to the West. In 1972, Sadat expelled the fifteen-thousand-man Soviet military contingent that Nasser had invited to Egypt. A year later, he won Egypt's heart by successfully sending its army across the Suez Canal, regaining a segment of the Sinai, which Nasser had lost in 1967. Building on Egypt's recovered self-esteem, he initiated the process of peacemaking which culminated in his trip to Jerusalem in 1977 and the Camp David agreement a year later. Meanwhile, he instituted a liberalization which he hoped would revive a stagnant economy and, without departing significantly from one-man rule, reinstated some of the attributes of a free society; he lifted censorship, licensed opposition parties, restored the integrity of the courts and diminished the presence of the secret police in daily life.

"Sadat moved us back toward democracy, though I don't know whether he believed in it or not," Mahfouz told me. "What he gave us was far from real democracy. It was controlled and disciplined, and it still contained authoritarian traces. But it was a change of direction which, with some setbacks, has continued. And for a while we felt relieved. Sadat's great contribution was to turn the country to constructive goals and values. The most important was to bring Egypt peace."

Mahfouz told me that he had begun thinking of peace after the defeat of 1967, while Nasser still ruled. Peacemaking was not a course that he could explore openly, though he said he talked about it with Hakim, and both agreed it was senseless for Egypt to be mired in Nasser's posture of no-war, no-peace. "I witnessed five wars in my generation," he said to me. "After every one, we had to start from zero to rebuild our country. That's why I was against war. Sadat knew we could not wage another war, and so did Nasser. So why not peace? Unlike some, I did not believe it would destroy Arab pride."

After Nasser's death, talk about peace intensified in the cafes, Mahfouz recalled. In the ministry of culture, where he worked, quasi-official meetings among the senior civil servants were occasionally held to explore alternatives to war. Mahfouz told me that once he was bold enough to convey his thinking to Sadat, who answered with public mockery: "Mahfouz and Hakim want me to negotiate peace. God forbid!" In a novel called *Love in the Rain* (no English translation), which appeared in serialization in late 1972, Mahfouz hinted, though timidly, of his concern. One passage read: " 'But where is this world heading?' asked Aliyyat. This was the question he collided with everywhere and all the time. Where indeed! War or peace? And the storm of rumors?" Then, after the canal crossing in 1973, Sadat himself embarked on peacemaking and began looking for allies among Egypt's intellectuals.

A month after the 1973 cease-fire, Mahfouz in *Al-Ahram* called on Arabs everywhere to concentrate on developing their countries instead of making war. "The Arab East," he wrote, "has to be transformed into a land of civilization before its natural resources are depleted; otherwise it will wake up, after briefly living in a dream-like world, to find itself back in the stage of hunters and herders." Not long afterward he gave an interview to a Gulf paper which scandalized many Arabs in its advocacy of peace. "The Arabs didn't like it when I told them to spend their money on culture rather than on arms," Mahfouz said. When Sadat journeyed to Jerusalem, the Arab world broke all relations with Egypt and relocated the Arab League from Cairo to Tunis. Mahfouz's work was blacklisted in many Arab countries, and he personally was ostracized by Cairo's pro-Moscow and Nasserite intelligentsia.

Sadat, Mahfouz said to me, was "a man who did great things—but who also made big mistakes." His biggest triumph was peace with Israel; his biggest mistake was rehabilitating the Muslim Brotherhood, with which he had flirted in the 1930s and which he was sure he understood better than anyone. The Brothers had survived Nasser's ban by going underground, and regularly performed vicious acts of violence. Sadat, respectful of the Brothers' austerity and anxious to exploit their zealotry, proposed to return them to mainstream Egyptian life and tacitly lifted the ban. He did not underestimate their seditious appeal to Egyptian soldiers, a large majority of whom were practicing Muslims from the countryside. But he thought he knew how to keep them focused on religion rather than politics—a belief that events proved grievously wrong.

Mainly, Sadat wanted the Brotherhood to serve as a counterweight to Egypt's leftists, who were cold to his pro-Western, pro-peace policies. With tacit government sanction, Brotherhood gangs did indeed terrorize Marxists on campuses and in union halls, and then they went further in putting the torch to Christian churches, nearly igniting a civil war. Far from staying out of politics, the Brothers angrily denounced Sadat's economic liberalization, his rapprochement with the West and his peacemaking with the Jewish state. By 1980, the Brotherhood was out of control, and in September 1981, using tactics that outdid Nasser, Sadat arrested sixteen hundred dissidents in a single night. Not all were Muslim fanatics; every real or illusory foe Sadat could find—politicians, professors, journalists—

was rounded up. Embarrassed, Egypt wondered whether its president had lost his senses. On October 6, military members of an extremist Muslim group called Jihad shot and killed Sadat while he reviewed a parade commemorating the eighth anniversary of the canal crossing.

"Unfortunately for Sadat," Mahfouz said, "the last deeds he performed are the ones for which he is remembered." In contrast to Nasser, almost no Egyptians shed tears for the slain Sadat. It was to examine why Sadat was unmourned that I made my trip to Alexandria, where I had met Hakim and Mahfouz nearly a decade before. My hosts that day admitted they were themselves puzzled, but they shared with me some of their speculations on what disturbed Egyptians so much about their slain president.

While making much of his humble peasant origins, they said, Sadat wore flashy uniforms and lived in conspicuous luxury. He extolled liberty but brutally suppressed dissent. Nasser was direct and honest; Sadat was deceitful and hypocritical. In contrast to Nasser's suppression of the rich, Sadat's policy of liberalization restored their privileges, encouraged high living and promoted corruption, from which even members of his family profited. He proclaimed a deep dedication to Islam but communicated a non-Islamic worldliness. He allowed his wife to conduct herself arrogantly, even immodestly. Why, she even kissed President Jimmy Carter, on the tarmac of the Cairo airport, on television!

"What I utterly reject," said Mahfouz, "is the claim that the assassination was a popular repudiation of Sadat's policy of peace. I was there the day Sadat returned from Israel in 1977. Five million people showed up, and their enthusiasm was genuine. There was no doubt they were ready for peace. Egyptians are deeply disappointed that what the peace promised it failed to deliver—a settlement for the Palestinians and prosperity at home. But I know of no one who regrets that we are at peace."

Sadat's assassins explained their case in a document entitled *The Neglected Duty*, which held that a Muslim had the responsibility—including the use of violence, if necessary—to establish an Islamic state. Among the sins they attributed to Sadat was his proclamation that religion and government were separate domains, a contention that clearly contradicted Islamic doctrine. Such notions, to the extremists, constituted apostasy, requiring Sadat's death. Though they were profoundly opposed to the state of Israel, its existence was less objectionable to them than the more immediate enemy in Cairo. The assassins had made no plans beyond the killing of Sadat, but the evidence presented at the trial suggested a conviction that once they had inflicted their punishment, God would transform Egypt into an Islamic state.

"Sadat's killers were unquestionably opposed to peace with Israel but they were an exception," Mahfouz said. "They knew that his popularity had collapsed. They killed him thinking this was Islam's big chance to seize power. But they botched the job."

VI THE BROTHERHOOD AND THE MOSQUE

THE RISE OF the Muslim Brotherhood, like Nasser's revolution, was a popular reaction to the Liberal Age. British teachings had produced a series of Muslim thinkers, more or less liberal, who devised systems to reconcile Islam with European values and institutions. They distanced themselves from Islamic tradition, and the distance increased with the victory of the Western democracies over the Ottoman empire in World War I, followed by Turkey's abolition of the caliphate. Self-nominated candidates to replace the sultan—including Egypt's King Fuad I and, later, his son King Far-ouk—were plentiful, but worldwide Islam was unable to agree on whether a new caliph should be selected, much less on who it should be. Meanwhile, Zaghlul's liberal, secular government had demonstrated its inadequacy to meet popular needs. It was in this gloomy atmosphere, with Islam un-moored and no anchor for Egypt to grasp, that the Muslim Brotherhood was born. It became, as one historian noted, "the first mass-supported and organized . . . effort to cope with the plight of Islam in the modern world."

The founder of the Muslim Brotherhood was Hassan al-Banna, who was born into a religious family in the delta in 1906. While still a young man, he studied at Al-Azhar, became a Sufi and acquired a teaching post in Ismailia, capital of the Suez Canal region. The British occupation there provided a fertile ground for converting workers, a mission on which he embarked in 1928. Al-Banna's condemnation of Egypt's elite for embracing Western ways found sympathetic audiences and within a decade, the move-ment had five hundred branches; by 1949, it had two thousand, with an estimated half-million adherents. In a few more years, over the resistance of every Arab government, it had spread throughout the region, its organi-zations in the various countries mutually supportive in challenging the political and social status quo.

The foundation of the Brotherhood was Egypt's clerics, the *ulema*, a body known and esteemed by Egyptians generally. Though the *ulema* was never a formal priesthood—Sunni Islam has no formal priesthood—during the long centuries when Egypt was ruled by foreigners it served as the people's advocate, seeking to mitigate the harshness of whatever regime was in power. Its character was never revolutionary, and since Mohammed Ali it had become increasingly identified with the interests of the state. Nonetheless, the imams, with popular roots in the mosques, and at least some religious education, retained a reputation as the people's protectors and conveyed an authority to which Muslims deferred.

Al-Banna, who himself claimed the high title of *sheikh*, invoked the tradition of the politicized clergy in organizing the Brotherhood. He had no use for political parties, or for democracy itself, on the grounds that they divided the Islamic community. Instead, he organized a fascist-style mass movement, centered on his own charismatic personality. Though most of the Brotherhood's members came from the urban working classes, he also attracted a large number of Western-educated professionals, a sign of the rising xenophobia of the Egyptian middle class.

Al-Banna's goal was to transform Egypt into a Koranic society but, to start, he invoked the popular issues on the national agenda. He led protests against Britain's occupation of Egypt; he promoted the cause of the Arabs in Palestine. He was hostile to foreign control over Egypt's economy, as well as to Egypt's Christians. In 1948, the government dissolved the organization for the first time. Three weeks later, a member of the Brotherhood assassinated Egypt's prime minister; shortly after that, al-Banna was himself murdered, presumably in retaliation by the Egyptian secret police.

Nasser, a practicing Muslim, had enlisted the Brotherhood's help in 1952 but the Free Officers' coup d'état went so smoothly that he did not need it, which left him with no Islamic debts to repay. The regime's motto, "Religion is for God and the Nation is for All," was a clear expression of church-state separation, an idea which Muslim thinkers had promoted since the Liberal Age. Nasser continued the monarchy's policy of suppressing the Brotherhood, but the neutrality of religion was not enough for him. More totalitarian than Muslim, he reshaped the Islamic establishment to place religion more directly than ever at the service of the state.

But Nasser's secular policies disintegrated with his armies in the Six-Day War, permitting Islam to renew its courtship of the masses. The Brotherhood declared the defeat to be an expression of God's wrath toward secularism (in Israel, Orthodox rabbis credited God with the victory) and demanded a rebirth of state support for the mosques. On the campuses, young women put on long dresses, and among young men Islamic-style beards became the fashion. What Sadat failed to appreciate in turning the Brotherhood loose a few years later was how aggressive Islam had become. Though a majority was probably law-abiding, a minority of breakaway extremists accepted no restraints on the right to seize power; in 1974 and again in 1977, the government turned to force, including executions, to put down popular insurrections. In 1979, Khomeini's bloody victory in Iran provided Islamic extremists with both a tactical and a political model. Two years later, fanatics killed Sadat. More recently, they have threatened the life of Naguib Mahfouz.

"Young people feel the system has failed them, and that things are getting worse," Mahfouz said; "First democracy, then Nasser, then Sadat failed them, and the Brotherhood has come along to give them another way, which is to go back to their Islamic ancestors. The Khomeini revolution, although it was Shiite, made a big impression on them. The Brotherhood worships Khomeini, or at least worships his triumph. He has given a big boost to the Islamic movement.

"The *shari'a* is just a symbol of what they want, however. It's been applied by secular governments in the Arab world throughout history. In fact, ninety percent of the laws that Egypt lives under overlap the *shari'a*, and if the remaining ten percent were added, the country would not be ruined. The true battle is over power. The Muslim Brothers are an opposition force. Their slogans say 'Islam is the solution' or 'Apply *shari'a*,' but what they really mean is 'We want to be in power to make the rules.' They are getting stronger every day, and though I don't think they will win, before they are finished they'll do much damage to the country. If we had a Berlin wall across our minds to keep out foreign ideas, I think most Egyptians would be tearing it down; the Brotherhood would be building it back up."

One evening I called on Ahmad Baha al-Din, a well-known columnist for *Al-Ahram* and a strong critic of the Islamic movement. He lived in a high-rent quarter called Dokki, just west of the Nile, near the new opera house that the Japanese have built. Many diplomats and business executives lived nearby. So did Jihan Sadat, the unloved widow of the late president. Notwithstanding the high rents, the streets were muddy and covered with rubble. Predictably, the hallways of the apartment building were unlit and difficult to negotiate. Standing in some dark, ill-kept hall in an Arab city, I am often astonished, when a host opens the door, at the tastefulness of the apartment inside. Baha al-Din, a bent man in a blue blazer and heavy spectacles, showed me into a huge living room with polished wood floors, modern paintings and many linear feet of books.

"The fundamentalists are furious with me," he said over coffee. "I make the argument every day that the Koran is liberal, that Islamic values are consistent with modern life. But even if the Koran gives women full rights, so what? Our societies have never permitted them to practice these rights. The Koran talks of democratic rule, which was applied in the first two or three decades after the Prophet, but has not been applied in the fourteen centuries since. We all recognize that Islam requires respect for human rights, but no Arab regime cares about them. The Prophet commanded his followers to make this a better world. The fundamentalists have interpreted this command to justify their taking the law in their own hands, to attack Christian churches or coed parties at the university—or to threaten the

life of Mahfouz. They demand that the university stop teaching the works
of Islam's liberal philosophers.

"But I think it is important to make distinctions within the Islamic
community. The Brotherhood itself is willing to work through the political
system. It is now more than a half century old, and it has been mellowed,
by exile or jail or whatever. It is no longer secret. Its writers make their
arguments in the press. It even has members in Parliament. It has become
respectable. The extremists, generally grouped under the name Jihad, are
newcomers. They are disciples of Sayyid Qutb, a Muslim absolutist who
was arrested and executed in connection with the plot to kill Nasser in
1965. His works did for contemporary Islam what Vladimir Jabotinsky did
for Zionism—that is, he made it much more militant, intolerant and
violent. Sadat's indulgence encouraged them. Sadat did not recognize their
rise before they killed him and, unfortunately, neither did the rest of us."

While we talked, Baha al-Din's wife, elegantly dressed, came in, and the
two discussed a dinner party they were to attend later in the evening. Baha
al-Din apologized for the interruption before continuing.

"The relationship between the branches of the Islamic movement is not
clear. Jihad sneers at the Brotherhood for being collaborationist, and the
Brotherhood is angry at having to pay for Jihad's extremism among people
who oppose violence. They ostensibly hate each other, and I have no doubt
that the moderates are afraid they will be swept away by the extremists.
But some say the Brotherhood is the civilian and Jihad the military branch
of the same organization. Clearly, Jihad's recruiting is made a lot easier
by the grass-roots organizing of the Brotherhood.

"The problem is that no influential Muslim calls for what I believe is
necessary: a basic overhaul of Islam. Islamic thinkers even in the Liberal
Age were, at best, tinkerers. If Islam is to go modern, it must take a
revisionist view of its history and its roots. Muslim writers today express
a diversity of views but none attack this issue courageously. When I
criticize Islam in the newspaper, the sheikhs in Al-Azhar call me to say
they are with me, but they consider it too dangerous to say what I say.
What happened to Islam's freedom of speech? My reading of history is
that Christianity did not come out of the Dark Ages until it undertook a
full reexamination of its own thought. That's what the Renaissance was
all about. In our time, Khomeini is Savonarola; instead, we need a Jan
Huss or a Luther. It has to be done if Islam is to lead the Muslims into
the modern world."

Baha al-Din inspired me to pay a visit to the Mufti of the Republic,
whose name is Mohammed Tantawi and who, it is said, had memorized
the Koran by the age of twelve. Born in 1928 in a village in Upper Egypt,
he was a dean and professor at Al-Azhar before Mubarak appointed him

to his present post in 1986. His duty is to provide official interpretations of Islamic law. He and the more conservative Sheikh of Al-Azhar are the twin pillars of Egypt's Islamic establishment, but they disagree over such questions as whether family planning and government bonds (Islam forbids the payment of interest) are legal. Of the two, the mufti, who routinely supports Mubarak, is the government's favorite. He also tours the country denouncing Jihad. I found him, to my surprise, in a dingy tenth-floor office in a neighborhood of rundown buildings. He had sleepy eyes and unshaven cheeks, and on his head he wore a white turban with a red crown. A servant brought me a cup of tea, into which he stirred a teaspoon of sugar before handing it to me.

"The politician and the religious man have different responsibilities toward the state," said the Mufti, after delivering a condemnation of Jihad and sectarian violence. "That is not to say we accept the separation of the state and religion. We hold that they are one. But the politician specializes in politics, the religious man in religion, and each to his own realm. If either transgresses, it leads to mistakes. We differ with the Shiites, who see no problem in the clergy being involved in politics. We believe religious men should not be ignorant of the world but should not try to run it. I haven't studied politics, so how can I practice it?"

Prodded by Baha al-Din's comments, I inquired of the mufti about the limits he placed on examining the precepts of Islam. Are you, I asked, and is Al-Azhar willing to go back to the Koranic roots of your faith?

"Religion comes from heaven like rain," he answered, lowering his hand evocatively from eye level to his desk. "What comes down is clear and pure, but when it hits the earth it becomes mixed with dirt and refuse. So people all over the world—Muslims or Christians or whatever—need to take it while it is still in its pristine state. Unfortunately, many people do not. They use religion to advance themselves but they, and not religion, are to blame. Religion is innocent. That is why we must go back to the original texts, to relearn the tenets that exalt the best qualities of mankind."

This answer, if I understood it aright, showed some willingness to sweep away the man-made strictures that, over the centuries, had come to clutter Islam. But never having spoken to a mufti before, I was unsure how far I could press him. When I asked why Salman Rushdie had been condemned for examining the roots of religion, he answered without any sign of distress.

"It is not right to slander God and the Prophet. I myself am against spilling any blood, but I think Rushdie should be brought before a neutral panel and, if it is decided that he should be killed, the judgment should be made scientifically."

Of more immediate interest, I asked whether he supported Al-Azhar's continuing ban on *Children of Gebelawi*, which, according to my reading, was Mahfouz's effort to reexamine religion starting with its pristine state. The mufti, I knew, had courageously defended Mahfouz when he was threatened with death by the fundamentalists.

"Though only God knows for certain what is inside a man," the mufti replied, "I consider Naguib Mahfouz a good Muslim. But being human, he can make errors. Many people argued that he slandered the Prophet, but he said that was not his intention. His other books have posed no problem. I hope Mahfouz will rewrite *Gebelawi* and make the necessary changes. Then, perhaps, he and Al-Azhar will be able to negotiate a reversal of the ban."

Next on my list of Islamics to see was Mohammed Abdul-Kuddous, an active Muslim Brother. A few days before my visit, the Cairo newspapers reported a possible attack—the facts were not quite clear—on Zaki Badr, who as minister of the interior was Egypt's chief policeman. Badr was known as the scourge of the Brotherhood, and the papers the next day were filled with dutiful statements from prominent supporters of the movement, distancing themselves from the incident. Each in his own words insisted that no good Muslim would ever contemplate such a dastardly act.

Abdul-Kuddous, forty-two, was a regular among Badr's targets. A lawyer and a writer for *Al-Dawa* ("The Call"), the main Islamic newspaper, he was the son of Ihsan Abdul-Kuddous and Rose al-Youssuf, both prominent literary figures, both secularists. Mohammed received me in his father's apartment in fashionable Zamalek. He wore the obligatory beard and told me that, in his fifteen years as a Brother, he had been jailed twice for his beliefs. Besides writing for the paper, he said, he preached in the mosque on Fridays and proselytized among students, professionals and workers. He is, he said, a "soldier for Islam," and he contended disdainfully that the Badr incident had been trumped up, to embarrass the Brotherhood.

"Though we are tolerated, the Brotherhood is still not legal," Abdul-Kuddous said. "This is common in Egypt, that a practice goes on openly that is not legal. As everyone knows, the Brotherhood has several dozen members of parliament who were elected on the ticket of another party. But we're under surveillance all the time. Under emergency laws that have been in force since Sadat was killed, our people are regularly arrested and tortured. Our paper is often confiscated. At this moment, there are secret police standing on the sidewalk. I can be taken in any time." Amnesty International essentially confirmed these statements in one of its reports. "The government knows it can't crush us. It knows any serious attempt would backfire. It is also afraid that revolution could erupt at any moment because of worsening economic conditions. The government thinks it needs absolute power to survive. It's been that way since the Pharaohs."

Abdul-Kuddous insisted that most Egyptians share his deep Islamic faith. Only a few are willing to put themselves at risk for it, he said, but most would vote for the Brotherhood in an honest election. His goal, he said, is a free election, which would give the Brotherhood enough votes to form either the government or a major opposition force in the parliament.

"Tactically, we disagree with Jihad," Abdul-Kuddous said, "which wants violent revolution. Islam has never been spread by the sword. Our goal is to change Egypt through political means. But the government wants Islam out of politics altogether. Perhaps if Al-Azhar were more than just another state bureaucracy, our work would not be so necessary. If it had been doing its job, Hassan Al-Banna would not have seen a need for an Islamic movement. Al-Azhar tolerates the foreign idea that religion is a private matter between man and God. We think that all of day-to-day life is attached to religion. Work is a form of worship. We think men should run the family, and though we know that injustice exists in husband-wife relations, if a man is a true Muslim, he respects his wife. We believe injustice could be overcome if most men prayed as they should. The separation of religion from politics and life may work in the West; it does not work in the Islamic countries."

The Egyptian government never clarified what happened in the Badr incident, but with time more and more people acquired doubts about the original story. A few months later, the Egyptian Organization for Human Rights released a report criticizing Badr's widespread use of torture, mostly against Islamic activists. The next day, Mubarak dismissed him and replaced him with a professional policeman who urged dialogue with Islamic groups. The Brotherhood greeted Badr's dismissal as a victory, as did Western governments and human-rights organizations. But for some fundamentalists, it was not enough. In the heavily Islamic city of Asyut, scene of frequent antigovernment protests, an unruly crowd demanded that Badr be put on trial. In suppressing the crowd, the police arrested twelve and killed at least one person by gunfire. More significantly, within a few months, human-rights organizations were reporting that, under Badr's successor, torture continued much as it had been before. Since that time, the conflict between the government and the Islamic movement has intensified, and violence by both sides has steadily increased.

VII   THE MAHFOUZIAN PRESIDENT

PUBLIC LIFE IN Egypt calmed down after Mubarak succeeded Sadat in 1981. The new president, who was seated next to Sadat when the shots were fired, immediately reaffirmed Egypt's commitment to the peace with

Israel. He released the political prisoners whom Sadat had imprisoned, and he named a new government of reconciliation, which included several Christians. Mubarak also promised to curb the Islamic extremists, a policy to which he has adhered throughout his years in office. As vice-president, Mubarak had opposed the freedom to make trouble that Sadat, in effect, had extended to the militants. After the assassination, he arrested several hundred of them, and he cashiered a hundred more from the armed forces. A month later, the government tried two dozen Muslim extremists on charges of murdering Sadat, and executed five of them.

Mahfouz told me that Egyptians quickly took to Mubarak because he was a humble person. "Nasser thought he was a god," Mahfouz said, "and Sadat thought he was a Pharaoh. No one could ever touch either one of them. No one could put an arm around the shoulder of either one without feeling his hand would be cut off. That is not our way." Egyptians also liked Suzanne Mubarak, the president's half-English wife, he said, and saw her modesty as reflecting well on her husband. Perhaps the highest compliment Mahfouz paid Mubarak was to say he would feel comfortable sitting in a cafe drinking coffee with him.

I interviewed Mubarak three years after he took office, in a small European-style palace in suburban Heliopolis where he liked to receive guests. The security was heavy, but Mubarak was relaxed and he frequently reached his hand over while we talked, as Mahfouz suggested he would, and placed it on my shoulder.

"My term as president is completely different from other terms," he said. "After the revolution, Nasser had his own ideas about pan-Arabism and the glory of Egypt. Then Sadat came. He had to lift the Israeli occupation of the Sinai and take us to peace, then start developing this country with its big population that is steadily increasing. Now I have to start again. I have to look for stability in this country first. We must try to find solutions for the problems existing inside Egypt. Nasser and Sadat were interested in foreign affairs. Now we have to look internally. The people want housing. The people want infrastructure. The people want to eat and they want clothing. If I did not pay attention to these demands, I would not be able to stay as president. My job presents great difficulties. To deal with foreign affairs is much easier than looking after internal problems."

I have since often thought back on this declaration of Mubarak's, with its implicit confidence and optimism, and the contrast it presents with Egypt's stark reality. It is a country whose population has soared from twenty-two million at the time of Nasser's revolution to sixty million in our own time. Its supply of arable land has long since been exhausted. Its natural resources, apart from some oil in the Sinai, are negligible. The state has only a modest income at its disposal. I remember an official who once said to me, "No matter how many schools we build, or clinics, or factories, we cannot keep pace with the growing number of mouths we must feed." Even the most efficient government would find the obstacles to solving Egypt's internal problems to be monumental. Under Mubarak, these problems have grown steadily worse.

I asked Mubarak about his attitude toward democracy.

"I think I've started the country on the way to real democracy," he answered. "We tried a totalitarian regime under Nasser. Then we tried some kind of democracy during Sadat but he made many mistakes, as any leader might. I have to build democracy because it's the only way to govern this country. I can't go back. In a totalitarian regime, you never know the mistakes that are made. But in democracy, if anybody does something wrong, against the will of the people, it will float to the surface. The whole people are looking. Democracy has its drawbacks, just as totalitarianism does. But democracy is much, much better, especially in a developing country."

Mubarak argued that democracy—specifically, the right to express ideas freely—would help satisfy the fundamentalists and discourage violence. The country, he said, should have an ongoing dialogue with fundamentalism, in the form of debates between its proponents and "the Al-Azhar people, the scientists of Islam." As for his own religious practices, he said, "Sometimes I go to the mosque. Usually, I pray in my house, but I'm a very modern man. I'm not so tough in this direction." He insisted I could take his word that Egypt would not adopt the *shari'a*, would not ban interest on loans and would not proscribe alcohol. "I'm not going to punish you because you drink alcohol," he said. "It's between you and God." He said he was trying to set an example in lowering his voice on matters of religion, in the hope of softening the confrontation. He also hoped he could redirect the fundamentalists' energies into legitimate channels, he said, by giving them fair access to the electoral system.

The fundamentalists were in fact treated fairly by Mubarak, at least according to secular observers, but over the years their relations with the state grew increasingly embittered. With the decline in Egypt's economic condition, fundamentalism found more converts who accepted its argument that Islam was more important than prosperity. Without prospect of material improvement, more Egyptians seemed willing to substitute religious gratification. Fundamentalist leaders, growing stronger, became more audacious, directing physical attacks on Christians and nonbelievers, and even on foreign tourists. Repeatedly they called for the death of Mahfouz. In response to this violence, Mubarak turned increasingly to police and military oppression, while the traditional tolerance of Egyptian life ebbed.

"In the armed forces we had democracy," he said, in responding to my question about where he acquired his political views. After I scoffed, he smiled and went on to explain. "We really do have democracy. Whenever you adopt any decision in war, you have to listen to all the specialists who argue, who argue with the leader. We look at the alternatives. We have to discuss everything openly and deliberately. Then the commander makes his decision, on the basis of the information he receives. I'm used to meeting all the people in the air force and listening to them tell me what's right and what's wrong. Sadat did not do that.

"I'll tell you what else Sadat did not do. I lived all my life on an air base, though I had a house in Cairo. I passed most of my life among the working people of the air force, not just the officers but the sergeants, corporals, soldiers. When I was commander of a base, I used to get up at five o'clock or six o'clock and make a tour, to see that the sentries were eating well, to see that the people guarding the important posts understood their responsibilities. I liked to speak with them. What's your mission? Are you eating your food? I asked them about personal things. How many children do you have, are you married, did you receive your new shoes, how is your family, do you have sons, are you tired, do you have a problem with the job? This is the soldier who is guarding the mess or guarding the planes, a very simple man. I look out for the lower ranks more than the higher. I found a soldier whose father was very ill, and he was sad that nobody was looking after him, and I said, 'Go sit with your father, and if you need anything just let me know.' "

Mubarak's idea of democracy obviously contained a stronger commitment to paternalism than to the right of self-government. In Islam, after all, sovereignty belongs not to the people but to God; as a military officer, Mubarak was prepared to do God's work. What he called democracy was a vehicle for realizing the Egyptian dream, dating back to Mohammed Ali, of creating a modern state. But Mubarak's vehicle had strict limits. Mubarak offered considerable freedom of the press and a multiparty parliament, but retained all major decision-making in the presidency. Charitably, the system has been called "guided" democracy. Some Egyptians say it is so paternalistic that it is not democracy at all.

"I'm meeting with people all the time," Mubarak continued, "lots of telephones from all over the country, until my head gets like this"—and he separated the palms of his hands to about the length of a watermelon—"at the end of the day. The style of Nasser and Sadat suited the specific needs of the time. Now it is another era and I must deal with the country differently. Nasser and Sadat did not accept freedom and democracy. I do."

Whatever Mubarak's domestic concerns, his greatest triumph has been in restoring Egypt's standing among the Arab states. It is a goal he has pursued diligently. Even the "Order of the Nile," an award presented to Naguib Mahfouz in recognition of the Nobel Prize, was made to serve this vision. In presenting the award, Mubarak repeatedly referred to Mahfouz as "our Egyptian-Arab writer." One day I asked Mahfouz what Mubarak had meant by that curious phrase, and he shrugged. I finally decided that, to Mubarak, the term—crediting Arab culture with an Egyptian achievement—served as one more step in Egypt's tortuous journey to reestablish its preeminence in the Arab world.

Mubarak seems to see Egypt as entering a new era of history. In the Liberal Age, Egypt entertained the notion that it was a European power. Nasser proclaimed Egypt an integral part, in fact the predestined leader, of the "Arab nation." After the expulsion from the Arab League, Sadat testily declared that Egypt was a Pharaonic state, unique in the nature of its grandeur. Mubarak's goal has been to return Egypt to its Arab roots.

Mubarak, in his own way, accepts the concept of Arab nationhood. In extolling Mahfouz, he called Egypt "a part of the Arab nation, and everything Egypt contributed was presented to the larger family of that Arab nation." But whatever those anodyne phrases were designed to mean, his concept of the Arab nation is not one which subsumes Egypt's peculiar character. Mubarak has no use for the integrated pan-Arab state, a Nasserite fantasy that will never exist. The Arab nation, to him, is at most an amalgam of sovereign countries linked by cultural, economic and religious bonds. Within it, Egypt would be pre-eminent.

Naguib Mahfouz, on the day he received the Order of the Nile, paid Mubarak a mixed compliment. He thanked him for the effusive congratulations and commended him for encouraging Egyptian culture. Then he added that he hoped he would one day, in reciprocation, be able to congratulate Mubarak on a victory over the internal problems that face Egypt—poverty, overpopulation, a stagnant economy, no less crushing a burden after a decade of his presidency than they were before. It was a none-too-subtle slight, and an expression of Mahfouz's refusal to surrender his integrity as an Egyptian just because he had a ribbon and a medal draped around his neck. His audacity provoked a minor scandal in Cairo.

"Mubarak," Mahfouz said to me at the Ali Baba, "is sincere and honest. He has made a genuine effort to correct Egypt's past errors as a democracy. He has given journalists and artists full freedom of speech. He is a protector of free thought against the assaults of the religious extremists." (Mahfouz was, perhaps, being too generous; some censorship persists, and in 1991 a minor novelist was sentenced to eight years in prison on charges of slandering Islam.) "But, unfortunately, only those who need him for their own interests believe in him. Egyptians have no emotional attachment to him. Mubarak's concern is to open no new fronts in Egypt's war against backwardness. That's not enough, and I'm afraid it is the thinking of a man of weak character.

"But, ironically, his very weakness of character gives room for Egyptian democracy to assert itself. We are fortunate in that what we need at this moment in our history is not so much charismatic leadership as popular involvement. Our problem is that the people have not been zealous enough about straightening out our government. We are not used to making our voices heard. The people want democracy but, at the same time, they fear it.

"We may still be a hundred years away from being able to cope with real democracy. A great deal of damage has been done by our history to our national spirit. The most recent decades have not been any kinder. I am confident that we have the potential to become a first-class country, but I'm afraid it will still take many more generations to overcome our handicaps."

CHAPTER FOUR

SYRIA

I SALADIN'S SCION

FROM A HILLTOP above Damascus, President Hafez al-Assad's palace, an intimidating symbol of power, looks down in the sunlight upon Syria's capital of three and a half million inhabitants. It is not a pretty place. The heavy stone facade and irregular, flat-topped silhouette made me think of a prison, and I wondered why Assad had chosen such an austere design. A Syrian friend speculated that it was drawn from the twelfth-century fortress of Saladin, a great hero of the Arabs. Traveling in the mountainous north of Syria, I once came upon that magnificent fortress, whose powerful walls and distinctive square turrets command the valley routes of ancient invaders, and I understood the inspiration. But what explained why the palace, finished in 1989, had never been occupied? When night falls on Damascus, it vanishes, without even a light as a reminder of its presence.

Assad has surely faced the temptation to compare himself with Saladin. He was brought up in a village called Qurdaha, a few miles from Saladin's citadel. No doubt he played among its ruins. Qurdaha is a seat of a dissident Muslim sect called Alawites. The sect takes its name from the Prophet's son-in-law Ali, but its polytheistic doctrines are so far removed from the rigorous monotheism of Islam, whether Sunni or Shiite, that most authorities—though not the Alawites themselves—hold that it is not Muslim at all. Within Arab culture, Alawites are decidedly outsiders.

Saladin, a Kurd, was an outsider too. Nonetheless, he founded an Arab dynasty, reunited the divided Arab world and in 1187, having defeated the Crusaders, restored Jerusalem to Arab control. Though Hafez al-Assad reveals little of himself, having been raised in the era of colonialism he has to have been inspired by Saladin's humbling of the intruders from the West. Imbued with talent and ambition, he has embraced the dream of making the Arabs powerful again. Can an Alawite, measuring himself against Saladin the Kurd, aspire to less than winning Jerusalem back for the Arabs?

Unfortunately for Assad, however, he is running well behind schedule.

Saladin had stopped the Crusaders cold by the time he was fifty; Assad, now over sixty, is still far from matching that achievement. Even when he had the Soviet Union as his patron, Assad failed in his bid for strategic parity with Israel, and, with the Soviet Union gone, he has had to acknowledge Syria's permanent military inferiority. His relations with the West have remained tense, despite joining America's war against Iraq in 1991 and his participation in the peace process with Israel. Does an encroaching sense that he is only a shadow of his great exemplar explain why Assad has continued to govern Syria from a modest villa in downtown Damascus, leaving the fortress on the hilltop dark and empty?

In Syria, it is difficult to get answers to even innocuous questions, much less to those that trespass onto the personal domain of the president. Damascenes do not consider it unusual that they are told little or nothing about the operations of the state. The standard reporter's queries—Who designed the palace? How much did it cost? Who paid for it? Why has it remained vacant?—are treated by officials as an assault. In the rumor mill around the city I learned that the building was designed by a Japanese architect, that the cost exceeded $3 billion, that the Saudis paid the bill, that Assad will not budge because he considers the finished product to be ugly. But I could not confirm any of this information, and much less was I able to penetrate the veiled personality of the man behind it, a man for whom an air of enigma is an instrument of state.

Intrigued by the mystery of the palace, I went several times in search of information to the presidential villa. President Assad's two closest aides received me graciously, but it was obvious that they had no authority to tell me anything. Apart from Assad himself, it has been said, the only men who exercise power in Syria are the heads of military intelligence and the secret services, all of them Alawites like himself. Rifat al-Assad, his younger brother, once also belonged to the power elite, but he showed himself greedy for money and status, and was sent off into exile. More recently Assad's son, Basil, has been climbing up the rungs of the hierarchy, and Syrians look upon him as the heir apparent. In the Syrian system, the prime minister and his cabinet are no more than administrators. It is the security junta, men who never appear in public or speak for publication, whose words have meaning. The president's personal entourage, the men I went to visit, were well-meaning, but their real role was to shield Assad from the outside world.

The offices in which Assad Kamal Elyas and Joubran Kourriya received me were tiny, and crowded with cardboard cartons that overflowed with files. Elyas was the president's chief speech writer, Kourriya his press aide. They offered me coffee, and spoke with eloquence of their patron's multitude of virtues. But when I asked some specific questions about the president's relocation plans, I did not get so much as a cliché. "Why would you want to know that?" said Elyas, a septuagenarian who has spent decades at Assad's side. I replied that he might himself want to know, in view of the obviously overcrowded conditions in which he worked. Will it not take considerable planning, I asked, to transfer the presidential office to a new site? Elyas shrugged. "This matter is of no concern to me," he said, scarcely able to contain his irritation. "When the president's ready, he'll let us know. We'll move when we're told." He had never discussed the new offices with the president, he said, or even set foot in the new palace. He clearly thought I was being obsessive and, after a time, I began to wonder whether he was right.

The presidential villa was in Malki, a handsome neighborhood favored by diplomats, high officials and the prosperous bourgeoisie. Malki was part of the new Damascus, which spreads from the walls of the Old City across the fertile plain called the Ghouta and climbs the flank of Mount Qassioun, a hinge of the range that makes up the border with Lebanon. The Ghouta, washed by the waters of the Barada River, made Damascus a legend among the Arabs even before the advent of Islam. New Damascus is built on a design drawn by French urban planners during the mandate. Its wide avenues, spacious parks and circular intersections with fountains and statues evoke L'Enfant's design for Washington, D.C. Trees shade the streets and behind high walls stand elegant mansions. Malki contains Damascus's boutiques and restaurants, filled each night with well-dressed couples speaking many languages. During the early 1980s, an insecure period for the regime, machine-gun posts stood at many of its intersections. In the succeeding years the level of armament dropped, and security for the president's house and the nearby embassies was turned over to young men, casual in manner, who wore automatic weapons over their shoulders.

With Assad firmly in power, Damascus seemed to have banished politics from its mind in the hot weeks of the recent summer of my visit. Day dawns in Damascus in the darkened *souk* and the narrow streets of the Old City, which the Romans laid out some two thousand years ago. In the cool early light, the streets erupt into a vast market, with thousands of carts appearing, bearing fresh vegetables and fruit. By ten or so, the shops have opened. In both the new city and the old, the small merchant reigns; Damascus still has no department stores. Until one o'clock or so, commerce is intense, the traffic choking and the coffeehouses full, mostly with old men smoking and playing backgammon. Then, with the sun approaching its zenith, shopkeepers lower their shutters, government offices empty and taxi drivers speed past prospective riders, waving apologetically as if to say, "Excuse me, but my wife has lunch on the table." During the afternoon, the city sleeps, awaking again as the sun goes down and the temperature, responding to the dry desert climate, abruptly drops.

In the evening, when the shops and offices of the new city reopen, Damascus seems ready to play. Promenaders turn the downtown into a family playground—window-shopping, nibbling pastries from open trays in the pastry shops, sipping coffee or sodas in the cafes. Unshaven teenage boys of the working class, wearing worn jeans, loiter at orange-juice bars or on the terrace of cheap restaurants. The student set, flirtatious in their Riviera fashions, crowds ice cream parlors and fast-food shops. As night falls, the movie houses draw the promenaders away for lurid Arab love tales, grade-B thrillers from Europe or America, kung-fu flicks or some Hollywood oldie. At eight the offices close, and secretaries and clerks pour out to compete—quite politely, as a rule—for taxis (only the poor seem to ride in the ancient buses) and by ten or so, after the store windows darken, parents and their children head home. But the city's life rolls on. In the nightclubs—from chic for the Saudis to shady for the soldiers—the gyrations of belly dancers start only after midnight. And in an open-air officers club just below my hotel window, couples danced to alternating Western and Arab rhythms until well after I had switched off my light.

Yet, there was an undercurrent of tension in the city. Great artillery battles were raging that summer in Beirut, barely an hour away by car, between Christian forces hostile to Syria and the Syrian-supported Muslim coalition. The Assad government was silent about the fighting, but not because Damascus was indifferent. Except for those born too late to have savored it, all Damascenes speak lyrically of a Beirut that they had known since childhood. With cafes, beaches and a night life, with a free press and political tolerance, Beirut was the lung through which Damascus long breathed the air of liberty. Many Damascenes had attended Lebanese high schools, or the American University of Beirut, in an era when there was little education at home. More than a few had kin in Beirut, and many had weekend apartments there. The reports of Beirut's agony evoked deep feelings among them, but the government yielded no clues about what was happening.

Its silence, however, did not mean that the city was uninformed. There were foreign broadcasts, and a grapevine that passed through sons and husbands in the army. Refugees regularly crossed over the mountains into Syria. Damascenes could even learn something from decoding dispatches in the nightly television news, in which the world was packaged in party-line platitudes and presented amid camera shots of officials meeting with foreign dignitaries. Repeatedly, I was asked, "What do you think is happening in Lebanon?" or, sometimes, "What do you think we should do about Lebanon?" But these questions did not reflect a lack of information, much less any special confidence in me. They were expressions, I think, of a widespread frustration at being closed off from involvement in crucial events. They reflected a deep anxiety, if not distrust, about what the government was saying and doing.

Though the West also had serious concerns, the Assad regime was not without legitimate justification for its policy in Lebanon. Its problem was that any brain cells that its officials had ever applied to candor had long since atrophied, leaving only those that summoned up party slogans.

Once, on an earlier trip, I sat in on a briefing given to an American delegation by Vice-President Abdul Halim Khaddam, who was in charge of Lebanese affairs. A small man with a sly look, Khaddam, a lawyer, was widely known for an acid tongue. ("As many years as you've been coming around here," he once said to me, prior to an interview in his office, "why do you still speak such lousy Arabic?" He was right about my Arabic, but the remark struck me as a ploy to put me on the defensive.) Occasionally, however, he did his best to be charming. At the briefing in question, he spoke uninterruptedly for an hour, spinning out one banality after another. In concluding, he said, "I'm sure that if the American people could only hear me explain our position, they would agree with it." At that point, the woman sitting next to me (she happened to be my wife) leaned over and whispered, "I think that if the American people ever heard him, they'd declare war." The truth is that, whatever the intrinsic merits of the positions presented by Syrian officials, their humorless, rigidly ideological, and self-righteous delivery of their arguments inevitably alienates their listeners.

"To understand Assad and his people," said Dr. Antun Makdissi, "you must see them as a link in the chain of Syrian peasants who lived with the Ottoman pashas for centuries. The Syrian peasant is never spontaneous; he is always calculating, always suspicious. The European, in dealing with others, learns to ask, 'What does he mean?' The peasant asks, 'What does he want and how can I use it to my advantage?' His reflex rejects unguarded honesty. He is trained to play the parties he deals with against one another, so that he winds up on the side of the winner. In Syria, man is not young or innocent or naïve. Man is old and cynical. In that sense, the Assad regime is totally Syrian."

I had gone to Makdissi, a retired scholar trained in philosophy in Paris and Beirut, in search of information on the residual influence of the Ottomans in Syria. The subject had turned out to be more complex than I foresaw. Scholarship was not only lacking but distorted by politics. Committed Muslims feel a nostalgia for the caliphate, for a society shielded from Western contact, for the rule of Islamic law, and so they speak positively of the Ottomans. Strong nationalists, on the other hand, denounce the Ottomans, placing themselves on the side of secularism, social reform and an Arab renaissance. Makdissi, being Christian, seemed detached. I met with him in a simple office in the ministry of culture where he worked several hours each day, largely for his own pleasure, translating from French into Arabic books that were to be published by the government press.

"Thoughout the Ottoman period," Makdissi said, "Syrians, like other Arabs, identified themselves only by their religion. The Ottomans were seen not as occupiers but as fellow Muslims. Only in the empire's dying years did an Arab consciousness—the seeds of nationalism—begin to emerge, as a reaction to the efforts of reformers in the Ottoman army to Turkify the society. The transition to nationhood is still not complete. Even now, many people in the street, especially the Muslim believers, think of Syria as a transitional concept.

"The sense of nationhood, furthermore, is being undermined by our confessional practices, which are a vestige of the Ottoman empire's old *millet* system. As a Syrian, for example, I cannot have a civil marriage. As a Christian, I must marry in my church, and if I have a fight with my wife, I don't go to a state tribunal but to a church court, which settles our differences according to Christian law, which might be very different from Muslim law. In personal matters, like marriage and inheritance and in some measure education, a citizen is not a Syrian first but a Muslim or a Christian or a Jew. The system splinters us, though not as badly as in Lebanon, where it has run amok. Assad understands the danger and would, I think, like to banish the system, both here and in Lebanon. But Islam is a powerful seducer, and Assad is no Ataturk. Maybe if he were a Sunni he could do it, but he is an Alawite, and therefore suspect."

Confessionalism, as inherited from the Ottomans, was an approach that accorded substantial authority in the provinces to religious leaders. The sultans, though remembered as oppressors, usually exercised only weak control on the margins of the empire, and they willingly allowed power to devolve where it would, not just to religious authorities but to tribal chieftains and feudal landowners. They asked the provinces only to provide soldiers and pay taxes, which the Arabs, to preserve the barriers against the Christian West, were willing to do. In the nineteenth century, the reforms imported by the Ottomans from Europe failed to tighten Istanbul's control. By the twentieth century, the rise of local consciousness fractured the system even more.

It is a paradox that though the Arabs were never really governed from Istanbul, neither did they ever govern themselves. They lived, under the Ottomans, in a culture of neglect. Until the nineteenth century, writes the

Arab-American historian Hisham Shirabi, the Ottomans' Arab provinces "consisted of fragmented and isolated groupings of decayed cities, stagnant villages, impoverished peasantry and marauding bedouin." Commerce was negligible, industry confined to a few crafts, education practically nonexistent. Only as the empire tottered did a few Arabs begin to contemplate an alternative to Ottoman ascendancy. In their last desperate decades, the sultans themselves offered their subjects an experiment in constitutionalism and democracy, and in 1908, seventy-two Arabs were elected and briefly sat in a parliament in Istanbul. The experience gave the Arabs a brief exposure to the process of self-government. But after centuries of misrule, it left them still without an inkling of how to run a state.

II THE REALITY OF THE STATE

HISTORIANS TELL US that the Mediterranean rim, until the rise of Islam, was a single civilization, the empire of Rome. Its inhabitants had grown accustomed to the concept of a universal state. Reinforcing it was the practice of Christianity; bonding it was the flourishing trade conducted across the waters of the inland sea. Of the great traders, the Syrians, a seafaring people then, stood in the highest rank, maintaining links with the east and the south, managing an entrepôt in Aleppo and Damascus of spices, ivory, papyrus and wines.

In the view of the French historian Henri Pirenne, neither the conquests of the barbarians nor the schism between Rome and Constantinople in the early centuries of the Christian era shattered the Mediterranean's essential unity. But the Arabs' conquests of the seventh and eighth centuries, which established their control over much of the Mediterranean shoreline, did. "A complete break was made," writes Pirenne, "which was to continue even to our own day. Henceforth two different and hostile civilizations existed on the shores of *Mare Nostrum*." In the east, this polarization severed Syria, as well as the more distant Islamic lands, from Western commerce and, in time, from Western ideas. In the west, it cut off the barbarians from their contacts with North Africa and Spain. Rome was no longer a power. The Arab conquest launched continental Europe into an era of separate development which, ultimately, produced the institutional and intellectual structure known as the nation-state.

The idea of the nation-state—where a set of laws applies within a fixed territory—was devised by the Greeks. When Rome unified the Mediterranean, the concept went into eclipse, but it had taken root in Europe and never disappeared. During the Dark Ages, the continent continued to render homage to the universal state. Charlemagne claimed to rule the

Roman empire, the myth of which had survived its destruction. The papacy insisted upon its right to apply God's law throughout Christendom, a notion that was so close to Islamic thinking that Muslims referred to the pope as the caliph of the Franks. In reality, however, Europe in the centuries after Rome broke up into self-governing tribes.

By the twelfth century, tribal organization in Europe had largely evolved into kingdoms, with strong central rule. Passing through channels set up by the Arabs, the political scriptures of classical Greece and Rome were once more in circulation, and with time, the individualist impulses that gave rise to the Renaissance transformed political thought. Patriarchy and the hierarchical relationships that originally characterized the tribe gradually gave way to the obligations of citizens, which became the seeds of democratic doctrine. Then, during the Protestant Reformation the myth of the universal state died, and Europe recognized that it was actually a collection of diverse secular sovereignties, relating to one another as equals through the developing rules of international law.

Islam evolved in a totally different way. As a political leader, Mohammed's genius was to retain tribalism and reorganize it into the *umma*, the Islamic community. In *Neopatriarchy*, Shirabi explains that, in response to the military and commercial requirements of the time, the Prophet created the *umma* as a supertribe. At the base of the *umma* was a series of patriarchically organized families, and at its summit was God, the patriarch of them all. This structure satisfied the individual's basic needs— shelter, security, identity—and elicited his most basic loyalty. Cultivating dependency, it demanded submission and shaped personalities whose identities were not individual but grew within the framework of the collectivity. The Arab personality, Shirabi contends, is much the same today.

Doctrinally, Mohammed's Islam was, like Christianity, a universal religion—that is, it offered its benefits, through conversion, to all people. But where Christianity accepted its followers' allegiances to diverse states, Islam defined its believers by membership in the *umma*, in which all stood before God as equals. To Islam, the state as a geographical concept was simply not relevant. The Islamic world was known as the *dar-al-Islam*, and Muslims, wherever they resided within it, were subject to the same codes of conduct. Indeed, Muslims have historically changed residences, often traveling long distances over land or sea, without ever feeling they were leaving the *umma*. The good Muslim was barred from living only in the *dar-al-harb*, the "realm of war." Its name was drawn from the Muslim's duty to vigorously offer his faith to the non-Islamic world.

In practice, however, the "realm of Islam" over the centuries often split into rival political regimes, some of which looked very much like states, although a common recognition of the supremacy of the caliphate preserved the formal unity of the *umma*. Under the Ottomans, Arabs never thought of themselves as living under foreign rule. They identified themselves only as an afterthought by a place of residence, an ethnic group or a tribe. Until the last, rather disorderly years of the empire, Arabs thought of themselves as the equal of Turks within the *umma*. No sense of Arabism, much less Arab nationalism, existed.

In addition to Islamic doctrine, historians have noted other obstacles to development by the Arabs of a sense of the state. "Islam," writes the historian John A. Armstrong, "is the only civilization created by nomads." While the Europeans, tilling the soil, were settling into fixed territories, paying growing attention to legal boundaries, the Arabs remained under the influence of their nomadic heritage, even while living in cities. The emblem of the Arab civilization has long been the camel; even today, Arab culture looks upon the farmer with some disdain. Throughout history, boundaries in the desert made as much sense to Muslims as boundaries in the sea; both were arbitrary, indiscernible and scarcely worth heeding. Islam's concept of the *umma* is consistent with this notion; it is essentially a bedouin concept.

Yet the reality of Islamic civilization has always been at odds with its nomadic myths. The Prophet himself was a city-dweller. The centers of Islamic learning were cities. As much as Arabs revere their bedouin roots, their image of paradise is Damascus, with its green and fertile gardens.

But unlike the cities of Europe, Arab cities did not dominate great hinterlands. The great Arab capitals—beginning with Mecca, and going on to Damascus, Cairo and, in some measure, even Baghdad—were oases, at the edge of if not within the desert, enjoying only a narrow economic base. They did not serve as economic and social hubs for farmers and villagers, as Europe's cities did, generating regional loyalties. The bedouin was hostile to the city-dweller; urban Arabs saw the bedouin as an enemy, moving lawlessly over the trackless sands, interrupting communications, sometimes attacking the city itself. Within Arab civilization, the nomad was an obstacle to the realization of unity within the *umma*, and only in modern times have the cities succeeded in subduing him. His psychological presence was—and to a degree remains—a strong impediment to the development of any idea of an integrated state.

As a people, the Arabs were introduced to the idea of the state only with the collapse of the Ottoman empire. The transition began on the eve of World War I, when the Young Turks replaced the long-standing sultanic tradition of tolerance of ethnic diversity with a policy of Turkification, which they applied with particular rigor to their Arab subjects. Their actions provoked an awareness of Arabism, and the establishment of a small nationalist movement, centered in Damascus. The movement, such as it was, did not break down into Syrian or Iraqi or Palestinian components. The Arab leadership, accustomed to thinking in terms of an *umma*, embraced an ideology that was trans-Arab; from it, by an organic process, emerged the idea of an Arab nation. But when World War I began, this vision was still in a nascent stage.

At first, the war looked to Arabs like simply another round in the ongoing struggle between Islam and the Christian West. Few Arabs sensed an impending political change and, when the fighting began, nearly all Arabs lined up obediently behind the Ottoman flag. The Young Turks appraised this loyalty badly, however, and responded to the occasional outbreaks of Arab nationalism with brutal repression. As a consequence, Arabs, for the first time, began to express reservations about their allegiance to Istanbul.

Curiously, the leader who chose to take responsibility for the nationalist movement was not, as one might have expected, a Damascus intellectual, but a sheikh from conservative Hejaz, the western half of Arabia. Sharif (the title signifies a descendant of the Prophet) Hussein, who administered the holy places of Mecca and Medina in the sultan's name, was from Mohammed's family, the Hashemites. Proud of his autonomy, which he openly aspired to extend to all of Arabia, he saw the Young Turks as menacing, and the menace was increased by the impending extension of a railroad from Istanbul as far as Mecca, which meant that Ottoman troops could move quickly into his domains. Sharif Hussein had the support of two strong and ambitious sons, Abdullah and Faisal, who had made contact with both the nationalists in Damascus and the British in Cairo, even before the war. After the war broke out, father and sons saw an opportunity to make a move.

Sharif Hussein provoked the Young Turks from the start by refusing to join in declaring a *jihad* against the West. Turning secretly to the British, he claimed that he could bring the Arabs over to their side. By 1915, the sultan's army had stopped Britain's grand assault at Gallipoli and was threatening the Suez Canal; at that juncture, the British were willing to leap at almost any chance to weaken the enemy by getting his Arab units to defect. London disliked Sharif Hussein's terms: the establishment of an Arab nation after the war, under a Hashemite throne. Such ambitions conflicted with its own imperial designs, and the understandings it had reached with its allies on carving up the Ottoman domains. Britain did not deal straightforwardly with Hussein's demands. In an exchange of correspondence known as the McMahon Letters, it conveyed a vague promise of Arab independence, knowing that it did not have either the power or the will to deliver on the pledge. It was also true, however, that Sharif Hussein lacked the power to deliver the Arabs to the Allied side.

By late 1915, Turkey had caught wind of Hussein's intrigue with the British. The Turks also executed several dozen nationalists in Damascus on charges of conspiracy. In June 1916, Sharif Hussein finally proclaimed the shift in allegiance that would go down in history as the Arab Revolt. Yet, to most Arabs the call to fight the Ottomans on the side of the West was tantamount to declaring war on Islam. The only forces that responded positively were a few thousand Arabian tribesmen, faithful to the Hashemites, most of them already receiving a British dole. These tribesmen went on the attack against Ottoman garrisons in Hejaz but, given their lack of discipline, they had no success. Nonetheless, in November 1916, Sharif Hussein proclaimed himself King of the Arabs; except in Hejaz, his appeal received no support anywhere in the Arab world.

By this time, the British and French had expanded their previous understandings into a secret pact—the Sykes-Picot Agreement. It totally ignored Hussein, dividing up the Ottomans' Arab provinces among themselves. The agreement gave the French Lebanon, where they had longstanding ties, as well as Syria and Mesopotamia, as far west as the Persian border. (Britain later took over Mesopotamia for itself.) The British, asserting claims for themselves to the south of the French sector, were to assume control of what was loosely called Palestine, a swath of land from the Mediterranean to the Gulf. On November 2, 1917, Britain went a step further by issuing the Balfour Declaration, which promised to the Jews a national homeland in Palestine. The Sykes-Picot Agreement left the Arabs with nothing.

To the Arabs, Sykes-Picot, along with the Balfour Declaration, established a pattern of deceit from which the West has rarely departed. Is it any wonder that since then they have perceived Western conspiracies wherever they look? The Arabs scoffed at Britain's postwar assertion that Sykes-Picot somehow complemented the McMahon Letters, and that together they would lead—in due course—to full Arab independence. In the crumbling of the Ottoman empire, what they experienced was not liberation, much less unification, but a Christian takeover of the Arab realm, with some help from the Jews. Arab civilization had been transformed— but nothing in Arab experience or doctrine had prepared them for the new era. The West now occupied the Arab heartland; the Crusaders, by duplicity, had triumphed.

Of all the Arabs, it was the Syrians who felt the most aggrieved. Historically, Syria had included the expanse from the Taurus Mountains in the north to the Sinai in the south, the landmass that has since become Lebanon, Jordan and Israel, as well as Syria itself. Under the Ottomans, the term "Palestine" had rarely been used; the region was known as Southern Syria. After the war, the West coined the term "Greater Syria" to refer to Damascus's territorial aspirations—but until then the whole area was simply "Syria," and nationalists in Damascus believed they were entitled to rule it in its entirety. Had Syria not fathered the idea of Arab nationalism, they asked, and sacrificed many sons in its name? To this day, on the slightest pretext, Syrian officials launch into bitter denunciations of Sykes-Picot, of the wartime Allies and of the fraud of the postwar settlement.

Before the war in the Middle East was over, Sharif Hussein's bedouin forces had made a noteworthy contribution to the Allied victory. Reinforced by Arabs from the Ottoman army—many of them defecting prisoners of war, preponderantly Iraqis—they became disciplined fighting units. Some fought as regulars with the British; others, under the command of Faisal, the sharif's youngest son, served as guerrillas, helping to clear the Arabian Peninsula, then drive the Turks steadily northward. They conducted harassing operations, often behind enemy lines. Fighting as bedouins have long fought in the desert, they inflicted heavy losses on the Turks.

Damascus fell on September 20, 1918, ten months after the Allied capture of Jerusalem. After four hundred years in occupation, the Ottomans quit Damascus precipitately, leaving behind a serious vacuum of authority. In the confusion, Faisal, backed by the celebrated British officer T. E. Lawrence, proclaimed an "Arab constitutional government . . . fully and absolutely independent," having authority over "all Syria." The Damascenes seemed satisfied enough to have an Arabian prince in command, but the grip of the new regime was fragile. The French at that point were less worried about the Arabs than about Britain, whose presence in Damascus, they feared, might serve as a wedge in their long-standing colonial competition. The French took for granted that Faisal would not long remain in power.

"I was thirteen when I saw the camel caravan carrying Faisal arrive in Damascus in 1918," said Bedreddin Shellah, who at the time we spoke was the dean of the Damascus commercial community. Eighty-four years old, he looked decades younger in an elegant white suit, which he wore each morning to the office of his import-export company in the Old City. "It was an hour of great jubilation. We had had mixed feelings about the Ottomans. Because they were Muslims like us, we had not considered them a colonial power, and we had counted on them to protect us against czarist Russia and European secularism. But they governed badly. Most of our people were poor and only a handful were educated, nearly all of them at Islamic schools. It was a pity that while Europe was having a golden age, the last years were so bleak in Syria. We saw the Ottomans as a barrier to progress and prosperity, but we parted with them only when they hanged our patriots in 1916. After that, there was no going back.

"Still, when Faisal arrived, most of our people were bewildered. Only a few were nationalists. Our young men were off fighting in the Ottoman army. The masses welcomed Faisal, not out of patriotism, but in the hope of seeing an end to wartime suffering."

Though they abandoned Sharif Hussein as soon as the fighting was over, the British acknowledged a debt to the Hashemites and consented to name Faisal as king in Damascus. Under the best of circumstances, Faisal would have had a daunting task. He ruled over a people with little sense of national identity and no experience in self-government. He himself, a foreigner and a bedouin chief, evoked some apprehension. The old merchant class, to which Bedreddin Shellah's father belonged, had been the backbone of the Ottoman administration; it asked only for a license to run its own affairs and stay rich. But the city's Arab nationalists had been joined by a cluster of radical intellectuals, many of them from Palestine, and they had captured the country's emotions. In mid-1919, Faisal convoked a parliament in Damascus that contained representation from all of historical Syria. Its members had no use for the Sykes-Picot Agreement and challenged not just French but British designs over the land it considered their own.

Faisal himself spent late 1919 and early 1920 in Paris, negotiating desperately with the Allied leadership at the peace conference to salvage his kingdom. To please the British, he made a deal with the Zionists in which he endorsed Jewish immigration to Palestine in return for an acknowledgment of Damascus's sovereignty. He also agreed to swallow French preeminence in Syria in return for recognition of Syria's independence and unity. After returning to Damascus, he submitted these and other proposals to his parliament, contending that Syria's only hope for avoiding permanent colonization lay in compromising with the French and retaining the support of Britain. The parliament, however, passed resolutions that not only rejected French involvement but insisted on full authority within Syria's historical boundaries, which meant the nullification of the Balfour Declaration. A victory for the radicals, the resolutions meant the doom of any hope of Britain's help in stopping France.

Actually, no matter what it did, it is unlikely that Damascus could have stopped France. A French army of nearly two hundred thousand men had already landed in Beirut and, in July 1920, began moving east. Faisal's cabinet organized a ragtag volunteer force which met the invaders at the border town of Maysaloun. Historians say that at most a skirmish ensued, but Syrian schoolchildren are taught that it was a great battle, a heroic, if vain, assertion of Syria's right to independence. After the encounter, Faisal abdicated and fled, and those of his supporters who did not follow him were either executed or jailed by the French.

France's occupation put an end to the vision of an Arab nation. Britain and France proceeded to impose on the Middle East a system of nation-states modeled after Europe's, which they, for the time being, controlled. From it ultimately emerged sovereign Syria, Iraq, Jordan and Israel, as well as a sliver of territory still in dispute that may become a state of Palestine. Arabs came increasingly to recognize unity as an ideal—which, in reality, it probably always was. In our own time, most Arabs acknowledge that the dream is not likely ever to be achieved. But the dream persisted for decades, and even now is not totally extinguished.

Shellah recalled for me that by 1920 his family had decided to put its business interests above politics—as it does to this day—and he was absent from Damascus when the French army marched in. His father, he said, had sent him off to sell watermelons in Tulkarm, a market town in what is now the West Bank. In those days, it was still normal to travel by train throughout the region, without passport or other documentation. On the return trip, he recalled, the train was stopped by remnants of the Maysaloun volunteers searching for Syrians who had collaborated with the French. When they refused to let the train proceed on its way, he said, he went back to Tulkarm, then on to Cairo, where he bought cotton for sale at home. By the time he got back to Damascus, his family had joined with other merchants in searching for an accommodation with the French.

"The occupation was not oppressive on the whole, but still it was an occupation, and it was Christian," Shellah said to me. "Faisal, though he was a stranger to us, was liked but the government was a mess, and the French came along and provided stability. They set up schools and hospitals, administered the country well and organized a strong police force. Damascus had barely changed in a thousand years. It still had only two hundred thousand people, all of them living in the Old City. The French planned its growth into a modern city. They also established a system of recording land surveys and titles, which was important for business. Industries were founded, including our family's canning factory, and, at least until the depression of 1929, Syria was prosperous. Our family gave financial support to the nationalist resistance, including the fifty-six-day strike of 1936, when all of the city was closed, but we were too busy to get deeply involved in political affairs. We never doubted, however, that our people wanted independence, and were not going to rest until it came."

It took the turbulence of another European war to enable Syria to wrest free of France. By then, the French had long since made Lebanon a separate state, with boundaries that went well beyond the lines of the old Ottoman province. Pursuing a divide-and-conquer strategy, the French had also established autonomous principalities—although they were later abolished—for the Alawite and Druze minorities. On the eve of World

War II, they further depleted Syrian territory by ceding the northern province of Alexandretta to Turkey to forestall a Turkish alliance with Germany; the cession left Syria with no major port. Only in 1946, after heavy local fighting and under severe international pressure, did France withdraw its occupying army and acknowledge Syrian independence.

Syria at that time was a shaky parliamentary republic, its unity in doubt, its economy undeveloped, its population still largely illiterate. Its leaders, products of the French, were heavily committed to the interests of a Sunni landholding class. Its army, though small, was disproportionately Alawite and Druze, the disadvantaged minorities that the French had favored; clearly it was a rival to the government itself.

At the same time that Syria struggled with republicanism, its neighbors, Iraq and Jordan, were governed by Hashemite monarchs, with close ties to Britain. Iraq, where the British had placed Faisal after the French deposed him, now had Faisal's grandson on the throne; Jordan was still ruled by Abdullah, Faisal's older brother. Each of the Hashemites thought of his own realm as temporary and artificial, a stopgap until the issue of unity, the real business of the Arabs, was resolved. Both Faisal and Abdullah, like their father Sharif Hussein, dreamed of a single Arab nation, over which he himself would reign. Indeed, the belief was widespread among the Arabs that the states created after World War I were simply political subdivisions of a more legitimate Arab whole. Of the three, the weakest country at the time of independence was thought to be Syria, which political observers were convinced would be unable to resist absorption by one Hashemite king or the other.

III   ASSAD AS LEADER

IN 1949, the Syrian republic survived its first coup. It came when the Arabs were searching widely for scapegoats to explain the defeat in the war with Israel. Over the following decade, the regime weathered repeated attempts to overthrow it, proving remarkably resilient. But the ongoing conflict with the Jewish state was, in the long run, more than it could withstand. Power inevitably gravitated toward the army, and when the Cold War reached the Middle East in the mid-1950s, tensions sharpened. While Hashemite Iraq pulled the Arabs toward a Western alliance, Nasserite Egypt pulled them toward Moscow. Surrendering to anticolonial passions after the Anglo-French attack on Suez in 1956, Syria finally lined up with Nasser, who had seduced its officer corps with visions of East-bloc arms. In 1958, Syria's parliament submitted to the army's demands to form a Syrian-Egyptian union, then agreed to dissolve itself. The union lasted only three years, but it left Syria an army-ruled state and a dependency of the Soviet Union.

The 1950s were also the years in which Syria's Baath Party grew from a handful of high-minded partisans clustered around Michel Aflaq into a major political movement. It is no coincidence that Aflaq was a Christian, or that a large proportion of his followers were, like him, outsiders in a Sunni society. Syria had Alawite, Christian and Kurdish minorities, each roughly 10 percent of the population, as well as smaller communities of Druzes, Ismailis and Jews. Both the Ottomans and the French had cultivated differences between them; Aflaq's Baathism sought reconciliation, by emphasizing the Arabism they shared. Not surprisingly, Aflaq's program was most warmly received in impoverished rural Syria, where the minorities were strongest—and in the armed forces, which ambitious young Alawites and Druzes had made into a vehicle of social advancement.

"We start as Baathis from the historical reality that the Arabs are one nation," said Saber Falhout, president of the Syrian Journalists Union and director of the Syrian Arab News Agency. Falhout, a white-haired Druze in his fifties, was often called the poet of the Baath revolution—though his poetry is hard to distinguish from partisan propaganda. We spoke one evening in his dimly lit office at the news agency in Midan, an industrial quarter of Damascus, adjacent to the Old City walls. Though not all experts would accept as "historical reality" Falhout's assertion that the Arabs are a single nation, I chose not to interrupt him. "During the Omayyad period," he said, "the Arab nation was ruled from Damascus. It was the center of the Arab world. We want to regain that unity, and that leadership. This idea may seem romantic to you, but we believe that one day we will achieve it. You're not a real Baath party member unless you believe it."

Hafez al-Assad joined the Baath Party at the age of sixteen. Born in 1928 into a family of Alawite peasants, he was the ninth of eleven children. Only a few years before, the French had built a school in his village, and he was the first of his family to attend it. At age nine, he was sent down the mountain to a school in Latakia, the Alawites' seaside capital, and in 1942, after passing a formal exam, he went on to secondary school. Class-conscious and aggressive, he became national president of the Union of Syrian Students and, despite his antiregime politics, he was admitted in 1951 to the army's flying school at Aleppo. On graduating in 1955, he was already at a professional and social level that few Alawites before him had attained.

Sent for advanced flight training to Cairo, Assad was personally exposed to the magnetism of Nasser. On his return, he became Syria's foremost pilot but, more important, he joined four fellow officers—two Alawites, two Ismailis—to form a secret Military Committee to reshape the Baath

Party. Defying Aflaq, they envisaged the party not as civilian, parliamentarian and liberal but as military, radical and authoritarian. Nasser's Free Officers were their model, and in 1963, having already participated in one failed coup, the Committee became the hinge of a coalition that overthrew the government. After months of violent factional fighting, Assad emerged as a major figure in the regime. Though only thirty-five and a captain, he personally controlled the air force, and through it he extended his influence into the other armed services. Then, in a bloody coup in 1966, the Committee captured the Baath Party, put an end to meaningful elections and drove Aflaq into exile. The Committee also named Assad minister of defense.

The chief of the government after 1966 was Salah Jadid, a fellow Alawite and one of the five founders of the Military Committee. A few years older than Assad, and substantially more radical, Jadid governed with a tyrant's hand. It was Jadid who directed the elimination of the Druzes as rivals to the Alawites in the military hierarchy. He also presided over nationalizations, confiscations and land reform, shifting wealth from the Sunnis who had been Syria's aristocracy since Ottoman times to the rural peasantry and urban middle classes, preponderantly of minority stock. Brutally, Jadid implemented the program of Baathi socialism. It was a revolutionary triumph of Syria's perennial have-nots.

Jadid, however, then had the misfortune of presiding over Syria's disastrous defeat in the Six-Day War. Assad, as defense minister, should have known better than to permit his disorganized armed forces to challenge the Israelis, but he avoided the blame, charging that Jadid's radicalism had weakened the country. Determined to seize power from Jadid, he initiated another savage struggle, and when it was over, two of the Military Committee's five founders had vanished into exile (one was later murdered) and another had committed suicide. Jadid, along with dozens of highly placed Baathis, wound up in prison. In 1993, a handful of those locked up in 1970 were released, but an estimated ten or twelve, including Jadid, remained in prison. Jadid died in August of that year. The battle—Baath Party ideologists call it the "corrective movement" of 1970—ended in Assad's taking full charge of the party and the regime, which he has run without challenge ever since.

Historians have debated why Assad has succeeded where all his predecessors failed, in bringing stability to Syria. But he came to power when Syrians had tired of disorder, and his calls for national reconciliation were greeted with relief. In naming himself president, he proclaimed that he was not beholden to any junta, and he imposed his own strict control over the armed forces and the secret services. To please the Sunni majority, he pronounced himself a Muslim—a dubious assertion for an Alawite—and accepted a constitutional provision that the president must be faithful to

Islam. He also reached out to the urban bourgeoisie, softening some of Jadid's harsh economic strictures. But he did not weaken the benefits aimed at the rural poor: school and hospital construction, electrification and the extension of piped water. After years of revolving-door leadership, Syrians gratefully embraced what Assad set out to do, and the strength he demonstrated in doing it.

They also approved of his personal modesty. In a culture of pompous chieftains, Assad shunned the creation of a personality cult. It is true that his photographs were widely disseminated, but what they showed was an avuncular man with tired eyes, concealing baldness by brushing his hair sideways, barely smiling. Aloof by nature, Assad rarely appeared in public, though Syrians were reminded of his presence each evening by TV footage of his reviewing troops or meeting dignitaries. Hardworking, he was untainted by scandal and said to be considerate to his family and staff. Syrians never forgot that he was an Alawite, or that Alawites controlled the state, but they regarded him as fair in distributing government bounties and they respected him. Even after twenty years, they did not forget the regime that preceded him, and they were grateful that political life in Syria had become low-key, stable, predictable.

Yet Assad's record of achievement was not spectacular. Throughout the 1980s, the economy stagnated. Assad, apprehensive of political repercussions, was reluctant to authorize the liberalization that economists urged. The country suffered from a chronic shortage of hard currency, evident from the ancient buses and taxis that cruised the streets, and the relative absence of gadgets in the stores. Hopes for a boom based on oil discoveries were unrealized. Some government critics insisted that corruption was rampant, and particularly that top military officers were skimming off fortunes in smuggling and drug operations in Lebanon. Economists knew that Syria supported a thriving underground economy; its magnitude was unknown, but the young men hawking smuggled American cigarettes on street corners in downtown Damascus were testimony that something was amiss. In the 1990s, Assad changed his mind on reforms and the economy picked up momentum, but Syrians were slow to feel the impact.

It was no secret that Syria suffered from conspicuous economic inequalities. A few old business families with close connections to the government live very well. During a gaudy wedding party that I observed around the Sheraton pool one night—the host, I was told, was an old provincial landowner—an employee standing near me snarled, "Some socialist regime!" At the other end of the spectrum, I stopped at a village near Aleppo, having been struck by the intriguing beehive design of the mud houses I saw from the road. Two parents and eight children, who shared the complex of structures with an assortment of farm animals, received me warmly.

They were all neatly clad—mother and daughters in gaily colored peasant dresses—and looked amply fed and healthy. It was primitive living, without piped water or electricity; the children took turns riding a donkey to a well about a mile away. But the village had a school and a clinic, which meant that the children had the prospects for a better life that come with being able to read and write.

In between these two extremes was a modern middle class, which the economic data suggested was hard-pressed but which somehow rode in taxis, went to the movies, got its children educated and consumed plenty of food and drink. The middle class had also replaced Beirut as a summer resort with Latakia, the largely Alawite city on the north coast, where I spent several days at a beach hotel which had been hastily erected a few years before to accommodate the Mediterranean Games, a regional version of the Olympics. Part of a complex that included a high-rise condo with a swimming pool, the hotel was tacky and uncomfortable, but jammed with families who had arrived by car from Damascus and Aleppo. The scene looked authentically European: a sandy beach blanketed with sun-worshippers, who each evening dined on the patio at a fine buffet, with wine, to the sounds of a rock band. A few women dressed in accordance with Islamic standards of modesty, but, to my surprise, many moved about in swimsuits, not just on the beach but in the hotel lobby. No one I spoke to claimed to know the source of the money for such recreation, but most credited the black market generated by the Lebanon war.

On several occasions, I was invited to join Syrian friends at Bloudan, a mountain resort that was a one-hour drive from Damascus—past government reforestation projects, suburban housing developments and luxuriant fruit orchards—on good highways. The rich have villas in Bloudan; middle-class families enjoy long lunches and dinners in outdoor restaurants shaded by awnings, with views across the mountains into Lebanon. Most of the women I saw in Bloudan were in pretty summer dresses, though a few wore Islamic headscarves or even robes. The men were in sport shirts; none wore a uniform. Children ran between the aisles, or played in a small playground outside the restaurant door. The food was standard Middle East fare: tasty salads, roast chicken and kebabs, washed down with beer or arak. Most of the parties consisted of families—Syrian social life still revolved around the family—sitting at tables of a dozen or more. These luncheons were not inexpensive but, my friends told me, the tables were booked up weeks in advance.

Though Assad had set Syria on the course of economic development, his real interest was security policy, of which he considered himself a master. Ironically, his failures in this domain were more glaring. Having helped provoke the Six-Day War in 1967, he was far from blameless in the poor showing against Israel on the battlefield, and he blundered again in 1970 by sending tanks to help the PLO in its "Black September" fight against King Hussein, only to have them scurry home in the face of Israeli intimidation. In the October war of 1973, Syria's army, after a string of early victories, was again beaten by the Israelis. In 1976, Assad entered Lebanon's civil war, and for many years helped to limit the scope of the violence, without bringing it to an end. Since 1990, Lebanon's factions have observed a truce, underwritten by Syria, which has imposed on the country the status of political dependency. Over the long run, Syria's relationship with Lebanon is likely to turn on the terms of an eventual settlement with Israel. But until then, Syrian forces are likely to remain in the eye of a storm—one whose winds are constantly shifting.

As for Assad's grand strategy to rid Arab soil of the interlopers—the Saladin dream—it was also stalled. With help from the Soviet Union, Assad had long aspired to "strategic parity" with Israel, a term he never precisely defined but which seemed to go beyond weaponry. His plan, like Saladin's, was to make Syria the linchpin of an Arab front stretching from Egypt to Iraq, which ultimately would be strong enough to triumph. But in 1977 the front began to fall apart when Assad failed to stop Sadat from going to Jerusalem to initiate peace talks with the Israelis. Three years later, he alienated Baghdad by allying with Teheran in the Iraq-Iran war. Damascus's Iranian bond offended the Arab world generally—many Syrians included—and helped Egypt to recover the influence it had lost by its treaty with Israel. The magnitude of this error became clear in 1982, when Syria had to stand alone—Assad's worst fear—against the Israeli invasion of Lebanon, in which it was badly beaten once more. In 1988, Assad's anti-Iraqi gamble seemed altogether lost when Iran turned out to be the loser in the Gulf. To compound the decline, the Soviet Union, Syria's longtime patron, after several years of steady retreat from the Middle East, ceased to exist. The collapse forced Assad to draw closer to the American orbit, and in 1990 he renewed his anti-Iraqi militancy by supporting Washington in the war over Kuwait. But even in subscribing to Washington's Middle East peace initiative, he labored under the burden of strategic inferiority to Israel, and the promise of rewards was slow to present itself.

IV   THE *MUKHABARAT* STATE

IF SYRIANS FELT critical of Assad for his failures, they expressed themselves in muted voices, because the freedom promised them by the Baath Party was never granted. The *mukhabarat*—the secret police—was the state's most powerful institution. It is true that Assad, unlike Saddam

Hussein, did not allow oppression to become part of life's routine; the Syrian Baathis ruled with a lighter hand than their Iraqi counterparts. It is also true that Assad maintained a facade of political diversity by tolerating an elected parliament—though only Baathis and their supporters were eligible to run for it. He built a network of ostensibly democratic unions—women, doctors, farmers, journalists—all controlled by the party. And in conversations at home, even in front of foreigners, Syrians often vented critical feelings. But one Damascene I knew, fearful that his home was bugged, believed he avoided retaliation by talking politics only in the privacy of his car.

If the Assad regime seemed to ignore Syrians who engaged in malicious small talk, it was merciless with those it considered dangerous. In reporting on Syria in the 1990s, Amnesty International spoke of "thousands of political prisoners, including prisoners of conscience" detained in jails, most of them without trial, many tortured. A human-rights report by the State Department, though less sweeping, charged Syria with "pervasive denial of human rights, including widespread torture and denial of freedoms of speech, press and association." (In December 1991, after the Gulf war and the Madrid peace conference, Assad pardoned nearly three thousand political prisoners, presumably to win favor with the United States.)

To obtain some perspective on the opposition to Assad, I made a visit to Paris, home of a community of political émigrés from Syria. I had a few phone numbers in my pocket, and over the course of a week, I met with a dozen of its members, whose stories recalled to me novels whose authors and titles I had long since forgotten, about disillusioned political exiles, mostly Russians, who marched up and down unfamiliar boulevards. As I recalled these characters, most were impoverished, frustrated, pitiful, commiserating with one another on how bad conditions were, waiting for something to happen. In Lenin's case, of course, something did happen, and he raced home to take command of a revolution. My impression of the Syrians I met in Paris was that they all dreamed of becoming Lenin.

The opposition that I found was—not surprisingly, considering Syria's recent history and the experience of exile movements generally—badly splintered. It had a top layer of former presidents, ministers and generals who had lost out in one or another power struggle and escaped with their lives; their role was symbolic, since most were now too old to be active participants. On the functional level, the movement divided into left and right. The left was divided into roughly a dozen factions. The Baathis, for example, had their Aflaq and Jadid wings; the Communist left had Gorbachev, Brezhnev and Berlinguer tendencies. (Enrico Berlinguer was an Italian proponent of "Eurocommunism.") On the right, the Muslim

Brotherhood stood more or less alone, though even it was split between pro-Saudi and pro-Khomeini sympathizers.

The movement was divided not only ideologically but according to geography and money as well. There were the Paris groups, whose members insisted they depended only on Syrians for support, and the Baghdad groups, who were presumably kept by Assad's enemies, the Iraqis, and of whom the Paris people were disdainful. In some instances, the same faction had both Paris and Baghdad offices, but the Parisians claimed to be more pure, while the Baghdadis defended themselves as more effective. In the atmosphere of suspicion in which the exiles lived, they routinely accused one another of being tools of the CIA or the KGB or Iran. More convincing was their claim that dozens, maybe hundreds, of their members inside Syria had been imprisoned and were subjected regularly to torture.

Perhaps it should be noted that Rifat al-Assad, the president's brother, was also in Paris. In a manner of speaking, he too was an opposition figure. Owner of two Arabic-language magazines and much property, he did not live in the shabby conditions of those I had gone to see. Rifat, who still held the title of vice-president of Syria, declined to meet with me, but an aide invited me to his richly decorated office, then took me to lunch, for the obvious purpose of promoting Rifat's ongoing campaign to return to his brother's good graces. He argued strenuously in behalf of Rifat's reputation, insisting that the charges of smuggling and graft and, particularly, of power-grabbing were untrue. Rifat, he claimed, thinks only of serving his brother. Though Hafez had sent his brother off in disgrace, he had never denounced him publicly. Syrians told me that Rifat retained important connections inside the security apparatus and was still a major contender to succeed his brother.

Ahmad Mohafel, an Aleppan in his mid-fifties, could be considered a more authentic opposition figure. A Communist, he told me he had left Syria in 1976 with the aim of unifying the democratic, secular opposition to Assad.

"As an opposition," Mohafel said in our talk, "we have been in existence for nearly twenty years, and frankly we are getting nowhere. If anything, Assad's terror is moving us backward. I suppose that's why he leaves us alone in Paris. We have so far failed to harmonize our actions with the internal life of the country, so that we can isolate the regime from the people. We had a written program in 1980, which was passed around from hand to hand, until the government began making arrests. Now we are back to debating how we can become a mass movement. We have got to find a way to attract the people into our camp, without falling into bloody adventurism. But we are not yet ready."

When I asked how I could reach the Muslim Brotherhood, which had no representatives in Paris, Mohafel put me in touch with a Syrian student, with whom I fixed a meeting at a metro station near the suburban university at Nanterre. Mohammed, as he called himself, said I could see the Brothers only in Amman, Jordan, which surprised me, since some years before, Assad had accused King Hussein of providing the Brotherhood with facilities for terrorist activities, which the king angrily denied. But I agreed to the proposal and, in Amman, went first to see a well-informed official who told me that the king had been deceived by his own intelligence services, which had indeed tolerated Brotherhood operations against Syria. The king had reprimanded the intelligence agencies, he said. Nonetheless, Hussein continued to grant asylum to the Brothers, because in the 1970s he had extradited several of them on Assad's promise of a fair trial and, instead, they were summarily shot. The next morning, three Brothers in Western dress arrived at my hotel in Amman, and suggested we talk in my room, where we would not be observed.

The delegation leader identified himself as Ali al-Bayanouni, head of the Syrian Muslim Brothers in Jordan. A tall man who wore dark glasses and played with worry beads, Bayanouni told me the Brotherhood was established in Syria soon after its founding in Egypt in the 1920s, and as a parliamentary party it had enjoyed some early electoral success. He himself, he said, had been elected to parliament in 1963. But in that same year the Baathis took power and "put an end to civilized dialogue" on Syria's future. By then, he said, the Brotherhood was Syria's strongest political movement, and so the regime vowed to destroy it.

"In 1964," Bayanouni said, "the Syrian government began jailing the Brothers and suppressing the Islamic press. When Jadid came to power, it started torturing and killing Brothers in prison and in 1973, after Assad took over, it adopted an openly leftist, antireligious line. Remember that Assad is an Alawite, far removed from Islam. He calls himself a Muslim but we do not agree and, since he took power, the Sunni-Alawite conflict has been getting worse. I was imprisoned from 1975 to 1977 and was lucky to get out alive. The Assad government is not just against the Brotherhood. It is against all Islam."

Bayanouni said that what the Brotherhood wanted in Syria was a modern, democratic state, with freedom of speech and religion. Women would be the equal of men, he said, though he acknowledged that they would be expected to cover their hair, and although they would be permitted to take jobs, they would have to respect Islamic tradition—which probably meant working only at home. When I asked his position on the Salman Rushdie case, he replied much as had the Egyptian moderates: no government should sentence a man to death without trial, but Rushdie should be brought before an Islamic court. "Islam respects all religion," he assured me, and in an Islamic state, Rushdie would be prosecuted for offending religion. But he insisted the prosecution would be conducted fairly.

"The Brothers," Bayanouni went on, "began their counter-campaign of resistance in the 1970s. Assad's chief of police in Hama was assassinated, and the military school in Aleppo was bombed, killing many students, mostly Alawites. These acts were a declaration of war, although the Brotherhood, as a party and as a movement, condemned violence and denied responsibility for any killing. Under a new law, Assad retaliated in 1980 by sentencing our supporters to death, and by executing our leaders in exile in Europe and the Arab countries. Then the massacre in Hama came. We now have seven to ten thousand members in prison, and we are preparing for a long struggle. We are weak and have stopped all violence, but we will rise up at the right political moment."

The massacre in 1982 at Hama, a midsized Sunni city on the plains of central Syria, was a defining moment in the war between the Assad regime and the Muslim Brotherhood. Long an Islamic stronghold, Hama was treated as a kind of test tube by the Brotherhood, which began reaching out for power there as early as 1964, claiming a Sunni right of ascendancy over the Alawites. Throughout the 1970s, as Bayanouni made clear, the Brotherhood waged a vicious campaign, aimed chiefly at Alawites, taking hundreds of lives, once narrowly missing Assad himself. The Baath's counterattacks culminated in a full-scale military assault on Hama, in which as many as twenty-five thousand people died. By chance I visited Hama in the spring of 1982, two months after the massacre, and found barely half the buildings standing; when I returned six years later, few signs of the carnage remained, though the psychological scars were still far from healed.

In Paris, Mohafel, the secularist, told me he thought that Assad had tricked the Brothers into a violent confrontation in order to crush them. It was the kind of deceit, he said, in which Assad excelled. Though never officially acknowledged, the story of Hama was known to all Syrians, and few, whether Sunni or not, forgave Assad for his excesses. Nonetheless, the ruthlessness had its impact: Mohafel said the massacre had intimidated not only the Brotherhood but the secular resistance as well. Since Hama, there has not been in Syria even a hint of rebellion.

Dr. Jamal al-Atassi had been recommended to me by dissidents in Paris as Syria's most outspoken and courageous *résistant*, and he received me at twilight in his dingy office in downtown Damascus. A psychiatrist, about seventy at the time, Atassi was among the founders of the Syrian Baath Party and served briefly as minister of information after the 1963 coup, resigning, he said, to protest the party's turn to oppression. Later, he founded a Nasserite party, explaining to me that he admired Nasser's populism, though not his authoritarianism. In 1970, after Jadid's downfall, he became an advisor to Assad, but he resigned once more when Assad violated the promises he had made to democratize the system. Since 1973, Atassi said, he had been openly in opposition.

I asked Atassi the obvious question: Why did Assad tolerate his opposition, rather than putting him in prison with other dissidents? He answered that, during the 1980 crackdown, the government had taken away his work and blown up his car, and since then, had kept him under constant surveillance, but, probably because of his age and poor health, had otherwise left him alone. He had no ties with Iraq, the Muslim Brotherhood or any organized resistance group, he said. Though he was still head of the Nasserite party, he said, its ranks were so infiltrated that the *mukhabarat* knew more about its activities than he did. Though free to speak as he liked, Atassi said, he had no idea how long this freedom would last.

"Assadism," said Atassi, "is a false nationalism. It is the domination of a minority, and I'm not talking just of the Alawites, who control the society's nervous system. I include also the army and the *mukhabarat*. Assad has a huge army and hundreds of thousands of police, and in the university twenty or thirty percent of the students work for him. The national assembly, the multiparty front, the popular associations and the labor unions are phantoms, under the *mukhabarat*'s control. And despite its socialist slogans, the state is run by a class that has made a fortune without contributing—a *nouvelle bourgeoisie parasitaire*. The Syrian people know all this. In private, they criticize but they are afraid. Assad is tenacious, but without real contact with the people, and his regime is reaching the limit of popular tolerance. I don't think it can last another decade."

Mamdouh Adwan is Syria's best-known poet and playwright, a gray-haired man of fifty or so who chain-smokes and drinks a great deal. An Alawite, Adwan insisted his people were maligned by the assumption that they were uniformly supportive of Assad. Many were in Assad's prisons, he said, and maybe one day he would be, too. Adwan's most celebrated play, called *The Night of the Slaves*, deals acidly with Islam's transition from an underground movement to the state religion. It was banned by the government after one performance, he said, on the grounds that it was a thinly veiled satire of the Baath Party.

Adwan invited me to dinner one evening at the Writers Union, which he distinguished from other unions in that four or five rebels, of which he was one, sat on the board of directors, constituting a hard core of dissenters to official policies. In 1976, the dissenters protested the decision to go into Lebanon. In 1979, they urged the regime to settle its dispute with the Brotherhood without resort to force, although three years later they were too frightened to criticize the massacre at Hama. "Any government that makes the decision to blow up a city will not worry about a few intellectuals," Adwan explained. "It will blow them up too." Adwan said the dissenters aspired to keep alive at least a flicker of light in the darkness of Syrian politics.

Adwan told me that, since the start of the Lebanon war, the ranks of intellectual dissidents in Damascus had swelled to about fifty. The Syrians, he said, had been joined by Palestinians and Lebanese, even an Iraqi and a Saudi, fleeing from the violence in Beirut. Novelists, poets, film directors and painters, they were all secular in their religious orientation, and have made Damascus an unlikely center of Arab creativity. Being Western in outlook, Adwan said, they were considered enemies by the religious right. "We are, of course, influenced by Western culture and Western values," he said. "We could not be of the modern world if we were not." But Adwan argued that, in its earliest days, Islamic history was tenanted by dissident intellectuals, including companions of the Prophet. These were the models, he said, of the secular intellectuals within Islam today.

A few months before, Adwan and his band had issued a manifesto endorsing Salman Rushdie's "concern for freedom and the right of free men to live outside the walls of repression, ignorance and hunger." The manifesto exalted Islam's Golden Age, when thinkers criticized conventional theology "without having their blood spilled or being hanged," and attacked Khomeini for being "among those who consider Rushdie's book a greater danger to Islam than contempt for basic human needs, . . . who are not moved when the heritage of Islam is defamed every hour by hunger, ignorance, jails and the domination of imperialist corporations . . . and who forget the violation of human dignity trampled by the rulers of every Islamic community." The statement was one of the few in Rushdie's defense that came out of the Muslim world. Adwan said the signers understood the jeopardy in which they placed themselves, particularly since much of the criticism—hardly by accident—applied equally to the Assad regime. Predictably, the manifesto was not published in Damascus and was scarcely noticed elsewhere in the Arab press. But Arab intellectuals everywhere, Adwan said, knew of and applauded it.

The *mukhabarat*'s response to this protest was related to an interview with Assad published at about the same time in *Time* magazine. In the interview, Assad strongly backed Khomeini. "I consider Salman Rushdie a bad man . . . ," he told *Time*. "In his book, he exceeded his personal freedom and his right to write what he believes. . . . He should know that the mission of literature is not to insult people, let alone a prophet or a holy book. . . . Were Rushdie a Syrian citizen, I would certainly put him on trial before a court." Adwan said the *mukhabarat* wanted to know whether the manifesto was written after the publication of Assad's state-ment—which would have made it a criminal affront. Fortunately, he said, he proved during several hours of questioning that it had been written before, and so the *mukhabarat* dismissed the episode as a minor cultural spat.

Ideologically, Mohafel, Bayanouni, Attasi and Adwan had little in com-mon, and there seemed small likelihood that they could ever unite around a democratic regime. Syrians do not share a common concept of the state— as Americans share a constitution or the British the monarchy—and even less do they share a commitment to democratic procedures. And so these men waited for Assad to go away, hoping that in the struggle for succession the pieces would somehow fall favorably for their own beliefs.

Neither Baathis nor anti-Baathis pretended to know how the succession would go. One possible scenario held that the top men in the security services would each mobilize their allies for a showdown, but none would be strong enough to win without calling for help. The democratic forces reasoned that, were they able to mobilize enough followers, they would be rewarded for providing the margin of victory. That was the way, they said, that democracy was restored in Spain after Franco and in Greece after the junta. The prospect of its happening that way in Syria, where the security services appeared so strong, seemed more remote, but no one would know until the time arrived.

One evening, I returned to see Saber Falhout, the putative poet of the revolution, and told him I wanted to discuss the freedom that was part of official Baathi doctrine. Syria had embarked on independence, I said, with institutions, however fragile, that were free and democratic. Is there a prospect, I asked, that at some point it will return to this heritage?

Falhout feigned bewilderment before speaking, as if the answer were obvious. "We have been moving toward democracy since the 'corrective movement' in 1970," he said finally, "but democracy is not simply a book in a library that you open up, then implement. Every country has its own destiny to address and must select its plan for democracy according to the level of its own people. We believe that Syria tops the list of developing countries in implementing democracy. I will not say that support is unani-mous but the government has a huge majority. I don't see the point to your question. Syria already has democracy."

If I found his answer unsatisfactory, I found it also characteristic of party ideologues of any and all shades of opinion, and I wondered, as I have so often when confronting the species, whether he was being deliberately disingenuous or actually believed what he was telling me.

V THE JEWS OF DAMASCUS

A FEW YEARS AGO, on a Saturday afternoon in Damascus, I found myself with no appointments, and so I decided to seek out the city's central synagogue and attend the end-of-Sabbath service. To do so, I had to overcome some trepidation, brought on by repeated charges made by American Jewish groups of the persecution of Syria's Jews. (That very week in the *New York Times*, the Anti-Defamation League ran an ad saying that "Syria holds her Jews under the harshest conditions . . . literally hostages in their own land.") Though I carried directions written in Arabic, it turned out that finding the synagogue was not easy. Synagogues in the Arab world, unlike mosques and churches, tend to be hidden behind high walls, and even the best of taxi drivers may be unacquainted with the sites. Only after a half hour of driving through the labyrinth of the Jewish Quarter, at the eastern end of the Old City, and making a dozen inquiries at shops and cafes, did the driver locate the right alley, at the end of which was a gate, and behind it the synagogue courtyard.

Several men and many boys, all wearing suits and ties, stood chatting beneath a grape arbor, waiting for the service to begin, and when I made my identity known they welcomed me, though with some obvious discomfort. "Do you have permission from the police?" I was asked by a clean-shaven man in his forties, who I later learned was Avraham Hamra, Syria's chief rabbi. "Since when does one need permission to pray?" I asked with slightly feigned indignation. "Here you do," he told me, warmly but firmly.

He then assigned an amiable young fellow named Victor to join me on the journey through the narrow streets to the neighborhood police station. There Victor explained my presence to two plainclothes policemen sitting at an ancient desk. They listened respectfully, then made some phone calls, and within a few minutes, a voice at the other end of the line was politely questioning me, in good English. Finally, the voice said, "*Ahlen*—you are welcome. I hope you have a nice evening." The words were friendly, but on our way back Victor and I were joined by one of the cops.

When I reentered the synagogue, the rabbi beckoned me to sit among the elders. The synagogue was an eighteenth-century building with a wooden roof supported by three pairs of stone arches. It was newly painted and in excellent repair. The well-worn floor was white marble mosaic. The men among whom I sat whispered warm greetings, and when the service was over they crowded around me but, aware of being observed, they said little, except to invite me to a wedding the next night, provided the authorities concurred. When most of the men had drifted away, Victor led me to a busy thoroughfare at the edge of the quarter, and waited until a taxi cruised by to take me back to the hotel.

The Jewish population of Syria, which dates back to Biblical times, was about thirty thousand at the end of World War II. At the time of my visit, the Jewish community in Damascus had been reduced to three thousand. There were an additional five hundred Jews in Aleppo, and about one hundred seventy in the town of Qamishly on the Turkish border. Most of the Jews recognized that Middle East politics were bringing their community to an end, but at the time, Damascus still had eighteen working synagogues, full- or part-time, and several kosher butchers.

The next morning the ministry of information gave me permission to attend the wedding, and in the evening I returned to the synagogue. The event was elaborate, with the bride in an embroidered gown, the family in formal wear, the wedding party fashionably dressed, a boys' choir singing and a photographer snapping tirelessly away. Later, I attended the reception at a fashionable downtown hotel, where several hundred guests ate, drank and danced until the early morning. But before going downtown, Abu Khalil Jajati, Victor's father, invited me for tea at his home. (Men in the Arab world often take the name of their first-born son. Jajati, born Youssef, is usually called Abu Khalil, "Father of Khalil," who was Victor's oldest brother.) On the short walk from the synagogue, we stopped for a *shawarma*—a sandwich of grilled meat served on pita, a regional favorite—which he said was kosher. The non-Jews in the quarter were mostly Palestinian, refugees of the 1948 war, who took the homes vacated by Jews who had fled to Israel. The two peoples, he said, had since become cordial neighbors.

Since Roman times, historians tell us, the eastern sector of Damascus's Old City has been reserved for minorities. Paul of Tarsus, newly converted, entered the city through the eastern gate and met with the Christian community before going off to proselytize. Christians, a third of Damascus's population, still predominated in the quarter. Next to them, the Shiites had a small quarter, where visiting Iranians tended to gather, while other dissident Muslim sects clustered nearby. Abu Khalil's house, a few steps from the Street Called Straight, was in the traditional Damascene style, two stories high, built around an open courtyard, shaded by trees, with a fountain at the center. Divided into apartments, the house now accommodated several branches of Jajatis. Abu Khalil told me he was born in this house, which had been in the family for as many generations as anyone knew.

When I revisited Damascus the following summer, Abu Khalil urged me to attend a Sabbath service, which happened to fall on the eve of Tisha

B'Av, a fast day commemorating the destruction of both the First and Second Temples in Jerusalem. Sitting on the bench next to me, he pointed with a sardonic smile to the Torah passage that the rabbi was reading. It was a quote from Moses—"Turn you . . . and go into the land of the Canaanites . . . Go in and possess the land." Abu Khalil and I had never discussed Israel. Damascene Jews, I found, generally adopt the safe course of avoiding the subject. In translating, Abu Khalil seemed to be telling me that the Torah passages affirming the claim of the Jews to Palestine summed up the dilemma of being Jewish in an Arab land.

Historians agree that Jews who lived in the Arab world never experienced the anti-Semitism that, in the Christian West, produced the Inquisition, the pogroms and the Holocaust. Like Christians, Jews under Islamic law were assigned a rank inferior to Muslims and suffered various painful indignities. But anti-Jewish brutality was unusual and when it did occur could often be traced to the incitement of anti-Semitic Christians coming from the West.

In Syria, the most celebrated incident of anti-Semitic violence took place in 1840, when the French consul accused local Jews of the ritual murder of a Capuchin monk. Before the Ottoman governor called a halt, dozens of Jews had been tortured and killed. Unmentioned in any guidebook—I was told by a Damascene Christian—the monk's remains lie in a crypt in the Roman Catholic church in the Old City, where a wall inscription in Italian, dated February 5, 1840, states: "Here lie the bones of Father Tomaso of Sardinia, Capuchin Missionary, Killed by the Jews." Similar though less serious incidents occurred sporadically for the remainder of the century, corresponding with the rise of anti-Semitism in Europe and the decline of order in the Ottoman empire. Then, in the twentieth century, the bloody violence began between Jews and Arabs over the rights to Palestine. Its roots, however, lay not in religious prejudice but in ethnic politics.

Ethnic bloodshed reached a peak after World War II, when Arab mobs responded to the impending establishment of Israel. A second wave followed Syria's defeat in the Six-Day War, when fifty-seven Jews were killed in Qamishly, and the government passed laws forbidding Jews to travel, to transfer property or to attend the university. Many Jews were locked up without charges or trials. It was only after Assad became president, proclaiming reconciliation, that the imprisoned Jews were amnestied and conditions improved. In the October war of 1973, as the Israeli army drew close to Damascus, Assad actually sent troops to protect the Jewish quarter against angry crowds. In 1974, he received Jewish leaders at a formal meeting to hear their grievances, and two years later he repealed the remaining anti-Jewish codes. Jews have since been legally equal to other

Syrians, with one crucial exception. The new law gave to the *mukhabarat* the duty to monitor all Jewish rights, and the power to suspend those that it deemed threatening to Syria's security.

Abu Khalil, with the authorities' consent, invited me to his home to meet the Jewish community leaders a week after the Tisha B'Av service. Dr. Nissim Hasbani was the chief lay official. About fifty, he told me he was the first Jewish graduate of the Damascus University medical school. He arrived with Rabbi Hamra. The evening was balmy, so we climbed to the roof of the house and talked while looking out on the city's flickering lights.

"We have a branch of the *mukhabarat* which deals exclusively with us," Hasbani said. "We have ambiguous relations with them. They can be very hard on us. But they also help us solve problems when we go to them. They think of us as their clients, and they sometimes act as our advocates with the bureaucracy."

The power of the *mukhabarat*, Hasbani said, was applied most sternly to Jews seeking to travel abroad. In general, the government granted visas to Jews for foreign travel, but on condition that they left behind a deposit of money, to be forfeited if they did not return. Characteristically, the *mukhabarat* did not permit an entire family to travel together; someone had to stay home. (Hence, the charge by the Anti-Defamation League that Jews were "hostages in their own land.") When someone failed to return, the *mukhabarat* sometimes applied a penalty, depending on whether it regarded family members as accomplices. The restrictions were hard on Jews with relatives living in Europe or America; they could be dire for those with relatives in Israel.

"We are troubled, of course, that our people are singled out for penalties," Hasbani said, "but Syria, understandably, is very sensitive about contacts with Israel. In most matters, the *mukhabarat* is not much tougher with Jews than non-Jews. As you know from your experience with us, we can't talk with any foreigner without being questioned, but that rule applies to all Syrians. The difference is that because Syria is at war with Israel, we find it prudent to be a little bit more careful."

At the beginning of 1989, Amnesty International condemned the imprisonment of ten Syrian Jews in connection with foreign travel. Three years later, all but two—middle-aged brothers who had visited their parents in Israel—had been released. Shortly thereafter, they too were released.

Brushes with the *mukhabarat* aside, Damascene Jews led reasonably normal lives. They faced no restrictions on religious practice; they had, besides their synagogues, two religious schools, and were building a community center. They made their homes where they liked, and though the young had begun to move out of the Jewish Quarter, most remained within walking distance, to be near the synagogues and kosher butchers. The marriage rate was healthy, the birthrate was high and Jewish living standards were, on the whole, well above the Syrian average. Hasbani told me the community, at that time, had fifty doctors, ten dentists, thirty pharmacists, two lawyers and many successful businessmen, including Abu Khalil, who owned Damascus's most stylish men's clothing store. There were, however, also working-class Jews with modest incomes, he said, most of them in traditional crafts.

When we talked in 1989, Hasbani estimated that not more than a third of Syria's Jews would leave if restrictions were lifted, and even fewer if they were free to make regular visits to relatives abroad. At the time, the Jews assumed they would not be permitted to emigrate until peace was reached with Israel, which seemed a dim prospect. But in October 1991, Syria attended the Middle East peace conference in Madrid, and hopes soared.

In April 1992, Assad stunned the world Jewish community by having the United States declare that Syria's Jews would henceforth be allowed to emigrate. It was odd that Assad had chosen Washington to make the announcement, but the information was authentic. Still, the Syrian government, chronically short of hard currency, set a limit—the same imposed on all its citizens—on the funds that Jews could transfer abroad, effectively barring them from taking their capital with them. It also established a series of bureaucratic obstacles which slowed the process. Nonetheless, within a few months, nearly half the Jews in Syria had left, and the remainder were expected to follow in short order. Some two thousand years of Jewish history in Syria was quickly drawing to a close.

VI   ASSAD ON PEACE

FOR MORE THAN TWENTY YEARS, Hafez al-Assad would not make clear whether he was prepared to join in a Middle East peace settlement. When the question was put to him, he treated it with some irritation, arguing that there was hardly much point to his contemplating peace with Israel, since Israel rejected peace with the Arabs. "Do you think," he asked in one interview, "that peace can be achieved while Israel continues to behave like a big power in the region? Any such belief is lacking in logic and objectivity." Assad was convinced—really convinced, I believe, not just pretending—that Israel would rest only when its frontiers extended from the Nile to the Euphrates. He argued that this goal was inherent in Zionist doctrine and apparent in Israel's aggressive behavior.

Similarly, when Assad was asked if he planned to build a Greater Syria, he pretended to be baffled. There is no *Greater* Syria, he answered, only *Syria*, which was divided and subdivided by the Allies after World War I. Greater Syria, he said, is a term the Allies invented to conceal this partition from the world and convey the impression that whoever sought to reunite the country was somehow an aggressor. Assad maintained that Syrians, Lebanese, Jordanians and Palestinians were actually one people, with a single language, a single culture and interlocking family ties. He never acknowledged having a plan to reunite this population, deprecating the notion of *Syrian* unity in favor of the grander Baathi vision of *Arab* unity. But the obstacle to peace, Assad argued, is not Greater Syria at all, but Greater Israel.

I asked many of Assad's supporters in Damascus, over the course of many visits, whether his designs to unite the Arab world were not incompatible with hopes for a Middle East peace. The answers were uniformly negative. Baathis proclaim that the Arab world cannot be unified by force, which is why, they say, no effort has been made to abolish Syria's border with Lebanon. Their statements are Baath Party dogma, of course, but what begins as slogan often becomes doctrine. Uniformly, Syrians— whether party members or not—proclaim that peace in the region, at least as an immediate goal, holds a higher priority than Arab unification.

In talks in Damascus, Western diplomats maintain almost unanimously that Assad recognizes that Syria is too weak to take on Israel in another war. They acknowledge that he will drive a hard bargain, but when Israel is ready to withdraw from the territories occupied in 1967, and particularly the Golan Heights, he will seize the opportunity. Patrick Seale, Assad's biographer, argues that Syria, as a condition of peace, will insist not only on the return of territory but on the restoration of national honor, through Israeli recognition of Syrian preeminence among the Arab states in the region. But, in fact, Syria already enjoys such preeminence, and Israeli evacuation of the Golan, whatever the terms, could only enhance its stature.

What Assad dreads, all agree, is a settlement between Israel and the Palestinians that ignores him. He has yet to recover from what he regards as Sadat's betrayal, and in 1982 his worst fears were realized when the Israelis, free of worry about the Egyptians at their rear, invaded Lebanon, and he stood alone to face them. Though he renders lip service to a Palestine state in coexistence with Israel, he is not enthusiastic about this prospect. He resents the independence of Arafat's PLO, and sees a prospective West Bank–Gaza Strip state as another nibble out of Syria's real territory, and one more violation of the principle of Arab unity. He would no doubt contemplate such a state as part of a regional arrangement that includes Lebanon and the Golan. But without such an arrangement, he will persevere in his effort to frustrate any peacemaking, which he would see as an Israeli stratagem to isolate him further.

Assad's antagonism toward the PLO has left the Palestinians living in Damascus in a quandary. Nearly three hundred thousand live in the city, one in ten of the population. Most occupy the quarter called Yarmouk, a refugee camp in the late 1940s that was swallowed up and digested by urban sprawl. Yarmouk, day and night, is a bustling suburb of shops, movie houses, restaurants, offices and workshops—a testimony to Palestinian energy and achievement. It is also an index of Syria's generosity in opening up its economy to the Palestinians. Notwithstanding this generosity, Syria deals with the Palestinians much as it does with the Jews: it subjects them to the relentless scrutiny of the *mukhabarat* on the premise that their loyalty is not to the regime. Long gone are the days when Damascus was the center of PLO activity. Since Assad's break with Arafat in 1982, only PLO dissidents occupy the shabby and untidy offices where flags of Palestine hang on the walls. The dark-eyed young men who run these offices know they have a dual mission—to be true to the homeland while staying in the good graces of the Assad regime.

Abu Moussa—Said Moussa Mahmoud, age sixty-two, commander of the PLO forces in south Lebanon at the time of the Israeli invasion—heads one of the two Palestinian groups in Damascus that are still categorized as "rejectionist." Leader in 1982 of the unsuccessful uprising of PLO forces against Arafat, whom he regards as too soft, he condemns all peace initiatives as betrayal of the Palestinian people. "We recognize that if we keep the pure line of the revolution," said Abu Moussa, a tall, husky man in military uniform, "we will not get quick results. We also won't be popular, like Arafat. But what's the use of being popular if we don't get our national territory back?" Abu Moussa said that Syria gave his group "strong political support," but his vagueness suggested to me that he was far from satisfied with the actual extent of that support.

Another "rejectionist" group in Damascus is the Popular Front for the Liberation of Palestine, General Command, led by Ahmad Jibril. This is the group that Western governments initially held responsible for bombing Pan American's flight 103 over Scotland in 1988. Later, the West shifted the blame to the Libyan government, but without exonerating Jibril. Assad's hospitality to the General Command, and several similar organizations, keeps Syria on the State Department's list of countries supporting terrorism. I met with Jibril's spokesman, known as Abu Firas, in a shabby basement office in a run-down neighborhood. A small, round, nervous man with sixties-length hair, Abu Firas chainsmoked as we spoke.

When I asked Abu Firas what his organization would do if the PLO reaches a peace settlement with Israel, his expression turned melancholy.

"We will go on with our armed struggle," he answered. I then asked whether Syria supported this hard line. He deliberated before replying: "We have no pledge from Syria on holding out. The Syrians have never made an explicit statement, but Assad has officially accepted UN Resolution 242 and the compromise settlement plan of the Arab Summit at Fez in 1982, and we have rejected them both. We simply have different policies on this point." I asked Abu Firas whether he thought that, ultimately, Assad would abandon the rejectionists, leaving Jibril alone. He stopped again, took a long drag on his cigarette and answered mournfully, "Yes, I think he will."

A FEW DAYS BEFORE LEAVING SYRIA, I drove down the old Damascus-Jerusalem road as far as the Golan Heights, the object of the diplomatic struggle between Israel and Syria that began at Madrid, and still a likely flash point for any future Syrian-Israeli war. The drive, across utterly flat terrain, without natural barriers, lasted barely an hour, which revealed much to me about why the Syrians are terrified of an Israeli army based on the Golan. On the right side of the road, in the middle distance, was Mount Hermon, site of ferocious battles in 1967 and 1973, where Israel was said to have installed enough electronic gear to hear Assad tossing in bed. The villagers who walked along the road near the border were mostly Druze refugees; they have waited for a quarter century to return to their homes, either in Israeli-occupied territory or in the no-man's-land adjacent to it.

The principal city of the Golan is Quneitra, which now is a silent sea of rubble, leveled to the ground by Israeli forces before they withdrew under the terms of the disengagement agreement that followed the Yom Kippur War. A monument in what was once a bustling marketplace commemorates Assad's hoisting of the Syrian flag on June 26, 1974. For a bird's-eye view across the mined fields around Quneitra, I climbed to the roof of a gutted building, identified by a sign which read: "Golan Hospital, Destroyed by the Zionists." From it, I could see a burned-out mosque with no roof, a church with a decapitated steeple, and a wrecked movie theater named Al-Andalus (Andalusia), a reminder of the days of grandeur when the Arabs ruled Spain. I could also see an Israeli jeep patrolling along a road that paralleled the line which separated the armies. I drove as far as the last Syrian outpost, where I was stopped by a thick barrier of barbed wire with tiny purple wildflowers growing among the strands.

Further down the road I saw a small United Nations installation and, beyond it, a guard post flying a blue-and-white flag with a Star of David. Above it flapped a banner that read "Welcome to Israel." The banner was meant ironically, no doubt. Apart from a few UN vehicles, the border had been closed since 1948. But could some contingent of Israeli soldiers have seen the future? I allowed myself to think the banner might be an invitation, not just to me but to the Syrians on the cease-fire line. It is only an hour's drive from Quneitra to Haifa, two to Jerusalem or Tel Aviv. One day, I thought, the border will surely be open. After so long appearing hopeless, can peace really be near?

CHAPTER FIVE

LEBANON

I THE CHRISTIAN ENCLAVE

At FIRST GLANCE, Lebanon looked peaceful enough—hardly a country defined by death. It was dawn, and the *Empress*, a shabby old ferry that I had boarded the night before in Cyprus, was steaming into the port of Juniye, a few miles to the north of Beirut. The ferry was the only available transportation into Lebanon. The airport, though open, lay in West Beirut, under the control of the Iranian-backed militia known as Hezbollah, who were at that moment holding nine American hostages; it would have been hubris to land there. The seven-hour boat trip, though uncomfortable, was at least safe.

As the *Empress* approached the dock, I watched with pleasure as sailboats, and even a seaplane, bobbed at anchor in the harbor. My eye fell on a series of seaside hotels, their patios ready to serve a clientele at tables shaded by cheerfully colored umbrellas. I saw modern apartment buildings and handsome stone structures with arched windows and red tile roofs, which I took for old Turkish villas. But mostly, my eye confronted Mount Lebanon, known everywhere here as "the Mountain." The country's dominating physical feature, heavily wooded, it descended abruptly from high above to within what seemed like a few steps of the water's edge. Its flanks were neatly terraced, and dotted with structures of every sort. At its summit I spied the domed silhouette of a large church, with a cross and bell tower reaching dramatically toward the sky. The silhouette seemed to validate the historical role of the Mountain, ancestral home of Lebanon's powerful Christian community, which I had come to examine. But before I disembarked from the *Empress* I was abruptly introduced to the venomous politics which in the years just past had left one hundred and twenty-five thousand Lebanese dead. The purser informed me apologetically that, unlike my fellow passengers, I would be unable to retrieve the passport I had left with him the night before until I had been questioned by representatives of the Lebanese Forces.

I had not expected to be greeted by the Lebanese Forces, a self-appointed

Christian militia independent of the Lebanese government, just as Hezbollah was a militia of Lebanon's Shiite Muslims. Some months before, when I had begun thinking about visiting Lebanon, I called on the country's ambassador in Washington, Dr. Abdallah Bouhabib, who said that while West Beirut, and particularly the sector to the south held by Hezbollah, was very dangerous for foreign journalists, East Beirut, where the Christians ruled, was safe. He seemed relieved that I planned to write chiefly about the Christians—he being one of them—but he insisted I would be well advised, nonetheless, to allow his government to handle my security. After some reflection I agreed to the condition, and Bouhabib, an energetic man in his fifties with a Ph.D. from Vanderbilt, informed me that I would be met at the dock by a Lebanese government delegate. The delegate was indeed waiting when the *Empress* docked, but I could not get to him until the Lebanese Forces finished with me.

The interrogation, conducted by two young men in T-shirts, was gracious enough. They asked what I, as a journalist, planned to do in Lebanon, and whether I intended to see the Lebanese Forces' spokesmen in Beirut. When I assured them I was willing to see anyone, they said they would be happy to organize my visit. I did not know what to make of it when they invited me to appear at their headquarters the next morning at nine.

Only after they returned my passport and sent me ashore was I approached by a slim, blue-eyed, elegantly dressed man in his forties who introduced himself as Samir Fares, aide to Amin Gemayel, the president of Lebanon. Apologizing for the inconvenience, he led me to his car. "Naturally, the President doesn't consider the Lebanese Forces as legal," he told me as he settled in behind the wheel. I knew that, though they were both Christian, the Lebanese Forces took a much harder line in the civil war than Gemayel. "We stay on good speaking terms with them, but we don't deal with them directly. You noticed I hesitated to have any conversation with them. We try to keep their forces off the streets, to keep a civilized face to the outside world." To leave the port, Fares and I had to pass a checkpoint manned by uniformed youths of the Lebanese Forces, carrying automatic weapons. We were waved through with an indifferent nod. Then, with the Mountain on our left, we turned south toward Beirut, along a highway choked with traffic that ran parallel to the beach.

Though I had visited Beirut several times since the civil war began in 1975, I never ceased to be surprised at the spirit that imparts an air of normality to the city. Battered as it was, Beirut had a life-goes-on look about it: men and women munching pastries and drinking coffee at an outdoor restaurant, a sporting-goods store promoting surfboards, movies with the latest American films, farmers selling fresh produce from truck beds, billboards featuring a seductive woman advertising brassieres, a flower shop soliciting customers with the sign "Liven up your balconies with our annuals." Some buildings carried on their facade larger-than-life posters of President Gemayel in a white suit and tie; others offered up his brother Bashir, who had been elected president and assassinated before taking office in 1983. Unlike the more conventional Amin, Bashir—shirt unbuttoned at the throat, sleeves rolled up to his biceps—had been known as the rough-and-ready type. After fifteen or twenty minutes of driving, Fares turned off the highway onto the mountain, and we wound upward until we reached his splendid home in Rabbieh, an upper-class suburb. There we sat on his balcony and ate a Lebanese breakfast of olives and cheese, listening to Beethoven and gazing out over the Mediterranean.

As we ate, Fares told me he had arranged with a rental agency to provide me with a car and an experienced driver at a fair price. As for bodyguards, he said, he had consulted with the government's security office and concluded that they were unnecessary. He made clear he was willing to defer to my wishes if I felt otherwise, but he said kidnappings were unheard of in Lebanon's Christian sector and bodyguards were likely only to attract attention. I replied that, being unfamiliar with Lebanon's security conditions, I was quite willing to be guided by the experts. That seemed to settle the matter. When we had finished our last cup of coffee, Fares introduced me to Roni, my driver, and instructed him to take me to Broumana, a town located a few miles higher up on the mountain, where I had reserved a room. My hotel had a classical, European look. After unpacking, I decided to phone the U.S. embassy, to announce my presence in town.

Checking in with the embassy is by no means customary for correspondents visiting foreign capitals, but Beirut was different. Because of the ongoing hostage crisis, Lebanon was then off limits to holders of U.S. passports. The State Department had granted me a waiver, but it was not enthusiastic about my itinerary. The last thing the embassy wanted was another American hostage—a concern I fully shared.

I was a bit surprised that the voice at the other end of the line told me the ambassador would be pleased to see me that very afternoon. Under the circumstances, it seemed only reasonable to comply. I was familiar with the old embassy in West Beirut, which had been leveled by a bomb in 1983 at a cost of sixty-three lives. The new embassy was in the foothills of the Mountain in East Beirut and, when I reached the gate, the security astounded me: a tank surrounded by armed guards with their fingers on the triggers of their automatics, huge concrete blocks and traffic bumps to slow approaching vehicles, metal detectors and heavy wire-mesh doors through which visitors had to pass, an electrically operated steel barrier on the road inside the gate as a second line of defense and, surveying the entire scene, sharpshooters seated in two tall towers. I had to acknowledge that these safeguards, given the recent history of the embassy, were not excessive. Since the start of the civil war, a U.S. ambassador had been murdered, and a year after the embassy in West Beirut was destroyed, another car bomb exploded at the presumably safer site in East Beirut, killing eight. This was the third site, and inside the embassy compound the security system generated an atmosphere of unremitting tension.

Nonetheless, the ambassador, seated in an easy chair sipping a soft drink, appeared relaxed when I entered his office. John Kelly, who in his twenty years in the Foreign Service had served in a variety of military and intelligence posts, fit at a glance no diplomatic stereotype; he looked more like an Irish bartender. Forty-eight years old, he had a prominent belly and a shock of unkempt hair that kept falling over his forehead, and he seemed a bit uncomfortable wearing a business suit. During several visits over the next few weeks, I would come to appreciate Kelly's sure grasp of the intricacies of American and Lebanese politics. But that day Kelly's concern was my safety, and when I told him that Fares had decided I did not need bodyguards, he scowled.

Kelly's memory was still fresh of an incident two weeks before on the streets of East Beirut, when he was challenged by several carloads of gunmen during the journey from his residence to his office. As ambassador, Kelly habitually traveled through the city in a convoy led by a vehicle with a machine gun on the roof. He himself rode in an armored limousine, followed by two more carloads of bodyguards waving automatic weapons out the windows. The routine is admittedly provocative, particularly on streets crowded with militiamen, private bodyguards and divers other young studs who, as a matter of course, carry lethal weapons. That morning, Kelly's convoy apparently antagonized some headstrong youths of unidentified allegiance, who engaged his car in a dangerous game of high-speed tag for ten minutes or so on Beirut's boulevards, while Kelly, on the orders of his security chief, lay cramped on the floor. Accounts differ as to whether shots were fired at all, but the two sides apparently did not shoot at each other, and the episode was not regarded as either an assassination or kidnapping attempt. Nonetheless, it upset Kelly enough to persuade him that I should not be cruising around Beirut unattended. In passing, he said that the murder a few months before of three French embassy guards might well have been averted had they not been so arrogant as to go shopping alone. Kelly said he would phone at once to urge Fares to assign bodyguards to me. Under the circumstances, I did not object.

The next morning, five athletic-looking men appeared in Broumana, at about the same time as Roni arrived in the rental car. When I saw them waiting in the hotel lobby, it seemed to me that Fares had overdone it, but the team's chief, who introduced himself as Elie, assured me that the number was routine. Before setting out for the day's appointments, he explained that I would ride in the back seat of Roni's car while he rode shotgun in the front, and that the others would follow directly behind in the security car. I felt overwhelmed by the arrangement, especially after I spied the mean-looking automatic that Elie cuddled between his knees, but I confess that it took very little time before I got used to the arrangement. On the first trip down the Mountain, I had some trouble with Roni, whose restraint at the wheel vanished in the presence of his macho companions— he was steering the car around curves as if it were an Olympic bobsled. When I stated crisply that I had no need of bodyguards if we were to careen off a mountain road, Elie agreed, and Roni resumed the more reasonable driving style that he had exhibited the day before.

As Ambassador Bouhabib had promised, I never felt in jeopardy in the Christian enclave. As Lebanon's Christians so often were quick to point out, hostage-taking was a phenomenon of West, not East, Beirut. A few weeks after my arrival, I did an interview with Simon Kassis, the chief of Lebanon's counterpart to the CIA, who told me his agency followed the Western hostages wherever they went, charting their movements, snapping their pictures. All were heavily guarded by Hezbollah militiamen loyal to Iran, he said, and were kept in areas under Syrian control, either the south suburbs of Beirut or to the east in the Beqa'a Valley. Any attempt to rescue them, he told me, would bring thousands of armed defenders to the site within minutes, and he had advised the interested governments to contemplate no military operations, out of a likelihood that the hostages themselves and hundreds of others would be killed in the fighting. Besides, he said a bit meekly, even if the hostages were rescued, Hezbollah would simply go out and seize new ones the next day.

Yet, safe as East Beirut may have been, it was always tense, and I was grateful for the company of Elie and his team. Elie knew every street in the city, as well as every road on the Mountain, which was reassuring in a country where few walls were unmarked by the scars of war, where prudent storekeepers kept their wares hidden behind sandbag ramparts, where security men examined the trunks of cars for bombs at all public and many private buildings. In spite of these precautions, attacks continued. One morning we drove by the smoking hulks of cars scattered across the road by a bomb (twenty injured, none dead, the newspaper said the next morning) that had exploded fifteen minutes earlier. Somehow, the traffic still flowed smoothly. Though traffic lights had long before ceased to function, and one-way signs were routinely ignored, Beirutis had improvised workable rules of the road, and drivers regularly yielded at intersections—perhaps because each knew that the other driver might well be carrying a loaded firearm. If I was in a hurry to make an appointment, Elie rolled down his window and, with an air of authority, signaled that we were seizing the right of way.

I saw him defied only once, by a pretty young woman who smiled slyly as she maneuvered her car in front of us, causing Elie to break out in laughter. The only other time I saw him defeated was when a guard at the Lebanese Forces office told him he would have to leave behind the .45 he carried in his belt—though he could keep his walkie-talkie—if he wanted to accompany me inside. Muttering, he handed the gun to one of his deputies, reasoning, I suppose, that he preferred defending me with his bare hands to leaving me unattended, at the mercy of his foes.

11   MEETING THE MARONITES

FATHER ETIENNE SACRE, a Maronite priest in his late sixties, had been recommended to me as a good place to begin to understand Christian Lebanon. Educated at a Jesuit college in Strasbourg in Alsace, holder of a Ph.D. from the Sorbonne in Paris, he was a member of the Order of Maronite Monks, which he said was the largest monastic order in the East. Father Etienne spoke French rather than Arabic, and preferred the French spelling of his name, which translates as "rite," to the conventional Arabic spelling, Saqr, which means "falcon." A short, rotund man, he wore a dark caftan and smoked cigarettes as he answered my questions, with great serenity at first but with increasing animation as we moved more deeply into politics.

Father Etienne had served for six years as rector of the University of the Holy Spirit, which was where we met, in the seaside town of Kaslik, north of Beirut. The university was founded in 1962 to train novices for the priesthood. It nonetheless offered a full curriculum, he said, in fulfillment of its role as a guardian against the anti-Lebanese ideologies spreading through the country, and as a preserver of Maronite culture.

The Maronites are the principal Christian sect in Lebanon, and were a crucial element in the conflict that had been raging since 1975. By best estimates, of Lebanon's total population of three million, the Maronites—at the start of the war—numbered about 900,000. By adding some 250,000 Greek Orthodox, 200,000 Greek Catholics and 125,000 Armenian Orthodox, it was possible to claim that nearly half of the population was Christian. Since then, about a third of these Christians are believed to have left the country, perhaps permanently. But numbers were never more than a secondary concern in Christian claims upon Lebanon, and on Maronite claims to preeminence among the Christians.

The Maronites have been an identifiable community in Lebanon since breaking away from Byzantium's authority in the seventh century. Though they adopted the Arabic language, they have fiercely resisted, from their bastion on the Mountain, both the Islamic religion that the Arab conquerors brought with them thirteen hundred years ago and affiliation with what is sometimes known as the Arab nation. Over the centuries, the vanguard of their resistance has been the Maronite priesthood, dozens of whose monasteries still hug the Lebanese slopes. Maronites note with pride that, in contrast to the other Christian sects, they have been a part of Lebanon throughout their entire history. They are, Father Etienne said, the incarnation of "Lebanonism."

In the eleventh century, the Maronites—then as now a Christian island in a Muslim sea—sided with the Crusaders in their assault upon Islam and, by reliable accounts, provided vital assistance in the capture of Jerusalem. For this, Father Etienne noted, "the Arabs have never forgiven us." With the Crusaders as intermediaries, the Maronites established ties with the Papacy and, by the thirteenth century, they had submitted themselves—while retaining much of their doctrinal peculiarities—to the authority of the Church of Rome. In the sixteenth century, the Ottoman Turks overran Lebanon, but they left the Maronites largely to themselves, preserved from Islamic ways. Shortly afterward the caliph signed a "capitulation," which granted to France the right to protect the Christians within his realm, confirming France as the dominant influence on Maronite culture. Beginning with Louis XIV, the French, as part of their *mission civilisatrice*, offered reduced boat fares and free tuition to generations of Maronite students in France. Such policies Westernized the Maronites, at a time when their Muslim neighbors, under Ottoman rule, were becoming increasingly insular.

In the seventeenth century, the Maronites began moving down from the Mountain, west into the coastal areas that were home to Sunni and Shiite Muslims, and south into the hilly region occupied by the Druzes, a highly individualistic community of Islamic schismatics. In 1820, the Maronite-Druze collision sparked a series of ferocious wars, now deeply embedded in Lebanon's collective memory, which culminated in 1860 in the massacre by the Druzes of twelve thousand Christians. In response, France landed troops and imposed on the Ottomans a system of government for Lebanon based on an autonomous communal life for Christians, Muslims and Druzes, with a power-sharing formula which left the Maronites dominant. When their own regime replaced the Ottomans after World War I, the French perpetuated the principles of this system—known now as "confessionalism." In 1920, they enlarged the territory of their Lebanese Mandate, creating a "Greater Lebanon" by attaching to the

Mountain the Syrian port cities of Beirut, Sidon and Tripoli, all heavily Muslim, as well as Syria's almost totally Muslim Beqa'a Valley.

Nationalism among the Arabs, meanwhile, had emerged as a major political phenomenon in the Middle East, and the Arabs of Lebanon— that is, the Sunnis and Shiites—were among its leaders. Inside Greater Lebanon, the Arabs turned aggressively eastward, chiefly toward Damascus, in search of communal relations. Meanwhile the Christians, heavily dependent on France, faced resolutely west.

In 1926, France declared Lebanon an independent republic, and bestowed on it a confessional government, which the Maronites were to dominate through permanent tenure of the key posts. To the Muslims, the system was obviously unsatisfactory and in 1943, after acrimonious discussions, an unwritten understanding was reached, known to all Lebanese as the National Pact, in which the Christians renounced dependence upon the West in return for Muslim renunciation of union with Syria or any other Arab state. The National Pact preserved confessionalism as the basic constitutional principle and reaffirmed the Maronite claim to the presidency, the command of the army and other top positions. Parliamentary seats were allotted in a ratio of six to five in favor of the Christians, as were the bulk of civil and military posts. But the Maronites conceded the office of prime minister to the Sunnis and the speakership of the parliament to the Shiites.

No Lebanese ever claimed that the National Pact established a democracy, at least in the majoritarian sense. On the contrary, it was designed to assure Lebanon's Christians that they would not be engulfed by Lebanese Islam. In fact, early in the republic's history, it became apparent that the Christians had become the minority, and to avoid facing up to this troublesome development, Lebanon simply stopped taking censuses. In 1945, the Muslims were thrown a bone, when the country asserted its Arab identity by joining the Arab League—the only member led by Christians. After that, Lebanon attempted to straddle the two worlds, a posture that became steadily more precarious.

"We don't want to be the enemy of the Arabs," Father Etienne said to me. He was talking heatedly by now. "But we're afraid that Lebanese Muslims who talk about Arabizing the country really want to Islamize it. We want to be open to dialogue with the Arab world without the Arabs imposing any condition that shuts out other influences. We are surrounded by Arab countries but, as Christians, we Lebanese do not want to wear an Arab label.

"If Lebanon had a Muslim president, he would have to govern according to the Koran, and we could not accept that. In Jordan and Egypt, King Hussein and President Mubarak are more or less liberal, but the Christians in those countries are not the equals of the Muslims. We cannot live like the Copts in Egypt, without rights. We know the Arabs. We are convinced they want to make us second-class citizens (*dhimmis*) within the Islamic community (*umma*). We are willing to live in a secular state, but we think that if Lebanon had unrestricted majority rule, the state might start out as secular but would soon become Islamic. That is the nature of Islam. So we cannot stray too far from the guarantees of the National Pact. Lebanon is our country. The Christians are the heart of it, and we have been here for thirteen hundred years. I think we can live together with the Muslims, but we cannot agree to changes that will require us to give up our way of life and our traditions."

LEBANON IS A COUNTRY of roughly four thousand square miles, slightly smaller than Connecticut, of which the Christian enclave—the Mountain and the shoreline from East Beirut to Byblos—occupies about a fifth. Many Christians live outside the enclave, in villages scattered throughout the country. But in fighting since 1975, hundreds of thousands of Christians fled to the enclave from basically Muslim regions. Conversely, many Muslims live under Christian control. East Beirut, for instance, contains a substantial body of Sunnis, and Byblos for centuries has had a community of Shiites. Still, the Christian enclave, and particularly the Mountain, is socially and politically different from the rest of Lebanon. The visual evidence alone confirms that it is part of the West, not of the Arab world.

I caught my first glimpse of the Christian civilization on the Mountain in the early 1980s, traveling by road from Damascus to Beirut. The driver, to avoid unfriendly checkpoints on the Damascus-Beirut highway, turned north in the Beqa'a Valley and then west into the hills, winding upward along the ridges from one Christian village to the next until his descent to the narrow coastal plain just above the capital. I was astonished then at the handsome Italian look of the villages, in contrast to the rather nondescript Arab villages I had seen during visits in the south of the country. The resemblance to Europe, I later learned, was a product not of coincidence but of the Maronites' fascinating history.

Lebanon's Christian builders have been inspired by European models since the Crusades, and art historians identify a particular affinity between traditional Mountain design and Venetian architecture of the Middle Ages. The influences, in fact, moved both ways. The Crusaders probably brought the concept of the pointed arch back home with them from the Arab world, whence it was integrated into European gothic. But the idea appears to have returned via Venice to Lebanon, where the motif of the pointed triple arch became characteristic of local design. Unlike the Europeans, however, the Maronites put their best design into their homes rather than their churches, which play only a modest role on the Mountain. This may be because Lebanese villages, adapting to the sharp perpendicular drop of the Mountain, tend to be linear, leaving no space for a church-dominated central square. Maronite convents, usually located in remote recesses or on distant heights, are more common as expressions of religious faith. In the villages, churches generally are hidden among the houses and, except for the bell towers, are architecturally indistinguishable from them.

On the Mountain, the traditional house is lovingly crafted of a clear, white stone, with a balcony placed to look out upon an exquisite panorama, either of valleys and peaks or the Mediterranean Sea. Social historians say this design reflects the Maronites' cultural independence of the Arabs, a flatland people who made their houses of mud, as well as of the Turks, who usually built of wood. They say the Maronites' traditional house—almost invariably small, detached and with little external ornamentation—reflects a rough egalitarianism, and a way of life based on the nuclear family, also uncharacteristic of Muslims. The ensemble conveys to the villages of Mount Lebanon a solid, prosperous, bourgeois quality, which is probably an accurate reflection of the Maronite community until recent times.

Unfortunately, commerce has transformed these handsome villages in the modern era, as it has the aesthetics of much of the Western world. During my visit to the Mountain, automobiles rode bumper to bumper, day and night, on narrow, winding roads. Elegant shopping centers, with chic boutiques and movie houses, fast food and video shops, had largely replaced the family store. Broumana had become famous for its brightly lit restaurants and open-air cafes, where loudspeakers playing rock music competed against the roar of hot-rodders each night in keeping me awake.

Relative to the lowlands, the Mountain was free of the damage of war, but not the neglect. Much was in disrepair. The real change, however, derived from the migrants who had fled from Beirut's tension to the Mountain's tranquillity. Residential building had boomed, and the entire region—perhaps for the first time in history—conveyed a sense of crowdedness. At the same time, the decline of government opened the door to the depradations of laissez-faire capitalism. Cardboard signs and billboards of every size intruded upon rural roads. Cement and steel replaced hewn stone in the construction of new buildings. Filling stations supplanted traditional houses as village landmarks. The banality of modern design increasingly obscured the dignity and charm which earlier generations of Maronite builders imparted to the eye, and thus to the quality of daily life.

Beit Shebab, where I spent several afternoons, was among the few villages that had preserved its prewar flavor. Fastened to an especially steep flank of the Mountain, slightly off the beaten track, Beit Shebab had ten thousand residents, nearly all of whom traced their roots to seventeen families who settled there five hundred years before. Built on a site once inhabited by Romans, if not by Phoenicians before them, Beit Shebab saw Crusaders pass, then Mamluks and Ottomans and Egyptians and French. It had been twice destroyed and abandoned, but both times its original families returned to rebuild. Each of them now had its own church, a small architectural treasure of clear stone embedded in the wooded landscape, and each had its own cemetery, except for eight families who decided early in the century to share a crypt. Many of Beit Shebab's residents had, like other Lebanese, emigrated in the twentieth century to Africa, Europe and the Americas to make their fortune. Most sent money to the families they had left behind, and most over time returned to vacation, to marry, to die. Their contributions, I was told, made Beit Shebab, notwithstanding the war, richer than it had ever been.

My host in Beit Shebab was Emile Bejjani, a descendant of one of the original seventeen and a successful lawyer, who each morning descended fifteen miles down the Mountain to his office in East Beirut. The decor of his house, with its antique furniture and heavy drapes, reminded me of bourgeois villas in the French countryside. It was a few steps from an outdoor market, an area of a hundred square yards or so covered by a nineteenth century roof that was supported by wooden pillars and pointed arches. Herds of goats often passed on the narrow, cobblestone street in front of Bejjani's house.

Bejjani one afternoon took me to visit Beit Shebab's major "factories," vestiges of an industrial system that was once the Mountain's economic backbone. I watched a potter fashion clay jars on a wheel he turned with his foot and a weaver produce intricate designs in cotton cloth with a nineteenth-century machine imported from France. I also took a lesson from eighty-year-old Shibli Nafa'a on how to make and repair church bells, a craft he said his ancestors had learned on a visit to Orthodox priests in Russia four hundred years ago. Though each of these artisans would like to pass on his craft, Bejjani noted, their outmoded techniques were obviously doomed.

In addition to its industry, Beit Shebab was known for a rehabilitation center for handicapped victims of the war. Shortly after the fighting began, a group of Maronite monks recognized the need and founded the center in their seventeenth-century convent. Father Antoine Achkar, another member of Beit Shebab's seventeen families, became the director. A robust and handsome man, he led me on a tour of the modern hospital, a few steps from the convent, that had recently been built. In the space between the buildings, patients were sitting in wheelchairs, enjoying the sun. In 1982, Father Antoine said, a shell, presumably fired by Syrians from over a nearby ridge, landed in that space, and it was only a miracle that none of the patients was struck.

Another afternoon, Bejjani invited the principal of a local high school to join us for tea. English is growing in importance, the principal said, while French declines—"The seduction of the dollar," Bejjani quipped—but the village retains the French orientation it has had for centuries. Most of the young people, on their way to the university, still attended French-language lycées rather than the Arabic-language public schools. The traffic signs were in French. Like the French, Mountain people loved to eat and drink, and fine restaurants were scattered throughout the region. Maronites still felt at home in France, Bejjani said, and many of his friends now lived there. In France, he noted, many took up with right-wing political parties that promote anti-Islamic doctrines. Out of nostalgia, he said, a large number are even royalists.

"We Maronites are Mediterraneans, not Arabs," the principal said. "Our civilization is Greco-Roman. Our back is toward the desert, our face is toward the sea." Bejjani remarked that the reason the Syrians made so much trouble in Lebanon was that they were jealous of the prosperity and the liberty of the Christians. "We're sorry the French ever left us," the principal said. "We miss them. For us, France still represents an ideal."

One Sunday when I had no appointments, Roni and Elie took me on a tour of the Mountain. They drove me to the marvelous ruins of a first-century Roman religious site at Fakra, where families were picnicking in the shadow of ancient stone pillars and altars. They showed me a natural bridge over a raging stream, which my 1912 Baedeker said was longer than the famous Natural Bridge in Virginia; beneath it, a dozen or so teenage boys and girls in jeans were singing lustily as they cooked up lunch on a smoky grill. We drove past a ski resort, which was waiting for the first snowfall; past country restaurants, surrounded by the parked cars of mid-day diners; even past a pinball parlor, filled with long-haired young men.

Later, we called at the Convent of the Annunciation, where in the nineteenth century fifty nuns lived cloistered from the outside world. Though it is at the end of a deep valley, it commands a view all the way to the Mediterranean. In 1950, the convent was transformed into a fortress by the Lebanese army, and in 1975, it was seized by a Christian militia. In the mid-1980s, the nuns regained possession and transformed it into a home for children orphaned by the war. Its long halls with ceilings of crisscrossed stone arches had been transformed into brightly lit playrooms and dining rooms, and the austere nuns' quarters of bygone days had become the cheerful bedrooms of children.

That was the day that I attended mass in Bikfaya with President Gemayel. A handsome village of about twenty thousand, Bikfaya is the seat of the Gemayel clan. At its southern gate stands a larger-than-life statue of Pierre Gemayel—known to most Lebanese as Sheikh Pierre—placed there by his son, Amin. Pierre Gemayel was a pharmacist who in 1936 attended the Olympic Games in Berlin; inspired by fascism, he returned home to found an ultranationalist political party which he named the Phalange. Out of it grew the first Christian militia.

Although Sheikh Pierre never attained his ambition of becoming Lebanon's president, he had two sons elected to the office. Bashir was now dead. Amin, the survivor, spent most of the time in the village, where he felt more secure than at Baabda, the presidential palace in Beirut. His Bikfaya office, the *sérail* of a regional governor in Ottoman times, had been renovated and combined with a family house that was built a few steps away. Linking them was an old stable, adapted for use as a dormitory for the presidential guards. Though the residence had a second-story chapel, it was too small to accommodate a Sunday mass. The rite I attended was held on the ground floor, in a brightly lit corridor transformed by adding an altar and chairs into temporary duty as a church.

The controversial president, then in the last year of his term, sat in the front row, wearing a conservative blue suit. Next to him sat his attractive wife, Joyce, dressed in bright yellow. The service was conducted in Arabic by an elderly priest in raiments of white; at his side stood a choir of six young women in knee-length dresses and high heels. The audience seemed to consist chiefly of local people, neighbors of the Gemayels, except for a handful of monks and nuns, and though not all of the fifty chairs were occupied when the mass began, a crowd of more than one hundred, seated and standing, had soon assembled.

President and Mrs. Gemayel took communion at the end of the service, followed by about twenty others, then thanked each member of the choir with a handshake. Adjourning to a nearby room, he and his wife formed a receiving line, while servants passed coffee and cookies from silver trays. The atmosphere was informal; if there were bodyguards about, they were inconspicuous. The president seemed to recognize nearly everyone who approached him, and he addressed most of them in French. He grasped hands warmly and kissed some women on both cheeks, taking sips of coffee in between. My impression as I stood watching was of a melancholy man, with sad eyes. After an hour, the receiving line broke up, and the president circulated among his guests, sitting with them singly or in groups of two or three. I was told he rarely missed a Sunday in Bikfaya. Since Sheikh Pierre died in 1983, Amin has been head of the clan, which to the local people may have been more important than his being president.

III   DOWN FROM THE MOUNTAIN

THE NATIONAL PACT OF 1943, the formula of political accommodation between Lebanon's Christians and Muslims, worked for more than thirty years. For the Arabs of the Middle East, these were trying times. Emerging from centuries of colonialism, the new nations were thrashing about in search of useful institutions. The kings of Egypt, Iraq and Libya were overthrown. Syria went from one bloody coup to the next. Meanwhile Lebanon was a model of stability. Not only did its confessional system provide social order but its capitalist economy brought a substantial measure of prosperity. Whatever its peculiarities, Lebanese democracy was the freest in the Arab world, and Beirut the freest city, a great metropolis where international businessmen, journalists and scholars amiably rubbed shoulders with fun-seeking Arabs escaping from the rigid conformism of Islamic culture.

Only one major crisis marred the period. In 1958, responding to Nasser's strident nationalism and the bloody coup in Iraq, Lebanon's Muslim masses under the leadership of local Sunni radicals tried to force the government to join with Cairo and Damascus in the newly founded United Arab Republic. Two thousand Lebanese died in the ensuing civil struggle, which ended with the intervention of U.S. Marines, dispatched at the request of the Lebanese government by President Eisenhower. The conflict, though quickly resolved, left Lebanon's Christian community skeptical about the Muslims' commitment to the Lebanese state, and nervous about how they would react to the next Arab demagogue who came along.

Historians can, more or less, identify the missteps which, during these relatively halcyon years, led to the unraveling of Lebanese society. Without much enthusiasm, Lebanon joined the Arab nations in 1948 in going to war against Israel. When several hundred thousand Palestinians arrived as refugees at its borders, Lebanon opened its gates to let them in. Most Lebanese figured they did not have the political or moral option of turning refugees away, but few suggested that they should. In response to the infusion, however, Lebanon's rulers had the duty to strengthen the state, and particularly the army. Instead, they chose, quite deliberately, to make the state weaker.

The most plausible explanation for this course was that Lebanon's leaders feared one another more than they did the Palestinians, and feared to create an apparatus which might wind up taking sides if conflict broke out among them. The Lebanese state evoked no strong allegiance. Lebanese were loyal first and foremost to their religious communities, and within these communities to their clans. Even the Maronites, most "Lebanese" of the sects, felt little attachment to the state; the Muslims felt even less. From this attitude emerged a strategy summed up in a slogan credited to Sheikh Pierre. "Our strength lies in our weakness," he said, which meant that the Lebanese would be spared from fighting by being too weak to threaten their neighbors, or one another.

The naïveté of this view was demonstrated in December of 1968, when the Israeli army raided the Beirut airport, symbol of Lebanon's sovereignty and prosperity, in retaliation for acts of terrorism committed by Lebanon-based Palestinians. While the Israelis were destroying thirteen airplanes belonging to Middle East Airlines, Lebanon's flag-carrier, the government remained paralyzed, incapable of ordering the army to action. The anger and humiliation provoked a popular demand to allow a free hand to the Palestinians to wage war against Israel from Lebanon's soil.

The episode was also a measure of the strength of the Palestinians. During their first twenty years of residence, Palestinian refugees had not been a major problem, but after the Arabs' devastating defeat in the Six-Day War, their political arm—the Palestine Liberation Organization— decided to initiate terrorist warfare, which it euphemistically called "armed struggle," on its own. Under pressure from the Arab League, and particularly from Nasser, Lebanon gave the Palestinians a large measure of autonomy. In the Cairo Accords of 1969, Lebanon ceded to the PLO authority over the refugee camps, and the power to build military bases within striking distance of the Israeli frontier. Some Christian Lebanese allege that the Cairo Accords were a plot by the Arab League to Islamize the country. But the agreement was endorsed by Lebanon's parliament, the Christians included, with only a single dissenting vote.

The following year, Lebanon began paying the price of its passivity. Unlike Lebanon, Jordan vigorously resisted the ambitions of the PLO, and in "Black September" 1970 it thrashed the *fedayeen* soundly. Summarily evicted from Jordan, the PLO's military units showed up on Lebanon's doorstep, and the Lebanese government was too weak to send them away. Once they established residence, they rearmed themselves and carved out a state-within-a-state in South Lebanon and the Beirut suburbs, while their raids into Israel increasingly exposed innocent Lebanese to Israeli retaliation. The process aggravated Lebanon's polarization: Muslims blamed Israel for the havoc and gravitated toward the Palestinians; Christians, irritated by the liberties the Palestinians were taking, sympathized with Israel and looked to it for support. As the months passed, tolerance between Christians and Muslims steadily faded. Each community took to recruiting its young men into militias and to buying arms in anticipation of battle.

The fighting finally broke out on a Sunday in April 1975, when unidentified gunmen fired at Sheikh Pierre after mass outside a church in the Beirut suburb of Ain Rummaneh, killing his bodyguard and two others. That afternoon, Phalangist militiamen ambushed a bus passing through Ain Rummaneh and massacred its twenty-eight passengers, most of them Palestinians. As if by some prearranged signal, the combat spread, with the Christians throwing down the gauntlet before the combined forces of the Palestinians, their Muslim allies and the heavily armed Druzes, ever ready to even scores with their traditional Maronite enemy. Of the parties to the early combat, only the PLO seemed prepared to back away, their leader Yasir Arafat claiming he wanted nothing to do with a war between Lebanese. The others took up the battle zestfully, with no obvious concern for the consequences.

Rival militias quickly turned downtown Beirut into a battlefield, where they savagely killed and maimed one another, along with thousands of bystanders. Looking anarchy in the eye, the Lebanese government talked on and on and did nothing, not even when the army began fragmenting into segments favorable to one faction or another. The old godfathers who had successfully shared the helm of state since negotiating the National Pact three decades before had run out of expedients. The killing intensified in spurts over more than a year, finally reaching a peak in the summer of 1976, when the Christian armies besieged the Palestinian camp of Tel-Zaatar, home of thirty thousand refugees, while PLO-Sunni forces advanced into the Maronite homeland on the Mountain. At that point, the Lebanese turned outward for help. What they found were the Syrians, who regarded Lebanon as their stolen province, and who were ready for a role for which they felt history had destined them.

Lebanese, and especially Maronites, like to say that the war they fought was not a civil war at all. They prefer to see their country as a playground for foreign forces, particularly Syria's, manipulating them cruelly. They tend to forget that Lebanon had created a system of government characterized not only by political paralysis but by social indifference. The ruling elites, Muslim and Christian alike, exploited the country mercilessly. The working class got little reward, the poor not even pity. The state, unable to provide for public safety, was no better in providing education, health care and other basic human services. Beirut was surrounded by a chain of shantytowns known to everyone as the Misery Belt. In this explosive mix, the Palestinians were a catalyst. But their presence does not explain why the Lebanese went after one another in such bloodthirsty fashion. It was the Lebanese themselves who in 1975 and 1976 did most of the fighting and the killing. It was also the Lebanese, Christians and Muslims alike, who acknowledged that they could not stop the killing on their own, and called upon the Syrians to save them from themselves. Only then did their territory become the arena for wars that were not their own.

The Syrians sent their first contingents into Lebanon in January 1976, and by the summer their strength had reached about thirty-five thousand. Impotent itself, the Arab League legitimized the Syrian presence retroactively. No one had illusions that Syria's motives were disinterested. The Syrians coveted Lebanon, believing sincerely that it had been scissored away from its rightful place under their flag. They had never formally recognized Lebanon's sovereignty and independence, and had never had an embassy in Beirut. The Maronites understood that, once in the country, the Syrians were unlikely ever to leave. Having joined in summoning the Syrians, they were scarcely surprised to find later that they were in no position to send their benefactors home.

It is ironic that Syria's first military operation was to rescue the Maronites by clearing the Mountain of Palestinian invaders. The message Damascus sent was that it would not permit the PLO, any more than the Christians, to take over the country. Syria's strategy, soon apparent, was to maintain a balance among the Lebanese factions, so that it could itself be the arbiter of Lebanon's future. Until the Israeli invasion of 1982, Syria presided over an uneasy truce, which kept the killing in Lebanon at a far lower level than it was before. After the invasion, the Israelis, still occupying a strip of South Lebanon, became Assad's excuse for staying. Syria's relationship with the Christians—and, less openly, with the other Lebanese—was at best adversarial. Having come as a peacemaker, Syria permitted Lebanon to retain many of the trappings of independence, but its actions made clear that it intended to retain the last word on Lebanon's fate.

IV   BASHIR

IN RETROSPECT, it was inevitable that the Maronites, at some point, would make common cause with the Israelis. Both regarded themselves as a beleaguered minority in a sea of Muslims. Both took pride in a culture that is alien to the Muslim region. Both cultivated a nationalism based on a common historical, religious and even ethnic identity, and both had coreligionists around the world to help them preserve this identity. Politically, they shared a strong animosity toward the Palestinians. Many Maronites, to be sure, were critical of the Israelis for seeking to overpower rather than resolve the Palestinian problem, leaving some four hundred thousand embattled refugees to run loose inside Lebanon. But at the same time they envied in the Israelis the determination that was so wanting in themselves to organize against external foes.

Israel's presence sharpened the debate among Lebanese Christians on their relations with the Arab world. Though it was often said that they were different from other Arabs only in religion, that was not how most Maronites saw themselves. Emotionally they were not, and historically they had never been, Arabs. For reasons of expediency, they had at times made common cause with the Arabs. But, as Muslims have never forgotten, they supported the Crusaders centuries ago, and they scarcely concealed their sympathy for the Israelis. In diplomacy, they formally endorsed Arab positions on the Palestinians. But they failed the crucial test of Arabism: Maronites regarded the Palestinians as "them," not "us."

During my weeks in Lebanon, what I seemed to hear in the voices of Maronites talking about Israelis—or, more specifically, about Jews—was unique. On this topic, the Arab voice is forever weighted with the stark anger of decades of struggle and frustration; the Western voice carries the complex burden of centuries of guilt, condescension and awe. The tone of the Maronites seemed to me refreshingly direct, matter-of-fact. The Jews? "They're that tribe down the road," they seemed to say. "They moved away for a couple of thousand years, but they're back now. And they're bringing up the neighborhood."

As long ago as the 1950s, the Israelis looked into the prospect of promoting the establishment of a Maronite republic as their ally in Lebanon. But, in those days, the National Pact worked satisfactorily and the Maronites were not interested. Then, after the start of the civil war, when Syria's domination of the country loomed, they took another look. According to Ze'ev Schiff and Ehud Ya'ari, Israeli writers on military affairs, one of the first contacts took place in late 1976 on an Israeli missile boat in the Mediterranean, when Yitzhak Rabin, then Israel's prime minister, met with Sheikh Pierre and his two sons, Amin and Bashir. Though Sheikh Pierre reproached Rabin for Israel's clumsy handling of the Palestinian problem, Schiff and Ya'ari write, the two men acknowledged a common danger in the PLO. Within months the Maronite militias were receiving military materiel—tanks, rifles, artillery shells, antitank rockets—from the Israelis, most of it made in the United States.

By 1977, with Syria entrenched in Lebanon, Israel had established clandestine relations with Bashir Gemayel, who was in the process of fusing the diverse Christian militias into a single powerful force. Proclaiming a new era of Christian power, Bashir was tough, brash, courageous, and contemptuous of his father's generation, the source of Lebanon's woes. He had been a soldier all his life, in contrast to his older brother, Amin, who had made his career in Parliament. Amin was cautious, conformist and aloof, and seemed at best to be a transitional figure between the generations. Bashir was the new generation incarnate. He frequently traveled secretly across the border as a guest of Israeli prime minister Menachem Begin, to cajole arms and to argue for Israeli strikes against the Syrians. He got his way in 1978, when Israel conducted a major raid against the PLO in South Lebanon. Bashir saw this as a warning to Syria. He credited the raid with persuading the Syrians to exclude from their military occupation of the country the Christian redoubt in East Beirut and the Mountain.

Meanwhile, Bashir, as commander of his father's Phalangist militia, spared no blood in extending his control over Christian forces. His first target was the most pro-Syrian and anti-Israeli of the Christian factions, the rival family led by the old patriarch Suleiman Franjieh, Lebanon's president when the war began. In June 1978, Phalangist forces directed by Samir Geagea, a young disciple of Bashir's, attacked Franjieh's stronghold in the north and killed Tony Franjieh, the patriarch's eldest son, along with Tony's wife and child, and thirty followers. A year later, Bashir's own daughter died in an ambush, probably at the hands of the Franjiehs, but he forged on with his plans. In 1980, he went after an old Gemayel ally, the Chamoun family, and defeated its militia, called the Tigers, in a ferocious battle. As his power grew, several smaller militias voluntarily came to his side. Bashir called his organization the Lebanese Forces; being its leader made him a major figure not only in Lebanese but in Israeli calculations.

After Begin's reelection in 1981, Israel's calculations became grander. Ariel Sharon, the new defense minister, dreamed of making the entire Middle East an Israeli sphere of influence, and tantalized Bashir with the prospect of a position of leadership in it. Sharon's design provided for an Israeli invasion of Lebanon that would shatter the PLO's military power, humiliate the Syrians and create a Maronite-dominated state prepared to negotiate a Lebanese-Israeli peace. Bashir would be elected president, and Lebanon would openly become Israel's ally.

Accordingly, in June 1982, Sharon sent the Israeli army into Lebanon and quickly won his military objectives. Though the Lebanese Forces disappointed Sharon by hanging back from the battlefield, he proceeded with the execution of his plan. Bashir was elected president but, on September 14, a few days before his scheduled inaugural, he was assassinated by a bomb placed in his headquarters, presumably by the Syrians. Two days later, a Lebanese Forces unit commanded by a young officer named Elie Hobeika, by agreement with the Israelis, entered the Palestinian refugee camps of Sabra and Shatila to search for PLO stragglers; it stayed to slaughter more than a thousand (the exact number is disputed) men, women and children. On September 20, the Lebanese parliament unanimously elected Amin Gemayel, who was free of ties to Israel, as president. In the confusion that accompanied the presidential succession, and the international uproar over the massacre, Sharon's grand design for Lebanon collapsed.

"We made a mistake to send our people into Sabra and Shatila immediately after Bashir's assassination," said Fady Frem, who at twenty-nine succeeded Bashir as the Lebanese Forces' commander. A small, stocky man, he had enlisted in the Phalange militia as a teenager and worked his way up the hierarchy. "The Israelis said the operation was necessary to make sure the PLO was gone, to secure their flanks. Our people did not hold the PLO to blame for Bashir's death, but the Palestinians nonetheless became the target of our rage. I don't think anyone intended a massacre. We made a mistake. We also made a mistake in refusing to accept responsibility, but that may be part of our Lebanese mentality. There should have been an investigation, but we acknowledged nothing. The Muslims wanted to blame the Israelis, and Amin allowed them to do it. The Israelis were furious at taking the blame. It changed their attitude toward the Lebanese Christians, and vice versa. It helped turn everything around."

By then, twelve hundred United States Marines had come, left and returned to Lebanon. With Israel's consent, they first landed in August 1982, along with contingents from France and Italy, to supervise the evacuation of the PLO's forces from captured Beirut. Having left after the Palestinians, they came back in the wake of Sabra and Shatila. Their mission was unclear, even to themselves, but their presence generated some hope among the Lebanese for Western help in reestablishing the state. The Israeli invasion had loosened the bonds of the Syrians, who had retreated to the Beqa'a Valley, and the Israelis themselves were negotiating terms of withdrawal. Under the eyes of the Western forces, the barriers between East and West Beirut abruptly came down and the Lebanese army began cautiously to extend its authority from the city into the countryside. Overcome with wishful thinking, the Lebanese began thinking that Washington would be the intermediary in restoring Lebanon's sovereignty.

"Bashir had a vision," Frem told me. "He wanted Lebanon to be an American ally; he also favored a peace agreement with Israel and continuous coordination with it in regional affairs. As he saw it, driving Syria out of Lebanon would be followed by the creation of a U.S.-Israel-Lebanon axis, with all its strategic ramifications, and at the time the plan looked feasible. The Shiites in the south had welcomed the Israelis as their savior from the Palestinians. The Sunnis were happy to get the Palestinians out of West Beirut. The Muslim leadership knew Bashir wanted to get rid of the Syrians, and it elected him president anyway. Syria, which had lost much of its support in the moderate Arab states for supporting Iran in the Gulf war, was weak then. The moderate Arabs admired Bashir's dynamism. Building on Israel's military momentum, we could have pulled it off, but only if Bashir had lived."

When I met with Elie Salem, at the time a close advisor to President Gemayel, he confirmed Frem's account of Bashir's vision. But he said Frem's view of how it might have played out was fantasy. He contended that prior to his death, Bashir had begun moving away from the Israelis. On September 1, Bashir had a tumultuous argument with Begin and Sharon in Nahariyya, an Israeli seaside resort, over the delivery of a Lebanon-Israel peace treaty. "Bashir discarded political opinions like autumn leaves," Salem said. Had the Lebanese relied on Israel to drive out the Syrians, he said, they would have been condemned as traitors by the entire Arab world. Bashir was not prepared, he said, to sever ties with the Arabs to become an appendage of Israel and of Western military strategy.

On becoming president, Amin Gemayel, anxious to restore Lebanon's Arab orientation, notified Washington that he was shifting the government away from its dependence on Israel. He refused to deal directly with high-ranking Israelis, as his brother had done, and described Israeli soldiers as occupiers, not liberators. He proceeded, however, with peace talks with the Israelis, hoping negotiations would result in the withdrawal of both the Israeli and Syrian armies. The talks, which began in the fall of 1982, dragged on into 1983, when the United States stepped in as intermediary. Curiously, the parties never brought Damascus into the proceedings, though the Syrians were obviously in a position to veto the outcome. While the three delegations talked, Moscow went about rearming Syria, while Khomeini's Iran, Syria's ally, set up bases in the Beqa'a.

On May 17 an agreement was signed. In return for Israel's withdrawal, Lebanon agreed to end the state of war, but it did not consent to a formal peace—an arrangement that was far less than Israel had anticipated when Bashir was in power. Then, after the negotiations ended, Jerusalem declared it would not withdraw from Lebanon unless Syria withdrew first. In all of this maneuvering, Assad saw the United States not as an intermediary but as an instrument of the Israelis and, through them, of the Gemayel government. He had no intention of leaving Lebanon and characterized the agreement as a Lebanese "capitulation to Israel." And so the agreement was never carried out. Lebanon's parliament ratified it but Gemayel refused to execute it, and a year later, Lebanon officially rescinded its approval.

By then, the U.S. Marines were gone for good. In the second half of 1983, they had become targets of intensifying sniper fire from Syrian positions above the airport and had virtually ceased patrolling. Meanwhile,

Israel evacuated the Shouf mountains south of Beirut, the first step in their withdrawal from all of Lebanon, save for a "security zone" several miles deep which they established along their own northern frontier. In the race to take over behind the withdrawing Israelis, the Druzes defeated the Lebanese Forces in a series of bloody battles. Then, on October 23, 241 Marines died in their barracks in the explosion of a car bomb, and on the same day 59 French soldiers were also killed by a bomb. In retaliation, the American battleship *New Jersey* lobbed a few shells at Syrian targets, and French aircraft dropped some explosives, but the Western governments were not interested in intervening on the ground. Damascus had won the contest to control Lebanon. The surviving Marines packed up and went home, leaving America's reputation in the region in shambles.

"I think Washington never really grasped what Lebanon was about," Elie Salem told me. "America promised that it would stand with us, and it did not. If the May 17 Agreement could not be implemented—that is, if Washington could not convince Syria to withdraw—then we should never have been asked to sign it. Lebanon is too small and exposed to make a peace with Israel on our own. The day before we signed, George Shultz [The U.S. secretary of state] said Syria would come around in four or five weeks, and he could not have been more wrong. Then the Americans left, and the Syrians concluded that they could do what they wanted in Lebanon. They still feel that way. Amin Gemayel survived as president only by a miracle. The French were ready to evacuate him, and when he decided to remain, the Americans told him how courageous he was. Big deal!"

After the American withdrawal, the wave of euphoria that had passed over Lebanon vanished. Violence grew worse than ever, with not only Christians and Muslims shooting at each other but Muslims shooting at Muslims, and Christians at Christians. East and West Beirut were again separated, and the militias resumed their control. Amin Gemayel, as president, split with the Lebanese Forces over their refusal to sever ties with Israel. Behind his back, they mockingly called him "Mohammed," for his policy of maintaining ties with the Arabs. In August 1984, Sheikh Pierre died, and Amin tried to take over his father's party, and through it to impose some discipline over the Lebanese Forces. But Samir Geagea of the Lebanese Forces, who had been in charge of the murderous operation against Tony Franjieh, took hold of the party and then he was deposed by Elie Hobeika, the commander at Sabra and Shatila, who was considered among the most anti-Syrian of the Christian leaders.

Whatever Hobeika's reputation, however, shortly after seizing power he entered into secret talks with Syria with a view to ending the civil war. A militia commander himself, he purported to speak also for the Shiite and Druze militias, and for Damascus to negotiate with him rather than with Gemayel's legal government was highly irregular. Syria's defenders argue that Gemayel had failed to establish ascendancy over the factions, so why not turn to the militias, where the power lay? Indeed, though Lebanon's old power-brokers remained in regular contact, they could not agree on how to restore the supremacy of the state. With public order once again disintegrating, Hobeika traveled to Damascus, and on December 28, 1985, he and his fellow militia leaders signed a document known as the Tripartite Agreement.

The Tripartite Agreement proposed to replace the National Pact of 1943 with "deconfessionalization," a system of one-man-one-vote democracy that would wipe away the guarantees which the Christian community considered essential. It also proposed to give Syria huge powers over Lebanese affairs, effectively placing Lebanon's military, educational and foreign policy, and particularly its relations with the Arab world, in Syria's hands. For a decade, the Lebanese had wondered what the Syrians really wanted; the Tripartite Agreement told them. It confirmed that even if Syria did not formally annex Lebanon, it planned to control the country as a satellite. The Tripartite Agreement would have tied Lebanon tightly to Syria's aspirations to dominate the region. Lebanon's Muslims and Christians alike were dismayed by the message.

Hobeika's motives in negotiating the agreement are a puzzle, even today. Did he come to understand, as admirers say, that the interests of Lebanese Christians would be better served by ties to Syria than to Israel? Hobeika's detractors say he was bought, and that he may even have been a Syrian agent as far back as 1982, when he was in charge of Bashir's security, and when he led his men into Sabra and Shatila. Was he seduced by the promise of becoming Lebanon's president? Whatever the explanation, the Lebanese Forces responded quickly to what they considered a betrayal. At dawn on January 15, 1986, Samir Geagea, supported by units loyal to Gemayel, mounted an attack on Hobeika, and after fighting that left more than one hundred dead, Geagea prevailed. Hobeika departed with his loyalists to Cyprus, and soon thereafter showed up in the Beqa'a Valley, fighting for Syria.

Gemayel had no intention of giving his backing to the pro-Syrian Tripartite Agreement, any more than he had to the pro-Israeli May 17 Agreement. His aim was to kill it, while maintaining decent relations with Syria, objectives which were probably incompatible. He achieved the first, but in retaliation Syria demanded that Lebanon's Muslim ministers boycott the presidency, and for the remainder of his term, Gemayel never met with the Lebanese cabinet. In February 1987, Syria, at the "invitation" of Lebanon's Muslim leaders, moved its army back into West Beirut, from which it had fled before the Israelis five years earlier. These moves were no doubt revenge for Gemayel's rejection of the Tripartite Agreement. But the punishment was not paid by the Christians alone. By all the evidence, the Muslims were hardly any happier to have the Syrians back in charge.

V EAST BEIRUT, WEST BEIRUT

FROM THE MOMENT I stepped off the boat at Juniye, the Lebanese Forces people had been phoning to remind me that I had promised to spend a few days talking to their representatives and inspecting their installations. They were right, and after we fixed a date, they mentioned casually that I could release my security guards, since they would take care of me during the visit. When I told this to Elie, my bodyguard, he said, "No way," and over the course of a half-dozen phone calls I was unable to resolve the disagreement. So at 8:30 on the appointed morning, two sets of bodyguards pulled up at the door of my hotel, ready for trouble. I note with some pride that there then ensued, under my presidency, what may have been the most successful negotiation since the start of the civil war. It took a half hour, but when it was over Elie climbed into the front seat of *their* car, in the back of which I rode with the guide from the Lebanese Forces, a pretty twenty-four-year-old woman named Carole, while their man sat next to Roni in the front seat of *my* car. Since it may be a useful lesson, I would also note that by late that first morning, the two sets of bodyguards had become buddies, and by the end of my stay, after an itinerary that covered much of East Beirut, the seacoast and the Mountain, they embraced warmly in parting.

The first stop was at the Lebanese Forces headquarters at the Karantina, which was near the green line, the division between East and West Beirut. The Karantina—once the quarantine area of the port—is a section of docks, warehouses and two-story office buildings that lies behind a wall, the gates of which were guarded by heavily armed men. The surrounding area had been bulldozed clean; it was once a crowded Palestinian slum, and the site of one of the early battles of the civil war. In the Karantina, Christian militiamen defeated a stubborn Palestinian and Shiite force, while gratuitously slaughtering several hundred noncombatant women and children. The massacre helped set the standard of brutality which prevailed thereafter in nearly all the fighting in Lebanon.

At the Karantina, I met with Karim Pakradouni, a small man in his mid-forties who, behind horn-rimmed glasses, conveyed a manner that seemed far too easygoing for the times. Pakradouni, who was not Maronite but Armenian Catholic, told me he had become involved in Phalangist politics as a student and was now a kind of intellectual-in-residence of the Lebanese

Forces, a post he had held since Bashir's day. The Lebanese Forces, he said, were convinced that the Syrians wanted no solution to the Lebanese problem. Lebanon, he argued, was no more than a lever that Damascus operated to get back the Golan Heights from Israel, subdue the Palestinians and suppress dissent in Syria itself. The Christians would offer peace only if Syria acknowledged Lebanon's sovereignty and agreed to relations of equality, permitting it to deal with Israel. These were terms, he said, to which the Syrians were unlikely ever to agree.

"The Muslims of Lebanon claim they have been dominated by the Christians," Pakradouni continued, "but in fact they have more power than we do. They have an Arab Lebanon with a Christian face; what they want is an Arab Lebanon with an Arab face—and that's bad. President Gemayel had the courage to say 'no' to the Tripartite Agreement, but he is nonetheless a proponent of Lebanon's historic compromise, in which Christians and Muslims share the power. His problem is that the Muslims do not want to reciprocate. He held his hand out to them, and they held out their hand to Damascus, preferring Assad to him.

"We Lebanese need to have the Syrians out of Lebanon to achieve our reconciliation. Even then, it will not be simple, but we will find a compromise in which Islam accepts Christian power, and we will concede the Arab character of the state. But an Arab state is not the same as an Arab people, which we are not. The Muslims would like Lebanon to be like the other Arab lands, and that is impossible. That's why Lebanon remains like a gas-filled room: light a match any time and it will blow up."

During my tour over the following days with the Lebanese Forces, I visited offices where young volunteers worked on computers to process applications for public assistance. I saw clinics distributing medicines to the chronically ill, and I talked to officials whose work was to appeal to Lebanese Christian expatriates for funds for the needy. I inspected accommodations provided to Christians displaced by the war ("600,000 . . . driven from their homes by the enemies of Christianity," said one publicity circular), and though as refugees they complained bitterly of their misfortunes, and even of the inadequacy of the efforts made on their behalf, I found their lodgings far better than any available to Palestinians in refugee camps throughout the Middle East. All of the displaced Christians I talked to said they wanted to return to their villages, now in the hands of Syrians or Druzes or Shiites—but few were optimistic about the prospect.

Early one morning, three young officers in olive drab met me at a Lebanese Forces command post under a highway bridge in downtown Beirut and took me by jeep to the green line. There I saw the rubble of what was once the city's animated center—the famous Martyrs Square, a mélange of burned-out movie theaters with names like Radio City and

Roxy and Rivoli still visible over their grand entrances, and of badly punctured facades of art deco and fin de siècle French architecture. A big electric sign advertising Orient watches, having somehow eluded destruction, stood guard over the mess. Instructing me to keep my head below the level of the window sills, my guides led me through a labyrinth of gutted buildings, where young soldiers slept on camp cots, to look across the dividing line at a mirror image of destruction on the West Beirut side. Climbing over the debris, Elie mentioned softly that it was here that his best friend was killed fighting next to him in a battle in 1981. Later, on the abandoned street below, a sign caught my eye; it offered the services of a Dr. Jean Ma'alouf in surgery of the genito-urinary tract, and I wondered what had ever become of Dr. Ma'alouf.

That same morning, my guides took me to the shrine that marked what was once the Lebanese Forces headquarters where Bashir Gemayel died. Over it loomed a ghostly ten-foot cardboard silhouette of Bashir. Where there had been ruins from the explosion of two hundred pounds of dynamite, there was now a rose garden, containing an eternal flame and a granite stone inscribed in Arabic with the names of the victims. Three young guards in T-shirts sat in a concrete kiosk nearby, automatic weapons slung over shoulders, keeping a wary eye on the mourners.

The following Sunday, I was driven high up on the Mountain to Jhosta, site of an eleventh-century Maronite convent which had become the Lebanese Forces' military academy. We arrived during mass, which was conducted by Father Antoine Achkar, whom I had met when I visited the hospital for the handicapped at Beit Shebab. Father Antoine, who greeted me warmly, had brought forty of his patients with him for the Lebanese Forces' annual tribute to wounded veterans. After mass, the patients reviewed the cadet corps, before sitting down to lunch. I had a chance then to interview Lieutenant Selim Khoury, the director of training at the academy, who said the student officers at Jhosta—of whom forty entered each year, for three years of study—were taught "Fort Benning" techniques, designed to transform the militia ("highly motivated but unorganized, unprepared for protracted war") into a real army ("highly organized, hierarchic, disciplined"). "If this war isn't settled soon," Khoury said, "we're going to have to face the Syrian army, and we'll need all the training we can get."

MARWAN HAMADE WAS a Druze with good family connections and a political history that included several ministerial posts. He had been recommended to me as Syria's man in Beirut by Abdel Halim Khaddam, the Syrian vice-president who was responsible for Lebanese affairs. During a visit to Damascus, Khaddam even gave me several telephone numbers for reaching him. That the telephones worked from East to West Beirut was astonishing, in view of the mutual hostility of the regimes that administered the two sides of town. One of the peculiarities of Lebanon at war, however, was that a single ministry continued to run the phones, just as single ministries—with on-and-off reliability—ran the electricity system, the post office, the banking structure, the television. I reached Hamade at one of Khaddam's numbers, and he invited me on a visit, to talk not only with him but with other prominent leaders in West Beirut.

Hamade and I fixed a time when he said a car would be waiting at the Villa Mansour, the Lebanese parliament, a neoclassical building located at the checkpoint where cars and pedestrians crossed the green line. Known as the Museum Crossing, the checkpoint was named for the badly battered Lebanese Museum which stands nearby. Hamade, too, said his people would take care of my security while I was in West Beirut. I notified Samir Fares of my plans, and he warned me that going to West Beirut was dangerous for an American. How dangerous?, I asked him. He thought a minute and replied that there was one chance in ten thousand I would not come back. I said I thought the odds were good enough, and he raised no further objections.

At 8:45 on a Friday morning, Roni pulled the car up in front of the Villa Mansour. This was no-man's-land, and Elie, visibly nervous, apologized repeatedly for being unable to accompany me the rest of the way. I was not the only one crossing, of course; many Lebanese, with special permissions, made the trip daily, almost casually, to school or work. Dozens of cars were lined up, their drivers waiting patiently to show their papers; hundreds of people were making the journey on foot. Hamade's car, followed by a Land-Rover full of armed men, was already sitting in the parking area, its motor running. As I climbed in, Elie and the driver settled amiably on the hour of my return.

It took Hamade's driver only a moment to get the car out of no-man's-land and into West Beirut, where the atmosphere was clearly different. Posters of Assad replaced those of the Gemayels. There was more Arabic, less French, in the signs over the shops. Syrians in shabby khaki uniforms and scuffed boots stood at the street corners. The destruction was far greater, the debris more prominent. With the help of a siren and a flashing light on the Land-Rover, my driver forced his way through the heavy traffic and delivered me to a shabby apartment building on a narrow street, where a dozen heavily armed men seemed to be waiting for me. One of them begged pardon that the elevator was not working, and he accompanied me up the staircase to the door of Hamade's apartment on the third floor.

Hamade greeted me with a warm handshake. He was a small man, with a soft and delicate face, and he wore a fashionably cut, light blue suit with a shirt and tie. The living room of his apartment, with handsome paintings on the wall and Oriental rugs on the floor, conveyed a threadbare elegance, and adjoining it I saw a library stocked with books. As we sipped the obligatory coffee, Hamade asked my forgiveness for not inviting me to lunch. "Two or three hours in one place would permit them to locate us, and I'd be nervous," he said quietly. I did not know who "them" were, though I assumed he meant hostage-takers, so I forgave him. Hamade was known to be well connected in political circles, though his relations with the Syrians were unclear. We talked about President Gemayel, whom he said he disliked and distrusted, and about "deconfessionalization," which he said must be Lebanon's goal, though it need not be attained overnight. After chatting for an hour, we went down the stairs to his limousine, which he assured me was fully armored, and drove to the prime minister's house, a few blocks away.

Salim Hoss, a Sunni, was acknowledged by all Lebanese as prime minister, which was testimony to a consensus that the state should be preserved. The Lebanese parliament had been elected in 1972, and though its mandate had long since expired, it remained the country's recognized legislative authority. Hoss, who served as prime minister from 1976 to 1980, was renamed to the post in June 1987, after Rashid Karame, his predecessor, was assassinated. His cabinet was never formally confirmed, and because of the Muslim boycott of Gemayel, it had never legally met; ministers fulfilled their duties individually. Hoss, without a formal office, worked out of his rather modest apartment, where I found the rooms crowded with petitioners. There, Hoss conducted consultations and did his paper work. The decrees and other documents that the law required him to sign were sent across the green line, in a bizarre effort to preserve constitutionality, to the presidential palace in East Beirut, for countersignature by Gemayel.

A tall, cordial intellectual with a Ph.D. in economics from Indiana University, Hoss in our talk criticized Gemayel for the rejection of the Tripartite Agreement and blamed him for the Syrian-imposed boycott. He said he and the other top Muslim leaders, after discussions in Damascus, had planned to take the text of the agreement to the cabinet for amendments, and ultimately the parliament would have had a chance to amend it further. But the Maronites sank the agreement, Hoss said, because it would have put an end to their claims to the presidency and to the most powerful posts in the administration—and he cited commander-in-chief of the army, head of military intelligence, director of immigration, chief justice and governor of the central bank. It is unfortunate, Hoss said, that Gemayel was under the influence of Geagea and the right wing of the Lebanese Forces.

"I had reservations of my own about the Tripartite Agreement," Hoss said. "But I think we should have sat around the table to amend it. We are a country without authority, and we need the Syrians here. I am not happy about their negotiating the agreement with the militias. I'd be among the first to object to any reduction in our sovereignty, to any compromise in Lebanon's independence. But reconciliation is not a push-button affair. We have to get off the military track and back on the track of democratic struggle. Once we took the text of the Tripartite Agreement into official channels, I think we could have reconciled Syrian designs with Lebanon's conception of statehood. Amin's blanket condemnation settled nothing."

After the meeting with Hoss, Hamade took me in his car on a tour of West Beirut's decimation. The celebrated district of seaside hotels, which I had seen in its gaudy prime, was an assortment of twisted steel skeletons and heaps of rubble, overgrown by vegetation. The American University of Beirut remained an island of tranquillity, though many had died there too. A Ferris wheel in an amusement park by the sea, which for some reason remained fixed in my memory, was still turning. But no effort had been made to repair the old U.S. embassy, bombed out in 1983, or the neighborhood around it. In all, the eye was offered little relief from the destruction of war.

In a final swing, Hamade drove me through ruins where, he said, Shiites from the south had found refuge from the Palestinians and Israelis, only to live like rodents in the capital. Hezbollah—kidnappers of foreigners, especially Western journalists—controlled the sector, he said, and if his intention was to scare me, he succeeded. Clad in rags, sallow-skinned women and gaunt-eyed children stared at our armored car as we rolled through the debris of the neighborhood. A few minutes later, when the car returned me to the Villa Mansour, Elie was waiting and—proof that all is relative—I felt stunning relief in getting back to the safety of East Beirut.

VI   AMIN

WHEN I REPEATED to President Gemayel what Hoss had said of his rejection of the Tripartite Accord, he replied disdainfully, "How could he say otherwise? The Syrian system is built on terror, and our Muslims are scared. They criticize me for refusing the Tripartite Agreement, but they know I had to do it, and they are grateful for my courage. To say, as Hoss does, that the Lebanese could negotiate with Syria over the terms of the Tripartite Accord is to believe that a woman can be a little pregnant. The

Muslims would not dare to convoke parliament to discuss the agreement, because the Syrians know it would not survive an open discussion. Hoss goes for everything to Khaddam, who is a very tough guy. Khaddam seems to be receiving Lebanese all day long. It's a wonder he has time for anything else. Hoss and the other Muslim leaders are terrorized."

I met Amin Gemayel in the presidential palace in Baabda, a sprawling L-shaped building of glass and marble panels, finished just before the war. Surrounded by woods on a low hill at the southern end of Beirut, the palace overlooks the airport to the east, the Shouf hills to the west. It was held by the Israelis when Gemayel was elected president in 1982—he moved in only after they left—and was shelled by the Syrians a year later, after Lebanon approved the May 17 Agreement.

Gemayel and I were alone in our talks, which began in his ceremonial office, a high-ceilinged, angular room, decorated with two clay vases from Lebanon's prehistory and a shelf of books that appeared too new to have been read. Chain-smoking Gitanes, he grew fidgety as the hours passed, and we moved into a smaller room nearby. Only one phone call—which I took from the paternal tone to be from his children in Bikfaya—interrupted us. The president's style was more aggressive than I had anticipated, and when I asked him about the charge, made by both Lebanese and outsiders, that at the start of his term he had missed through indecision opportunities to end the civil war, he defended himself vigorously.

"I would have liked to move more quickly toward national reconciliation," he said, "but we had to finish the difficult negotiations with Israel first. Moreover, after eight years of war, we were a very sick and divided country. I invited the major Muslim and Christian leaders to meet in the palace but, unfortunately, events ran away from me. I had problems with the Lebanese Forces. There was the pact with Israel, and then the war in the Shouf between the Lebanese Forces and the Druzes. And there was the biggest battle of all, between us and Syria over the Tripartite Agreement. Assad wants to arrange the region so that neither the Lebanese nor the Palestinians can deal with their national affairs without Syria. He hated the fact that we were negotiating with Israel without him, though I kept him apprised of every development. When we signed the May 17 Agreement, he considered it a *casus belli*, and he had Moscow and Iran behind him. In effect, Assad declared war on Lebanon."

Gemayel acknowledged his differences with extremists in the Christian community, particularly with the Lebanese Forces. The basic dispute, he said, was over the relations between Lebanese Christians and the Arab world. He believes, Gemayel said, that it would be a grievous mistake for the Christian community to try to create a nation that was alienated from its Arab roots.

"We Lebanese Christians have a unique culture," he continued, "but we also belong to a country. That country is very cosmopolitan; it has great religious and cultural diversity. The other Arab countries are one-dimensional. Lebanon is multidimensional, and it has a diverse history. The Arabs remain very sensitive about the Crusades, though not all Lebanese Christians were with the Crusaders. Lebanon's factions, the Christians included, have overreacted in their distinct nationalisms—pro-Syrian or pro-Israeli or even pro-Iranian. But there is also a patriotic feeling among Lebanese, and it is not marginal. In a nation of their own, a few hundred thousand Lebanese Christians would be quickly absorbed by Europe, but in the Arab world we are vital as a bridge between East and West. That is our essential role. Whatever the extremists say, the Christian community cannot live as a ghetto nation. It is in our fundamental interest as Christian Lebanese to be Arab."

I asked the president to compare himself with his late brother, Bashir, whom the public perceived as a stronger leader.

"My perception is not different from Bashir's, and before he died, he adopted positions that were close to my own. The day after he was elected president, Bashir became Amin. He recognized that Lebanon could not live without a national consensus, which means Muslims and Christians together, and though he wanted to maintain his relations with the Israelis, he made a one-hundred-eighty-degree change. The Americans persuaded him to exercise the Arab option, even at the cost of the strategic alliance with Israel. Bashir was comfortable with this idea, because it permitted him to preserve our traditional relations. I think that even the Lebanese Forces now accept this position.

"But there was one difference between us: I don't believe in the language of arms, and I would use arms only for legitimate defense. Bashir, as a militia leader, was ready to use arms but, as president, he would have tried to bring the Lebanese together. There are extremists, of course, in the Lebanese Forces who want the Christians to set up their own state. I find them not evil but foolish. They may call me 'Mohammed' for my views on reconciling with the Arabs but as I see it, wanting to go it alone is like believing in Santa Claus."

Gemayel was among those—and they included both Muslim and Christian Lebanese—who insisted that the blame for the civil war should be laid on outsiders. It is true that the prospect of settling the civil war was enormously complicated by the interests established in Lebanon by Syria, Israel and Iran. But that was after the fighting started. Gemayel, like many Lebanese, defended the dubious thesis that the differences between the factions could have been resolved, had Lebanon only been left alone.

"The Lebanese were marionettes," he stated, "manipulated by exterior powers. Arafat started the war. His objective, in alliance with the Druze leadership, was to use Lebanon as a weapon against Israel. My brother Bashir, frustrated at being unable to control the Palestinians, turned to Israel, which was ready to provide him with arms. Then Syria, and later Iran, began to feed the war. Today no militia could last for more than a few days without arms and munitions from outside.

"Once the state is restored, the militias will have no more access to money, and they'll have to bow to lawfulness. We will have to reform the government, to have more decentralization, which is necessary for a diverse society, but we must hold Lebanon together. As for 'deconfessionalization,' we can set it as a goal. In fact, it was always looked upon by the Lebanese as temporary. But we can't eliminate it in our texts until we have eliminated it in our mores, in our ways of thinking. Political reform yes, but not 'deconfessionalization,' at least not yet. I don't want to underestimate our responsibility as Lebanese for all that has happened to us, but I don't want to overstate it either. If it were not for the conspiracy against us, Lebanon would never have had these problems. And that conspiracy comes from abroad."

I WAS INDEBTED TO the Lebanese Forces for providing me with the means to leave Lebanon by a different route from the one by which I arrived. As part of its social-welfare work, it ran a ferry service from Beirut to the Israeli security zone in the south, where many Christians still lived. Inside the Karantina at four o'clock one morning, I embraced my friend Elie and his men, and mounted the gangplank to go aboard. Looking barely seaworthy, the boat—a caricature out of a Conrad novel—was named *Gray Wing*. Eighty feet in length, it carried some one hundred fifty passengers, splayed out all over the deck, among cardboard suitcases, plastic sacks and handbags which said, "Adidas" and "World Cup, Spain, 1985." The passengers ranged from the very old to couples carrying babies to students headed home for the summer.

Gray Wing hauled anchor under twinkling stars, took a wide swing seaward to avoid the guns of West Beirut, then turned south, out of sight of land. Security, the friendly young man at the wheel told me, determined both the hour of departure and the course we followed. The sea was calm and a cool breeze blew, for both of which I was grateful as the hours passed and the sun rose higher. The passengers, without food or accessible toilets, were amiable but increasingly restless. After some six hours at sea, an Israeli patrol boat, its guns trained menacingly, approached and circled within about fifty feet, then shadowed us for a half hour more. At eleven o'clock, the *Gray Wing* finally tied up at Nakoura, and under the watchful eye of Israeli soldiers, its exhausted passengers disembarked.

Nakoura is a Lebanese fishing village three or four miles north of the Israeli border crossing of Rosh Hanikra. A few years earlier, the Israelis laid a huge concrete slab perpendicular to the beach, and thereby made the village into a commercial port. A good-sized container ship was tied up at the pier as we pulled in and, after we landed, neither the Israelis nor the Lebanese merchants who milled about the dock were reluctant to talk about it. The ship was one of several, they said, which shuttled regularly, by arrangement between the Lebanese Forces and Israel, from Nakoura to East Beirut, carrying a variety of Israeli products, chiefly food. The morning of my arrival, Israeli farm trucks sat on the dock, while their cargo of watermelons was transferred to large metal containers, which were then lifted aboard the ship by cranes. A merchant told me that from East Beirut, where the Lebanese Forces collect port taxes, the food is distributed throughout Lebanon. Much of it, he said, also finds its way surreptitiously into Syria, and from there it may go as far as the Gulf.

As I left the port area, my passport was checked by an official from the South Lebanese Army, the Israeli-supported militia that patrols the security zone. From there I hitched a ride to the Israeli border post, crossed on foot and found a taxi that took me to Jerusalem.

VII SINCE AMIN

ABOUT A YEAR after I left Lebanon, President Amin Gemayel's term of office expired. The Lebanese constitution provided that a successor must be elected by a two-thirds vote of the parliament, and that a president cannot succeed himself. In practice, however, Syria, not the parliament, was the central player in the selection, while Israel reserved a right of veto. And, after four years of absence, the Americans reentered the game, serving as intermediaries in an effort to defuse tensions between the contending parties.

The Americans involved were Richard Murphy, assistant secretary of state for the Middle East, and April Glaspie, then director of the State Department's bureau of Syrian and Lebanese affairs. They shuttled between Beirut and Damascus, carrying proposals not just for the choice of president but for reforms in the distribution of power between Christians and Muslims. None of the parties sought to overturn the tradition, written into the National Pact, of having a Maronite in the presidency. All acknowledged, furthermore, that reforms were necessary. But the Muslims, seek-

ing to curb the president's powers, wanted agreement on the reforms before the election; the Christians wanted the election before the reforms.
As for the Syrians, they remained attached to the Tripartite Agreement,
including the principle of deconfessionalism, even though none of the
Lebanese were interested in it.

Throughout the first half of 1988, the talks had made no progress,
though all sides—sensitive to preserving the facade of the Lebanese state—
avowed a commitment to a constitutional succession. In late July, as a
cease-fire to the Iran-Iraq war was about to take effect, Glaspie went off
to her new post as ambassador to Baghdad, leaving Murphy alone. The
Syrians about that time suddenly realized that the end of the Gulf war
was likely to bring Iraqi intervention in Lebanon. Their fear apparently
persuaded them to insist on having a president they could fully trust, and
they named as their candidate Suleiman Franjieh, the seventy-eight-year-
old patriarch of north Lebanon, the most pro-Syrian of all the Maronite
leaders. The Franjieh family, however, had a long-standing blood feud
with the Gemayels, and the old man hardly made his candidacy more
palatable by announcing that, if elected, he would invite Syria to occupy
Lebanon's Christian enclave.

Franjieh was more extreme than most Christians could take and, notwithstanding Syrian threats, they united bravely to defeat him in a parliamentary vote. Washington, endearing itself to neither side, bumbled about
in a last-minute effort to find a compromise candidate but failed to salvage
the election. On September 22, Gemayel's term expired, with no successor
chosen.

Under Lebanese law, Gemayel was then required, as his last official act,
to select a prime minister to head a caretaker government, and he chose
General Michel Aoun, the Maronite commander of the army. Hoss protested that the choice violated the National Pact, which held that only a
Sunni could be prime minister. Gemayel replied that since there would be
no president, the old rule did not apply. But Hoss refused to resign and,
for the first time, Lebanon ended up with two governments, one in West
Beirut, the other in the Baabda palace.

I had met Aoun during my visit in Lebanon. A career soldier, he was
not a member of one of Lebanon's grand families. I remembered him as a
stocky man with a substantial belly, unimpressive in his camouflage fatigues, and without a hint of fanaticism. My notes of our conversation
revealed a sympathetic understanding of the pressures imposed by Damascus on the Gemayel government. "We have to have security arrangements
that satisfy Syria," he said, pointing to the flaw in the May 17 Agreement
with Israel. Yet, once in office, Aoun set out to extend the power of his
regime to all of Lebanon, an objective that was, ironically, applauded by

some Muslims as well as many Christians, but which predictably ran into a Syrian roadblock.

In February 1989, Aoun, with Iraqi support, embarked audaciously—foolishly, many said—on a "war of liberation" against the Syrians and the Muslim militias. A thousand more Lebanese died in the fighting. This was the fighting that caused Damascenes so much consternation during the summer that I spent in Syria. So destructive was it that the war spurred the Arab states to action, and in September they succeeded in brokering a cease-fire between the two sides. The Arab League then convened a meeting of the Lebanese parliament in Taif, a resort town in Saudi Arabia, for the purpose of its drafting an accord for a lasting peace.

To widespread surprise, the Lebanese actually hammered out an agreement at Taif, and it won Syria's approval. It was far from deconfessionalism, which Damascus had promoted, but it equalized Christian and Muslim representation in the parliament, and shifted some power from the Maronite presidency to the Sunni prime minister. It resembled the Tripartite Agreement, however, in providing for "distinctive relations" between Syria and Lebanon, to be defined in subsequent negotiations, which Damascus would obviously dominate. Though it required a pullback of the Syrian army to the Beqa'a Valley within two years, it otherwise legalized Syrian military presence in Lebanon. In effect, the document formalized Lebanon's status as a Syrian satellite, but to most Lebanese this seemed, after a decade and a half of civil war, to be no more than inevitable.

Aoun, however, rejected the agreement, and issued a decree—which the deputies ignored—dissolving the parliament. On November 5, the parliament, with Syria's approval, elected René Mouawad, a Maronite, as president. Though the election restored a semblance of constitutional legality, Aoun refused to recognize it. Seventeen days later, Mouawad was assassinated; like most killings in Lebanon, it was only perfunctorily investigated and never solved. Elias Hrawi, another Maronite, was elected in Mouawad's place. Again Aoun refused to resign, setting the stage for still another round of strife, with the Christians divided between Aoun and Hrawi, rival claimants to Lebanon's leadership.

In standing up to the Syrians, Aoun found a constituency—not limited, it should be noted, to Christians—but it was obvious from the start that he was not strong enough to prevail. The Syrians could have crushed him sooner, but delayed acting out of uncertainty at how the Israelis would respond. The procrastination came to an end late in 1989, when Samir Geagea brought the Lebanese Forces to the support of Hrawi and the Taif Agreement, tipping the scales. Aoun then launched a war against the Lebanese Forces, which lasted four months and killed still another thousand Lebanese. His aggressiveness cost Aoun the support of the international community, including Washington, and helped set the stage for Syria's participation at America's side in the war over Kuwait. On October 13, Syria launched a military assault against Aoun, which raised no protests in the West. The Christian enclave fell quickly, though Aoun escaped and took refuge in the French embassy. He remained there for nearly a year, until Syria finally permitted him to leave for permanent asylum in France.

Since Aoun's fall, Syria has continued to strengthen its hegemony in Lebanon. With Syria's backing, the Lebanese government reclaimed control of most of the territory that had been held by the independent militias. Only Hezbollah and the Palestinians, insisting on the right to contest Israel's occupation of the security zone, remained armed; the other militias, including the Lebanese Forces, gave up their weapons to the state. But Syria controlled the state, and not even the Western powers protested its hegemony. The United States was rewarded when the remaining Western hostages were released, with Syria's intermediation. And shortly afterward, Syria delighted Washington by participating first in the war to liberate Kuwait, then in the Middle East peace talks that convened in Madrid. Syria still had not withdrawn its forces to the Beqa'a Valley, as promised in the Taif Agreement. Lebanon nonetheless signed a "Treaty of Brotherhood, Cooperation and Coordination" in May 1991, which set up a formal structure by which it would answer to Syria in its political, military, economic and internal security policies. The long era of Christian domination of Lebanon was over. Lebanon was now, by treaty, a Syrian client, the status Damascus had sought since the Tripartite Agreement in 1985—and had certainly dreamed of since the mandate of the French.

CHAPTER SIX

THE PALESTINIANS

I THE MOUNTAIN VILLAGE

AN ISRAELI SOLDIER, a machine gun slung over his shoulder, waved my rental car, displaying a yellow license plate, through the military checkpoint on the Nablus Road. My guide, Nasser, a twenty-eight-year-old Palestinian, was at the wheel. It was a warm, clear day in the spring of 1990. As we entered Jerusalem's Arab suburbs, heading north through the West Bank toward Ramallah, Nasser pulled a black and white checkered *kuffiyeh* from underneath the seat and placed it on the dashboard.

Nasser and I had discussed this routine the night before, when we were planning the trip. The *intifada*—the uprising of Palestinians in the West Bank and the Gaza Strip—had created a dilemma for us. If I rented a car with the blue plates of the West Bank, the Israeli soldier, assuming we were Palestinians, would stop us to examine our identity papers, search the trunk for guns or leaflets and ask a lot of questions. Discovering that I was a journalist, he might even say the territories were closed to outsiders—often they were, in times of disorder—and force us to turn back. Renting a car with yellow Israeli plates would give us the look of Jewish settlers on our way home from an innocent shopping trip to Jerusalem. Displaying yellow plates, on the other hand, could make us a target of the *shebab*, the young Palestinian rebels whose stones, flung by hand or by sling, exposed Jewish settlers in the territories to injury, or worse, every day. Finally, we chose a compromise, deciding to go Israeli, while bringing along the *kuffiyeh* to signal to the *shebab* that, whatever the color of the plates, we were not enemies in the ongoing conflict over Palestine.

The *intifada* had been raging for several years when Nasser and I set out on our excursion. The uprising began in early December 1987, after an Israeli was stabbed in the Gaza Strip. Within the context of twenty years of military occupation, a stabbing was not an unusual event; throughout the West Bank and the Gaza Strip, territories occupied in the June war of 1967, violence between Israelis and Palestinians was commonplace. But this stabbing did not reduce itself to a simple statistic confirming the horrid relations between adversary peoples. It proved to be the spark that lit the powder keg. When an Israeli truck the next day slammed into two cars carrying Arab workers, killing four and injuring seventeen, rumors raced through the Gaza Strip that the driver was a relative of the stabbing victim, intent on revenge. The Israeli police then made the mistake of dismissing the driver with a traffic citation, inflaming the Palestinian sense of injustice. Later that day, young Palestinians in the Jabaliya refugee camp went on a rampage of protest, which rumbled irresistibly across the Gaza Strip and, from there, into the West Bank.

Confident of the efficacy of harsh measures, the Israeli army reacted with the insensitivity that generally characterizes military occupation: it sent heavily armed soldiers to put down the disorders. But this time, the harsh measures did not restore its authority, and as steadily harsher measures were applied, the more the protests spread. Young women joined young men in the ranks and, in unprecedented numbers, Palestinians of every age seemed prepared, for the first time, to defy the Israelis, risking serious injury, even death. Within a few days it became apparent that the clashes were not a passing phenomenon. Few observers asked why they had occurred. The answer seemed obvious. Relations between the soldiers and Palestinian civilians had been antagonistic since the Israeli army arrived, and in recent years the occupation had grown more oppressive. The pertinent question was: why had the blowup occurred at that moment?

Part of the explanation surely lay in the exultant feelings of Palestinian teenagers in the territories over the feat of a guerrilla who some weeks earlier flew from Lebanon into Israel in a motorized hang glider and killed six Israeli soldiers on an army base in the Galilee. The message of this exploit, in which the guerrilla also died, was that the Israelis were not invulnerable to Palestinians who were willing to stand up to them.

But a longer view would take into account the observation among Palestinians that they were steadily being abandoned by outsiders—the Western powers, the Soviet Union, even their Arab brothers—whom they had hoped would accomplish their liberation. No doubt Palestinians should have learned by this time that the outside world would not assume the burden of their cause. They had been confronted with this truth repeatedly over the course of the twentieth century, but they had done little about it. Young Palestinians over the years had shown scant taste for combat. Only a handful were willing to accept the sacrifices that national liberation required. Unlike the Algerians, for example, the Palestinians never forged a mass movement of resistance. Much as they loved the land, they had never before seemed willing to die for it.

In 1982, when Israeli forces invaded Lebanon to crush what little military power the PLO had managed to muster, the Palestinians were reminded of how alone they were. Not a single Arab state stepped forth to help, while the outside world turned its back. By 1985, the Israelis had withdrawn from all but a sliver of Lebanon, but it was largely by dint of the harassment of Israel's soldiers by Lebanese guerrillas, not by the intervention of the Palestinians, much less some external power.

The Americans, in fact, not only made no protest against the Israeli invasion but had made clear over the years their indifference to the Palestinians' right to self-determination. In 1981, Saudi Arabia's King Fahd proposed an eight-point peace plan which included recognition of Israel in return for its withdrawal from the occupied territories, but neither Washington nor Jerusalem disclosed any sign of interest in it. In the mid-1980s, a squabble between the PLO's Yasir Arafat and Jordan's King Hussein put an end to Palestinian hopes of an international peace conference, in which even Israel had shown some interest. Then, in the fall of 1987, the Arab heads of state, meeting in Amman, publicly placed the settlement of Palestinian claims against Israel behind a settlement of the Iraq-Iran war in their list of priorities. Somehow, the message the Palestinians were getting was that they had to create the opportunity themselves if they were ever to be free.

Israeli officials, proceeding on their usual assumptions, initially blamed the PLO for the spreading disturbances in the occupied territories. But, to everyone's surprise, the PLO claimed none of the credit. On the contrary, the evidence indicated that it knew no more about the uprising than what it learned over Israeli radio. It took several weeks of relentless disorders for the Israelis to admit that they faced a *popular* movement which was out of control. New to Arab-Israeli relations, the movement took the name *intifada*—meaning "shaking off"—which the world quickly accepted.

What threw the Israelis off stride was not only the commitment of the Palestinians but the tactics they adopted, more by happenstance, it seems, than by any prearranged design. These tactics fell loosely under the rubric of nonviolent protest, a doctrine that had recently been introduced by Palestinians familiar with the civil rights and anti–Vietnam war movements in the United States. By the standards of Gandhi and Martin Luther King, the *intifada* was never nonviolent. Its tactics were based on the ancient Arab tradition of protest by stone-throwing which, when transposed to the streets of the West Bank and Gaza, took a form that should more accurately be called "nonlethal." These tactics neutralized the Israeli army's heavy weapons, forcing it to commit manpower which it could not afford. Even without heavy weapons, however, the "passive resistance" of the *intifada*, designed for television cameras, forced Israel into responses whose disproportionate nature chilled many of its friends and alienated much of international public opinion.

Deciding they could not permit the *shebab* to set the terms of the battle completely, the Israelis routinely used gunfire—if not massive force—against the demonstrators. In five years, while a few dozen Israelis died, the Palestinians suffered upwards of a thousand dead. Many of the fatalities were at the hands of other Palestinians, sometimes in a settling of private scores, often as a punishment for alleged "collaboration" with the enemy. But most of the victims fell before Israeli bullets. Many of them were children, or bystanders to the conflict.

In addition to the casualties in the field, the Israelis inflicted other heavy costs. Tens of thousands of young men were imprisoned without trial. Income in the territories fell by more than a quarter. Unemployment surpassed a third of Palestinian breadwinners. Yet, never had the Palestinians shown themselves so prepared to endure whatever personal pain and hardship the occupiers could inflict. A young Palestinian may have overstated in telling me during the heyday of the *intifada*, that "Suffering is not a limiting factor any longer," but he was not far afield. At times, there would be a lull, when the army would conclude that its tactics were working, and an Israeli general would declare the uprising crushed. But then the *intifada* would break out again, often with amended tactics, requiring further Israeli adaptation.

The young leaders of the uprising, calling themselves the Unified Command and communicating with one another secretly, understood that Israel's soldiers could not be everywhere at once, and kept them constantly dashing about suppressing demonstrations throughout the length of the territories. For a time, for example, the *shebab* frustrated the soldiers by declaring "free villages" in the rural sectors, raising the green, red, white and black Palestinian flag on the public square. Army units, on arriving, would arrest a few youths, only to have the village declared "free" again when they left. Every refugee camp, town and village in the West Bank and the Gaza Strip was caught up in the dynamism of the revolt.

The Palestinians who believed that the *intifada* would in itself bring liberation deluded themselves, however. The uprising was never a military threat to Israel. It was a political exercise, forcing Israel to recalculate whether the benefits of the occupation justified the costs. It gave Israelis new respect for the courage and convictions of Palestinians. It also caused a deep rift within Israeli society over the moral issues raised by the oppression of another people. Finally, it kept the Palestinian cause on the global agenda, in a far more sympathetic manner than the assassinations, the hijackings and the other outrages that terrorist bands had perpetrated in the past. The *intifada* gave the Palestinians a new image.

On the morning that Nasser and I crossed the checkpoint on Nablus Road, we were headed for Kafr Ain, a mountain village north of Ramallah.

Its name comes from the Canaanites and, in Arabic, translates as "Village of Spring Water." To get there, we traversed El-Bireh, the town where Nasser was born. His father was its mayor when, in 1973, the Israelis deported him for his nationalist leadership. From 1967 until 1992, the Israelis deported sixteen hundred Palestinians, in what was generally recognized as a violation of international law. Nasser told me he had seen his father only twice since he was put on a bus and dumped at the Jordanian border. (Abdel-Jawad Saleh Atta, Nasser's father, was returned to the West Bank in an Israeli-Palestinian deal during the peace talks in 1993.) Passing through El-Bireh, I recalled a military observation post on the roof of a stone house at a curve in the road; it looked down on a refugee camp called Jalazone, where five thousand Palestinians lived. I had first noticed it in the 1970s. Seeing it again reminded me that, *intifada* or not, the occupation hovered relentlessly over the lives of Palestinians.

North of El-Bireh, we followed a new, multilane highway, and as we drove I was struck by the number of Israeli settlements built since my previous visit, two years earlier. Their crisp, modern design distinguished them from the nearby Arab villages, identified by soaring, sculptured, ancient minarets. The new highway was constructed for the Israeli settlers, to permit them to avoid Arab villages and towns where they were routinely stymied by roadblocks or pelted with stones. Its exits led directly to the Jewish settlements, bypassing Arab life.

Turning west from the highway, we passed through groves of thick, gnarled olive trees that the Arabs call *rumani*, a word suggesting that they could be traced back to Roman times. Red and purple wildflowers covered the shoulders. The flanks of the mountains, which would grow parched and brown in a month or two, had been turned a sparkling green by the recent spring rains, and from the distance, the blossoms of almond trees looked like puffs of white smoke. As we wound upward through the mountains, I took note across the valleys of the concentric rings of carefully tended stone terraces, most of them dedicated to olive culture, the West Bank's economic backbone even in Roman times.

By the time we entered Kafr Ain (population: about one thousand) the pavement had given way to a rutted dirt road. Nearly all the buildings on its single street—the old ones of neatly trimmed stone, the newer ones of ugly cement block—were defaced by spray-painted graffiti, which Nasser translated for me into pro-PLO and pro-*intifada* slogans. Small Palestinian flags hung from utility poles. Clusters of young men sat around in front of houses, listening on their transistor radios to the groan of Arab music. Nasser stopped the car so I could examine a large, unusual building, domed in the Ottoman style. A half-dozen donkeys grazed at its door. Its dimensions suggested that Kafr Ain was once a place of some grandeur; its crumbling facade indicated that the time was long past. Curious, we asked an old woman, dressed in a traditional embroidered gown, carrying a pot of vegetables on her head, what it was. She shrugged, as if to say, "What a silly question!" Except for Koranic history, Arabs, in my experience, do not have the fascination that most Westerners have for history, not even their own. The most the woman allowed was that she had lived her whole life in Kafr Ain, and the building was there long before she was born.

Khader el-Alem, whom I had come to see in Kafr Ain, was absent when we arrived. He had been delayed by an errand in a neighboring village, we were told, and to pass the time I chatted with his eldest son, Hazem, who was twenty-two, and son-in-law, Wasfi Kharma, who was a decade older. Both had served time in Israeli detention camps for rebellious activity and admitted that they had given up, at least for the present, any hope of productive careers. Both worked occasionally in the olive groves, and the rest of the time were idle. They said that before 1967, the young men of Kafr Ain typically migrated to Jordan, the Gulf and even to the United States. Many of them were now prospering, Wasfi said. But they themselves would stay, to help safeguard the land against absorption by Israel.

"The Israelis want us to leave," he said, "to make it easier for them to confiscate our property. But as long as we keep our fields in cultivation, we make it hard for them to establish a legal claim." Neither denied that their lives were abnormal and generally grim but, said Wasfi, who had a university degree, "for now, we must put our dreams on the back burner." Weeks went by, he said, when all they did was sit around, smoking and grumbling on the front stoop of the house.

Khader el-Alem (known to all as Abu Hazem) drove up a few minutes later in a noisy old car and apologized for his tardiness. He began telling me about the village by claiming that he could trace his family back eight generations there. Sixty-two years old, he was Kafr Ain's unofficial mayor—unofficial, in that he was not recognized by the military administration. Throughout its history, he said, Kafr Ain had been a center of olive cultivation. He himself owned olive trees and managed the village's marketing cooperative. He was also a lifelong nationalist, he said, and had passed on his beliefs to his three sons. A round man with missing teeth, Abu Hazem wore a shabby blue suit and sunglasses. His wife, a woman equally shapeless, looking ageless and wearing a traditional scarlet gown and a black headscarf, silently served tea.

Until the automobile came into use on the West Bank, Abu Hazem said, Kafr Ain was an important stop for travelers journeying on foot or by donkey between the cities of Nablus and Ramallah. The building which aroused my curiosity, he said, was erected near the end of the Ottoman period and served as a *diwan*, where travelers would not only eat and sleep but carry on their business, most notably the purchase of olive oil. In those days, he said, Kafr Ain was twice its current size, and a major commercial center. Even now, it was prosperous, he said, though most commerce had shifted to the cities. More important than the automobile in changing the life of the village, however, was the fall of the Ottomans in 1918, which subjected the region successively to British, Jordanian and Israeli rule and made it, in the process, the victim of wars and political disarray.

"Up here in the mountains," said Abu Hazem, "we didn't feel the presence of Jews in the early days. Once I saw them on the coast when my father sent me down to Haifa on some business, but in our village we considered the British our enemy. I was very young when I joined the anti-British resistance, and in 1944 I was arrested and sent to prison in Jerusalem. The experience opened my eyes. Many Palestinians were there, for participating in the wars against the Zionists in the 1930s. And many Jews were there for fighting the British in the underground. Though we were segregated from one another in the prison, we met and could talk during the exercise hours, and I came to know many of the Zionist leaders. We didn't hate each other. We even had a common interest in opposing Britain, though we recognized even then that we had conflicting aims. I was released in November 1947, while the United Nations was debating the resolution to partition Palestine. The struggle between Arabs and Jews was just coming to a climax.

"I belonged then to a Marxist group that supported the UN partition resolution," he said. "I know that seems strange, but Moscow also supported a Jewish state, believing it would undermine the British empire, which it considered still powerful. Our group was not bound by Moscow, but we knew the Palestinian side was weak and we reasoned that if we rejected partition, we would lose everything. Our position was realistic then, and it still is. We were suspicious of the Arab governments during the fighting in 1948. We knew they had their own goals, not ours, in mind. Jordan's annexation of the West Bank proved we were right, and after that, Jordan treated the Palestinians like second-class citizens. That's why so many of our people left to work in the Gulf. In 1957, I was sent to jail with hundreds of others for opposing the Jordanian occupation. We were beaten and tortured. I was kept in handcuffs and legcuffs for eight months. In all, I spent eight years in Jordanian prisons, and later I was confined under town arrest. Then, in 1967, the Israelis arrived."

True to his rebellious nature, Abu Hazem said, he was imprisoned by the Israelis four times, for periods ranging from weeks to months, between 1971 and 1988. The process in each case was "administrative," which meant incarceration without charges or trial. He was beaten each time, he said, and still suffered from some of the bruises. His last jailing, just two years before, was the product of a screaming argument with an officer of the Shin Beit, the Israeli security police, he said, over the abuse of several young political activists from the village. In retrospect, Abu Hazem said, he was ashamed, at his age, of having lost his temper.

Israeli army units, Abu Hazem said, had raided Kafr Ain forty-three times since the start of the *intifada,* and still visited every month or so, by day and by night. The villagers used to be forewarned by engine noises or headlights as the soldiers approached across the valley, allowing the young men time to run into the fields and hide among the olive trees. Later, airborne units swooped down from behind the mountain in helicopters, leaving no time to escape, so many of the *shebab* slept at night in the fields. After arriving, he said, the soldiers tore down nationalist symbols, forced whatever young men they found to paint over the graffiti, and barged into homes in search of guns or leaflets. Sometimes they beat up a few villagers before leaving, and they almost always arrested some young men, claiming—rightly or not—that they were *shebab.* "It used to be," Abu Hazem said, "when the soldiers came to the village they were looking for me. Now, they had to look for everyone." Every male in Kafr Ain, he said, had been jailed at least three times.

"The big difference between the Israeli and Jordanian occupations," he continued, "is not the physical cruelty. It is that Israel wants to change the identity of the land. Israel is trying to destroy our sense of nationhood and substitute its own, within a territory that we have inhabited for more than a thousand years. The Jordanians did not tamper with our landholding. We sensed, with Jordan, that we would ultimately succeed in gaining control here, and that we needed only to be patient. Under the Israelis, half the population of Kafr Ain has fled, not because they're so anxious to earn money in Jordan or the Gulf, but out of fear, and a recognition that they have no future in this land. We believe that one day our men and women will choose to return, but unless we succeed quickly against the Israelis, there will be nothing to return to."

II   THE TRAGEDY UNFOLDS

THE PALESTINIAN TRAGEDY, like so much that has happened in the Middle East, had its roots in the disintegration of the Ottoman empire. Under the Ottomans, Palestine had lost its identity and even its name; it was known among Arabs as South Syria. But Palestinian Arab society nonetheless possessed its own distinctive character within Arab culture, shaped as it had been not by the desert and nomadic life but by bustling towns and flourishing agriculture, by exposure to the West, and by the eminence imparted to it by the holy city of Jerusalem. At the time of the Arab Revolt, its population was probably seven hundred thousand—nine-tenths Muslim, one-tenth Christian—and Zionist immigration, though still a trickle, was already bringing changes in agriculture and commerce. Then, in November 1917, the old world came apart. The Turkish army fled before the advancing British, whose Balfour Declaration had recently pledged Palestine as a homeland for the Jews. Within a year, the Ottoman empire had vanished, and the struggle against both the British and the Zionists had begun. No longer Ottomans, the Palestinians started to shape an Arab identity, while the Jews arrived in increasing numbers to stake a claim to their patrimony.

At first, most Palestinians turned instinctively for deliverance to the Arab government that the Hashemite prince Faisal had established in Damascus. Faisal had raised the flag of the Arab Revolt in the name of pan-Arabism; Arab visionaries spoke of a single state from the Atlantic to the Persian Gulf. To Palestinians, pan-Arabism seemed prospectively a shield against the intruders. The British tried to persuade Faisal that pan-Arabism was fantasy, that the Arab future lay in nation-states on the Western model. But even as Faisal's hold was weakening, young Palestinians, dazzled by the pan-Arab vision, flocked to Damascus to assist in the founding of a new regime.

Soon, however, the Palestinians found themselves squeezed between British and French ambitions in the Middle East. Britain, Faisal's only hope of survival against the French, was also the chief sponsor of Zionism. To gain British favor, Faisal negotiated a deal with the Zionist leader Chaim Weizmann, waiving Arab objections to Jewish immigration to Palestine. The Palestinians were stunned. The British applauded Faisal's move, but as a party to the Sykes-Picot Agreement they could not accept Faisal's condition: the revocation of France's claim to Syria. Britain did nothing to stop the French from taking Damascus in 1920. With Syria under France, Palestine embarked on its own historical course under the rule of Britain, a Christian power whose first obligation was, paradoxically, to the Jews. Isolated, the Palestinians were left to nurse a sense of betrayal, against both the West and their brother Arabs.

Alone, the Palestinians were never able to put up an effective fight against either the British or the Zionists. The Jews had their own conflict with Britain, which was anxious to preserve its privileged position in Palestine and at times came close to repudiating its Zionist pledge. But the Jews worked relentlessly to build their strength, and in the three-way contest for power the Palestinians held the weakest hand. Although all Palestinians opposed Zionism, their sense of allegiance did not extend much beyond their individual families and villages. Two-thirds were *fellahin,* working the land. Most were illiterate, suspicious of townspeople and resentful of the landowners among their own people. The landowning families, faced with the loss to outsiders of power and status, turned on one another, forswearing the obligations of leadership. The Muslim majority, humiliated at being colonized by Christians, grew wary of its own Christian minority. Until the end, the Palestinians conducted their affairs as clusters of feuding sovereignties. Palestinian nationhood was an alien notion, and they never rallied to defend it.

Unlike the Zionists, the Palestinians created no political institutions to deal with, much less supersede, the mandatory authority. The British refused to recognize any body that did not accept the mandate's "principles," which included the Balfour Declaration; obviously, this was a step the Palestinians could not take. So they were trapped and, unable to extricate themselves, were denied the practical benefits of access to power, as well as preparation for self-rule. By the 1930s, Palestine alone among the Arab lands did not have even a nominal legislative body. While Zionist leaders presided over a small but steady immigration, the relentless purchase of land and the recruitment and training of a secret army, the Palestinians had no strategy but to resort to periodic violence, itself random and undirected.

During a general strike that began in 1936, the Palestinians made their only real try at political organization. Hitler's rise to power in Germany had doubled the size of the Jewish population in Palestine, to about three hundred seventy-five thousand. In an effort to coordinate protests, the major Palestinian families agreed to form the Arab Higher Committee, and chose as its president the Mufti of Jerusalem, Hajj Amin al-Husseini. Member of an eminent clan, Husseini brought to the struggle a religious zealotry that was uncharacteristic of Palestinian society.

The general strike mobilized thousands, from all sectors of Arab society, and after a year the British agreed, in return for a truce, to name a body of inquiry—the so-called Peel Commission—to go to Palestine to reexamine the conflict. Incomprehensibly, the Higher Committee boycotted the commission's deliberations, giving the Zionists an uncontested forum. The outcome was a recommendation for the partition of Palestine into separate Jewish and Arab states, which Britain endorsed, signaling its willingness to abandon the mandate and leave Palestine. Neither the Arabs nor the Jews were satisfied with this compromise, but common sense dictated that any party rejecting it be powerful enough to enforce its own will. Reluctantly, the Jews accepted the proposal; the Arabs under Husseini vetoed it outright.

The Higher Committee's decision led to outright war in Palestine, but a war was also approaching in Europe. Britain, deeply involved in the Arab world and bowing to its own strategic interests, set the partition plan aside in a celebrated White Paper, and imposed severe limits on Jewish immigration. The Zionists responded by redoubling their military preparations and pleading for support from Jews overseas. The Higher Committee leading them nowhere, in contrast, fomented anti-Jewish riots in Baghdad, Cairo and Damascus. To stop the Higher Committee, Britain arrested its leadership, but the mufti escaped and made his way to Europe, where he proclaimed his support of Nazi Germany. The Higher Committee survived into the postwar era, by which time Britain had reached a decision to quit Palestine, come what may. As for Husseini, he was now too tainted to help the Palestinians in the postwar diplomacy over Britain's departure, and too weak to lead them in what had become an inevitable war against the Jews.

On November 29, 1947, the United Nations General Assembly voted to partition Palestine between Arab and Jewish states. The British, anxious to wash their hands of the dilemma, refused to take responsibility for implementing the resolution, and as they withdrew, Zionist bodies moved in to fill the administrative gap, while Palestinians watched with dismay. The Jews systematically mobilized their forces, but the Palestinians brought to bear only a fraction of their manpower. In early 1948, several thousand volunteers from the Arab states, the so-called Arab Liberation Army, arrived to complement the Palestinian irregulars. The British, while imposing a general arms embargo, left the bulk of their weapons to the Arabs.

In the end, however, the assistance made little difference. Arms superiority persuaded the Arabs that they could and would crush the enemy, but their internal squabbling, low morale and poor leadership left them totally outclassed. In the early spring of 1948, the Jews went on the offensive and won a series of important battles. Military defeat resulted in the Palestinians' social disintegration. In the course of the fighting, ordinary citizens, accompanied by their mayors, policemen and *mukhtars*—the traditional village leaders—fled from their towns and villages. Panic was widespread. So was hunger, following the breakdown of services. Arab commanders did nothing to stop the flight and may even have encouraged it. But recent scholarship, chiefly Israeli, has also made clear that the Jewish forces had orders to scatter the Palestinians, seeing in the chaos of battle an opportunity to drive the local population from the land. The Palestinian flight was sudden, and it is unlikely that many of the refugees regarded it as permanent. But none returned, and to this day their homelessness hobbles efforts to find a resolution to the Arab-Israeli conflict.

The war, however, was not yet over. The Jewish victories of early 1948 roused the nearby Arab states and, after the last of the British withdrew in May, they rushed to Palestine. For the most part, their motives were less than pure. Their objective was less to help the Palestinians than to salvage for themselves what they could from the debacle. The most inter-ested party was Jordan's King Abdullah, older brother of King Faisal, who made no secret of his loathing for Hajj Amin, or of his intention to annex what he could of Arab Palestine. Syria had designs on territory in the north. Lebanon, Iraq, Egypt and Saudi Arabia all sent troops, chiefly to maintain a front of Arab solidarity. None supported the Palestinian state proposed in the UN partition resolution. By the end of 1948, Israel had defeated them all.

When the cease-fire became final, the holdings of the Arabs in Palestine had been reduced to the West Bank, occupied by Jordan's army, and the Gaza Strip, occupied by Egypt's. The Jews had enlarged their territory by 20 percent, and though they were strong enough to drive out the remaining Arab forces, the new Israeli government decided against it, largely to avoid British wrath. By now, roughly 650,000 Palestinians had fled their homes—240,000 to the West Bank, 60,000 to Jordan's East Bank, nearly 100,000 to Lebanon, 70,000 to Syria. In addition, some 180,000 had crossed the Egyptian lines and settled in Gaza. Life for the refugees was everywhere horrid, but nowhere was it worse than in Gaza. "Refused employment and resettlement by Israelis and Egyptians alike for the next generation," the Zionist historian Howard Sachar wrote of the Gaza refugees, "they were destined to vegetate in a confinement even more tragic than that endured by the Jewish displaced persons in Europe between 1945 and 1948."

III   GAZA

IT IS A DRIVE of about an hour and a half from the mountains of the West Bank—across Israel's rolling green countryside—to the bleak, seaside flats of the Gaza Strip. A half century ago, there was no West Bank, there was no Gaza Strip; both were part of the undivided land of Palestine. But the Balfour Declaration promised a Jewish homeland, and within scarcely more than a generation the Jews had established a state in the heartland of Palestine. All that remained of the claim of the Palestinians were these two districts—some 22 percent of the land, on the periphery.

Arabs today—having lost both the West Bank and the Gaza Strip in 1967—have for some years spoken of uniting the two into a Palestinian state. The vision is more modest than the one they were offered and rejected in 1948. The prospect of a West Bank–Gaza state is obviously complicated by the contrasting topography and geographical separation of the two districts. The West Bank, furthermore, is underpopulated, rela-tively prosperous and economically and psychologically oriented toward the Arab hinterland to the east. Gaza, besides being overpopulated and impoverished, looks toward the Mediterranean and is psychologically bound to Egypt, which ruled it between 1948 and 1967. It is not easy for Palestinians to dream of making a nation of these two disparate tracts; still, given the options, many Palestinians dream of little else.

According to records kept by the Israelis, about three hundred and fifty Arab towns and villages in what is now Israel were depopulated during and immediately after the war of 1948. Most of them were systematically destroyed after the residents fled. As a matter of routine, the Israelis leveled every building in these communities. It seems from the evidence that the practice of deliberate destruction was initially adopted to deny shelter to Arab soldiers wandering in the rear areas. Later, the practice became a convenient way to wipe out all traces of Arab habitation, making return impossible.

The population of the Gaza Strip, about 80,000 at the time of Israel's independence, has since grown to at least 700,000 and continues to rise naturally at the rate of 30,000 a year. Gaza's population density is some fifteen times that of the West Bank. Historically, the Gaza area was known for its orange groves, and thrived on the fruit that it exported to Europe; once foreigners and Arabs alike were lyrical about Gaza's beauty. But the orange groves have steadily vanished under the relentless pressure of the exploding population. A half million Gazans are registered refugees, and half of this number live in the squalid camps that are supervised by UN-RWA, the United Nations Relief and Works Agency, founded after the first Arab-Israeli war in 1948. The poverty is appalling, misery is widespread and rage is endemic. Since taking control in 1967, Israel has had increasing difficulty keeping the Gaza Strip pacified, but it was not much easier for the Egyptians, when they were in charge. It is no surprise that the *intifada* started there.

To enter the Gaza Strip during my most recent visit, I had to pass through an elaborate security system set up by the Israeli army at the northern gate. Just beyond, I ran into the labor exchange, an open field—called, by Arabs and Israelis alike, the "slave market"—where Israeli employers picked up men for day work. Before the *intifada*, some fifty thousand Gazans commuted daily to Israeli cities and farms; their labor was Gaza's principal source of income. Most of their jobs have since disappeared under intensified security regulations. Some have gone to recent Jewish immigrants from Eastern Europe. As an additional burden, the Gulf war wiped out the employment of several hundred thousand Palestinians, most of them in Kuwait, who had sent home millions of dollars annually. The consequence of these changes has been devastating. Few of the lost jobs, in either Israel or the Gulf, have much chance of being restored. The loss has left growing hardship, and though few Gazans go hungry, thanks largely to UN relief, many children are said to be suffering from malnutrition.

A few miles beyond the gate, the city of Gaza, a seaport dating from Biblical times, gave indication—in its public parks, movies, a beach front—of having once been a pleasant place to live, but it was crumbling from the strain of too much use and too little maintenance. Huge mounds of trash were everywhere; the beaches were ugly with litter. Many streets were unpaved; all were badly rutted. As in Kafr Ain, graffiti covered every exterior wall. Most of it consisted of anti-Israeli slogans, but much reflected the rivalry between the Palestine Liberation Organization and Hamas, an organization of hard-line religious fundamentalists who were trying to Islamicize the *intifada* in the hope of one day establishing an Islamic republic in Palestine, modeled after Khomeini's state in Iran.

In the city center was a crowded market, not distinguished by cleanliness, where men and women in Palestinian dress shopped for fresh fruits and vegetables, and for meat cut from the carcasses of beef and goat that hung from hooks. While I was browsing through the stalls, the street silently began to empty, leaving me bewildered. Within fifteen minutes, only the merchants remained, pulling down their shutters. Closing the market, I was told, was an act of protest directed against an Israeli announcement of the deportation of four *shebab*, who would be taken by helicopter into Lebanon the next day and forbidden to return.

One morning, I paid a call on Abu Fayez Okasha, a *mukhtar* who had fled to Gaza from Dimra, a village that the records show once stood just west of the border of the Strip; it no longer exists. In the spring of 1948, most refugees, looking for shelter after their flight, clustered with their neighbors and their kin, and in some measure rebuilt in the refugee camps the social structure they had left behind. The *mukhtar* was the core of that structure. The post is usually hereditary, but a *mukhtar* must also have a talent for social relations. His duties are to solve disputes between families, serve as a link to other villages and perform a variety of ceremonial functions. He also represents his village before the authorities—which, since the *intifada*, has often led to accusations of collaboration with the Israelis, and more than a few assassinations. Some observers say the *intifada* has made the *mukhtars*—of whom there are some two hundred in Gaza—obsolete, but Okasha, who was sixty-nine at the time of our meeting, has stayed at his post.

Okasha presented a marked contrast to most of the *mukhtars* I had met, who dressed in shabby Western clothes and lived like other refugees in tiny cement-block houses with roofs of corrugated iron, lit by bare bulbs. Okasha received me on the porch of a villa surrounded by a wall, with palm trees and a garden in his front yard. Barefoot, wearing a belted black robe and a white *kuffiyeh*, he was tall and dignified and seemed a throwback to an earlier, better day. He invited me into his *diwan*, a large receiving room with red plush easy chairs. Before reaching Gaza, he said, his family had inhabited Dimra "for generations beyond remembering."

In 1948, Okasha said, Dimra was a village of a thousand inhabitants; the survivors have now grown to a community of four thousand, most of them living in the Jabaliya camp. His father, Okasha said, had been the *mukhtar* and principal landowner, and managed to bring a few head of cattle along with him during the flight. From this base, and a parcel of land that he rented, he gradually rebuilt his wealth. Okasha said that he had himself worked as a teacher and became *mukhtar* when his father died, a decade before. He noted with pride that he had sent all four of his sons to the university. Three were now in business in Abu Dhabi, while the fourth was studying computer technology in the United States. Four years before, they pooled their savings to buy him the house in which he currently lived, but none of them, he said, is likely ever to see Gaza again.

Abdul Fatah Othman Abu Zaida had nine children—six sons and three daughters—but he had been less lucky with them. He lived near Okasha, but his house was inside the boundaries of the Jabaliya camp, and he lived in a quite different style. In March of 1987, soldiers arrested his second son, Nasser, a student at Gaza's Islamic University, and, in searching the house, they found anti-Israeli pamphlets. Nasser was sentenced to four months in prison, and for the same offense Abu Zaida was fired from his job as a policeman. He has since been on relief. Three years later, another son of Abu Zaida's, twenty-year-old Kamal, a member of the Islamic underground, was arrested for throwing a gasoline bomb at an Israeli jeep. A few days before my visit, soldiers had come and bulldozed the family's house to the ground. (Home demolition, a form of collective punishment, was a standard deterrent to insurgency. In the first three years of the *intifada*, some five hundred homes were demolished in the territories, and about three hundred more sealed shut.) Besides Nasser and Kamal, two other sons had each served six months, in what the army called "administrative detention."

When I approached Abu Zaida, a rotund man of fifty-five in a well-worn leisure suit, he was wandering aimlessly among the ruins of his house. In the debris, I could see an old soccer ball, some plastic food containers and the remains of a hot-water heater. As we spoke, an Israeli army personnel carrier, carrying six heavily armed soldiers, the barrels of their guns pointed outward, drove slowly down the narrow dirt street. The grimace on their faces recalled to me a UN official's observation that the soldiers and the *shebab* were locked in a common fear. A handful of women, shelling peas, barely looked up as the soldiers passed, but dozens of teenage loiterers suddenly disappeared. The younger children playing in the street—young children were everywhere in Gaza—hid in doorways. Only when the vehicle was out of sight did the rhythm of the street resume.

Abu Zaida's story was much like that of other Gaza refugees. He arrived from a nearby village called Bureir, which the records show was captured by the Israelis on May 12, 1948. Son of a farmer, he talked to me of a happy childhood spent playing in the fields, attending school and participating in the festivals that were a part of rural life. In the spring of 1948, he said, the Egyptian army turned and fled in the face of an Israeli attack, and in what the survivors still referred to as "the massacre," one hundred and twenty villagers were killed. As a teenager, Abu Zaida said, he worked for a few years in the citrus groves, then found a job with the British police at the Suez Canal. When he married at twenty, he joined the Egyptian police in Gaza. After Israel's occupation, he stayed at his post, against the objections of some of his neighbors to his serving the Israelis. The issue became moot, however, when the Israelis dismissed him on the grounds that his sons made him a security risk. Later, after the *intifada* began, he said, the three hundred Palestinians who remained on the Gaza force resigned, leaving no local policemen at all.

Abu Zaida said he had no idea that his house had been targeted for demolition until the soldiers arrived early one morning. The officer in charge gave the family a few hours to remove its belongings, suggesting that furniture be stacked in the kitchen, which he said would be preserved. By noon, the soldiers had leveled the bulk of the house, and the family was making plans to use the kitchen for sleeping. That evening, another army contingent came by, announced that a mistake had been made and proceeded to destroy the kitchen. Abu Zaida said that he and his family had since been staying with neighbors; only through mutual support, he said, can the Palestinians survive. I asked Abu Zaida whether he was angry with his sons for being the source of the family's misfortunes. He answered that, much as he would like to have his job and his home back, he was proud of what his sons had done to challenge the occupation.

During my stay in Gaza, I also called on Sheikh Ahmed Yassin, widely regarded as the leader of Hamas. His home was in a depressed corner of the city, but in the shadow of a new and handsome white-domed mosque. Yassin had been imprisoned by the Israelis in the 1980s for hiding arms in his home. Victim of a paralytic illness, he was extremely frail. He spoke in a thin voice, his misshapen body curled in a wheelchair, wrapped in warm clothes, next to a narrow hospital bed. Four middle-aged men in shabby native dress, drinking tea and eating pastries, were sitting in a circle around him when I entered, and stayed for our meeting. The room was small and dark; its roof of corrugated iron was held in place by wooden posts. Outside a window, goats bleated. Only Sheikh Yassin's beatific smile brought some cheer to the setting.

"The objective of any Muslim," he said, "is to establish an Islamic state, whether there is an *intifada* or not. But under the present circumstances, we have a special responsibility. The Palestinian people are one body, and we all support the PLO in its struggle to end the occupation, but most of us do not accept the PLO's indifference to an Islamic system. On a temporary basis, it is feasible to live with a secular state in Palestine. We can even endure living with the Jews. But in the long term that is not satisfactory. Palestine is a holy land. When I say that, I mean it is part of our faith, and our faith cannot be divided. Now the Palestinian people are oppressed because they are weak. But the weak will not be weak forever, and neither will the strong [be strong]. And so, if I support the PLO, it does not mean I will be satisfied to live in a Palestinian state governed by the PLO, unless it agrees to respect Islam."

Shortly after my visit, the Israelis returned Sheikh Yassin to prison, where it was expected he would remain until the *intifada* had run its course—or they themselves left Gaza.

IV ABDULLAH'S DREAM, ARAFAT'S VISION

KING ABDULLAH'S ARAB LEGION was in command of what was to become Jordan's West Bank when the fighting stopped at the end of 1948. The Arab League, dominated by Egypt, had no sympathy for his expansionist vision and had created an administrative council in Gaza as a putative step toward Palestinian statehood. The only claimant to lead it was Hajj Amin, who was living in Cairo. Inside Palestine, however, Hajj Amin had little support; outside, he was reviled. The Arab states did not support him. The British, who still had forces in the Middle East, were so dismayed at the prospect of Hajj Amin at the head of a Palestinian government that they withdrew their support for Palestinian statehood. As for the Israelis, they found Abdullah, the only Arab leader with whom they had cordial relations, preferable to any Palestinian regime, particularly one led by the mufti. Many Israelis reasoned that under Abdullah, the Palestinians would in time adopt a Jordanian identity and forgo irredentism. Abdullah, pressing his advantage, proposed that the Arab League add the Gaza Strip to Jordan's holdings, but such a claim was too much for the Arabs. In the end, rule over the residual Arab domains in Palestine was determined by the path of least resistance: the Egyptian army stayed in Gaza, just as the Jordanian army remained to control the West Bank.

To legitimize his rule, Abdullah convoked a conference of three thousand influential Palestinians in Jericho on December 1, 1948. On the same day, Hajj Amin called a rival meeting in Gaza, where he had established an "All-Palestine Government," but his effort quickly petered out. The Jericho conference, controlled by Abdullah's supporters, "petitioned" for the unification of Palestine and Jordan under the Hashemite crown. Britain supported the merger, and Israel raised no objections. The Palestinian people, still in shock at losing their homeland, responded with mixed emotions. Many felt that though they had been betrayed by Abdullah's ambitions, incorporation into his kingdom was now inevitable. In contrast to Abdullah, Egypt waived annexation of the Gaza Strip, declaring its occupation temporary. All the Arab regimes, save for Hashemite Iraq, protested the West Bank's annexation, and never recognized it as a legal part of Jordan.

Nonetheless, the territory's integration into Abdullah's realm proceeded rapidly, with the replacement of military rule by civilian government, the appointment of Palestinians to high posts in Amman and the removal of border controls across the Jordan River. "Palestine" was banned from official usage in favor of "West Bank," all residents of which were declared Jordanian citizens. In April 1950, elections to Jordan's parliament were held, with the West Bank assigned half the seats, and among the winners were several opponents of Abdullah's rule, including supporters of a Palestinian state. Over the ensuing months, resistance to Jordanian rule continued and, on July 21, 1951, Abdullah was shot to death at the entrance to the Al-Aqsa Mosque in Jerusalem. His assassins included relatives and known followers of Hajj Amin, though the mufti himself was never implicated. News of the assassination is said to have brought public rejoicing among the refugees in the camps, and quiet satisfaction elsewhere in the Palestinian community.

After the interval of a year, Abdullah's grandson Hussein succeeded to the Jordanian throne. Hussein followed, with greater success, his grandfather's practice of cultivating the loyalty of West Bankers. He offered them high government offices and access to education and business opportunities, and though he favored the long-standing elite families over the *fellahin*, he helped generate a new social fluidity, which brought advantages to Palestinians at every level. It is true that Palestinians never obtained top military and security posts in the Jordanian government, and suffered heavy-handed repression for political dissidence, particularly in the late 1950s, at a time when Egypt's Nasser was feuding with the king. It is also true that the bulk of available development funds was spent on the East Bank rather than the West. Nonetheless, thousands of Palestinians became doctors, professors, engineers and bankers. Benefitting from education, hundreds of thousands gravitated to jobs in the Gulf, where many grew rich creating modern institutions in Saudi Arabia, Kuwait and the Emirates. And in Jordan, Palestinians were the engine of a dynamic free-enterprise economy. The king's policies helped, as much as anything, to transform the Palestinians from farmers and shopkeepers into a community prepared for leading positions in the modern economic culture that was spreading worldwide.

Yet, in their hearts, few Palestinians ever became Jordanians. Their loyalty to the king was always, at best, qualified. Most Palestinians today speak with resentment of the period under Jordan's rule; some even call it the "Jordanian occupation." It is now clear that in these years, nascent Palestinian nationalism, paralyzed by the shock of 1948, was reemerging. The Palestinians never seriously challenged Jordanian rule, but by the time the Israelis arrived in the West Bank and the Gaza Strip in 1967, nationalism was ready to explode as a major political force.

THE PALESTINE LIBERATION ORGANIZATION, which Egypt's President Nasser founded in 1964 as one more weapon in his arsenal to dominate Arab politics, became the vehicle of that nationalism. Promising to free all of Palestine of Israeli rule, the PLO was an exile body, and made little effort in its early days to recruit followers from inside the territories. The leadership argued that the constituency it served was the total Palestinian community, spread all over the Middle East, and it was instrumental in provoking a war in 1967, which it was convinced would lead to Palestine's liberation by Nasser's legions. But within six days the Arab armies went down to devastating defeat, and even the most hopeful Palestinians had to face the harsh truth that the Arabs might never be strong enough to free them. The disaster, however, did emancipate the PLO from Egyptian control. The PLO reorganized after 1967, to become independent, nationalist and militant.

Under the leadership of Yasir Arafat, the PLO adopted terrorism as its principal tactic for expelling the Israelis from Palestine. Its bloody guerrilla raids, hijackings, bombings and assassinations put it constantly in the news, keeping the Palestinian issue on the international agenda. But there is no evidence that the strategy actually advanced the cause of liberation. Some thinkers in the occupied territories, freed of the constraints that inhibited them while Jordan ruled, began during this period to rethink the maximalist doctrines of the PLO; they talked of accepting partition, of cutting ties to the king to form a Palestinian state on the West Bank, and perhaps in the Gaza Strip. But the PLO remained stubbornly committed to the liberation of all Palestine, a doctrine that was far removed from both its military potential and the hardships of life under Israeli occupation.

Slowly, however, the PLO changed. In 1970, it reached its military pinnacle with 30,000 armed *fedayeen* based in Jordan, but they were more menacing to the king, their supporter, than to Israel, their enemy. Finally, King Hussein dispatched his forces against them, and in the ten days of bloody battle known as "Black September," the PLO's military power was crushed. The survivors straggled into Lebanon, where Arafat tried to rebuild an army. But he understood by then that the PLO was unlikely ever to liberate Palestine on the battlefield.

I first met Arafat in the summer of 1981 in Beirut, when the city was at its most lawless. Diverse militias reigned in every neighborhood, some of them no more than criminal gangs. Waiting in my hotel room, I received a call one evening after dinner instructing me to be ready to meet the chairman at midnight. The hour was not negotiable; the chairman was a night owl. The PLO headquarters in those days was in Fakhani, a district inhabited mostly by Palestinians. Inside, it was safe; getting there, through a half-dozen unfriendly checkpoints, was a problem. The taxi driver I hailed outside my hotel agreed to take me only after I placed a sizable bill in his hand.

The street was silent when the cab pulled up outside the PLO headquarters. Having visited before in daylight, I ducked knowingly behind a wall of sandbags and climbed the four floors to the information office. It was strewn as usual with dirty coffee cups, old newspapers and overflowing ash trays. In a corner was a shelf of spent shells, mementoes of lost battles. On the walls were posters proclaiming the cause of Palestinian liberation amid photos of sunken-eyed youths, whom the PLO called "martyrs," lost in battle.

Two PLO functionaries waited for me and, after drinking a coffee, we set out in search of the chairman. As we walked, our footsteps rang on Fakhani's deserted pavement. At the door of a seedy apartment building, indistinguishable from the others we passed, stood some young men in uniform. We entered, climbed to the third floor and were seated in a shabby office, where we were served tea. An electric fan played on us. After a half hour, I heard a commotion in the hall and saw the well-known *kuffiyeh* and unmistakable half-shaven face rush by and out the door. I was told that for reasons of security, Arafat never spent more than an hour or two in any one place, and that he slept every night in a different bed. With my companions, I descended the staircase and marched for another ten minutes through the silent caverns to another indistinguishable building.

The next door that opened admitted me to what I assumed was Arafat's private apartment. Its decor evoked the pages of an old Sears Roebuck catalogue, an Arab decorator's fantasy of Western elegance. The rooms still smelled of wallpaper paste and paint. With a dozen Palestinians, I sat around a plastic-topped table, sipping fruit juice. When summoned, my two companions and I entered a library, obviously the creation of the same decorator. New books glittered on the shelves, and a wood carving of the map of Palestine shone on the wall. Behind a polished desk sat the chairman, chatting amiably with a colleague.

On seeing me, Arafat tactfully broke off the discussion. It was now nearly two a.m., and an aide, reminding me that it was Ramadan, said the chairman would be taking a break for supper, since he would be fasting from sunrise to the following sundown. It was Arafat who invited me to join him, waving me into another room, where a table was set with olives, fruits and cheeses. Surrounded by his associates, I sat in the next chair as the chairman talked, mixing Arabic with broken English, meanwhile scooping up his supper in pieces of flat bread, Arab-style. His voice was deeper than I had expected, his hands more delicate, his skin lighter and, though there was no concealing his homeliness, his eyes sparkled and he flashed a radiant smile.

Over supper, I said to Arafat that I wanted to explore with him the origins, the personal relationships and the structure of the PLO, of which little had then been written. An aide kept interrupting, "Let's concentrate on the political issues," but Arafat nodded his head as if to say he concurred with me. After supper, when we returned to the library and took comfortable chairs, I turned on the tape recorder and opened by asking him to tell me about his boyhood and his early years in the resistance. "Those are the most difficult questions for me," he answered in English. "It is a rule of our revolution not to speak about personal matters." An aide chimed in to say that the revolution discouraged any personality cult. "We prefer," Arafat said softly, "to speak about our freedom fighters, our heroes, our martyrs."

For the next few hours, the chairman and I maneuvered over what he would and would not say, while the tape rolled. He was gracious, even playful, shifting out of English and into Arabic whenever he could. The aides translated, but they were more than interpreters. They discussed his answers with him, often volunteered their own opinions, sometimes corrected his and, though a shade deferential, were obviously unintimidated. Arafat was clearly most comfortable making political pronouncements, most of which I had heard before. But he also tried to honor his commitment to me, and little by little he sketched out the outlines of his life and the movement.

Though his past remains shaded in some mystery, it seems that Arafat was born in 1929 in Jerusalem. His father belonged to a Gaza merchant clan, his mother was a Husseini, distantly related to Hajj Amin. As a teenager Arafat was already a nationalist, and when the war in Palestine began in 1947, he joined the staff of another kinsman, Abd el-Kader al-Husseini, the Arab commander of Jerusalem. After the defeat, he took up residence in Gaza, where he finished high school and, in 1950, he went to Cairo to study civil engineering. It was in Cairo in 1954 that he and some friends met secretly to found the General Union of Palestine Students, the first organization of Palestinian resistance. In 1958, while working in Kuwait, they organized Fatah, to spread the message of resistance; in 1967, when the PLO was reorganized to purge Egyptian influence, Fatah became the dominant body in the PLO coalition.

"When we founded the movement," Arafat said, "we were all excited about the political revolution of Nasser, which then was two years old. We were trying to face our tragedy as Palestinians, but we were forbidden to organize ourselves in any way, not only under the Israeli occupation but in the Arab countries too. After we started, many of us left Cairo to organize underground, inside the occupied territories, but also in Iraq, the Gulf and Saudi Arabia. Everywhere it was forbidden. It was not easy."

Fatah's doctrine was a dramatic challenge to the myth of the Arab nation. "The ideology we adopted was unique in the Arab world," Arafat said. "We were not Baathis, not Muslim Brothers, not Communists, not pan-Arab nationalists. We were not part of any existing parties." Fatah's ideology, he said, was Palestinian nationalism. Fatah was a Palestinian movement to liberate Palestine, and it carried that doctrine into the PLO.

"We had counted on the Arabs, our brothers, to liberate us," he said, "and I don't want to say too much about them now. But I remember being surprised and disappointed when Nasser himself, in 1957, said to a delegation of Palestinians from Gaza, 'I don't have any plans to liberate your country, and you should not believe anyone who tells you there is a plan to liberate your country or to solve the Palestinian question.' We organized Fatah because we knew we had to do it ourselves."

By 1974, when the Arabs officially recognized the PLO as the spokesman for the Palestinians, it had begun moving toward a doctrine of compromise settlement. The United Nations Security Council had set the stage after the Six-Day War in Resolution 242, which established the principle of Israel's exchanging land for peace. President Sadat had moved the process along by publicly renouncing the goal of destroying Israel, insisting that the Arabs would be satisfied to regain the territory lost in 1967. Two weeks after the Arab summit in Rabat, Morocco, which declared the PLO "the sole legitimate representative of the Palestinian people," Arafat was invited to address the General Assembly of the United Nations. In November 1974, he promised the UN that the PLO, for the sake of peace with Israel, would settle for "a little homeland of our own," and declared, "I have come bearing an olive branch and a freedom fighter's gun. Do not let the olive branch fall from my hand." In the high-powered diplomatic campaign that followed, the PLO gained observer status at the UN and official recognition from dozens of governments.

Within the PLO, strong opposition remained to the retreat from maximalism. But in 1982 the hard-liners suffered another setback: Israel defeated a tenacious PLO army in Lebanon, making clear that Palestine was unlikely ever to be liberated by force. Under the terms of the ceasefire, the PLO contingents defending Beirut were evacuated to Tunis. The remaining Palestinian units split between Arafat loyalists and Syrian-supported rebels, between moderates and rejectionists, who over the ensuing months fought a nasty civil war in the north of Lebanon for control of the PLO.

I met Arafat again in the fall of 1983 in his battlefield headquarters, an old brick warehouse in the northern Lebanese town of Tripoli. As we talked, shells from the rejectionists' guns rained down around us, and I remember wondering what my good Jewish mother would say to her friends if I were to be found together in the rubble with the PLO's infamous chief. The interview that day was not especially noteworthy, except for a comment by Arafat that came back to me only quite recently. Not only was he committed to making peace with the Jews, he told me, but he would be willing to start by setting up an independent Palestinian homeland on any part of the territory from which Israel withdrew, and he specifically mentioned Gaza and Jericho. His comment had no meaning for me then; in those days, it was normal to greet Arafat's statements skeptically. But a decade later, when the PLO and Israel signed a peace agreement based on the notion of "Gaza and Jericho first," it became clear to me that the idea had been important, and that it had long gestated in Arafat's mind.

With the evacuation of its forces from Beirut, the PLO transferred its headquarters to Tunis and began to move away from the policy of "armed struggle." Over the next few years, the Palestine National Council, the Palestinians' "parliament-in-exile," passed a series of resolutions calling for Palestinian-Israeli negotiations to establish a state in the West Bank and Gaza. Without ever winning over the hard-liners, Arafat formally renounced terrorism, recognized Israel and accepted its right to live in the Middle East in peace and security.

Israel, during this same period, was moving in another direction. Persuaded that the West Bankers, if not the Gazans, were reconciling themselves to the occupation, it agreed in 1972 to sponsor municipal elections; to its dismay, the result was a huge victory for candidates loyal to the PLO. Disdainful of the reported softening of the PLO's line, Israel began deporting Palestinians who proclaimed a nationalist allegiance; Nasser's father, the mayor of El-Bireh, was among those caught in the net. Notwithstanding the deportations, the PLO in the territories kept growing stronger, while ironically the deported leaders, representing in PLO councils abroad the interests of the Palestinians at home, hastened the shift to the two-state position. Then, in 1977, Menachem Begin's Likud Party, committed to achieving a Greater Israel, was elected to power, dealing a severe setback to peace prospects between Israel and the Palestinians.

THE MASRIS OF NABLUS were one of the families that was converted during the occupation to Palestinian nationalism and loyalty to the PLO. Nablus had long been a cauldron of Palestinian emotions. A major city since the days of the Canaanites, though always in Jerusalem's shadow, it was the center of a rich agricultural region, and a site of industry and commerce. Under the Ottomans, prominent Nabulsis, designated as "notables," served as liaisons between the imperial government and the people. The Masris say their rise began only after the Ottomans left.

Under the British in the 1920s, Taher Masri, having acquired some wealth selling farm products to the Syrians, sent his son Hikmet to the American University in Beirut to acquire a degree in business. A decade later, Hikmet built a mill to grind grain, and, in succession, factories to process olive oil into soap, to manufacture matches and to refine vegetable oil. Collateral branches of the Masris, meanwhile, founded other businesses. But the family always found members to serve in Nablus's social institutions and public offices. Mayor Ma'zuz Masri entertained King Abdullah at home in Nablus on the day the king was assassinated; Mayor Zafer Masri was himself assassinated in 1986 by rejectionists within the PLO.

One morning, I drove with Nasser to Nablus, where I met with Salah Masri, Hikmet's forty-year-old son, at the cooking-oil factory, which was near an Israeli checkpoint at the edge of the city. His stylish plaid sports jacket and gray slacks gave him the look of an American college professor; his attire seemed incongruous in a city that was also a center of Islamic traditionalism. Salah drove me in his car along Nablus's unkempt boulevards, through an agglomeration of gray buildings, dark workshops and cheerless stores, to his spacious apartment on a hill in what looked like an upper-class quarter. There, among old-fashioned European furnishings, we met his elder sister, Nihaya, who taught English at Al-Najar University, which the family had helped to found. I would not have guessed that Salah, who seemed so easygoing, had been released only a few weeks before after six months of administrative detention, during which, he said, he was at times beaten, insulted and denied food and toilet facilities.

Salah and Nihaya talked to me of the accommodation made by the

Masris with the Hashemites in Amman after the war of 1948. Like most Palestinians, the family felt embittered toward the Arab states, but Jordan's occupation of the West Bank left it no option but to cooperate. Hikmet was elected in the 1950s to the Jordanian parliament and subsequently became its speaker, while the rest of the family developed close business and personal ties with Amman.

By the mid-1950s, however, the Masris had had enough of Jordan's oppressive style of rule, and in 1965 they shifted their support to the PLO. (Some of the Masris remained loyal to King Hussein; in fact, Salah's cousin, Taher Masri, served as Jordan's prime minister in the 1980s.) When the West Bank fell in 1967, Israel permitted the family to keep its factories, though the restrictions imposed on their operations ultimately forced the closing of two of them. When I spoke to the Masris, they were obviously still prosperous but, I was assured, were nonetheless strong supporters of Palestinian nationalism and the PLO.

Salah told me that after getting a business degree at Cairo University, he worked in Saudi Arabia for ten years and returned home in 1987, on the eve of the *intifada*. From the start, he said, the family sympathized with the uprising, and sent many of its sons into the street to throw stones. Of the extended Masri family—which he estimated at three thousand— six have died in the struggle and dozens have been imprisoned. The family fortune, he said, had been much depleted helping *intifada* victims. In September 1990, he was himself arrested, after nearly three years of deliberately intrusive surveillance. Salah acknowledged being a PLO member, but said he had never been active in the resistance. Though not charged by the Israelis, he was sentenced to six months in prison; when he emerged, he was more determined than ever, he said, to fight for a Palestinian state.

"Outsiders criticized the Palestinians in the territories for cheering when Iraq's Scud missiles fell on Israel during the Gulf war. They insisted it wasn't natural," Salah said. "Can't they understand how we feel after decades of oppression, occupation, demolitions, torture, expulsions? We saw the rockets as a message to Israel, a brief exposure to the suffering that we have experienced for so long. The missiles destroyed some apartments in Tel Aviv, and that is regrettable. But how many houses have been destroyed here and no one has paid attention? Our young people saw all roads toward freedom and a decent life blocked in front of them. They have become desperate. That is why they started the *intifada*."

When we finished talking, Salah and Nihaya took me to visit Hikmet, the patriarch, whose home was downtown, in a neighborhood of shade trees and large villas. Nihaya told me in the car that, until 1927, the family had lived in the Kasbah, the Nablus of ancient stone houses and narrow, winding streets. It was only after a devastating earthquake in 1927 that the family built a new house in the Turkish style outside the old city walls. This house had since become the headquarters of a foundation that the Masris established, Salah said, to help needy citizens. In 1950, Hikmet moved his family to a new villa, designed to announce the importance of the man who lived within. The entrance, behind a locked gate, was through a portico supported by six pillars, reached by climbing a steep staircase. Hikmet himself welcomed me at the entrance and led me to a small receiving room furnished with a fireplace mantel carved in granite, a crystal chandelier and overstuffed chairs upholstered in pink satin.

Incongruously, I found Hikmet an unpretentious man. At eighty-five, he was slim, healthy-looking and elegantly dressed in a dark suit and Italian loafers. He had fine features and bright blue eyes—the Crusader influence, Palestinians always say of blue-eyed countrymen—and the only concessions that age seemed to have elicited from him were a hearing aid and a trembling hand. Seated in the receiving room when I entered was his cousin, Wasfi Masri, a lawyer, who was about the same age. Hikmet interrupted the visit to talk to me. His manners were exquisite and his English was excellent.

"Israelis say the land belongs to them because they had it three thousand years ago," Hikmet said, without anger. His tone suggested that he had spoken the same words many times before. "The Jews were a part of Palestinian history for about a century, under King David and King Solomon. They base their claims on their sacred book, the Bible. But we have lived here for the last fourteen centuries. Our entire history is here, and our sacred book, the Koran, also stakes its claim. But why, I wonder, should either of us look back? Israel exists, and we can't ignore it. All we ask is the share of the land attributed to us by the United Nations, not in 1947 but in Resolution 242 of 1967. These boundaries give us twenty percent of Palestine, and we ask only that the Israelis withdraw to them. That is the position of the PLO, and I support it. It is the safest basis for our relationship. If they settle with us, we'll have a peace treaty, and no more war."

V BARAMKI AND RADA

IT IS FAIR to say that the Palestinians on the West Bank, even those living in the refugee camps, enjoy a better life than those in the Gaza Strip. There is more space, and a better climate. Places of employment are more accessible on both sides of the green line, the Israeli-Jordanian border that was wiped out in the Six-Day War. Even when the army closes the territories, keeping men from their jobs, West Bankers, with greater reserves of food and money, fare better than Gazans. Relations with Jordan over the Allenby Bridge, a crossing to which Israelis generally permit access, provide a feeling of connection with the Arab world. Urban life is relatively developed, meaning that residents of the refugee camps—about 100,000 of the total West Bank population of some 1.2 million—have modern amenities within reach.

The negative side for West Bank Palestinians is that more than one hundred thousand Jewish settlers live in close proximity, generating relentless tension. During the first decade of the Israeli occupation, the Labor Party government discouraged Jews from settling in the territories, except in a few peripheral areas that were said to be important for security. On the whole, the army kept order with a light hand. But in 1977, after the victory of Begin's Likud, the government began the active promotion of Jewish settlements. Gaza was too crowded for much activity; the West Bank was not. From the start, the Likud government made it clear that if it had its way, Israel would annex "Judea and Samaria," the Biblical names for the West Bank, ending Palestinian life there forever.

In this struggle, the Israeli army, the source of order in the territories, was not an impartial force; it was, naturally, on the settlers' side. With no available recourse to authority, the Palestinians felt thwarted and frustrated. Relations between the local inhabitants and the settlers deteriorated steadily, and with the start of the *intifada*, they entered on a steep downward spiral. Since then, civility on the West Bank, no less than in Gaza, has all but disappeared.

I caught a glimpse of the deterioration on a visit to the West Bank as early as 1980 while reporting on strife between the army and students at Birzeit University. The Palestinians, having been wrenched from their agrarian roots in 1948, had turned increasingly to education as the safeguard of their future. Having been cut off from East Bank institutions in 1967, they began building and enlarging their own universities, five of them on the West Bank, one in the Gaza Strip. Birzeit, located in a village some twenty miles north of Jerusalem, was the best known among them. At the time, it had about a thousand students. Its president, Hanna Nasser, was among the Palestinians deported in 1973 for showing sympathy to the PLO. (He was also among those repatriated by the Israelis during the peace talks in 1993.) Nonetheless, during the first decade of the occupation, Birzeit was a fairly quiet place and made few problems for the authorities.

That is not to say that Birzeit students were passive. Several times a year, usually on the anniversary of some lost battle, students would march through the streets for an hour or two before returning to class. While they threw some stones or burned a tire, the military administration would look the other way. This tolerant attitude changed when radical settlers established a community up the road and began passing regularly through the village to reach their homes. Students and settlers quickly fell into the practice of mutual provocation, to which the army could scarcely remain neutral. Soldiers now tear-gassed, beat and occasionally fired on students, and in a demonstration in November 1980 eleven young men and women were shot in the legs.

The facts in the ongoing strife between the army and the Birzeit students were not in dispute. The army acknowledged that, in repeated searches, it never uncovered revolutionary cells, discovered weapons or even found stores of incendiary tracts. The university, for its part, admitted that the students were turbulent, threw stones and objected to the occupation. The dispute, however, was not placed for resolution before an impartial judge. The army was in charge, and it fell into the routine of closing Birzeit, for days or weeks, at the slightest provocation. Its argument was that its first duty was not to justice but to the security of the settlers and the preservation of order.

In January of 1988, a few weeks after the start of the *intifada*, the Israeli government permanently closed the occupied territories' six universities, claiming—probably correctly—that the *shebab* were using them as centers for recruitment and organization. On the same grounds, it also shut the elementary and secondary schools, which it permitted to reopen sporadically over the next four years. The universities, however, remained closed. Birzeit, in response, set up a temporary office in Ramallah, which the army tolerated, and which was where I talked with Dr. Gabi Baramki, the acting president since Hanna Nasser's deportation. Baramki's daughter, Haniah, was among those wounded in the 1980 shooting. A tall, round-faced man of rather formal demeanor, he insisted to me that there was no way that either he or the army could keep young people from expressing their concerns with politics, or with the future of their country.

"We are trying to act in some fashion as the Hebrew University did in the early part of the century," said Baramki, referring to the Israeli institution that has grown to several campuses in Jerusalem, with stately buildings and an undisputed reputation for excellence. "The Hebrew University set out deliberately to give a national identity to the Jews. I wish we could be as successful.

"We don't encourage politics. Since the military government makes it illegal, we don't allow open politicking on the campus. But, like other universities, we value our freedom and think that students should be free to choose their own direction. The Israelis say that everyone in Birzeit is a radical, and therefore dangerous. If the army means by that a person who feels a strong identity with his own people, then the university, the students, all the Arabs on the West Bank are radicals. But if it is talking about someone as irreconcilable, as uncompromising, then such students are a small minority, though I think their numbers may be growing as the occupation drags on."

The university, Baramki told me, had interpreted the army's shut-down order as a ban on campus meetings, but not as a bar to teaching or to studying. It continued to conduct classes, serving about half the student body, he said, in the homes of teachers, in mosques and churches, and even in apartments and in stores that it rented. The army did not object, he said, but he did not think this approach satisfied the needs of the university or the West Bank population. First, he said, the rules kept Birzeit from enrolling freshmen, meaning a suspension of higher education in the years to come. Second, students were not allowed the use of such university facilities as the library, the most extensive in the West Bank, which is on its rural campus. Third, during the Gulf war, he said, many students were cut off from even their improvised classes by an order requiring special permission to enter Jerusalem, a transit point for all north-south roads. Most important, Baramki said, Palestinians saw the closing of the universities as an effort to suppress their culture and keep their children from education, their most important resource.

"We think Israel is being terribly short-sighted," he said. "Israelis think of the Palestinians only as a source of cheap labor, as a dependent people. But the universities can bring the creative elements of the two societies together, setting a tone for stability. They can be a bridge, a step toward coexistence. Keeping them closed is criminal; it is not even wise."

IF BARAMKI'S CONCERNS about military rule were long-term, Rada Sliman Ramahi's were immediate, and very personal. The mother of nine sons and two daughters, she had been exposed all her life to harshness in the relations between Arabs and Jews. In 1948, when she was seven, her family, frightened by the fighting, fled from its home near what was now Tel Aviv's Ben-Gurion airport. She remembered stopping near a spring, in an olive grove west of Ramallah, she said, and then living there for a year under the trees without as much as a roof for protection. By then UNRWA had set up a refugee camp in Jalazone, and the family was assigned a tent, which was its home until cement-block houses were introduced three years later. Rada learned to read and write at an UNRWA school, to which she walked barefoot, but ended her education with the fifth grade, which was the school's highest class. By then, she said with a blush, she was a pretty young woman with hair to her waist and she agreed to marry Wajdeh Mustafa Abdullah Ramahi, whose brother had married her sister. She told me she was fifteen at the time.

Her husband had spent six years in Amman working as a baker, saving money for their marriage while supporting his own family in the Jalazone camp. The two had a traditional wedding, she recalled, with seven wonderful days of singing, dancing and feasting. When it was over, he returned to Amman and she to Jalazone, to await the birth of their child. After Wajdi was born, she rejoined her husband—who proudly took the name Abu Wajdi—but when her father died the three of them came back to the West Bank and moved in with her mother in the Jalazone house. This was the house in which, nearly thirty years later, I interviewed her. She was without several teeth now, and had gained some pounds, but she was impressively tall and possessed a handsome, even radiant face. She wore gold rings on her fingers and a Palestinian gown of red velour over what seemed like pajamas. Her youngest son, Ghassan, who was eight, stood shyly at her side. Murad, who was twenty, brought in cups of tea.

The thirty years had not been easy, Rada said. It was not so much living in the camp that was hard; the camp-dwellers had created a large-hearted community and made their dwellings reasonably habitable. Most houses had been improved with indoor kitchens, toilets and additional rooms. Many had porches or flower gardens. Most families, with multiple earners, had found the means to buy refrigerators and television sets. UNRWA paved the streets, collected the trash and maintained decent school and health systems. Mosques had been built with private contributions, chiefly from the Gulf states. Over the years, the West Bank camps had come to look much like the nearby villages.

But Rada said she rarely felt financially, much less physically, secure. When the occupation started, Abu Wajdi, attracted by higher wages across the green line, worked as a maintenance man in a religious school in Jerusalem, then as a laborer in the Tel Aviv suburb of Holon. He lost both jobs to immigrants from the Soviet Union, she said, and was now unemployed, though occasionally he found work as a baker, his boyhood craft. Her sons, she said, were deeply involved in anti-occupation activities and, though they took occasional jobs, had not embarked on careers. Seven of them had served prison terms, and at one point, five were locked up simultaneously. On the day we talked, she said four were in prison and one in hiding. In 1983, Wajdi, her first-born, was shot in the leg. Murad, when he was twenty, was shot in the stomach by a settler and almost died. Rada told me that she herself fell and broke a leg in 1985, trying to save one of her sons from a beating by soldiers.

Even her daughter Wajdan, who was twenty-two, had participated in the *intifada*, Rada said, throwing stones at soldiers. It was not unusual for women to serve in the ranks, and she noted with satisfaction that she was herself once involved, functioning as a link in a signaling system that warned of the approach of army units. Routinely, she said, she helped to hide *shebab* during the soldiers' searches. Wajdan was now less involved, she said, having earlier that year married a carpenter from the camp. But, Rada noted, Wajdan did not have a wedding like her own, more than thirty years before. The family had no money now for such a celebration, she said. Besides, she added, it did not seem like a time to celebrate.

While we talked, Rada's twelve-year-old daughter Olla entered the room and stood quietly nearby. With large brown eyes and an innocent face, she seemed unscarred by the hardships of camp life and the occupation. Olla's lot, it seemed, was to stay at home, taking care of her father and her brothers. When I asked why she had dropped out of school, Olla, though obviously bashful, said clearly that she would prefer to have gone on, but that her parents would not permit it. Rada's explanation led us into an examination of the army's treatment of Jalazone's women. Given the protectiveness that Arab culture accords to the modesty of its daughters, I asked, was there not some reluctance to expose them, as activists in the *intifada*, to the Israeli soldiers? Rada answered the question with no apparent embarrassment.

"Before the *intifada*, the soldiers were quite respectful of women," she said, "but that has changed, and there is some abuse. Most commonly, the abuse is verbal. The soldiers can be very obscene, especially if they speak Arabic, and it frustrates our men to hear them. We know of a few cases of sexual abuse, though none of rape. Increasingly, however, women are being beaten. It never happened to me. I hide when the soldiers come to our house. But young women who laugh at the soldiers or try to protect the *shebab* are beaten these days, and sometimes they are sexually mishandled.

"When the army began raiding schools, I had a discussion with my husband about Olla's future. Olla is very pretty and looks much older than her age, and her father was worried that she might be abused, so he decided to keep her home. Our men worry about that sort of thing more than the women do."

In June 1989, an army unit knocked on Rada's door and announced that, based on the participation of the children in the *intifada*, it was about to demolish their house. After some debate, the unit commander agreed to spare one room because the house remained, after forty years of camp life, registered in the name of Rada's mother. After the demolition, Rada said, the entire family—she and Abu Wajdi, her mother, whatever sons were not in prison, two daughters, a daughter-in-law and two grandchildren— all lived in one room. Finally, with the help of several sons, Abu Wajdi built an additional room on the second story. Normally the army bans all construction on demolition sites, Rada said, but so far it had allowed them to keep the room.

Rada insisted that, among the families living in the camp, hers was not unusually political. Throwing stones—or, occasionally, something more lethal—is what the children of this generation do, she said; it was their vocation, and there was not a single family in the camp whose sons had not been imprisoned. But, she told me, it was not something to which she had grown accustomed.

"As a mother, I worry about my children all the time," Rada said, "but it is right that they believe in our cause. I had hoped by now that they would be into their lives and on their own, but in fact I spend much of my time looking after them. I spend hours talking to their lawyers, though it does no good. I visit three of them, traveling back and forth on the bus to the prison, carrying food and gifts. Unfortunately, I am not allowed to visit the fourth, my son Sofian, who is nineteen and is in the third year of a five-year sentence for throwing a Molotov cocktail. I have not seen him at all. So my life is very difficult. My soul is a circle of torture. When I cook or clean the house, I am reminded that four of them will not be home for dinner or to sleep tonight, and I begin to cry. But I am very proud that they are taking their place in the struggle with the other shebab."

Interestingly, Rada showed no resentment at the harsh treatment her sons endured while locked up. She talked of how the guards shouted insults at them, how the food was inadequate, how the heat and cold were often intolerable. But she added, shrugging, "The Israelis are our enemies. What do you expect?" She even smiled occasionally as she talked, as if to convey sardonically, "That's our lot!" But she did indicate that, since the start of the intifada, the army's intrusion into the daily life of the camp—with middle-of-the-night raids, random beatings, routine identity checks and patrols through the streets by heavily armed soldiers—had intensified from month to month and had now become virtually unbearable. Rada said the people of the camp would do almost anything—except give up their struggle for independence—to get the army out of their lives.

When I asked Rada if the intifada was worth all the suffering it had imposed on her and her family, she answered unequivocally that it was. The Palestinian people have no choice but to try to end the occupation, she said, so they can get on with living normal lives. But what would a normal life be, I asked, for herself and her family?

"Like all Palestinians," she answered, "I dreamed of some day returning to my village. When my children were young, I talked of it all the time to them, just as my mother had talked to me. But several years ago I crossed the green line to make a visit to the village, and nothing remained of it. Not a building was standing. I was sad that none of my children would ever see where I was raised, but the Jalazone camp is now our home.

My children were born here and my daughter's baby will soon be born here. I realize now that we will never go back to my village, and so I've decided I'd like to stay here—without the Israelis, of course—and build a new house for my children and my grandchildren. What I mean is that I want my children one day to be living in freedom, like other people in other places, in peace, without beatings or jail, and with hope for the future."

VI WHO DECIDES

IT IS NOT EASY to know who exercises power in Palestinian society now in its third decade of military occupation.

The Israelis have been inconsistent in their governing tactics: they have, at times, sponsored elections, permitted ad hoc leadership organizations to function, allowed strong statements to be published in the press or spoken in the mosques, tolerated the existence of political and religious parties and labor unions. But they have also dissolved organizations, suppressed political speech and deported strong figures, as part of a policy designed to keep the community off balance and permit no mobilization of political power. Given the fact that the Palestinians have never had a tradition of strong leadership, much less institutional mechanisms for collective expression, it is surprising that they have found a voice at all with which to deal with the world. They have done better than they did in the 1930s and 1940s. They have run an *intifada* and organized an impressive delegation to negotiate with Israel. Yet it is difficult to know who is in charge.

Faisal Husseini is widely regarded as the representative of the PLO, but it is not clear whether he is the leader of the Palestinians in the territories. Some observers think the real leaders are the anonymous young people of the Unified Command, the shadowy body that is said to direct the *intifada*. Others insist that major political decisions are made only at PLO headquarters in Tunis. Husseini himself disclaims leadership, insisting he is just an activist. A mild-mannered man, considered even by his friends to lack charisma, he does not have the air of a chief. But he is a Husseini, from the family of Hajj Amin, and he is the son of Abd el-Kader al-Husseini, an authentic Palestinian hero, killed in the war of 1948. He is also thoughtful and soft-spoken and has spent nineteen months in Israeli prisons, a prerequisite for leadership in these times. Whatever his disclaimers, many Palestinians feel that Faisal Husseini, born to a sense of duty, must inevitably lead.

I interviewed Husseini in late 1991 in the living room of his modest house at the foot of the Mount of Olives, on the summit of which is the oldest campus of the Hebrew University. At the front door, two or three young men, apparently bodyguards, stood empty-handed—Palestinians are not permitted to carry weapons. They looked good-natured rather than menacing. Husseini was fifty then, balding and a bit overweight. He wore an ordinary dress shirt, the sleeves buttoned at the wrist, without a tie. The furniture that surrounded us was rickety. Arabic-language newspapers stood in dusty stacks on plastic stools, and two amateurish paintings of Husseini's father hung on the walls. Husseini's English was hesitant, but he managed to convey his message clearly enough.

He talked of the changes over the previous decade in the PLO, which had decisively shifted its strategy to the two-state solution, and he credited Arafat with persuading not only the organization but the bulk of the Palestinian people to accept the new direction. He complained that the Arab states had repeatedly disappointed the Palestinians in their liberation efforts, and had even reneged on promises of money to improve conditions in the territories. Arafat, he said, had the loyalty of the *shebab*, who endorsed his strategy, but he cautioned that some of them were growing impatient with nonviolence, and a few regarded partition as only a temporary step en route to statehood in all of Palestine. "They think differently from me on these matters," he said, "but I would not expect seventeen- or eighteen-year-olds to think as I do." The anger behind this thinking, Husseini warned, made very clear that the *intifada* would turn to deadlier weapons—which, indeed, it has—if negotiations with Israel did not soon produce results.

"The Gulf war," he said, "proved that Israel's occupation of the West Bank and the Gaza Strip has not enhanced its security. Israel's extended borders offered no protection against Iraqi missiles. Israel's army kept the territories quiet, by imposing a twenty-four-hour curfew, but that was a temporary expedient. As the *intifada* shows, controlling two million angry Palestinians against their will is not easy. Had Israel been fighting an enemy at its borders, the territories would have been in flames and guerrillas would have diverted several divisions from the battlefield.

"The Palestinians suffered a setback in the Gulf war in that Iraq, Israel's only military rival in the region, was defeated. The hundreds of thousands of our people working in the Gulf were expelled and mistreated by the states which they had done so much to create. The war diverted attention from the *intifada*, even for us. But the defeat will contain a silver lining if its result is real progress toward a settlement. Popular frustration has not diminished, and the *intifada* is not over. It will not be over until the occupation ends, and our political goals are satisfied."

I ran into Husseini not long afterward at the Madrid conference of October 1991, in which formal peace negotiations finally started. The

Israelis had backed away from their early opposition to a separate Palestinian delegation—they had argued that Jordan should represent the territories—but they imposed several conditions on the delegation's membership.
Designed to underscore the exclusion of Jerusalem's status from the
agenda, they barred Jerusalemites from participation. They also barred
Palestinians publicly identified with the PLO. Husseini fell into both cate-
gories, and so had no official post, but he was there, nonetheless. The
Palestinians insisted that he was their real leader, which was their way of
asserting that they were not Israeli pawns and, no less important, that the
"inside" was now an equal partner with the PLO's established leadership,
the "outside," in making decisions. Husseini said publicly at Madrid that
he talked strategy daily with Nabil Shaath, Arafat's representative in Madrid, as well as with Arafat himself by phone. The Israelis, though annoyed
at the arrangement, limited themselves to a feeble protest.

"I see Madrid as a triumph of the *intifada*," Husseini said to me. "It is
a huge popular victory, and all the people of the occupied territories share
in it. We still have serious problems to settle with the Israelis, and when
I return home, I must go around the territories to tell people their expectations must not be too high, as they were when the *intifada* began. But I
must also work to keep up the momentum that we gained in Madrid."

Husseini, however, made no effort to conceal from me that there was a
palpable tide of opposition to the negotiations on the West Bank. Some of
it came from the old rejectionist wing of the PLO, though the principal
rejectionist leaders had promised to give Arafat's policy of negotiations a
chance to prove its worth. Greater opposition was generated by Hamas,
the Islamic fundamentalists, who had no sympathy for negotiations at all.
Hamas's position was clear: Palestine was a Muslim land, and the Jews
had no business there. Husseini said that fanatics within these groups—
and, perhaps, among Israeli extremists as well—were capable of trying to
assassinate him, with the aim of terminating the peace talks. The fact
that Madrid had a generally positive outcome put the opponents on the
defensive, he said, but they could be counted on to bounce back at the first
sign of failure.

Nabil Shaath, the liaison between the Palestinian delegation and the PLO
headquarters in Tunis, made no public appearances during the negotiating
sessions at Madrid. A large, round-faced man who expresses himself volu-
bly, he was uncomfortable maintaining a low profile, but it was considered
prudent not to rub the noses of the Israelis in the PLO's presence. After
the meetings were over, he was more than willing to talk. Shaath readily
acknowledged that Husseini and his colleagues on the Palestinian delegation had—to the dismay of some of the PLO's old-timers—come into their
own as sources of power.

"Since the *intifada* began, there has been a reformulation of relationships," he said, "with concomitant tensions. This isn't new in the history of the PLO. There was a similar shift when the organization had to move from Jordan to Lebanon in 1971, and when it moved from Lebanon to Tunis in 1982. At one time, the centerfold of our movement was the guerrilla with the Kalashnikov rifle. Then it became the young kid throwing stones in the streets of the occupied territories. Now it is shifting to somber political operatives like Faisal Husseini in the territories. The emphasis of the movement is no longer on armed struggle. Now we are into diplomacy, with less reliance on the Arab countries—whom we have not been able to count on—and more on ourselves. The rejectionists are dinosaurs, relics of another era. Faisal represents the rejuvenation of the PLO, in the era of diplomacy."

But Shaath also had to acknowledge the rising menace of Hamas, whose quarrel with the PLO was over the very nature of Palestinian society. Islam was not a new factor in Palestinian politics. In the 1930s, a band of *fellahin*, preaching Islam, gave themselves a place in history by rebelling against the British and the Jews. In the 1940s, Egypt's Muslim Brotherhood began recruiting in Palestine, and, though its efforts collapsed after 1948, a few cells survived to function in secret. The years after 1967 were marked by the steady growth in popular allegiance to the PLO's secular and nationalist doctrine, but the shift to the two-state solution was more than many traditionalists, both Islamic and secular, could take.

Ironically, the Israelis gave the Islamics a big boost, hoping to divide the opposition by tolerating a wave of recruitment by the Brotherhood; only in 1990 did they change this policy. At the start of the *intifada*, Hamas, heir to the Brotherhood, was a PLO ally of some consequence, and the Unified Command was glad to get its support. But as the fighting dragged on and the peace talks faltered, Hamas set itself up as a rival, taking positions on both tactics and goals that were more extreme than the PLO's. Now part ally, part foe of the PLO, Hamas has since grown steadily, principally in the Gaza Strip, where Israel's suppression has been the harshest.

"With Hamas growing stronger, our margin of maneuver is getting narrower and narrower," said Mustafa Baghoudi, a doctor who runs a public-health center in an Arab suburb of Jerusalem and who serves on the steering committee that helps shape Palestinian negotiating policy in the peace talks. "Saudi Arabia has been supporting Hamas for some time, and recently we think Iran has moved in. They are building mosques and clinics, and they provide funds for social welfare, all of which Hamas uses to strengthen its political position. Hamas has no program for dealing with the occupation; it offers only God, though to some Palestinians, that's enough. We have invited Hamas to join our advisory bodies, but it insists on our changing our political line, which we cannot do. Hamas is very secret, and we're not always sure what it wants, but we know that if negotiations fail, it will have a big popular surge.

"We are prepared in the negotiations to make concessions to Israel. But if we are pressed too hard, at some point we will have to say, 'We can't go on.' We have basic needs. Satisfying these needs does not weaken Israel's security; they have to do with our identity and dignity. We and Israel will both lose if Hamas supersedes us. I hope the Israelis can understand this."

Hanan Ashrawi, the dark-haired spokeswoman for the Palestinian delegation to the peace negotiations, lives in the outskirts of Ramallah, fifteen minutes north of Jerusalem. The modern stone house that she shares with her husband and two daughters, Zena and Amal, is across the road from an Israeli army headquarters and prison. Ashrawi was born in Ramallah of a deeply rooted Christian Arab family. Her father was a doctor who, contrary to custom, gave his five daughters the same education as boys receive, and she ultimately obtained a Ph.D. in the United States. I first met Ashrawi in 1979, when she was teaching English literature at Birzeit. I remember her telling me she was writing a novel, and my asking her—rather naïvely, I suppose—whether it was political. She gave me the withering smile that has since become familiar to television audiences and said, "In the West Bank, everything is political."

Ashrawi could, no doubt, have left the West Bank long ago, as have so many Palestinians. Her hometown, gracious and sophisticated, even liberal, in her youth, had become, under the impact of refugees from the countryside, poor, overcrowded and increasingly fundamentalist. Since 1967, much of Ramallah's well-to-do population, most of it Christian, had left. Throughout the West Bank, in fact, the Christian population since the Six-Day War is believed to have fallen from 15 to 3 percent, and I sometimes wondered why Ashrawi stayed. Recently, I came across a pamphlet in my files that she wrote at Birzeit in 1976. It was entitled "Contemporary Palestinian Literature under Occupation," and in it, she said of writers: "Such a tremendous responsibility is placed on their shoulders, burdened with the aspirations of a whole nation, that they are no longer free agents or individuals." It seemed to me that in those words I had found the answer.

Since I have known her, Ashrawi has articulated the philosophy of the West Bank's nationalist mainstream—that is, she favors the recognition of Israel on the condition that it withdraws from the territories occupied in 1967, and though she insists on the right to establish a Palestinian state, which would be democratic and secular, she agrees, as a practical matter, to accept autonomy in the territories during a period of transition.

In the summer of 1992, her goal seemed a step closer to realization with Likud's defeat in Israel's parliamentary election. Labor's Yitzhak Rabin, the newly installed prime minister, promised to negotiate autonomy for the occupied territories without delay. His pledge—in lending immediacy to the prospect of an Israeli-Palestinian agreement—intensified the conflict between the PLO and Hamas. Fighting between the two moved into the streets, and both sides suffered fatalities. The pressure of the PLO-Hamas conflict made it more imperative than ever for the PLO to come up with some tangible results to justify its involvement in negotiations. It seemed possible that breakdown of the talks would spark an explosion, in both the West Bank and the Gaza Strip, that would become a Palestinian civil war.

Ashrawi and I talked in her Ramallah home about what Rabin's election offered to the peace process. We sat on easy chairs in her study, which looked out over the Judean hills. Nearby was a bookcase containing the works of Chaucer and other medieval English writers, and some volumes on the Crusades, the relics of her academic past. Ashrawi was, as usual, carefully coiffed. But the international press had criticized her clothes as dowdy, and she wore a light blue jacket with a pastel, flowered skirt, as if in response. We sipped coffee as we spoke, and she smoked one cigarette after another.

"We were encouraged, of course, by Rabin's offer to meet at once for negotiations, and to continue negotiating without a break. Likud had no intention of negotiating at all. It had created insuperable obstacles in its program of building settlements, and in its violations of Palestinian human rights. We had hoped Rabin would remove these obstacles before we sat down to talk. We wanted to go right into talks on elections and the self-governing authority.

"Our plan was to start with the withdrawal of the Israeli army. We proposed a total transfer of authority to the Palestinians, with negotiations over the exceptions, basically in the areas of Israeli security. The Palestinians must replace the military government as the source of law. We know the settlers don't want any of that, and they have their own military guard, with plenty of guns. Israel, unfortunately, has created a class of people that defies its laws; now it does not know what to do with them. If the army wants to stay in the territories and maintain law and order in our behalf, that's all right. But the army has got to get out of our lives, to end the brutality, violence and daily intrusion of the occupation. We entered the peace process to end the occupation, not to beautify it."

I mentioned to Ashrawi that all the Arab regimes seemed to have chosen to stress their disappointments with the Rabin government. I asked whether she was not overstating her grievances, and failing to give Rabin credit for positive steps. Like the Palestinians, I said, the Israelis must also take local political pressures into account.

"I don't want to give you the impression that everything is negative," she answered. "We recognize Rabin's political problems, but we disagree on how he is handling them. He was elected on a promise of new priorities, and we feel that he is now catering to Israel's right wing. We have our extremists, and they are very threatening to us. But we haven't indulged them, and we don't think that Rabin ought to indulge his. I don't feel pessimistic. We are not without power. We are willing to be reasonable in dealing with the Israelis, and we will acknowledge positive moves, but we must also be realistic. We're dealing with the fate of our people, and we have to be careful."

I did not think that Ashrawi was fully honest in saying that the Palestinian side in the peace talks had not been indulging its extremists. In fact, the Palestinians negotiators in 1993 were taking a much tougher line than they had taken in Madrid in 1991. The change might be explained, at least in part, by the rigid stance adopted by the Labor government elected in Israel in 1992, which was supposed to be more "dovish" than its Likud predecessor. Instead, Labor not only made no new concessions in the talks but, equally important, did nothing to lighten the heavy hand of the occupation. Under these circumstances, the Palestinians seemed to have no choice but to show themselves equally stubborn. Whatever Israelis might do, however, the PLO's freedom of action was limited by the knowledge that Islamic fundamentalists were standing by ready to exploit any sign of weakness. The Palestinian delegation, as Ashrawi said, had to be careful, but the danger faced in the negotiations was probably less from the Israelis than from Hamas, whose demagogy threatened to deprive the PLO of its very mandate to make peace.

CHAPTER SEVEN

KUWAIT

I Carrying a New Flag

THE GULF WAR of 1991 will no doubt be recorded as a critical juncture in the history of Arab relations with the West. For the first time since the system of sovereign states was established after World War I, one Arab country, Iraq, tried to swallow another, Kuwait. In the ensuing war of liberation, Saudi Arabia, the most Islamic of the Arab states, served as the base of operations for the West. Two major Arab states, Egypt and Syria, both secular, became the West's military allies. In contrast, most Arabs on the street, whether Islamic or secular, brushed sovereignty concerns aside to give emotional support to Iraq for standing up to the West; they were impotent to give anything more. For both Easterners and Westerners, the Crusader reflex was reborn.

For Arab society, it was civil war, and since then, the breach has shown few signs of healing. The war left the notion of Arab unity—to say nothing of the "Arab nation"—in shambles. Many have attributed the calamity of the Gulf war solely to the evil spirit of Saddam Hussein, the Iraqi despot. That is surely an oversimplification, which ignores the highly intricate context in which this Arab tragedy took place.

The war would not have happened but for the involvement, at many stages, of the United States. On the one hand, Washington saw a need to preserve the international order based on the sovereignty system. On the other, it worried about damage to its interests in the Gulf. Washington had clearly signaled this concern during the Iraq-Iran war, when it agreed to accept the consequences of its placing the American flag on the oil tankers of Kuwait's merchant fleet. Its solicitude was not so much for Kuwait for as the Gulf's oil, an indispensable asset to the West's industrial culture.

During a visit to Kuwait in February 1988, I discussed the "reflagging" of the tankers with Saoud al-Osaimi, then the minister of state for foreign affairs. We met in his office in the Sief Palace, a complex of sand-colored buildings stretching along the seafront. A relic of old Kuwait, the palace was also the working quarters of Kuwait's emir, Sheikh Jabir al-Sabah. Fortresslike in design, it was checkered with courtyards and gardens, and the only signs of security that I saw were two light machine guns facing out across the water. Osaimi was dressed in a *dishdasha*, a floor-length robe worn invariably with a flowing *kuffiyeh*; the fashion is white cotton in summer and muted shades of wool in winter. Kuwaiti officials never dress in anything else. Osaimi played self-consciously with the tails of his *kuffiyeh* while we talked.

"The story really opens in 1983," Osaimi said, "when the Iraqi air force started doing serious damage to Iranian shipping in the Gulf. Iran talked of closing the Gulf in retaliation, declaring that it would be for everybody or for nobody, and in April 1984, the Iranians began attacking neutral shipping, including ours. Remember, all our oil, which represents ninety percent of our income, is exported through the Gulf. Almost all of our food is shipped in through the Gulf. At first, we speculated that Iran wanted us to pressure Iraq to ground its planes, but we had no power in Baghdad. We talked to the Iranians, directly and through intermediaries. We worked through the Islamic Conference, the Nonaligned Movement and, finally, the United Nations. We got the Security Council to pass Resolution 552, which called on Iran to stop bombing the harbors and boats of countries uninvolved in the war. But none of these efforts worked."

Osaimi reminded me that Iran's attacks on Kuwait were not limited to Gulf waters. In 1983, partisans of Iran bombed the American and French embassies, killing six people and wounding eighty. In 1985, an attempt was made on the life of the emir. Repeated sabotage was committed on installations in the Kuwaiti oil fields. Kuwait did not like to acknowledge that more than a few of those arrested for these acts were Kuwaiti nationals—Shiite Muslims sympathetic to the message of Iran's Ayatollah Khomeini. But it had no doubt that Iran was behind them.

Iran's complaint against Kuwait, it should be said, was not frivolous. Kuwait, notwithstanding its official neutrality, was giving important assistance to the Iraqi war effort. It provided loans estimated at a billion dollars or more a year, in addition to an annual subsidy of several hundred million in the form of Kuwaiti oil marketed on Iraq's account. Iraq needed this help desperately in the early years of the war, after the destruction of its port facilities; later, the construction of new pipelines permitted Iraq to bypass the Gulf in exporting its own oil and so restore its earnings. Until the end of the war, however, Kuwait served as a depot in the overland supply line between the Gulf and Iraq. These services angered Iran and put Iraq deeply in Kuwait's debt.

By the second half of 1986, Osaimi said, Kuwait had come to recognize that it could not deal by itself with Iran's attacks—that it would have to "internationalize" its defense. Its first stop was the Gulf Cooperation Council, a body consisting of Saudi Arabia, Kuwait, Bahrain, Qatar, Oman and the United Arab Emirates, the sheikhdoms bordering the Gulf. The GCC was formed in 1981, shortly after the start of the war, to shape common security policies. But Saudi Arabia had not assumed the leadership that had been expected of it in dealing with Iran, while Oman and the Emirates showed more interest in maintaining their Iranian trade than in responding to any Iranian threat. In war or peace, Iran was the region's most powerful nation, and the GCC, unwilling to invite a confrontation, rebuffed Kuwait's plea.

"We decided then to go to the UN Security Council, to facilitate its task of keeping peace in the world," Osaimi said. "After all, the Gulf is considered an international waterway, where the rights of free navigation are confirmed in international law. Part of the Security Council's responsibility for keeping the peace is to protect such waterways. Our first talks on this subject, in late 1986, were with the Soviet Union."

Kuwait's itinerary indicated no pro-Soviet bias. Osaimi said that Kuwait, feeling desperate, knew that Moscow could act more quickly than Washington. Moreover, at that very moment the press was spreading the details of the Reagan administration's secret deal to send arms to Iran—later known as Irangate—and the Kuwaitis were uncertain whether Washington, though ostensibly pro-Iraq, was in reality promoting the military designs of Iran. Irangate added major confusion to America's Gulf policy which for decades had lacked clarity.

America's interest in the Gulf began with the first shipments of oil after World War II, but its involvement was delayed until Britain, in 1971, ended more than a century of hegemony in the region by withdrawing its last contingent of soldiers from the Emirates. The United States took over Britain's naval station in Bahrain and brought in a few small ships to steam around, proclaiming its presence. For real power, Washington turned to the shah of Iran, pledging whatever arms he fancied in exchange for his safeguarding Western security interests. The arrangement worked satisfactorily until 1979, when the shah fell and the Soviet Union invaded Afghanistan, a twofold policy debacle. Not only did Moscow appear to be on the march toward the Gulf, but Iran was no longer available to stop it.

In 1981, in his last State of the Union address, President Jimmy Carter declared, in response to the Soviet presence in Afghanistan, that "An attempt by any outside force to gain control of the Persian Gulf region will be regarded as an assault on the vital interests of the United States . . . and will be repelled by any means necessary, including force." These words, known as the Carter Doctrine, were a clear warning to Moscow, but without American forces to back them up, no one could say whether or not they were a bluff.

Washington was fortunate that Afghan resistance blocked the Soviet option of moving on the Gulf. It was not so fortunate with Iran. Khomeini's revolution was committed not only to exporting its stern Islamic ideology into the Arab world but also to striking blows at the West, especially the United States, which it called the "Great Satan" for having corrupted the regime of the shah. When the Iraq-Iran war started, Washington had been on bad terms with Baghdad since the Six-Day War a dozen years before. But it was on even worse terms with Iran, which at the time held fifty-two Americans captive in the Teheran embassy. Neutral at first, Washington extended agricultural credits to Iraq in 1982, and by 1984 the two countries had agreed to resume diplomatic relations. Two years later, Washington openly proclaimed its preference for Iraq in the war.

In January 1987, when Kuwait disclosed its reflagging plan, President Reagan at first balked at the idea of American involvement, but changed his mind after learning that Moscow had agreed to provide armed escorts for Kuwaiti tankers. Although Kuwait was a practiced hand at playing big powers against one another, Osaimi denied that the Moscow deal was meant to smoke Washington out. In May, after Reagan endorsed the plan, Kuwait formally declined Moscow's help. Reagan's move meant more than American protection for Kuwaiti ships; it meant, as well, putting American weight on Iraq's side to end the Iraq-Iran war.

By early 1988, though the war still raged, Kuwait pronounced the "internationalization" policy a strategic victory. Britain, France, Italy and Belgium had followed the American lead by sending warships to the Gulf, and relative calm had been restored to the shipping lanes. Teheran's war effort was clearly winding down. Then in the spring, Iran launched a last-gasp offensive, mining convoy routes and firing on Kuwaiti land positions. After hitting an American ship, the so-called "tanker war" flared up, in which the U.S. Navy destroyed two of Iran's oil platforms and crippled or sank six of its ships. A few weeks later, Iraq retook the Fao peninsula, just across the water from Kuwaiti territory. The hostilities were still going on when I asked Osaimi whether his government would call on Washington if Iran invaded Kuwait.

"Right now, the United States is not defending Kuwait; it is defending its own flag," he answered disingenuously. "I don't want to talk about something that we hope will never happen. I know that the subject of a long-term military relationship has come up in your newspapers, and your congressmen have mentioned it during visits here. But we've had no official discussions on the issue, much less on such specific questions as bases in our territory. The guiding principle of our foreign policy is nonalignment, and that is what it will remain. After the Iraq-Iran war, we don't know what the Americans will do."

In fact, Kuwait had already established a close relationship with the United States. State Department officials told me when I returned home that American and Kuwaiti strategists regularly discussed the security problems of the Gulf region and said that the discussions were growing increasingly candid and intimate. This relationship did not end with the cease-fire in the Iraq-Iran war. In fact, it grew more intense over the years that followed. When Iraq invaded Kuwait in August 1990, the relationship that began with the reflagging of the tankers three years before was put to its severest test.

II   OUT OF THE DESERT

THE ARABIAN DESERT has for millennia been the home of nomadic tribes, dependent upon the camel for their meager existence, jealous of their freedom, constantly at war with one another. In the eighteenth century, one of these tribes migrated toward the northeast, in the direction of the Gulf, under pressure from marauding rivals. The tribe was the Bani Utub, and on reaching the Gulf it found that Europeans had established trading posts along the shore. The opportunities for commerce the Europeans offered induced the Bani Utub to adopt a new way of life, and after a search they chose a site—a natural harbor, with fresh water, in the northwest corner of the Gulf—which had long been a crossroads for caravans. There they built a town surrounded by walls—"Kuwait" is derived from the local word for "fort"—and established a society based on seafaring, pearling and trade with the bedouin tribes of the interior. Until the oil age, through cycles of boom and bust, the economy and character of this society remained fundamentally unchanged.

To cope with problems that were far more complex than those of the desert, the Bani Utub devised a unique political system. Historians believe that the tribe's three chief families negotiated a contract which provided for a division of labor. The Khalifas took responsibility for commerce and the Jalahimas for the seafaring trades. The administration of the town was left to the Sabahs. Historians disagree on whether to attribute this assignment to the Sabahs' preeminence, to the good relations they maintained with the tribes of the interior or to the indifference of the money-makers to local government. Kuwaiti legend holds that the Sabahs, never warriors, were known even then for their bargaining skills, which they put to use extracting from the other families of the tribe the money needed

for municipal expenses. This practice evolved into a political system dominated by the ruling family but based nonetheless on widespread consent.
Great merchant families arose as a check on the authority of the Sabahs.
Over time, Kuwait became a kind of constitutional monarchy, which gave
it, alone among the Arabs, an indigenous foundation for building a democracy. Its original social contract grew into a tradition of popular participation that has persisted for more than two centuries, and of which Kuwaitis
remain extremely proud.

Throughout the early years, the Sabahs used their diplomatic skills to
maintain Kuwait's independence from stronger rivals. Rarely did Kuwaitis
go to war, and then to fight only brief skirmishes. Kuwait relied on a
policy of calculated neutrality, tilting now toward one power, now toward
another. It never fell under the control of the Saudis, the tribe which
ultimately came to rule nearly all of the Arabian peninsula. It was lucky
to stay clear of the Persians who, throughout most of Kuwaiti history,
were too busy defending themselves from the czars. Nor did it ever submit
to the Ottomans, who claimed a sovereignty over Kuwait that they were
unable to enforce. Because it depended for much of its wealth on the
Ottoman port of Basra, at the confluence of the Tigris and Euphrates,
Kuwait did its utmost to keep on amicable terms with Istanbul. Only when
the Turks in the 1890s eyed Kuwait as the Gulf terminus of the Berlin-
Baghdad railway, a joint Ottoman-German project, did Kuwaitis grow
nervous and turn to Britain for help.

The British navy, to protect the empire's lines of communication to
India, first entered the Gulf in 1805, and a few years later deployed a
permanent naval squadron there. Within a few decades, the Royal Navy
had established its ascendancy in the Gulf, but the British worried about
Russia's southward moves. These moves persuaded them that keeping
Kuwait in friendly hands was imperative. In 1841, a British official, exploring the Gulf, sent his government the following dispatch on Kuwait:

> Its harbour . . . is certainly an exceedingly fine one, capable of
> holding the navy of Great Britain, but so far as my observation goes,
> it possesses no other advantage. The country around is a salt and
> sandy desert, of the most barren and unhospitable description, with
> not a tree or shrub visible as far as the eye can reach, excepting a few
> bushes which mark the wells. From the taste and quality of the water,
> I feel almost certain that it would not agree with the constitutions of
> either Europeans or Indians. . . .
> [But] the town presents a singular instance of commercial prosper-
> ity. . . . The energy and courage of the people, who are closely united
> and free from feuds and factions, render them respected by all the

other maritime tribes . . . The government of Shaikh Jabir is of a truly mild and paternal character. [He] and his sons are perhaps among the worst dressed and most ill lodged residents in the place. Excepting a small duty levied upon the sales and purchases of the bedouins who resort to his town, the Shaikh collects no taxes or customs. . . . This liberality, together with the utter absence of all pretension of outward superiority, renders him . . . most popular among his subjects, who are consequently devoted to him in an unusual degree.

Attentive to the sensibilities of the Ottomans, in whose lands they owned extensive date-palm groves, the Sabahs declined to consider at that point a British proposal to establish a base in the town. It took Britain until the reign of Sheikh Mubarak al-Sabah to achieve this objective. Mubarak had ascended to the throne in 1896 by assassinating his two half brothers. His bloody coup stands out as an exception in a history virtually free of dynastic violence. Kuwaitis rarely discuss the episode and would no doubt prefer to excise it from their collective memory, particularly since Mubarak's reign is otherwise regarded as illustrious. But for the Ottomans, the murders became a pretext for threatening to occupy Kuwait, and so Mubarak signed a treaty with Britain that made his realm a protectorate. The treaty shifted Kuwait's political alignment away from the Ottoman empire and opened a window to the West that has never been closed.

Badr Khalid al-Badr, a former Kuwaiti ambassador to the Gulf states, reminisced with me about the days of his boyhood, when Sheikh Salim, Mubarak's son and the ninth Sabah to rule, routinely wandered through the *souk* on horseback. Badr was born in 1912, into a prominent merchant family. After his retirement, he published a memoir of his early life and acquired a reputation as both a historian and a storyteller. We talked on a chilly February afternoon, with an electric heater warming the living room of his medium-size house. Badr wore a heavy sweater over his *dishdasha* and wool slippers on his feet. A small pot of coffee, heavily laced with cardamon, stood beside a dish of Arab cakes and candies on a low table before us. Periodically, he filled my tiny cup and urged a sweet on me.

"In the morning," Badr recalled, "the emir worked in the Sief Palace, where he received visitors and mediated minor disputes. When he finished his work, he made a tour of the *souk*, surrounded by a handful of retainers. He wore ordinary Arab dress. Kuwait was a small place then, and he knew most of the people. In those days, Kuwait still felt like a family, or at least a tribe. But it was tolerant. Bedouins, drawn by our prosperity, settled in the town and were quickly assimilated. We had communities of Christians and Jews. But the atmosphere was harmonious, and the people working or shopping in the *souk* rose to greet the sheikh, without class resentment, respectfully, but as if he were one of them. Often he rode with a junior member of the family, who would stay behind to listen to whatever the shopkeepers had to say. After his tour, he went to a coffee shop named Abu Nashi—it's not there anymore—near the big mosque. Anyone could approach him and talk to him. That was our tradition. But mostly, he received his friends—distinguished merchants and other notables—and together they conducted the business of the state."

Over the years, Badr said, trading patterns changed but the *souk* remained the same labyrinth of shops shaded from the sun by flimsy roofs of whatever materials were available. Fresh fish was always abundant, brought in daily by local fishermen. Bedouins brought in meat, the best of it after the spring rains, when the desert was green and the animals were fat. Persians imported rugs and other fine items; they were the first Shiites in the society, he said, and some became extremely rich. The Jews specialized in importing European fabrics, which attracted the stylish ladies; they had a synagogue and were permitted to make, but not to sell, an alcoholic drink, the product of fermented dates. Kuwait was then known in the Gulf for its graceful dhows, built by its craftsmen of Indian teak, Badr said, as well as the *boum*, a larger ship of similar design, to ply the high seas. Maritime products—ropes, sails, nets, anchors, pulleys—made up much of the *souk*'s business. Every day, caravans arrived from as far away as Baghdad or Damascus, and ships pulled up to the dock. Kuwait, Badr said, was then among the most prosperous, most cosmopolitan communities of the Arab world.

"For me, as a young boy," he said, "the last day of the pearling season, usually at the end of September, was the most exciting day of the year. The ship captains would agree in advance on the day and send a courier home from the sea to notify the town. All the women waited on the shore with their children, and as the flagship came into sight, it fired its guns. It was the end of four months of hard work—of diving from dawn to dusk, with breaks only to sleep, eat and say prayers. In the year I was born, eight hundred ships went to the sea for pearl fishing, averaging thirty-five men, each of whom received a share of the profits. When the fleet docked, the pearl brokers were waiting in the *souk* to bargain for the catch, which they sent to Bombay or to Paris. And when the men came ashore their earnings were waiting for them, and they joined the townspeople in a huge celebration that lasted all day long."

THE GOLDEN DAYS came to an abrupt end after World War I. Though economic distress was worldwide, Kuwait was hit particularly hard. The

Japanese discovered how to produce cultured pearls, and the British introduced the steam freighter, which made a relic of the sail-powered dhow.
Kuwait was no longer queen of the Gulf, and its decline only aggravated
the historical rivalry between the Sabahs and the merchant elite. Over the
years, the merchants had learned from the British about political democracy, and they undertook a campaign—reminiscent of the demands of
thirteenth-century English barons on King John for a charter—to institu-
tionalize their traditional rights. The struggle reached a climax in 1938,
when the merchants convened an assembly which declared the people to
be the source of authority in Kuwait. The Sabahs, while acknowledging
the principle of power-sharing, defended the family interests by arresting
and beating their opponents. When the assembly barricaded itself in its
chamber, the emir sent his tribal militia to break it up, and two assembly
members were shot, one fatally. But there was no civil war. The people
did not support the merchants, and the Sabahs emerged triumphant.

What the rebellious merchants did not know was that events they could
not control had already transformed the terms of the struggle. In 1934,
the emir, Sheikh Ahmad al-Sabah, had signed an agreement giving an oil
concession to the Kuwait Oil Company, a consortium made up of Gulf Oil
and British Petroleum. The terms treated Kuwait as the emir's private
domain, with all income going directly to him. The merchants, failing to
grasp the full significance of the contract, never challenged it. The deal
emancipated the al-Sabahs, making it likely that any future sharing of
power would be the product not of negotiation between partners, as it had
been for two centuries, but of the largesse of the ruling family.

The Kuwait Oil Company in 1936 dug its first well, which two years
later led to the discovery of one of the world's largest oil fields. World
War II halted production, but by the 1950s Kuwait's annual oil income
had reached $16 million, which gave the state ample resources to carry out
its functions. In the ensuing decades, income would rise a thousandfold,
tempting the Sabahs to rule like absolute monarchs. By then, every member of the Sabah family, of which there were thousands, received a substantial state stipend. Yet plenty of wealth remained for successive emirs to
spread around. They saw to it that the merchant class benefited hand-
somely, and when radical Nasserism struck Kuwait, they were ready to
buy off the general population, offering an open-handed social-welfare
program—education, health care, housing, utilities and water, all free, as
well as a guaranteed government job at a decent salary. Notwithstanding
this generosity, the Sabahs by the 1980s controlled financial reserves believed to be in the range of $100 billion, nearly all of it invested in the
West. Under the circumstances, it is astonishing that Kuwaitis did not
forgo completely their historical attachment to democracy.

In 1961, Kuwait regained its independence in a treaty with Britain, and soon afterward Sheikh Abdullah, the reigning emir, bestowed on the country a constitution which included provisions for an elected assembly and a free press, but which also banned political parties and imposed strict limitations on the franchise. The barriers were designed to produce a compliant assembly, but in the first election under the constitution, the voters elected a noisy opposition bloc of a dozen Nasserites. Despite government manipulation, the assemblies elected in 1967 and 1971 also showed a surprising spirit of independence. In 1975, the assembly, with strong popular and press support, launched an outspoken attack on the ruling family's favoritism to the rich in the allocation of revenues. The strife made clear that much of the country was dissatisfied with Kuwait's hierarchy of privilege. Dismayed by this audacity, Sheikh Sabah al-Salem, Abdullah's successor as emir, dissolved the assembly and suspended the constitution. But, whatever their power, the Sabahs were not able to eradicate dissent, and the struggle continued.

III   UTOPIA IN THE SANDS

FEW CITIES HAVE burgeoned with the same momentum and rapidity that Kuwait has," an urban visionary wrote in 1964, commenting on how a modest town sitting on the shoreline between the desert and the sea had been transformed by oil. "The impact of revenue on landscape is, in Kuwait, perhaps more dramatic than anywhere else. The Kuwaitis have chosen so far to build everything urban . . . en masse: roads, houses, schools, hospitals, mosques, warehouses, public utilities. . . . To get this huge job done, Kuwait recruited engineers, technicians, white-collar workers, and laborers literally by the thousands, till the corps of employees in the building of Kuwait exceeded in number the armies of many an Arab country. . . . The development craze had reached such a high pitch by June, 1960, that . . . urban suicide was incipient . . . Kuwait literally exploded from a small village into a fast-urbanizing regional metropolis.

"Townscape here is baffling, scale overwhelming. . . . The streets—more like superhighways—are wide and long, and buildings rarely bear any architectural relationship to them. The art of walking has been lost. The speed of this unique urban explosion, the momentum propelling it into a chain of explosions, the ambitious drive behind the fast urbanization, and the vast revenues making all this possible are, perhaps, unprecedented in urban history. They are certainly unprecedented in any harsh desert locus. . . . Millions of cubic meters of sand have been removed from the city, exchanged for 'sweet' soil and planted until several areas in and around the city have been transformed into parks, gardens and green strips. The effort expended on confronting the desert in Kuwait is a gigantic, ruthless, unrelenting, courageous and determined effort: a unique Arab effort."

These words are from a memoir by Saba George Shiber, an architect and urban planner who was born in Palestine and educated at universities in Beirut, Cairo and the United States. Summoned by the emir in 1960 to guide the city's growth, he was—as the memoir reveals—both exhilarated and appalled by what he found. He never succeeded in his goal of checking "all the parasites profiteering from too rapid growth," largely because profiteering was part of the emir's program of indulging the merchant elite. He did manage to impose some standards of urban planning, keeping the disorder from becoming worse than it might overwise have been. But he failed totally in making Kuwait "the renaissance city of the century," which had been his dream. The Kuwait of the 1960s that he described was materially too rich, and culturally too impoverished, and it had no desire at all to change. That is precisely what Kuwait has remained.

Modern Kuwait is a land created for the automobile and the air-conditioner. At its core is the old town, once squeezed between the sea and a semicircular mud wall of which nothing but the gates remain. Within it are the *souk*, the Sief Palace, a new Grand Mosque, a mélange of multistoried bank and government buildings, and countless parking lots in the spaces where for centuries the homes of Kuwaitis stood. The new downtown that surrounds the old town mixes luxury hotels with shabby, low-lying commercial buildings that have shops on the street level and apartments for foreign workers, mostly of the managerial class, up above. Beyond, following the contours of the old wall in widening half-circles are sequentially numbered ring roads, which intersect in the desert with superhighways radiating outward like spokes. At some of these intersections are communities of slums, the residences of foreigners who do Kuwait's menial work. Kuwaitis themselves inhabit villas of varying degrees of sumptuousness, and every morning and evening they jam the roads from and to monotonous suburbs, which are as much as an hour's drive from the city's commercial hub on the sea.

"In the 1960s, every Kuwaiti wanted a Western-style villa," said Ibraheem al-Shaheen, the American-educated head of the National Housing Authority, the agency with responsibility for filling out these suburbs. "Then, in the seventies, people began to ask for old-fashioned Islamic arches and traditional Arab lines. Now the trend is toward a Kuwaiti style—simple houses, the rooms opening on a courtyard, with small windows to keep out the sun."

Shaheen told me that a Kuwaiti couple, on getting married, acquires the right to a house of two living rooms, five bedrooms, five bathrooms, and a maid's quarter. Though most couples now live in a Western manner— that is, women are not walled off into a *haram*—they also exercise their right to a traditional *diwaniyah*, a room set aside in most Kuwaiti homes for men to gather for convivial talk. Over the years, Shaheen said, Kuwaitis came to take for granted not just their free housing but the "total welfare system" as a right of citizenship.

"Our way of life," Shaheen said, "has probably substituted psychological problems for the society's old economic problems. That explains the changed taste in architecture. There is a new emphasis on heritage. The demand for the *diwaniyah* suggests a drifting back to the old order of values. It was especially apparent after the start of the Iraq-Iran war, which spread a sense of insecurity. The notion of returning to our roots became a system of defense against the danger from outside."

By the early 1980s, the Kuwaiti government, having completed a modern infrastructure, had put its mind to providing amenities for the city. It laid out parks with trees, lawns and flowers, to which the local population responded by planting gardens around their own homes. An American woman long married to a Kuwaiti told me that over a quarter century the face of the city had been transformed from an ugly, depressing brown to a cheerful, almost European green. The government also renovated the seafront, where many Sabahs have splendid homes and where young princes drag-race their roadsters late at night; it constructed promenades, playgrounds, a sailing marina, restaurants and outdoor cafes. It has also built a network of sports clubs and, some miles from the city, an Arabized version of Disneyland for children.

But providing an atmosphere of sociability was not easy in a culture committed to the rather austere version of Islam that the Bani Utub brought from the desert, and it was made more difficult by the Kuwaitis' taste for self-segregation. Kuwait had a few concert halls, theaters and cinemas, but they were patronized nearly exclusively by foreigners. It had book stores, but no literary tradition, and collections of Islamic art, but no artistic tradition. Kuwaitis liked family camping in the desert, and a Westernized segment was known to hold elegant dinner parties, with whiskey and wine. Kuwaiti men enjoyed gathering in one another's *diwaniyah*, and the women, it was said, liked nothing better than shopping, practiced in air-conditioned supermarkets and malls filled with luxury imports. Kuwaitis also congregated to watch television and videocassettes, a particularly favored diversion because it was exercised in the sanctuary of the home, where foreigners could not intrude.

The first wave of outsiders to arrive in Kuwait were the Palestinians, and until the Iraqi invasion in 1990 they made up a community of three hundred and fifty thousand, second in size only to the Kuwaitis themselves. Their services became available in 1948, just when Kuwait required manpower to launch its expansion. Israel's victory had left hundreds of thousands crowded into refugee camps, in desperate need of work. Many came as simple laborers, but others had the skills to be administrators, teachers, doctors and lawyers, craftsmen, businessmen. Kuwait was glad to have them, and the Palestinians in turn found the regime of the Sabahs no harsher than Israel, or than the Arab regimes they had left behind.

The Palestinian community thrived in Kuwait. Yasir Arafat, an engineer trained in Cairo, was among those who gravitated there, and found likeminded young Palestinians with whom he formed Fatah, the backbone of the PLO. The Sabahs encouraged the Palestinians in their dreams of regaining their homeland; it diverted them from designs upon Kuwait. For years, Kuwait was known as the most generous supporter in the Arab world of Palestine liberation and the PLO.

The former oasis of Hawali, three or four miles across the desert from the Sief Palace, was the center of Palestinian life in Kuwait. Its small restaurants and coffeehouses, the color photos of the Dome of the Rock in the shop windows, the peeling paint and laundry hanging from the balconies, all conveyed the feeling of a Palestinian town. The day I visited Hawali in 1988 had been chosen by the PLO to celebrate the local Palestinians' solidarity with the *intifada*, which was then several months old. Outside the PLO headquarters, parked buses crowded the narrow street, while inside an auditorium overflowed with women wearing Palestinian folk costumes and singing Palestinian songs. Elsewhere in town, meanwhile, a rambunctious band of Palestinian university students paraded without a permit until, I learned later, the police stopped them and arrested a few on charges of provocation. Kuwait, in those days, imposed one stringent rule on the Palestinians: Stay out of Kuwaiti politics. Unwilling to challenge the rule, PLO leaders chose not to come to the students' defense, and simply let them spend a few days in the lockup.

From the time they began arriving in large numbers, foreign workers were denied most of the privileges, and nearly all of the rights, that Kuwaitis enjoyed. A foreigner, no matter what his length of residence, was not permitted to own a house, or a plot of land, or more than a minority share in a business. No foreigner was given a work or residence permit without a Kuwaiti sponsor, to whom he was beholden, and though immigrants with professional status were permitted to bring wives and children, they were required to leave promptly at the loss of employment, even for retirement. Barred from all social benefits except health care, foreigners even had to pay to send their children to school. Their wages were set by international supply and demand, which meant they received a fraction of a Kuwaiti's pay for equal work, and for housing they had to go to the free market, with the result that many lived in slums. Foreigners had some access to the courts, and were only rarely subject to police harassment, but they were faced with expulsion for the slightest infraction of rules, a powerful weapon to ensure good behavior.

In the late 1960s, Kuwait began shifting its migration policy away from Arabs, in favor of Asians. The government, officially, insisted that it was only following the labor market. Having skimmed the available skills of the Arab world, officials said, they were turning to Asians, who accepted lower wages for the same qualifications. Most observers, however, believed the real reason for the shift to be the growing fear in which Kuwaitis held other Arabs. As members of the *umma*, Arabs could make claims on Kuwait, and as Kuwaitis grew richer they became increasingly sensitive to the prospect of other Arabs seeking to share their wealth. The issue came to a head at the time of the Six-Day War.

Pan-Arabism had unleashed turmoil in Kuwait, and the Nasserites in the national assembly were at the peak of their power. After the Arab defeat, the government took in a substantial number of refugees to appease them, but announced that it was henceforth looking elsewhere for foreign workers. Since then, only Egyptians—considered the most malleable of the Arabs—have been freely admitted to the country, and the percentage of Arabs among the foreign work force has steadily declined.

By the 1980s, more than a hundred thousand Indians worked in Kuwait, along with large numbers of Pakistanis, Bangladeshis, and even Thais and Chinese. It was the Indian government that first set a limit on the emigration of nationals, by imposing a ban on young women migrating for domestic service. Too many women, the Indian government decided, were being physically and sexually abused. Indian women were replaced chiefly by Sri Lankans and Filipinos, who suffered the same treatment but whose societies, as their diplomats conceded, were too poor for the luxury of such protests. Even Kuwaitis acknowledged the abuse of foreign workers, and a few were sent to jail for it, but Kuwait did not take the objections of non-Arabs seriously, and since that time the abuse, particularly of women, has grown worse.

Many Kuwaitis have long recognized the risks of decadence in a society where the natives have no obligation to work. "In the fifties and sixties, we had to employ others to execute our massive development programs," said Fuad Mulla Hussein, the secretary-general of the government's Higher Planning Council. "But now we persist in the same practice. Kuwaitis have become spoiled children. They want a job only if they can be directors or managers. The government would like to make hard work socially acceptable again. We have got to have Kuwaitis repairing cars, running retail shops, operating computers. We have a master plan, but at best it will take time to transform our consumer culture, our *rentier* society. And even if our best projections work out, Kuwaitis will be thirty-nine percent of the population in the twenty-first century and will still hold only 25 percent of the jobs. The truth is that we're not sure we know how to get Kuwaitis to work. How do you motivate someone who has everything?"

Shiber, the city planner, described the problem in 1961, and proposed a radical solution. "When everyone in Kuwait owns a villa or two, four cars or five, and has more than enough of all that the U.S.A., Europe and Japan manufacture, what then?" he wrote. "When all the schools and hospitals and fire and police stations, the corniche and the government center, as well as the regional highway network and . . . the international airport are all built, what then? . . ." Shiber envisioned Kuwait as a kind of Los Angeles of the Gulf, welcoming a wide range of Arabs to citizenship. Were not the Arabs, he reasoned, one people? Islam, the unifying faith, did not recognize borders. Had not Arabs wandered from the Atlantic to the Gulf, without passport or visa, throughout most of recorded history? Before the oil boom, Kuwait absorbed Syrians and Iraqis, bedouins, Jews and Persians. Shiber saw a wider citizenry as enriching Kuwait's economic base and creating healthy intellectual and social diversity. Influenced by patterns of life that he saw in the United States, he argued for a cosmopolitan city, a "great oasis" of three million Arabs.

But the Sabahs would have none of it, and on this issue the native Kuwaitis supported them overwhelmingly. A consensus in the country— from which only the few Nasserites dissented—held that enlarging the popular base would cause political instability. Reacting like an embattled tribe, the Kuwaitis perceived other Arabs not as brothers with whom to share their good fortune but as rivals threatening to steal their financial birthright. Whatever their rank or class, Kuwaitis liked their closed world, and they invited neither Arabs nor anyone else to join it.

Outside Kuwait, most Arabs sensed this attitude, and resented it. In fairness, it should be noted that not all of Kuwait's riches were pocketed. The government made regular grants of foreign aid, most of it to other Arab countries. In fact, as a percentage of gross national product, this aid was higher than that of any industrialized country. Yet it never won Kuwait many friends. Few Arabs complained audibly; no recipient was prepared to bite the hand that fed it. But in private conversations with Arabs, I often heard angry and disdainful judgments. It was said that Kuwaitis were parasites living off the labor of others, violating the egalitarian doctrines of the *umma*. I heard officials in finance ministries throughout the Arab world grumble at the emirs' placing their fortunes in Western banks and stock markets, rather than making them available for Arab economic development. Oddly, the Kuwaitis themselves never seemed to pick up these signals, and when they desperately needed help at the time of the Iraqi invasion, they were astounded at the number of Arabs who deliberately turned their backs.

IV   STRANGE NEGOTIATIONS

KUWAITI SOCIETY HAD been at ease with itself—self-satisfied, many said—until the Iraq-Iran war, which generated a significant rise in tensions. Sunni fears of the Shiite minority, after a long decline, rose sharply in the face of widespread Shiite sympathy for Iran. Sunni fundamentalism, till then virtually unknown in the country, made its appearance and established its first foothold in national politics. In 1985, parliamentary elections once more brought in an outspoken opposition, which provoked a crisis by charging the ruling family—apparently with good cause—of profiting in the scandal of the Souk al-Manakh, a local financial market that for some years had been ruled by unrestrained speculative greed; its collapse had caused losses of tens of billions of dollars. Sheikh Jabir al-Sabah, the emir, responded to the attacks, as had Sheikh Sabah al-Salem a decade before, by dismissing the assembly and suspending the constitution. This time, the opposition mobilized to challenge the suspension, and by the winter of 1989 it was rallying thousands of protesters in downtown Kuwait for weekly demonstrations. The government broke up some of them by beatings and tear gas.

Respect for the Sabahs was in obvious decline when I visited in 1988. In a speech during my visit, the defense minister, a member of the ruling family, evoked derision in vowing that Kuwait's ten-thousand-man army, "the nation's sword," would defeat any aggressor. "Kuwaitis are not fighters—it's as simple as that," a European military advisor to the army told me, and as evidence he pointed out that Kuwait had not even bothered to build fortifications on its northern frontier, a few miles from the war zone. Though the reflagging agreement had raised the country's morale, Kuwaitis were not yet sure what to make of of their new protector. Sheikh Nasser al-Sabah, the minister of labor, expressed his concerns to me one evening at his *diwaniyah*. "Right now, we are getting along fine with you, but Kuwait can't depend on you Americans," he said. "No country can. We read history. You abandoned Marcos, Sihanouk, Haile Selassie, South Vietnam and the shah of Iran. If the going gets rough, I don't believe we can count on your assistance." But other Sabahs, with more critical responsibilities than his, were more confident of American protection and conducted the business of state accordingly.

Few Americans thought much about the United States–Kuwaiti relationship after the Iraq-Iran war ended. Nor did Kuwaitis think about it much more. Knowing of Baghdad's historical claims on Kuwait, I had occasionally asked in the course of several wartime visits whether the government anticipated problems with Iraq once the fighting was over. The reply was invariably negative. Every Kuwaiti said that, after years of alliance with Iraq, it was unimaginable that the old differences between the two countries would be resurrected. But in early 1990, Western newspapers began carrying accounts of disputes between the governments, and in the spring, Saddam Hussein made a series of threatening statements, followed by the deployment of troops on the Kuwaiti border. Washington, like every other capital at the time, was fixated on the impending collapse of the Soviet Union and the reunification of Germany. The building blocks of four decades of cold war were rapidly disintegrating, and few Westerners were diverted by what looked like a petty spat in the Gulf.

But early on August 2, 1990, Iraq invaded and within a few hours had conquered Kuwait, putting the emir and his entourage to flight. President Bush promptly condemned the invasion, embargoed Iraqi trade and persuaded the United Nations Security Council to demand Iraqi withdrawal. Britain, France, the European Community, the Soviet Union and Japan all instituted sanctions, which the UN strengthened on August 6 by voting an international embargo. When the Saudis asked for help, Bush began to move troops toward the Gulf, and as the world geared up for war, Baghdad formally announced Kuwait's annexation, an action which the Security Council declared null and void.

The Iraqis had long advanced a plausible argument for annexation. Kuwait, they said, had belonged to the Ottoman province of Basra, which after World War I became a part of Iraq. Kuwaiti independence was an artificial creation of British imperialism, they contended, designed to sever Iraq from access to the waters of the Gulf. Indeed, in redrawing the Middle East map, Britain took over Iraq and prevented its reunion with Kuwait out of fear that Iraq might one day become a power with its own regional ambitions. Iraq staked a formal claim to Kuwait as early as 1932, when Iraqi independence was still only nominal. In 1961, when Kuwait became independent, Iraq voted against admitting it to membership in the Arab League. Iraqis often told me that they were routinely taught in school that Kuwait belongs to them.

As soon as the British left, Iraq's Qasim regime published an edict of annexation of Kuwait. Though it sent no troops, the Sabahs called for help, and Britain returned with a military contingent, which was replaced a few months later by an all-Arab force. In 1963, the newly installed Baath regime—the direct antecedent of Saddam Hussein—ended the confrontation by recognizing Kuwait's sovereignty. But in 1975, Iraq reopened the issue by occupying a Kuwaiti frontier post and demanding cession of the Kuwaiti islands of Bubiyan and Warba. The Baathis backed off under pressure from the Arab League, but the Kuwait-Iraq frontier remained tense until Saddam turned eastward in 1980, with the start of the war against Iran.

Whatever the historical merits of the Iraqi claim, however, there was also a rebuttal. Throughout Ottoman history, Kuwait had been only a gleam in Istanbul's imperial eye. Ottoman mapmakers placed Kuwait in Basra province, but no Turk ever governed there. Only the Sabahs ruled in Kuwait from the time the Bani Utub came out of the desert, and even under the British their legitimacy was not disputed. Culturally as well as politically, Kuwait never belonged to Iraq. Muslims might contend that, as an Islamic state, Kuwait has no right to nationhood, and after Saddam's annexation, some made precisely that argument. But every Arab state, Iraq included, ignores Islamic strictures and has adopted the Western-born sovereignty system. The Arab League is itself an association of sovereign states, of which Kuwait, notwithstanding the Iraqis, is one. By universally accepted standards, Kuwait's sovereignty was unchallengeable.

YET SADDAM'S INVASION raised other questions, unrelated to historic claims. Jordan's Crown Prince Hassan first brought them to my attention during a stopover in Amman on trip I made to Iraq about two weeks after the invasion. He said the evidence suggested collusion—deliberate or inadvertent—between the United States and Kuwait during the previous spring and summer. Having heard many conspiracy theories in the Middle East, I have learned to be skeptical. Nonetheless, this one did not seem so farfetched.

The Prince noted that the entire Arab world had been bewildered by Kuwait's defiant behavior toward Iraq over the course of their disputes in early 1990. The squabbling began with Kuwait's overproduction of oil, which coincided with a fall in the world price far below the target set by OPEC (Organization of Petroleum Exporting Countries). Oil economists pointed out that, as a country of a half-million citizens, with foreign investments that generated a huge income, Kuwait could afford a major price drop, while seeking greater international consumption and a larger market share. Iraq, a country of seventeen million, was, by contrast, deeply in debt from eight years of war and desperately short of cash for reconstruction. Though Kuwait's policy might make economic sense, the prince said, governments do not normally make decisions without considering their political consequences, and certainly no responsible regime could fail to take account of the disparity in military power that existed between Iraq and Kuwait.

What was the explanation? Late in the Iraq-Iran war, Kuwait and Saudi Arabia, both supporters of Iraq, had pumped oil in significant excess of market demand, bringing about a collapse in prices at the very moment when Iran was running out of financial reserves. Some experts argue that it was this action, as much as Iraq's victories on the battlefield, that forced Khomeini to his knees. In 1992, United States government documents released under court order revealed that the Reagan and Bush administrations, at a time of soaring trade deficits, had routinely urged the Saudis and the Kuwaitis to overproduce to force oil prices down. The documents revealed no explicit animus toward Iraq, but they did not have to. It was enough that in the spring of 1990, Washington and Baghdad had categorically opposite objectives in the oil market. Whatever America's role, Kuwait's oil policy severely weakened Iraq.

The possibility of collusion was fed by information pointing to American anxiety about Iraqi aims. Washington was the source of charges of Iraq's chemical genocide against the Kurds, of secret construction of a supercannon with a range of hundreds of miles and of the theft of krytons to build nuclear weapons. These charges generated demands in the press and in some political circles for action to destroy Iraq's swelling military capacity. In Israel, the government leaked warnings of an imminent clash with Iraq, to which Saddam responded by warning that if the Israelis attacked, he would retaliate by incinerating half their country. His choice of words served only to exacerbate anti-Iraqi sentiment in the United States.

Moreover, Washington was concerned that Iraq was emerging as a strategic power in the Gulf. The Iraqis were transforming Um-Qasr, a fishing village on its narrow Gulf coastline, into a major naval facility. Linked by a deep-water canal to Basra, Um-Qasr needed only Bubiyan and Warba, uninhabited Kuwaiti islands at the mouth of the port, for its security. The Iraqis asked Kuwait either to cede the islands or to lease them, but Kuwait refused any agreement at all. Meanwhile, with Soviet power slipping rapidly, Washington could, for the first time since Britain's departure, contemplate keeping a permanent fleet in the Gulf. Many Arabs wondered whether Kuwait's hard line on the islands was meant to assure American naval supremacy in the Gulf.

During the negotiations in early 1990, in fact, Kuwait offered concessions on nothing, including division of the Rumaila oil fields on its boundary with Iraq, a dispute dating back to colonial times. What is more, Kuwait raised the ante by demanding repayment with interest of loans it had made to Iraq during the war, loans which Iraq had assumed would be forgiven. Iraq's answer was to demand compensation for some $2.5 billion in oil that it accused Kuwait of stealing by slant drilling into its Rumaila wells. To make matters worse, the Kuwaitis were said to have twice offended Iraq by sending home emissaries who had come for prearranged meetings with the emir. Even disregarding the snub, most Arabs agreed that Kuwait was being imprudent.

"We couldn't put together the pieces of the mosaic," said an advisor to Prince Hassan, "but we were suspicious. The Kuwaitis were very cocky. They told us officially that the United States would intervene. We don't know where they got that impression, from the United States itself or from another party, like the British or the Saudis. But they said they knew what they were doing. They seemed to think they were safe."

IN BAGHDAD, where I flew directly from Amman, Tariq Aziz, the foreign minister, made no effort to conceal the seriousness with which Iraq took the confrontation with Washington over Kuwait. "This is more frightening to Iraq than the eight years of war with Iran," he said. It was a statement that surprised me, given the bravado with which Saddam embellished the growing prospect of a war with the West.

Aziz described Iraq's seizure of Kuwait as "what the West calls aggression," and though he made no effort to justify it as anything else, he complained of Washington's unwillingness in the preceding weeks to accord a hearing to Iraq's case, much less to do anything about it. Three days before the Iraqi army made its move, he said, Saddam Hussein summoned April Glaspie, the U.S. ambassador, and gave her a full account of how Iraq's accumulating grievances against Kuwait were leading to a showdown. Saddam assured Glaspie, he said, that Iraq would not attack—but only as long as negotiations held out some promise of resolving the dispute. After the invasion, he said, President Bush distorted this assurance—conveniently forgetting the condition attached to it—to accuse Saddam of lying.

"For ten years, Iraq was rich, though not in the style of the sheikhs of Saudi Arabia and Kuwait," said Aziz, puffing on his cigar. "We spent our wealth for schools, houses, hospitals, roads and bridges, and industrial complexes, not villas on the Riviera like the Saudis and Kuwaitis. Since our revolution of July 1968, we have been working day and night to improve the standard of living of our people. Then Khomeini came along, threatening to destroy all that we did. We had to defend our country and our achievements. But in protecting ourselves, we also protected the people—as well as the sovereignty and wealth—of the Gulf States, which were more vulnerable to Iranian subversion than we were. The Kuwaitis accumulated fortunes while we saved them with the blood of our sons. They invested tens of billions in the West during the war and, though they provided us with financial help, we spent it to fight, not to promote our economy. The Gulf states kept the more than forty billion dollars that they sent us on the books as a loan. We thought of it as their contribution to a common cause. Frankly, we are now stunned at the Kuwaiti insistence that its share be repaid.

"Besides the Arab debts, we owe an equal amount to the West. This year's state budget required seven billion dollars for debt service, which was a huge amount, leaving us with only enough for basic services for our country. Our budget is based on a price of eighteen dollars a barrel for oil. But since the Kuwaitis began flooding the world with oil, the price has gone down to eleven dollars. No government, neither ours nor the Americans', could sustain a loss of one-third of its income. We sent emissaries to the Kuwaitis, and they replied that they would do what they liked. The Kuwaitis are all millionaires. Some are billionaires. Kuwait has some two hundred and twenty billion dollars in assets in foreign countries. There are many theories about why they forced down the price, but it came down to one thing. They did it to satisfy their own greed, and in the process they were destroying Iraq."

Aziz said that in May, Iraq convened an Arab summit in Baghdad, where Saddam was very conciliatory. Appealing to an Islamic sense of fairness, he told the meeting that Kuwait was waging a war of economic sabotage against poor Arabs. But, Aziz said, nothing changed.

"After the summit, Saddam proposed a meeting of the oil ministers, who got together on July tenth and assured us of some relief. But the Kuwaiti oil minister promised to refrain from overproduction for only two months, which meant nothing, since the market was already glutted. On July fifteenth, Saddam sent a list of grievances against Kuwait to the secretary-general of the Arab League. He said that Kuwait's actions were the equivalent of aggression. He warned that Iraq was desperate and could not pay its bills for food imports. It faced a starvation war. When do you use your military power to preserve yourself? Iraq will not become a beggar state. We are a dignified people with a five-thousand-year civilization. Obviously, none of those leaders who denounce us now seemed to care about finding a solution.

"We concluded that this was a conspiracy to destroy Iraq. But Kuwait was too small to do this without backing from a superpower. Weren't the Kuwaitis supported and encouraged by some other country? Who was the backer? We saw a conspiracy to bring about the economic collapse of Iraq, followed by its political collapse and a change of regime. This was more threatening to us than an attack by Israel, to which we could retaliate. We had to challenge this conspiracy. We tried until the summit of July thirtieth at Jedda to settle this matter without force, and then we acted."

I had traveled to Baghdad in a party that included Jesse Jackson, who at the time was the host of a televised talk show. During the visit, Jackson was invited to a private meeting with Saddam, and afterward told me that the subject which evoked Saddam's greatest passion was America's refusal, announced by President Bush, to discuss Iraq's grievances with him. Saddam said that he had announced a negotiating proposal that had taken him to the "limits of his creativity," and was aghast when the U.S. embassy in Baghdad, ignoring common diplomatic courtesy, did not even request an official translation of his statement. Saddam said the United States had adopted the pose of an imperial power dealing with a colony.

A day later, the minister of information left a message at the hotel saying that he would send limousines to pick up a delegation from our party at seven that evening. In his spacious office, he subjected us to the slogans that in official Iraqi circles pass for small talk, while aides mysteriously shuffled in and out, handing him memos. After fifteen minutes, he stood up abruptly and said we were all going on a tour of Baghdad, and for an hour, we drove aimlessly through the busy city, its animated streets showing no signs of preparation for war. Finally we passed through a gate, followed a long driveway that intersected illuminated gardens and pulled up to the portico of a palace that, I later learned, had been built to house Iraq's Hashemite kings. It was still not finished when the last of them was murdered in 1958. It was now the palace of Saddam Hussein.

We entered a huge rotunda with a dome of carved white stone, then were shown into a ballroom, set up for a TV interview, with wood mosaic floors, Oriental carpets, glittering chandeliers and French inlaid furniture. A few minutes later, Saddam entered from an adjacent hall, surrounded by uniformed men. He proposed that, before turning on the cameras, we have tea in another room. He wore a handsome blue suit and a matching blue tie, above shoes that were well worn and unshined. His face was paunchier than I had remembered from his pictures, and his voice, at a middle pitch, was thinner than I had anticipated. Still, there was something about him which evoked the strength of a lifelong revolutionary, a man who had volunteered at twenty-two to assassinate the head of state, then lived for years in hiding. Saddam looked distracted when he sat down to sip his tea, but somehow he noticed that I was taking notes on the back of an envelope. He motioned to an aide, who a few minutes later reappeared carrying a pad, which he quietly handed to me.

In the interview with Jackson that followed tea, Saddam performed poorly. His expression was relentlessly deadpan. Obviously tense, he shifted his eyes back and forth in search of familiar faces around the room. His posture was poor. What was worse, he made his points badly, often falling back, like so many Baathis, on clichés and jargon. Saddam's case for Iraq consisted largely of fulminations against conspiracies on the part of Americans, Kuwaitis, Saudis and, of course, Zionists.

Saddam argued that, far from plotting Kuwait's annexation, Iraq entered the dispute with Kuwait with the simple goal of ending the harmful manipulation of oil prices. Had the Sabah family acted in a spirit of Arab brotherhood, he said, there would never have been an invasion. As for Saudi Arabia, it was not in danger. "Saudi Arabia," he said, "is an independent sovereign state, as independent as Iraq. Unlike Kuwait, there was never a time when it was part of Iraq. . . . We have a nonaggression pact with Saudi Arabia, which we fully respect. . . . Within a few days after we entered Kuwait, the Iraqi armed forces took defensive positions, which the U.S. satellites could easily detect. The Americans knew that we did not mean to invade Saudi Arabia." Saddam declared that the claims of an Iraqi threat to Saudi Arabia were simply a pretext for the basing of American forces in the Gulf.

IN MID-JULY, with Iraqi troops arrayed on Kuwait's border, a State Department official in Washington stated at a press conference, "We do not have any defense treaties with Kuwait, and there are no special defense or security commitments to Kuwait . . . [but] we remain strongly committed to supporting the individual and collective self-defense of our friends in the Gulf with whom we have deep and longstanding ties." The statement echoed what Washington had said at the time of the reflagging. The next day, Saddam Hussein summoned Ambassador Glaspie to interpret it. He was told that Iraq's dispute with Kuwait was an Arab, not an American, affair, a disclaimer that has left historians debating whether he took what he heard as an invitation to Iraq to swallow its neighbor.

By that time, the Kuwaiti government knew, from both American satellite photos and its own agents in Basra, that Iraq's army was poised to advance. Its response was to turn its back. The Sabahs clearly believed that the Iraqis might, at worst, seize a swath of territory which contained the disputed oil wells and the two islands, much as they had in the crisis of 1975. Sheikh Sabah al-Ahmed, the foreign minister, compared the situation publicly to a "summer storm," and Sheikh Nawaf al-Ahmed, the defense minister, actually downgraded the army's level of alert, permitting many officers to go off on leave. Except for those who monitored foreign radio broadcasts, the Kuwaiti public knew very little, because censorship had banned all mention of the crisis in the press and on television. No one entertained the possibility that Saddam might grab the whole country.

Many Kuwaitis first learned of the invasion from relatives who phoned with the news from Europe or America early in the morning of August 1. The government permitted an announcement of the attack only several hours later, by which time many civilian installations had been bombarded, and tanks were filing down Kuwait's boulevards. But by then the emir was safely across the border in Saudi Arabia. So was the defense minister, though he was in command of the army. Sheikh Fahd al-Ahmed, a younger brother of the emir, stayed to fight alongside his troops at the Dasman Palace, the emir's official residence, and he was killed. It was the only resistance put up by the army, and Sheikh Fahd was unique in sacrificing himself for his country. The other senior members of royal family all ran away.

"The government never brought the realities of the crisis to the people," said Ahmed Sadoun, during a visit I made to Kuwait after the war. A former speaker of the national assembly and a leader of the democratic opposition, Sadoun had not forgiven the emir for suspending the constitution in 1986. We spoke in the elegant *diwaniyah* of his spacious home. "The government chose to keep us in the dark. The international media were warning us of danger, and several of us who were following the story often discussed it, but the government kept insisting that the Iraqis were bluffing. There was nothing we could do.

"In earlier times, the Sabahs were known as skillful diplomats, able to maneuver to keep the country's enemies at bay. These skills kept Kuwait free from more powerful neighbors—the Iraqis, the Iranians, the Saudis, and earlier the Turks. In our two-hundred-year history, Kuwait was never invaded and never had a real war. But the diplomacy of the early Sabahs was the product of an open society, when the public had some influence. Kuwait lost everything with the end of democracy. The opposition doesn't challenge the right of the Sabahs to govern. There is no sentiment for a revolution or a coup. But we do challenge its autocracy, its insistence on running everything alone. Two or three men make all the decisions, and they inevitably make mistakes. If you provoke the Iraqis, you'd better figure out a way to diffuse their anger. I believe we could have avoided this catastrophe. Taking the Iraqis on was a bad mistake."

Abdullah al-Nibari, another ex-parliamentarian, was even harsher in his criticism. Educated at the University of Cairo and at Oxford, he now edits an opposition newspaper and works at organizing democratic Kuwaitis. Nibari invited me to his large and comfortable home, where we talked—

interrupted now and then by little children and their Asian nannies—in a parlor decorated with traditional Arab furniture and desert landscapes.

"We believe the government should have stayed in Kuwait," he said. It was a position widely shared by the Kuwaitis I met. Many said it was proper for the emir, as the symbol of the state, to flee, on the grounds that his freedom sent a message to the world that Kuwait still lived. But it was widely agreed—at least, among those who had stayed behind—that the government, and particularly its Sabah members, should have been in Kuwait to share the people's fate.

"The army, thanks to the minister of defense, and the police, thanks to the minister of interior, both members of the ruling family, were left without orders. Some of our reserve soldiers put on their uniforms and rushed to the camps, ready to fight, and no one was there to give them assignments. The Sabahs abandoned the people in the first hours. They played into the hands of the Iraqis, who wanted all of us to get out of the country. Many Kuwaitis would have stayed if the government had remained, and morale would have surged. Most Kuwaitis think the government was unwise. Many believe it was cowardly."

V KUWAIT UNDER THE IRAQIS

THE HISTORY OF KUWAIT under the occupation is likely to be written and rewritten in the years to come. It is the history of two hundred thousand Kuwaitis, roughly a third of the population. An equal number of Kuwaitis were vacationing abroad at the time of the invasion, and did not return; about the same number left after the Iraqis arrived. The occupation has given rise, as in Europe after the Nazis, to a range of myths, many of them self-serving, some of them hotly disputed. Most notably, the Muslim fundamentalists, having organized clandestinely into the Islamic Constitutional Movement (suggesting a linked dedication to religion and the constitution), claim to have been the spearhead of resistance. Secular Kuwaitis insist the claim is, at best, exaggerated. Substantial evidence, however, makes one clear point: any resistance that took place was generated from within, by the Kuwaitis who stayed and not by those who left. A second conclusion, for which I believe there is abundant evidence, is that the Kuwaitis who remained inside conducted themselves, on the whole, honorably and even valiantly toward the invaders. They demonstrated a genuine sense of patriotism and redeemed in substantial measure the humiliation of an army that laid down its arms, and a government that ran.

The resistance started from the first days, while the Iraqis labored to set up a quisling regime. Saddam apparently believed—knowing of the angry street clashes over the constitution the previous spring—that Kuwaiti democrats would rally to his side. Proclaiming himself Kuwait's savior, he went looking for sympathizers. He found none. The Iraqis tried blackmailing at least one prominent opposition figure, to no avail. They seized Faisal Saneh, who was known openly as a Baathi, and when he refused to join their scheme, they took him away, presumably to an Iraqi prison; he was never heard of again. Ahmed Sadoun told me he went into hiding, where he remained for several weeks, before escaping across the border. Finally, Iraq announced seven names, apparently army officers, as the new cabinet. Unknown to the public, they were all bedouins, far removed from the political mainstream. But the cabinet never took office. Soon afterward Saddam announced that Kuwait would be Iraq's nineteenth province, and he sent one of his relatives to run it.

Kuwaitis say that in the first weeks, armed bands, composed mostly of teenagers, fought Iraqis throughout the city, firing at trucks and jeeps. Young women were as active as young men. Initially, the occupiers took only defensive measures, apparently in the hope of winning over the population, but by the end of August it was clear they had failed, and they began to pick up hostages, more or less at random. Some of the hostages simply disappeared. Others were tortured and released, to convey a lesson. In September, the Iraqis adopted the tactic of arresting suspects, torturing them, bringing them home for a momentary family reunion, then shooting them and leaving their bodies on the sidewalk. This grisly procedure took forty or fifty victims, of both genders. Within a few weeks, the brutality had made its point, and organized resistance came to an end. Free-lance car bombing, exacting a heavy toll in Iraqi lives, continued for another month or so. But by November, it also petered out.

Meanwhile, Kuwaitis organized themselves for passive resistance, which the Iraqis seemed resigned to accept. With few exceptions, Kuwaitis boycotted their workplaces—including banks, hospitals, municipal services and the police—and refused to send their children to school. They painted out street signs to confuse the occupiers. They produced counterfeit identity papers to protect individuals, including some of the younger Sabahs, whom the Iraqis sought. It was said that a few Kuwaitis, using satellite telephones and fax machines, even passed information of military value to offices in Saudi Arabia.

After the war, the resumption of political rivalries made it hard to identify the heroes. But one of them certainly was Sheikh Ali Salem al-Ali, a thirty-four-year-old cousin of the emir, who deliberately returned to Kuwait two days after the invasion. Another was Abdul Aziz Sultan, a banker and member of a prominent merchant family. There were many leaders, however, and their work was made easier by a popular consensus to give the enemy no cooperation. So Kuwaitis willingly did things they had never done before: collecting trash, baking bread, driving trucks, cleaning streets, manning counters at the retail-sales co-ops. Women, it was said, even did housework. Those who shared this experience insisted that popular morale had never been so high, and that Kuwaitis never enjoyed such a feeling of bonding.

The chief problem was to keep people fed, in a country where no food is grown, and to provide currency for daily requirements, at a time when no one was working. To meet these needs, leaders set up semisecret networks, through neighborhood mosques and *diwaniyas*, to distribute money for the purchase of necessities—taking pride, it should be noted, in keeping careful accounts for later settlement. At first, they used currency from internal stocks made available by rich Kuwaitis, and disbursed it only to the indigent. But in September, when both food and money ran out, they made contact with the government-in-exile in Saudi Arabia, which responded by smuggling currency in on a regular basis, for distribution to all Kuwaitis. The Iraqis sent in food from the Basra region and kept the marketing structure intact, enabling them to get their hands on some of this money. It was a tacit deal. The contraband currency benefited the Iraqis, while providing Kuwaitis with the means to live, as well as to pay occasional bribes to soften the edges of military rule.

The system was barred to non-Kuwaitis, however. Several hundred thousand, early in the occupation, took the Iraqi offer to leave. But some two hundred thousand Palestinians, most of whom knew no other home, remained. Despite the central role they played in the country, these Palestinians were forgotten when rich Kuwaitis began distributing funds. Their needs were also dismissed when the government began sending currency from abroad. Kuwaiti functionaries who boycotted their jobs were given to understand that their salaries would be paid; Palestinians, who for four decades had been the backbone of the Kuwaiti economy, were told clearly that theirs would not.

Part of the reason that Kuwaitis turned their backs on the Palestinians was that Yasir Arafat and the PLO had made the mistake of standing publicly by Saddam after the invasion. How could they betray us, Kuwaitis asked, after our long and faithful support of their struggle? It was hard to make the case to Kuwaitis that Palestinians were reacting not against Kuwait but against America's long-standing preference for Israel over their own cause. Kuwaitis had never sensed, furthermore, the resentment that Palestinians felt toward the condescension and want of generosity they had so long experienced in Kuwait. Without income, most Palestinians during the occupation went to their jobs and sent their children to school. Some unquestionably helped the enemy. A few joined in the looting of stores, identified Kuwaiti fugitives, backed up the Iraqis at checkpoints. But there were also many Palestinians who protected the businesses of their Kuwaiti employers, moved contraband around the city in their cars or hid in their own homes private treasures that would have been stolen or destroyed. On some occasions, Palestinians saved Kuwaiti lives. But Kuwaitis were convinced that the Palestinians prospered under the occupation, while they alone were in torment.

Samer—he asked me not to use his last name—told me he stayed home like the Kuwaitis, until his boss called. Thirty years old, he was born in Kuwait, the sixth of nine children of West Bank parents. His father had worked in Kuwait's ministry of justice; his mother was a teacher. Determined to have their children educated, they had to send them abroad, Samer said, because places for Palestinians at the university were limited. Then, in 1984, Kuwait—stepping up its campaign to get rid of Palestinians—barred the return of any non-Kuwaiti who was out of the country for more than six months. The rule, Samer said, spread his brothers and sisters all over the world. He and I met in a Hawali restaurant called Sultan Salem, where he told me that, after finishing school in the United States, he had got back into Kuwait under a loophole in the rule, and now worked in a small factory servicing machinery.

"My boss said he wanted to reopen his business," Samer said, "but he didn't want to work himself, so his Palestinian employees ran the shop. We even slept there, to keep it safe at night. I'll admit that for us life was more or less normal under the Iraqis, but we didn't want to live under Saddam either. If Iraq stayed, I planned to leave. But, meanwhile, we Palestinians kept Kuwait going, while the Kuwaitis boasted about their boycott, collected money from the government every month and stayed home. I think, in our way, we suffered as much as they did."

The Iraqis, on arriving in Kuwait, stormed through the stores, taking everything in sight. They even invited civilians from Basra to join the looting. As a gesture of defiance toward their chief antagonist, they burned American properties; Safeway supermarkets, for example, were demolished. They also confiscated houses, many of them along the seashore. Anticipating invasion, they dug trenches or built fortifications in the gardens; invariably they plundered the interior. After the first weeks, tensions dropped. The Allies tightened their economic embargo, and the Iraqis settled down for what promised to be a prolonged standoff.

Then, on November 8, President Bush changed the rules, announcing that American troop strength in Saudi Arabia would double to four hundred thousand, providing an "offensive military option." In Kuwait, the American buildup was mirrored in increasing daily pressures. Surly Iraqis imposed rigorous measures at checkpoints, enforced nightly curfews stringently and stepped up house searches, arbitrary arrests and the random confiscation of goods, especially cars. Encouraged by the Iraqis, more and more families fled the city, leaving behind houses that were routinely stripped of valuables and turned into squalid barracks. Kuwaitis who stayed told me of pleading with neighbors not to abandon their homes and their country. Departure meant that more soldiers came and went in the neighborhood, intensifying surveillance and the risk of unforeseen confrontations. But the Kuwaiti government made clear that fleeing families would get a check each month, a policy which gave them the choice of living comfortably abroad or in an atmosphere of permanent fear at home.

"I can't forgive those who left," said Badr al-Baijan, an executive of the Kuwait Petroleum Company, in whose office we spoke after the war. Baijan, married with children, was among those who stayed. His views were characteristic of Kuwaitis who had endured the occupation. "For myself, I decided it was better to die in dignity than live as a refugee. You have only one country, and if you run you're like tumbleweed. For us, it was the violation of an Arab proverb which says that if you abandon your house, you deserve the contempt of your neighbors. I understand that people were scared out of their skin; that is why the Iraqis harassed us. Their goal was to replace us with Iraqi families, so we really would be the nineteenth province, and some Iraqi families actually moved into our homes. But the Kuwaitis who left made it easier for them. They breached the walls of our solidarity. I was ashamed to read stories in the newspapers later about Kuwaitis dancing in the discos of Cairo and London. I know the government is now trying to soften the bitterness between those who stayed and those who left. But I lost my respect for our people."

VI THE GOVERNMENT OF EXILES

THE GOVERNMENT-IN-EXILE decided in the third month of occupation to make a show of national solidarity. Under the emir, it had installed itself in the luxury hotels of Taif, the resort town in the mountains of Saudi Arabia. From there, it issued a call to Kuwaitis of every social and political stripe to come to a conference from October 13 to 15 at the Red Sea port of Jedda. Prominent Kuwaitis—male Kuwaitis, to be precise— were invited, and some thirteen hundred, their airline tickets and hotel bills prepaid, turned up. They met at Jedda's Palace of Conferences, lent to the Sabahs by the Saudi royal family.

With the allied armies assembling for Kuwait's liberation, the government wanted to make the meeting a manifestation of support for Sabah legitimacy. The Kuwaiti opposition, however, had other ideas. Since the invasion, some of its leaders had conferred regularly in London, and in late August they issued a statement reaffirming their backing of the emir as the head of state, while adding, "The Kuwaiti constitution does not permit absolute rule, and clearly identifies the nation as the source of authority." The opposition's interest was to turn the conference into a rally for Kuwaiti democracy.

The government may not have understood the gamble it was taking. Kuwaitis wanted to know why Kuwait had been so intransigent in the pre-invasion bargaining with Iraq, why the army had not fought, why the cabinet fled on the day of the invasion and why, after the occupation, Kuwait endorsed Western military confrontation with Iraq without attempting to negotiate a voluntary withdrawal. Many also wanted to ask who would control, and benefit from, the estimated $100 billion in Kuwait's overseas investments if there were no longer a country. Some opposition leaders even proposed that the cabinet, to promote national unity, resign in favor of a government of technocrats. At meetings behind closed doors, the debate was lively, and at times even acrimonious, but in the end the Sabahs won the gamble. The government continued unchanged, with the opposition agreeing to defer debate of sensitive matters until the return home. In exchange, the emir made what the opposition considered a solemn pledge to restore the constitution immediately upon liberation. The meeting ended with a unanimous show of support for the Sabahs, and the opposition pronouncing itself satisfied with the outcome.

But within a few weeks, bickering resumed. Ahmed Sadoun told me the emir promptly violated a commitment to establish planning committees, with opposition participation, for the postliberation period. By the start of 1991, the government had made clear that, on its return, it would not reconvene the national assembly or call new elections, and it talked openly of imposing martial law, at least temporarily, to replace the departing invaders. Abandoning a self-imposed silence, the opposition issued a series of angry protests. After the liberation, Kuwaitis said publicly that they had been deceived at Jedda, and that the ruling family never intended to restore democracy at all.

On the eve of their withdrawal from Kuwait, the Iraqis did their best to finish the pillage and destruction on which they had earlier embarked. They torched virtually every building in which the government had an interest: the ministries, the headquarters of Kuwait Air, the international hotels, the palaces, the parliament, the major shopping complexes. They wrecked the airport, sabotaged the public utilities and sank ships to block the channels into the ports. They transformed the oil fields into a blazing inferno. They also blew up the complex of buildings that made up the National Museum, Kuwait's pride, and burned to cinders an outdoor collection of ancient dhows. Their work assured Saddam Hussein a place in history near Hulagu Khan, the Mongol conqueror who in 1258 sacked Baghdad.

Three days after the Allies began their ground offensive, the Iraqi army withdrew from Kuwait. Saddam's brazen claims that he would wage the Mother of Battles vanished in the soft footsteps of his retreating columns. A month earlier, as the air attacks intensified, Iraqi soldiers had begun arresting Kuwaitis at random. On February 21—which Kuwait calls Black Thursday—Iraqi soldiers, anticipating the ground assault, seized and dispatched twenty-five hundred hostages toward the north; some were never heard from again. One Kuwaiti who had been arrested—and had bought his way out with some cash he had sewn into the pocket of his *dishdasha*— told me he heard Iraqi officers boast that they were leaving for just a few days. On February 28, with Kuwait free of Iraqis (except for a few in hiding), President Bush declared a cease-fire. The Iraqi army, though decimated by Allied fire, had not been destroyed, however, and many Kuwaitis believed it might come back. Some believe it still.

The twenty-eighth was also the day when Sheikh Sa'ad, the crown prince and prime minister, left Taif for Dammam, on the Saudi coast, several hours' drive from Kuwait. Over the following days, seven or eight ministers—none of them Sabahs—returned home, but the crown prince remained in Dammam and the ministers, without a leader, were unable to carry out their duties. (During World War II, Europe's governments-in-exile returned on the heels of the liberating army, to avoid a hiatus of power.) The crown prince never explained his delay, leaving most Kuwaitis to assume he was frightened for his safety. Suleiman Mutawa, who was then the planning minister, told me many Kuwaitis in the city sneered, "After losing the country, you persuaded the world to get it back for you. Now you behave as if you're afraid to take it." The Allied command inside Kuwait embarked energetically on restoring municipal services, but took the position that state administration and the maintenance of public order were not its job. Martial law was in force when Sheikh Sa'ad finally came home on March 5, but for nearly a week the country had been left with no one in charge.

Nine more days passed before the emir himself returned and, with characteristic condescension, he made no statement to justify his absence. Observers said that as he stepped out of the Kuwait Air jet that carried him home, he brought his hands to his face, presumably to hide his tears. After descending the stairway, he knelt and touched his forehead to the ground. Airport security permitted only a few officials to greet him on his return, but Kuwaitis were invited to hail him on his ride into the city. The streets, however, were all but deserted.

The surly reception mirrored the prevailing mood. The city had no water or electricity, and much less food than was available during the occupation. (For a time, bread was rationed, with non-Kuwaitis receiving one half the Kuwaiti allotment.) But Kuwaitis were also feeling out of sorts toward the emir personally. An introverted, reclusive man with little formal education, he had never reached out to his subjects and, at sixty-four, could tap no reservoir of good feeling after seven controversial months of absence. Kuwaitis were unwilling to forgive his dallying in Taif, or a later stop in Mecca; "a little danger is part of the job description," one said. Even before the war, the emir was far from popular. Kuwaitis, who like to think of themselves as modern, had grown increasingly uncomfortable at making excuses for his practice—though technically sanctioned by the Koran—of marrying and divorcing a succession of young girls, numbering perhaps in the hundreds; observers of the royal family estimated that he had fathered at least seventy children. Many Kuwaitis were also uneasy with his demand for luxury, so inconsistent with the tradition of austerity that the Bani Utub brought from the desert. Before he took up his temporary quarters at the Bayan Palace, crystal chandeliers were strung, gold toilet fixtures were installed and a shipment of gold-braided cushions, monogrammed Irish linen and writing tables with inlaid leather was unloaded from Saudi Arabia. Though some Kuwaitis fired guns to celebrate the emir's return, most spent the day in line with buckets to get their daily water ration.

Notwithstanding martial law, security in Kuwait broke down in the early days of liberation, but when Hamad al-Jouan, a government critic, was wounded in an assassination attempt and left permanently paralyzed, many Kuwaitis concluded that the Sabahs were not the targets but the instigators of the breakdown. Bands of young Kuwaitis, many of them armed with weapons left by the Iraqis, waged a campaign of terror, abducting and inflicting kangaroo justice on alleged collaborators, most notably Palestinians. Most Kuwaitis believed the adolescent gangs had the endorsement of Sheikh Sa'ad, who had declared while still in Taif that he was planning to "check on . . . some of the Palestinians." A few days after liberation, Kuwaiti tanks surrounded Hawali while vigilantes conducted house-to-house searches. Dozens of Palestinians were beaten and hospitalized, and scores—one government official said the toll might be as high as a thousand—were summarily executed. On March 11, three days before the emir's return, Abdullah al-Nibari, speaking for an opposition coalition, told a press conference that six members of the royal family—he did not name them—had organized the vigilantes, which he said were intimidating not only Palestinians but prodemocracy activists. Despite official denials, most of the opposition was convinced that the government was behind the witch hunts, in an effort to divert criticism from its own embarrassing record.

The allegations of collaboration against the whole Palestinian community became the lever for implementing a policy long dear to the Sabahs: driving the Palestinians from Kuwait entirely. Within weeks of the liberation, the government made its intentions clear. Having insinuated that all Palestinians who had remained in Kuwait were collaborators, it announced that no Palestinians who had fled the occupation would be permitted to return. It terminated the employment of all non-Kuwaitis in the public sector, which had long been the Palestinians' domain. And while it did not bar Palestinians from private-sector jobs, it prohibited enrollment of children who had attended school during the occupation, which effectively drove out their parents. It even issued a regulation authorizing the deportation of non-Kuwaitis—that is, Palestinians—for traffic offenses! Perhaps most shamefully, it expelled from the country, without trial or any other legal procedure, any Palestinian who had been arrested or tortured for alleged collaboration. For weeks, caravans of buses, each carrying dozens of Palestinians, regularly made the trip to the Iraqi border, where they unceremoniously disgorged their cargo on the other side.

It took about three months for the lawlessness to run its course. The Allied military command and the American embassy applied strong pressure on the government, and in April, Secretary of State James Baker stopped in Kuwait and personally delivered a stern admonition of his own to the emir. The warning that Kuwait was squandering its international support seemed to have an impact. Sheikh Sa'ad leaked word that the family's younger sheikhs were to dissolve their bands, in itself an admission of Sabah involvement, especially since his own son, Fahd, was acknowledged to be among them. Unless they put an end to their violence, he said publicly, he would "hang them from the lampposts for all the people to see."

The Iraqis had been gone for five months when I arrived to see how Kuwait was faring. The airport where I landed was still not fully operational, but a few weeks before it had not been operating at all. Driving into the city, I noticed graffiti on a concrete barrier that said, TANK U AMERICA . . . MERCI MITERANT . . . THANK TATCHER, but it seemed to me that, whatever the joy at liberation, Kuwait looked grim. The vacant dwellings on both sides of the freeway, shabby enough to have been inhabited by foreigners, testified that its population had declined to a fraction of the prewar level. The burning oil fields, visible as the plane descended, produced a heavy, sooty air, aggravated by the 120-degree temperature of the summer afternoon. The greenery of which Kuwaitis were inordinately proud had all but disappeared. Later, I learned that the Iraqis never bothered to water the lawns and the trees, delivering the city back to the desert, which was a major victor in the war.

Driving around downtown over the next few days, I saw relatively little damage, though half of the small shops—where crowds of foreigners had shopped for shoes and clothing, fast food, airline tickets, videos, jewelry— were shuttered tight. Most of these shops had been run by non-Kuwaitis, chiefly Palestinians, and I wondered whether they would ever reopen. Still, over the course of my visit, Kuwait got closer each day to the place I knew before the war: more shops doing business, another international airline flying out of the airport, new bottlenecks on the freeways. The supermarkets were quickly stocked with imports; the European designers were arriving at the malls with their fall lines. One afternoon, I looked out my hotel window and saw speedboats and water skiers in the marina, a sign that the good times were back. According to one Kuwaiti, an even better sign was the crowds shopping every evening in furniture stores, buying essentials for homes and apartments that the Iraqis had plundered.

On August 2, the first anniversary of the invasion and the 150th day after liberation, the American embassy issued a press release listing the achievements of the U.S. Army Corps of Engineers in restoring Kuwait. Its scoresheet noted the furnishing of electric power to 98 per cent of the population, the replacement of fifty-four hundred miles of electrical transmission lines, the pumping of fresh water to every house, the removal of twenty-eight hundred wrecked vehicles from roads and streets, the resumption of operations of all eight commercial banks, the repair of seventy public buildings and the reopening of Kentucky Fried Chicken, Arby's, Hardee's, Pizza Hut and Baskin-Robbins.

Later, an Army spokesman told me that the Corps, at the President's instructions, had been laying plans for the reconstruction since October of 1990. Some damage, particularly of communications facilities, had been caused by American bombing. Most of it, he said, was the product of the Iraqis' theft and sabotage but, because of the haste in which they departed, it turned out to be only a fraction of what had been feared. Reconstruction costs, placed at $100 billion in early estimates, were subsequently recalculated at about $20 billion over a five-year span. With the help of Palestinian technicians, the only ones who knew the equipment, the repairs of the power plants were accomplished in thirty days, a far shorter time than anticipated. By then, one of Kuwait's three ports, vital for the importation of food and equipment, was in operation. In another thirty days, all municipal services were functioning. By the end of May, the emergency phase of the reconstruction was declared over.

As most of the world's television watchers knew, the most dramatic and devastating damage was done to the oil wells. One morning I drove south from Kuwait City to Ahmadi, the company town that administers the Burgan field, the country's largest. I remembered Ahmadi from earlier visits as a green and cheerful place, a relocated slice of America with a town center where the kids of the managers and technicians stopped for ice cream after school. This time, I found the town brown from desiccation and gray from the particles of burning oil that had settled on it. Most of the shops were closed; the kids had gone home. I had to stop at a company office to pick up a guide to take me to the oil field, where I was not at all sure I wanted to go. I had already read more than enough about it, and seen too many grotesque pictures. But the inferno in the oil field was like the Eiffel Tower, in that if you happened to be there, you would miss something if you did not go for a look.

I climbed into the passenger seat of the four-wheel drive, and we headed straight into the desert, passing on the way a junkyard of wrecked Iraqi military vehicles, then the storage lot for the firefighting equipment. The initial teams of firefighters were American, but a dozen teams from several nations were by then in the Kuwaiti fields, and there were to be twenty-seven working by October. As we drove, my guide told me the far-off white smoke I saw was actually the condensing water of an extinguished but still simmering well. Entering the wellhead area, we drove along the dikes containing oil lakes, literally huge, ugly puddles produced by gushers that had failed to ignite. Then we turned onto a desert track and drove to the rim of a well from which brilliant flames spewed forty feet into the sky. Above the flames billowed thick black smoke, meandering southward with the breeze. Parked at the wellhead, among tractors and hoses, was a pickup truck marked "Boots and Coots."

Coots Matthews of Houston, described on his calling card as a "blowout specialist," was talking with his crew chief while his men directed thick streams of salt water, pumped in from the Gulf, into the well. I could feel the heat from the flames on my face as I eavesdropped on heavy Texas accents. Coots, a leathery-looking man of sixty-eight, had been one of the first to take on the dangers of extinguishing the oil-field fires, and when we talked, he expressed awe at the systematic efforts the Iraqis had put into starting them. They had painstakingly packed explosives around a thousand wellheads, piled sandbags around to direct the explosions downward, then wired the network electrically to central detonating units. Nearly three-fourths ignited, said Coots, a good record. "They couldn't fight worth a shit, but they sure knew how to blow up wells," he observed with grudging admiration.

The team I was watching had already extinguished twenty-six fires, he said, and Coots' Company, among its three crews, had put out seventy. In all, some three hundred fires had already been quenched of the seven hundred that had been ignited. By the end of August, some pumping had resumed, and it seemed likely that within a year the fields would be nearly restored to their prewar productivity.

SULEIMAN AL-SHAHEEN'S OFFICE was in the desert, but well to the north of the Burgan field. His ministry—he was undersecretary of foreign affairs—had been housed on the seaside in the Sief Palace, which the Iraqis had gutted. Temporarily, its home was the Bayan Palace, where the emir also was lodged. A cluster of apartment-style buildings, about twenty minutes from downtown, the Bayan Palace had been designed to provide a suitable setting and luxury accommodations for delegates to the Islamic Conference of 1988. Its hub, now incinerated, had been a structure of some grandeur, incorporating a large theater, a library and a reception hall with a lofty ceiling and huge chandeliers. The retreating Iraqis had put an artillery shell through its roof, which collapsed into the theater, and set fire to the library, from which the flames spread out of control. When I visited, charred books were still scattered amid overturned shelves; the shattered windows had not yet been replaced; the ornate ceiling of the reception hall lay in heaps on the marble floor; soot covered the exterior walls. Awaiting the restoration of the Sief Palace, the Kuwaitis refitted the apartments with desks and telephones for the staff of the emir and the foreign minister. The offices were a bit cramped, but they all had bathrooms with marble tubs and gold-plated fixtures.

Kuwaitis, Shaheen said, felt the war had left some troublesome matters unresolved. They were not convinced that Saddam Hussein had been defeated and feared that, as long as he stayed in power, his army might return. Shaheen's assertion corresponded with many other conversations I had in Kuwait. Even in victory, Kuwaitis remained frightened of Saddam's revenge, which they expected might be fiercer than his earlier visit, and they cited as evidence of his power his brutal repression of the post-war Kurd and Shiite rebellions. Moreover, Shaheen said, every Kuwaiti worried that the next time, the West would be under less resolute leaders than George Bush and Margaret Thatcher. Kuwaitis suddenly felt insecure, though he added that only part of their concern was based on uncertainty about the West. What worried Kuwaitis even more was the disdain for their welfare that so many Arabs had shown.

"We keep asking ourselves," Shaheen said, " 'Why did this happen?' We were brought up believing that Arabs were the brothers of Arabs, that the large countries would protect the small ones—as Iraq protected us from Iran. Our elite certainly believed it. Then this terrible attack came, with its savage and cruel treatment. And on the first day of the occupation, we learned that the Arabs in Yemen and Jordan and Tunisia were cheering Saddam and denouncing us. Why were they asking for our destruction? Why did they march in the streets shouting that our wealth belonged to all Arabs? This reaction had a huge psychological impact on us, on the people and on their leaders.

"The Palestinians who worked among us for so long say they had a right to share in our land, in our sovereignty. They say they built this country, and most of the Gulf states, with their brains and their muscles. My answer is that they came here to sell us their services as doctors, teachers and engineers, and they took our money in return. They didn't come here as prophets. If all they wanted was to build a civilization, why didn't they go to Mauritania or Sudan? In demanding that we share our wealth with them, they were asking us to betray our sovereignty."

It seemed to me, in listening to Shaheen, that he was caught in the trap set by history for Arab thinkers. A modern man, he was comfortable with the doctrine of the state system; a Kuwaiti, he liked the money that citizenship bestowed on him. But the *umma* and the Arab nation, values imparted to him in his upbringing as a Muslim and an Arab, clashed with the notion of the state imported from the West. This caused him pain.

"It is true that all Arabs are taught, in our schools and by our religion, that we are one people, one nation, and that we have an obligation to share our good fortune with our brothers. On the other hand, we are an independent state, with every right to use our riches as we choose. Others don't have claims on our wealth. That is the essence of sovereignty. Our dilemma, as Arabs, lies in trying to harmonize those two concepts. Arab civilization has got to set some sort of balance between Islamic and modern concepts. We cannot continue to live on two planes, one moving in contradiction to the other."

As Shaheen went on, his words made clear that his pain reached to still a deeper level. "We were humiliated by the Iraqis in a brutal, primitive way," he said. "The experience of the invasion and the occupation changed us mentally and has affected our behavior. I know we did not have it as bad as other countries that have been occupied for decades"—he was referring, as any Arab would, to Palestine—"but it is hard for us to get back into our old routines, back to our old lives. Now we have many experts coming here, many advisors on reconstruction, but we haven't yet had a psychiatry mission to tell us what's wrong among our people."

Shaheen's grimaces left me in no doubt about his psychological disarray. In the short time I had been in Kuwait, I thought I had seen such expressions on other faces. Listening to Shaheen helped me clarify an impression that Kuwaitis, who had always seemed so self-assured, even rather cocky, had become grievously disoriented by the experience of the invasion. The months of occupation were not simply a political aberration; they were a personal trauma. Never before had I encountered questions from them that cast doubt on the validity of their whole culture of privilege; and though, by the end of my stay, I had concluded that they would probably wind up changing little or nothing, it was apparent that the inquiry caused real anguish. As Shaheen talked, I wrote in the margin of my note pad "looks bewildered."

"If you look at an average Kuwaiti family, by which I mean one that is fairly rich," Shaheen went on, "you find that we have always been served by others. When I was a child, my mother prepared all the meals for my brothers and me, but my wife has never had to cook and doesn't know how. A family with three or four servants is normal. I can bring in a Sri Lankan to work in my house for a tiny fraction of my salary. It solves my problems, and the Sri Lankan's, so why shouldn't I do it? During the occupation, most non-Kuwaitis left, and the availability of servants has not returned to what it was. Without them, my children ask, 'Who does the laundry?' and 'Where is the driver?' After the liberation, we needed volunteers to paint over the Iraqi graffiti that covered the schools in my neighborhood, and many came forward, but none of them had ever held a paint brush. So the government organized courses on how to paint, but soon foreign workers began flooding back, and the volunteers lost interest.

"We've been transformed by forty years of easy living. We think money is to buy luxuries. Read Kuwaiti folklore: the fortunate people always have slaves, women, land, jewelry. That is our traditional way of thinking. In your society, a rich man uses his money to develop hobbies, build a library, teach his child piano. In Kuwait, our goal is two or three cars, a television in every room, three or four servants. We use money to provide physical gratification; it's the only way we know."

VII   POSTLIBERATION NORMALITY

DESPITE THE ANGUISHING of Kuwaitis like Suleiman al-Shaheen, Kuwait after liberation was no clearer about the direction it should take than it had been before the war. The perspective of the royal family did not go much beyond the preservation of its power, but the opposition was hardly more farsighted. It exalted democracy, on which it sought to build a consensus, but it rarely mentioned what democracy was meant to achieve. Much of the reason was the sharp cleavage between seculars and Islamics, who deeply distrusted each other. The seculars were convinced that, for the Islamics, democracy was merely a way station, to be scrapped at the earliest opportunity in exchange for a coerced religious conformity. Many Islamics admitted that they were right, but correctly pointed out that the seculars offered no conception of a social system at all.

Ironically, both causes were discredited by the war. The seculars were embarrassed at being invaded by Iraq, the most secular of the Arab states. The Islamics had trouble explaining why Arab Islamic movements rallied to Iraq. Both had responded patriotically to the invasion, though in fact neither's doctrine was much imbued with Kuwaiti nationalism. In theory, both thought in terms of a wider community—the seculars of an Arab nation, the Islamics of a Muslim *umma*. In reality, both were essentially tribal in outlook, and after the liberation, neither was of a mind to contemplate subsuming national sovereignty under a wider framework, whether secular or religious.

The war, however, did resolve, at least for a time, the persistent hostility between Sunnis and Shiites. Kuwait is a Sunni state; its royal family is Sunni; its roots in the Arabian desert are Sunni. The 30 percent of Kuwaitis who are Shiite are migrants, some from Iraq, most from Iran. The early arrivals thrived. The more recent migrants have tended to drift into the lower class, though, having arrived before the oil boom, they have been accepted as Kuwaitis. Always tense, relations between the Sunnis and Shiites grew edgier during the eight years of the Iraq-Iran war, but the pro-Khomeini explosion that many Sunnis feared never came. Then, suddenly, Khomeini died, Saddam invaded, and Iraq replaced Iran as the principal source of trepidation.

"After the invasion," said Mohammed Ashkanani, a thirty-four-year-old Shiite active in the human-rights movement, "the Shiites' long opposition to Saddam Hussein was thrown into a different light. The Shiites could make the claim that they had been right all along about Iraq and, memories being short, many Sunnis were ready to agree. At the same time, the Shiite fanatics, witnessing Khomeini's failure in the war, adopted a lower profile. Sunnis and Shiites worked and fought side by side during the occupation and were killed by the Iraqis with the same indifference. Now the great Shiite merchant families want to show that they are better Kuwaitis than the Sabahs, and relations between Sunnis and Shiites have never been better.

"But the Sabahs have always used their powers to divide Kuwaitis, and playing Sunnis and Shiites against each other is a way to break up democratic solidarity. As a minority, Shiites have an interest in democracy, though they are very Islamic, because they recognize they are safest in an atmosphere of tolerance. They don't join Sunni fundamentalist parties, and the Sunni Islamics do not consider them allies. Shiites generally like the constitution, where their rights are spelled out. The Sabah strategy is to get them to forget the constitution and depend for their well-being on the ruling family. Most Shiites understand that the Sabahs manipulate their rights according to political needs, and they see the constitution as an anchor. But they certainly expect the Sabahs to test their loyalty again."

As the euphoria of the liberation faded, and the Allied contingents left Kuwait, apprehension rose over how the country would defend itself in the next crisis that came along. Egypt and Syria, members of the coalition that defeated Iraq, offered to contribute their armies to an Arab security force, but most Kuwaitis lumped Egyptians and Syrians with the Palestinians, as Arabs looking for some sort of handout. In *diwaniyahs* all over town, Kuwaitis debated putting the country under American protection. Many favored such a course, but they had concerns about Americans, too.

I spent one evening at the *diwaniyah* of Issa al-Shaheen, a heavily bearded man of forty-five, and a fundamentalist who is active in the Islamic democratic movement. He is also the brother of Suleiman al-Shaheen, the foreign ministry official. Not all the men in the room—a modest, middle-class *diwaniyah*—were Islamics. Issa's *diwaniyah* was considered highly intellectual and attracted men, both secular and religious, from a wide range of Kuwaiti professional life—teaching, journalism, business, government and medicine. The participants spoke with intelligence and wit, choosing their phrases carefully. These were some of their observations:

"Our needs are permanent, not temporary. The next Iraqi regime may be as dangerous as Saddam. Or the danger may come again from Iran. Only a long-term arrangement with the United States can satisfy them."

"Why not have the Americans here? What damage have they done to Great Britain or Spain, Germany or Japan? Their bases will protect us. They will present no danger."

"If we agree to have them, the Arabs will criticize us for submitting to Christianity and Western colonialism. On the other hand, if we don't, they will not come to protect us at all."

"We must think of the threat to our daughters. An American soldier will go out with a Kuwaiti girl, and we'll shout, 'Go home, Yankee!' "

"Let's be honest, the war has already brought American influence here. Think of the young men who have abandoned the *dishdasha* and are wearing T-shirts and shorts. Suddenly, we're seeing all those hairy young legs. I'm not used to it and I don't like it."

"It is too simplistic to approach the question as if we face the choice of American occupation or Iraqi conquest—between colonialism and submission. What about some middle ground, like UN troops? Besides, the United States doesn't need our permission to protect its interests here."

Another evening, I listened to a debate at the hot and stuffy *diwaniyah* of Mubarak Duella, an ex-parliamentarian. It was shabby, among *diwani-*

yahs, and the *dishdashas* worn by many of the men who attended were soiled or wrinkled. Most were in chairs lined up against the walls, but about thirty sat barefoot and cross-legged on the floor. They had the faces of men who worked outdoors in the sun. They were bedouin tribesmen—that is, they had come from the desert only in the past generation or two and lived in unfashionable neighborhoods—and though not intellectuals, they listened carefully. As I arrived, a fiery young orator named Nasser al-Masri, a small man with a carefully trimmed beard, had the floor and he was denouncing the emir. Later, he told me he had recently been dismissed as a police officer for his attitude.

"Kuwait must be like Israel," al-Masri declared, paying a compliment that I had rarely heard in Arab lands. "Kuwaitis are not respected by their government, as are all Jews in Israel, even *falashas*. The Israelis are trained to defend themselves, to use weapons. The government has confidence in them. The Kuwaiti government does not want Kuwaitis to defend the country, but people who do not defend themselves do not deserve to survive. Kuwaitis who stayed during the occupation organized and resisted the Iraqis, which proves that Kuwait has the potential to fight. But the government does not appreciate this potential. It is afraid of its own citizens. It is determined to rebuild the army as it was, empty and useless. The people have got to be ready, or Iraq will come again. They only need to be trained. When the Iraqis came, the government ran but the people fought. The lesson is that Kuwaitis must be prepared to defend themselves."

A few Kuwaitis, even if they did not fully agree with al-Masri, worried that the government, as it moved toward increasing reliance on the United States, had learned the wrong lesson from the war. Immediately on its return, the Kuwaiti government embarked on a program of punishing the Arab leaders who had not fully supported its positions, most notably Jordan's King Hussein and the PLO. I heard little willingness to inquire whether there were not good reasons for questioning the wisdom of the war on Iraq. Certainly, none accepted King Hussein's claim—which the record sustained—that, far from endorsing the invasion, he had urged only that a greater diplomatic effort be put into reversing it, before inviting in the Western armies. Even among the democratic opposition, support was almost total for the policy of vindictiveness, initiated by the Saudis, which the Sabahs followed. Only a few Kuwaitis argued for a tolerant view of Arab deviation, in the interests of reconciliation within the Arab world.

"We can't live in a hostile neighborhood," said Abdlatif al-Hamad, scion of one of the great merchant families and one of the rare dissenters. Al-Hamad is chairman of the Arab Fund for Economic Development, which directs investment into Arab countries. "It's time to start on a healing process. In the crisis of 1961, the Jordanians were our strongest supporter; enemies today may be friends tomorrow. We must share more of our wealth, not less. What the government should stop is the practice of buying off corrupt leaders by giving money to numbered bank accounts. We are still rich, and we cannot turn our backs on so many Arabs who are poor. The incompetence in policy-making in recent years has fed the image of the ugly Kuwaiti. We have bragged about our opulent displays of wealth, when we could have created an image of Kuwait that was gentle and humane. We must adopt a long-term view. We will be living with the Arabs for the rest of our history."

Fuad Mullah Hussein, secretary-general of the Higher Planning Council, reckoned that the Sabahs were buying off the entire Kuwaiti population. The five-year plan that was drafted by his office, putting emphasis on education and manpower development to prepare Kuwaitis to take control of the civil service and the economy, was languishing. Since the war, he said, it had been amended to put more Kuwaitis into security posts, to restore the confidence of the public and private investors. But Kuwaitis could hardly take it seriously, with the government encouraging them to hasten back to their old big-spending, no-work habits.

"The government," Hussein said, "began pouring money on the people after the liberation, paying all back salaries, cancelling debts. Now the supermarkets are overflowing. Medical treatment is better than ever before, because of the population decline. Savings accounts have been refilled, and Kuwaitis can leave the country for a holiday whenever they like. The government has encouraged them to resume the easy life. They're all importing two or three servants again. The people in power refuse to think ahead to a self-reliant society. They extol the principle that Kuwaitis must be a majority in their own country, but more foreigners are pouring in, some legal and some illegal, as we go back to pursuing only personal enjoyment. The government, dismissing the five-year plan, knows that it can buy power with money. Giving comfort to the people also brings loyalty to the state."

(The Arab Economic Report of 1992, an annual study financed in part by the Arab League, stated that the war had cost Kuwait $160 billion. Although the government kept its books closed, it was believed that two-thirds or more of the $100 billion in reserves that Kuwait kept in the West had been depleted, by mismanagement and corruption as well as by the war and reconstruction. In 1993, the Arab Monetary Fund estimated the costs to the entire region of the Gulf war at $676 billion, not counting damage to the environment and diminished economic growth. The reforms following this decline in wealth, however, have generally been limited to cutting back on foreign assistance, in Saudi Arabia as well as Kuwait.)

VIII HOLDING TO ACCOUNT

LESS THAN A WEEK after the emir returned, his cabinet resigned in response to a mounting popular clamor. The opposition suggested the moment was now right for Sheikh Sa'ad, the crown prince, to give up his long-standing claim to the office of prime minister. It argued that democratic reforms should begin by divorcing the royal family's prerogatives from political control of the country. The Sabahs, on the defensive but barely scratched by any of the opposition's attacks, rejected this proposal out of hand. Sheikh Sa'ad retained his cabinet post, while the family mounted its counterattack.

On the last day of Ramadan, 1991, the emir spoke on television; it was his first statement to the public in the six months since liberation. He announced in his talk that he would ask the United States to keep troops in Kuwait, to defend it against the continuing threat from Saddam Hussein. It was in this speech that he wiped out the commercial debts and the mortgage loans of all Kuwaitis, "in recognition of the hardships to which our citizens have been exposed." He also made a pledge to hold parliamentary elections in 1992. "Consultation and popular participation in the affairs of state have always been characteristic of life in our country," he said, a bit disingenuously. "It can take many forms, but the restoration of parliamentary life is what we agreed to at the popular conference in Jedda."

The prodemocracy faction did not concur that the emir had delivered on the Jedda agreement. It considered 1992 much too far away for the election. It also regarded the debt forgiveness, whatever its social justification, as a political bribe, in violation of the constitution. The forgiveness was not decided in the cabinet; it was the emir's decision alone. The opposition hardly exaggerated in charging that the emir used the state treasury as a personal campaign fund, answering to no one for the expenditures. But it had been like that since oil was discovered.

On April 20, Sheikh Sa'ad announced the composition of the new cabinet. It was known that he had consulted with a range of technocrats and opposition figures in an effort to give the new government more variety, but had declined to accept any dilution of the Sabahs' powers. Nonetheless, some fresh names appeared, some old ones were dropped, and a few of the Sabahs were moved to new posts. Kuwaitis took to their tea leaves to interpret the changes, and a few concluded that the emir, in his own dark way, was taking a measure of responsibility for the disaster. Others dissented. But one thing was clear: the Sabah family remained in command. Humbling the opposition further, the government banned a press conference that some leading democrats had scheduled to protest the choices.

Kuwaitis, meanwhile, continued the postmortem on the events preceding the invasion. One evening, Dr. Mussama al-Mubarak, a professor of political science, said in a talk show on local radio that the government, by stubbornness or inadvertence, had misled Saddam Hussein into the blunders that culminated in the attack. Given the seriousness of the charge, it generated remarkably little fuss, probably because Kuwaitis, and particularly the intellectuals, had been saying that kind of thing in dinner-table conversations for some time. When I tracked Dr. Mubarak down at the university, she was quite willing to elaborate on her ideas.

"Many Kuwaitis think the government should have been more flexible in dealing with Iraq's demands during the negotiations last spring," she said. "I'm talking about Iraqi claims of money and oil wells, and even the islands of Bubiyan and Warba. None of their demands violated our fundamental national interests. I agree it's possible that Saddam, being greedy, might only have responded to concessions by asking for more, but we don't know that. If the government had read Iraq's statements carefully, it would have understood how serious Saddam was. I don't know why the government adopted an extremely hard line. It makes me think the decisions were not Kuwait's alone. I assume that, on such matters, Kuwait would have consulted with Saudi Arabia and Britain, as well as the United States, none of which wanted the status quo in the Gulf to change in Iraq's favor. Kuwaiti chauvinists supported this hard line but, in reality, Kuwait miscalculated on its own interests. Many Kuwaitis are convinced that the government took a dangerous negotiating position, which cost us very dearly."

At about the same time, Dr. Jassem Sadoun, a highly regarded economist and business consultant, was involved in a dispute with the ministry of information over a column he had submitted for publication to the newspaper *Al-Qabas*, the most outspoken of the Kuwaiti dailies. The column severely criticized the government for, among other failings, "following the wrong oil policies, thereby provoking a maniac who only understands the language of violence." In a talk with me, Sadoun argued that the roots of the problem with Iraq lay in the arrogance and incompetence of the government, particularly Sheikh Sa'ad, the prime minister, and Sheikh Ali al-Khalifa, who successively headed the ministries of oil and finance. When the information ministry's censors barred publication of the column, Sadoun circulated it by *samizdat*, while threatening to sue the information minister.

"Let him take me to court!" said Dr. Badr al-Yacoub, the information minister, when I visited him one evening in his office. "I didn't suppress the column; I only told him to remove a few offensive words, and he refused. I won't allow the publication of something that's not true, and it is simply not true that the government made mistakes in its policies before the invasion."

Ali al-Bedah, a business consultant by profession, spent most of the occupation in London organizing democratic opposition to the government. "My personal feeling is that the war was planned as a way to get rid of Saddam," he told me in his office in a downtown building that still showed damage from the war. "I don't think there was a major conspiracy, with planning committees and the exchange of papers and the rest. In my judgment, the situation was ripe and the United States was determined to make the most of it. I think that if the Americans had not pushed, the royal family would never have taken the steps that it did to provoke Saddam. The Kuwaiti government, using psychology, got under his skin and he was stupid not to see what was happening. Then he was hit by the United States, not because he seized Kuwait but because he became too powerful in the region."

After listening for several weeks to critics of the Sabahs, I had to acknowledge that I had no smoking gun to support the hypothesis that Washington and Kuwait had actually *conspired* in the destruction of Saddam Hussein. Yet it was clear that Kuwait had bearded Saddam in the spring and early summer of 1990, serene in the conviction that it would not pay a prohibitive price. Esteemed for centuries for their diplomacy, had the Sabahs, sapped by power and greed, lost their touch? Critics of the Bush administration have argued that Saddam, having been "coddled" by the White House, was led to believe he might actually get away with taking over Kuwait. A greater weight of evidence, however, leads to an opposite conclusion: that the Sabahs believed that, whatever they did, the United States would back them up. And so they were careless, offering pretexts to Saddam to do his dirty deed.

Some months after the Gulf war, I interviewed an American diplomat who had served in a senior post in Kuwait prior to the invasion, and had been among those trapped in the embassy when the Iraqis arrived. The diplomat, who declined to be identified, said the embassy had repeatedly assured Kuwaiti officials that the United States would stand up for Kuwait's sovereignty and territorial integrity, as it had at the time of the reflagging. "We thought that Kuwait was bargaining in good faith," the diplomat said, "and we told them we would do what we could to help. At no point did we get involved in the substance of the negotiating. We talked about it a lot, and concluded it was like the haggling over a carpet in the *souk*, and that ultimately Kuwait and Iraq would reach an agreement. We sent warnings to Washington in late July that the situation was getting tense, but frankly we didn't foresee an invasion, even after Iraqi troops moved to the border. We certainly didn't think that Saddam would swallow the whole country. In any case, no one in Washington was paying attention. Everyone was focused on the cataclysm in Europe." Late in July, with the pressure rising, the diplomat said, the United States offered to fly missions over Kuwait, as a show of American support, but the Kuwaitis were so confident they could handle the situation that they declined.

Among the crucial players in the period before the invasion was General H. Norman Schwarzkopf, who in 1990 was to become the commanding general of Desert Storm. Two years earlier, just after the Iraq-Iran war came to an end, Schwarzkopf had been appointed chief of the U.S. Army's Central Command, which had direct responsibility for military security in the Gulf region. Schwarzkopf, unlike those American leaders whose eyes were then fixed exclusively on the Soviet dissolution, was sensitive to the problem of the vacuum of Western power in the Gulf. He recognized that with Iran out of action, at least temporarily, Saddam would be tempted to become the Gulf's master, and only the United States stood in his way. Schwarzkopf transformed the Central Command, which had been established in 1983 to counter a Soviet threat, to confront the Iraqis, who he believed had become the real enemy in the region.

"Schwarzkopf was here on visits before the war, maybe a few times a year," an American diplomat in Kuwait told me after the liberation. "He was a political general, which was in itself unusual. He kept a personally high profile, and was on a first-name basis with all the key ministers. He had good political instincts, and though there were no agreements or commitments, when the invasion occurred he already had the ties that he thought he needed. The Kuwaitis feared that when they called, we wouldn't come. Schwarzkopf insisted—explicitly or not—that we would. Some Kuwaitis, of course, remained skeptical. They were impressed by our support during the reflagging episode, but they could not forget that we had abandoned the shah of Iran. I think Schwarzkopf finally convinced most Kuwaitis that if Iraq came in, we'd be there."

In his own book, Schwarzkopf essentially confirms these observations. Like any good general without battles to fight, he was in search of a mission, and as early as July 1988, he writes, he worried that the war's end had "left Iraq with a million-man army and an economy too weak to absorb the soldiers back into civilian life." The war also ended with Basra a wreck, forcing Iraq to pressure Kuwait for Bubiyan and Warba, the islands it needed to make Um-Qasr into a viable port. At the time he assumed his post with the Central Command, Schwarzkopf writes, he was ordered to scale his forces back to the level preceding America's intervention in the "tanker war" of 1987 and 1988. The instability in the Gulf, he declares, persuaded him instead to petition the Pentagon to strengthen the forces under his command.

Schwarzkopf acknowledges that he toured the Gulf giving out warnings on Iraq. He found the sheikhs "highly cultured," in contrast to Saddam, a "thug," and he exulted in his intimacy with Kuwaiti officials, relating with delight how, on one trip, he attended an official dinner wearing Arab robes, in the manner of T. E. Lawrence. Schwarzkopf does not challenge the legitimacy of Saddam's concerns over money and the islands, but defines his own mission as one of persuading the Gulf Arabs that Iraq had superseded Iran as their chief threat. In retrospect, the issue is not whether Schwarzkopf was right or wrong, but whether his tactics helped touch off the chain of events that fulfilled his gloomy prophecy.

When I put this notion to Sheikh Ali al-Khalifa, he denied that Kuwait, in negotiating with Iraq, was influenced by the prospect of American military support. A handsome man of about fifty, with wavy black hair, al-Khalifa is a luminary of the international petroleum culture and an inveterate jet-setter. As minister of oil, he was credited with being the architect of the reflagging policy, and he was known as a ceaseless advocate of close Kuwaiti relations with the United States. A cousin of the emir's, he had been implicated in the Souk al-Manakh financial scandal in 1985, and on the night we spoke he was still nursing the loss of his post as finance minister in the recent cabinet reshuffle. His huge home, where we met, had been occupied for six months by Iraqi soldiers who, he said, had left with most of the furniture. With eloquence, Sheikh Ali offered me the party line on Kuwait's preinvasion dealings with Iraq: since Saddam had long before made up his mind to swallow Kuwait, it hardly mattered what transpired in the negotiations. But his story showed inconsistencies, and in the end it seemed to me to confirm the contention that America's military guarantees were crucial to Kuwait's negotiating posture.

"It never entered anyone's mind here, after the help we gave the Iraqis during the war, that they would turn against us," he said. "The border problems that separated us were small, a half mile here or there. The essential thing for them was to gain the confidence of the Gulf—and they obviously failed.

"During the meetings we had with them in 1990, their demands were invariably unreasonable. They were shooting for the moon, but we took that as normal tactics. They made threatening speeches, of course, but we were used to that, and until July, there was no prospect of a serious rift. They said we were overproducing on our oil quota, but so was everyone else in OPEC. We had a saying in OPEC: 'Those who could did, those who couldn't complain.' Iraq had technical problems. Their oil fields were not properly maintained. They couldn't expand production. But I don't think Saddam ever understood that. The information was no secret. It was in the international technical press. But I think he found it easier to blame his problems on Kuwait. Our overproduction was quite small—about two hundred and fifty thousand barrels on a quota of one and a half million. Those few barrels were not responsible for the drop in international prices.''

Experts I later talked with generally supported Sheikh Ali's arguments, declaring that the drop was the reflection of a softness in the international market. Daniel Yergin, an American specialist, predicted in July of 1990 that prices would fall to the thirteen to fifteen dollar range, because the United States was sliding into a recession. Saddam thought he should get 50 percent more and tried to intimidate OPEC's producers, when in fact prices were being set by conditions beyond his control. But Saddam might not have understood the problem, one expert said, since his ministers were probably too frightened to tell him the truth.

"Saddam Hussein's problem was that he wanted more of everything," Sheikh Ali continued. "He wanted to build an incredible army, costing billions. He wanted a strong industrial base, even if it was underutilized. He wanted unlimited personal expenditures; he was building palaces all over Iraq, at a cost of $500 million to $1 billion each. And he wanted to bring prosperity, or at least a higher standard of living, to Iraqis. Saddam did not understand the economics of his aspirations. No matter what he did, his ambitions were bound to bankrupt him, and he looked to the Gulf to give him the money to keep afloat.

"Finally, Saddam thought he could annex Kuwait, and bleed Saudi Arabia without invading, and that he would solve everything that way. But *the American policy was clear. I spent too much time in Washington to make a mistake and received a constant stream of American visitors here. We understood it but Saddam didn't. We knew the United States would not let us be overrun* [my italics].''

A couple of days later, I met with Sheikh Salem, the foreign minister, and was able to take up with him the issue of the security relations between the United States and Kuwait. I had seen him from a distance at a session of the national council, where he delivered a droning speech in which he reaffirmed Kuwait's vow to punish the Arab states that had sided with Iraq and restated Kuwait's preference for the West over an Arab alliance as guarantor of its security.

By the time we met, the international newspapers had carried stories, datelined Washington, giving the general outlines of an impending United States–Kuwait security pact. It provided for the positioning of American weapons in Kuwait and for joint military exercises but not for the stationing of American troops, which the Sabahs had hoped for. An American diplomat in Kuwait told me that the U.S. army simply did not want to take on the burden of dealing with Islamic sensibilities, particularly after Saudi Arabia had already rejected military bases. The agreement, which was made public in September, went a long way toward relieving Kuwaiti uncertainties, however, by reaffirming that the United States would treat the Gulf region as a national security concern.

Sheikh Salem, who received me in the Bayan Palace, said that he was willing to discuss security affairs but that, first, he had other matters on his mind. "I know you have been hearing complaints about the Sabah family," he said. Sheikh Salem, who is considered second in the line of succession, is scarcely regal in appearance—a small, squat man, with dark hair and dark eyes. (Sheikh Sa'ad, who is first in line, has slightly buck teeth and pop eyes, and looks even less regal.) His English was fluent, and he sat relaxing on a soft easy chair as he spoke.

"We consider the complaints about us to be normal. Kids don't approve one hundred percent of what their fathers do. Kuwaitis may have something against us as individuals, but not against the family. In the bottom of their hearts, even the opposition doesn't want to be rid of us. But because Kuwaitis love the Sabahs, they want us to be perfect. We can't be perfect. We have our ups and downs. Perfection, alas, is limited to Almighty God."

Sheikh Salem then launched into a rambling discourse in condemnation of Saddam Hussein, whose presence, not surprisingly, he called an obstacle to regional stability. He suggested that if the international community kept the pressure on Iraq, "two or three young officers with guts" might be disposed to change its direction. He did not say precisely what he meant by those words, but he added approvingly that ordinary Kuwaitis in their *diwaniyahs* think the CIA should identify such officers and give them some training. "It would open a new page in history," he said. When he finished talking about Saddam, Sheikh Salem asked me to excuse him for fifteen minutes so he could say his prayers. He returned about an hour later, apologizing for the delay.

"Before the Iraqi invasion," he said, resuming, "the leftists in Kuwait were trying to blacken America's reputation by calling it imperialist. They created a controversy over the reflagging, though the level-headed people were all in favor. It was all political. They were determined to make an issue for the next elections. That's the difference between democracy in the West and in the Arab world. You are a mature democracy, we are not. As Sabahs, we are for democracy. We practice democracy. But we want a well-guided democracy that will mature and last.

"Since the liberation, the hatred toward America that they tried to provoke has been transformed by Kuwaitis into love. I now see something I thought I'd never see—American flags all over Kuwait, flying from houses, displayed on cars. In the *diwaniyahs*, I see as many pictures of President Bush as of Sheikh Jabir. Now is the time for you to capitalize on this popularity. Your people want contracts in Kuwait. There are economic benefits here. I remember when Kuwaitis blamed Britain for every problem in the region, even if it was only two fish fighting in the sea. I hope we don't start blaming the Americans. My advice is that you don't interfere, that to get what you want you deal with the authority that exists. Don't push us too hard on democracy, or the wind might blow the wrong way on your ship. Democracy is now on the shelf. In the election next year, I do not see a big surge away from the family. The people will support the Sabahs, out of a zealous concern for the interests of Kuwait."

(The election took place as scheduled in October 1992, and a majority of the fifty seats in the national assembly were won by opposition candidates, either democrats or Islamics. Ahmed Sadoun and Abdullah al-Nibari both won, as did Hamad al-Jouan, the victim of the assassination attempt in 1991. Since the election, the national assembly, replying to the reports of financial scandal in high places that have outraged Kuwaitis, has put most of its energy into trying to take the control of public finances out of the hands of the Sabahs. Among the charges made in the assembly was that funds were removed from Kuwait's overseas accounts to buy votes in the UN Security Council during the debates over the Gulf crisis. One of the few officials with the power to transfer such funds, it was noted, was Sheikh Ali al-Khalifa, then the finance minister.)

Sheikh Salem and I had by now been talking for a couple of hours, and though he showed no signs of tiring, I was becoming worried that he might at any time bring the meeting to an end. To press him on my own agenda, I shifted the subject and asked him to review Kuwait's relations with the United States since the end of the Iraq-Iran war. Before long he was telling me what I thought I might hear about Kuwait's expectations of the United States in the months prior to the invasion.

"Our close relations with the United States began with the reflagging," he answered, "and they never declined. The reflagging opened the door for us, and after that we always had in the back of our minds that if anything happened to us, we could turn to the United States.

"When I was minister of interior, I consulted with the Americans on intelligence. Later, we had exchanges with the United States about the growing danger of Iraq. The United States knew that something was going to happen. Iraq had military camps in Safwan, Basra and Fao, very near to our borders, and after the Iraq-Iran war there was a great deal of movement in the region. We had question marks about how normal this was, and there were even several border incidents, which we suspected were military probes. General Schwarzkopf came here a few times and met with the crown prince and minister of defense. These became routine visits to discuss military cooperation and coordination.

"By the time the crisis began in early 1990, we knew we could rely on the Americans. There was an exchange of talks on the ambassadorial level just before the invasion. No explicit commitments were ever made, but it was like a marriage. Sometimes you don't say to your wife 'I love you,' but you know the relationship will lead to certain things [my italics]."

Sheikh Salem did not state directly that Kuwait's expectations of American support determined the intransigent positions it took in the negotiations with Iraq. As minister of interior at the time, it is possible that he was not even involved in the talks. But, like Sheikh Ali al-Khalifa, he left no doubt that the government did not consider itself alone in confronting Iraq. Near the end of our talk, he made clear that he believed the postwar security agreement, though not everything the Sabahs wanted, left Kuwait stronger than ever.

"The agreement was drawn up by the both of us," he said, "and it is for the benefit and interest of the United States as well as Kuwait. It is true that most Kuwaitis would have preferred to have American troops on the ground, but we agreed together that this was not advisable. Any group of soldiers here would be mingling with the people. Daily irritations would build up. Suppose an American soldier got killed, for whatever reason, by a Kuwaiti or a non-Kuwaiti; it would create a major incident. Even a car accident would require us to deal with questions of immunity and responsibility. Your boys wouldn't be able to go into town and drink beer, and they would grow restless. But we are confident, even without your troops, that Kuwait is secure. If another crisis occurs, there will be time for proper measures. What matters is that the basic relations between Kuwait and the United States are strong. As our arrangements become more explicit, we believe our friendship will grow still closer."

SHEIKH SALEM'S STATEMENT to me, in conjunction with Sheikh Ali's, left me convinced that in the spring of 1990 the Kuwaiti government felt itself free to take a dangerous position in confronting Iraq. As a graduate student long ago, I was taught a rule of statecraft that went: "Little states don't play tricks on big powers." That is precisely what the Kuwaiti government did.

The Kuwaitis played their tricks because Washington, deliberately or not, had conveyed the message to them that they could. If Kuwait misunderstood its intent, then Washington had the responsibility to take corrective action. It had opportunities before the invasion; even after the invasion, opportunity was not foreclosed. Was President Bush unaware of the background to the attack on Kuwait? Or had his plan always been, as so many Arabs suspect, to reduce Iraq to a choice between its own economic collapse and aggressive war against Kuwait? Far from trying to undo the effects of the message conveyed to the Kuwaitis, the United States stood defiantly behind it. Kuwait, as the victim of aggression, paid heavily for this course. Iraq, as the aggressor, paid more heavily still. From the perspective of 1993, with Saddam still in power and the Gulf region less stable than before, it is not even clear what the rewards of the war were for the United States.

CHAPTER EIGHT

JORDAN

I FRIENDS OF SADDAM HUSSEIN

It was just an ordinary Friday evening in Amman—as ordinary, that is, as most evenings in the fall of 1990, after the palpable tension of the Gulf crisis descended—and among the ordinary events on the schedule was a homily to be delivered by Abu Zant at the mosque of the Islamic College. Sheikh Abdul Mun'im Abu Zant was known as Amman's most outspoken cleric, a fiery orator, born in the West Bank city of Nablus, given to colorful turns of phrase, and occasional rabble-rousing. He was also a member of Parliament, one of the victors in the semi-landslide of the Muslim Brotherhood in the fall of 1989, when Jordan held its first parliamentary election in twenty-two years. It would be an exaggeration to call Abu Zant a popular leader; notwithstanding the election results, Jordanians did not seem much tempted by Islamic radicalism. But Abu Zant nearly always drew a crowd on a Friday at a mosque.

So, shortly before seven o'clock, I set out from my hotel on a short walk through modern Amman. I proceeded first along a wide avenue heavy with the aroma of *shawarma* shops and the charm of florists. Then I circumnavigated a traffic circle with a gushing fountain and a banner which proclaimed in Arabic, "The Arab Peninsula will become Another Vietnam." I continued past a series of bland public buildings and handsome stone villas, some of them embassies. Finally I arrived at a low-lying structure surrounded by a ten-foot wall. Its obscure entrance was on a narrow side street about a dozen steps from the avenue; I would have missed the mosque had I not followed the gathering crowd.

Emulating the worshippers, I took off my shoes in the doorway and tucked them under my arm, then proceeded into a large room, bare except for Oriental rugs covering the floor. The men, nearly all in Western clothes, were arranging themselves in parallel lines, facing east; I found a place near a pillar at their edge. The entering women, wrapped in head-scarves (a few also wore veils), moved quickly to a section concealed behind a curtain. A high proportion of the worshippers were young people, in their teens or twenties; some had come with their parents, others as couples, with their children. The variety of dress suggested that much of Amman's social structure was represented. Around the walls, policemen with black hair and neatly trimmed moustaches, wearing berets and navy epaulets on light blue shirts, stood by unobtrusively. By 7:20 or so, the mosque overflowed with what I estimated to be about three thousand people. The men responded to the crowding by tightening their ranks, keeping their prayer lines as crisply parallel as a marching team on a parade ground. The women were hidden from view.

The prayer service, during which the men dropped at intervals to their knees and lowered their heads to the floor, lasted only a quarter hour and was followed by Abu Zant's warm-up speaker, who proceeded to entreat God to send snakes, flies and other pests to attack the infidels whose occupation of Arabia had placed the holy Muslim shrines in jeopardy. Abu Zant himself opened with more restraint, praying to God to send the foreigners home regretting their intrusion. A small man shaped like a jelly roll, Abu Zant frequently lifted his short arms in a choppy motion for emphasis. Dressed in a black robe and a white turban piped with red, he spoke with rising passion, in the end reaching a high, almost screeching pitch, made more acrid by a very scratchy amplifier system.

"The battle is not between Iraq and America," Abu Zant declared, "but between Islam and the Crusaders. It is not between Bush and Saddam but between the leaders of infidelity and the Prophet of Islam, Mohammed, peace be with him. . . . Why is Iraq the focus? Because the Zionist and American enemies don't wish to see the Arabs or the Muslims possess any power that can stand against Israel. The ambitions of the Crusader invasion are to contain the Islamic awakening, safeguard oil which is the new god of the West, and protect Israel, which is the fifty-second [sic] state of the United States of America. . . . The Saudis have lost their credentials as Muslims by allowing foreign forces to come to our holy land, which only God can protect. They have brought the Americans, and what the Americans have brought to the holy land is VD and AIDS. The royal family of Saudi Arabia is a traitor to Islam. Mohammed's army will be back to drive them and the infidels out of the holy land, and out of Palestine, too."

The assembled men seemed to find Abu Zant's performance more entertaining than rousing. In response to obvious cues, they dutifully shouted back, "God is great . . . the Koran is our constitution . . . Holy War is our plan . . . to die for the cause of God does not frighten us." After fifteen minutes or so of solemn listening, the attention of the children flagged, and more and more of them began to wander around, joining up with one another in corners of the mosque to romp and frolic. After a half hour,

Abu Zant recognized that he was losing his audience and prudently brought the talk to an end. Another speaker then took over, but the men, hardly interested in him, turned to chatting among themselves and, in the growing disarray, women with their children in hand appeared on the floor to summon their husbands home.

By the end of the second speech, the mosque was half empty. As those of us who had persevered straggled out, a muezzin chanted, his melancholy voice wafted over the rooftops of the neighborhood by a loudspeaker attached to the minaret. On the street, the departing crowd seemed in an affable mood, more exhilarated, I suspect, by the prospect of supper than of holy war in the Gulf.

ABU ZANT AND his Islamic companions were not the only supporters in Amman of Saddam Hussein. On a bright morning about a week later, a three-day congress opened that brought together nationalist and leftist forces from around the Arab world in solidarity with the Iraqi leader. The congress was held at the Royal Cultural Center, a monument to the wealth that had filtered into Jordan since the oil boom in the 1970s. A large auditorium of modern design, the Center is part of an oil-built neighborhood of new office buildings, mosques, shopping centers and luxury hotels. The University of Jordan, the Royal Scientific Society and the University Hospital were nearby. Written on a banner in front of the Center was "Arabs and Muslims Unite Against the American and Zionist Invaders." Another fluttering nearby proclaimed, "A Victory for Iraq is a Victory for Palestine."

The congress had been organized by a coalition that called itself JANDA, for Jordanian Arab National Democratic Alliance. It had emerged out of a dozen political associations and parties, all secular. Clandestine for decades, they had surfaced since the election and were building support. At the congress, they were testing their strength. King Hussein had agreed to place the meeting under his patronage—a conventional gesture in Jordan, well short of an endorsement—but had disappointed the sponsors by sending a low-level surrogate to make the keynote speech. Saddam supporters from North Africa, Sudan, Lebanon, Yemen and the Palestine Liberation Organization were present, representing, according to a press release, more than one hundred organizations. The newspapers also promised delegations from Egypt and Syria, whose governments had joined the West's anti-Saddam coalition, but when I entered the crowded lobby, I was handed a hastily printed notice which said the Egyptians were "detained at the Cairo airport and prevented from flying to Jordan." To no one's surprise, the Syrians did not show up either.

The stars of the congress turned out to be the veteran terrorist leaders George Habash and Nayef Hawatmeh, heads respectively of the Popular Front for the Liberation of Palestine and the Democratic Front for the Liberation of Palestine, minority organizations within the Arafat-dominated PLO. Both men had been expelled from Jordan after the PLO's "Black September" uprising in 1970. They had since renounced terror and adopted a tolerant attitude toward Arafat's peace overtures to Israel, but neither had, until now, been permitted to return. As I entered the main hall, decorated with photographs of King Hussein and Crown Prince Hassan, both wearing the *kuffiyeh*, the crowd was cheering for the Jordanborn Hawatmeh, who stood in the aisle, his arms raised high in a "V for victory" sign. The cheers were even lustier for the more charismatic Habash. As Habash entered, limping slightly from a stroke he had suffered a few years before, the galleries erupted with the rhythms of PFLP slogans. Arafat himself never appeared, and when I inquired of some of his supporters, I found that they were as surprised as I was, since it was rather unlike him to leave such public acclaim to his PLO rivals.

By the time the program began, the audience had reached some two thousand, about four-fifths of it men. Most seemed by their dress to be Western-oriented intellectuals, though a sprinkling of Islamic and traditional costumes conveyed a sense of wider representation. None of the speakers was electrifying; a few descended into conventional demagogy. But, on the whole, they were not so much anti-American as profoundly opposed to the American military intervention in the Gulf. As a signal of solidarity, the women regularly emitted ululations, time-honored among Arab peasant women, though it was doubtful that there were any peasants among them.

King Hussein at this point was seriously at odds with President Bush, who had delivered to Saddam Hussein an ultimatum to withdraw from Kuwait, on which he would admit no negotiation. The king still favored a meeting of Arab heads of state to negotiate Saddam's withdrawal. On the king's behalf, Suleiman Arar, the speaker of the parliament, told the congress that "the Gulf crisis could have been solved if it had not been for American involvement. The Americans made a serious mistake in rushing to Saudi Arabia. A military outcome is not the answer. The Arab solution is best, and it can be achieved at the least cost." There was no knowing, of course, if the "Arab solution" would work. But it seemed only logical to many Arabs that, before the killing started, the proposal deserved a try.

Many of the speakers expressed variations of this theme. According to Hawatmeh, "The Gulf crisis is purely an Arab problem, and the United States has nothing to do with it." Habash struck a note that I had heard repeatedly, saying "At first, I was opposed to Iraq's invasion, but now I consider the American intervention a much greater threat to the Arab people and I support Iraq one hundred percent." The climax of the three days was an audience granted to a delegation that included Habash and Hawatmeh, in which King Hussein reaffirmed his commitment to a negotiated resolution of the crisis. The congress ended with a communiqué calling, in florid language, for American withdrawal and further Arab diplomatic efforts.

A couple of days later, I called at the office of Dr. Mamdouh Abaddi, executive director of JANDA. Abaddi, a bedouin by origin, was an ophthalmologist, trained in Istanbul and London; he was also president of the Jordan Medical Association. JANDA's congress, he said, had helped establish ties around the Arab world which would not only enhance popular support for Iraq but for multiparty democracy. In Jordan, he said, JANDA's objective was to promote representative government and human rights, both of which had made major advances in recent years, and to build up the strength of the democratic left for a challenge of the Islamic parties in the next elections.

Many of JANDA's activists, he said, had been imprisoned over the years for political reasons; most of them had had their passports confiscated. Abaddi lamented that the Western countries, having created the model for democracy, were now allied with such antidemocratic regimes as Saudi Arabia and Kuwait. The JANDA congress, he stressed, had been called not to support the leadership of Saddam, whose human-rights practices he deplored, but to express the resentment of Arabs toward Western meddling in Arab affairs.

In Washington, meanwhile, the State Department, to rally support for the impending Gulf war, expressed "dismay" at Jordan for hosting JANDA's meeting, at which it said Arabs threatened American interests and displayed "overt anti-Americanism." I did not find evidence to support this prickly allegation. "We are appalled," the department added, "by the statements that were made."

Echoing this line, the *Washington Post* published an editorial entitled "King Hussein's Party," blasting the Hashemite monarch personally for giving "a stage, sounding board and personal audience to the conferring Arab radicals, people who can only have contempt for a leader like him whose sources of power are largely foreign and whose principal goal is to preserve his throne. It was a pathetic performance. It is tempting to write off this exasperating figure. . . ."

The *Post's* overstatement, reproduced in the *International Herald Tribune,* which was available at the city's newsstands, produced shock waves in Amman, not only in official circles but among the normally imperturbable foreign journalists who had gathered to cover the crisis. Most assumed the

Bush administration had inspired the *Post's* invective, which for a couple of days was the talk of the town. Replying to reporters, Jordanian officials said that JANDA had obviously forced Washington, which for years had been pressing for wider freedom of speech in the Arab world, to swallow some of its own medicine. My own reaction was that the White House had deliberately inflated the importance of the congress, in order to coerce King Hussein into joining the anti-Saddam coalition. The king, however, continued on the course he had staked out.

THE BEQA'A CAMP IS about fifteen miles from downtown Amman, on the Damascus road. Established in the wake of the 1967 war, the camp provided shelter for refugees of the Israeli occupation of the West Bank. It was in the countryside then; now it is at the northern edge of the swelling city.

Though the tents that once accommodated refugees have given way to cement-block houses, the camp retains a feel of impermanence. The residents, whether born on one side of the Jordan River or the other, never forget that they are Palestinian, and still talk, though wistfully, of going home. By conventional estimates, more than half of Jordan's population of three and a half million are Palestinians. Almost all hold Jordanian citizenship and exercise the same political and economic rights as native Jordanians, except perhaps for access to membership in the country's ruling elite. During "Black September," they reciprocated Jordan's decent treatment by supporting the king against the PLO. About two hundred and twenty thousand Palestinians live in refugee camps; Beqa'a, with a population of seventy-three thousand, is the largest. The other Palestinians inhabit Jordan's towns and cities. Amman, a preponderantly Palestinian city, is home to many who have become very rich.

Amer Salti, the manager of an Amman bank, lived with his wife, his mother, his children and an Asian maid in a modern stone house in a neighborhood of fine villas. He was among the Palestinians who had made it. Born of middle-class parents from Safad, now an Israeli city, he fled to Syria with his family in 1948, then migrated back to Jericho when it was still part of Jordan. Both his father and his grandfather, he said, died of the anguish of losing everything in the upheaval, and he was raised by his mother and an older sister, who set up a dressmaking business that prospered. Salti attended mission schools, excelled in his studies and obtained a scholarship to Brigham Young University in Utah, before returning to Jordan with an American wife and a Ph.D. In his early fifties, Salti climbed the professional ladder of the Citibank branch in Amman, until he and some friends joined together in 1989 to organize a bank of their own.

"Anyone with an education was welcomed here," Salti said. "The king gave Palestinians every encouragement to build the private sector. In tough times, when jobs were scarce, the Jordanians grumbled about us, because we controlled much of the economy, but they made up for it by monopolizing the top jobs in the army and the civil service. Only the Palestinians who were political—that is, with ties to the PLO or to more radical groups—had problems. They were sometimes harassed by the *mukhabarat*. But the rest of us were accepted.

"Amman was a good place to do business. The government paid for the city's infrastructure, with a minimum of kickbacks and corruption, and we did the building. We got investment capital from Palestinians working in the Gulf, principally Kuwait, where they made a lot of money but were not really wanted, so they built their homes here. Amman was a good city to live in—clean, well governed, good schools, maybe a little stodgy but with wholesome values. The Palestinians made it what it is today because, living with permanent instability, we had stability here."

In Beqa'a, there was stability, too, but no maids. Though administered by UNRWA, the United Nations agency, the camp was under Jordanian civil authority, which meant that the police and the *mukhabarat* had the last word. Normally, these authorities required prior permission for a visit, though Jordanians are not sticklers for rules. I had heard, however, that procedures were tightened after the *intifada* started, out of a nervousness that disorder might cross the river. So, on arriving one morning, I went directly to the headquarters of the camp-services officer, UNRWA's administrator, where a plainclothesman or two were usually in residence. The UNRWA chief, a Palestinian, was hardly delighted to see me, and turned to the policeman seated near him when I asked whether I could make a tour. On receiving an affirmative nod, the UNRWA man sent me on my way, with a guide who he said was provided by the government's Office of Palestinian Affairs. I took that to mean he was an agent of the *mukhabarat*.

With my guide at my side, I walked first to a new school which the Chinese government had donated to the Palestinians: they built it with Chinese labor and stocked it with Chinese equipment. UNRWA had designated it a girls' preparatory school, and in the schoolyard I found a hundred or so well-scrubbed, healthy-looking preteens in gray-green smocks, most of them wearing scarves to conceal their hair, playing and talking with great intensity. After a swing through the halls, which were covered with patriotic, nostalgic posters about Palestine, and an inspection of some classrooms, where the girls giggled self-consciously in the presence of a strange man, several of the teachers invited me for coffee, and in our conversation I learned that twenty new students had recently arrived from Kuwait, in flight from the Iraqis. The new arrivals had sharpened the interest of the student body in the Gulf crisis, the teachers said, though as Palestinians, the girls had all, no doubt, imbibed an interest in politics at home. Their remarks opened a political discussion in English, which my "guide" either did not understand or chose to ignore.

King Hussein for many decades had refused to authorize parliamentary elections, they agreed, for fear of a contest for power between Palestinians and Jordanians. In 1989, he reversed himself, and the PLO responded by advising its followers in Jordan not to offer a slate of candidates. Only the fundamentalists ignored the advice, and their votes elected several Palestinian Islamics, including Abu Zant; most Palestinians, however, abstained from voting to avoid dividing the country. When Saddam invaded Kuwait, the Palestinians understood that Washington had put the king under great pressure to condemn Iraq. The Islamics among them wanted the Americans off sacred soil; the non-Islamics, angry at America's pro-Israel bias, saw Saddam as a powerful defender of their cause. Palestinian morale soared, they said, because Saddam had restored some motion to the long stalemate in the Arab-Israeli conflict. King Hussein's refusal to bow to America's pressure, they said, earned him much of the credit.

After I left the school, I wandered around the camp, which evoked the intensity of the towns across the river. Its heart was an outdoor market, crowded with mothers and their children shopping for food from stalls roofed with corrugated iron. Nearby, peddlers sold clothes, shoes, hardware and medicines from rickety pushcarts. At the edges of the market were barber shops, video shops, camera shops and music shops playing the latest cassettes from Cairo. A few steps away from it was an open-air bus terminal, where hundreds of Palestinian men, talking and smoking cigarettes, waited for transportation to jobs in the city. Kids kicked soccer balls between the ruts of adjacent streets, where industrious men in tiny workshops repaired cars and bicycles, or built doors and cabinets and sofas. Beyond were the residential neighborhoods, rows of cement-block houses, some decorated with flowers or vines, or occasionally a tree, all grim to the Western eye, though no worse than the homes of the poor in the West Bank. Yet, despite the solidity of the houses, the refugees nearly unanimously insisted that their residence in Jordan was temporary.

When I returned to the UNRWA office, sitting with the camp-services officer and the policemen was a tall, wrinkled man with gold teeth, gray stubble and a black cape edged in silver that he had draped over his dark blue suit. Introducing himself as Sheikh Abdul Razak Weheidi, he said he was a *mukhtar* of the Beqa'a camp. The refugee camps, I knew, were organized around the villages from which their residents originated. Each village unit—like those in the West Bank and Gaza—was headed by a *mukhtar*, who served as a source of information for the police, while at the same time standing between their people and the authorities. In the occupied territories, the *mukhtar* networks largely disintegrated during the *intifada*, but in camps in the Arab countries they remained intact. Beqa'a had some fifty *mukhtars*. Sheikh Weheidi, a bedouin born in Beersheba in 1931, told me he had fled to Gaza in 1948, before making his way to the West Bank and, in 1967, to Jordan. As *mukhtar*, he said, he was responsible for some five thousand refugees with Beersheba roots.

"All the people in this camp are ready to fight the Americans," Sheikh Weheidi volunteered when I told him where I came from. His tone, far from hostile, was straightforward, as if he were reporting on a disagreement between two Beersheba families. "All the people inside the camp are with Saddam Hussein. We care nothing for the Kuwaitis. All the money they have given the Arabs is not worth one-millionth of their total wealth. Kuwait sent its money to the West, and then the Americans sent it to Israel. That tells me that Kuwait is an ally of Israel. We are not against the American people, but we are hostile to American policy. As a Palestinian and a refugee, I have been the victim of American injustice. The Americans want to wage a criminal war against the Arab nation. The honorable leaders among the Arabs—and I place King Hussein at the top of that list—will soon declare a holy *jihad* against America, and anyone who dies in the struggle will be a martyr and go to paradise."

11   AMERICAN QUEEN, ARAB HOME

QUEEN NOOR AGREED TO see me after I had been in Jordan for a couple of weeks. Normally, she is more accessible, but with the United States building up its forces in Saudi Arabia, the Gulf crisis was in suspended animation, and dozens of reporters were prowling around the city in search of stories. I had to wait my turn. At the designated hour, a young soldier at the wheel of a black limousine picked me up at my hotel. He was listening to the wail of Arabic love songs on the radio when I climbed into the back seat. As we pulled out of the driveway, out of earshot of bystanders, he switched the dial to an Israeli station that played rock and roll.

From the car window, the view before me was a reminder that Amman is a handsome city, with sharp slopes dropping into deep ravines, with up-to-date people surrounded by vestiges of ancient days. The city was founded beside a riverbed, now paved over, in the widest of these ravines. Old Amman contains a magnificent amphitheater built by the Romans two millennia ago, and a labyrinth of tiny shops along streets laid out by the Arabs who arrived early in this century. Modern Amman is on the crests of the hills, linked by wide boulevards with soaring overpasses and tile-lined tunnels. The roller-coaster geography creates curious sensations: the dome of a mosque that appears to be on the next street might take ten minutes of circuitous driving to reach, because it is really on the summit of an adjacent hill; driving along a busy street of stylish shops and medium-rise office buildings, I could look into a valley floor at Biblical-era bedouin tents, and shepherds tending flocks of goats.

My driver's destination was the rear entrance of the palace grounds, which took us out of the settled city, past patches of farmland and antiaircraft missile installations. The palace, a complex of low-lying, neatly tended, closely guarded buildings, spread over a forested hilltop on the eastern end of Amman. King Abdullah, founder of what was then Transjordan and the grandfather of King Hussein, built a small palace on the hill in 1924 after spending the first few years of his reign in a simple house in the town center. During the colonial era, which outlasted World War II, the British Resident lived near him, in quarters since occupied by Crown Prince Hassan and his family. After Abdullah, King Hussein added buildings for living and working, all of them on a restrained scale. Though each was different, they were rendered collectively harmonious by a simplicity of design and a modesty of ornamentation, by the lush gardens in which they were set and by the white stone, native to the hills which run from Jerusalem to Amman, of which they were all built.

King Abdullah, after World War I, rescued Amman from the obscurity into which it had fallen over the centuries. First settled in the Stone Age, the city took its name in Biblical times from the Ammonites, a tribe about whom a testy God once instructed Moses (Deuteronomy 23:6), "You shall never seek their welfare or their good will all your life long." During the Roman era it became a wealthy market town, and with the coming of Christianity it served as the seat of influential bishops. After the Muslim conquest the city had a resurgence, then a gradual decline, until it was abandoned in the fifteenth century to famine and plagues. In the nineteenth century, the Ottomans settled several thousand Circassians—Muslims from the Caucasus, in flight from the Czar—near the Roman amphitheater, and the town remained Circassian until the building of the railroad to Mecca, which brought with it several thousand Arab laborers. When King Abdullah decided to make it his capital, Amman began to grow. After the war against Israel, he added the West Bank to his realm, changing the country's name to Jordan and doubling its population. The war of 1948 also brought in the first wave of refugees, and the war of 1967 the second, each influx one hundred thousand or more. In the 1980s, the population of Amman reached a million, a figure it has since surpassed.

During my visits over the years to Amman, I have always been astonished at how well put together the city is. It is free of the unsightly improvisation of other Third World cities that have suddenly exploded in size, and shows little of the shabbiness and squalor that characterizes the other capitals of the Arab world. It seems, in short, to be remarkably well governed.

"The state made a deliberate effort to create a new urban culture in Amman," said Abdel Rauf Rawabdeh, who, as mayor from 1983 to 1989, earned high marks for successfully coping with population growth. "We set out to disprove the belief that Arab cities necessarily are dirty. We established a policy we called 'Clean Amman,' consisting of house-to-house collection of garbage, regular street sweeping and the distribution of free garbage bags. We even cleaned vacant lots, until the people themselves began to keep them clean. We talked up the importance of trees, which are alien to our civilization, and sometimes we had to plant three or four times before the people would let them grow, but now we are a city not only of trees but of flower gardens and parks. We made a policy of restricting building heights to take advantage of the sunlight and airiness of our climate. We insisted that buildings be white, and that all construction in some neighborhoods be of stone. We built bridges and tunnels, but we refused to decimate the city by superhighways. We now have good water and sewerage systems and we are expanding our street lights. The people, seeing where their money goes, willingly pay their taxes. It also matters that King Hussein provides stability and service, and the people have responded positively."

The hill on which the king's compound stood is just above the old Circassian village, not far from the depot where the Arab workers arrived. The Nadwa Palace, the family residence, is a few minutes' walk from the *diwan*, the royal court. It was there that I met the queen the first time, in the early 1980s. She had been married five years and had three little children, and outside the window of her living room I could see a small garden, with a standing swing and overturned tricycles. On this visit, we met in her own office, a small room decorated in Islamic fashion with an elaborately carved desk in the center and Koranic calligraphy on the walls. With the children in school, she said, her maternal duties were less consuming. She was conservatively dressed, in an American style, with an aqua blouse and a beige skirt, and only simple jewelry. Her blond hair, which fell nearly to her waist, was pushed straight back. On every surface of the office were photographs, most of them of her and the king, sometimes with dignitaries, more often with the children.

The queen was a trifle upset the day we met. The *International Herald Tribune* carried a column written by her father, Najeeb Halaby, who lived in Washington, where she spent her adolescent years. Halaby, son of a

Syrian immigrant—the family name means "of Aleppo"—was a former test pilot, graduate of Stanford and Yale Law School, head of the Federal Aviation Administration under President Kennedy and ex-chairman of Pan American Airways. The queen, who was born Lisa Halaby, was extremely devoted to him. I remembered her telling me in an earlier meeting that though she was not raised with much Arab consciousness, she felt a mystical attachment to her Arab roots. Now, having been a Jordanian for more than a decade, she said she disagreed strongly with her father's scriptural assertion that "the United States and the West have reacted righteously" to Saddam Hussein's invasion of Kuwait by mobilizing "a magnificent coalition against aggression." The queen repeated the Jordanian position that President Bush overreacted to Iraq's incursion by dispatching too many troops too quickly, giving Arab diplomacy no opportunity to negotiate a solution.

"My father, as a first-generation Arab-American," the queen said, "has been dedicated for many years to improving relations between the United States and this part of the world. He grew up privileged. He was accepted. He enjoyed the best in education and rose very high. He's never denied his Arab roots, but he has never forgotten how much he owes his country. He and I agree that Saddam Hussein acted illegally and immorally in invading Kuwait. But, like President Bush, he is so outraged by the aggression that he is incapable of looking behind to understand it within its historical context. Maybe he's overcompensating. Maybe you have to be in the Arab world, even if you have an Arab background, to understand the sensitivities of the Arabs. The problem as we see it is that most Americans don't want to know how we feel."

The queen spoke softly but with greater confidence than she had in our earlier meetings. She had gone through a "long process of discovery," she said, from the graduate of Princeton with a degree in architecture in 1974, to the young bride and mother, to the self-assured consort of the leader of three and a half million Arabs. She had changed her name (Noor means "light" in Arabic), converted to Islam and acquired Arabic, which she now spoke fairly well. In learning her duties, she was educated by her husband in Jordanian and Arab politics, she said, while yet "shaping a perspective of my own with the benefit of my American education." Noor acknowledged that there were strains in the fairy-tale life that she lived, but they did not seem to have hardened her. Lisa Halaby, as Noor, seemed to me to have grown wiser and more composed, but remained unmistakably American in her view of the world.

"I was targeted from the start," she said, "by those who wanted to get at the king but found me easier to strike. I was careful: I never made a public statement in disagreement with policy or tried to establish myself as an autonomous political figure. But the Islamic fundamentalists were never comfortable with me as a Western woman and they questioned my Islamic convictions. I guess I feel I had to take certain risks for my beliefs, but the printing presses were always running and, obviously, some of the comments hurt. One claimed that I bought a brooch and some earrings at auction in Europe for twenty million dollars. That came after the revelations of extravagant spending in the Imelda Marcos scandal, which was a period of economic recession in Jordan. They said the charge proved I should not be making policy, but it was damaging, and also ridiculous. I am far from being a policymaker.

"Yet I stand for a certain ideology. I make no secret that I favor an openness of the political system, with press conferences and television appearances by the king. I also favor a greater role for women, an open door for Western culture and interaction with the rest of the world. I suppose the Muslim Brothers think they are defending Islamic tradition by attacking me."

Noor said that Americans harmed themselves by accepting the stereotypes of Arabs and Arab culture: Too many false notions were perpetuated by television and the press—persuaded, for example, that democracy was alien to Arabs, they had dismissed Jordan's new democratic experiment. Jordan, she said, was poised at the leading edge of change in the Arab world; its democracy had provoked bitter protest not only from Saddam's Iraq but from Saudi Arabia, America's ally in the Gulf.

"Saddam Hussein reinforces the Arab stereotype," she said, "but in Jordan we live next to him, so we have had to work with him. Americans are unable to see Saddam's action, and Jordan's reaction, within the context of decades of erosion of their own credibility among Arabs. We wish he hadn't invaded Kuwait. On the other hand, he has helped to focus attention on issues, like the Palestinians, that America has ignored for a very long time. He may be an aggressor but he is also a catalyst, and his audacity, if we can call it that, has touched a sensitive chord here."

A few days after our meeting, the queen invited me to join her on a visit to the Azraq camp, where some twenty thousand evacuees from Kuwait—Indians, Bangladeshis, Sri Lankans and Filipinos—were waiting for transportation home. I met her at her office, where a car waited to drive us a few hundred yards to a helicopter that was standing by. She had her hair in a long braid, and wore a beige blouse, a skirt that came below her knees and high leather boots. Accompanying us in the air-conditioned, comfortably appointed six-seater aircraft was Salameh Hammad, the general secretary of the ministry of interior, who was overseeing the refugee evacuation.

During the half hour in the air—Azraq is about fifty miles east of

Amman, on the desert road that leads to Baghdad—she and Hammad reviewed the day's computer printout on the status of evacuees. In all, some six hundred and fifty thousand foreign workers and dependents, more than half of them Egyptians, crossed the border from Iraq and left for home during August and September 1990, most of them remaining in Jordan for three or four days. An additional one hundred and fifty thousand evacuees with Jordanian passports also entered; about a third went on to homes in the West Bank, while most of the rest stayed. From the helicopter window, the cultivated land on which Amman sits disappeared quickly, replaced by caramel-colored dunes as far as the eye could see. Finally Azraq, a tract of square white tents pitched in dozens of parallel rows, appeared on the horizon, a kinetic patch on the lifeless landscape.

An honor guard of a few uniformed men stood on the pad as the helicopter settled to the ground. An army officer approached and saluted when the queen descended, then escorted her to a Land-Rover parked a few yards away. He knew her routine. She jumped in behind the wheel, offered her guests the backseats and joyfully drove off across the hard, trackless sand, followed by two or three police jeeps at a discreet distance.

The day was hot but a crisp wind blew, infiltrating clothes and hair with sand, making conversation impossible at less than a shout. Occasional gusts blew grit into our eyes. The queen stopped first at a large tent marked with the insignia of the Red Cross and its Islamic counterpart, the Red Crescent. A receiving line of about twenty doctors, nurses and medical aides had formed, and she marched stolidly along, shaking each hand, asking the proper questions, usually in English, occasionally in hesitant Arabic. Meanwhile, several hundred Indians, mostly unshaven young men in soiled working clothes, gathered outside the tent and were being held at bay by a line of soldiers. On emerging, the queen, to the dismay of the officers, barged in among them, grasping hands as if she were running for alderman in Chicago. After extricating herself, she made for a hospital tent, where she comforted mothers and cradled infants, inquired about food to eat and water to shower, and promised to search for more blankets for nights which had already turned cold. Then she climbed back into the Land-Rover and drove to another part of the camp to repeat the experience.

From what I saw at Azraq, it was apparent that Jordan's hospitality to the evacuees was both generous and well administered. To be sure, much of the cost of the rescue was picked up by international agencies, as part of a global effort, and not surprisingly, there was institutional competition for credit and publicity. Some foreigners reproached the king for selecting the interior ministry—which meant the security services—to oversee operations. In fact, the government's concern was not so much security as the possibility that evacuees would slip away from the camps and throw themselves onto an already explosive job market. The rescue operations cost Jordan $30 million, but that was only a small part of the economic strain that the crisis had imposed. From the day Saddam invaded Kuwait, Jordanian analysts recognized that the crisis could lead, quite literally, to the country's economic collapse.

At its best, Jordan's economy has never been a powerhouse. Only 6 percent of its land is arable and its only natural resources are phosphates and potash from the Dead Sea. With its industrious Palestinian population and excellent educational system, it once dreamed of becoming the "Singapore of the Middle East," or the new Beirut, but that proved an illusion. In 1978, after Egypt withdrew from the struggle against Israel, Jordan's Arab neighbors in the Gulf agreed to give it an annual subsidy of $1.25 billion in recognition of its service as a "front line" defender—a buffer between them and the powerful Israelis. But they never paid more than a fraction of the pledge, and in recent years have paid almost nothing at all. What saved Jordan was the export of its skilled Palestinians, three hundred thousand of whom worked in the Gulf, who sent home more than a billion dollars a year, out of the total national income of $4 billion. The Gulf crisis was expected to cut these funds at least in half.

In addition, the UN embargo on exports to Iraq—which Jordan honored despite its reservations—cost the country several hundred million a year, as did the end of transit traffic from Jordan's port of Aqaba to Iraq. With the collapse of tourism, the government counted total losses at more than half of the GNP, which proportionally was far greater than the losses of any other country. Economists spoke of prospective unemployment of 35 percent. In theory, the rich countries were supposed to provide Jordan with compensation. But President Bush was unwilling to direct funds to a government that had not supported his coalition, while the Saudis, a traditional benefactor, abandoned Jordan on the grounds that the king sympathized with Saddam. (Unforeseen, the Jordanian economy was rescued for a year or two by the savings that the Palestinians expelled from Kuwait brought home with them, but it was considered likely that this stimulus would soon peter out.)

In all, Queen Noor spent about an hour at the Azraq camp before climbing into the Land-Rover for the bumpy drive back to the helicopter. By then she was sweaty, her hair was disheveled and her face was reddened by the sun and wind, but she was clearly satisfied with the work she had done. "With each new crisis in the Middle East," she grumbled after we climbed aboard, waiting for the pilot to get underway, "the circle of people who suffer expands. This is a man-made problem. This suffering is not the result of a freak natural catastrophe. This crisis did not have to happen. And Jordan, more than any country, has been asked to pay for it."

The queen closed her eyes for a few minutes of rest after takeoff, then resumed her conversations with Hammad, the ministry official, offering him ideas on what the camp needed. When the helicopter touched down in the palace compound, a car was waiting on the pad. Noor hastened down the stairway and waved good-bye as she was whisked away, explaining that her children were waiting for her in the family quarters.

III DEMOCRACY AND FUNDAMENTALISM

KING HUSSEIN HAD something of a scare from within the country in April of 1989—and, in reacting positively, he transformed and, according to some, saved his regime. Since the start of the *intifada*, he had worried about the Palestinians, especially the poor who were crowded into the refugee camps. His concern was they would turn not on him but on Israel, thereby destabilizing a frontier he had long sought to keep calm. The Palestinians, however, never went beyond an occasional parade to show solidarity with the occupied territories.

Instead, the king was surprised by a round of street protests by Jordanians, emulating the *intifada*, that broke out in the southern town of Ma'an. At the source of the protests was the decline of Jordan's economy. When oil prices fell drastically in the early 1980s, and the Gulf states cut their subsidies, Jordan had turned for help to the International Monetary Fund, which had insisted on a succession of belt-tightening reforms. The king happened to be visiting the United States when his government announced a major increase in the price of gasoline and other basic commodities. No one had anticipated that Ma'an would respond with riots, which in a few days killed eight and injured more than fifty.

The king was particularly upset because Ma'an was the hub of a tribal region that had long been the bedrock of Hashemite support. During the Arab Revolt of World War I, Ma'an was Abdullah's first stop after leaving Hejaz, before setting up his capital in Amman. The bedouins of Ma'an, romanticized by T. E. Lawrence, had fought with the Hashemites from Mecca to Damascus and stood by them against Saudi incursions into Transjordan in the 1920s. But years before, overpopulation had exhausted the desert's potential to sustain nomadic life. After that, construction of the railroad to Mecca deprived bedouin raiders of their annual quarry of pilgrims, and in the 1930s Abdullah decreed an end to raiding for good. To retain the bedouins' allegiance, Abdullah dispensed to them posts in the government and the army, a practice that King Hussein preserved. Though their lives settled down, bedouins continued to identify with their tribes and retained many of their old desert values, including their loyalty to the king. In contrast to the Palestinians' loyalty, theirs was unambivalent, and King Hussein knew that he dared not jeopardize it.

I spent an afternoon with the Bani Hamida tribe, some thirty-five hundred people who inhabited a string of villages scattered over a mountain ridge north of Ma'an, overlooking the Dead Sea. Though their cement-block houses had electricity and water, many said they preferred sleeping bedouin-style, in tents which they pitched in adjacent fields. Most of the men held menial jobs in nearby towns. About half of the women wove traditional rugs as part of a self-help project sponsored by Save the Children, an American development agency. A few families had planted olive trees, and some tended sheep and goats, but the dry, rocky soil yielded very little for the handful that farmed. None of the Bani Hamida, not even the children, wore Western clothes while I was there, but neither were the women veiled. The children all attended school, I was told, and many went on to the university. The older inhabitants readily shared memories with me of life on the move with camels, but acknowledged that their current life, with radios and clinics and cars, was far less onerous.

In Ma'an, the transition to modern living had transformed several thousand nomads into truck drivers. Most owned their trucks, and had prospered during the Iraq-Iran war carrying food and arms from Aqaba, Jordan's Red Sea port, across the desert to Iraq. Even after the war ended, they thrived on overland hauls to the Gulf. So when the government, at the insistence of the IMF, announced a big increase in the price of gasoline, without permitting a commensurate rise in transit fees, they felt deceived and abandoned.

Characteristically, the target they chose for their wrath was not the king, who was untouchable, but his prime minister, Zeid Rifai, for whose resignation they clamored. When their community leaders joined their cause, the demands escalated to include a shift away from state authoritarianism. Though far less oppressive than its Arab neighbors, Jordan still allowed the *mukhabarat* to control political life and intimidate the press. "Down with Rifai," the crowds shouted, while standing behind Rifai, inviolable, was the personage of King Hussein.

In the king's absence, Prince Hassan flew to Ma'an, where he invited a delegation of protesters to meet with him in the governor's office. The protesters, perceiving the governor to be hostile, countered with an offer to meet at a local mosque, but the crown prince, at the urging of his bodyguards, refused. The decision was afterwards debated at length; many Jordanians say the king, a notably brave man, would have accepted the offer. The crown prince's decision provoked stoning and looting. Though Prince Hassan was said to have imposed restraints on the security forces, they attacked the crowds and arrested some local political leaders. One widely accepted account held that the king, on learning what had happened, admonished his brother by phone, then boarded his plane to return home.

Back in command, the king fired Rifai, a boyhood friend, then turned his attention to the protesters' grievances. In addition to granting economic concessions, he relaxed press censorship, released those arrested in the rioting and limited the application of martial law. He also announced that free parliamentary elections would be held by the end of the year.

Jordanians were not, however, fully convinced by the vow. Elections in Arab countries, when held at all, had a way of being rigged. But by election time in November 1989, Jordanians acknowledged that the king had kept his promise: the balloting was the freest ever held in Jordan, perhaps in the Arab world. Recalling the king's unhappy experiences in the fifties and sixties with pro-Nasser, anti-Hashemite parliaments, many Jordanians wondered why he had chosen the course of democracy. Some speculated that Queen Noor was the catalyst. Publicly, the king said that he felt the time had come for democracy to unite Jordanians against both internal division and external threats. After the election, he stated with evident satisfaction that Jordanian democracy would serve as a monument to Hashemite rule, and a model for the region.

"We are not a powerful country, and we don't proselytize among our neighbors," Prince Hassan told me one day, elaborating on the king's thinking. "We are not in the business of destabilizing regimes. But we are a relatively established society, with a ruling family that has played a role in the Arab world since well before the Prophet Mohammed, and people do listen to our ideas. We are trying to persuade Arabs that they can be for democracy without being seditious. We would like human-rights norms recognized throughout the Middle East, including Israel. Participatory government is something we consider crucial to the future of Jordan, and the entire Arab world."

From the Communists to the fundamentalists, all candidates for the eighty-member parliament pledged their support to the king, to multiparty democracy and to human rights. Beyond that, their differences were substantial, but the government did not intrude in the campaign debate. Left-wingers and nationalists, whose activities had been illegal for three decades, suddenly emerged as candidates. Through gerrymandering, the southern tribesmen probably enjoyed a slight advantage, at the expense of Amman. Some interpreted this as a move to limit Palestinian influence, but most Palestinians abstained anyway. If any group had an advantage, it was the Muslim Brotherhood, whose control of the mosques gave them the only real political organization. Still, the candidates debated openly before large and enthusiastic audiences in clubs, theaters and homes. Though few women were candidates, they were as active as men in the campaigning. The press covered accurately and commented vigorously, and the *mukhabarat* was hardly ever seen.

Though he remained at a discreet distance, near the end of the campaign the king expressed some criticism of religious extremism, which was interpreted as a blow at the Brotherhood. Ironically, the sanction he had given to the Brothers over the years to organize the mosques, aimed at countering the leftists, provided them with a vital edge. The leftists won only a dozen seats. A majority went to unaffiliated centrists, mostly tribesmen loyal to the king. The Brotherhood, however, emerged very strong. Electing twenty of its own members, it had the additional support of a dozen independent Islamics, which gave it the parliament's largest organized bloc.

The king made no secret of his displeasure with the Brotherhood's power in the parliament. In an interview shortly after the voting, he said the division of Jordan along religious lines "is something I shall never permit as long as I live." Religious rivalries, he said, were responsible for the catastrophe in Lebanon, and were they to spread, they would destroy Arab claims to Jerusalem. After the election, the Brotherhood was prudent and made no effort to enact an Islamic program. The seculars warned, however, that the Islamics were only waiting for the right moment.

Abdel Latif Arabiyat, head of the Brotherhood's parliamentary bloc, met me one afternoon at the office of the Islamic delegation in downtown Amman. Wearing a blue suit, Arabiyat, who has a Ph.D. in education from Texas A&M, looked very secular, but told me he was never comfortable in the United States, and since his return had worked to Islamicize his country. Mild in style and appearance, he came across as unthreatening, even boring, which may explain why the parliamentary majority, with a minimum of controversy, elected him as speaker at its opening session.

Arabiyat described to me a Brotherhood program which was barely distinguishable from that of the centrists, or even of the left. He wanted, he said, laws to punish corruption and promote human rights. He would not impose veils on women and would add only a prayer or two in the public schools. He would ban alcohol only for Muslims, he said, though he held even this in low priority. (In 1993, the Brotherhood introduced a general antialcohol law.) What troubled him more than secularism at home, he said, was the presence of foreign forces in Jerusalem and, referring to the Gulf crisis, in proximity to Mecca and Medina, "which didn't even happen in the Crusades." As for the Brotherhood's commitment to democracy, Arabiyat insisted that it was intrinsic to Islam, and that he was ready to follow the people's decision anywhere. "But we are confident they will turn to Islam," he said. "Why not? We know the time is not yet ripe here to practice the *shari'a*. But Islam is good for everybody."

Azzam Tamimi, director of the Islamic delegation's office, took a purer line than Arabiyat in talking to me. "King Hussein is not as Islamic as we'd like," he said. "As a descendant of the Prophet, he'd prefer not to offend Islam. He prays and performs the *hajj*, which are good signs. We don't mind whom he married; Muslims are not forbidden to marry Christian or Jewish women. But we think he should apply a more Islamic context to the society. We'd be happier with him if he enforced Islamic law, and we will not hesitate to take positions in opposition to him."

Tamimi, who was in his thirties, confirmed that the Brotherhood had campaigned in the election in favor of banning alcohol and usury, Islamicizing the school and tax systems, promoting Islamic dress and restricting women to work only in places where they would not routinely encounter men. He added that the Brotherhood was "not ready" to have women in electoral office. As for Israel, "we have not adjusted to its existence. We cannot recognize a Jewish state on Palestinian territory, and we oppose the efforts of the king and the secular Palestinian movements to make a compromise peace. Our sublime goal is the application of the *shari'a* and the restoration of the caliphate, as it was under the Abbasids and the Omayyads. We'd even welcome King Hussein, as a Hashemite, in the post. But we're in no hurry. We can wait."

Among the losers in the election was Toujan Faisal, a slim, long-haired woman in her early forties with an incredible story that, in checking, I readily confirmed. Faisal, wife of a gynecologist and a mother of two, as well as a university graduate in English literature, told me she was working as a television reporter when her editor assigned her to a new beat, covering women's affairs. Though never a feminist, she said, from 1988 to 1989 she was the hostess of "Women's Issues," a weekly series. "It turned out to be the most controversial program in the history of Jordanian TV," she said. One broadcast, dealing with the physical abuse of women, stirred up particular frenzy. "The fundamentalists," she said, "tried to have it banned even before it went on. They maintained that it was men's God-given right to beat women, and that my program challenged God's commands. Afterward, the station received hundreds of letters from men, many of them unbelievably sadistic."

Muslim marriage, Faisal said, placed women in a state of total economic dependency by giving their husbands possession of their property. A husband can keep three or four wives. He can divorce any one of them at will and throw her out of her house, leave her destitute and even deprive her of her children. In practice, women of every social rank are in jeopardy as husbands move up the economic ladder, taking and disposing of wives.

The Koran—she became a Koranic student, she said, in order to reply to the fundamentalists' attacks—nowhere authorizes such behavior; men, supported by the religious leadership, have sanctified these rules in their own interest. "I rebutted them within the context of Islam," Faisal said. "I quoted directly from the Koran and the sayings of the Prophet. But the fundamentalists said I was a heretic, and that I wanted four husbands for myself." After a year of threats and denunciations, the ministry of information took Faisal's program off the air.

It was then, she said, that she decided to run for a seat in Parliament, from Amman. She took a few thousand dollars of her own money out of the bank, she told me, half of which went for filing fees, and placed some ads in the newspapers soliciting volunteers. She was deluged, she said, with offers to ring doorbells, make phone calls and conduct coffee klatches, as well as to design, print and distribute leaflets.

Her platform proposed to amend Jordanian family law to give greater rights to women. This so infuriated the fundamentalists that they brought charges of heresy against her in a religious court. The penalties for conviction, she said, included dissolution of her marriage, separation from her children, and—under the rule applied by Khomeini to Salman Rushdie— an invitation to all Muslims to assassinate her. The first judge to hear the case threw it out, but her foes shopped around and found another who was willing to rehear the charges. The ensuing trial, in which she had to be protected by the police from screaming zealots, ended in a guilty verdict, which she immediately appealed. During all of this, Faisal said, her husband and her family were subjected to relentless harassment and intimidation, and he ultimately had to close his clinic. Meanwhile, surrounded by volunteer bodyguards, she continued her election campaign.

Just before election day, a delegation of secular-minded intellectuals called on King Hussein to protest Faisal's treatment. The king had always been sympathetic to women's rights, she said, and specifically endorsed women's suffrage, but his aides had not told him about her problem with the zealots, and the press, intimidated by them, had largely ignored the affair. After learning the facts, she said, the king made an election-eve statement criticizing religious extremism. But even he—much less the queen, whose hands were tied by their fanaticism—was not powerful enough to confront the fundamentalists head-on.

Faisal came in third among five candidates for the contested seat and claimed she was cheated of the victory. Her district, she said, was the only one in Jordan where announcement of the results had been delayed for a day, and one of only two with demonstrable irregularities. "The fundamentalists will do anything for the sake of power," she said. "The people are passive, both women and men, and they still see the world in religious terms. And the government is afraid, knowing the fundamentalists may resort to violence one day to get what they cannot get in elections."

Since the election, she said, the cold war against her had not relented. Taken away from the religious judges, her case went to the state system, where an appeals court found her innocent, but Islamic leaders continued to denounce her from their pulpits. Some of the imams, in fact, publicly reaffirmed the death sentence. "It wouldn't even help to surrender to them," Faisal told me. "I never thought they would go this far. But they do not forgive." Faisal's husband had gone abroad for work, while she stayed in Amman, taking care of the children. Resigned to unemployment, she passed the time studying for a master's degree in English literature.

"Most Jordanian women are brainwashed," Faisal said; "They lack confidence and know nothing of their rights." Unfortunately, she said, it seemed unlikely that her candidacy would set a precedent. On the contrary, the abuse she had suffered was likely to discourage other women from running for office. "I believe I am fighting for human rights," she said, "but in an Islamic country like ours, human rights often begin with the fight for women and children, and we are not making much progress."

Yet most Jordanians seemed to think that the government's handling of human rights, since the incident at Ma'an, had kept pace with its encouragement of democracy. Even in the worst of times, it should be noted, Jordan's oppression was not on the scale of Syria's or Iraq's. During the Nasser era, a period of great stress, King Hussein probably turned a blind eye to the excesses of the *mukhabarat*, but he did not inculcate Jordan with the kind of fear present under the regimes in Damascus and Baghdad. The *mukhabarat*, dominated by Jordanians, maintained tight surveillance over Palestinians, and was tough on many leftists. According to international human-rights organizations, it seldom engaged in killing, and though it arbitrarily imprisoned and sometimes tortured prisoners, its most common instrument of control was to deny passports to citizens who wanted to travel abroad. At its worst, Jordan remained committed to law, and since 1989 the *mukhabarat* has assumed a much lower profile in daily life.

"We used to have about one hundred and fifty persons a year who were prosecuted for speech violations," said Asma Khader, one of a dozen or so lawyers in Amman who specialize in human-rights cases, "but since democratization we've had only a handful. Martial law, though in force for several decades, is rarely invoked. The *mukhabarat* is still tough on Palestinians who are tied to the extremist wings of the PLO, and it treats Communists very arbitrarily. Recently it's been getting down on the violent factions in the Brotherhood and imposing stringent rules on dissent in the universities. Anyone arrested can spend as much as a week in detention or get sentenced to seven years in prison, usually without trial. I try to defend them, but I've had hardly any success. Lawyers are never allowed to talk with *mukhabarat* officials.

"Still, King Hussein, who used to be above the struggle, has recently been supportive of human rights. He encourages organizations for human rights, and we have established groups affiliated with Amnesty International, Middle East Watch, the Lawyers Committee for Human Rights and some new Arab human-rights organizations. The bar association has a human-rights committee, and so do many of the professional associations, particularly the journalists. The people are conscious of human rights, and are acquiring the courage to go to court when they see these rights abridged. Recently Amnesty International published a report on abuses in Jordan. The *mukhabarat* acknowledged its accuracy, and the newspapers published comprehensive stories about it. That's a sign that things really have changed."

In his speech opening the newly elected parliament, King Hussein declared that he "had not found a contradiction between protecting national security and giving the utmost care to the matter of public liberties," and he avowed his "faith in the principles of human rights." Within a month, several hundred confiscated passports had been returned, and Jordanians to whom passports had been denied were invited to reapply. A year later, at the opening of the second parliamentary session, the king announced that "martial law has been frozen in preparation for its eventual cancellation," and he reported that the government had "freed all political detainees, reemployed civil servants who had lost their jobs because of their political affiliations and safeguarded the freedoms of work, travel and movement. Media credibility has risen, while the press has assumed its role in a positive climate of freedom and sense of responsibility." Few Jordanians were disposed to dispute his statement.

The enthusiasm with which King Hussein gave himself to democratization suggested strongly that it was not a passing fancy. That the program has so far worked successfully is surely due to several factors, not the least of them that the Jordanians of today—many of them educated, traveled, sophisticated and middle-class—bear little resemblance to the Jordanians of the 1950s, when Nasser's pan-Arab radicalism was riding high and democracy and human rights were at their nadir.

The king also benefited, paradoxically, from the Gulf crisis. "The crisis has given breathing space to Jordanian democracy," Queen Noor said to me. "The people are rallying around the king as never before. There is a real sense of family now."

It helped, too, that the crisis preoccupied the Saudis, active opponents of democratization, who abandoned their usual meddling in Jordan's affairs. "The success of Jordan's democratic experiment will have an influence on many of the countries bordering Jordan," Sa'ad al-Din Ibrahim, a well-known Egyptian sociologist, wrote recently. "Anything that happens in an Arab country has a chain reaction." Ibrahim predicted—with a bit too much optimism, I thought—that, with Jordan as the model, the 1990s would be "the decade of democratization in the Arab world."

IV   CRITICAL DAYS

KING HUSSEIN'S CLOSEST confidant on state affairs has for many years been Crown Prince Hassan, his younger brother. Jordanians speculate that at some point the king will be tempted to choose one of his sons as his heir. But having designated Hassan as his successor, he has shown no disposition to replace him.

Educated at Oxford, Prince Hassan is intellectually more gifted than his brother, though less well endowed in political instincts and personal charisma. A Jordanian once said to me that, unlike the king, it was hard to imagine the prince on a camel in the desert in a sandstorm. The prince is sensitive to such criticism; he once chided me for the criticism I reported of his actions in Ma'an in 1989. Still, Jordanians hold him in esteem. Prince Hassan lives on the palace grounds with his wife and four children. He is a small, stocky man whose joviality belies his fierce eyes, and whose weakness for broad, sometimes vague pronouncements has been the bane of journalists, though it is much softened by a wry, self-effacing wit. During my 1990 visit, the crown prince was among several palace advisors willing to discuss the king's reaction to Saddam's invasion of Kuwait, but he was the only one I was free to identify.

Prince Hassan said that King Hussein was awakened at six o'clock on the morning of August 2, 1990, by a phone call from Saudi Arabia's King Fahd. "Have you heard?" the Saudi king asked, "The Iraqis are within a few kilometers of Kuwait city." King Hussein was dumbstruck, the prince said, though he had been in regular contact with Saddam in an effort to mediate the Iraqi-Kuwaiti dispute. It was the king's view, Prince Hassan said, that the invasion was a last-minute decision by Saddam, made in anger at the Kuwaiti walkout in Jedda.

But what surprised the king even more—at least in retrospect—was that King Fahd did not at that time demand a total Iraqi withdrawal. Instead, he proposed that the Iraqis pull back to the disputed border areas, a compromise that would have left Iraq in possession of the Rumaila oil field and the islands of Bubiyan and Warba. Whether that represented to King Fahd the limit of the possibilities, or the limit of his aspirations, was not clear. But, significantly, he did not at that time express any fear that Saddam Hussein would order Iraqi troops beyond Kuwait into Saudi Arabia. Two days later, in fact, King Fahd sent a high emissary to Amman, who repeated that he saw no threat of an Iraqi invasion. King Hussein and his circle were confident that Saddam told the truth—and that King Fahd knew it—in saying he never had plans for entering Saudi territory.

After King Hussein ended his wake-up conversation with King Fahd, he embarked on a flurry of activity to head off what he saw as a looming Arab disaster. He placed a call to Baghdad and talked to Foreign Minister Tariq Aziz, and in the early afternoon reached Saddam himself. Both Saddam and Aziz told him that Iraq, having invaded to teach Kuwait a lesson, planned to withdraw over the weekend. Saddam warned, however, that any public censure or threat to Iraq from within the Arab world would, by conveying the impression that he was caving in to pressure, seriously complicate the execution of his withdrawal plans.

In response to a summons by the secretary-general of the Arab League, the Arab foreign ministers had by then assembled in Cairo, and it seemed likely that they would censure Iraq. Recognizing the dangers that such a motion would pose to a quick solution, the king phoned President Mubarak, who was vacationing in Alexandria, and in the afternoon flew to meet him there. The two placed a call to President Bush, who was upset by the invasion; though noncommittal about his intentions, he agreed to give King Hussein forty-eight hours to settle the crisis. They then called King Fahd, who urged that King Hussein fly to Baghdad to reassure Saddam that the Arabs would, for the moment, withhold any denunciation. The three also agreed to convene promptly a limited Arab summit—Saudi Arabia, Egypt, Jordan and Yemen, as well as Saddam and Sheikh Jabir, Kuwait's emir—to settle the Iraqi-Kuwaiti dispute once and for all. With the approval of both Mubarak and Fahd, King Hussein then sent his own foreign minister, Marwan Qasem, who was with him in Alexandria, aboard Mubarak's private plane to Cairo. His assignment was to forestall the passage of an anti-Iraqi resolution.

The next day, Friday, August 3, King Hussein met in Baghdad with Saddam, who agreed to attend a summit meeting, which they fixed for Sunday, two days later, in Jedda. Kuwait, however, had already gone to the UN Security Council and obtained approval of a motion demanding Iraq's withdrawal. President Bush, meanwhile, had been told by the Pentagon that satellite intelligence showed three Iraqi divisions heading for the Saudi border, with four more behind them. Though the photos left Iraq's intentions undeciphered, Bush shared the information with Prince Bandar bin Sultan, the Saudi ambassador in Washington, who conveyed it back home. Shortly afterward, Bush announced the dispatch of American war-

ships to the Gulf and a freeze on Iraqi assets. By the time the king returned
to Amman from Baghdad, near midnight, his plan for summit negotiations
was in shambles. Mubarak that afternoon had publicly denounced Saddam,
explaining to the king by phone, without elaborating, that "I am under
tremendous pressure." Also that day, the Arab foreign ministers, in a split
vote, approved—with Jordan in dissent—a condemnation of Iraq.

When Saddam learned of these actions, he withdrew his promise to
attend the summit, asserting that he had been prejudged. On Sunday,
President Bush, having spent the weekend lining up allies, held an im-
promptu press conference. He referred to the Iraqis as "international out-
laws and renegades," and added, clearly referring to King Hussein, "I was
told by one leader I respect enormously—I believe that was back on Friday—that they needed forty-eight hours to find what was called an 'Arab
solution.' That obviously has failed." But the evidence suggests strongly
that Bush's racing to condemn Saddam had helped to make it fail. Instead
of the Arab summit, the Security Council met on Sunday to consider the
American proposal to impose an embargo until Iraq withdrew from Kuwait.
The crisis then assumed the character of a face-off between two stubborn
men. Bush rejected negotiations with Saddam, and Saddam adopted a
posture of intransigence.

The king's advisors did not claim to have hard evidence that Bush had
leaned on Mubarak and King Fahd over the weekend, but that is certainly
what they believed. Nor did they claim to know that Saddam, with some
face-saving, would have withdrawn. None denied the gravity of the diplomatic problem, but they observed with considerable irritation the intem-
perance of Bush's statements, which evoked the worst in Saddam. It made
them suspect that American policy had long been directed toward destroying Iraq's war-making potential.

"It seems to us that the position of the Americans has been war, war,
war, from the very beginning," the crown prince told me shortly after
the invasion, "and they dismissed the Arab role. I think King Hussein
could have had an Arab solution that weekend and the Americans decided
against it."

President Mubarak's foreign-policy advisor, Osama el-Baz, in a talk
some time after the war, gave me an account of the crucial days after the
invasion that reflected Egypt's position. He said that, though Mubarak was
willing to attend an Arab summit, Saddam refused the precondition that
he promise to withdraw from Kuwait. In Cairo at the foreign ministers'
meeting, Saddoun Hammadi of Iraq, who had conducted most of the negotiations during the spring with the Kuwaitis, declared the seizure "an
irrevocable act." In Alexandria a few days later, Izzat Ibrahim, Saddam's
second-in-command, met with Mubarak to say that Kuwait was "legally,

politically and morally part of Iraq," and that Saddam would not be moved. Baz said he was present at the meeting, in which Ibrahim said, "Iraq has liberated Kuwait; withdrawal is not on the agenda." Mubarak was not under pressure from Bush, he said, and had not acted impulsively. Egypt's president concluded from the Iraqis themselves that the prospects for negotiations were hopeless, said Baz, and decided to follow the course Bush had set.

King Hussein, however, came to a different conclusion about Saddam's intentions and continued to work diligently to keep alive the prospect of an "Arab solution." On August 16, he made a visit to Kennebunkport, where he was notably unsuccessful at persuading Bush to be more flexible, but mostly he worked on the Arabs, aiming particularly at a coalition with the North African countries, to bring pressure on Saddam and King Fahd to find an acceptable negotiating formula. But, his advisors told me, he was consistently thwarted by Washington and Riyadh.

"The Americans may be too fickle for us to deal with," one advisor said, presumably reflecting the thinking of the king. "We studied in your schools, where you told us that in dealing with Israel we had to learn to compromise, but now *you* reject compromise. You've told us since 1967 it was crucial to accept the principle of a negotiated settlement, but now *you* deal with Iraq by ultimatum. You told us we needed to practice more democracy and extend greater human rights, and now you are supporting this spendthrift, reactionary, uncultured family that rules Kuwait.

"Everyone understands that Iraq has to withdraw; the world needs it as a precedent. But in Saudi Arabia and Kuwait, America is tying itself to the ugliest image of nondemocracy in the world. You are not protecting a society; you are protecting a class, or maybe a family business. Knowing that your talk of democracy sounds foolish, you have shifted to talk of legitimacy. Is this a notion that the Saudis have thrust on you?"

Dismayed as they were by Washington, the men around King Hussein did not exempt the Saudis from blame for the catastrophe, and their words foreshadowed how the divisive consequences of the Gulf crisis would linger in the Arab world.

"We feel that the Saudis went beyond the red line, in calling the Americans to come in," one of them said. "At the grass-roots level, long-submerged feelings of resentment on the part of most Arabs toward the Saudis and Kuwaitis are now out of the bottle. We resent the fact that they buy everything—technology, protection, ideas, people, respectability. We are upset that the Americans sneer at us, but we are outraged that the Saudis punish us because we are seeking to avoid an inter-Arab war. Most Arabs now say Saudi Arabia has turned its fate over to the Americans, who alone are running things in the Gulf. We see Bush on television almost every day, but we almost never see King Fahd. The military action in the Gulf is American, not Saudi. For years the Arabs have resented America's unlimited support of Israel; now they are saying that the United States and Saudi Arabia are indistinguishable, and from this they conclude that the Saudis are backing Israel, too. Have the Saudis no shame? The Saudi monarchy, when this crisis is over, will find it very difficult to shake that association."

"Every time the king and other leaders say they have a package," Crown Prince Hassan said sardonically, "the Americans knock it down, maintaining that nothing short of complete and unconditional Iraqi withdrawal is acceptable. His Majesty never saw himself as an ally of Saddam Hussein. As an Arab, he considers himself a friend to the Iraqi people, and he wanted to serve as a mediator. We have paid heavily for that offer." In a series of trips to the Middle East to deal with the crisis, Secretary of State Baker and Secretary of Defense Richard Cheney deliberately bypassed Amman to signal their disapproval of the king's course. Commenting on Washington's reaction, Prince Hassan quipped, with some bitterness, "It was as if we were being punished as wogs who didn't know our place and have stepped beyond our bounds." Then he chuckled dryly at his own joke.

V. KING, FROM BOY TO MAN

KING HUSSEIN IBN TALAL IS, by family reckoning, in the fortieth generation of descent from the Prophet Mohammed. Mohammed's tribe was the Quraysh, whose seat was Mecca, a spiritual center even before the advent of Islam; by dominating the caravan trade, the Quraysh became the most eminent, and probably the richest, tribe of Hejaz. Within the tribe, Mohammed's clan was the Hashemites, and in the tenth century the clan took over Mecca, thereby acquiring responsibility for its religious shrines. The Hashemites were dislodged from this high position only in 1924, when the Saud family consolidated its conquest of the peninsula and assumed for itself the guardianship of the holy sites. Whatever the effort to dissemble their disappointment, the Hashemites have never recovered from this loss.

The Hashemites' departure from Hejaz may, in part, be attributed to their sacrifices for the Arab cause. In igniting the Arab Revolt, King Hussein's great-grandfather, Sharif Hussein, believed he would become the leader of a united Arab nation, but events turned out differently. His two sons, Abdullah and Faisal, achieved great eminence in the Arab world. But the family, in the course of pursuing its aspirations abroad, was so weakened inside Hejaz that it fell with hardly a struggle to its rival, the Sauds. From his seat in Transjordan, Abdullah fought an intermittent border war against the Sauds and only in 1948 did the two families formally make peace. Sharif Hussein, who was never reconciled to his loss of Mecca, lived his final years in exile under the British in Cyprus.

After World War II, Transjordan won its independence from Britain, and Abdullah took the title of king. In the Arab-Israeli war of 1948, he alone among the Arabs emerged successful, if not victorious, enlarging his realm by seizing the West Bank of the Jordan River. But Abdullah's ambitions were not limited to the kingdom. Like his father, he thought of himself as the leader of the Arab nation, and he aspired mightily to unite Jordan, Syria and Iraq into a single state under his rule. To achieve this goal, he was willing to lay aside the conflict with the Jews. Few Palestinians—few Arabs—shared his priorities, however, and in 1951, Abdullah was assassinated by a Palestinian nationalist at the door of Jerusalem's Al-Aqsa Mosque.

Hussein, Abdullah's grandson and protégé, became Jordan's king after only a year of service as king by his infirm father, Talal. He was then sixteen. While never renouncing the ideal of an Arab nation, Hussein nourished the *Jordanian* idea, and in his time the notion took root of a Jordan—without history, without even a geographic identity—as a separate Arab sovereignty. Some Arabs argue that Hussein's lineage, fortified by the Hashemites' nationalist credentials, makes him the only legitimate ruler in the Arab world. Some fundamentalists say he would qualify as caliph if he were only more religious.

I once asked King Hussein how it felt to be a descendant of the Prophet, with the religious and political burden of centuries upon his shoulders. I had always found the king an exquisitely polite man but a trifle distant and, I thought, consciously regal. As befitted a graduate of Harrow and Sandhurst, his English was excellent, even if his phrases were sometimes foreign, and though his voice was deep and resonant, he spoke so softly that my tape recorder barely picked up the words. It was clear from the drawn muscles of his face and his taut lips that the king was a man who did not easily relax. But what most remained with me was the sadness in his eyes, and after rereading his answers, I could see threaded through them a melancholy that seemed to be his constant companion.

"We are a family that has been a part of the Arab struggle throughout its history," he said. "We have a position, and a responsibility, regardless of the demands of the day. My great-grandfather [Sharif Hussein of Mecca], my grandfather [King Abdullah], my great-uncle [King Faisal of Iraq] all understood that, whatever the aspirations of the nation, they were Hashemites and that they belonged to the House of the Prophet. But, in terms of our role, what we have experienced is that the dreams and hopes are far greater than what is permitted by the realities, which are very, very distressing, and have been throughout our history.

"My concept of my rule is that I am a Hashemite and a proud servant of the people. Throughout my years of responsibility, I have not thought that Arab unity could be achieved through the old approach, linked to a single individual or family. For me, all that remains in the way of an objective is to try to leave something behind which would mean greater security, greater stability, greater continuity. The Arab world is a cross-roads, a link between two continents, with enormous energy resources and much to look after. I would feel I had succeeded if what I did meant that the Arab identity was not lost in an area which is seeing a struggle [Arab-Israeli, presumably] for its domination. There have been many shocks. There have been many disappointments. All Arab leaders must do what-ever they can do to ensure a better future. But my challenge is that I live up to all that my family has achieved in doing its duty."

I knew that the king's father had been ill throughout his childhood, and that the dominant influence in his life was Abdullah, who had groomed him for the succession, and so I asked him to describe for me the relation-ship between grandfather and boy.

"I did not know him at the beginning," he answered, "but toward the end of his life I had the privilege of being with him, being very close to him, practically all the hours of every day. To me, he was a father, the father probably that I didn't have as much as one would normally have a father. He was the head of the family, with a great love for his people, and he suffered so many setbacks in his life. The whole Arab Revolt was for the defense of Arab identity, to secure Arab freedom and Arab unity. To see the Arab world occupied, to see it divided, was a very great shock to his hopes and aspirations and dreams. The Arab movement did play an important role in the First World War, and the abandonment by the Allies of their commitment to the Arab cause was unethical. But all of that never affected his commitment or his determination to continue to the end to serve his people honestly. He was a good man and he represented goodness to me."

I asked the king what he had learned from his grandfather about dealing with Israel.

"I believe that accommodation was his objective," he said. "That was his advice to the Arabs during the period that preceded the partition plan [of 1947]. Then, when things went down in 1948, he had to take a stand, but still his approach was different from that of the rest of the Arabs. If there was some way of putting together an equation that would last, which people on both sides felt they could live with, he would have tried his best to achieve it. That has been exactly my approach as well.

"It is unfortunate that we Arabs are being held to account for the many tragic things that befell the people of the Jewish faith in Europe, though we and the Jews lived together for generations in this area in calm. We are the victim of events that did not have anything to do with us. What I will never be able to understand is how a people who have suffered so much could inflict so much suffering on others. This is a tragedy that I must live with. My grandfather experienced it before me."

The early decades of King Hussein's reign were tumultuous. The 1950s marked the rise of radical Nasserism, Jordan's formal break with its British patrons, the reverberations of the bloody overthrow of the Hashemites in Baghdad, the short-lived Egypt-Syrian union and a series of failed coups directed at his own regime. The 1960s were hardly better, with the founding of the Palestine Liberation Organization, the campaign of terrorism and reprisal on the Israeli border, and the Arab catastrophe in the Six-Day War, which included Jordan's loss of the West Bank.

Many Western critics considered participation in the war a blunder by the king, who, knowing he would lose, nonetheless forswore neutrality. "I knew exactly what the price would be," he said when I asked why, "but we had to honor our commitment to our Arab allies. If we had not entered the war, our country would inevitably have broken in half, Jordanian and Palestinian, and our army, too. The Israelis would have found an excuse to move in any event, and I would have been portrayed as a traitor, an accusation which I had already suffered over the years for counseling caution."

For a quarter century, the king has dealt with the consequences of the defeat—the refugees, the unresolved status of the West Bank, the rivalry with the PLO. Black September in 1970 was a direct result. Though most of Jordan's Palestinians supported him, Egypt and Syria refused to forgive him for the punishment he inflicted on the PLO's forces. The United States, which saw his triumph as a defeat for Moscow, rewarded the king by refitting his army, which only intensified Arab suspicions. In 1973, Egypt and Syria launched the October war without him. "I was seated with Queen Alia in the garden when a guard rushed up and told us of the attack," King Hussein told me. "I was completely surprised." Jordan later contributed a token military force to the fighting, but its isolation deprived it of the benefits of the postwar diplomacy, undertaken under American auspices, in which Israel returned to Egypt and Syria some of the land they had lost in 1967. In 1974, an Arab summit meeting at Rabat delivered another blow, naming the PLO to replace the king as the "legitimate representative of the Palestinian people."

In 1977, President Sadat traveled to Jerusalem to meet with the Israeli government, a prelude to the Camp David accord. King Hussein refused to embrace the settlement subsequently negotiated by Sadat, on the grounds that it left Israel as master of the West Bank. In the mid-1980s, the king embarked on a peace campaign of his own, designed to involve Jordan and the PLO in talks with Israel, but he failed to reach an accommodation with Arafat, at least along lines that Israel would accept. Frustrated by the failure, and by the Palestinians' suspicion that his objective was to thwart the establishment of a Palestinian state, he washed his hands of the West Bank, announcing on July 30, 1988, a formal renunciation of any further claim on the land. Meanwhile, the Iraq-Iran war had once more divided the Arabs. Though Syria supported Khomeini, the king gave his full support to Iraq, out of a belief in Arab solidarity; the move forged a tie that left him in a profound dilemma when Saddam invaded Kuwait.

When I saw the king in the fall of 1990, it was in the *diwan,* his working quarters in the Basman Palace. The halls were patrolled by ceremonial Circassian guards, wearing black uniforms with silver trim, high black boots, fur hats, and daggers in their belts. Waiting in a dingy anteroom, I cast my eye on an old photograph hanging on the wall. It recorded the king's first trip to Washington, and showed two men wearing the funny, outsized overcoats which were then in fashion; they were reviewing a guard of honor. One was a frowning vice-president in his mid-forties, nearly a head taller; the other was a frail-looking youth wearing an expression of delight. The photo was signed "With admiration for his magnificent courage and with appreciation for the leadership he has given the free world. Richard Nixon." I found the inscription ironic, in the context of the beating the king was then taking from President Bush. After a few minutes, I was ushered into a small, undistinguished office, where the king sat alone behind a desk, smoking a cigarette. He was heavier, grayer, more somber than the slim youth in the photograph, but no less courteous than I had remembered him.

"Iraq emerged from eight years of war a new phenomenon in the region," the king said, "but it was unable to gauge the mood of the world. In Kuwait, it acted in a way that caused others, particularly the Saudis, to panic. I had been to Kuwait during the negotiations. I begged the Kuwaitis to be conciliatory but I came back with an uncomfortable feeling. The Saudis didn't think there was any crisis, and then after the Jedda meeting, on which everything depended, the Iraqis overreacted. We raced to try to slow the situation down, and I think a solution was almost in our grasp in the first days. But in the atmosphere of suspicion that existed in the region, the Saudis and the other Gulf states quickly seized on the opportunity for foreign intervention.

"I can't understand the attitude of the Egyptians, whom I helped to return to the Arab fold after the Camp David agreement. They have fanned the fires. They even told their workers that there will soon be jobs in the Gulf to replace the Palestinians who were driven out. Mubarak is poisoning his reputation in the Arab world. At Kennebunkport, I sought assurance from President Bush that he would not act militarily, and I got a bit of hope from him. But he was influenced to take this intransigent line. I don't know if it's the Saudis, but we in this region have fallen into a trap and now the walls are closing in on us. We are in a dash toward a disaster of the greatest magnitude."

The king's words were grim, but I had the feeling in talking with him that his morale was higher than at our previous meeting, when the Iraq-Iran war seemed stalemated, when the peace process with Israel was paralyzed, when the problems of the region seemed to linger without prospect of resolution. The king was a man of action, who liked to get out-of-doors, bivouac with the troops, mount a camel, fly a plane, race a car. It was my sense that he tended to depression if left too long with his own reflections. Though the dangers of the Gulf crisis made him edgy, they had also aroused him. He seemed excited at having a hand to play, and whether or not he succeeded in averting war, he had a measure of control over the outcome.

It was impossible for the king not to see the confrontation in the Gulf within the framework of the Arab-Israeli conflict, which had dominated his reign, indeed his life. How can you expect us, he asked, to be enthusiastic about Security Council Resolution 660 which requires Iraq to quit Kuwait immediately when Security Council Resolution 242 requiring Israel to evacuate the occupied territories has been on the books, unenforced, for twenty-three years? How can you counsel us to be serene about a war between Arabs which Israel, whose officials refer to Jordan as a Palestinian state, might well seize upon as a pretext to invade us? Why can't Washington understand how its indifference to the plight of the Palestinians frustrates us, and poisons our feelings toward the presence of Americans on Arab soil? Even if the crisis is resolved without war, how can any agreement last which the Arabs look upon as imposed by outsiders—outsiders known to be friends of Israel and hostile to us? Wouldn't any settlement have a better chance of promoting stability in our region if the Arabs themselves, rather than the Western powers, took responsibility for it?

"I travel now in the Arab world more than ever before," the king said, "looking for an Arab solution. There is so much talk about 'a new world order'; is its meaning that we Arabs are to do exactly what the Great Powers say? We cannot waste time with more wars in this region, we have too many things to do. Many borders may have to be reexamined that were left to us by the colonial powers. We have to reduce the gaps between the haves and the have-nots by embarking on a meaningful development plan, beneficial to all. We must bring more democracy and more concern for human rights to the region.

"I am not fooled by the Iraqis. Remember that my whole family in Baghdad was wiped out by these people in 1958, but I don't look back. I came to power when Truman was president. I'm not here for four years or eight years like your leaders. The United States always talks about things in the short-term perspective, and it's nice for a politician to have people react promptly and tell you you're right. Your people say it is not enough that Jordan is upholding the UN sanctions, despite the huge cost to us. They want us to abandon our long-term responsibilities for peace in the region. They tell us to join the majority in the Arab League in condemning Saddam. I wonder if the United States also rigs the elections in the Arab League. I'm in this office for the long haul, and I can't forget that I'm an Arab and a Hashemite. I hope people remember me for having made some enduring contribution after I'm gone.

"Grim as this crisis is, something positive can come out of it. The germs of a solution of the Arab-Israeli conflict are contained in it, I believe. If we can restore stability, we can resolve the oil problem to the satisfaction of the industrial powers. More than that, I think we can even get to the issue of arms control—nuclear, chemical and biological weapons, even missiles—in the region, if we put both Arab and Israeli arms on the table. War can't possibly be to the advantage of the United States or anyone else, not even Israel. We can't foresee what will happen once a war starts. Will the Arab world even survive? I'm not sure I know. For me, I'll continue to play my role, whatever intimidation I face, from inside or outside the region. I will fulfill my responsibility."

VI   MEETING THE ISRAELIS

KING HUSSEIN WAS right in predicting that "something positive" could come out of the war against Iraq, though the form probably surprised him. Shortly after the fighting stopped, U.S. Secretary of State Baker renewed an effort to which he had already given some attention: bringing Israel and its Arab neighbors together over the bargaining table. The time was propitious.

The outcome of the war, on the heels of the Soviet collapse, had confirmed the United States as the world's only superpower. Washington had always maintained that peace could be negotiated only within the context of Israeli security. It had not wanted Israel to take sides in a war between

Arabs, and so Israel remained a spectator. But with Iraq defeated, and the Soviet Union no longer available as an arms supplier to the Arabs, Israel had never been more secure. Syria, without Moscow, admitted a need to negotiate, and Jordan and Lebanon, as always, were more than ready. As for the Palestinians, their support of Saddam had cost them the backing of the Gulf Arabs, and discredited them in Western eyes. The *intifada* had given them negotiating leverage, but they nonetheless had to participate on terms that Washington, on Israel's insistence, imposed. None of the parties was completely happy with the arrangements, but all seemed ready to talk.

The negotiations opened at Madrid in October 1991. They soon bogged down, however, with posturing on the part of the participants, and the effective departure of the Americans, who became consumed by their own election campaign. I met King Hussein again late in 1992, while the parties to the talks waited for the new administration in Washington to take office.

It had not been a good year. The king's relations with the Saudi and Kuwaiti monarchs were still strained, and his relations with the United States had not been fully repaired. The Muslim Brotherhood's parliamentary bloc had openly challenged Jordan's involvement in the peace talks, and in November, two of its members were tried and convicted of Iranian-backed subversion, raising the prospect of domestic unrest. The king himself had been touched by the scandal of an alleged affair with a young woman in the palace entourage. More important, he had had a brush with mortality; in an operation performed in the United States cancerous organs were removed. Though pronounced recovered, he had been told to return regularly for medical checkups.

Not surprisingly, when he stated in a televised speech on November 9, 1992, that "the life of an enlightened people and a vibrant nation cannot be measured by the life of an individual," Jordanians feared that he was preparing them for the worst.

Jordan did not take the prospect of succession indifferently. During his long reign, the king had passed through many images. In the fifties, he was still the pawn of the British and of Jordan's colonial past; in the sixties, he was the pillar of traditionalism in the conflict with Nasserism; in the seventies, he was the West's tacit ally in suppressing Palestinian radicalism; in the eighties, he was trying desperately, within the context of peacemaking, to maintain his claim to his West Bank provinces. In each of these personae, the king found it harder to please the Palestinians than the Jordanians. It was only in the nineties, having democratized politics and stood up to the West in the Gulf crisis, that he seemed finally to have brought satisfaction to both segments of the national community.

Pleased when the king renounced his claim to the West Bank in 1988, the Palestinians found even greater satisfaction in the king's refusal to pressure in any way the Palestinian delegation to the peace talks. "If the Palestinians are unhappy, everyone in the region will be unhappy," said Foreign Minister Kamel Abu Jabber, an old-line Jordanian, articulating Jordan's new sensitivity. "If they don't get reasonable terms, no one will have peace." When the king returned home from his surgery in September 1992, a million subjects—nearly a third of the population of the kingdom—showed up along the parade route to welcome him. Observers said the overwhelming majority of them were Palestinians.

"After the king severed his ties to the West Bank, the Palestinians began to feel more relaxed, and relations between us improved," said Hanna Nasser, the president of Birzeit University, who had lived in Amman since his deportation in 1973. "Then, during the crisis over the invasion of Kuwait, the king became heroic in Palestinian eyes, up there with Saddam Hussein, as a man of daring. Both defied the United States and, by extension, Israel. Few Palestinians had any feeling for Kuwait, which they considered an American colony. All Palestinians appreciated that the king had counseled the Arabs not to be hasty in making war on Saddam, that they should try negotiations first. In retrospect, maybe that wasn't the wisest course in dealing with the West, for either the Palestinians or the king, but it has paved the way for a major reconciliation of the two banks of the Jordan River."

By the early 1990s, it had become apparent that, notwithstanding the PLO's demand for an independent state, the East and West Banks of the Jordan were destined, once the occupation ended, to associate under a single flag. Arafat even proposed agreeing to a confederation in advance. Given Israel's aversion to an independent Arab Palestine, he said, such an agreement would facilitate the talks. But the king, never totally comfortable with Arafat, saw the proposal as a maneuver to promote PLO power in Jordan after confederation, and he declined, saying he would prefer to make the decision later, with a legally designated Palestinian authority. Washington, it was said, endorsed the king's position.

"The king is being very discreet," said Taher Masri, one of the few Palestinians with deep roots in Jordanian politics. Scion of the Masris of Nablus, he had served at times as prime minister and foreign minister to the king. "The king knows that the West Bankers have never quite forgiven him for misunderstanding them before 1967, and for leaving them to the Israelis after 1967. He wants them to take the initiative in whatever involves them in the peace talks, including confederation with the East Bank. He doesn't want to take responsibility for any compromises that are made with the Israelis. This lessens Jordan's role in the negotiations, of course.

But the king is walking on eggs. He knows he has to let the Palestinians do what they have to do. In the long run, that's his safest course."

As the peace process unfolded, King Hussein increasingly distanced himself from Saddam Hussein. His damage-control teams adopted the line that his speech of November ninth was meant not to foreshadow his own death but to exhort the Arab world to build political institutions that do not depend on the life of a single leader. The words suggested a scarcely veiled criticism of Saddam, which the king took no pains to deny. The palace let it be known that the king felt he had already squandered too much of his international credibility on Saddam.

During my visit in late 1992, King Hussein summoned me to the palace shortly before I was to leave Jordan. He did not look like a man at death's door. Sitting over coffee, he seemed more relaxed than he had the last time I'd seen him, in the midst of the Gulf crisis. Since it had been so widely discussed in the newspapers, I deliberately did not ask about his health, but he volunteered ten minutes of assurances that he was in no danger.

Making clear that the success of the peace talks was his highest priority, the king said he had done as much as he was going to do for Saddam Hussein. He acknowledged that he worried about his differences with the fundamentalists over a possible agreement with the Jewish state—"misunderstandings with some segments of the Jordanian political spectrum," he insisted on calling them—but he declined to voice any criticism of them. He spoke respectfully of the PLO and even positively of the Israelis. The peace talks, he said, are "a chance that must be taken, that cannot be missed." My sense was that he saw them as the climax of his four decades on the throne, and the last, best hope for a renaissance of the Arab world. I also sensed that he would do virtually anything to have the talks succeed, except abandon what he saw as the responsibilities of a Hashemite to the Arab nation.

CHAPTER NINE

IRAQ REVISITED

I OVERLAND TO BAGHDAD

It was five in the afternoon when the taxi, a lumbering 1974 Dodge, pulled into the driveway of Baghdad's Al-Rasheed Hotel. The journey—sixteen hours across the desert from Amman—had not been pleasant. In the night hours the temperature was bitterly cold, and the car had no functioning heater. After the sun rose, the air turned hot and dry, and the water that we carried aboard in plastic bottles, by now lukewarm, was barely drinkable. The driver, an elderly Jordanian named Mohammed, chain-smoked to stay awake, and played wailing Arab music on cassettes that competed with the rumble of the ancient engine to grate on my taut Western nerves. The car's suspension system, stiff with age, magnified every bump. I had not anticipated being nostalgic for the bland experience of air travel, but Iraq had lost the war and the United Nations' embargo was in force, so I had no choice. Only by an overland route, in a caravan without camels, could a traveler get to Baghdad.

I arrived in the second wave of journalists after the war. The first consisted entirely of television teams. In response to the demand for visas from the paper-and-pencil contingent, the Iraqi embassy in Amman had simply shrugged, pointing out that the decisions were made at the ministry of information in Baghdad. The embassy, like most others in Amman, was a handsome building hidden behind a high stone wall, but, in almost certain violation of some zoning statute, its wall had been refaced with a garish plaster replica of the gate to Nebuchadnezzar's Babylon, to which Saddam Hussein had at times compared Iraq under his own rule. Such kitsch might have been tolerable for a triumphant Iraq; it seemed ludicrous after the recent defeat. Defeat, however, had not humbled the functionaries within, who dealt with reporters as if they were awarding free vacations to a Caribbean paradise. Since the journalists were in Amman only to get on to Iraq, however, they swallowed their annoyance and waited.

I got lucky during my first weekend in Amman, when Nizar Hamdoon showed up at the hotel where the foreign press was lodged, on his way home from a conference in Africa. I had known Hamdoon during the years when he was Iraq's ambassador in Washington, and I had seen him several times since in Baghdad, where he later served as deputy foreign minister. Hamdoon agreed to transmit an endorsement of my visa request, but he pointed out that administrative procedures, never very efficient, were now additionally burdened by the destruction of Baghdad's telephone system. Papers moved around the city only by messenger, he said, and the list of approved visas had to be sent to Amman by courier.

Hamdoon did not know that while he was away, the process had been speeded up with the help of the Western TV crews who had arrived in Baghdad carrying satellite telephones, which they offered for the ministry's use. About ten days after my talks with Hamdoon, the satellite beamed to Amman a list of approved visas, and about ten o'clock, while I was seated at dinner in the hotel, an Iraqi official called me to say that my name was on it. My instructions were to get to the embassy as quickly as possible for the paperwork, since I was expected to be on the road at three in the morning, in a convoy of taxis heading for Iraq.

Only a few of us that morning were in "print." The TV people going along carried tons of bulky equipment, the transport of which had required days of advance planning and the hiring of special vehicles. Traveling alone, I packed all I thought I needed in a shoulder bag, and made a last-minute arrangement to ride with a newspaper reporter from Turkey named Ali, who had already reserved a car.

Fortunately for me, Ali was an old hand in wartime travel to Baghdad. He said that the Iraqis, hoping to fan antiwar sentiment in Turkey, had, in the weeks before the fighting started, been openhanded with visas to Turks; this was his fifth trip into Baghdad in two months. Ali said that during the weeks when the bombs were falling, Jordanian drivers routinely charged $18,000 for the Baghdad run, and a Japanese television crew, ill at ease with the local custom of bargaining, was known to have paid $30,000. With satisfaction, he noted that the market collapsed after the cease-fire; we were riding for a mere $500, which we would split two ways. Ali acknowledged that our car was uncomfortable, but it was big enough to handle the supplies that he said our stay in Baghdad would require. Assigning me the front seat, he climbed into the back with six cases of bottled water, two of assorted canned foods, one of cigarettes and a large plastic bag of flat bread. I felt embarrassed at traveling empty-handed but, even if I had known the routine, I had been notified too late to get to a grocery store. Dismissing my concerns, Ali said we would share whatever he had—which, I found later, was the rule within the community of journalists in Baghdad after the war.

Reassured by the provisions stacked in the back seat, I watched with a quite different feeling while Ali and Mohammed packed the trunk with jerricans of gasoline. Though one of the world's major oil producers, Iraq had been without gasoline since the destruction of its refineries early in the war. Most of what we carried, Ali said, was needed to get the car to Baghdad and back. He said he had also calculated having one jerrican left over, which he planned to present to a local driver at the Al-Rasheed, to assure his transportation needs around Iraq. The cargo filled the car with fumes and left me with the uneasy sense of riding in an outsized Molotov cocktail.

Once settled into the taxi, I fell into an uneasy sleep, fighting the chill night air and the bumpy pavement but, heading due east, it was only an hour or two before we were looking directly at a rose-colored light which displaced the new moon and the glittering stars. It was dawn, and I came fully awake. The land was flat and ugly, lacking even the vegetation to feed the sheep and goats that supported bedouin life in much of the Middle East desert. We drove through a few run-down oasis towns, slowed at the warnings of camel crossings and, at Jordanian army checkpoints, halted for inspections of our papers by soldiers wrapped in red-checkered *kuffiyehs* for protection against the cold. Just before the Iraqi border, we queued up with some two dozen trucks for a final fill-up at a ramshackle gasoline station. Most of the trucks were lightweight, which suggested they were carrying to Iraq the food and medicines that had recently been exempted from the embargo. More than a few, however, were gasoline trucks, and I could only surmise that, in violation, they were delivering to Iraq the trickle of fuel that kept the economy alive.

At 7:45 we reached the Jordanian border, where we spent a quarter of an hour on formalities before heading into the forty miles of no-man's-land that separated the two countries. Halfway in, I saw the light blue flag of the United Nations waving over a neatly laid-out camp, a remnant of the summer's massive international effort to rescue the hundreds of thousands of foreign workers caught in Kuwait by Iraq's incursion. At nine, we rolled into the Iraqi border post, an unkempt assemblage of one-story buildings, bleached by the relentless sun into the color of the surrounding sand. Our car had arrived an hour late for the rendezvous with the other members of the convoy, though we were a quarter hour ahead of the last straggler. Both the drivers and the passengers who preceded us, basking in the early morning sun, seemed grateful for the break. Also waiting for us at the border was a representative of the ministry of information, who had been assigned to take care of our paperwork, then escort us into Baghdad. While he worked to clear our passports, Ali and I munched a breakfast of flatbread and cheese. Mohammed, meanwhile, heated some water for tea on a portable gas burner he extracted from the trunk. After an hour, the ministry official rounded up his scattered charges and got us back on the road.

Inside Iraq, the terrain remained the same but the road changed into a newly finished, six-lane, divided superhighway. It did not take long before the first sign of war appeared, a series of communications towers snapped near ground level, their wires lying in a heap in the sand. Every few miles thereafter, the burned-out carcass of one or two trucks lay pathetically at the side of the road. Ali was not shocked, as I was. The Iraqis, he said, had worked hard at clearing away wreckage; a month before, the roadway had been littered with such junk.

The superhighway itself was not badly damaged. Open craters in the shoulders and the median strip testified to near-misses, and here and there the pavement itself had been hit, but most of the pits that were left had been filled. The overhead bridges had, curiously, been spared. The first serious damage I saw was at Ramadi, about seventy-five miles west of Baghdad, where a bridge over the Euphrates had been struck, but it was still in use. Mohammed, familiar with the route, followed the roller-coaster pavement, supported by twisted girders, as it dipped almost to the surface of the river; after circumventing a wide hole, he brought the car up sharply to reach the level of the roadway on the other side.

Ramadi was the dividing point between the desert and the sown. We entered there historical Mesopotamia, with its fertile fields and palm groves. Just beyond the damaged bridge, we found peasant women in the fields, harvesting spring vegetables in their brightly colored costumes. It was enough to make us forget, momentarily at least, our tired bones and even our preoccupation with the war.

The diversion ended abruptly at the Baghdad suburbs, where we encountered the first of a series of checkpoints manned by the Republican Guards, the Iraqi army's crack units. Clean-shaven, their uniforms neatly pressed, wearing their berets at a rakish tilt, the Guards looked in no way like a defeated force. They were courteous in asking to see our passports, and said "welcome" in returning them. Not far into the suburbs was the wreckage of the Abu Ghraib factory, made famous by a dispute over whether it manufactured arms, as the Allies insisted after their bombs struck, or powdered milk, which was Iraq's claim. Ali, who had visited the site after the bombing, told me that he leaned toward the milk. Advancing on the city center, I saw machine-gun posts at intervals along the road, and antiaircraft batteries on nearby hilltops; but the casual bearing of the soldiers that manned them conveyed the sense that they considered the war behind them.

Once inside the city, however, the security structure became more stringent. Though there were no machine-gun posts, such as I had seen in

Damascus and Cairo in times of tension, checkpoints had been erected every few blocks, manned by surly-looking fellows, many of them in scruffy civilian clothes, with cigarettes drooping from their lips, cradling Kalashnikovs. These men, Ali said, belonged to the Popular Army, composed of Baath Party members or candidate-members, who were more loyal to Saddam Hussein than to Iraq. The only function these checkpoints served, I surmised, was to keep an army of the faithful at the ready in the event of trouble from the Baghdadi masses.

Still, my first impression of Baghdad was that the masses were not looking for trouble. The streets on the way to the Al-Rasheed looked very much as they had during my visits in previous years; only the traffic was sparser. The passersby seemed well washed, neatly dressed and amply fed, and conducted themselves in no unusual way. The city was damaged, of course, but little ruin leaped into view. The in-town airport, where I had boarded planes for short hops within Iraq, had been leveled; two bridges over the Tigris were knocked out; the convention center across from the Al-Rasheed had been blown up. But the railroad yards were untouched, most of the bridges remained intact and the stadium looked ready to receive a soccer crowd.

I thought I might see fewer panels than before carrying the face of Saddam Hussein. But there he was—in his field marshal's uniform, his bedouin robes, his Italian designer suit, his party greens—laughing as usual, as well he might, since the war was over and he was still in power. It took me some days of watching and talking to pin down a sense of what was different in Baghdad since the defeat.

Having reached the Al-Rasheed at last, Mohammed parked in the driveway, and while I unloaded the gear, Ali went to the reception desk to register. He returned to quote for me the daily room rate, which not only was high but payable in advance, in weekly installments, in American dollars. Accustomed to the luxury of traveling on credit cards, I had brought nowhere near the amount of cash I needed. I should have remembered that, under the embargo, Iraq was barred from credit-card transactions, but the cash crunch did not account for the astronomical prices we faced not only at the hotel but almost everywhere else we turned. Journalists, it appeared, had become Iraq's chief source of hard currency, and each night, it was said, the finance ministry scooped up our cash and rushed off to settle its bills with the *contrebandiers*. Ali made me a bridging loan to cover the first week's hotel charges, but I would have been in a serious fix had not the manager of the CNN office kindly agreed the next day to exchange many thousands of the company's dollars for my personal check. By the time I left the country, nearly all of those dollars had been spent.

But Ali also came back with some good news: the hotel's generators now provided electricity more or less around the clock, and its restaurants were plentifully stocked with beer and victuals. As for running water, Ali mentioned that during his previous visit, the showers were turned on only between five and six in the evening—the one hour that the satellite phone was available to him for filing his stories to Istanbul. Ali said he had been told that all water restrictions were now lifted. He was looking forward to making this a more well-showered visit.

II BAGHDAD IN PAIN

IN THE DAYLIGHT HOURS, the war did not seem to have exacted a heavy toll on Baghdad. Saddoun Street, the city's main thoroughfare, was vibrant with pedestrians. In the *souk*, neatly dressed Baghdadis, most in reasonably up-to-date Western styles, moved through the aisles emanating good humor. Beneath the arcades of Rashid Street, the little department stores, the shoe shops and the bookstores were crowded with shoppers. Moviegoers lined up for films from Egypt and India. Grammar-school children in neat scholastic uniforms made their way home in clusters, carrying book bags. A policeman wrote tickets for doubleparkers. One night, at the Hotel Al-Rasheed, the wartime suspension of weddings came to a dazzling end, when eighty couples—the brides all in white, the grooms in tuxedos—celebrated marriage with feasting and dancing.

Baghdadis, in contrast to other Arabs, and even to other Iraqis, tend to carry their religion lightly, and though it was Ramadan, there were few signs of fasting. The street-side restaurants suffused the air with the spicy aroma of grilled kebab. Old men sat sipping tea in seedy cafes; younger men drank beer and whiskey in darkened bars. The bake shops offered pastries for the *iftar*, the meal after sundown, when Muslim families meet to take their first sustenance of the day. Clearly, many of the pastries did not make it to the dinner table.

One afternoon, in an informal survey of available food, I noted that grocery stalls were offering a wide range of fruits and vegetables, and that fresh carcasses of lamb and beef hung from the hooks of butcher shops. I saw plentiful supplies of flour, rice, noodles, spices and cooking oil, and throughout the city people were carrying home cartons of eggs. I found tinned peas from Bulgaria, beans from Jordan, olives from Iran, crackers from Turkey, cookies from Great Britain and jars of garlic powder from Canada. A merchant told me these products were from prewar stock. He said no imports had reached the market since the embargo started six months before. But it looked from the labels as if some items had been pilfered from Kuwait. And, according to reports in the international press, smuggling from Jordan, Iran and Turkey was thriving.

But if the street scene suggested normality, on a second look it was clear that the wreckage left by Allied aircraft was huge. The raids had crippled Baghdad's physical infrastructure. At night, blackouts engulfed whole neighborhoods, revealing the amplitude of the damage. But it seemed there was no urban destruction on the scale of World War II, notwithstanding the tons of explosives that fell. Instead, with meticulous care—one might almost call it artistry—American aircraft took out telecommunications facilities, transportation links, key government offices and, most painful of all, electrical-generating plants.

A report made by a Harvard study group soon after the cease-fire said that eighteen of Iraq's twenty power plants had been knocked out. The central post office was struck with such exquisite accuracy that three of its four brick walls remained standing, while the interior was transformed into a maze of twisted girders. Some of the targeting seemed arbitrary. Why, for example, were the ministries of justice and local government on stately Haifa Street targeted? Why the convention center, asked a local wag, when the pompous monuments that Saddam had built to himself were spared? Judging from the ruin made of the palace, the bombers had tried to get Saddam. But, apart from a direct hit on a shelter in a residential suburb, killing more than two hundred sleeping people, they made a deliberate effort to keep civilian casualties and random destruction to a minimum.

The invisible damage was the most dangerous. The mayor of Baghdad, for instance, warned during my visit of the likelihood of epidemics, because sewerage and water-purification systems were unable to function without electricity. His words were confirmed in the report of the Harvard group, which predicted that at least one hundred and seventy thousand children under five would die unless prompt improvements were made. According to the report, serious epidemics of cholera, typhoid and gastroenteritis, all water-borne diseases, were already underway. Hospitals, short of power, had to cut back their services; vaccination programs for children were abandoned; all incubators had been laid aside.

Baghdadis, with food to eat and water to drink, complained little, but the absence of gasoline made it hard to get provisions home. Interestingly, the poor had it easier; being crowded into neighborhoods in the city center, they generally found necessities within walking distance. But the well-to-do, as in modern cities throughout the world, lived in distant suburbs, among open spaces and avenues unblighted by common commerce, and without gasoline they scrambled to do their daily chores. One Iraqi told me he walked a half hour to catch a bus that passed only at irregular intervals to take him into town, then turned around with his bag of groceries to retrace the journey. The government, to ease the hardship, had cut down the standard working day, providing more time for household duties. But, in fact, without telephones, and with power supplies severely curtailed, most offices had little work to do, anyway.

Meanwhile, inflation and unemployment were growing. The government instituted rationing, which limited increases on basic commodities, assuring to the poor a floor for their daily diet. But most families received too few calories to thrive and turned to the black market to survive. The government made no wage adjustments to compensate for the new price levels; it had no money to pay for them. Then, it began laying employees off, adding to the thousands already idled by the embargo and the destruction of workplaces. Yet, recognizing inflation and idleness as incitements to unrest, the government exempted the army and the police from its salary freeze.

In retrospect, it is evident that a United Nations survey in 1991 overstated the case in describing Iraq as relegated "to a pre-industrial age," with "near-apocalyptic destruction." Indeed, the Iraqi government, using its own resources, had made a remarkably good start on restoring the essentials of daily life. But as late as 1993, a UN humanitarian mission concluded that the conditions of life within Iraq, still subject to international embargo, were continuing to deteriorate. "For most of the Iraqi civilian population, whether urban or rural," the report stated, "living conditions remain extremely precarious: health care, nutrition, education, water and sanitation and other basic services are minimal. Price inflation of basic commodities on the open market, increasing unemployment accompanied by only modest rises in incomes, have increased the numbers of the population registering for destitute status and have caused the living standards of the population in general to drop even further in the past year. Malnutrition has apparently increased among women and children as per observation of cases admitted to hospitals. . . . Cases of kwashiorkor and marasmus [nutritional-deficiency diseases occurring primarily in children] are reported to be 24 times higher than the levels in 1990." Notwithstanding these conditions, the international community continued to make clear that, as long as Saddam Hussein remained in power, it would make no more than minimal efforts to relieve the suffering.

The war, then, had initiated an abrupt reversal of Iraq's steady progress toward becoming a modern country. Though Iraq had always been stingy with statistics and had become almost maniacal in its secrecy once the war started with Iran, the upward trends were clear from UN indicators. In the decade or so prior to the war, infant mortality dropped by two-thirds, life expectancy rose from forty-eight to sixty-five years and adult literacy nearly tripled to 90 percent. Though food was still imported, production rose substantially, even as urbanization doubled to four-fifths of the population. Eighty-seven percent of Iraqis had access to clean water and ninety-three to health services. School enrollment of children was 98 percent, and the average daily caloric intake was 124 percent of needs.

The changes went beyond statistics, however. While the status of women remained frozen in neighboring Saudi Arabia, emancipation in Iraq progressed steadily. And though Saddam adopted a facade of piety during the war, the better to connect with the masses of the Arab world, he had over the years followed a determinedly secular policy, freeing Iraq's civil life from clerical control.

In the words of a Baghdad intellectual trained in the West, Iraqis had a social contract with Saddam and the Baath Party in the decades after their coming to power; the people endured dictatorship and the absence of human rights in return for modernization and economic development. The war over Kuwait, he said, had breached that contract.

Saddam Hussein, however, was hardly one to recognize such a contract. Though not religious, he was the product of conventional Islamic thought. The caliphate, with its religious prerogatives, was of no interest to him, but the sultanate was. Its doctrines denied to the people not only rights but citizenship itself. The notion of a contract between the ruler and the ruled—which found its way into Western political theory only in the seventeenth century—had no meaning to most Arabs. An Arab ruler derived his legitimacy from his power; he owed his allegiance only to God. The duty of the people was submission, in the temporal no less than in the religious domain. Saddam ruled by that principle; most Iraqis—particularly the Sunnis—consented to be governed by it.

III   THE SURVIVOR

YET I WAS SURPRISED, on returning to Iraq after the war, to find how open criticism of Saddam and his regime had become. It was as if the grievances of decades were suddenly pouring forth. The anger of people I had known for years, and from whom I had never heard a word of dissent, could not be contained. One friend, mocking Saddam's boast that his army would fight "the mother of all battles," referred wryly to the war as "the mother of all defeats." Taxi drivers and storekeepers and even government functionaries—all total strangers to me—seemed ready to complain at the slightest sign of interest. In a downtown shop where I stopped to have a shirt mended, the tailor, after his store emptied of other customers, blamed

Saddam for the loss of his son, his son-in-law and two nephews in Kuwait. But do not identify the shop, he implored me, or there will be no men left in his family at all.

It was obvious to me that the war had cost the regime the support of the intellectual class—artists, writers, professors, professionals. Many spoke of emigrating, temporarily or permanently; yet, when the government opened applications for exit visas, most Iraqis took it not as a gesture of liberalization but an effort to get rid of troublemakers. During a visit to Baghdad University, I was told that the student body had lionized a young woman who was expelled for declaring, "I love my country but we have got to get out of Kuwait in order to save ourselves." If the theory of the historian Crane Brinton is valid—that the flight of intellectuals from support of the state portends revolution—then Saddam was in big trouble. But then, Brinton may never have studied a regime as repressive as Iraq's.

Indeed, the fear of the secret police, of listening devices and of pervasive informers remained as great as ever. Baghdadis still spoke with some caution, taking care not to be overheard. One intellectual, referring to the Prague precedent, called the postwar period "Baghdad Spring," heady but short-lived, waiting for the *mukhabarat* to strike back. But as never before, Iraqis seemed to revel in the danger that they knew was inherent in defiance.

Every critic blamed Saddam personally for the catastrophe of the war. Some acknowledged sharing the patriotic elation that accompanied the occupation of Kuwait. Many endorsed Saddam's claim to Kuwait, and his impulse to punish Kuwait for its greed. But few regarded the annexation as worth a war, and none claimed to understand how Saddam could have calculated that Iraq was capable of defeating the United States, the world's mightiest power, as well as the thirty nations that were allied with it. Even if Saddam had been justified in occupying Kuwait, Iraqis said, he had no right to reject demands for withdrawal, given the consequences which anyone could foresee. The adjectives I heard to describe him—stupid, arrogant, stubborn, self-deluding, even crazy—echoed those used by American editorialists. I listened to more than a few Iraqis argue that the government would never have got itself into its fix had it been a democracy, in which the leadership had a duty to pay heed to the people.

Curiously, Iraqis expressed virtually no anti-American feeling. It seemed as if they were so angry with Saddam that they had no emotion left to condemn their attackers. A woman who told me how saddened she was by the destruction of the Jumhuriya Bridge, where she had played as a child, added that she understood why the Americans might think it necessary to impair Baghdad's transportation system. Some hacks in the bureaucracy, of course, felt it was their duty to make anti-American declarations, but even they spoke with notably little conviction. After a tour of a hospital ward, for example, a young administrator said to me, "See what Mr. Bush did to us!" When I muttered under my breath, "With a little help from Saddam Hussein," he paused a moment, then smiled and responded, "With a big help."

I found Iraqis, on the whole, remarkably tolerant of the Allied bombs that destroyed homes or killed civilians. They referred to them as "mistakes," a term which acknowledged that American pilots had not deliberately sought out civilian targets. I also heard Iraqis speak with appreciation of the decent treatment their sons and brothers who were taken prisoner had received at American hands. I encountered only one genuinely anti-American incident during my visit. Traveling with other journalists to the south of Baghdad, our car stopped in a village with a small tractor factory that had been demolished. With us was a French photographer named Fifi, who was snapping pictures of the marketplace when an old peasant woman with a tattooed face, dressed all in black, leaped at her shouting, "Foreigners go home. You are the enemy. You killed our people." Several young men standing nearby, looking embarrassed, gently took hold of the old woman and led her away, explaining to Fifi apologetically that her home had been destroyed and her son killed in the attack.

It was no less ironic to Iraqis than to Americans that though the war had been lost, the country ravaged and many thousands killed, Saddam Hussein, who started it all, was still in power. "At least Nasser had the good grace to resign," an Iraqi said to me, referring to the aftermath of Egypt's defeat in 1967. Saddam, in contrast, assumed no personal responsibility. He showed no sign of remorse, or of being chastened by the experience. At one point, he tried blaming the Baathi bureaucracy for the defeat, but the idea played poorly and he did not repeat it. Saddam never apologized; he did not even bother to make excuses. He surely understood that the West would not restore normal relations with Iraq as long as he remained in office, but he gave not the slightest hint of a willingness to go. Officials, asked whether the regime had not made grievous errors, answered that a study on this question was underway and would be finished in a few months. There was an eerie quality altogether in the demeanor of the government, which in many ways behaved as if the war had never taken place at all.

After the defeat, Saddam replaced some of his ministers, but his purpose was not to open the government to greater diversity. On the contrary, the new cabinet included his son-in-law, Hussein Kamil Hassan, as minister of defense, and his cousin, Ali Hassan al-Majid, as minister of interior, the post that controlled the *mukhabarat*. A torturer by reputation, al-Majid had run Kurdistan, and after the invasion was put in charge of Kuwait.

Saddam's son Qusay was made head of the security police, while another son, Uday, was given control of youth programs. Saddam also spread his brothers around as watchdogs in key agencies. The most influential, Barzan, had supervised the failed discussions with Secretary of State Baker on the eve of the war. The new government reflected Saddam's disposition—not uncommon in tribal culture—to trust only those linked to him by blood. His changes made the rule of Iraq more than ever a family affair.

An exception to family rule was the appointment of Saddoun Hammadi as prime minister, a post that had not been filled before the war. Hammadi, educated in America, was known for many years as the liberal in ruling circles, though his circle was not the innermost. Iraqis considered him decent and well-intentioned but weak. As prime minister, Hammadi promised democratization, including elections within a year. But he convinced no one, and his words were interpreted as an effort to polish Saddam's international image. Though the Iraqis I knew yearned for freedom, after two decades of tyranny they doubted whether Saddam had the will, or even the psychological capacity, to loosen the reins.

At a meeting with Hammadi in Baghdad, I asked whether it was possible for Iraq to embrace democracy or to persuade the United Nations to lift the economic embargo, as long as Saddam was in power. He answered with obvious irritation:

"Who is president of a country is a sovereignty issue, a national issue, not for the United Nations or any foreign state to decide. The president will be chosen by the Iraqi people. I don't agree that our system is currently a dictatorship. It is a one-party system but, in fact, now we are moving toward greater democracy. Our plans for democracy are not new. There have been discussions within the leadership since the early 1980s to adopt constitutional institutions, which include civil liberties, a free press and multiparty elections. We believe in democracy as a matter of principle, and if we have not implemented our plans until now, it is not because we have gone back on our promises. It is that circumstances, principally the Iran-Iraq war, have prevented us. After that war, a draft law to change the system was prepared, but the present crisis caused our plans to be postponed again. We are unwavering in our commitment. I'd like to say with emphasis that no leader is more attached to the principles of democracy than President Saddam Hussein.

"Now we are prepared to forget the recent past, to turn over a new page. We can't remain entangled in this crisis. Those who say they are not ready to cooperate with Iraq until it changes its government, until it replaces Saddam Hussein, are making a serious mistake. Countries talking about what kind of government we should have are embarking on a dangerous trend in international relations. Iraq has had the same stable government since 1968. We have had good relations with the Western countries. Iraq's leader is popular and he has historical achievements. Now I am confident that the time has come for this government to realize its commitment to democracy. I can't tell you how long it will take. It won't be done in a few months, but it won't take decades either. I think it will be a few years. But I believe we will be able to do it."

If Hammadi believed what he was saying, he was unquestionably engaged in wishful thinking. The Iraqi people, in their skepticism, understood the regime better than he did. Saddam never gave democratic ideas a public endorsement, and he soon brought Hammadi's tenure as prime minister to an end. Elections were never held, and not even a glint of liberalization has since been instituted.

After the defeat, Saddam seemed to concentrate on nothing weightier than his own survival, and did not emerge from his hiding places. He was said during the war to have, like Arafat, slept in a different bed every night, and to have avoided using the telephone for fear American electronic devices would find him. For six weeks after the cease-fire, his appearances, staged for the television crews that accompanied him, were all unannounced and without crowds.

The first time he showed up he was in the Kurdish city of Arbil, where he delivered a brief homily before some adoring party functionaries, then went off to a mosque for some on-camera religiosity. Wearing a uniform and a pistol on his hip, he knelt praying, his knees on a colorful Oriental prayer rug, his hands raised toward heaven, his face assuming a putatively beatific expression. A few evenings later, he was filmed at a refinery, where he listened to a team of engineers in hard hats talk of getting the machinery back in operation. In the background, employees cheered on cue, but none was permitted by his bodyguards to get close enough to touch him. Saddam's followers used to acclaim his personal courage, but he amply demonstrated on television that he did not have the heart, even with a large security contingent around him, to present himself in person to the Iraqi people.

Iraqis saw pictures of Saddam every evening on television, stock footage or interior shots of visits with officials or foreign dignitaries. The TV was part of the cultism that placed his portrait on most street corners, in every morning newspaper, in all offices and restaurants, even in many private homes. But television did little for Saddam. At the refinery, and at the Arbil meeting, his eyes wandered back and forth, and his hands fidgeted. He reminded me of Richard Nixon in his absence of spontaneity, in the smile that invariably seemed forced. In Arbil, Saddam was caught by the camera beneath a portrait of himself, grinning from ear to ear; live, he was unable to emit more than a scowl. His face seemed scarred not by war but by stage fright. Not even his propaganda apparatus was able to persuade him to lay aside his suspicions and deal with television, much less the political environment, as if it were a friend.

Though I left Iraq before Saddam celebrated his fifty-fourth birthday on April 28, by chance I was in on some of the preparations. I was standing at a side door of the ministry of information about a week before the festivities when a truck pulled up and unloaded tens of thousands of freshly printed, poster-size Saddam portraits, which were to be distributed around the country. As I watched, a ministry employee leaving the building stopped next to me and, looking at the posters, whispered hoarsely, "Our biggest movie star! He used to play Rambo. Now he's playing in a new hit called 'Desert Storm.' When he finishes, we hope he'll retire." Then, without another word, the whisperer walked away. After my return home, I read in the newspapers that, at a televised birthday reception, Saddam, wearing an immaculate white suit, was passionately embraced by government officials. But the celebration was closed to the public and the press. The government never said where it took place, nor why Saddam failed to show up at any of the public ceremonies held on the occasion.

Saddam was probably wise to be careful about his security. He had lost the backing of Iraq's Shiites and Kurds, and the very foundation of his power, the support of the Sunnis of Baghdad, had seriously eroded. But why, I wondered, were the Baghdadis so passive? In the time of Nuri Said, for example, they took to the streets when conditions became intolerable. Why did I not see so much as a symbolic protest—a defaced portrait of Saddam, for example—much less an overt act? I did not hear even a rumor of revolt, nor a word about a possible coup by the Sunni-dominated army, which was the scenario that President Bush envisaged when he stopped the war. With uprisings raging north and south, there had been some talk—never confirmed by the government, of course—of attacks on the Baghdad police. But these incidents were believed to have happened in Shiite neighborhoods, and the violence did not spread. During my visit, Baghdad appeared totally secure.

Why, if Saddam had squandered his mandate, was Baghdad quiet? Though Baghdadis were scared, only part of the answer lay in the mechanism of repression. At least as much of the answer lay in the structure of Iraqi society. Iraq is a nation of seventeen million people. Between 55 and 65 percent are Shiites. A quarter are Kurds. Apart from a handful of Christians, the rest are Sunni Arabs—but, though they may be the smallest of the three major elements, they have been politically dominant at least since the Ottoman era. One of the hidden factors in Iraqi politics was the effort by the Sunnis to remain in control.

The Sunni concept of the nation, furthermore, differed from that of the

Shiites and Kurds. Most Kurds dreamed of uniting with their brethren in Turkey, Syria and Iran to establish a state of their own. Most Shiites, following religious strictures, aspired to establish an Islamic state, modeled generally after Khomeini's Iran. These visions, though vaguely separatist, did not necessarily compel either to divorce themselves from the Sunnis or from Iraq. Save for the pure romantics, Kurds recognized the political complications of becoming a nation-state, and were willing to settle for political and cultural autonomy. The Shiites' beliefs were more closely linked to the idea of the *umma* than to nationhood; they viewed themselves as Iraqis more or less by default. Tactically, both Kurds and Shiites were willing to turn to Teheran for help—though both saw Iran ultimately as a foreign enemy—because their immediate foe was Saddam. It was against him, not against Iraq as such, that their uprisings were directed.

In contrast to Kurds and Shiites, Sunnis considered themselves pure nationalists, the heirs to the Abbasids. They claimed an Iraqi identity with a thousand years of history. Their highest goal was the preservation, within the Arab community, of an Iraqi state, independent and secular. They tolerated Shiites, with whom they shared their Arab ethnicity, and Kurds, whose Islam was Sunni like their own. But it was imperative to Sunnis that, if the vision of Iraq held by Kurds and Shiites was not identical to their own, it had at the very least to be reasonably compatible.

It was hard to imagine how democracy might reconcile these three diverse visions. In exile, Kurd, Shiite and Sunni dissidents had failed miserably to find anything more than a mutual loathing of Saddam on which to coalesce. It was unlikely that the three, living in Iraq, could agree on more. Precisely because the Kurds and Shiites were rebelling against Saddam—with conspicuous help from Iran—the Sunnis did not. And though the Kurds and Shiites rebelled simultaneously, their rebellions had little to do with each other.

In the Sunni view, Saddam represented the Iraqi nation, not a particular population group. Sunnis saw the Baath Party—for all that it was a slightly corrupt, self-serving bureaucracy—as a unifying force, making non-Sunnis into Iraqis. The Sunnis, unlike the Kurds and Shiites, reproached Saddam for jeopardizing the nation's integrity by going to war against the West. But abandoning him, they reasoned, would weaken the state even further. Much as they detested Saddam personally, the Sunnis would not join in an action to smash the state—and the Iraqi nation—into fragments.

Ironically, the concerns of the Sunnis were the same as those that paralyzed American policy after the fighting ended. President Bush, though obsessed with getting rid of Saddam, had to recognize the danger of regional instability if Iraq were to disintegrate. This danger, of course, was, or should have been, just as apparent on August 2, and ought to have imposed on Bush greater caution in rushing into war in the first place. Indeed, the strategic need to have Iraq as a balance to Iran forced Bush, in the end, to forgo the overthrow of Saddam, the villain of the piece. Some Iraqis argued that the Baghdad mobs would take to the streets as soon as the Shiite and Kurdish rebellions were crushed, and the nation was no longer in danger. Their case was not convincing: by then, it was obvious the regime would be far too well reestablished to be challenged at all. Saddam, in defeat, had the last laugh on Bush. Because Sunnis—and many other Iraqis, as well— preferred Iraq intact *with* him to an Iraq dismembered *without* him, they would not rise up to drive him from power.

IV   TARIQ AZIZ SPEAKS

TARIQ AZIZ, the most worldly member of Saddam's entourage, lost his post as foreign minister after the war and instead was named deputy prime minister. Iraq's chief spokesman during the Gulf crisis, he was said to have warned against the course that led to defeat. But Saddam, in tribal fashion, preferred the advice of loyal family members and old comrades-in-arms. Like him, these men knew precious little about the outside world. Some observers predicted that after the war Aziz—a Christian, thus without a power base of his own—would disappear from public life. But he remained a member of the Revolutionary Command Council, the state's highest policy-making body, and continued as a prominent player in government councils.

For a journalist, an interview with Aziz was consistently illuminating. He had a thorough grasp of English. He listened carefully to questions and addressed them directly and at length. He was courteous and knowledge-able, and once you had him in front of you, he showed no impatience to get away. Most important, he was unlike many high Iraqi officials in that he did not babble slogans; he conveyed the impression of telling the truth—at least, his view of the truth. Some subjects were exceptions: Aziz was evasive about differences within the ruling circles, and especially differences between himself and Saddam. Sometimes I wondered whether he knew everything that was going on. But based on my own experience, he did not often mislead his questioner and, when checked against other sources, his words proved to a high degree reliable.

I met with Aziz in the spacious town house where he worked after leaving the foreign ministry. It was in Baghdad's al-Qadisiyah district, part of a walled compound of official residences, a large section of which had been destroyed by bombs. I asked him to give me his account of how relations between the United States and Iraq, which only a year before had seemed so cordial, turned sour and ended in war.

Aziz said that the United States, after increasingly warm relations with Baghdad during the Iraq-Iran war, shifted suspiciously in its attitude as the fighting drew to a close. The Irangate affair, which revealed secret sales of arms to the Khomeini government, was extremely disturbing, Aziz said, even though Washington later apologized for it. Irangate was followed by Washington's angry accusations—which Aziz said were not true—that Iraq used poison gas against the fleeing Kurds in the summer of 1988. After that, he said, the Iraqi government began receiving information from officials of the Gulf states—Kuwait excepted—that American diplomats were spreading a warning that Iraq was dangerous, and advising caution in relations with Baghdad. (General Norman Schwarzkopf's autobiography leaves no doubt that this was true.) Later, Aziz said, his government was informed that the CIA was contacting Iraqi dissidents, both inside and outside the country, and telling them that the Saddam regime had to fall.

"I went to Washington in the fall of 1989, at the time of the General Assembly session in New York," Aziz said, "and I raised our concerns with Secretary Baker. [The State Department confirmed the general lines of this account.] I spoke to him in a very businesslike way, not at all hysterical. We had a talk of fifty minutes, and it was very substantive. I told him that we were working for the stabilization of the region, and that we were discussing procedures with our neighbors to settle disputes. [Iraq formally supported moves toward Arab-Israeli peace talks in 1985 and endorsed Yasir Arafat's recognition of Israel in 1988.] We felt that after eight years of war, we needed stability, to rebuild our country and our depleted wealth. Later, we signed nonaggression pacts with Saudi Arabia and Bahrain. We made the same offer to Kuwait, but its government was not interested. [The Kuwaitis did not dispute this statement.] I also told Baker that we were disturbed by obstacles to our efforts to renew our soft-loan agreements by which we bought American food on favorable terms.

"Baker denied that his government was looking for trouble with Iraq. On the contrary, he said, the United States wanted good Iraqi relations, and he promised to do his best to renew the soft-loan deal. In February, Kelly came to Baghdad and saw Saddam Hussein, who raised the same questions that I had spoken about with Baker. [John Kelly, former ambassador to Lebanon, at the time assistant secretary of state for Near Eastern affairs, reported on his return that Saddam expressed concern about Washington's growing military strength in the Gulf, and rejected criticism of Iraq's human-rights record, especially toward the Kurds.] Saddam also protested that the United States had done little to put a formal end to the

Iraq-Iran war, and he raised the question of whether American policy was no-war-no-peace, to keep us weak. Baker, by the way, did follow up on the soft-loan problem; he got half of the deal through, but in April 1990, it was suspended by your government, just when we critically needed barley. By then, relations between our countries were becoming more complicated."

Aziz recalled that months before the crisis, at a summit in Amman, Saddam irritated Washington by stating that, with Moscow in decline, the United States was planning to project its power increasingly into the Gulf, in violation of Arab interests. He also repeated the charge that Washington was behind press reports of Iraq's construction of a supergun, a long-range artillery weapon, and its illegal purchase of krytons, sophisticated electronic devices for use in guided missiles and nuclear bombs.

In February 1990, Saddam became indignant about an Arabic-language broadcast over the Voice of America which said, "The 1990s should belong not to the dictators and secret police but the people"; he took it as a call to the Iraqis to revolt. On March 15, over British protests, Iraq executed Farzad Bazoft, an Iranian-born journalist traveling on British papers, on spying charges. "He *was* a spy," Aziz said. "We are very sensitive about security matters in our region. We react strongly, but that is how we are. Bazoft was tried in a security court, in the presence of a British official. We punished him as we punish others for this crime." Aziz said that Iraq was bewildered by the fierce reaction of the West.

This was at the time, Aziz continued, that the Western press began speculating about a new Gulf war, though there was no discernible crisis at all. He acknowledged that Iraq was buying arms, because it was unsure whether its war with Iran was really over, but he said its military budget was decreasing and that Iraq had demobilized fifteen divisions, reducing its army to half of what it was in 1988. (American sources contradicted these claims.) The heated atmosphere, Aziz said, reminded Iraqis of the period preceding Israel's bombing of the nuclear reactor in Baghdad in 1981, and the government began wondering whether a similar attack was planned. "In 1981, being at war with Iran, we could not retaliate," Aziz said. "But we were not that weak any longer. We talked it over in the leadership, and we decided a strong speech would be a deterrent." So Saddam publicly declared that if the Israelis attacked, he would incinerate half their country. Washington, ignoring the provocation perceived by Saddam, professed shock at this vitriolic statement, and relations between the two countries became only worse.

"One important unresolved question for the region," Aziz went on, "was that of loans made to Iraq during the war, by Saudi Arabia and Kuwait, and by all of the Emirates. These governments acknowledged that

Iraq had protected them against Iran. They thanked us publicly. Our problem, after the war, was that we were deep in debt not only to our neighbors but to the outside world. Since the loans from the Arabs were for our mutual benefit, we asked that they be forgiven. The Arabs didn't say no; they just passed the buck back and forth. We brought it up when King Fahd visited Baghdad, and when Saddam made a reciprocal visit to Riyadh, but though the king made promises, he did nothing. We did not think we had real problems then, even with the Kuwaitis, to whom we also offered a settlement of our border differences. This was the period when we were concentrating on improving relations in the Gulf, looking for a new start."

Aziz stopped here and chuckled bitterly.

"Then the oil crisis with Kuwait began. In December 1989, oil was selling for twenty-one dollars a barrel, and people were talking of the price rising to twenty-five. Iraq took a rational attitude. We needed cash badly, but we did not want a big jump. That's when the big pumping started in Kuwait and the Emirates, with the price dropping until it reached eleven or twelve dollars. Our economic situation worsened very dramatically. We talked to the Kuwaitis and the Emirates. We also talked to the Saudis, who seemed to agree with us but were indecisive. The Americans understood the problem. We weren't the only ones being hurt. Mubarak told me Egypt had lost seven hundred million dollars. Algeria and Iran lost billions. But, because of our vulnerable condition, we were the worst victim.

"Oil is our chief source of income, and we faced a budgetary shortfall of seven or eight billion dollars. We were near the point of economic collapse, and in May, Saddam Hussein brought up the issue before all of the Gulf heads of state at the summit in Baghdad, where he accused Kuwait of waging economic war. Yet nothing changed. Until the end of June, we were still thinking in terms of reaching a financial and border settlement with Kuwait, but then we began to wonder whether Kuwait was deliberately trying to destroy us. The Kuwaitis were very strange, very pompous, very obstinate. As for the United States, we figured that our two countries were engaged in a peaceful competition for influence in the Gulf, but we committed no acts against American interests, and we saw no reason for conflict."

Aziz recalled that on July 11 the oil ministers of Iraq, Kuwait, Saudi Arabia and the Emirates met in Jedda and reached agreement on limiting production in order to get the price back up to eighteen dollars a barrel. "When our oil minister informed us of the outcome of the meeting," he said, "we thought it was too good to be true. In fact, it was." In announcing the agreement the next day, Kuwait added the stipulation that it would review and possibly reverse its commitment in the fall. (Aziz's assertion was confirmed in published statements of Sheikh Ali al-Khalifa, the Kuwaiti oil minister.) Demand for oil in the summer months was always slow, Aziz said, and the statement by Kuwait tipped off major buyers to wait until October, when the price was sure to drop again. In effect, he said, Kuwait killed the agreement. At the OPEC meeting a few days later, he said, Kuwait repeated its intention to observe the limitation only until the fall, and it took the same position at the Jedda meeting on August 1, the eve of the invasion.

"President Saddam Hussein had no intention of invading—he didn't even think of it before the end of June," Aziz said. "It was never discussed at any level of government. After Saddam's speech at the Baghdad summit, we desisted from further threats to Kuwait. The issue of the Rumaila oil fields and our border demands became a part of our talks with the Kuwaitis only in late June, by which time we had concluded that they had joined some sort of conspiracy to destroy our regime.

"I have the impression that in Washington, at the time, there were two contending schools of thought. One held that Iraq was a tough partner to deal with but responsible; the other held that Iraq was dangerous and had to be checked, even if it meant conflict. And you know who controls the balance in situations like this." Aziz at this point raised an eyebrow, which was meant to tell me that his reference was to the Israeli government and its Washington lobby. (Contemporary press reports confirm that Israel had for more than a year been urging the Bush administration to impose economic sanctions on Iraq.) "We didn't ourselves go to Washington with our complaints. Maybe it was a missed opportunity. We didn't see much use; we assumed that if the Israelis were involved, the Americans were right behind them. Finally, in mid-July, we decided to dispatch troops to the Kuwaiti border, hoping it would make the Kuwaitis change their minds."

The Iraqi troop deployment was so open that not even Kuwaitis doubted that its aim was to send a political message. In tough language, Saddam declared that his army would advance if the Kuwaitis continued to violate their production quota. At the same time, he publicly condemned Washington for inspiring Kuwait. On July 23, the Pentagon, as a warning to Iraq, sent two aerial tankers and a cargo transport plane on maneuvers over Gulf waters; the navy dispatched six warships to positions closer to Kuwait.

On July 24, Saddam received Egypt's President Mubarak on a mediation mission. Aziz said that Saddam told Mubarak, "Don't comfort the Kuwaitis," but he also pledged to take no military action as long as negotiations continued. Mubarak, on reaching Kuwait, offered his hosts the misstatement that there would be no invasion under any circumstances, which Aziz said only made Kuwait persist in its intransigence. (Mubarak's reputation as a well-meaning bumbler extends to diplomacy; a high-level Egyptian source acknowledged the accuracy of this account.) Mubarak, Aziz sneered, was the Americans' man and followed American instructions. After the invasion, Mubarak accused Saddam of lying about his intentions; according to Aziz, it was Mubarak who spoke falsely, deliberately or not, on a point that was crucial to Saddam's negotiating position.

A day after Mubarak's visit, Saddam summoned April Glaspie, the U.S. ambassador, for their now celebrated meeting. The State Department acknowledges that in the course of the meeting, Glaspie told Saddam that the United States regarded the Iraqi-Kuwaiti dispute as none of its affair. Intentionally or not, the United States misled the Iraqi government about its policy, and for that Glaspie's statement will be remembered in diplomatic history. Many Arabs see it as a trap meant to lure Saddam into the invasion; many Americans see it either as a terrible blunder on Glaspie's part or as proof that the Bush administration was soft on Saddam. Some critics have said that the State Department, in refusing to defend Glaspie, made her the scapegoat for a major breakdown in American diplomacy on the eve of the invasion.

Glaspie's report of the meeting to senior State Department officials, excerpts of which were later published, makes it possible to reconstruct much of the exchange. Saddam complained about the American maneuvers in the Gulf, which he said—correctly, as Kuwaiti officials have made clear—encouraged Kuwait's hard-liners. He also said that Iraq's "financial situation is such that the pensions for widows and orphans will have to be cut," and she observed, "At this point, the interpreter and one of the note-takers broke down and wept." Glaspie's notes say that she asked Saddam why Iraqi troops had taken positions on Kuwait's border, but they do not reveal the warning—that Washington would not stand for aggression—which Glaspie told a Senate committee she delivered. Saddam, according to her notes, said that if Washington continued to use Kuwait as a "spearhead" for its ambitions, "Iraq will have to respond . . . Iraq knows the United States can send planes and rockets and hurt Iraq deeply . . . and asks that the United States not force Iraq to the point of humiliation, at which logic must be disregarded."

Meanwhile, the Iraqi foreign ministry released its own transcript of the meeting. It covered more ground than Glaspie's account, and though she characterized it as incomplete, the State Department never challenged the accuracy of its content.

"Yours is a society which cannot accept ten thousand dead in one battle," Saddam said, according to Baghdad's text, providing a clue to why he thought Iraq could stand up to American military power. Elaborating on Glaspie's notes, the Iraq transcript offered a further clue to Saddam's motivation. "When we feel," Saddam said, "that you want to injure our pride . . . then we will cease to care and death will be the choice for us. Then we would not care if you fired one hundred missiles for each missile we fired. Because without pride, life would have no value." The statement was one of many Saddam made during the confrontation emphasizing the centrality of self-esteem in his policy decisions. Saddam argued, in the Baghdad text, that the source of the crisis was America's encouragement of Kuwait "to harm Iraq's interests." It was in reply to this charge that Glaspie made her controversial disclaimer of American interest in the Iraq-Kuwait dispute.

A well-informed State Department source insisted to me that Glaspie's statement to Saddam had been generally misunderstood. It was not made within the context of possible military action, and did not imply American indifference to a possible Iraqi invasion. Glaspie, in fact, had no instructions on what to say about Saddam's military threat to Kuwait. The highest echelons of the State Department were too preoccupied then with the rapid changes taking place in Europe to focus on the Gulf. Glaspie did, however, have standing instructions on an answer if Saddam asked for American mediation in the negotiations with Kuwait. Following these instructions, she told Saddam that the dispute was not an American concern. The Iraqi transcript substantiates the accuracy of this interpretation.

The transcript has Saddam complaining about the costs to Iraq of Kuwait's manipulation of oil prices. "I know you need funds," Glaspie responds. "We understand that, and our opinion is that you should have the opportunity to rebuild your country. But we have no opinion on the Arab-Arab conflicts, like your border disagreement with Kuwait." Glaspie goes further to say, "I was in the American embassy in Kuwait during the late 60s. The instruction we had during this period was that we should express no opinion on this issue, and that this issue is not associated with America. James Baker has directed our official spokesmen to emphasize this instruction." Far from getting the ambassador's sanction to invade Kuwait, Saddam got nothing. He certainly did not get Glaspie to promise American intercession in the negotiations with Kuwait, which it seems clear that he wanted.

When I asked Aziz how he interpreted Saddam's meeting with Glaspie, at which he was present, he took a surprisingly detached view. He did not claim that Iraq had been misled in any way about American intentions. "Having been a foreign minister, I understand the work of an ambassador," he said, "and I believe Miss Glaspie's behavior was correct. She was summoned suddenly. The president wanted to tell her that the situation was worsening and that our government would not waive its options [vis-à-vis Kuwait], and he wanted to add that Iraq was not hostile to the United States. We knew she was acting on available instructions. She spoke in vague diplomatic language, and we knew the position she was in. Her behavior was a classic diplomatic response, and we were not influenced by it."

Aziz told me that Saddam's decision to invade was made only after the collapse of Iraq's final negotiations with Kuwait on August 1 in Jedda. (In *The Commanders*, Bob Woodward, a journalist with excellent sources in the Pentagon, corroborates this assertion, based on American satellite photos of Iraqi war preparations.) Aziz said the Kuwaitis were surprised only by the scope of the operation, which they expected to be limited to the disputed border areas, specifically the Rumaila oil field and the offshore islands. Arab observers had predicted such an incursion, reversible in nature; it even had precedent in Iraqi-Kuwaiti history. Schwarzkopf, who was sending intelligence reports to Kuwait on Iraqi deployment, says in his memoir that, though he anticipated Iraq's invasion, he too was convinced that its objectives would be limited.

Saddam, according to a high Jordanian official to whom I later talked, decided to go the whole way only after receiving information that Kuwait planned to invite an American army to land in the unoccupied part of the country. Convinced that the Saudis would not allow foreign forces on their territory, the Jordanian said, Saddam calculated that he could thwart the Americans, denying them bases, by taking all of Kuwait.

Aziz did not confirm the Jordanian's assertion but said that Saddam made the shift to a plan of full occupation only at the last minute. The decision, he said, was based on the government's belief that it would make no difference whether Iraq chose to take part or all of Kuwait. Saddam by then was convinced, he said, that the Americans had decided to crush Iraq, and that there was nothing his government could do to change their minds.

"We expected an American military retaliation from the very beginning," Aziz said. "We knew the Americans would not be caught by surprise. I have no conclusion about what might have happened if we had engaged in a limited incursion, but within the leadership, we had no dispute; we agreed that we had to go all the way. As foreign minister, I was convinced that in April the Americans had stopped listening to us and had made up their minds to hit us. Senator Dole met with Saddam Hussein and said he thought the United States could do business with Iraq. [Bob Dole of Kansas, visiting Iraq with four other senators, had a cordial meeting with Saddam on April 12, in which the looming crisis was never discussed.] But no one in Washington was interested in what Dole said. After the collapse of Communism and of eastern Europe, the Americans became more and more arrogant."

Aziz lamented that, after the invasion, whenever his government tried to find a resolution of the crisis, it found itself trapped by the American determination to wage war. He had not anticipated the almost total political boycott which Washington succeeded in imposing, he said, and which closed all normal diplomatic channels. Old friends like the French and the Germans would not even talk to Iraqi emissaries; as for the Russians, he said the proposals which they made to reconcile the parties had no real authority behind them. By December, after repeatedly failing in its peace efforts, he said, the Iraqi government decided to stick to its positions, to make no concessions and to see what would happen.

When he finally met with Secretary of State Baker in Geneva in January, Aziz said, Baker opened by saying, "You think we are bluffing." Aziz told me he answered, "No, we take you very seriously." But the Iraqi government, he acknowledged, had decided not to meet the condition—withdrawing unconditionally from Kuwait—that Bush demanded as an alternative to a Western attack.

Now, Aziz said, he looks at the whole episode philosophically, and what he sees is that the West was unwilling under any circumstances to accept Iraq as an equal partner in a negotiation, or in any sort of relationship. Furthermore, Washington was not prepared to tolerate the rise of a strong, modern, assertive, developed country in the Arab world. What Aziz seemed to be saying was that the United States refused to treat Iraq with the respect that Saddam felt his country deserved. Could the drama have ended differently if Bush and Baker had adopted a less belligerent tone in their public pronouncements? President Bush never deviated from his vow not to negotiate with Saddam over withdrawal from Kuwait. Aziz told me he had no choice but to believe that the Western assault on Iraq was what America wanted; in that sense, it was foreordained.

"I'm not a strong believer in conspiracies," Aziz said, "but they do exist. And they exist more in our part of the world than elsewhere because we have oil, a strategic position and Israel. Our people have been frustrated for decades. War seems to come, whatever we do. It seems to be our historical tradition to suffer and to fail. We felt fatalistic. That is the mood that governed our judgment here."

Incredulous at these remarks, I told Aziz I did not understand the passivity which he attributed to his government. Even if a thread of fatalism was woven into the fabric of Islamic culture, I said it had never before seemed to impede Saddam Hussein, whose regime, whatever else it might be, had probably been the most dynamic in the Arab world.

Like others, I was bewildered in the months preceding the outbreak of the war by the clumsiness of Iraq's diplomatic moves, by its failure to create or to seize opportunities to put Washington on the defensive, by its unwillingness to slip out of the trap that Bush, wittingly or not, had set for it. I had assumed there was some design, however hard to decipher.

Was Aziz now saying that Saddam's pride had been so deeply wounded that he preferred almost certain defeat to diplomatic maneuver, to say nothing of compromise or retreat? Did Bush deliberately strike at Saddam's self-esteem as a way of barring a peaceful solution to the crisis? Did he foresee that Saddam, subjected to a psychological barrage, would willingly stumble into a war he could not possibly win? Was Saddam, as Aziz was suggesting, a helpless, even a willing, victim? Even now, I find myself disturbed by the conception that Aziz seemed to be articulating: Iraq as a cork upon the waves unleashed by the West. I weighed the possibility that this was a loyal retainer's way of excusing his leader's costly mistakes. Whatever it was, the hard facts left little doubt that Iraqi diplomacy was paralyzed as the war neared. Aziz seemed to be confirming that Iraq marched knowingly into the cannons, with no real policy at all.

v   PROVINCIAL SPRING

THE DAY AFTER the cease-fire on February 28, the Shiites in the south rose up; a few days later, the Kurds in the north followed them. It would be too much to say that Iran provoked these rebellions; both Shiites and Kurds had ample reason to rebel. But Iran, having much to gain by the uprisings, gave impetus to both; neither insurrection is likely to have taken place without its support.

By historical standards, the moment was ideal. Like Czarist Russia in 1917, the Iraqi government, its armed forces vanquished on the battlefield, seemed to have nothing left to protect it. Besides, had not President Bush indicated repeatedly in his public statements that he would not permit the government of Saddam Hussein to survive? The leaders of the two rebellions smelled success, and by the middle of March, while the defeated army was still in positions around Kuwait, most of the major cities in the north and south of the country fell into their hands.

Then, with Iraq on the verge of disintegration, Bush came face to face with what he had wrought. Iran, having been beaten back by Iraq's army only two years before, was once again in a position to threaten much of the Arab world, a landmass extending from the Gulf to the Mediterranean. Even with Khomeini dead, the Iranian regime was hardly a more reliable friend of the West than Saddam's Iraq. If protection of the Gulf's oil was Bush's interest, had not the Iraqi army been America's first line of defense against revolutionary Iran? A successful uprising, whether of Kurds or Shiites, would reduce Iraq to a shell, leaving Iran the dominant force in the region. Suddenly, the prospect presented itself that the American army might be caught in the web of regional animosities, from which it would be unable to extricate itself. President Bush had second thoughts about his victory and decided to let Saddam regroup.

Once the Iraqi army had withdrawn from Kuwait, neither the Shiites nor the Kurds proved nearly as strong as their early triumphs had suggested. Nor was Saddam nearly as weak. A few units of his army defected to the rebels; most stayed loyal to the regime. Bush drew the line at Saddam's using fixed-wing aircraft and poison gas against the rebels; otherwise, without fear of American intervention, the Iraqis were free to use whatever equipment they had salvaged from the defeat.

Saddam turned first on the Shiites, then on the Kurds. His units moved quickly across the countryside, over a road network many said he had built precisely to meet such a contingency. He used his advantage in weaponry, especially tanks and artillery, devastatingly. The rebel forces could not stand up under the fire of his helicopter gunships. Poorly led, the rebels also lacked a strategic plan. In retrospect, it is clear their leaders had acted quixotically in taking to the battlefield without real preparation. When the Iraqi army reappeared, the Shiites fought, the Kurds fled. But whether they stood or ran, the rebels were devastated by Saddam's army. By the end of March, at most a few guerrilla bands remained in the field, capable of no more than an occasional raid. After less than a month of fighting, the civil war was over.

It is hard to say whether, of the two losers, the Kurds suffered the greater catastrophe, but their condition received by far the greater attention. Encamped in the mountains on the Turkish and Iranian frontiers, they were accessible to the world's press, in contrast to the Shiites, who fought in the interior of Iraq, hidden from view behind borders that Saddam had sealed shut. Hundreds of thousands of Kurds—some reports said as many as two million—took flight. Television gave constant coverage to their wretchedness. The newsweeklies had a field day in laying the tragedy out as the latest horrible example of the brutality of the Saddam regime. The real story of the relationship—in which virtue had been in short supply on the Kurdish no less than on the Iraqi side—was complex, and scarcely told at all.

It is worth recalling that in 1970, Saddam Hussein himself took the initiative to end decades of warfare between Baghdad and the Kurds by negotiating an agreement that established a Kurdish autonomous region. Though in spirit he violated the accord, by placing the Kurdish regime under the control of the Baath party, he nonetheless delivered far more rights than Kurds enjoyed in Syria, Turkey or Iran. What was missing from both sides in Iraqi-Kurdish dealings was trust. Saddam's duplicity was equalled by that of the Kurdish leader, Mustafa al-Barzani, who for decades maintained secret military relations with Iran directed at Iraq.

Though most Iraqi Kurds were loyal to the government during the Iraq-Iran war, some—chiefly Barzani's guerrillas—served Iran's army across the mountainous frontier. Saddam's brutal efforts to stamp out the rebels, which included the forced migration of Kurds into "resettlement villages" and possibly the use of poison gas, had by the end of the war brought Kurdish relations with Baghdad to an all-time low. When the Gulf crisis began, in August 1990, it was predictable that the Kurds, at any sign of Iraqi weakness, would rise up again.

When I arrived in Baghdad after the American victory, the Kurdish uprising was said to have been suppressed, and the ministry of information set up tours for journalists to demonstrate that the region was calm. Getting to Kurdistan required several hours of tedious driving across the Mesopotamian flats, where occasionally we spied a factory that had taken a hit, or a burned-out truck that no one had bothered to haul away, but the signs of war were few. We had no sense that anything was unusual until, inside Kurdistan, we passed a string of resettlement villages, normally bustling with activity, and did not see a soul in any of them. The region was still heavily armed, with machine-gun posts and tanks at many road junctions. But the soldiers who passed in open trucks appeared relaxed, more as if they were going on leave than deploying for battle. The fact that we saw no military equipment at all heading north seemed to confirm that the fighting was over. It was only the presence of the Saddam portraits, pockmarked with bullet holes and splattered with mud, which reminded us that a few days before the region had been in rebel hands.

Our Iraqi guides knew exactly where they wanted to take us when we reached Sulaimaniya, the capital of the governorate. We stopped first at the edge of the city where several hundred men and women, some in Western and some in traditional dress, were queuing up in a vacant lot to receive government food rations. Most spoke only Kurdish, a language related to Iran's Farsi, which our translators did not understand. In return for ration coupons, the people were getting sacks of flour, a jerrican of cooking oil and cases of assorted tinned foods from functionaries stationed at the tailgates of open trucks.

From there, we drove to a hillside a mile or so away, where men with shovels, wearing surgical masks or kerchiefs tied across their faces, were working with a tractor to excavate a mass grave. When a body was exhumed, they placed it on the ground and washed it with hoses, before placing it in a refrigerated truck which stood nearby. A crew leader told us that 120 bodies—later raised to 370, by officials in Baghdad—had been found, all members of the Baath Party organization that had ruled the city. From the visit, I retain a vivid memory of a uniformed man of about twenty-five, sitting on the ground weeping inconsolably after finding his brother among the dead.

Arbil, the seat of government of the Kurdish autonomous region, was one of the few cities in the north that had been damaged in the fighting. A tank had punched a hole about six feet wide in the outer wall of the principal government building during an attack on rebel forces, and the interior was badly burned. The damage had forced Saddam's man in Arbil, Sirwan Abdullah Jaff, to move to a Baath Party building, where he received us in a small library. When I reminded Jaff that in an interview a few years before he had assured me that, with few exceptions, Iraq's Kurds were satisfied with their lot, he answered with a touch of wrath. "This unrest was another phase of the international conspiracy against Iraq," he said. "Kurdistan was the target of troublemakers who came here from Iran and other countries in huge numbers. Most of our prisoners are Iranian, which proves what I say. They had machine guns, mortars and heavy weapons. They were here for twenty days, but they could not win. The Kurdish people under the leadership of Saddam Hussein have all of their civil and patriotic rights. That is a major contrast with the Kurds in Turkey and Iran. Now, based on the instructions of Saddam Hussein, we are working to reconstruct the services that were destroyed by the enemies of Iraq and of God. Everyone who understands diplomacy and politics knows that what has happened to Iraq is part of a big conspiracy." Jaff's line was one we were to hear often, from party functionaries who seemed indifferent to whether or not we believed them.

On another day, we drove far to the north, almost to the Turkish frontier, to the mountainous region around the towns of Zakho and Dohuk, later to be taken over by the United States army as a protected haven for Kurdish refugees. At a checkpoint on a road coming down from the mountains, a small contingent of Iraqi soldiers, backed by two party officials, greeted an occasional truck or private car jammed with unwashed, bedraggled-looking refugees, returning to the lowlands carrying pots, pans, bedrolls and babies. In the distance, we could see American cargo planes flying at low altitude, parachuting supplies into the Kurdish camps.

The returning refugees talked to us of how miserable they had been in the mountain camps, from rain and cold, hunger and filth and tainted water, but they said most of the people there were still too frightened of Saddam's revenge to go home. Though they had heard of the amnesty the government had offered to returnees, they said they did not trust it. The soldiers at the checkpoint gave them some food, then examined their ID cards and and marked down their names. In reply to my question, a party official said he was recording names to track the number of returnees, not to exact retribution against the cardholders. He claimed the refugees had fled out of fear of being caught in the crossfire between the rebels and the army, and that the government was now trying to convince them that it was safe to go home. But the rebels, he said, had made the refugees into political pawns and were holding them against their will. Though the army had the capacity to go into the mountains and defeat the rebels, he insisted, the soldiers were held in suspicion by the Kurds. To spare the refugees anxiety, he said, the government had no choice but to wait until some understanding with the Kurds was worked out.

Zakho and Dohuk, where we stopped after leaving the checkpoints, looked much like the ghost towns of American Westerns. Both had been evacuated without a fight. Destruction was negligible. All but a few shops were shuttered. No traffic moved on the street. Apart from some old men smoking in a coffee shop, I saw almost no signs of life. In Zakho, the only working building appeared to be the Baath Party headquarters. In Dohuk, the party headquarters had been torched to the ground.

While I was looking around Dohuk's main street, a couple of teenage boys walked by, and on the chance that one of them spoke English, I asked why everyone had suddenly fled. "Kurds are Kurds," one boy replied with a shrug, "and will always remain Kurds," which seemed about as good an explanation of the Kurdish sense of separateness as I had heard. He told me he had remained behind because his father had doubts about the rebel leadership. "They promised an independent Kurdistan after the revolution," he said, "and people believed them. They said the government would use poison gas, napalm and even missiles on us, and the people were frightened. Half of the leaders came from outside the region and spoke Farsi [meaning, presumably, that they were Iranian], and the people stopped believing them. But the people are afraid of the government, too, and so they left and won't come back."

As we talked, a crowd of men, emerging from nowhere, gathered around. One, in particular, wearing a dark suit and tie, volunteered answers to my questions that were more faithful than the boy's to Baathi orthodoxy. After the boys left, he followed them, and before turning a corner he took the arm of the one who had talked to me and said something in his ear. The incident did not leave me with a good feeling.

On my last night in Baghdad, Jalal Talabani, one of the two chiefs of the coalition of Kurdish rebels, held a press conference at the ministry of information. For a week or so, the BBC had been broadcasting reports, based on Kurdish sources in London, that Talabani was in Baghdad meeting with Saddam. His presence seemed unlikely, given the depth of ill feeling between the Kurds and Saddam, and the ministry, in its characteristic fashion, claimed to know nothing. Then, about ten that evening, an official made a sweep of the Al-Rasheed, pulling all the journalists that he could find away from dinner to invite them to the ministry at once.

There, Talabani waited in the minister's large, luxurious office, sitting on a brown divan, directly beneath an oil portrait of Saddam. A round man with curly hair, he had a rather appealing face behind a pair of tinted glasses. He wore an all-beige designer version of traditional Kurdish dress, with tailored baggy pants, an open-throat shirt and a cummerbund. A lawyer and ex-journalist, he spoke a sonorous English in which the words tumbled grandly off the tongue. Talabani generally represented the leftist intellectuals and smaller tribes among the Kurds; Masoud Barzani, who had succeeded his father, Mustafa, drew his power from the major tribes. As nearly as an outsider could tell, the two men worked harmoniously together, and when Talabani talked, it was understood to be with the authority of the coalition.

Talabani said that he and Saddam had reached an agreement in principle in which the autonomy plan of 1970 would be reinstated, and administered according to its original intent. In effect, it would make Kurdistan self-governing. He dismissed differences over the rule of Kirkuk, a disputed city, and the revenues derived from the oil fields nearby, major obstacles in previous negotiations. The climate of the talks with Saddam, Talabani said, had been positive, frank and open. "Saddam tried to crush us and failed," he said. "We tried and failed to bring down his government. Now we are both looking for a political and peaceful solution. A new page will be turned in relations between the Baath Party and the Kurdish front." Talabani said that enforcement of the agreement would be based on common interests and democratic processes, not on international guarantees, which had not worked in the past. Kurds, who he said were faithful to Iraq, shared with Baghdad the conviction that foreign forces—by which he meant American—cannot remain in the country. Barzani, he said, would soon arrive in Baghdad to settle the agreement's final details.

Talabani's optimistic pronouncement left most of us skeptical. Taken at face value, it meant that Saddam had agreed to give up Baghdad's dominance of Kurdistan and allow a variety of Kurdish parties to compete for power there. After twenty-eight years of on-and-off negotiations, as Talabani himself said, he knew Saddam well. Saddam might be attracted to a Sunni-Kurd alliance to hasten the departure of the Americans. But Talabani said that the deal had been clinched on the basis of Saddam's agreement to democratize all of Iraq. Did he really believe that Saddam would keep such a deal? Baathis might swallow a coalition with Kurds, whose modern, secular values were much like their own. But in consenting to democracy for the Kurds, would not Saddam inevitably have to do the same for the Shiites, whose parties were fundamentalist? Such a concession to Iraq's majority would put Iraq on the road to becoming a *shari'a* state. To imagine Saddam sharing power at all was hard enough; to imagine his sharing it with a fundamentalist majority was inconceivable.

The next morning, Prime Minister Hammadi held a press conference, which the assembled journalists assumed would be the occasion for Iraq's confirmation of Talabani's report. But Hammadi said not a word about the Kurds in his opening statement, and in answer to a question, he replied simply, "I confirm that we are conducting this dialogue with sincerity and good intentions, and I have nothing more to add." It was hardly a ringing endorsement of Talabani's pronouncement, and left the journalists more doubtful than before. Barzani never got to Baghdad to nail down the details of an agreement, as Talabani had promised. In the end, the talks faltered over a variety of issues, most notably the geographical extent of the Kurdish domain. But more important, they gave way under the threat of American military action, which encouraged the Kurdish leadership to make demands going far beyond the 1970 autonomy plan.

Shortly after my visit to Kurdistan, the United States, Britain and France, concerned about Iraqi pressure on the refugees, made a "safe haven" of the region around Zakho and Dohuk. Though it was not authorized under UN resolutions, the Iraqis accepted it and withdrew from the area without a fight. In the months that followed, American air units, operating from bases in Turkey, enforced a "no-fly zone" over most of northern Iraq, and under their protection the Kurds rebuilt their armed forces. By the end of 1991, the Kurds were more or less in control of 80 percent of Kurdistan and had begun building political institutions that looked much like those of an independent state. Saddam's restraint left no doubt that he lacked the appetite for another fight with the Americans. His forces maintained an angry watch over the Kurds, however, and unless the United States was prepared to stay on indefinitely, it seemed only a matter of time before Iraqi-Kurdish warfare would be resumed.

HAVING VISITED THE NORTH, I headed south to see Karbala and An Najaf, the pilgrimage cities of Shite Muslims. I knew from reports that conditions were bad; without electricity and clean water, many people in both cities were said to have fallen sick. It seemed an ominous sign as we neared Karbala, which is an hour south of Baghdad, that groves of palm trees had been uprooted and were lying on the ground. My guide from the ministry said the Iraqi army had done it, to deny hiding places to rebel bands, remnants of which were still at large.

As we neared the city, the military units were much more alert than those I had seen in the north. By now, I had been conditioned by how few scars had been left by the civil war and the Allied bombing, so I was shocked by what I saw in the Shiite cities. The devastation was comparable to the leveled cities in World War II, and the damage to the great Shiite mosques more serious than that suffered by the great European cathedrals. What was more, the pervasive edge of tension in the cities made me wonder whether the fighting was about to start over again.

A manned Iraqi tank, its flag flying and its gun covering the roadway, greeted our car as we entered Karbala. As we approached the city center, pedestrians were negotiating their way amid piles of rubble. No neighborhood seemed exempt from destruction. The big holes in walls indicated tank fire; smaller holes, and chunks taken out of slabs of stone and cement, were the signature of lighter, automatic weapons. The debris suggested block-by-block, if not house-by-house, fighting, and many casualties.

Then, in silhouette, I saw the Mosque of Abbas, and at a distance it was resplendent. Occupying the equivalent of two or three city blocks, its size was in itself awesome, and above the encircling wall soared the twin gold-leafed domes and slim, piercing minarets that I remembered. As we approached, I spied the tanks parked at its gates, and a moment later I saw that the shrine was horribly defaced. Huge gashes had been taken out of its sides, and its heavy wooden doors were blown off the hinges. Graffiti had been painted on every surface, then painted over. "Long live the Republican Guard," said an outer coat in Arabic, but still visible was the message underneath: "Down with Saddam criminal." The archways leading into the courtyard had been badly hit. An officer invited us inside and, in what had been a religious library, showed us instruments of torture, and a noose from which he said Baathi officials had been hanged. The huge courtyard, where I remembered families picnicking, had become a campsite and parade ground for the army's guard unit. As we left to return to the car, soldiers carrying weapons slung over their shoulders looked down on us from the top of the wall. One of them smiled at me and, like a sports figure celebrating a triumph, gave me a thumbs-up gesture.

The Mosque of Hussein, which stands a hundred yards away, was in an even worse state. The *souk* and the plaza that lay between the two monuments had been reduced to dust. Ancient houses with overhanging *shanashils* had been leveled. Fifty-calibre machine-gun shells littered the ground. Several men were sifting through a mound of debris as I passed, and when I asked what they were doing, one replied, rather good-naturedly, that his jewelry shop had stood there, and he was trying to recover gold. Scattered over the pavement at the wall of the shrine were colorful mosaic tiles, slabs of granite facing and the ceramic grills that covered the windows. The dome, leafed in gold, had been damaged by cannon fire. Iraqi flags showed through breaches in the wall, but an officer on guard at the gate forbade us to enter. The wreckage took place during three days of battle over rebel positions in the courtyard, he said. Both sides were now trying to profit from the destruction; the government blamed the rebels for making a fortress of the shrine, while the rebels blamed the army for the gunfire that ultimately subdued them.

Barely out of Karbala, heading south, we were stopped at a roadblock, where a young police officer barred us from going on to An Najaf, which was another hour away. We argued with him, and even tried to get our guide to cite the authority of the ministry, but, apologetically, he declined. "I'm an Iraqi," our guide said; "Sometimes the police say yes, sometimes they say no. There is nothing we can do about it." He agreed, however, to take us to the office of Karbala's governor, where we hoped for an interview and, perhaps, an appeal on the An Najaf visit.

To our surprise, we were ushered immediately into the governor's office, a dark and gloomy room with a television set and no less than five portraits of Saddam on the wall. A tall, bald man wearing an olive-drab uniform with the insignia of a general of the police, the governor introduced himself as Abdul Khaliq Abdul Aziz Sayeed. Though he had been a Baath Party member for thirty-five years, there was something engagingly open about him, and he struck me as being much more honest than, say, Jaff, the chief functionary in Arbil.

Sayeed said that on March 1, with the army engaged in Kuwait, a band of Shiite fundamentalists under Iranian leaders raided the headquarters of the Karbala police and stole all of its weapons. A few days later, defecting army units joined the rebels—whom he referred to as "criminals"—to make up a force of about fifty thousand. When the army arrived from Kuwait, he said with grudging admiration, the rebels put up a tenacious fight, but they were weakened by the absence of a centralized command and strategic plans. About three thousand fighters, along with some civilian followers, retreated into the two shrines, thinking the army dared not attack them there. Only reluctantly, after the failure of a siege, did the army use its heavy guns, he said, which ended the resistance quickly. About six hundred people were killed, Sayeed said, most of them civilians—a figure which seemed low to me, judging from the devastation. In addition, three thousand, including sixty Iranians, were captured, he said. We thanked Sayeed for the account, then asked for permission to go on to An Najaf, and, to the dismay of our guide, he wrote out a paper that he said would get us through the checkpoint.

Our first impression of An Najaf came from a portrait of Saddam at the city gate: it had been penetrated by three well-aimed rockets to the face. An Najaf, however, was less damaged than Karbala. The Mosque of Ali, where the ayatollah Khomeini had prayed for fourteen years while plotting against the shah, had been hit by mortars but had survived better than the Karbala shrine. Through open doors, we could see signs of fighting inside the walls, but the guards would not allow us into the courtyard, or even to make a walking tour of the perimeter. In the normally busy marketplace adjacent to the shrine, we were struck by how few people we saw. Apart from a man on a street corner dispensing rations of water from a mule-drawn cart, there was no activity. We thought back to the effort made at the roadblock to keep us from reaching An Najaf, and we concluded that the city was on edge over a possible attack, but we left the site without seeing any military activity.

One reason I had been anxious to visit An Najaf was to call on Grand Ayatollah Abolqassem al-Khoei, a ninety-two-year-old scholar whom many Shiites venerated even more than the ayatollah Khomeini. Al-Khoei had appeared briefly in the news during the Shiite rebellion, when Saddam transported him to Baghdad to make a televised statement urging an end to the civil war. Later, Iran protested that he had been kidnapped and that his family was being held hostage. Our guide, agreeing to the visit, took us to a small mud-brick house away from the city center, where we found al-Khoei sitting in a shabby library, wearing a black turban and a brown wool robe over several layers of clothing.

The ayatollah seemed very frail, had trouble breathing and was sweating profusely. (He died the next year.) Questioned about the television incident, he replied, "I never asked for a *jihad* against Saddam Hussein. I am satisfied with the government. The rebels committed horrible crimes, and I asked Shiites to calm down." Then we asked him about his family, and as the words came out, our guide panicked. "My son, my son-in-law and others of my family—six persons in all—were arrested," al-Khoei said; "The president ordered them released, but up to now they haven't come back." At that point, the guide, with barely a thank-you, forcefully ushered us out of the house.

With the al-Khoei visit behind us, we headed out of An Najaf, taking one of Saddam's new highways, leading directly to Baghdad. Barely outside the city limits, we encountered a reminder of the earlier war. A bridge over the Euphrates blown out by American aircraft a few months before stopped our progress, and we were about to detour back the way we came when a man standing on the shoulder waved us down and suggested an alternate route. Following his instructions, we took a shaded dirt road along the river through a dense palm grove. About a mile downstream, we crossed on the top of a small dam, then headed back upstream. A mile or so beyond, a half-dozen women in long, colorful dresses stood knee-high in the river, washing clothes. It seemed like a glimpse of old Iraq—far from war and rebellion and Saddam—and it was pretty to see.

Minutes later, we regained the highway and turned north, and would have been back in Baghdad in an hour but for the indulgence requested by our guide. He wanted to stop to see his mother, who lived in a house beside the road, he said. Having forgiven him the incident in the al-Khoei house—he was, after all, doing his duty—we raised no objections. Since he invited us in, I suppose he had forgiven us, too. It was a charming house, with a grape arbor and a goat in the yard, and our guide's mother was a gracious, dignified widow who received us warmly.

Insisting on serving us tea, which she prepared over a portable gas burner, she apologized for her meager hospitality, explaining that she had no power in the house to cook. She invited us to return for dinner another time, when there would be electricity. I never saw her again, but I felt she was genuinely embarrassed at the condition in which her country and her kitchen had been left by the war, and that she really wanted us back to visit at a better time.

EPILOGUE

Unlike a book, a society is never finished. It always remains in process. The question posed by each is where it is going, and how fast. In our own time, we have seen major changes even in the highly developed societies of Western Europe, and the transformation in a few countries of East Asia has been dazzling. But most of the Third World has moved much more slowly. As for Arab society, it is not clear where it is heading, or at what speed. After three-fourths of a century, the Arab states remain on shaky feet.

The decades since the Ottoman collapse have, overall, not been gratifying for the Arabs. The parliamentary governments of the interwar period were a facade. The defeats by Israel have been humiliating. The relationship with Moscow led nowhere, and with it went the aspirations of Arab socialism. Nasser's promises of grandeur crashed in the debacle of 1967. The vision of an Arab nation has become an illusion. Most recently, the Gulf war sundered Arab society, leaving a major segment an international pariah.

As for democracy and human rights, it is apparent in retrospect that they were doomed from the start by the taint of their colonial origins. Arab scholars who sought to legitimize them by citing indigenous precedents, whether historical or religious, failed to persuade the multitudes. The idea of representative government was too unfamiliar. Even now, liberal values carry the burden of foreign rule, as well as of the West's insistent claim to ascendancy in the Middle East.

By and large, Arabs accept the judgment that their progress has been unsatisfactory. Some blame the Ottoman heritage, with its precedents of sultanic absolutism and public neglect; others, the sense of impotence left by the colonial experience. Many Arabs maintain that the West still conspires to keep them in a second-class status. Few Arabs like to hold themselves or their own culture responsible.

In fact, a strong argument can be made that Islam, the heart of Arab culture, sets the limits of personal and social development in the Arab world. Despotism, the Arabs' most pervasive political institution, is surely its offshoot, even though Islam has sometimes been at odds with its despots.

Is Islam also capable of producing offshoots that reflect liberal values? Arabs have been asking that question for a century or more. Like other religions, Islam is both theology and practice. As theology, it is probably no more limiting than the Western religions. But institutional Christianity and Judaism have retreated over the centuries before the assaults of reason, and made compromises with secular culture. Islam, however, had defeated secular, nationalist trends within its culture by the eleventh century, and has been successful ever since in fending off their rebirth. A few thinkers have argued that modernism, and even democracy, are compatible with doctrinal Islam. But whatever the implications in principle of its theology, traditional Islam prospers, promoting a stifling conservatism which preserves the social and intellectual status quo.

Influences from without still pour into the Arab world, of course. A major stratum of the population is acquainted with foreign languages and cultures, travels abroad, watches Western movies and television, follows the international press. An elite of no small number has been educated in universities in Europe and America. The language of human rights has been incorporated into Arab public discourse. Many women, and some men, have grown sensitive to the inequities of the social structure. The artifacts of wealth and technology have ignited the temptations of consumerism.

Still, the essence of Arab society has, withal, changed very little over the centuries. "The postindependence period," writes Hisham Shirabi in *Neopatriarchy*, "has produced scientists but not science, medical doctors but not medical science, social scientists but not social science." Arab culture, he tells us, continues to honor myth over reason, conformity over diversity, rhetoric over analysis. It has reached a certain level of imitation of the West, but it remains far below the level of Western creativity. An Arab professor at a West Bank university, a Muslim who taught for many years in the United States, told me that his Palestinian students, though more highly motivated and more conscientious than American students, were far more timid about exploring the bounds of knowledge. "They cannot free themselves from the habit of learning by rote," he said. "They are more sensitive to community opinion. They are more dependent on the teacher. Most striking to me, their training in the Koran teaches them that all knowledge is in the book. One can memorize the book; one can even interpret it. But a book is not a point of departure; one cannot add to it. The Islamic tradition holds that learning is fixed. My students resist going beyond the book, any book." His observations suggest why the Arabs, so adept at mastering the gadgetry of the modern world, still have trouble grasping its spirit.

In our own time, the influences arriving from the West have in fact provoked retreat. To most Arabs, Westernization means a relaxation in traditional dress codes, male-female relations, and patriarchal arrangements, all bruising departures from the status quo. On these matters, there has been some change. But intellectual rigor, the West's real gift to the modern world, has barely touched Arab civilization. While, as every Westerner knows, the consequences of this gift are by no means entirely positive, the fact remains that without it Arab society is unlikely to break the bonds of the past. Without an intellectual breakthrough, Arab society becomes increasingly hostile to foreign influences, and turns to fundamentalism as a barrier against the further bruises of change. Fundamentalism, solving nothing, offers the comforts of familiarity to a society that is reluctant to chart a new course.

Fundamentalists do not deign to engage in reasoned argument in their recruiting. Shirabi cites Egypt's Sayyid Qutb, a fundamentalist luminary, who criticizes secular values as a product of man's presumption: "Who is more knowledgeable," Qutb asks, "you or God?" Fundamentalists say that a return to the true faith will restore the putative paradise of an earlier age, and out of frustration and disillusionment millions of Muslims, in every country and social class, have taken them at their word. The few dissidents who have suggested subjecting Islam itself to a stern reexamination have been overwhelmed by the consensus on conformity. Blaming the West for every social ill, fundamentalism has become a massive movement, leading Arab society to the edge of an abyss of mindlessness.

Fundamentalism bespeaks rejection of the modern world—of the free intellectual inquiry that is intrinsic to modernism, and of the political pluralism that is basic to democracy. Is that what most Arabs want? Or, overwhelmed by the profusion of imported ideas, have they merely sought temporary refuge in fundamentalism in order to gain time to regroup?

A snapshot of the Arabs taken today shows a culture that, without much exception, offers its members a choice between secular and religious despotism. It seems possible that most Arabs have had enough of both, but see no middle ground. But a snapshot tells little of the past, and even less of the future. Surely, Arab society is still unfinished.

Indeed, in recent years more Arabs have come to recognize that building a civilization on tyranny or fanaticism, however indigenous they may be, is like building sandcastles. Human rights and the rule of reason, the foundation of modern societies, are as relevant to citizens of the East as to those of the West. The idea of freedom is unquestionably spreading, and here and there, Arabs are organizing, challenging, speaking out in its behalf. Few are optimistic that the idea will soon prevail. But it is much too early to despair; the process continues.

POSTSCRIPT

"A PLACE IN THE MODERN WORLD"

ON SEPTEMBER 13, 1993, a century of war in Palestine came to an end. To be precise, the day held out a promise of the end or, even more precisely, the beginning of the end. History, playing its customary cruel tricks, may yet consign the events of the day to the category of delusion. Still, many signs suggested that peace in the Middle East was truly, finally, at hand.

Before three thousand witnesses on the White House lawn, Yitzhak Rabin, Israel's prime minister, shook hands with Yasir Arafat, chairman of the PLO. They had come to celebrate the signing of an agreement reached in Oslo, but, more than the document, it was the handshake of these bitter enemies that betokened the new era. "We the soldiers who have returned from the battle stained with blood," declared Rabin, "we who have fought against you, the Palestinians, we say to you today in a loud and clear voice: 'Enough blood and tears! Enough!' " In response, Arafat stated: "Our people . . . , putting an end to their feelings of being wronged and having suffered an historic injustice, . . . want to give peace a real chance." The high drama of the moment was witnessed by a worldwide television audience, which included millions in Israel and the Arab lands. Many sobbed with emotion at the prospect of closing the book on an enmity that had appeared eternal.

There was neither winner nor loser among the parties that day on the White House lawn. Both had come to the table seriously wounded, one much more than the other, but each still wearing the psychological bandages of both old and recent wounds. Within each camp were partisans of fighting on, and in the hearts of Rabin and Arafat, warriors both, there surely lodged an unvoiced temptation to join them. But, aging veterans that they were, Rabin and Arafat were also weary of the struggle, and shared an understanding of how futile its prolongation would be. Their handshake, then, reflected not a sudden burst of friendly feeling, but a mutual recognition of the uselessness of further bloodshed, and a mutual choice to forswear maximalism in favor of a more constructive course.

For Rabin, the agreement was the culmination of wars won on the battlefield, then lost in the reality of the unequal relationship between Jews and Arabs in the Middle East. For Israel, the Six-Day War of 1967 was a military triumph of unparalleled magnitude. It forced the Arabs to acknowledge that the Jewish state was not the passing fancy of colonial powers, as they had so long been tempted to believe, but a presence which the Jews would fight to the death to preserve. To Israelis, victory demonstrated the limits of their military power. Israel was simply too small to dominate the Arab world. However powerful its army, it did not have the means to occupy Cairo and Damascus. And it could not prevent the Arabs from rising up from defeat to fight again and again. On the battlefield, Israel's armies repeated their triumphs in the Yom Kippur War in 1973, the war in Lebanon in 1982 and even the *intifada*; but taken together the victories only made clear that the Arab world had too much strategic depth, and that more wars awaited them. And so Rabin, the pragmatist, won out over Israel's romantics, whose visions of grandeur augured a fate of perpetual fighting. "Enough blood!" he declared, and opted for peace.

For the Palestinians, the wounds with which they entered on the course of peace were even more painful. They had not recovered from the loss of a land on which they lived for a thousand years. Only Israel's most rabid partisans would deny the validity of Palestinians' title deeds to this land, but of what use are such documents? Title deeds have never stopped the great migrations of history. Were the Arabs deterred in the seventh and eighth centuries from imposing their presence on the Middle East and North Africa? Did the Turks ask permission of the Anatolians whose lands they took a few centuries later? History assimilates its injustices and reissues them as new realities. The Palestinians could have battled on, but they too had learned the limits of their fighting potential. The *intifada* had been their most heroic moment, but it had exhausted them, and only the quixotics among them still believed they could liberate Palestine by force. Arafat, lamenting on the White House lawn the "historic injustice" that had smitten his people, was nonetheless wise enough to admit that it was irreversible. His decision was to salvage for the Palestinians what land he could.

The agreement signed in Washington had been reached in secret negotiations held in Oslo from January through August of 1993 under the sponsorship of the Norwegian government. Conducted directly between Israel and the PLO, the talks involved neither the United States nor the Arab states, and bypassed the elaborate procedures established at the Madrid conference in October 1991. Although Israel had tacitly acknowledged the PLO's presence at Madrid, at Oslo it recognized formally that the PLO spoke for the Palestinian people. The Oslo agreement fell substantially short of acknowledging the right to statehood that the Palestinians claimed. Nonetheless, it was an assertion of mutual recognition. It placed relations between Israel and the Palestinians on a level of juridical equality, thereby breaking fundamentally with the past.

The Oslo accord promised self-rule to the Palestinians in the occupied territories, an issue over which the two sides had been bargaining in vain for nearly two years. What surprised observers was the provision, never considered in the Madrid talks, that self-rule would start in the Gaza Strip and the Jericho area of the West Bank. The "Gaza and Jericho first" plan was to be the opening step in the transition, and a test of the change in the territories' status.

The accord, called a "Declaration of Principles," presented a general timetable and a set of political conditions for self-rule, the implementation of which would require still further negotiations. No one doubted that the bargaining over the specifics would be difficult. But a three-month deadline was set for the negotiators to reach agreement on the withdrawal of Israeli military forces, and the spirit in which the Oslo accord had been achieved suggested strongly that its terms would be met, perhaps even on time.

The agreement stipulated that Palestinian elections were to be held by mid-1994, by which time the occupied territories were to be free of the army, and self-rule was to apply. Israel, it was agreed, was to retain responsibility for external security, control of Jewish settlements in the territories and the governance of Arab Jerusalem. The Palestinian authority was to take responsibility for education, health care, social welfare, direct taxation and tourism, as well as the establishment of a Palestinian police force to be in charge of internal security. After the third year of self-rule, negotiations based on Security Council Resolutions 242 and 338 were to begin on a final settlement of outstanding issues. These were to include Jerusalem, the Palestinian refugees, the settlements, security arrangements, borders and relations with neighboring countries. A permanent peace agreement was to go into effect after five years of Palestinian self-rule.

The United States, which had known nothing of the Oslo negotiations, immediately endorsed the accord. The Palestinian delegation to the Washington talks, led by Haidar Abdul Shafi of Gaza, was clearly resentful at having been kept ignorant of the meetings but had no alternative to embracing the outcome. The governments of Syria and Jordan also expressed irritation at having been left in the dark. But King Hussein quickly dropped his reservations to support Arafat and, going a step further, announced his acceptance of a Jordanian-Israeli declaration of principles that had been negotiated earlier in Washington and kept pending. President Assad was characteristically more reticent, but he made no serious protest against the accord, and let it be known, moreover, that he expected his own negotiations with Israel to proceed.

Serious opposition was expressed by Hamas, the Islamic fundamentalist organization in the territories, and more vigorously by its military wings, the Islamic Jihad and the Izzadin el-Qassem Brigade, the latter named for the leader of an Islamic uprising in northern Palestine in the 1930s. Not surprisingly, the old-line rejectionist factions within the PLO, George Habash's Popular Front for the Liberation of Palestine and Nayef Hawatmeh's Democratic Front for the Liberation of Palestine, also vowed to resist the accord, and there was even some opposition within Fatah, Arafat's own faction within the PLO. But these groups, though capable of hampering implementation of the agreement, were not nearly strong enough to block it.

Surveys taken in September by competent Palestinian pollsters found that two-thirds of the residents of the territories favored the Oslo agreement, and that Fatah had overwhelming political support in both the West Bank and Gaza. Similar results emerged from polls of Israelis. Most seasoned observers, on studying the reactions of the principal parties to the conflict, came to the conclusion that the Oslo accord, the first compact ever between Israel and the Palestinians, had overcome the major barrier to an Arab-Israeli settlement, and that the parties would soon reach an agreement that would bring peace to the region.

GAZA, WHEN I ARRIVED a few weeks after the handshake on the White House lawn, was not the place I had known. It was not just the flags that struck me. The Israeli military administration, in anticipation of orders to withdraw, had dropped enforcement of the ban on the display of Palestinian flags, and from the rooftops of nearly every house flew the green, red, white and black banner that symbolized Palestinian nationalism. Their presence was a statement of hope that the occupation was about to end. But it took me a few days of driving through the city and the refugee camps to realize that the change in the atmosphere went deeper. Israeli army patrols, once ubiquitous, had virtually disappeared. The soldiers were still in their observation posts and barracks, surrounded by barbed wire. Army contingents still invaded homes in search of accused criminals, especially the killers of Israelis. But the remorselessly patrolling jeeps, carrying scowling young men in helmets and khaki nervously fingering the triggers of automatic weapons, were gone, palpably lessening the tension in the streets.

New concerns, however, were replacing the old ones. In the week or so prior to my arrival, three veteran leaders of the Fatah movement had been assassinated. All three had strongly supported the peace agreement. Since the start of the *intifada*, more Palestinians were said to have died at the hands of other Palestinians, whether in factional or personal disputes, than at the hands of Israelis. Fatah talked of setting up a secret police apparatus to protect lives, and Gazans could not help worrying whether the Israeli administration might be superseded by a Palestinian rule that presided over chaos. The assassinations spread deep forebodings.

Some Palestinians speculated that the killers were extremists from Hamas, fundamentalists prepared to do anything to scuttle the Oslo accord. Others pointed a finger at the Israelis, who in the past had been happy enough to foment discord within the Gaza leadership, although since Oslo they were apparently desisting from such agitation. But most regarded the assassinations as the product of differences among Gazans, if not disputes within Fatah itself. No one I met considered Arafat a suspect; most observers agreed that in dealing with Palestinians, Arafat was more a manipulator than a murderer.

One theory blamed the killings on the old bureaucrats at the PLO office in Tunis, anxious to eliminate rivals inside the territories. A second speculated that the *shebab*, the young men who had led the war against the army during the *intifada*, were now staking their claims against the older generation of leaders. A third saw the murders as the product of a long-dormant rivalry between clans of old Gazans and refugee families who had arrived in the Strip in flight from the Israelis in 1948. A fourth blamed class warfare, holding that Gaza's many poor were taking out their frustrations on the thin layer of the well-to-do, to whom the army accorded special privileges. Whoever was responsible, Gazans agreed that a struggle for position was underway in anticipation of the Israelis' departure.

"No one knows what's happening here. Everyone wants a piece of the action." The speaker was a native Gazan, a young man I had met on previous visits. He worked for an international NGO—non-governmental organization—that promoted better health care for Palestinians. Given the disorder in Gaza, he asked me not to use his name. But he was well connected, among both local and refugee families, and in the past I had generally found his perceptions sound. "Gazans are easily turned on and turned off," he said. "When the peace agreement was announced, they were euphoric. They were intoxicated at raising the flags, without understanding the problems they faced. Now they're beginning to understand what's ahead, and they've gone into depression.

"Everybody wants democracy, everyone talks about democracy. But for the past twenty-five years, we've had not only military occupation but the annihilation of our institutions. Not only have we had no government of our own, but no police, no courts, no administration of justice. Everyone applauds human rights but no one shows the slightest respect for anyone else's human rights. When the *intifada* started, strikes were directed against the Israelis. Now strikes are declared as a show of power by one faction against another, and it's the people who suffer. If a merchant doesn't observe the strike, his shop may be burned, or he may be beaten. He may even be declared a collaborator, which may imply a death sentence. If we are to stop the assassinations, we need a strong, well-trained local police force to keep order. But a more basic problem is that we have no respect in our culture for the freedom of others, no understanding of legitimate differences of opinion. If you don't agree, then you're an enemy.

"I expect a proliferation of militias after the Israelis leave. They're organizing already. There'll be money for economic development coming in from abroad, and they'll be competing for it. The old family feuds, which diminished during the *intifada*, are coming back. There are already plenty of handguns, maybe even a few machine guns. Some were bought from Israelis and smuggled in. Some were provided by the army to collaborators. What is more, people are hungry. The days of relative prosperity, when money was flowing in from Gazans working in Israel and the Gulf, are over, probably forever. Stress and depression have been intensifying. If the optimism of the peace agreement is not followed quickly by some real improvement in the conditions of life, anything might happen. The assassinations are a clue to what it might be. When the army goes, the lid is off."

Qassem Ali is a lean, bearded man of thirty-five, a journalist who dresses in blue jeans and earns a living as a free-lance producer for Western television networks. He told me he had been arrested five or six times by the Israelis for involvement in the *intifada*, and spent two-and-a-half years in Israeli jails. He came to visit me at the private guest house where I was staying; Gaza has no hotels. Though the city was still under curfew, the army had given him a pass in recognition of his duties as a journalist, and we were able to talk until late into the evening. Ali, too, had a grim assessment of conditions, but he saw some hopeful signs.

"The agreement didn't come a moment too soon," Ali said. "Gaza became a big jail in the last years of the *intifada*. The occupation was suffocating us. The sharing of hardship that accompanied the early fighting had disappeared. Under the curfew, people were confined to their houses, without social life. We felt that Gaza was getting smaller and smaller, that we were sliding downhill. The occupation took years from us. Everyone was paranoid. We were ready to grab at anything.

"The masses look back now and think they won a victory in the *intifada*, but it's hard to taste the fruits. The results are two or five or ten years away. But though our political differences are dangerous, I don't see a civil war. There will be victims, to be sure. There will even be more assassinations. But in time we'll settle down. Look at the problems that Russia has gone through in changing to a new regime. Look at Yugoslavia. Political transitions are hard everywhere. We won't realize democracy right away. We've learned something about the process from the Israelis. We've had the experience of elections on our university campuses and in our trade unions and professional associations. Our people have a high level of education, with practically no illiteracy. A great deal depends on the nature of the deal we strike with Israel. If Oslo is a first step toward freedom, then I think we'll go on to set up a stable society. But if it's a last step, giving a new face to occupation, then it's a catastrophe."

One morning, Haidar Abdul Shafi, the most respected public figure in Gaza, stopped by the guest house to have breakfast with me. A medical doctor, in his seventies and still practicing, Abdul Shafi was among the founders of the PLO in the 1960s, when Gaza was under the authority of Egypt. After the Israelis took over, he became inactive, but in 1991 he was selected as chief of the Palestinian delegation to Madrid, and remained in that post for the negotiations in Washington. But after ten rounds of talks in two years, he recommended that the Palestinians walk out, on the grounds that the Israelis were not negotiating in good faith. He had strongly protested the Oslo agreement when it was announced, in words that suggested that his reservations were based, at least in part, on his exclusion by Arafat from the negotiations. In our discussion he showed himself, like many Palestinians, to be in fact ambivalent toward the accord, but his influence was such that he could, if he chose, seriously undermine its implementation

Abdul Shafi told me his objections to the Oslo accord were based on PLO concessions to the Israelis which he said his delegation had resisted through dozens of Washington meetings. The most damaging, he said, was to leave the status of Arab Jerusalem and of Jewish settlements in the territories unresolved. He acknowledged that these items would be on the agenda for negotiating the territories' final status. He also conceded that formal recognition of the PLO made it possible, within the context of these negotiations, to put forward a demand for an independent Palestinian state. But then he returned to objections that were purely intra-Palestinian.

"I suppose my major concern," said Abdul Shafi, "Is that Arafat single-handedly made all the decisions. I protested his absolute rule long ago in Tunis, but nothing ever changed. I understand that as president Arafat should have certain powers, but we Palestinians are in the process of trying to get our basic rights, based on democracy and pluralism, and we have to have greater safeguards for them. Arafat is too accustomed to making all decisions himself, and the cult of personality that he has built up presents a danger. We can't leave our fate in the hands of Arafat alone."

Abdul Shafi said that under a system of democratic pluralism, he was confident that both Hamas and the PLO dissidents would become part of a healthy opposition to Arafat and Fatah's majority rule. He insisted that how well the Palestinians demonstrated their ability to run a democratic government would help determine the degree of support given by the world community to their demand for a state of their own. "I will not be an obstructionist to the agreement," he told me. "On the contrary, I am encouraging the people to take an active role in the new administration. My personal mood is not to participate myself, but I do not rule out running in the elections for the council that are to be held next year. It depends on how democratic the process turns out to be." But Abdul Shafi's final words were that he was not optimistic about the prospects for the transition to democracy.

At the headquarters of UNRWA one day, an official told me rather gloomily that he had recently been to see Arafat in Tunis to discuss the problems of the transition. UNRWA, under the mandate of the United Nations, has looked out for the needs of the Palestinian refugees, currently more than two million spread throughout the Middle East, for nearly half a century. It runs the camps, the schools, the relief programs and the clinics that serve the refugees, and it has the largest administrative staff in the Gaza Strip. This staff, nearly all of it Palestinian, will probably be absorbed into the self-rule administration. Now, in the hope that the refugee problem will at last be resolved, UNRWA is laying plans to phase itself out of existence; it has set a target of five or six years. But in the meantime, it is offering its experience and expertise to the Palestinians preparing for the new era. The UNRWA official whom I met told me he returned from Tunis very discouraged.

"The PLO never did any real planning for self-rule," he said. "By now, it should have made key appointments. We should know who's going to run the schools and the health care system. During all the decades under Egyptians and Israelis, nothing was built in Gaza. The place has only the most primitive infrastructure. It's in terrible shape. Obviously, Arafat is preoccupied by the talks with the Israelis over implementation of the Oslo agreement. Rebuilding Gaza must seem like a mundane administrative problem. But we have only a few months before the army is supposed to leave and the Palestinians take over. We haven't time to spare.

"What worries me even more than the delay is that Arafat has spent a lifetime making political deals, looking out for cronies, piling up political debts, and he may be too old to change his style. I urged him to apply a new set of standards, to appoint people for their competence. During the occupation, though the Israelis made the decisions, Gazans ran much of the civil service. They never went higher than mid-level in the bureaucracy, but some of these people are very qualified. Arafat also has a reservoir of highly experienced Palestinians who worked in the Gulf, particularly in Kuwait, and were driven out at the time of the Gulf war. They're available, and choosing the best of them could make a big difference to self-rule. Arafat told me he understood what I was saying. But so far he's given no clue to his plans."

One day I made my way to the Jabaliya camp, where I called on Abdul Fatah Othman Abu Zaida, whom I had visited after his home had been demolished by the army a few years before. At the time, three of Abu Zaida's six sons were in prison for involvement in the *intifada*. Two of them had now been released, leaving only Kamal, whose attack on an army jeep was cited as the reason for the demolition, still locked up. Four of the six, all stocky and thickset like their father, joined in on our talk. The weather was unseasonably warm, and the men all wore white cotton *galibiyas*, normally summer attire. We sat on the floor of the house which, contrary to army regulations, Abu Zaida had rebuilt. A Palestinian flag hung near the front door. Abu Zaida explained that a $3000 contribution from UNRWA gave him the means and, since his family had nowhere else to live, he took a chance and defied the regulations. Counting his wife, his sons and their wives, his three daughters and his grandchildren, twenty-five people were living in the three-room structure. If the soldiers returned to demolish the house again, he said, he would have no choice but to rebuild once more.

I had sought out Abu Zaida, a former policeman in Gaza, to inquire about his reaction to the peace agreement. I remembered him as a committed nationalist, who made no apologies for his sons' actions, even though their resistance to the occupation had cost the family its home. Before we settled in, Abu Zaida gave a sign to one of his grandsons, who a few minutes later appeared with a round of soft drinks. Abu Zaida's answer to my question was that the peace agreement was good if the Israelis left Gaza, but not so good if they stayed. His answer corresponded with what I heard from many Gazans, who had had too much of the occupation not to be skeptical of Israeli intentions. But as we talked, twenty-seven-year-old Nasser—uncharacteristically, I think, given the sternly patriarchal regime that obtains in most Palestinian families—asked if he might interrupt his father. Abu Zaida, an amiable man who was clearly proud of his sons, gave his consent.

"The Palestinian people have two opinions," said Nasser, the only son who wore a beard, "and the Islamic point of view is totally against the agreement. Islamic ideology holds that the Jews have no right to settle in

Palestine. They came from abroad to create their country, and they have no right to our land. The peace agreement is Arafat's surrender to Israeli power. I don't agree that it is a peace of the brave. Already the Israelis are showing their real aims by arguing for the narrowest possible interpretation of their obligation to withdraw their troops. Of the 13,000 Palestinians in Israeli prisons, only a few have been released. How can there be peace if this issue is not settled? I think that in the end, all Palestinians will find that the agreement is a hoax, and will be against it. And the reason I'm so sure is that I see who is behind this agreement—the great devil, the United States."

As we talked, Abu Zaida's wife meekly appeared at the door and handed in a tray with glasses of tea. Notwithstanding Nasser's harsh statement, the atmosphere was cordial, and I felt no discomfort in asking whether I could conclude from his statement that he belonged to Hamas. My question elicited howls of laughter from the assembled Abu Zaidas, suggesting that I had touched a sensitive spot. Nasser's older brother Azzedin explained that, while their father leaned toward Fatah, three of his six sons were for Hamas, a split which was unusual for Gaza families, who are normally all one or all the other. He added with a grin that the brothers routinely have loud, though not unfriendly, arguments over the dinner table.

"Peace depends on Israel's intentions," Abu Zaida said again. "The Israelis can't get rid of us, and we can't get rid of them. We won a great victory in the *intifada*, and now we have to get along with each other. I'd rather live with Israel, in fact, than with Syria, Jordan and Egypt. All of them have tortured and killed Palestinians. At least we know that the Jews are our enemy. The Arabs say they're our friends, and treat us worse than the Israelis do."

Nasser was quick to respond.

"I distinguish between Arab governments that collaborate with the West," he said, "and the Arab people, who suffer as we do. We are one people with the Arabs. We are all dedicated to Islam. We're part of the Arab people, but not of the Arab regimes. I believe that the Arab regimes are soft and weak and will disappear soon. In Algeria and Egypt, they survive only because they are protected by American tanks. America is also the source of Israel's power. I am a religious person, and it's true that my beliefs match those of Hamas. I don't believe that the peace agreement was the result of a victory in the *intifada*, though it was a great event in the life of the Palestinian people. The important thing is not to follow the *intifada* with surrender, but to make it work out into something good, and I don't think the peace agreement is good. I am convinced that Hamas's doctrine is the only way for us to get back our stolen land."

I asked Nasser whether it was not important to him to get the army out of the life of the Abu Zaida family, and to make sure that the soldiers did not return to demolish the house again. Nasser acknowledged that the army's departure was the highest priority, and said he would follow the Hamas doctrine of boycotting the self-rule authority, while doing nothing to impede Israeli withdrawal.

"I like Islam," Abu Zaida said, replying to his son, "and I'm proud to be a Muslim. But I also like reality. Can we now overcome Israeli power? The answer is no. That's reality. If peace can give us something at last, then we have to accept it."

Over the course of the next few days, I visited with several Gazans who were associated with Hamas. Almost all had done time in Israeli prisons, and were loath to admit their membership openly, pointing out that Hamas, unlike the PLO, was still illegal. They talked freely, however, and their hostility to the Oslo agreement, as well as to the larger principle of dividing up Palestine with Israel, was unequivocal. They spoke of creating an Islamic state in Gaza that would ultimately expand to include all of Palestine. Their war against the Israelis was not over, they agreed, and more violence was surely in store. "It's quite normal to spill the blood of Israelis," one militant said to me, "not because they are Jews but because they are occupying our country. The Oslo agreement has changed nothing." The men I spoke with took somewhat diverging positions on the level of cooperation they would give to the self-rule administration, including participation in elections. But what troubled all of them the most was the prospect that the PLO would use a Palestinian police force to suppress their resistance, provoking a communal war.

Wajdi Aqeel is a thirty-nine-year-old professor of botany at the Islamic University in Gaza, an institution known for its close ties to Hamas. We met in his apartment in a half-finished brick building that seemed planted in the Gaza sand. I had inadvertently arrived at the prayer hour, and Aqeel excused himself for a few minutes to finish praying. A handsome, graying man with a warm manner, he told me he had been educated at Al-Azhar, the Islamic university in Cairo, and had spent two years in Ketziot, the Israeli prison camp. He was a specialist, he said, in Darwinian theory, which he examined for inconsistencies with Islamic doctrine. He considered Darwinism to be sound for the most part, but a few of its tenets were in conflict with the Koran and so had to be rejected. Displayed on a wall of Aqeel's apartment was a certificate which he said came from the government of the United Arab Emirates in appreciation of his work in Darwinism. While we talked, his three little daughters played in an adjoining room.

"We will follow the same course as the Islamists in Cairo and Amman," Aqeel said. "We will be in opposition to the regime. We will obstruct the implementation of the Oslo agreement. But we will not use rifles against our fellow Palestinians. We will remind people every day that it was Rabin who ordered his soldiers to break our bones during the *intifada*. How can we forget that? And how can we forget the detention? I spent twenty-eight months in the desert without seeing my children. I don't think Arafat is a traitor. But he was losing support every day to the Islamic movement, and he was increasingly isolated in Tunis. The Oslo agreement, his only way out of the trap, was a mistake. Israel was losing ground in world public opinion. We could have continued in our *jihad*. The agreement gave us nothing.

"Now the conditions for our fighting the Israelis will be much harder. Israeli patrols will be fewer, and the Jews will remain inside the settlements. Without planes or mortars, it will be harder for Hamas fighters to reach them. What will be the effect of Palestinian policemen? Will they attack Hamas? No Palestinians can bear the thought of Palestinians killing each other. I can't imagine what will happen. Some PLO people say outright that the police will punish Palestinians who attack Israelis. Arafat has been more diplomatic. Maybe he'll order the police to say they didn't see the incident, or they can't control the people, or they can't find the culprits. In any case, there won't be enough police to control the resistance, no matter how many policemen Fatah recruits."

I pointed out to Aqeel that the scenario he described was a made-to-order excuse for the army to remain in Gaza. Attackes on the settlers, I said, would play into the hands of Israeli extremists, whose objective is to perpetuate the occupation.

"It's true," he answered. "It's a bad idea for Hamas to give Israel a pretext for continuing the occupation. If that happens, Fatah will proclaim, 'Hamas loves the occupation! Hamas loves the Israelis!' This would be a big loss for us. It's like a gamble between Fatah and Hamas. If peace succeeds in making conditions better in the occupied territories, Fatah gets the credit and lures away Hamas supporters. But if peace fails, the Palestinians will blame us. We are in a dilemma, and we have some important decisions to make. Even if we do not actively fight against it, I think peace will fail, but I can't be sure."

THE WEST BANK by its very nature is more relaxed than Gaza, but during the *intifada* it had been permanently on edge. I drove to Jerusalem after a week in Gaza, and I found that life on the West Bank was almost as I remembered it in the pre-*intifada* years. Jerusalem's Old City teemed with tourists, and Jewish and Arab merchants once again rubbed shoulders as they competed for customers. The restaurants of East Jerusalem had reopened, and even Israelis were beginning to drift back to sample the salads and kebabs. The universities as well as the schools were in full operation, and the students I met seemed intent on catching up on the studies they had missed during the years when the army kept the doors of their institutions closed. The West Bank's roads, winding through olive groves and across the summit of ancient hills, were relatively free of patrolling jeeps. Even the observation post overlooking the Jalazone camp in El-Bireh seemed at last to have vanished.

To be sure, a checkpoint that backed up traffic on the Nablus Road was a reminder that Palestinians still needed permission to enter Jerusalem. And, more painfully, seven Israelis were murdered in the territories in the weeks after the Washington ceremony, most of them by Hamas extremists, who in one case distributed a video boasting of their act. But—to the embarrassment of both Arafat and Rabin—at least one killing was by a band that the army described as Fatah irreconcilables. Not surprisingly, right-wing settlers responded to the murders by assaults on Arabs and violent demonstrations against the Oslo agreement. The reaction was no doubt what the killers wanted; the extremists on the two sides have always been tacit allies in opposing peace. The disorders were a reminder—if one was needed—that the road to peace was strewn with obstacles. And yet, the obstacles notwithstanding, West Bank Palestinians seemed convinced that the end of the conflict was near, and they conveyed, more than their brethren in Gaza, a sense of unwinding from the years of unremitting strain.

I drifted from Jerusalem down to Jericho one day to look for signs of the change. Jericho has the character of a town-that-time-forgot. From the hills that overlook it, its green fields and palm trees are visually exciting. Jericho, situated below sea level just north of the Dead Sea, is an oasis at the edge of the desert that extends as far as Mesopotamia. The Allenby Bridge, connecting the West Bank with Jordan, is ten minutes away by car. Jericho's trees yield oranges and bananas, and its fields produce almost every fruit and vegetable imaginable. After the 1948 war, the town became a bustling center of refugee life; in 1967, however, most of the refugees fled to the East Bank, reducing Jericho to some seven or eight thousand inhabitants, most of them dependent on field work. Once a warm-weather haven for Palestinians escaping the winter, and a favorite of Jerusalemites, the town has dozens of hotels and villas, but most have now fallen into disrepair. Jericho holds the ruins of a grand palace of the Ommayad period, but the walls blown down by Joshua have long since eroded away. Regarded by archeologists as the world's oldest settlement, dating to 8000 B.C., Jericho now waits to be rescued by the arrival of Yasir Arafat.

More or less at random, I picked out a merchant on the town square and made the mistake of asking how it felt to have his town selected as the capital of liberated Palestine. He immediately responded that Jericho was not a capital at all, that Jerusalem was the capital of Palestine. Standing amid boxes of eggplants and tomatoes, dressed in an apron and a *gabaliya*, he then allowed that the people of Jericho were proud that theirs would be the first town liberated on the West Bank, and he pointed through the trees with some disdain at the Israeli police post, surrounded by barbed wire, on the other side of the square. "Our police headquarters will be there," he said.

The merchant volunteered that Jericho expected to be well treated under self-rule because it was overwhelmingly pro-Fatah, with little support for Hamas. When I asked where the seat of Arafat's government would be, he shrugged, then said there was talk of the PLO's taking over and renovating the dilapidated Hisham Palace Hotel, with seventy rooms, on a nearby street. It was understood, he said, that the Spanish government had offered to donate the bulk of the money needed for the renovation, and that some engineers had come by to survey the site. The town had also been visited by PLO officials from Jerusalem, he said, asking about health care and unemployment problems. But the PLO and the Israelis, he pointed out, had still not reached agreement on how much of the area around Jericho would be placed under the authority of the self-rule regime. The previous week, the positive spirit of the talks had been soured by the murder of two young Israelis hiking in a nearby wadi. The people of Jericho were still hopeful about the peace agreement, the merchant said, but nothing had so far happened to improve their life.

On leaving the square, I made a tour of Jericho; it took only a few minutes to drive across the oasis from end to end. I was directed to a modest house in the hills, said to be owned by a cousin of Arafat, where the chairman was said to have originally contemplated establishing his residence. But instead he has apparently chosen a handsome villa behind a picket fence, near the middle of town, where he will be more accessible, and security will be less of a problem. I stopped for a soft drink at a restaurant that gleamed from a new paint job, and was told by the owner that he was anticipating a surge in tourists, but I saw no other place where pains were being taken to overcome years of neglect. It occurred to me that if Arafat wanted to receive visitors in a proper-looking governmental seat, it would take weeks of scrubbing just to get the graffiti off the walls.

Arafat's liaison to Jericho was operating out of a storefront headquarters on the main street, a few doors from the Hisham Palace. A ceiling fan was oscillating slowly overhead when I entered, stirring up the smoke of the half-dozen men, several of them in *kuffiyehs*, who sat around puffing on cigarettes, lazily reading newspapers. They seemed to have no other work to do. The office furniture was worn and shabby; an improvised partition, thumbtacked with photos of Arafat and other PLO notables, separated the front area from private quarters in the rear.

A small man with a Vandyke beard who told me his name was Jamil Kleifa occupied the only desk in the room. He insisted he was not in charge, however; no one is in charge, he said, and from the languid atmosphere I had no reason to doubt him. Kleifa told me the mission of the liaison was to prepare files for Arafat's arrival, and to offer itself to the people of the town as an alternative to the Israelis in dealing with problems. The power in Jericho was still exercised by the army, he said, and by a Palestinian mayor whom the army had appointed, and who was likely to remain in office until an election next year. Kleifa said he expected the Palestinian administration to be installed by January, bringing in its own people from Tunis. He said he had no idea where Arafat would live or work, nor did he convey much urgency about the need to decide such matters.

If there was any serious planning in the West Bank in preparation for Arafat's arrival, it was being done by a diverse body of specialists organized into "technical committees." These committees, with their headquarters in Jerusalem, had been formed at the time of the Madrid conference, to back up the Palestinian delegation to the peace negotiations. Having established a reputation for providing sound technical advice, the committees had gradually moved into planning for the post-occupation period.

"When the PLO's policy was to establish a single state of Muslims and Jews, it talked of a 'democratic and secular state' in Palestine," said Sari Nusseibeh, a philosophy professor at Birzeit and a member of one of Jerusalem's most distinguished families. Nusseibeh was the first chairman of the technical committees. "Then, with adoption of the two-state objective in the 1970s, the secular idea—which sounded antireligious to many Palestinians—was dropped. The democratic premise, however, remains. We all agree that what we will establish is a multi-party parliamentary system." That is the system for which the technical committees are currently drawing up plans.

"With the adoption of the declaration of principles at Oslo, we moved into a new era," said Hassan Abu Libdeh, who succeeded to the chairmanship of the committees in October, when Nusseibeh went abroad to resume his academic work. With an M.A. from Stanford and a Ph.D. from Cornell, Abu Libdeh is a professor of statistics at Birzeit and a consultant with an office in Jerusalem, which is where we met. "Instead of planning in a general way, we now have to focus on implementing the agreements that the Israelis and the PLO reach in their talks," he said. "We have about one hundred committees and subcommittees, and about four hundred experts at work, all volunteers. We are trying to prepare the documents that the emerging authority will need as it comes to confront such problems as water, transportation, energy, education and refugees. We're connected directly to Arafat's office, and we have representatives at the negotiations. But many aspects of our work can't be completed until we know the terms of agreement in each of the areas of responsibility.

"The transfer of authority will not be easy; it doesn't mean simply replacing an Israeli with a Palestinian in every office. It also means changing policies and objectives. In every field, we will have to review hundreds of military orders, many of which have been concealed from us. We have to look at the files that the army has maintained, and we have to ask many, many questions of the Israelis. We haven't yet begun working with them, but we've had some preliminary informal contacts, and the spirit has been quite satisfactory. The Israelis have agreed to cooperate, and we expect they will. But so far, Tunis has not named the people for the key posts in the administration. There's no one to give us policy guidance, or to take the work we've done and start building an administration on it. At best, the transition will be complex. We're only now beginning to understand its magnitude."

It troubles some thoughtful West Bankers that the Oslo agreement, in a sense, turned the Madrid process upside down. What began juridically as a negotiation between Israel and the territories to *avoid* PLO involvement, has been replaced by an agreement between Israel and the PLO. The change left the West Bank and Gaza with no legal standing of their own. The Oslo arrangement, of course, was what the Palestinians themselves asked for; in insisting on the PLO as their spokesman, they believed they were legitimizing a political authority that would, in time, become the government of a Palestinian state. But the absence of a formal place for the territories within the PLO structure has created misgivings. No Palestinian I encountered regrets the preeminence accorded the PLO. But some in the territories were getting nervous about being left out as they waited for Arafat to take over.

Haidar Abdul Shafi was not alone in suggesting that Arafat's triumph in Oslo had enhanced his belief in his own omniscience. Arafat negotiated the agreement without consulting the Palestinians under occupation. Now his people were negotiating the implementation of the declaration of principles without representation from the "inside," which was where the results would be applied. And, given Arafat's record, many people in the territories worried that he would ignore the work of the technical committees when he began setting up his administration.

Faisal Husseini, the Jerusalemite who was the PLO's man in the occupied territories before and during the Madrid talks, had helped Arafat to solidify his base of support "inside." In those days, West Bankers recall, the U.S. secretary of state would not talk to Arafat, but he would meet with Husseini in Jerusalem, as would other foreign luminaries. The Israelis talked to Husseini, they point out, not to Arafat. Now Arafat, enjoying direct access to President Clinton and world leaders everywhere, no longer needs Husseini, and is said to have dropped him from the inner circle. A few West Bankers went so far as to express alarm at the prospect that in place of the outsiders from Tel Aviv they were going to be ruled by the outsiders from Tunis.

"Remember that last summer the PLO seemed to have run out of options, and people were writing its death notice," said Daoud Kuttab, a veteran Palestinian journalist who contributes to a half-dozen Western publications. "It made a big comeback at Oslo, and maybe that's an illusion. The PLO thinks it has all the answers, but we're worried that it's a big mess. The technical committees have done more to plan the state in a few months of work than the PLO did in twenty years. Arafat was never good at details. He has tried to reassure the Palestinians about his competence by boasting that he once ran all of Lebanon from his little corner of Beirut. Is that what the Palestinians want? The PLO hasn't presented any political guidance from Tunis because it has no idea what's needed here.

"Arafat has an advantage because the opposition is in disarray. It has no leadership, and not a great deal of courage. It fears that if it participates in elections it wil be acquiescing in the Oslo agreement, and yet it is afraid not to. Hamas, which is much stronger in Gaza than it is here, might kill a few Israelis, but that's not a political program.

"The key to our political future is probably the *shebab*, the generation that cut its teeth on the *intifada* and is now waiting to get into politics. They all know something about the Israelis and learned Hebrew in their prisons, where they also developed strong organizational ties to the PLO. Arafat was very clever in identifying himself with their cause, and they remember that. Their targets are not Arafat himself but the old-timers who have been around him for decades. These old-timers don't want any elections, and they will try to find a pretext for cancelling, or at least postponing, them. Arafat has got to recognize that they're a liability. He once said that, if forced to make a choice, he'd choose what's best for the Palestinian people over what's best for the PLO. Does that mean he's ready to dump them? Arafat has survived all this time because he's a skillful politician. I think it's possible that when he makes contact with the people, and no longer needs the old-timers, we'll see them pensioned off.

"What concerns me is that a power vacuum is already developing in the towns and the camps. The Israelis are largely out and the PLO is not yet in. There are a lot of young men around with guns. They are not primarily political, but some of them are organized into vigilante bands, and they're dangerous. If the PLO is too slow in exercising its authority, it may find it's lost the chance to impose real restraints on them."

Most Palestinians agree that Fatah currently has a safe margin of political control in the West Bank. Hamas's appeal on the West Bank receded with the signing of the Oslo accord, and it seems unlikely that the Islamic extremists who are assassinating Israelis have contributed to the organization's support. The PLO's rejectionist factions, the Popular Front and the Democratic Front, had a following among among West Bank students and intellectuals attracted to their hard-line Marxism. But their long dependence on Moscow became a debilitating weakness when the Soviet Union dissolved. Still, there remain rejectionists faithful to the old line, hoping that a failure by Arafat will give them a renewed political life.

"I'm not opposed just to the Oslo agreement; I've been opposed to the peace talks since they started in the aftermath of the Gulf war." The speaker was Dr. Mohammed Jadallah, a fifty-two-year-old surgeon who, besides running a chain of clinics in the West Bank and Gaza, has long been a leader in the Democratic Front. Sitting with me over coffee in the garden of my hotel, he delivered harsh judgments, but so amiably that he seemed far from threatening. "I think this peace agreement is part of an American plan to reorganize the region in a way that serves U.S. interests," he said. "Israel is America's partner. It is the region's greatest military power. Now it is about to become a economic superpower. The economy of the territories will remain a captive of Israel's economy. This peace is America's way of imposing its own power in the area, and the stupid Palestinian side is falling into the trap.

"I say, what's in the agreement for us? Will it satisfy our national aspirations? Israel remains determined to block them. The Palestinians will have little power in the occupied territories, and Jerusalem, where I live, is a no-man's-land. There is no provision for the refugees living in foreign countries. I tried my best to find something positive in this agreement, and I found nothing. It might bring some temporary relief, but it is not a step toward a solution.

"Our problem, in the opposition, used to be with the Israeli army. Now we'll have a Palestinian administration to persecute us, in the name of democracy and peace. Instead of facing just Israel, we'll be squeezed between Israelis and Palestinians. Our task will be to keep ourselves alive.

"But we are too numerous to destroy. I myself may be too old to fight, but that is not true of my teenage sons, who don't believe in negotiations at all. They've been raised on the *intifada* and they are much more extreme than I. They threw bombs at the Israelis, against my wishes, and I didn't even know it until the army arrested them and sent them to prison. They think Israel will never leave without violence, and, much as I dislike what happened to them, I agree. If Israel withdraws and there's no more occupation, then I'll say I'm wrong. But I must be loyal to my fears."

The anger that Dr. Jadallah attributed to his sons, who are children of the West Bank elite, is surely no less than that of the sons of Abu Wajdi, offspring of the refugee camps. Abu Wajdi is the patriarch of the Ramahi family, whom I visited several years ago in the Jalazone camp, when four of his nine sons were in prison for *intifada* activities, and one was in hiding. All were now back home, he said, but one walks with a limp, another recently had back surgery and a third has a chronic stomach disorder, all from wounds received in encounters with Israeli soldiers or settlers. Rada, his wife, who once suffered a broken leg protecting one of her sons from a beating, said she was glad she no longer had to spend so much of her time visiting her children, bringing them books and home-made food, in prisons and detention camps in Israel and the occupied territories.

Abu Wajdi told me the Ramahi family had had one major run-in with the army since my previous visit. It had occurred two years before, when Jalazone was still a daily battlefield between the soldiers and the *shebab*. He was sitting on the threshold of his front door, he said, when an Israeli patrol came by and, without giving any reason, entered the house for a search. He said he resisted, and after the ensuing scuffle, in which several shots were fired, three of his sons were taken to a nearby military station. There, he said, he pressed a formal complaint against the patrol's behavior, and in response to his audacity a group of soldiers returned a few hours later and threatened to shoot him, leaving only after turning over the furniture in the house. A few days later, he said, the army filed against him the unlikely charge that he had attempted to take a gun from one of the soldiers. He told me he was imprisoned for a week, when the charge was dropped, but his sons remained locked up for three months.

Since the declaration of principles was signed, Abu Wajdi said, the army had cut back on its patrols and the Jalazone camp has been calm. On the day of my visit, it seemed almost sleepy. Two weeks later, however, I read in the press that Jewish vigilantes had retaliated against an attack on West Bank settlers by burning down a school in Jalazone. A spokesman for the settlers said the retaliation was the work of a minority, but that the settler community was supportive of such practices. Abu Wajdi's sons admitted that it would be hard for them to overcome the anger generated by their years of struggle with the settlers and the army.

"We've had too many broken bones," said Murad, who was twenty-three, and who noted proudly that the entire family was affiliated with Fatah. Two of the sons were wearing Fatah T-shirts, displaying crossed

Palestinian flags. Another shirt bore Arafat's face. "We've had too many demolished houses to forget the occupation," said Murad. "There's too much bitterness." Then, repeating the PLO line, he said, "But we don't want any more killing, any more war. The good thing is that now we're getting our independent state." Then he added wryly, "If we get it."

Abu Wajdi was more upbeat than his sons about the future. He was, in fact, much more assertive than he had been at our last meeting, when Rada had done most of the talking. My first thought was that his positive outlook was the product of his children's return. "I thank God none of my sons are in prison any more," he said at one point. But there was another factor. The last time I had seen Abu Wajdi he was unemployed, and now he was working as a guard, he told me, at a nearby UNRWA warehouse. None of his sons had jobs, nor did the family have money to send any of them back to school. Two of them did some part-time dishwashing in the kitchen of a Ramallah restaurant, but all of them carried green identity cards, which made them ineligible to cross into Israel for work. Abu Wajdi's first comment about the impending peace was that it was supposed to bring factories to the West Bank, which would mean jobs for his sons. But he clearly felt good at being the family breadwinner again, which may also explain why his wife was so much more deferential to him.

"I think this agreement is worth it, even though I can never forget my village," Abu Wajdi said. Both he and Rada, I recalled, came from a village near Lod, the site of Ben-Gurion Airport in Israel. "But if someone asked whether I'd favor Syria's getting my village back in a war, I'd say no. Sure, if the peace agreement stops at Jericho and we don't get back the entire West Bank, I'll feel differently. Then we'd have to resume the *intifada*, and though I would not want to endure again the suffering that our family has gone through, I would be proud to be the father even of forty sons in the resistance. But we don't want to make another war with Israel. We're tired.

"My sons are strong supporters of Arafat, more than I am. I'm willing to follow anyone who brings us peace with justice. But I remember that Arafat is the first man—after the Ottomans, the British, the Jordanians, the Israelis—to raise the Palestinian flag over Palestine. He deserves my support. He says we'll have a Palestinian state in five years. I will give my sons to his army—his police force. But a Palestinian army would not have the spirit of the *intifada*, and it would certainly not win a victory against Israel. Israel is simply too strong. Arafat had courage to negotiate with the Israelis, and I must follow him in getting back our territory by peace."

. . .

JORDAN WAS GETTING READY FOR PEACE, and a new election, when I made a brief visit to Amman for an interview with King Hussein. The date of the election was set last summer, and when the Oslo agreement was announced in September, there was speculation that Hussein would postpone it, to give himself time to rally support. The king, however, quickly sensed that the agreement was so popular that it would actually strengthen his hand. He placed some restrictions on public campaigning, in order to keep the anti-peace forces from massing in the streets. But the candidates rallied their supporters in indoor meetings and covered Amman with campaign banners, and when I arrived the city was reverberating with excitement. The press reported freely on the campaign, and for the first time lists were presented by organized political parties, of which there were no less than twenty-two on the ballot. On one level, the voting was to determine whether the Muslim Brotherhood would hang on to its control of a parliamentary majority. But effectively, the election was a referendum on King Hussein's support of the agreement to make peace with Israel.

While ostensibly neutral, the king—or, more precisely, the king's men—proclaimed loudly that peace with Israel was good not just for the Palestinians but for Jordan. In rural Jordan, the king could count on the votes of the tribesmen, who loyally delivered to Parliament a large body of pro-Hashemites. The swing votes were in Amman and other major cities, where political debate, particularly over economic matters, was intense. The king's officials argued that the Jordanian economy would enjoy a burst of new vigor under the impact of relations with the West Bank, and even with Israel itself. I found a clue that their arguments were working in an article in an Amman newspaper which said that, both at the university and in special institutes, registration had soared in classes teaching Hebrew. "Hebrew may not exactly be the language of love," wrote the reporter of the story, "but maybe it will be one of the languages of peace."

The election, which took place two weeks after I left Amman, ended in a severe defeat for the Brotherhood, which lost six of its twenty-two members of Parliament, including Abdel Latif Arabiyat, the mild-mannered leader of the Islamic bloc with whom I had had an interview on the eve of the Gulf war. Sheikh Abdul Mun'im Abu Zant, the fiery orator who had denounced American involvement in the Gulf during my 1990 visit, was reelected, but nine independent Islamic candidates, allies of the Brotherhood, were also defeated, breaking the fundamentalists' parliamentary hold. On the whole, the secular political parties also did poorly; most of the victors, even in the cities, were listed as independents. Among the winners were Taher Masri, kin of the Masris of Nablus and former Jordanian prime minister, and Abdul Rauf Rawabdeh, the former mayor of Amman. Most astonishing of all, however, the victorious candidates included Toujan Faisal, the feminist crusader whose life was threatened by the fundamentalists when she ran in 1989. I spoke briefly to her while I was in Amman, and she said she was still being targeted by the Brotherhood, but was confident of winning if the ballot boxes were not stuffed. None of the candidates claimed the elections were rigged, and she became the first woman elected to Parliament in Jordan's history.

It would be an overstatement to say that King Hussein, when I saw him, looked happy. As I have written before, he is a man who seems weighed down by the melancholy burden of the Arab past. But for someone who only last year had surgery for cancer, he appeared remarkably healthy. And if I were asked to assess the message transmitted by his eyes and facial expression, I would describe it as satisfaction. Why not? I thought. King Hussein had earned the right to feel that the impending peace had vindicated his life's work.

"My grandfather sought a solution to the Arab-Israeli conflict, and lost his life in the process," he said. We talked in a sitting room of the palace, furnished in easy chairs and Chinese vases, beneath a huge crystal chandelier. Wearing a blue blazer and gray slacks, the king spoke into a small microphone, which was connected to a tape recorder brought in by an aide. "My grandfather was an Arab nationalist," he continued, in his polite and formal way, "who contributed his utmost to an Arab revival. He was a pious man and, like everyone in our family, proud to belong to the oldest tribe in Arabia, the Quraysh, and to trace his descent to the Prophet Mohammed. The major problem encountered by him over the years was the tension leading to the establishment of Israel, and the violence leading to the first Arab-Israeli war.

"As a Hashemite and a Muslim, he considered it his duty—as I considered it mine—to do whatever was possible to achieve a solution to the problem. It was a source of instability in our entire region. As a Muslim, faithful to my religion, I cannot look at the Koran, the holy book treasured by all of us in the Arab world, without realizing that the essence of it is to recognize the rights of all the followers of the monotheistic faiths. My grandfather had a vision. He was humane in his approach, and he could see that the conflict was exploited by everyone who tried to climb the ladder of power."

I asked the king how he answers the fundamentalists who maintain that the Koran forbids surrender to the Jews of any Islamic lands, and particularly of Jerusalem.

"The fundamentalists are speaking nonsense," he replied with a slight nervous laugh. "That's their opinion, but that's not how it is. The Koran doesn't preach hatred and violence. It speaks warmly of Judaism and Christianity, the religions that preceded Islam. The Arabs and the Jews have a common history, and this problem arose only in the last century. It is an incorrect reading of the Koran to say that this little piece of land is Islamic, or that a Jewish state is not permissible in Palestine."

Regarding Jerusalem, however, the king took a sterner tone. Jerusalem, he said, was not a political question but a religious challenge to adherents of the three monotheistic faiths. He proposed working out Jerusalem's status in an interfaith dialogue. "The three religions can meet in love and awe of Almighty God, who alone is sovereign over the Holy Places," he said, and solve the Jerusalem problem, a solution that would take on meaning as a symbol of permanent peace.

The king called 1974 the turning point in Palestinian relations with Jordan. That was the year, he said, in which the Arab summit at Rabat, after a rancorous debate, designated the PLO as the Palestinians' legitimate representative, "freeing the Palestinians of the Hashemite regency." He acknowledged that this decision was a personal disappointment, even a reproach, but he said he accepted it, and worked over the years to persuade Israel to settle the conflict through the PLO. He tried to work with the Palestinians until 1988, he said, when he had to recognize that his efforts were leading nowhere, and that Jordan's total disengagement from the West Bank was the only sensible course.

"I carried a heavy burden in all these years," the king said, "seeing blood being shed and people suffering and wasted toil. Nothing was uglier than living with this agony day in and day out, night in and night out, year in and year out. The story to me is one of many lost chances. I think the Palestinians have long been ready to make peace. Now it's dawned on the Israelis too that this was the only way to go. The handshake in Washington meant that the two were finally able to meet in broad daylight. It's the breaking of a new dawn."

When I asked whether he agreed that he had been vindicated by the Oslo agreement, for both himself and his grandfather, the king answered with characteristic self-effacement. "I don't want to call it vindication," he said. "I did what I did because I believe in it. It is why I exist. It was my duty. I had to live with myself before God. I've tried my best." At that point, I thought I perceived one of the wry smiles the king occasionally permits himself, conveying exasperation at the world's misunderstanding of him.

The king distanced himself from his forebears only when I asked whether he now shared the dream of his great-grandfather, Sharif Hussein, who aspired to rule over the "Arab nation." "The Hashemites should rule the Arab world?" he asked rhetorically, with unusual emotion. "No way!"

He maintained that most of the recent attempts at Arab unity had come about "at the whims of leaders" who did not go deeply enough to create links between people. The destiny of the Arabs is not now the unity that was envisaged at the time of the Arab Revolt, but a unity of equals along European lines. The system of Arab states is here to stay, he said, and whatever leadership the Hashemites exert will be within that framework.

"When I saw the ceremony in Washington," the king said, "I reflected on how much we Hashemites had contributed to bringing the Palestinians to that point. I hadn't known about Arafat's negotiations. I was shocked initially. I was not pleased at having come out of meetings in which the Palestinians assured me that we Arabs were all coordinating our talks with Israel, then suddenly learning of this major step which I had known nothing about. Maybe if I were a different person, I'd do damage, but that's not my way. I called on the Palestinian people to come together to avoid fragmentation, and to support them I ratified our own agenda with Israel, on which I'd been holding off, waiting for the Palestinian negotiations in Washington to produce concrete results."

The king predicted that Jordan would serve as the anchor in the implementation of peace, protecting and helping the Palestinians. Denying the imminence of "confederation," he said it did not matter what political form the Jordanian-Palestinian relationship took, as long as both worked conscientiously toward erasing any divisions between them. Time, he said, would permit the issue of confederation to take care of itself; meanwhile, he looked forward to normal relations with Israel, including economic relations, within the context of peace. "I don't accept the argument that peace is dangerous because Israel is an economic powerhouse. We too have achieved something substantial, with very little." He said he was confident that Syria and Lebanon would soon be parties to peace, and he added the hope that Iraq would find its way back into the family of nations.

How will the Arabs respond, I asked the king, to the absence of the conflict with Zionism from their longstanding agenda?

"After the Arab revolt and the dissolution of the Ottoman empire, the dreams and hopes of the Arabs were shattered," he answered. "There was an association in the minds of many Arabs between this letdown and Zionism, one which we may finally be able to lay aside. In the absence of conflict, the Arab world will gain the opportunity to look inward. Zionism became the reason for the upheavals promoted by power-hungry groups. My late grandfather was a visionary, but others in the Arab world assumed power because of a hunger to assume power. The reason is now removed, and we must look at what has really been wrong with us.

"I foresee a revival of the spirit of the Arab people, much of which was lost after the Arab Revolt in 1917–1918. The Arabs never enjoyed the fruits of their revolt. Now I see the chance for the Arabs to regain a place in the modern world. Islam is a progressive religion. The Arabs in their history have contributed to human progress. My hope is now for a new openness to the rest of the world, to enrich others as well as ourselves. We need a sense of security, to know that we won't wake up in the morning to find war. But we will never have stability in the region without respect for the individual, and without the individual's knowing that he matters.

"Unless the Arab regimes understand the need to evolve and allow the people to shape their own future, they're in jeopardy. For too long, the Arabs have been ruled by governments which, if foreign, they'd have revolted against. Now we need pluralism, democracy, respect for human rights and the creation of institutions that by themselves will prevent the possibility of the kind of eruptions that this area has suffered for so long."

As he so often does, the king returned to the renaissance of democracy in Jordan, which he regards as a gift to the Arab world.

"I don't think we'd have survived here in Jordan, especially after the start of the Gulf crisis, without the rebirth of democracy. At a time when we were isolated, it gave us a sense of solidarity and of sharing. I'm tired of being asked if Israel is a threat. The basic threat to the Arabs is not Israel. The threat is our own doubts about our self-worth, our doubts about our ability to measure up with the rest of the world. Arabs are threatened by Arabs. If we succeed in our democratic undertaking here in Jordan, we will succeed beyond our borders. For the sake of the whole region, we don't want to fail."

Washington, D.C.
November 1993

Bibliography

Abdalla, Ahmed. *The Student Movement and National Politics in Egypt.* London: Al Saqi, 1985.

Abdallah, King. *My Memoirs Completed.* London: Longman, 1978.

Abu-Hakima, Ahmad Mustafa. *The Modern History of Kuwait, 1750–1965.* N. P., m.d.

Abujaber, Raouf S. *Pioneers over Jordan.* London: Tauris, 1989.

Ajami, Fouad. *The Vanished Imam: Musa al Sadr and the Shia of Lebanon.* Ithaca, N.Y.: Cornell, 1986.

Antonius, George. *The Arab Awakening.* New York: Capricorn, 1946.

Armstrong, H. C. *Grey Wolf.* New York: Penguin, 1937.

Armstrong, John A. *Nations Before Nationalism.* Chapel Hill: U. of North Carolina, 1982.

Armstrong, Karen. *A History of God.* New York: Knopf, 1993.

Badeeb, Saeed M. *The Saudi-Egyptian Conflict over North Yemen, 1962–70.* Boulder, Colo.: Westview, 1986.

Baker, Randall. *King Husain and the Kingdom of Hejaz.* Cambridge, Eng.: Oleander, 1979.

Baker, Raymond W. *Egypt's Uncertain Revolution Under Nasser and Sadat.* Cambridge, Mass.: Harvard, 1978.

Barakat, Halim. *The Arab World: Society, Culture, and State.* Berkeley: U. of California, 1993.

Barbir, Karl K. *Ottoman Rule in Damascus, 1708–1758.* Princeton: Princeton Univ., 1980.

Barreau, Jean-Claude. *De l'Islam et du monde moderne.* Paris: Le Pré aux Clercs, 1991.

Batatu, Hanna. *The Old Social Classes and the Revolutionary Movements of Iraq.* Princeton: Princeton Univ., 1978.

Bavly, Dan, and Salpeter, Eliahu. *Fire in Beirut.* New York: Stein & Day, 1984.

Becker, Jillian. *The PLO.* New York: St. Martin's, 1984.

Bell, Gertrude. *The Desert and the Sown.* Boston: Beacon, 1987.

Berque, Jacques. *Cultural Expression in Arab Society Today.* Austin: U. of Texas, 1978.

———. *L'Islam au defi.* Paris: Gallimard, 1980.

Bidwell, Robin L., ed. *Arab Personalities of the Early Twentieth Century.* Cambridge, Eng.: Oleander, 1986.

Birks, J. S., and Sinclair, C. A. *Arab Manpower.* New York: St. Martin's, 1980.

Brierly, J. L. *The Law of Nations.* Oxford, Eng.: Oxford U., 1955.

Bridge, Antony. *Suleiman the Magnificent.* New York: Dorset, 1966.

Bulloch, John. *The Persian Gulf Unveiled.* New York: Congdon & Weed, 1984.

——— and Morris, Harvey. *Saddam's War.* London: Faber, 1991.

Bronowski, J., and Mazlish, Bruce. *The Western Intellectual Tradition.* New York: Harper, 1960.

Chahin, M. *The Kingdom of Armenia.* New York: Dorset, 1987.

Cleveland, William L. *Islam Against the West.* Austin: U. of Texas, 1985.

Cobban, Helena. *The Palestinian Liberation Organization.* Cambridge, Eng.: Cambridge Univ., 1984.

Cohen, Amnon. *Political Parties in the West Bank Under the Jordanian Regime, 1949–1967.* Ithaca, N.Y.: Cornell, 1982.

Cohen, Roger, and Gatti, Claudio. *In the Eye of the Storm.* New York: Farrar, Straus, 1991.

Cooper, Mark N. *The Transformation of Egypt.* Baltimore, Md.: Johns Hopkins, 1982.

Coulson, Noel J. *Conflicts and Tensions in Islamic Jurisprudence.* Chicago: U. of Chicago, 1969.

Cottrell, Alvin J., ed. *The Persian Gulf States*. Baltimore, Md.: Johns Hopkins, 1980.

Crystal, Jill. *Oil and Politics in the Gulf: Rulers and Merchants in Kuwait and Qatar*. Cambridge, Eng.: Cambridge U., 1990.

Darwish, Adel, and Alexander, Gregory. *Unholy Babylon: The Secret History of Saddam's War*. New York: St. Martin's, 1991.

Dawisha, Adeed I. *The Arab Radicals*. New York: Council on Foreign Relations, 1986.

————. *Syria and the Lebanese Crisis*. New York: St. Martin's, 1980.

Dawisha, Karen. *Soviet Foreign Policy Towards Egypt*. New York: St. Martin's, 1979.

Darwiche, Fida. *The Gulf Stock Exchange Crash*. London: Croom Helm, 1986.

Dawn, C. Ernest. *From Ottomanism to Arabism*. Urbana: U. of Illinois, 1973.

Day, Arthur R. *East Bank/West Bank*. New York: Council on Foreign Relations, 1986.

Delafon, Gilles. *Beyrouth: Les Soldats de l'Islam*. Paris: Stock, 1989.

d'Entreves, A. P. *Natural Law: An Introduction to Legal Philosophy*. London: Hutchinson House, 1951.

Devlin, John F. *Syria: Modern State in an Ancient Land*. Boulder, Colo.: Westview, 1983.

Dietl, Wilhelm. *Holy War*. New York: Macmillan, 1984.

Djait, Hichem. *Europe and Islam*. Berkeley: U. of California, 1985.

Dockrill, Michael L. and Goold, J. Douglas. *Peace Without Promise: Britain and the Peace Conferences, 1919–1923*. London: Batsford, 1981.

Drysdale, Alasdair, and Hinnebusch, Raymond A. *Syria and the Middle East Peace Process*. New York: Council on Foreign Relations, 1991.

Dunn, Ross E. *The Adventures of Ibn Battuta*. Berkeley: U. of California, 1989.

Ebraheem, Hassan. *Kuwait and the Gulf*. London: Croom Helm, 1984.

El-Azhary, M. S. *The Iran-Iraq War*. New York: St. Martin's, 1984.

Elon, Amos. *Flight into Egypt*. New York: Doubleday, 1980.

Emerson, Gloria. *Gaza*. New York: Atlantic Monthly, 1991.

Enayat, Hamid. *Modern Islamic Political Thought*. Austin: U. of Texas, 1982.

Esposito, John L. *Islam and Politics*. Syracuse: Syracuse U., 1984.

Fahmy, Ismail. *Negotiating for Peace in the Middle East*, Baltimore, Md.: Johns Hopkins, 1983.

Farouk-Slugett, Marion, & Slugett, Peter. *Iraq since 1958*. London: Tauris, 1990.

Finnie, David H. *Shifting Lines in the Sand: Kuwait's Elusive Frontier with Iraq*. Cambridge, Mass.: Harvard, 1992.

Finucane, Ronald C. *Soldiers of Faith: Crusaders and Moslems at War*. London: Dent, 1983.

Fisk, Robert. *Pity the Nation: The Abduction of Lebanon*. New York: Atheneum, 1990.

Flapan, Simha, ed. *When Enemies Dare to Talk*. London: Croom Helm, 1979.

Freud, Sigmund. *Moses and Monotheism*, in vol. XXIII of The Standard Edition of the Complete Psychological Works of Sigmund Freud. London: Hogarth Press, 1964.

Fromkin, David. *A Peace to End All Peace: Creating the Modern Middle East, 1914–1922*. New York: Holt, 1989.

Funck-Brentano. *The Renaissance*. London: Centenary, 1936.

Gabriel, Richard. *Operation Peace for Galilee*. New York: Hill and Wang, 1984.

Gabrieli, Francesco. *Arab Historians of the Crusades*. New York: Dorset, 1989.

———. *The Arab Revival*. London: Thames & Hudson, 1961.

Gershoni, Israel, and Jankowski, James P. *Egypt, Islam, and the Arabs*. New York: Oxford, 1987.

Ghabra, Shaleeg N. *The Palestinians in Kuwait*. Boulder, Colo.: Westview, 1987.

Ghareeb, Edmund. *The Kurdish Question*. Syracuse: Syracuse U., 1981.

Gibbon, Edward. *Decline and Fall of the Roman Empire*. London: Everyman Library, 1900.

Gilmour, David. *Lebanon: The Fractured Country*. New York: St. Martin's, 1984.

Glubb, John B. *The Changing Scenes of Life*. London: Quartet, 1983.

———. *The Great Arab Conquests*. London: Quartet, 1980.

———. *A Short History of the Arab Peoples*. New York: Dorset, 1969.

———. *Soldiers of Fortune*. New York: Dorset, 1973.

von Grunebaum, Gustave E. *Islam: Essays in the Nature and Growth of a Cultural Tradition*. New York: Barnes & Noble, 1961.

Halsell, Grace. *Journey to Jerusalem*. New York: Macmillan, 1981.

Haim, Sylvia, ed. *Arab Nationalism*. Berkeley, Calif.: U. of California, 1976.

Halpern, Manfred. *The Politics of Social Change in the Middle East and North Africa*. Princeton, N.J.: Princeton U., 1970.

Hamidullah, Muhammad. *Muslim Conduct of State*. Lahore, Pakistan: Kashmiri Bazar, 1945.

Hammel, Eric. *The Root: The Marines in Beirut, August 1982–February 1984*. New York: Harcourt, 1985.

Hart, Alan. *Arafat*. London: Sidgwick & Jackson, 1984.

Heikal, Mohamed. *Autumn of Fury*. New York: Random House, 1983.

———. *The Cairo Documents*. New York: Doubleday, 1973.

———. *Cutting the Lion's Tail*. New York: Arbor House, 1987.

———. *The Sphinx and the Commissar*. New York: Harper & Row, 1978.

Heller, Mark. *A Palestinian State*. Cambridge, Mass.: Harvard, 1983.

Helms, Christine M. *Iraq: The Eastern Flank of the Arab World*. Washington, D.C.: Brookings, 1984.

Henderson, Simon. *Instant Empire*. San Francisco: Mercury House, 1991.

Heper, Metin. *The State Tradition in Turkey*. London: Eothen, 1985.

Hitti, Philip K. *Capital Cities of Arab Islam*. Minneapolis: U. of Minnesota, 1973.

———. *History of the Arabs*. New York: St. Martin's, 1970.

———. *Islam: A Way of Life*. Chicago: Regnery Gateway, 1970.

Hodges, Richard, and Whitehouse, David. *Mohammed, Charlemagne & the Origins of Europe*. Ithaca, N.Y.: Cornell, 1983.

Holt, P. M. *Egypt and the Fertile Crescent, 1516–1922.* Ithaca, N.Y.: Cornell, 1966.

Hourani, Albert. *Arabic Thought in the Liberal Age, 1798–1939.* Oxford: Oxford U., 1970.

———. *Europe and the Middle East.* Berkeley: U. of California, 1980.

———. *A History of the Arab Peoples.* Cambridge, Mass.: Harvard, 1991.

Hudson, Michael C. *Arab Politics: The Search for Legitimacy.* New Haven, Conn.: Yale, 1977.

Hurewitz, J. C. *The Struggle for Palestine.* New York: Norton, 1950.

Irani, George E. *The Papacy and the Middle East.* Notre Dame: U. of Notre Dame, 1986.

Ismael, Jacqueline S. *Kuwait.* Syracuse, N.Y.: Syracuse U., 1982.

Ismael, Tareq Y. *The Arab Left.* Syracuse, N.Y.: Syracuse U., 1976.

Issawi, Charles. *An Economic History of the Middle East and North Africa.* New York: Columbia, 1982.

———. *The Fertile Crescent, 1800–1914: A Documentary History.* New York: Oxford, 1988.

———. *Egypt in Revolution.* New York: Oxford, 1963.

Itzkowitz, Norman. *Ottoman Empire and Islamic Tradition.* Chicago: U. of Chicago, 1972.

Jansen, G. H. *Militant Islam.* New York: Harper, 1979.

Jansen, Michael. *The Battle of Beirut.* London: Zed, 1982.

Johnson, Maxwell O., "A New Assessment of the Arab Army's Role in the Great Arab Revolt, 1916–1918." M.A. Thesis, American University of Beirut, unpublished, 1974.

Kabbani, Rana. *Europe's Myths of the Orient.* Bloomington: Indiana U., 1986.

Karpat, Kemal H., ed. *Political and Social Thought in the Contemporary Middle East.* New York: Praeger, 1982.

Karsh, Efraim, and Rautsi, Inari. *Saddam Hussein.* New York: Macmillan, 1991.

Kays, Doreen. *Frogs and Scorpions.* London: Muller, 1984.

Kedouri, Elie. *Islam in the Modern World.* New York: Holt, 1980.

————. *Democracy and Arab Political Culture.* Washington, D.C.: Washington Institute for Near East Policy, 1992.

Kelly, Marjorie, ed. *Islam: The Religious and Political Life of a World Community.* New York: Praeger, 1984.

Kennedy, Hugh. *The Early Abbasid Caliphate.* London: Croom Helm, 1981.

Kepel, Gilles. *Muslim Extremism in Egypt.* Berkeley: U. of California, 1985.

Kessler, Martha N. *Syria: Fragile Mosaic of Power.* Washington, D.C.: National Defense University Press, 1987.

Khadduri, Majid. *Arab Contemporaries.* Baltimore, Md.: Johns Hopkins, 1973.

————. *The Gulf War.* New York: Oxford U., 1988.

————. *Political Trends in the Arab World.* Baltimore, Md.: Johns Hopkins, 1970.

————. *War and Peace in the Law of Islam.* Baltimore, Md.: Johns Hopkins, 1955.

Khalaf, Samir. *Lebanon's Predicament.* New York: Columbia, 1987.

Khalidi, Rachid. *Under Siege: PLO Decisionmaking During the 1982 War.* New York: Columbia, 1986.

Khalidi, Walid. *All That Remains: The Palestinian Villages Occupied and Depopulated by Israel in 1948.* Washington, D.C.: Institute for Palestine Studies, 1992.

————. *Conflict and Violence in Lebanon.* Cambridge, Mass.: Harvard, 1981.

Khoury, Philip S. *Syria and the French Mandate.* Princeton: Princeton U., 1987.

Kinross, Lord. *The Ottoman Centuries: The Rise and Fall of the Turkish Empire.* New York: Morrow, 1977.

Kunstel, Marcia, and Albright, Joseph. *Their Promised Land.* New York: Crown, 1990.

Laffin, John. *Rhetoric & Reality: The Arab Mind Considered.* New York: Taplinger, 1975.

Lamb, David. *The Arabs.* New York: Random House, 1987.

Laroui, Abdallah, *The Crisis of the Arab Intellectual.* Berkeley: U. of California, 1976.

Lawrence, Bruce B. *Defenders of God*. New York: Harper, 1989.

Lawrence, T. E. *Seven Pillars of Wisdom*. New York: Penguin, 1979.

Lenczowski, George. *The Middle East in World Affairs*. Ithaca, N.Y.: Cornell, 1980.

Lesch, Ann M. *Arab Politics in Palestine, 1917–1939*. Ithaca, N.Y.: Cornell, 1979.

———. and Tessler, Mark. *Israel, Egypt, and the Palestinians from Camp David to Intifada*. Bloomington: Indiana U., 1989.

Lewis, Archibald R. *Nomads and Crusaders, 1000–1368 A.D.* Bloomington: Indiana U., 1988.

Lewis, Bernard. *The Arabs in History*. New York: Harper, 1966.

———. *The Emergence of Modern Turkey*. New York: Oxford, 1968.

———. *The Muslim Discovery of Europe*. New York: Norton, 1982.

———. *The Political Language of Islam*. Chicago: U. of Chicago, 1988.

Lewis, Geoffrey. *Turkey*. New York: Praeger, 1960.

Lewis, Raphaela. *Everyday Life in Ottoman Turkey*. New York: Dorset, 1971.

Maalouf, Amin. *The Crusades Through Arab Eyes*. New York: Schocken, 1984.

MacDonald, Robert W. *The League of Arab States*. Princeton: Princeton U., 1965.

Maoz, Moshe. *Asad: The Sphinx of Damascus*. New York: Weidenfeld, 1988.

———, and Yaniv, Avner, eds. *Syria under Assad*. New York: St. Martin's, 1986.

Makiya, Kanan (Samir al-Khalil). *Cruelty and Silence*. New York: Norton, 1993.

———. *Republic of Fear*. New York: Pantheon, 1989.

———. *The Monument*. Berkeley: U. of California, 1991.

Mandel, Neville J. *The Arabs and Zionism Before World War I*. Berkeley: U. of California, 1976.

Mansfield, Peter. *The British in Egypt*. New York: Holt, 1971.

———. *The Arab World*. New York: Crowell, 1977.

Marr, Phebe. *The Modern History of Iraq.* Boulder, Colo.: Westview, 1985.

Masalha, Nur. *Expulsion of the Palestinians.* Washington, D.C.: Institute for Palestine Studies, 1992.

Matarr, Faoud. *Saddam Hussein.* London: Highlight, 1990.

Mattar, Philip. *The Mufti of Jerusalem.* New York: Columbia, 1988.

Maurois, André. *A History of France.* New York: Farrar, Straus and Cudahy, 1956.

McCarthy, Justin. *Muslims and Minorities: The Population of Ottoman Anatolia at the End of the Empire.* New York: New York U., 1983.

Melman, Yossi, and Raviv, Dan. *Behind the Uprising.* New York: Greenwood, 1989.

Metz, Helen C., ed. *Iraq: A Country Study.* Washington, D.C.: Government Printing Office, 1990.

Mishal, Shaul. *West Bank/East Bank.* New Haven, Conn.: Yale, 1978.

Middle East Watch. *Needless Deaths in the Gulf War.* New York: Human Rights Watch, 1991.

Miller, Judith, and Mylroie, Laurie. *Saddam Hussein and the Crisis in the Gulf.* New York: Times Books/Random House, 1992.

Morris, Benny. *The Birth of the Palestinian Refugee Problem, 1947–49.* Cambridge, Eng.: Cambridge U., 1987.

Mortimer, Edward. *Faith and Power: The Politics of Islam.* New York: Random House, 1982.

Muslih, Muhammad. *The Origins of Palestinian Nationalism.* New York: Columbia, 1988.

Newby, P. H. *Saladin.* New York: Dorset, 1983.

Nuseibeh, Hazem Z. *The Ideas of Arab Nationalism.* Ithaca, N.Y.: Cornell, 1956.

Nyrop, Richard F., ed. *Syria: A Country Study.* Washington, D.C.: Government Printing Office, 1979.

Ochsenwald, William. *The Hijaz Railroad.* Charlottesville: U. of Virginia, 1980.

Ostrogorsky, George. *History of the Byzantine State.* New Brunswick, N.J.: Rutgers, 1969.

Patai, Raphael. *The Arab Mind.* New York: Scribner's, 1976.

Payne, Robert. *The History of Islam.* New York: Dorset, 1959.

Pelletiere, Stephen, et. al. *Iraqi Power and U.S. Security in the Middle East.* U.S. Army War College, Carlisle Barracks, 1990.

Peretz, Don. *The Middle East Today.* New York: Holt, 1978.

Perlmutter, Amos. *Egypt: The Praetorian State.* New Brunswick, N.J.: Transaction, 1974.

Peroncel-Hugoz, Jean-Pierre. *The Raft of Mohammed.* New York: Paragon, 1988.

Pintak, Larry. *Beirut Outtakes.* Lexington, Mass.: Heath, 1988.

Pirenne, Henri. *Mohammed and Charlemagne.* New York: Barnes & Noble, 1992.

Pipes, Daniel. *In the Path of God: Islam and Political Power.* New York: Basic Books, 1983.

Piscatori, James, ed. *Islamic Fundamentalism and the Gulf Crisis.* Chicago: American Academy of Arts and Sciences, 1991.

Polk, William R., *The Arab World Today.* Cambridge, Mass.: Harvard, 1980.

———. *The Elusive Peace: The Middle East in the Twentieth Century.* New York: St. Martin's, 1979.

Quandt, William B., ed. *The Middle East: Ten Years After Camp David.* Washington, D.C.: Brookings, 1988.

———, ed. *The Politics of Palestinian Nationalism.* Berkeley: U. of California, 1973.

Rabinovich, Itamar. *The Road Not Taken.* New York: Oxford, 1991.

———. *Syria Under the Ba'th, 1963–66.* New York: Wiley, 1972.

Rahman, Fazlur. *Islam.* Chicago: U. of Chicago, 1979.

Randal, Jonathan C. *Going All the Way: Christian Warlords, Israeli Adventurers, and the War in Lebanon.* New York: Viking, 1983.

Reeves, Minou. *Female Warriors of Allah.* New York: Dutton, 1989.

Reich, Walter. *A Stranger in My House.* New York: Holt, 1984.

Richmond, J. C. B. *Egypt, 1798–1952.* New York: Columbia, 1972.

Ridgeway, James, ed. *The March to War*. New York: Four Walls, 1991.

Roberts, J. M. *The Triumph of the West*. London: BBC, 1985.

Rodinson, Maxime. *The Arabs*. Chicago: U. of Chicago, 1978.

————. *Islam and Capitalism*. Austin: U. of Texas, 1981.

Rosenthal, Erwin I. J. *Judaism and Islam*. London: Yoseloff, 1961.

Rubin, Barry. *The Arab States and the Palestine Conflict*. Syracuse: Syracuse U., 1981.

Rubinstein, Alvin Z. *Red Star on the Nile*. Princeton: Princeton U., 1977.

Saadawi, Nawal. *The Hidden Face of Eve*. Boston: Boston U., 1980.

Sadat, Anwar. *In Search of Identity*. New York: Harper & Row, 1978.

————. *Those I Have Known*. New York: Continuum, 1984.

Sadat, Jehan. *Woman of Egypt*. New York: Simon & Schuster, 1987.

Said, Edward W. *Covering Islam*. New York: Pantheon, 1981.

————. *Orientalism*. New York: Random House, 1979.

————. *The Palestine Question*. New York: Times Books, 1980.

Saint-Prot, Charles. *Saddam Hussein: Un Gaullisme Arabe?* Paris: Albin Michel, 1987.

Sahliyeh, Emile. *In Search of Leadership: West Bank Politics Since 1967*. Washington, D.C.: Brookings, 1988.

Salibi, Kamal. *A House of Many Mansions: The History of Lebanon Reconsidered*. Berkeley: U. of California, 1988.

Salinger, Pierre, and Laurent, Eric. *Secret Dossier: The Hidden Agenda Behind the Gulf War*. New York: Penguin, 1991.

Sanger, Richard H. *The Arabian Peninsula*. Freeport, N.Y.: Books for Libraries Press, 1954.

Saqqaf, Abdulaziz Y., ed. *The Middle East City: Ancient Traditions Confront a Modern World*. New York: Paragon, 1987.

Schiff, Ze'ev, and Ya'ari, Ehud. *Intifada: The Palestinian Uprising, Israel's Third Front*. New York: Simon & Schuster, 1989.

————. *Israel's Lebanon War*. New York: Simon & Schuster, 1983.

Schwarzkopf, H. Norman. *It Doesn't Take a Hero*. New York: Bantam, 1992.

Sciolino, Elaine. *The Outlaw State*. New York: Wiley, 1991.

Seale, Patrick. *Abu Nidal: A Gun for Hire*. New York: Random House, 1992.

———. *Asad: The Struggle for the Middle East*. Berkeley: U. of California, 1988.

———. *The Shaping of an Arab Statesman*. London: Quartet, 1983.

———. *The Struggle for Syria*. New Haven, Conn.: Yale, 1986.

Seurat, Michel. *L'Etat de Barbarie*. Paris: Seuil, 1977.

Shoukri, Ghali. *Egypt: Portrait of a President*. London: Zed, 1981.

Sifry, Micah L., and Cerf, Christopher, ed. *The Gulf War Reader*. New York: Random House, 1991.

Simon, Reeva S. *Iraq Between the Two World Wars*. New York: Columbia, 1986.

Sivan, Emmanuel. *Radical Islam*. New Haven, Conn.: Yale, 1985.

Smith, Jean Edward. *George Bush's War*. New York: Holt, 1992.

Smith, Wilfred C. *Islam in Modern History*, Princeton: Princeton U., 1977.

Sourdel, Dominique. *Medieval Islam*. London: Routledge & Kegan Paul, 1979.

Swallow, Charles. *The Sick Man of Europe: Ottoman Empire to Turkish Republic, 1789–1923*. London: Benn, 1973.

Tawil, Raymonda. *My Home, My Prison*. New York: Holt, 1979.

Timmerman, Kenneth R. *The Death Lobby: How the West Armed Iraq*. Boston: Houghton Mifflin, 1991.

Tucker, Robert W., and Hendrickson, David C. *The Imperial Temptation*. New York: Council on Foreign Relations, 1992.

U.S. News & World Report. *Triumph Without Victory*. New York: Random House, 1992.

Viorst, Milton. *Reaching for the Olive Branch: UNRWA and Peace in the Middle East*. Bloomington: Indiana U., 1989.

———. *Sands of Sorrow: Israel's Journey from Independence*. New York: Harper, 1987.

Wallach, Janet and Wallach, John. *Arafat*. New York: Lyle Stuart, 1990.

———. *Still Small Voices*. New York: Harcourt Brace, 1989.

Warner, Geoffrey. *Iraq and Syria, 1941*. Newark: U. of Delaware, 1974.

Weinberger, Naomi J. *Syrian Intervention in Lebanon*. New York: Oxford, 1986.

Winternitz, Helen. *A Season of Stones*. New York: Atlantic Monthly, 1992.

Woodward, Bob. *The Commanders*. New York: Simon & Schuster, 1991.

Yergin, Daniel. *The Prize: The Epic Quest for Oil, Money & Power*. New York: Simon & Schuster, 1991.

Zeine, Zeine M. *Arab-Turkish Relations and the Emergence of Arab Nationalism*. Beirut, Lebanon: Khayat's, 1958.

INDEX

Abaddi, Mamdouh, 289
Abbasid dynasty, 4–6, 8, 28, 29,
    39, 40, 67, 68, 304
Abdul Hamid, Sultan, 66
Abdul-Kuddous, Mohammed,
    115–16
Abdullah, King of Jordan, 20, 131,
    136, 205, 210–11, 294, 300,
    312–14
Abdul Shafi, Haidar, 363, 367–8,
    376
Abu-Alsouf, Bahram, 35–6
Abu Ghraib factory, 325
Abu Jabber, Kamel, 320
Abu Libdeh, Hassan, 375–6
Abu Zaida, Abdul Fatah Othman,
    208–9, 369–71
Abu Zant, Sheikh Abdul Mun'im,
    285–7, 292, 381
Achkar, Antoine, 168–9, 183
Adali, Sevki, 60
Adwan, Mamdouh, 146–8
Afghanistan, 47, 235–6
Aflaq, Michel, 28–9, 31, 137, 139,
    142
Ahmad, Sheikh Nawaf al-, 255
Ahmed, Sheikh Fahd al-, 256, 265
Ahmed, Sheikh Sabah al-, 255
Ahram, Al- (Egyptian newspaper),
    85, 88, 108, 112
Alawites, 29, 122, 127, 135,
    136–40, 144–6
Al-Azhar Mosque, Cairo, 88–90,
    92, 113–16, 118, 371
Alem, Hazem el-, 199

Alem, Khader el-, 199–201
Alexander the Great, 4, 91
Algeria, 340
Ali, 12, 15–16
Ali, Sheikh Ali Salem al-, 258
Ali, Qassem, 366–7
American University of Beirut, 125
Amman (Jordan), 293–5
Ammonites, 294
Amnesty International, 115, 142,
    152, 307
An Najaf (Iraq), 15–18, 352, 354–5
Anti-Defamation League, 149, 152
anti-Semitism, 151
Aoun, Gen. Michel, 191–3
Aqeel, Wajdi, 371–2
Arab Economic Report (1992), 273
Arab Fund for Economic
    Development, 273
Arab Higher Committee
    (Palestine), 203–4
Arabia, 12
Arabiyat, Abdel Latif, 303–4, 381
Arab League, 83–4, 120, 165, 172,
    174, 192, 210, 249, 253, 274, 318
Arab Legion (Jordan), 210
Arab Liberation Army, 204
Arab Monetary Fund, 274
Arab nation, see pan-Arabism
Arab Revolt, 20, 132, 202, 300,
    312, 314, 384
Arab Summit: Fez, 1982, 156;
    Rabat, 1974, 215, 315
Arafat, Yasir, 212–16, 227; Assad's
    break with, 155; and Gulf war,

Arafat, Yasir (*cont.*)
   259; Hussein and, 196, 316; in
   Kuwait, 245; and Lebanese war,
   173, 189; and peace process, 228,
   288, 320, 338, 361, 362, 367–80
   passim
Arar, Suleiman, 288
Arbil (Kurdistan), 18, 19, 349
Arif, Abd al-Salam, 24
Aristotle, 67, 68
Armenians, 60, 70–2
Armstrong, John A., 130
Army, U.S.: Central Command,
   278, 279; Corps of Engineers,
   266
art, Iraqi, 38–40
Ashkanani, Mohammed, 271
Ashrawi, Hanan, 230–2
Asilturk, Oguzhan, 81–2
Assad, Basil al-, 123
Assad, Hafez al-, 122–4, 126–7,
   137–48, 151, 153–6, 174, 178,
   182, 184, 187, 363–4
Assad, Rifat al-, 123, 143
Assyrians, 40
Aswan high dam, 104
Asyut (Egypt), 116
Atassi, Jamal al-, 145–6, 148
Ataturk, Kemal, 71–82
Atta, Nasser, 194, 197, 198
Attar, Leyla al-, 39–40
Austria, Ottoman empire and, 66
Autumn Quail (Mahfouz), 98
Ayyubites, 91
Aziz, Tariq, 22–25, 27–8, 42, 46–9,
   52, 252–4, 309, 337–46
Azraq refugee camp (Jordan),
   297–300

Baathism, 215; in Iraq, 18, 22–6,
   28–32, 40–2, 49, 249–50, 255,
   326, 330, 332, 336, 347–54
   passim; in Kuwait, 258; in Syria,
   137, 138, 142, 145, 146, 148,
   154–5

Babylon, 35–8
Badr, Badr Khalid al-, 239–40
Badr, Zaki, 115, 116
Baghdad, 3–9, 67, 68, 130; art
   center in, 38–40; Israeli bombing
   of, 339; Ottoman conquest of,
   54; postwar, 327–29; Shiites and
   Sunnis in, 13–15
Baghdad Pact, 21, 22, 25
Baghdad University, 331
Baghoudi, Mustafa, 229
Baha al-Din, Ahmad, 112–14
Bahrain, 46, 235, 338
Baijan, Badr al-, 261
Baker, James, 265, 312, 318, 332,
   343, 345
Bakr, Ahmad Hassan al-, 26, 27
Balfour Declaration, 132, 134, 202,
   203, 205
Bandar bin Sultan, Prince, 309
Bani Hamida tribe, 301
Bani Utub tribe, 237, 244, 250, 264
Banna, Hassan al-, 110, 111, 116
Baramki, Gabi, 221–2
Barzani, Masoud, 351
Barzani, Mustafa al-, 347, 351
Bashir, Munir, 37, 38, 51
Batatu, Hanna, 20
Bayanouni, Ali al-, 144–5, 148
Baz, Osama el-, 310–11
Bazoft, Farzad, 339
Bedah, Ali al-, 277
bedouins, 130, 240, 258, 273,
   300–1
Begin, Menachem, 176, 178, 217,
   220
Beginning of the End, The
   (Mahfouz), 98
Beirut, 125, 159–61, 166, 171,
   181–6
Beit al-Hikmah (House of
   Wisdom), 67
Beit Shebab (Lebanon), 168–9
Bejjani, Emile, 168, 169
Belgium, Kuwait and, 236

Beqa'a refugee camp (Jordan), 290–3
Berlinguer, Enrico, 142
Bible, the, 219
Bikfaya (Lebanon), 170, 171
Birzeit University, 220–1, 320
"Black September," 141, 172, 213, 288, 290, 315
Bloudan (Syria), 140
Bolsheviks, 70
Bouhabib, Abdallah, 159, 162
Brezhnev, Leonid, 142
Brinton, Crane, 331
Britain, see Great Britain
British Broadcasting Company (BBC), 350
British Petroleum, 241
Broumana (Lebanon), 167
Burgan oil field (Kuwait), 267
Bush, George, 249, 252, 268, 282, 286, 310–11, 332, 336–7, 342, 346; anti-aggression pledge of, 46–7; and Arab summit, 309–10; attempted assassination of, 40; declares cease-fire, 263, 335; Hussein and, 288, 290, 296, 299, 316, 317; and Israel, 341; and oil overproduction, 251; and reconstruction of Kuwait, 266; refusal to negotiate of, 254, 345; and troop buildup in Saudi Arabia, 260
Byron, George Gordon, Lord, 66
Byzantines, 54–6, 67

Cable News Network (CNN), 326
Cairo, 83, 96–100, 130; Ottoman conquest of, 54
Cairo Accords (1969), 172
Cairo Trilogy (Mahfouz), 93, 98
Camp David accords, 107, 316, 317
Carter, Jimmy, 49, 109, 235–6
Catholics, 55, 56, 64, 129, 151, 164, 181

Cemal, Hasan, 77
Central Intelligence Agency (CIA), 338
Chamoun family, 176
Chanson de Roland, 58
Charlemagne, 5, 57, 128–9
chemical weapons, 50–2
Cheney, Richard, 312
Children of Gebelawi (Mahfouz), 88–9, 105–6, 115
China, Palestinians and, 291
Chitchat on the Nile (Mahfouz), 106
Christians, 10, 19, 128–9, 131, 358; anti-Semitism of, 151; as Communist leaders, 23; in Egypt, 108, 111, 112, 117, 118; in Iraq, 28, 29, 31, 335, 337; Islam and, 58, 60; in Jordan, 294; in Kuwait, 239; Lebanese, 125, 158–76, 179, 182, 187–8, 191, 193; Nestorian, 37; Ottomans and, 54, 57, 61–3, 66, 67, 132; in Palestine, 203; Renaissance and, 69; social codes of, 88; in Syria, 127, 135, 137, 150; in Turkey, 81; in West Bank, 230; see also Catholics; Maronites
Circassians, 294
Civil War, American, 92
Clinton, Bill, 48, 377
Cold War, 22, 136, 249
Commanders, The (Woodward), 343
Committee of Union and Progress, 66
Common Market, 58–9
Communists, 215; Egyptian, 102, 103, 108; Iraqi, 21–5, 30; Jordanian, 302, 306; Syrian, 142, 143
confessionalism, 164–6; see also deconfessionalization
Congress, U.S., 51

Constantine, 55
Constantinople, *see* Istanbul
Copernicus, 69
Copts, 166
Crusaders, 55, 58, 61, 122, 123, 132, 164, 166, 168, 188
Ctesiphon, battle of, 4, 41

Damascus, 124–5, 130; French occupation of, 135; minorities in, 150; Ottoman conquest of, 54
Dark Ages, 68, 113, 128
Dateline (Turkish newspaper), 59
Dawa, Al- (Egyptian newspaper), 115
Decline and Fall of the Roman Empire, The (Gibbon), 57
deconfessionalization, 180, 185, 189, 192
Democratic Front for the Liberation of Palestine, 288, 364, 378
Desert Storm, *see* Gulf war
Dimra (Palestine), 207–8
Dohuk (Kurdistan), 349, 350, 352
Dole, Robert, 344
Druzes, 156; in Lebanon, 164, 173, 179, 182, 183, 187, 189; in Syria, 135–7
Duella, Mubarak, 272–3

Eastern Orthodox Christianity, 55
Egypt, 22, 28, 29, 48, 83–121, 171, 299; archeology in, 36–7; Christians in, 55, 165–6; Communists in, 23; fundamentalism in, 88, 109–16; in Gulf war, 233, 272, 287; Jordan and, 309–11, 317; Lebanon and, 168; under Mubarak, 116–20; under Nasser, 103–6, 136, 332; and oil crisis, 340; Ottoman empire and, 65, 70; Palestinians and, 205, 206,

209–12, 215, 229; political history of, 90–6; under Sadat, 106–9; Syria and, 136–7, 141, 315
Egyptian Gazette, 102
Egyptian Organization for Human Rights, 116
Eisenhower, Dwight D., 104, 171
Elyas, Assad Kamal, 123–4
Euclid, 67
European Community, 59–61, 81, 249
Evren, Kenan, 76

Fahd, King, of Saudi Arabia, 196, 308–11, 340
Faisal, King, of Syria and Iraq, 20–1, 28, 131, 133, 134, 136, 202, 205, 312
Faisal II, King, of Iraq, 21, 22
Faisal, Toujan, 304–6, 382
Falhout, Saber, 137, 148
Farah, Elias, 29–31
Fares, Samir, 159–61, 184
Farouk, King, of Egypt, 91, 103, 110
fascism, 170
Fatah, 215, 245, 364–5, 368, 373, 374, 378
Fatamids, 29, 91
Firas, Abu, 155–6
Foda, Faraj, 89
France: Arab invasion of, 57–8; Egypt and, 91–3, 104; Gulf war and, 249; Iraq and, 22, 52, 345; Kurds and, 352; Kuwait and, 236; Lebanon and, 164, 165, 168, 169, 177, 179, 193; Ottomans and, 64–6, 70, 71, 164; Palestinians and, 202; political émigrés in, 142–5; Syria and, 132–7, 151
Franjieh, Suleiman, 176, 191
Franjieh, Tony, 176, 179

Free Officers, 103, 111, 138
Frem, Fady, 177
French Revolution, 55, 64
Freud, Sigmund, 58
Fuad I, King, of Egypt, 95, 110
fundamentalism, 61, 236, 359; in
 Egypt, 88, 109–16; in Iraq,
 10–12, 25, 41, 354; in Jordan,
 297, 302–6, 321; in Kuwait, 257;
 Palestinian, 207, 228; in Turkey,
 75, 79

Galata (Turkey), 56
Galen, 67
Gallipoli, battle of, 71, 131
Gaza Strip, 194–7, 205–10, 212,
 216, 219, 220, 227, 229, 231,
 363, 364–72
Geagea, Samir, 176, 179, 180, 185,
 192
Gemayel, Amin, 159, 160, 170,
 175–7, 179–82, 185–91
Gemayel, Bashir, 160, 170–1,
 175–8, 180–3, 189
Gemayel, Pierre, 170–3, 175
General Federation of Iraqi
 Women, 32, 35
General Union of Palestine
 Students, 215
George, Donnie, 37–8
Germany: Iraq and, 345; Nazi, 21,
 203, 204, 257; Ottoman empire
 and, 66; reunification of, 249;
 Turks in, 59–61; in World War I,
 71; in World War II, 136
Gibbon, Edward, 57
Glaspie, April, 190, 191, 252, 255,
 342–3
Golan Heights, 154, 156, 182
Gorbachev, Mikhail, 142
Great Britain: in Baghdad Pact, 22;
 Egypt and, 91, 93–6, 102–4, 110,
 111, 131; Gulf war and, 249,
 252; hegemony in Gulf of, 235,

251; Iraq governed by, 7, 20–1,
 25, 249; Jordan and, 294, 313;
 Kurds and, 352; Kuwait and,
 236, 238–9, 242, 249, 276, 282;
 Ottoman empire and, 65, 66, 70;
 Palestinians and, 200, 202–4,
 209–11, 229; Syria and, 131–6
Greece, 60, 148; ancient, 55, 67,
 68, 129; Ottoman empire and,
 61, 66, 70–1; Turkey and, 72
Grunebaum, Gustave von, 69
Gulbenkian, Calouste, 38
Gulf Cooperation Council (GCC),
 235
Gulf Oil Corporation, 241
Gulf war, 32, 40, 43, 46, 193, 233,
 261–3, 357; aftermath of,
 263–84, 322–56; events leading
 to, 249–55; Jordan and, 269,
 285–90, 292–3, 297–300,
 308–12, 317, 318; occupation of
 Kuwait during, 257–61;
 Palestinians during, 206, 218,
 222, 227; Syria in, 123, 141,
 142, 193
Gunes (Turkish newspaper), 77

Habash, George, 288, 289, 364
Haig, Alexander, 47
Hakim, Tewfik al-, 85–7, 105, 106,
 109
Halaby, Najeeb, 295–6
Halefoglu, Vahit, 63
Hama, Syria, massacre at, 147
Hamad, Abdlatif al-, 273–4
Hamade, Marwan, 183–6
Hamas, 207, 209, 228, 229, 231,
 232, 364, 365, 370, 371–2, 373
Hamdoon, Nizar, 322–3
Hammad, Salameh, 297–8, 300
Hammadi, Saddoun, 49–50, 310,
 333–4, 352
Hammurabi, 4, 36
Hamra, Avraham, 149, 152

Hapsburgs, 64
Harun al-Rashid, Caliph, 5, 8, 67
Hasbani, Nissim, 152, 153
Hashemites, 7, 20, 131, 134, 136,
    202, 211, 218, 300, 302, 304,
    312, 314, 315, 321
Hassan, Crown Prince, of Jordan,
    250, 252, 288, 294, 301-2, 308,
    312
Hassan, Hussein Kamil, 332
Hawali (Kuwait), 245
Hawatmeh, Nayef, 288, 289, 364
Hebrew University, Jerusalem, 221,
    227
Hezbollah, 158, 159, 162, 193
Higher Education Council of
    Turkey, 76, 77
History of the Arabs (Hitti), 68
Hitler, Adolf, 203
Hitti, Philip K., 6, 67, 68
Hobeika, Elie, 176, 179-80
Holocaust, 151
Homer, 67
Hoss, Salim, 185-7, 191
Hrawi, Elias, 192
Hulagu Khan, 6, 263
Hurriyet (Turkish newspaper), 60
Hussein, King, of Jordan, 22, 141,
    144, 165, 196, 211, 213, 218,
    273, 287-90, 292-5, 300-21,
    363, 381-5
Hussein, Sharif, 131-4, 136, 312,
    313, 383
Hussein, Fuad Mulla, 246-7, 273
Husseini, Abd el-Kader al-, 215,
    226
Husseini, Faisal, 226-8, 376-7
Husseini, Hajj Amin al-, 203-5,
    210, 211, 214, 226

Ibrahim, Izzat, 310-11
Ibrahim, Sa'ad al-Din, 308
Ilah, Abd al-, 21, 22
India, 238
In Search of Identity (Sadat), 91

International Herald Tribune, 289,
    295
International Monetary Fund
    (IMF), 300, 301
intifada (Palestinian uprising),
    194-201, 206-10, 218-20,
    224-9, 245, 291, 293, 300, 319,
    362, 365, 366, 370, 372
Iran, 61, 111, 346, 355; Baathism
    and, 29; in Baghdad Pact, 22;
    Kurds in, 335, 336, 347, 349;
    Lebanon and, 158, 178, 188, 189;
    and oil crisis, 340; Palestinians
    and, 207, 229; and postwar Iraq,
    328; Rushdie and, 88; under
    shah, 17; Shiism in, 12; Syria
    and, 141, 187; Turkey and, 75;
    women in, 34
Irangate scandal, 47, 48, 50, 235,
    337
Iraq, 3-52, 91, 100, 135, 136, 146,
    171, 306; archeology in, 35-8;
    art in, 38-40; Britain and, 136;
    heterogeneity of, 9-19; Jordan
    and, 286, 289, 297, 309-10, 313,
    316; Kuwait invaded by, 40, 43,
    237, 244, 248-57, 292, 296, 299;
    Lebanon and, 192; occupation of
    Kuwait by, 257-61; in Ottoman
    empire, 6, 7, 19, 21, 44, 70;
    Palestinians and, 205, 211, 215;
    political history of, 19-31; post-
    war, 322-56; refugees from,
    297-9; Syria and, 141; United
    States and, 46-52, 337-45; U.S.
    war with, see Gulf war; war with
    Iran, see Iraq-Iran war; women
    in, 31-5
Iraq-Iran war, 11, 18-19, 27, 37,
    42-50, 250, 252, 278, 338-40;
    cease-fire to, 191; Jordan and,
    301, 316; Kurds during, 41, 47,
    50-1, 251, 348; Kuwait during,
    234-7, 244, 248, 249, 251, 271,
    282-3; reflagging of tankers

during, 233, 236, 237, 282; Syria during, 141, 178, 316

Ishaq al-Kindi, Yaqub ibn, 68

Islam, 129–30, 144–5, 357–9; in Egypt, 86, 88–90, 109–16; and Europe, 57–62; fundamentalist, *see* fundamentalism; Golden Age of, 147; Greek philosophy and, 68; in Iraq, 9–19, 31; Jews and Christians and, 151; in Jordan, 285–7, 296–7; in Kuwait, 244, 270–1; in Lebanon, 165–6, 171, 182, 190–2; Ottomans and, 54, 56, 57, 63, 69; Palestinians and, 203, 210; in Saudi Arabia, 233; in Syria, 122, 126, 127; in Turkey, 73–82; *see also* Shiites; Sunnis

Islamic Conference, 234

Islamic Constitutional Movement, 257

Islamic Jihad, 364

Ismail, Khedive, of Egypt, 92–3, 96, 100, 105

Ismailis, 137

Israel, 22, 24, 25, 62, 132, 134, 150, 245, 273, 312, 357; arms sales to Iran by, 47, 48; creation of, 202–5; Egypt and, 37, 83, 102–9, 111, 117; European Community and, 60; Gaza Strip occupied by, 206; and Gulf war, 259, 317; Iraq and, 51, 251, 339, 345; Jordan and, 294, 299, 302, 304, 311, 314–21, 363, 381–5; Lebanon and, 141, 155, 171, 172, 174–80, 182, 187–93; Palestinians and, 194–201, 206–13, 215–32, 290, 292–3, 361–80; recognition of, 338; Syria and, 123, 136, 141, 151–7

Istanbul, 53–7

Italy: Kuwait and, 236; Lebanon and, 177; Ottoman empire and, 70, 71; Renaissance in, 69

Jackson, Jesse, 254

Jadallah, Mohammed, 378–9

Jadid, Salah, 138, 139, 142, 144, 146

Jaff, Sirwan Abdullah, 19, 348, 354

Jajati, Yousef (Abu Khalil), 150–3

Jajati, Victor, 149–50

Jalahima family, 237

Janissaries, 63, 65

Jericho, Palestinian homeland in, 216, 363, 373–5

Jerusalem, 122, 132, 164, 202, 228, 303, 315, 363, 367, 372–3, 382–3

Jews, 10, 19, 221, 358; archeology by, 36; Balfour Declaration and, 132, 134, 202; as Communist leaders, 23; in Iraq, 25; Jordan and, 313, 315; in Kuwait, 239, 240; Ottomans and, 56, 61–3, 67; Palestinians and, 200, 202–5, 210, 216, 219, 220, 222, 228; social codes of, 88; in Spain, 61; in Syria, 127, 137, 149–53, 155; *see also* Israel

Jibril, Ahmad, 155, 156

Jihad, 109, 113, 114, 116

Jordan, 20, 48, 132, 135, 136, 165, 285–321; American queen of, 293, 295–300; Britain and, 136; democracy/elections in, 297, 300–8, 381; Gulf war and, 269, 285–90, 292–3, 308–12; Iraq and, 22, 328; Israel and, 286, 294, 299, 302, 304, 311, 314–21, 363, 381–5; Kuwait and, 273; Muslim Brotherhood in, 144; Palestinians and, 199–201, 205, 210–13, 218, 220, 223, 228, 229, 290–3

Jordanian Arab National Democratic Alliance (JANDA), 287–90

Jouan, Hamad al-, 264, 282

Kafr Ain (West Bank), 197–201
Kalaycioglu, Ersin, 65
Kara, Ismail, 80
Karame, Rashid, 185
Karbala (Iraq), 15, 16, 18, 100, 352–4
Kassis, Simon, 162
Kececiler, Mehmet, 79–80
Kelly, John, 161, 338
Khaddam, Abdul Halim, 126, 183–4, 187
Khader, Asma, 306–7
Khairallah, Adnan, 25, 26, 43–5, 52
Khairallah Talfah, 25
Khalifa, Sheikh Ali al-, 276, 279, 280, 282, 283, 341
Khalifa family, 237
Kharma, Wasfi, 199
Khoei, Ayatollah Abolqassem al-, 355
Khomeini, Ayatollah Ruhollah, 38, 49, 113, 207, 355; Baathism and, 29, 30; death of, 346; in exile in Iraq, 17–18, 354; Israel and, 48; and Kuwait, 234, 252, 271; revolution led by, 111–12, 236; Rushdie condemned by, 88–9, 147, 305; secret U.S. arms sales to, 338; and Syria, 178, 316; and war with Iraq, 11, 41–2, 46; women and, 34, 35
Khoury, Lt. Selim, 183
Kinross, Lord, 61
Kissinger, Henry, 47
Kleifa, Jamil, 375
Koban, Dogan, 54–7, 69
Koran, 57, 64, 76, 90, 97, 113, 264, 358; Christians and Jews and, 61, 382–3; as God's revelation, 10, 68; governmental system based on, 165; Greek philosophy and, 5; Palestinians and, 219; and Shiite-Sunni dispute, 11–12; women and, 77, 112, 305
Kourriya, Joubran, 123

Kurds, 122; as Communist leaders, 23; in Iraq, 11–13, 18–21, 24–6, 29, 122, 268, 335, 336, 338, 346–52; during Iraq-Iran war, 41, 47, 50–1, 251, 348; in Syria, 137; in Turkey, 11, 18, 51, 70–2
Kuttab, Daoud, 377–8
Kuwait, 233–84, 338–40; government-in-exile of, 261–2; Iraqi invasion of, 40, 43, 237, 244, 248–57, 292, 296, 299, 308, 316, 320, 324; Iraqi occupation of, 257–61, 332; Jordan and, 289, 319; modernization of, 242–4; and oil crisis, 340–1; Palestinians and, 206, 212, 244–5, 259–60, 264–6, 269, 272, 291, 293; political history of, 237–42; postliberation, 263–84, 346; United States and, 343–5; war over, see Gulf war; wealth in, 246–7
Kuwait Oil Company, 241

Labor Party (Israel), 220, 231–2
Latakia (Syria), 140
Lawrence, T. E., 133, 279, 300
Lawyers Committee for Human Rights, 307
League of Nations, 20
Lebanese Forces, 158–9, 163, 176, 177, 179, 181–3, 185, 187–9, 192, 193
Lebanon, 124, 132, 158–93; American hostages in, 47, 160, 162, 193; Christians in, 158–71; Communists in, 23; France and, 132, 135; under Gemayel, 186–91; Gulf war and, 187; Israeli invasion of, 141, 155, 174–80, 362; Palestinians and, 171–4, 196, 205, 207, 216, 229; peace agreement in, 192–3; and peace process, 319; Syria and,

139, 146, 154, 183–93; war in, 125–7, 140, 141, 147, 173–81, 303
Lenin, V. I., 142
Levantines, 56
Lewis, Bernard, 58, 65, 72
Libya, 171
Likud Party (Israel), 217, 220, 231, 232
Louis XIV, King, of France, 164
Love in the Rain (Mahfouz), 107

Ma'an (Jordan), 301
Madrid peace conference, 142, 152, 156, 193, 227–8, 232, 319, 362, 367
Mahfouz, Naguib, 83–100, 103, 105–13, 115, 117, 118, 120–1
Mahmoud, Said Moussa, 155
Majid, Ali Hassan al-, 332
Makdissi, Antun, 126–7
Mamluks, 91–2, 97, 103, 168
Mansur, al- 4, 5
Marcos, Imelda, 297
Maronites, 163–75, 181, 183, 185, 190–2
Marxists, *see* Communists
Masri, Nasser al-, 273
Masri, Taher, 217, 381
Masri family, 217–18, 320
Matthews, Coots, 267
Maurois, André, 58
May 17 Agreement, 187, 191
Maysaloun, battle of, 134, 135
McMahon Letters, 131, 132
Mecca, 130, 131, 294, 303, 312
Mecit, Sultan Abdul, 65
Medina, 131, 303
Mediterranean Games, 140
Mehmet VI, Sultan, 72
Mesopotamia, 132, 325
Middle East Airlines, 172
Middle East Watch, 207
Mitterrand, François, 52

Mohafel, Ahmad, 143–5, 148
Mohammed, the Prophet, 16, 29, 58, 100; as city-dweller, 130; conquest of Mecca by, 4; and democratic rule, 112; descendants of, 131, 312; and dissident intellectuals, 147; God's revelation through, 10, 68; Rushdie's "calumny" against, 89, 114; women and, 31–2, 35
Mohammed Ali, 65, 92, 93, 95, 110, 119
Mongols, 5, 6, 19, 40
Moses and Monotheism (Freud), 58
Motherland Party, Turkish, 78–9
Mouawad, René, 192
moulid (religious street festival), 100–2
Mubarak, Hosni, 84, 106, 113, 114, 116–21, 165, 310, 311, 317, 340–2
Mubarak, Mussama al-, 276
Mubarak, Suzanne, 117
mukhabarat (secret police), 141, 147–8, 152, 155, 291, 306–7, 331
mukhtars (village leaders), 207, 208, 292–3
Murphy, Richard, 190, 191
Muslim Brotherhood: in Egypt, 102–4, 108, 110–13, 115–16; in Jordan, 285, 297, 302–4, 306, 319, 381; Palestinians and, 215, 229; in Syria, 142–6
Muslim Discovery of Europe, The (Lewis), 58
Muslims, *see* Islam
Mustansiriyah, 6, 7
Mutawa, Suleiman, 263
Mutazilites, 68

Nablus (Palestine), 217–18
Nadim, Nawal el-Messiri, 99–100
Nafa'a, Shibli, 168
Naksibendis, 79

Napoleon, Emperor of the French, 65, 91

Nasser, Gamal Abdel, 28, 84, 91, 103–7, 109, 118–19, 357; Iraq and, 24; and Jordan, 211, 306, 307; and Lebanon, 171, 172; and Muslim Brotherhood, 110–12; and Palestinians, 211, 212, 215, 216; resignation of, 332; secularism of, 82; Soviet support for, 22; and Syria, 136–8

Nasser, Hanna, 220, 221, 320

Nasserism, 315, 319; Kuwaiti, 241, 242, 246, 247; Syrian, 145–6

nationalism: Egyptian, 95, 102–3, 171; Iranian, 30; Iraqi, 19–23; Lebanese, 165, 170; Palestinian, 215, 216; Syrian, 127, 130–4

National Pact (Lebanon), 165, 166, 171, 173, 175, 180, 190, 191

National Salvation Party (Turkey), 81

NATO, 61

Nazis, 21, 203, 204, 257

Nebuchadnezzar, 4, 36

Neglected Duty (terrorist document), 109

Neopatriarchy (Shirabi), 129, 358

Neo-Platonists, 67

Nestorian Christians, 37

New Jersey, U.S.S. (battleship), 179

New York Times, The, 149

Nibari, Abdullah al-, 256–7, 264, 282

Night of the Slaves, The (Adwan), 146

Nixon, Richard M., 316, 334

Nobel Prize, 84, 86–8, 90, 91, 94, 120

Nonaligned Movement, 234

Noor, Queen, of Jordan, 293, 295–300, 302, 305, 307

Nusseibeh, Sari, 375

October war, 84, 315

Okasha, Abu Fayez, 207–8

Oke, Kemal, 66

Oman, 46, 235

Omayyads, 11–12, 29, 137, 304

OPEC (Organization of Petroleum Exporting Countries), 250, 280, 341

Orientalism (Said), 58

Osaimi, Saoud al-, 233–7

Oslo agreement (1993), 362–4, 368–76 passim

Ottoman empire, 53–8, 61, 69–70, 76, 110, 130; collapse of, 12, 20, 70–3, 130–3, 357; decline of, 62–7; Egypt in, 91–3; Iraq in, 6, 7, 19, 21, 44, 249, 335; Jordan in, 294; Kuwait and, 238, 239, 250; Lebanon in, 164, 168; Palestinians in, 199–202, 217; Syria in, 126–8, 131–4, 137, 138, 151

Ozal, Korkut, 79, 81

Ozal, Semra, 79

Ozal, Turgut, 78–81

Pahlevi, Mohammed Reza Shah, of Iran, 17, 18, 34, 49, 235, 355

Pakradouni, Karim, 181

Palace Walk (Mahfouz), 94, 100

Palestine, 21, 36, 111, 132, 134, 135, 151, 361–80

Palestine Liberation Organization (PLO), 212–20, 226–9, 287, 316; founding of, 315; fundamentalist rivalry with, 207, 210, 231, 232; in Jordan, 141, 288, 290–2, 306; and Kuwait, 245, 259, 273; in Lebanon, 172–4, 176–7, 195; and peace process, 320, 321, 361–80 passim; and Syria, 154–5

Palestine National Council, 216

Palestinians, 48, 60, 109, 154, 175, 194–232, 297, 358; and creation

of Israel, 202–5; in Jordan,
290–3, 299, 301, 302, 304, 306,
313, 317; in Kuwait, 206, 212,
244–5, 259–60, 264–6, 269, 272;
in Lebanon, 171–5, 177, 182,
193, 196; in Ottoman empire,
199–202; and peace process,
319–20, 361–80; in Syria, 150,
155; uprising against Israel of,
see intifada
pan-Arabism, 22, 24, 25, 28, 202,
215, 246, 307
Paul of Tarsus, 150
Peel Commission, 203
Persians, 4, 11, 41, 238, 240
Phalange (Lebanon), 170, 173, 176,
177, 183
Pharaohs, 87, 90, 91, 115
Phoenicians, 168
Pioneers (Iraqi school of painting),
39
Pirenne, Henri, 128
pogroms, 151
poison gas, 50–2
Popular Front for the Liberation of
Palestine, 155, 288, 364, 378
Portugal, 60
Protestant Reformation, 129

Qadisiyah, al-, battle of, 41
Qasem, Marwan, 309
Qasim, Abd al-Karim, 22–4, 26,
27, 44, 249
Qatar, 235
Quraysh tribe, 14, 312
Qutb, Sayyid, 359

Rabin, Yitzhak, 175, 231, 361–2,
373
Ramahi, Rada Sliman, 222–5,
379–80
Ramahi, Wajdeh Mustafa Abdullah
(Abu Wajdi), 224, 379–80

Rawabdeh, Abdel Rauf, 295, 382
Reagan, Ronald, 47, 235, 236, 251
Refah party (Turkey), 81
reflagging of tankers, 233, 236,
237, 282
Renaissance, 55, 68–9, 81, 113, 129
Republican People's Party of
Turkey, 72
Respected Sir (Mahfouz), 98
Rifai, Zeid, 301, 302
Roland, Knight, 57–8
Roman empire, 55, 124, 128–9,
150, 168, 169, 293
Romanovs, 64
Rumaila oil fields (Kuwait), 251–2,
308, 341, 344
Rushdie, Salman, 69, 88–90, 114,
144, 147, 305
Russia, 238; exiles from, 142;
Ottoman empire and, 64, 66, 70;
see also Soviet Union
Russo-Japanese war, 83

Sabah, Sheikh Abdullah al-, 242
Sabah, Sheikh Ahmad al-, 241
Sabah, Sheikh Jabir al-, 234, 248,
282, 309
Sabah, Sheik Mubarak al-, 239
Sabah, Sheikh Nasser al-, 248
Sabah, Sheikh Sa'ad al-, 263, 265,
275, 276, 281
Sabah, Sheikh Salim al-, 239
Sabah family, 237–9, 241, 244,
245, 247–50, 255–8, 261–2, 264,
265, 271–7, 282
Sabra refugee camp, 176–7, 179,
180
Sacre, Fr. Etienne, 163–5
Sadat, Anwar, 36–7, 84, 88, 89, 91,
103, 106–12, 115–19, 141, 154,
316
Sadat, Jihan, 109, 112
Saddam Hussein, 17, 22, 46, 48,
52, 141–2, 233, 249, 252, 253,

Saddam Hussein (*cont.*)
256, 263, 271–81 *passim*, 322;
Aflaq and, 29, 31; Arab support
for, 269; Bush's refusal to
negotiate with, 254, 345; defeat
of, 268; and Iraq-Iran war, 11,
40–4, 50, 250; and Israel, 251;
Jackson interview with, 254–5;
and Jordan, 286–90, 292, 293,
296, 297, 299, 308–12, 318–21;
Kurds and, 18, 26, 50–1; and
Kuwaiti opposition leaders, 258,
277; Munir Bashir and, 37; and
oil overproduction, 280; and
postwar Iraq, 284, 326, 328–47,
349, 351–5; Reagan and, 47; rise
of, 25–8; Schwarzkopf and, 279;
secularism of, 82; and Shiite-
Sunni rivalry, 12
Sadoun, Ahmed, 256, 258, 262, 282
Sadoun, Jassem, 276–7
Sadr, Baqir al-, 41, 42
Sahin, Haluk, 59–60
Said, Edward, 58
Said, Nuri, 20–2, 24, 26, 335
Saladin, 122, 123, 141
Saleh Atta, Abdel-Jawad, 198
Salem, Elie, 178, 179
Salem, Sheikh, 280–3
Salem, Sheikh Sabah al-, 242, 248,
262, 263–4
Salih, Zaid Mohammed, 39
Salmawi, Mohamed, 87
Salti, Amer, 290–1
Saneh, Faisal, 258
Satanic Verses, The (Rushdie), 88,
89
Saud family, 312, 313
Saudi Arabia, 46, 61, 76, 90, 123,
192, 235, 238, 264, 276; Gulf
war and, 233, 249, 252–61
passim, 275, 280, 288, 289, 293,
299; Iraq and, 338–40, 344;
during Iraq-Iran war, 251;
Jordan and, 297, 300, 307–12,

316, 317, 319; Palestinians and,
196, 205, 212, 215, 218, 229;
women in, 329
Save the Children, 301
Sayeed, Abdul Khaliq Abdul Aziz,
354
Schiff, Ze'ev, 175
Schwarzkopf, Gen. Norman H.,
278–9, 283, 338, 344
Seale, Patrick, 154
Senate Foreign Relations
Committee, U.S., 51
Sèvres, Treaty of, 71, 73
Shaath, Nabil, 228
Shaheen, Ibraheem al-, 243–4
Shaheen, Issa al-, 272
Shaheen, Suleiman al-, 268–70,
272
shari'a (code of Islamic law), 12,
68, 73, 93, 112
Sharon, Ariel, 176–8
Shatila refugee camp, 176–7, 179,
180
shebab (Palestinian rebels), 194,
197, 207, 208, 224, 365, 377
Shellah, Bedreddin, 133–5
Shiber, Saba George, 243, 247
Shiites, 114, 122; in Iran, 41, 75,
112; in Iraq, 11–16, 19–21, 25,
26, 29, 30, 33–5, 49, 268, 335,
336, 346, 347, 352–3, 355; in
Kuwait, 234, 240, 248, 271; in
Lebanon, 164–6, 177, 179, 182;
in Syria, 150
Shin Beit (Israeli security service),
201
Shirabi, Hisham, 128, 129, 358,
359
Shultz, George, 47, 51, 179
shura (Islamic electoral body), 11
Six-Day War, 47, 111, 138, 140–1,
151, 172, 215, 219, 230, 236,
246, 315, 362
Souk al-Manakh (Kuwait), 248, 279
South Lebanese Army, 190

Soviet Union, 22, 23, 25, 357; Afghanistan invaded by, 235–6; collapse of, 62, 141, 249, 251, 278, 318, 339, 344–5; Egypt and, 104, 107, 136; Iraq and, 26, 47, 48; Jewish immigrants to Israel from, 223; Jordan and, 315; Kuwait and, 235; Muslim republics of, 11; Palestinians and, 195, 200; Syria and, 123, 137, 141, 178, 187; Turkey and, 61, 71

Spain, 148; Arab conquest of, 29, 57, 61; Inquisition in, 56, 151

State Department, U.S., 142, 155, 160, 190, 237, 255, 289, 338, 342, 343

Sudan, 287

Suez Canal, 92, 93, 102–4, 106, 131, 136, 209

Sufis, 79, 101, 110

Sugar Street (Mahfouz), 106

Sulaimaniya (Kurdistan), 348

Suleyman the Magnificent, 63

Sultan, Abdul Aziz, 258–9

Sumerians, 4, 40

Sunnis, 68, 122; in Egypt, 110; in Iraq, 11–13, 15, 19–22, 25, 29, 30, 33, 34, 330, 335, 336, 351; in Kuwait, 248, 271; in Lebanon, 164–6, 171, 173, 177, 185, 191, 192; in Syria, 127, 136–8, 144, 145; in Turkey, 75

Sykes-Picot Agreement, 132, 134, 202

Syria, 29, 122–57, 306; under Assad, 137–41; Communists in, 23; creation of modern state of, 131–6; Egypt and, 22, 136–7, 315; in Gulf war, 233, 272, 287; Iran and, 316; Jews in, 137, 149–53; Jordan and, 313; Kurds in, 11, 18, 335, 347; Lebanon and, 165, 169, 173–80, 182, 183–93; opposition in, 141–8;

Palestinians and, 202, 205, 290; and peace process, 153–7, 319

Taif Agreement, 192, 193

Talabani, Jalal, 350–2

Talal, King, of Jordan, 313

Talfah, Khairallah, 25

Tamimi, Azzam, 304

tankers, reflagging of, 233, 236, 237, 282

Tantawi, Mohammed (Mufti of Egypt), 113–15

technical committees, 375

terrorists: in Egypt, 88, 102, 109; in Jordan, 144, 288, 315; Palestinian, 172, 216

Tewfik, Khedive, of Egypt, 93

Thatcher, Margaret, 268

Time magazine, 147

Torah, 151

Tripartite Agreement, 180–2, 185–7, 191–3

Truman, Harry S., 318

Tunisia, 269

Turkey, 53–82; establishment of modern state of, 70–5; Iraq and, 323, 328; Islam in, 73 82; Kurds in, 11, 18, 51, 335, 347, 349, 352; Syria and, 136; *see also* Ottoman empire

umma (Islamic community of believers), 12, 129, 130, 246, 247, 271

Unified Command (of *intifada*), 197, 226, 229

Union of European Football Associations (UEFA), 59

Union of Syrian Students, 137

United Arab Emirates, 212, 235, 339, 340

United Arab Republic, 171

United Nations, 200, 204, 205, 208, 215–16, 318, 324; General Assembly, 338; and postwar Iraq, 322, 329, 333; Relief and Works Agency (UNRWA), 206, 207, 222, 291; Resolution 242, 156, 215, 219, 317, 363; Resolution 660, 317; Security Council, 215, 234, 235, 249, 282, 309, 317

United States, 22; Egypt and, 104; Gulf policy of, 235–7; Iraq and, 46–52, 337–45; Jordan and, 286, 288–90, 292, 293, 296, 297, 299, 300, 309–12, 315–18; Kurds and, 349, 351, 352; Kuwait and, 236–7, 248–55, 265–7, 272, 273, 275–84; Lebanon and, 171, 177–9, 188, 190, 191, 193; Palestinians and, 196, 199, 293; and peace process, 318, 320, 363; Syria and, 141, 142; war with Iraq, see Gulf war

Versailles conference, 70
Voice of America, 339

Wafd party (Egypt), 95–6, 102
Wahabi sect (Arabia), 12
Washington Post, 289–90
Weheidi, Sheikh Abdul Razak, 292–3
Weizmann, Chaim, 202

West Bank, 194–200, 205, 206, 211, 212, 216, 217, 219–22, 227, 230, 290, 294, 372–8 passim; Jordan and, 313, 315, 316, 319, 320
Wilson, Woodrow, 70
women: in Iraq, 31–5, 329; in Jordan, 304–6; in Kuwait, 246; in Turkey, 76–9
Woodward, Bob, 343
World War I, 7, 11, 20, 50, 54, 56, 66, 70, 71, 93, 110, 130–1, 164, 240, 300, 314
World War II, 21, 57, 97, 102, 103, 135–6, 150, 241, 263, 294

Ya'ari, Yitzhak, 175
Yacoub, Badr al-, 277
Yassin, Sheikh Ahmed, 209–10
Yemen, 105, 269, 287, 309
Yergin, Daniel, 280
Yom Kippur War, 156
Young Egypt Society, 102, 103
Young Ottomans, 66, 362
Young Turks, 66, 71, 130, 131
Yunis, Menal al-, 32–5

Zaghlul, Sa'd, 94, 95
Zakho (Kurdistan), 349, 350, 352
Zaman (Turkish newspaper), 80
Zionism, 30, 48, 134, 153, 200, 202–4, 255, 286

A Note About the Author

Milton Viorst, born in New Jersey in 1930, received his bachelor's degree at Rutgers and did his graduate work at Harvard, Columbia and the University of Lyon, France. He has been a professional writer throughout his life, and in recent years has appeared frequently on the op-ed pages of *The New York Times* and the Washington *Post*, and been on the staff of *The New Yorker*. He is the author of eleven books, among them *Hostile Allies: FDR and de Gaulle* and *Fire in the Streets: America in the 1960s*. In the field of Middle Eastern studies, in which he has specialized for the past two decades, he has written *Sands of Sorrow: Israel's Journey from Independence* and *Reaching for the Olive Branch: UNRWA and Peace in the Middle East*. Viorst lives in Washington, D.C., with his wife, Judith. They have three sons.

A Note on the Type

The text of this book was set in Aldus, a book version of Palatino, a roman type with broad letters and strong, inclined serifs. Both faces were designed in the 1950s by the German typographer Hermann Zapf, born in Nuremberg in 1918. Zapf has designed more than fifty typefaces, and has been a professor of typography and typographic computer programs, as well as a design consultant, in both Germany and the United States.

Composed by Crane Typesetting Service, Inc.
West Barnstable, Massachusetts

Printed and bound by The Haddon Craftsmen,
Scranton, Pennsylvania

Designed by Robert C. Olsson